2nd EDITION

Entrepreneur
MAGAZINE'S

ULTIMATE

Over
1,000
FRANCHISE
LISTINGS!

BOOK OF
FRANCHISES

From the Franchise Experts at
Entrepreneur *Magazine*

RIEVA LESONSKY
and MARIA ANTON-CONLEY

Ep
Entrepreneur®
Press

Entrepreneur Press
Editorial Director: Jere L. Calmes
Cover Design: Beth Hansen-Winter

Entrepreneur Magazine
Senior Art Director: Daryl Hoopes
Production Designer: Cheryl Fujioki
Articles Editor: Janean Chun
Listings Editor: Tracy Stapp
Editorial Assistant: Emily Weisburg
Designer: Annie Roach

This publication is designed to provide accurate and authoritative information in regard to the subject matter covered. It is sold with the understanding that the publisher is not engaged in rendering legal, accounting or other professional services. If legal advice or other expert assistance is required, the services of a competent professional person should be sought

Library of Congress Cataloging-in-Publication Data

Lesonsky, Rieva.
  Ultimate book of franchises : from the franchise experts at Entrepreneur magazine / by Rieva Lesonsky and Maria Anton-Conley. — 2nd ed.
    p. cm.
  Rev. ed. of: Entrepreneur magazine's ultimate book of franchises. c2004.
  ISBN-13: 978-1-59918-099-1 (alk. paper)
  ISBN-10: 1-59918-099-5 (alk. paper)
  1. Franchises (Retail trade)   I. Anton-Conley, Maria. II. Lesonsky, Rieva. Entrepreneur magazine's ultimate book of franchises. III. Entrepreneur (Irvine, Calif.) IV. Title.
  HF5429.23.L47 2007
  658.8'708—dc22

                                                                    2007007440

Printed in Canada

13 12 11 10 09 08 07   10 9 8 5 4 3 2 1

Table of Contents

SECTION ONE
How To Buy a Franchise

SECTION TWO
Ultimate Franchise Directory

Acknowledgements

THERE ARE MANY BOOKS THAT TELL you about franchising, but this is the only one to incorporate Entrepreneur magazine's acclaimed Franchise 500®, making Entrepreneur Magazine's Ultimate Book of Franchises the most comprehensive book about buying a franchise available anywhere.

It takes a talented, dedicated group of people to create a work of this magnitude, so we are grateful to all who have contributed. Several Entrepreneur magazine staffers went well above and beyond their job duties to make this book possible. There aren't enough words to properly thank book designer Cheryl Fujioki; articles editor Janean Chun, who edited this book with her usual flair; listings editor Tracy Stapp; editorial assistant Emily Weisburg; and designer Annie Roach. Also, thank you to senior art director Daryl Hoopes for his ongoing help coordinating the production of this book; and a special thank you to Matt Samarin, senior art director, and Marla Markman, managing editor of business guides and products, who provided additional guidance.

Every aspiring or current business owner needs a good accountant, someone he or she can trust without hesitation. And we have one. Many thanks to CPA David R. Juedes, who, as the former CFO of a franchise company, is especially qualified to review and rate the financials of the franchises in the listing section.

Many years ago, when *Entrepreneur*'s Franchise 500® was still young, we were lucky enough to meet Andrew A. Caffey, who, at the time, was an attorney for the International Franchise Association. Today, from his law practice in the Washington, DC area, Andy is a frequent contributor to *Entrepreneur*, using his years of experience as a franchise and business opportunity attorney to demystify the franchise buying process. The first section of the *Ultimate Book of Franchises* is adapted from Andy's book, *Franchise & Business Opportunities*. Without him, this book would not be worthy of the word "ultimate."

Rieva Lesonsky
Maria Anton-Conley

Introduction

I F YOU ARE LIKE MOST AMERICANS, chances are you or some member of your family spends time—and money—in a franchise nearly every week. Doubt it? Well, do you ever get gas? Stay in a hotel or motel? Get a cup of coffee at a place other than Starbucks? Pick up a fast meal at the drive-thru? Go to a staffing service in search of a job? Have your house (or office) cleaned? Think about buying or selling a house? Well, you get our point—franchising is a central part of our everyday lives. In fact, as an industry it generates more than $1 trillion in annual revenue.

Since you purchased the *Ultimate Book of Franchises,* you must want to be a part of it. You probably have at least considered buying a franchise. That's a good start, but to be a successful franchisee, you need to do more than just think about it—you need to actually get started. We can guess what you're thinking: "There are so many franchises to choose from, where do I even begin?" The obvious answer: right here. You can't start a business without doing your homework. Consider this book your cheat sheet—we've done a lot of the work for you.

First, a word about franchising. A type of business opportunity, franchises are essentially business packages that enable you to, as the franchisors say, be in business for yourself, but not by yourself. All franchises are offered with the same premise: "We (the franchisor) have already developed a successful business program. For your investment, we will provide you with all the tools you need to own and operate a successful business." All business startups entail some risk. But franchises generally are less risky to start: After all, you are buying a proven system. That's not to say there is no risk in franchising; obviously, there is. But you can mitigate that risk by knowing what to expect from franchisors, by understanding the rules and regulations that govern franchising and by getting the inside scoop on the hundreds of franchise opportunities available. And that's where we come in.

We are the folks who publish *Entrepreneur* magazine, and for 30 years we've been telling people how to start and grow their own businesses.

Since 1980, we've produced *Entrepreneur's Franchise 500*, the most authoritative and comprehensive ranking of franchise opportunities in the world. And we've taken the many months of research that go into the Franchise 500® and applied it to this book.

Ultimate Book of Franchises is divided into two sections. In the first section, "How to Buy a Franchise," Andrew A. Caffey—a franchise attorney, internationally recognized specialist in franchise and business opportunity law and former general counsel of the International Franchise Association—provides you with an overall look at the world of franchising. Here you'll find information on everything from researching a franchise on the internet to negotiating your franchise agreements.

An in-depth statistical overview of hundreds of franchises makes up the rest of the book. Organized by Maria Anton-Conley and Tracy Stapp, here you'll find the 411 on opportunities ranging from the tried and true, like Chem-Dry and Subway, to newer franchises, like Cereality and Environix.

While it's likely there is an opportunity just right for you, not all opportunities are suited for everyone. And chances are, you're going to invest a lot of your savings into your venture, so you need to invest wisely. As Chinese philosopher Laotzu said, "Every journey begins with a single step." So turn the page, and put your best foot forward.

How To Buy a Franchise

CHAPTER 1

So You Want to Own a Business?

T THE AGE OF 30, SUCCESS WAS ELUDING Jon, and he knew something was wrong. After a promising high school athletic career and a fair academic showing at his state's university, he bounced from one job to the next with no sense of purpose and without achieving the success he knew was in him. People liked him, and he was presentable, but his 30th birthday stopped him in his tracks. How and when was he going to realize his potential? He hungered for success but didn't quite know how to go about it. Somehow that part was not taught in school.

BUSINESS OWNERSHIP

The Advantages

Owning your own business—a sparkling, elusive goal of the American dream. It wasn't until Jon began considering starting his own business that he felt some optimism about his life's goals.

Business ownership seems out of reach to would-be entrepreneurs because it appears expensive, complicated and intimidating. Yet business ownership is the most common route taken by Americans to substantial wealth.

There are a number of advantages to owning a business:

- Small-business ownership can bring *independence*—no more punching a time clock and worrying whether your job will be there tomorrow.
- It can mean *flexibility* so that you are free to take time off and spend time with the ones you love.
- It can bring a *healthy variety* of daily tasks instead of the repetitive routines of so many workplace specialties.
- Business ownership can bring immense *pride in accomplishment*.
- Business owners make a *difference* in the lives of everyone involved, especially employees who depend on the owner's business savvy to keep their jobs.
- Owning your own business gives you the chance to do it *your way*. It gives you the chance to bring your pride, your style, your gifts to a business operation.
- Business ownership can bring *wealth*. You don't need to be Bill Gates to realize the

3

rewards of starting your own business. Ownership gives you the opportunity to build equity value over time, so that once your business is up and running, it will have acquired a substantial value. It puts to shame the apparent value of a week-to-week paycheck after those taxes are taken out.

The Challenges

Given these benefits, why don't even more people own their own businesses? It takes an enormous amount of work and drive to overcome the challenges of getting started. To many people, those challenges can seem insurmountable. Just take a look at what it was like for Jon:

Jon was practically in a panic: Look at this checklist! I can't do this! Borrow a quarter-million dollars? Who is going to lend me that kind of money? Quit my job and launch out on my own? What if I fail? The failure rates for small businesses are staggering. Am I nuts?! Even if I find the money, I will have to learn the traps of the business. Sure, there are lots of other businesses in my line I could talk to, but they are all competitors! No way are they going to tell me how to run this operation. I have to hire people, advertise, buy inventory ... I don't know how to do that. I'll probably get ripped off at every turn and lose my shirt.

In some ways, Jon is right. It is difficult to find the information you need to set up and operate a business, create the trademark and graphics, and amass the cash and borrowed funds necessary to get going. As they say, if it were easy, everyone would do it.

But owning a successful business is possible, and one way to make it a reality is to buy a franchise. The franchise concept is designed to help the average person overcome the challenges of small-business ownership and get into a proven business, while providing the type of training and continued coaching that is not available anywhere else.

There are lots of ways to skin the business cat, of course. Whether you choose a franchise or something else entirely, it must be a program that fits your needs and gets you on the road to building wealth through small-business ownership.

SUMMARY NOTES

✓ Avenues to success are often not taught in our schools.

✓ Business ownership is a proven pathway to success and wealth.

✓ You can overcome the intimidating challenges of business ownership.

✓ A popular way to get into business is owning a franchise.

Action PLAN

Write down on a single sheet of paper three goals of a business you would start. How do you imagine it would change your life? Then write down three aspects of business that appeal to you. If you have any general ideas of the type of business that would appeal to you, note them on the same sheet. Keep this paper in a folder labeled "Business Planning"; you will want to refer to it again.

CHAPTER 2

Organizing for Business

*O*NCE MERRY DECIDED TO GET INTO *business for herself, she realized that she didn't know much about business organization. She had heard the horror stories: A friend's dad had lost everything in a stupid business concept, and because of the liabilities of the business failure, the friend and her family had to move out of their house and into an apartment when she was in high school. Merry was determined to be smart about her own business, protect herself as best she could and build an organization that could stand on its own feet. However, despite her firm resolve, she didn't even know what questions to ask to get started.*

ADVANTAGES AND DISADVANTAGES OF DIFFERENT BUSINESS ORGANIZATIONS

One of the early decisions all businesspeople have to make is how best to organize legally to be in business. Do you form a corporation? Do you have to? Are there other choices? This can be confusing if you are new to business ownership. There are lots of choices and a number of concerns to consider as you sift through the options.

You can operate as a sole proprietor, a corporation, a partnership or a limited liability company. Even if you buy a franchise, you need to select a form of business organization. Take a look at each one.

The Sole Proprietorship

A sole proprietorship is a business owned directly by one person. This is the simplest type of business organization, and some may even find it hard to think of it as an "organization." However, some sole proprietorships may be large and complex with many employees. For now, think of a sole proprietorship as one person running the business as both owner and manager.

The greatest advantage to running the sole proprietorship is the ease with which it is formed. There are no papers to file or meetings to hold in order to keep it in existence. From an organizational point of view, you may simply start doing business as a sole proprietor with no further legal maintenance required. Of course, there may be licenses or permits required for the type of business you are starting, but the "organization" of your business is done.

The greatest disadvantage of the sole proprietorship is personal liability. The owner is required to repay any amount borrowed personally, no matter what happens to the business. This means they could lose more than their initial investment. There is no distinction between business and personal assets. A bank or other creditor may try to collect any money owed from the sole proprietor's personal assets if the business fails. You may obtain liability insurance, but it will not cover you if your business fails.

Another serious limitation for a sole proprietor is the inability to take on investors or partners. This may be unimportant for many businesses, but could make all the difference in financing others.

A lot of businesses start out as sole proprietorships and then morph into corporations or limited liability companies (LLCs). If you are buying a franchise, however, it may be important to consider forming a separate legal entity before you sign on to the franchised business, because it can be difficult to transfer the franchise rights to your new entity after you sign the franchise agreement.

Partnership

A partnership exists when two or more people agree to run a business together and share control and profits. Creating a partnership does not require any formal steps. The agreement to form a partnership may be either expressed or implied, oral or written. However, it is highly recommended that a written partnership agreement be prepared and signed by the partners.

The partnership agreement should cover such issues as the amount of each partner's contribution, how profits will be shared, what authority each partner has and how interests may be transferred. If a partnership is formed without a written agreement, the law will impose a series of standard terms that may not be intended by the partners. If you wish to have a partnership agreement, it is recommended that you consult with an attorney licensed in your state with some experience in the area.

Business partners should understand the significance the law places on sharing control. They may act on behalf of one another and the partnership in making agreements, incurring debt and taking any other action in the course of running the business. The obligations of the business become personal to all. State law will impose equally shared liability on each general partner, unless the partnership agreement states otherwise. For example, if your partner takes out a loan on behalf of the business and the business fails, the bank will seek repayment from both your partner *and* you. If your partner or the partnership has no assets to satisfy the debt, the creditor may look to you personally.

So far we have been discussing a general partnership; however, there is another form of partnership known as a limited partnership. A limited partnership has at least one general partner and one limited partner. The main difference between these two types of partners is that a limited partner has no liability for the debts of the partnership. Nor do they have rights to management or control of the business. The general partner controls the business and has unlimited liability. To form a limited partnership, you must carefully consult the laws of the state in which you do business and seek the assistance of a competent attorney. For accountability purposes, the partnership is required to report its income on IRS Form 1065.

Corporation

The corporation is radically different from the other forms of business organization. It is controlled by statute, and each state's laws vary to some extent. You should therefore contact the secretary of state's office in the state in which you incorporate for more information.

In the eyes of the law, a corporation is a legal entity separate and apart from its shareholders. It may buy, sell or inherit property; enter into contracts; and sue or be sued in court. It is also responsible for its own debts. If the corporation fails, creditors may not seek payment from investors in the company. The shareholder's liability is therefore limited to his or her initial investment.

Shareholders in a corporation are ultimately responsible for all corporate actions, somewhat like citizens in a democracy. Shareholders elect representatives to the board of directors, and the board of directors appoints the officers of the corporation to handle its everyday affairs. This three-tier structure applies to nearly all corporations, from GM to the smallest one-owner, homebased corporation.

If you form a legal entity like a corporation or an LLC, make sure that whenever you enter a business contract or other important obligation, you bind the entity to the obligation and not to yourself. To do this, make sure you sign in your official capacity showing your title, such as "President" or "Member." Make sure your title appears under your name and that you are committing the entity to the obligation.

Subchapter S Corporation

Most smaller businesses will benefit from selecting the tax treatment of a subchapter S corporation. A subchapter S corporation receives special tax treatment under the Internal Revenue Code and has some distinct advantages. These include:

- *No Double Taxation.* A subchapter S corporation sidesteps the principal disadvantage of the corporate form of doing business by receiving tax treatment that is similar to a partnership. It is not taxed at the corporate level, but the income of the entity is passed through to the shareholders and reported on each individual's personal tax return.
- *Ease of Election.* A new corporation or an existing corporation may elect subchapter S corporation treatment simply by filing IRS Form 2553.

In order to qualify for subchapter S corporation treatment, the corporation must be a domestic (U.S.) entity with one class of stock and no more than 35 shareholders. Its shareholders must be individuals, estates or certain trusts and not other corporations. Finally, it may not have a nonresident alien among its shareholders. Most personally owned and family-owned businesses qualify for subchapter S corporation treatment and should seriously consider electing it.

The drawback to a subchapter S corporation is that many of the corporate perks of a regular corporation may not be realized. For instance, a regular corporation can pay for the health plan of its shareholders, but a subchapter S corporation may not. There may be other drawbacks, as well, which you should review with your attorney.

Limited Liability Company

The limited liability company is a recently developed concept in business organization that has a number of significant advantages for small-business owners. Like a subchapter S corporation, a limited liability company (LLC) offers the liability protection of a corporation and the tax benefits of a partnership, but an LLC does not require compliance with the legal formalities that characterize a corporation.

Wyoming first adopted an LLC statute in 1977, but the concept really caught on in the 1980s. In 1988, the IRS ruled that an LLC under Wyoming law would receive tax treatment like a partnership (on a pass-through basis to individual managers), and its popularity has since soared.

An LLC has an enormous advantage over the corporation: flexibility in its management. Depending on the particular requirements of your state's law, an LLC is operated by either members or by appointed or elected managers. It may be structured for governance and economics by agreement of its owner-members, and there are few limitations on the way it is organized and operated. Most new business owners are well-advised to take a close look at the LLC concept.

For most small-business owners, the answer will be to stay a sole proprietor (and run whatever liability risks there may be), create a corporation and elect subchapter S treatment under the Tax Code, or form a limited liability company. Buying a franchise will accelerate your decision-making process, because the franchisor may demand you have your organization in place at the very beginning of the franchise term.

CONCERNS UNDERLYING BUSINESS ORGANIZATIONS

In order to make the right choice of business organization, it is important to consider the following:

Personal Liability

If you do not form any legal entity to hold your business, you will be operating under your own name, as yourself, and putting your personal assets on the line. Your form of business ownership will be known as a "sole proprietor," and you will have no protection from claims anyone may have against your business.

Here's a quick example. You start a business of buying and selling used videogames. It takes off like a jack rabbit, and soon you are dealing in large wholesale lots of games. You enter into a contract with a new local games store to buy all of its used games for a year at a negotiated price, a contract that you estimate is worth $25,000. You do this because you have a buyer lined up who tells you he will buy as many games as you can produce for him.

One bleak day, your buyer goes out of business and disappears. The games store expects you to continue buying from them, but you don't have the cash or the buyers to move the merchandise. When you don't buy the used games as required in your contract, the seller files a lawsuit on the contract, seeking $25,000 in damages. Your lawyer tells you that because you operate as a sole proprietor, all your personal assets are exposed to this claim, and you could lose your car and/or your house if you lose the case. If you operated as a corporation, he tells you, then it would be liable, and your personal assets would be out of your creditors' reach.

When someone talks about the disadvantages of operating under your own name, you need to weigh the potential liability that you could incur in the business. In large measure, your decision depends on the type of business (will you be entering into contracts for substantial obligations?) and the state of your personal assets (can you absorb all potential losses of the business?).

Taxation

This is a biggie. There are dramatically different tax consequences depending on the form of business organization you use. Taxation concerns drive a lot of the business organization decisions, and some of the legal forms available strike a balance between liability and taxation.

If you operate as an individual sole proprietor, then your tax picture is straightforward. You simply add a Schedule C to your annual personal return.

Corporations have another story to tell. The law (and the IRS) recognize that a corporation is a separate entity and must pay its own taxes on its own net income. Then, when the corporation pays out a dividend to its owners, the owners must pay taxes on that income when they file their personal returns. In an important sense, a corporation is taxed twice: once on its own revenue, and again when the owners take money out of the corporation.

A traditional answer to this double whammy is an IRS tax treatment as a "subchapter S corporation." This is a corporation that has met a series of qualifications (mostly as to size and the number of shareholders) and has elected to receive special tax treatment. As a result, the subchapter S corporation has the liability protection of a standard corporation but is not taxed twice. The IRS allows the corporation to pass through its revenues to its owners and the taxation on that revenue at the owners'

level. The subchapter S corporation does not pay taxes separately. The result: one-time taxation. Problem solved.

A partnership has always been taxed directly to the individual partners; it is not considered a separate entity for liability or taxation purposes. Limited liability companies have also solved the taxation problem by receiving single tax treatment.

Flexibility

This concern becomes evident when you are told what directors and officers you must have and what annual meetings you must conduct in order to maintain a corporation. The law imposes rather extensive rules on the owners of a corporation, and if the rules are not followed, the liability shield effectiveness is lost. Partnerships are quite flexible. So are limited liability companies. Sole proprietorships are the most flexible of all, of course, because there is no organization to nurture along the way.

Flexibility has another dimension. Say you want to take in other owners and give them different shares of ownership. You cannot do that if you are a sole proprietor, but the other legal structures are designed for multiple owners.

SUMMARY NOTES
- ✓ Business organizations will change depending on the needs of the business itself and the organizers.
- ✓ Limiting personal liability, maximizing tax benefits and flexibility are principal concerns.
- ✓ Understand the major forms of business organization before consulting with an attorney; it will save you time and money.

✓ One of the most attractive new forms of business organization is the limited liability company. It is fast becoming the leading choice of small-business owners.

Action **PLAN**

Make a checklist of goals for your business as well as concerns you may have about things like ownership and liability. Take the list to a good attorney, and ask what you need to do to form a solid business entity for your business plan.

CHAPTER 3

Understanding the Franchise Concept

*P*AUL HAD ALWAYS WANTED TO OWN HIS *own business, but the opportunity had just never presented itself. On a fishing trip to Minnesota, he came across a business concept that he could not get out of his mind. It was new and fresh, and he thought it had a huge market potential. He wanted to get in on the business somehow and learned it was being offered as a new franchise program. This might mean he could bring the concept to his hometown and open a sensational business. He had never considered a franchise. Where should he start?*

INDEPENDENT OWNERSHIP

Start at the beginning. A business format franchise is a long-term business relationship in which the purchaser (the "franchisee") is granted the right to operate a business under the trademark of an established business owner (the "franchisor") and use its business techniques. This franchise relationship gives the franchisee the right to start up a business concept that the franchisor has already invented and perfected, using an established trademark and a comprehensive set of operating techniques.

Once licensed to use the franchisor's trademark and business system, the franchisee has the right to set up a business—usually under the franchisor's close scrutiny—that looks and operates *exactly* like other franchises in the franchise network. The magic in this formula—the simple fact that drives the success of the entire concept of business franchising—is that *the franchise owner remains an independent businessperson*. A franchisee is never an employee and is subject only to the limited control exercised by the franchisor under the franchise agreement. Independence means that if the franchisee is very successful in operating the business, he or she will reap the financial rewards. And the rewards can be substantial: Franchising has created an untold number of millionaires (think McDonald's and Holiday Inn). Of course, the converse also remains true: If the franchised business is not successful, the franchisee absorbs the loss.

THE BUSINESS OF FRANCHISING

Contrary to the impression conveyed nightly by the business press, it is small-business ownership, not big business, that is the bedrock strength of the American economy. Franchising gives the individual investor the opportunity to own their own small business without having to go it alone or invent and perfect a profitable retail concept that is, statistically at least, doomed to failure.

The franchise relationship we describe here has been adopted by hundreds of successful business programs, many of which are familiar cultural icons: Burger King, Dairy Queen, Holiday Inn, Jani-King, Jiffy Lube, McDonald's, Midas, Quality Inn, 7-Eleven and Subway stores. Many American towns have strip malls and mile-long commercial streets that are dominated by such franchised businesses.

While quick-service restaurants may be some of the best known franchises, the franchise concept has actually been applied in more than 50 different industry categories. These include everything from children's fitness programs and dollar stores to automobile dent removal and management training businesses.

Are gas station dealers and automobile dealers part of business franchising? Yes and no. Most systems are made up of independent dealers licensed to operate under a particular company's trademark and are said to own "product franchises," but they generally do not pay the franchise fees described here. The traditional practice in these industries is for dealers to buy product from the manufacturer at wholesale and sell it through their dealerships at retail. In contrast, the McDonald's restaurant franchisee does not buy any product from the franchisor—not even one sesame seed. Supplies are bought exclusively from third-party suppliers approved by the company. Ray Kroc, the legendary founder of the McDonald's system, did not want any buyer/seller tension to creep into his relationship with franchise owners.

Franchising by itself is not an "industry," but a form of distribution. The franchisor is distributing products and services through licensed franchisees. This is important, because two businesses may be franchised—say, a convenience store and a hotel—but have absolutely nothing else in common.

In recent years, there has also been an explosive growth in international franchising. The McDonald's trademark has become nothing short of a symbol of American culture, the restaurant's golden arches established now in more than 120 countries.

THE FRANCHISEE VIEW

Consider three important measures of a franchise system from the franchisee point of view: independence, training and money dynamics.

Independent Ownership

This concept energizes franchising because of the motivation, commitment and drive of an on-site owner. An employee manager working on an hourly wage is usually not motivated to work as hard or as long as an owner. It's that simple: An employee is involved; an owner is committed. It is the lesson taught when a pig and a chicken form a partnership to produce a ham and egg sandwich. The chicken is "involved," but the pig is *committed*.

Training Says All

Training and support are keys to a strong business franchise. A well-established franchisor has something valuable to impart to the franchisee: know-how. It's one thing to perfect a business concept; it is quite another to transfer the essence of that concept to people who know nothing about the business and enable them to find success.

The strongest and best franchise programs are those able to convey know-how through rigorous training, often including classroom training at their headquarters and additional training when the franchisee opens for business.

How the Money Works

How does the money work in a franchise relationship? While there are no hard and fast rules, the franchisee generally pays the franchisor in three ways: the initial franchise fee, royalties and advertising contributions.

The *initial franchise fee* is a lump sum paid when the contract is signed. This payment can range from a few thousand dollars to as high as $50,000 or more. A typical initial franchise fee for a restaurant franchise is in the $20,000 to $30,000 range. This fee generally covers the franchisor's cost of recruiting franchisees and of initial services, like site location and training.

The franchisee also pays the franchisor a continuing *royalty fee*. This is usually calculated as a percentage of the business's gross sales, somewhere in the range of 3 to 8 percent. It is important to understand the significance of the royalty fee being calculated on gross sales rather than on a net figure or a flat-fee basis, such as $500 per month. Calculating the royalty on gross sales means that the percentage is measured on every dollar that comes in the door. Gross sales are those that are made by the business before any expenses, salaries, rent or other overhead is paid. They have nothing to do with the profitability of the business or with the net income

that the owner might take home. Naturally, the franchisor wants to see the gross sales of the franchise maximized, since this increases the level of royalties paid. However, the franchisee, like any business owner, wants to maximize profitability. The franchisor does not have a direct interest in seeing that the business is run efficiently or profitably. The cold reality is that the franchisor will be paid the royalty whether or not the business is profitable for the franchisee.

Finally, most franchisees pay *advertising fund contributions*. Many franchisors organize franchise owners in a particular market or region and have them pool their advertising money for coordinated expenditures that benefit all stores operating under the system trademarks. This fee is usually within a range of 1 to 4 percent of gross sales.

If those are all the fees paid to the franchisor, the rest of the business expenses must be assumed by the franchise owner, as with any other form of business. At the same time, the revenues from the business belong to the franchisee.

In business terms, then, a franchise is a form of joint venture, with the neophyte paying the experienced company for the right to conduct a business using all the techniques that made the experienced company successful. The franchisor has its arm around the shoulders of the franchisee, training and assisting, and showing exactly how to run the business. A good franchisor is a patient mentor, a relentless teacher and a demanding partner.

With such a robust market of franchisors, you can expect to find brand-new sparkling programs, fading giants, troubled systems with rebellious franchise owners, systems on the way up and systems crumbling under the weight of competition.

Be on the lookout for fad franchises that sound snazzy but probably won't be around long enough for you to get any return on your investment. My all-time favorite is the freestanding bungee-jump tower franchise of a few years ago; a close second is the corrugated cardboard coffin dealerships spotted at a franchise trade show in the late 1980s. Other fads might include laser tag games and low-carb stores. Also look out for businesses that may be eclipsed by fundamental changes in equipment or the marketplace. How would you like to have a franchise for the best typewriter repair shop in town? The internet is profoundly changing lots of businesses, such as travel agencies. Don't get stuck with a buggy-whip franchise. So before you invest in such a company, you owe it to yourself to do the research, just as you would before buying stock in a publicly traded corporation.

The underlying message here should be clear: You can get hurt financially if you invest in the wrong franchise.

THE ALL-AMERICAN HARD SELL

One feature of a robust franchise marketplace is that franchisors are under extreme pressure to make the franchise sale. They have invested heavily in their program (it takes a chunk of change to pull together the business organization and meet the legal requirements), and the sales process itself is difficult and time-consuming. The cost of the sale (representative's salary, trade show costs, advertising, promotional materials, etc.) can also be substantial. The result is often the all-American hard sell: sales representatives pressing too hard to move a vaguely interested prospect to make a commitment, selling a franchise to anyone with a heartbeat, and making untenable promises or inappropriate representations

about the financial potential of the business. Many franchisor sales specialists will employ crude closing techniques that would make a used car salesman proud.

Never allow yourself to be stampeded into making a franchise investment decision because of urgencies created by the sales representative. "Buy today before the price increase"; "Territories are going fast. Get in on this or the prime markets will be taken"; and "We only have a couple territories left" are just some of the claims you might hear. In all likelihood, these statements are entirely false. If you could see behind the curtain, you would understand that the salesman is scrambling to make his sales numbers, probably paid on straight commission and having a devil of a time closing on his leads. He wants to close you on his schedule, not yours.

INsight

Many franchise sales representatives are paid a large portion of their salary on commission, and will sometimes bring an overenthusiasm to their work that gets them in trouble with their employers, and sometimes with consumer protection agencies or franchise regulators.

Your best defense is to anticipate this hard sell and use it to your advantage. Learn to hear and appreciate a closing technique for what it is—a salesperson working hard to move you to commitment. Know that many franchise organizations would love to have you buy into their business concept, but in front of the curtain, they're cool about their eagerness. The better companies want to make sure that there is a great match between their concept and their franchisees and want to spend time exploring that match with a prospective investor. Ask them what qualifications they look for in a franchisee and what strengths among franchisees have led to success in their business. By listening closely during the sales process, you will learn a lot about the business of franchising.

Here is a little-known secret in franchising: The buyer has an enormous amount of control and power in the sales process. Many franchisors make buyers feel unworthy or poorly qualified to own and operate the franchise. They portray themselves as powerful trademark owners who control all aspects of their business, and they require detailed information in order for prospects to qualify for the right to buy a franchise. However, prospective franchisees actually have the greater power, since they can choose to invest or move on to the next opportunity. Experienced franchisors are aware of this, but you wouldn't know it from the noise surrounding most franchise sales.

The business of franchising is not slow, sedate and welcoming. It is fast, exciting, a hard sell and sometimes intimidating to the uninitiated. But read on. By the time you finish this book, you won't qualify as uninitiated anymore.

SUMMARY NOTES

✓ A business format franchise is a continuing relationship in which the franchisee is granted rights to operate under the trademark, business format and techniques owned by the franchisor.

✓ As a franchisee you are an independent business owner, never an employee. That includes risk and reward, success and failure.

✓ Franchisors like to say that in a franchise, you are in business for yourself, not by yourself.

✓ Training is one key to a successful franchise program.

✓ Initial franchise fees, royalties and advertising fees define your money relationship with the franchisor.

✓ Franchising represents a huge marketplace, so it takes some research to find a solid program.

Action PLAN

Identify as many franchises in your immediate market as you can, and list them. Ask the managers if the business is a franchise and where you can learn more about the program. Look up the businesses on the internet, and send away for franchise information of those business concepts you like.

CHAPTER 4

Buying Multiple Franchise Rights

*G*EORGE HAS THE HIGHEST CAREER *ambition of anyone in his family. He longs for a life of wealth and is determined to get there. Business ownership appeals to him, and he understands that most millionaires in the U.S. own their own businesses. He is interested in buying a franchised business but is already looking down the road to his second, fifth and 10th businesses. George never has done anything on a small scale.*

Investors like George and many franchise owners understand the real path to substantial personal wealth is ownership of multiple businesses. Many ultrasuccessful franchisees establish a profitable franchised operation and then go on to develop or buy a dozen other franchised businesses. Before they know it, they have built an empire.

Multiple franchise development is a challenging part of the franchising business and varies from one company to the next. Is it possible to purchase the right to develop an entire state or region of the country? Do you need to be a sub-franchisor or master franchisee for a region, or is there another way? What legal rights are granted for multiple franchise ownership? What if you want to purchase only two or three additional units?

TYPES OF MULTIUNIT FRANCHISE PROGRAMS

Let's start with a look at some of the basic concepts of multiple franchising.

Multiple Unit Ownership

This is when the same individual is granted franchise rights at more than one location. Most franchisors encourage multiple unit ownership once franchisees show they are capable of operating a successful business. Everybody wins under this arrangement. Franchisees expand their business one step at a time, as their resources grow. The franchisor enhances its relationship with successful franchise owners, rewarding those who prove themselves successful. The franchisor does not have the costs and risks associated with recruiting a new franchisee into the system. No special legal rights are created for multiple unit ownership. The franchisor simply grants standard unit franchise rights for newly identified locations or markets. Some companies will grant a right of first refusal, which says essentially, "We will give you the first shot at another franchise in this market if we want to grant one." Once George has established one territory, he requests the rights to another across town, and the franchisor decides to grant him a unit franchise agreement exactly like that of his first franchise. A year later he may want to go for a third.

Ask the sales representative what kind of multiple unit franchising the company has done in the past and what it offers now. You may find that a development agreement is included in the company's unit offering Uniform Franchise Offering Circular (UFOC). Other companies may have a separate UFOC for their multiple unit offering.

Area Franchise

Here the franchisor grants the franchisee, through a contract usually referred to as a development agreement, the right to develop a specified number of franchised units in a given territory. The development agreement details the time frame in which the units must be developed and opened for business, development quotas, the geographic area in which the franchisee has rights and the fee obligations that apply. This type of development agreement is essentially an option agreement with a development schedule; it grants the developer option rights to enter into contracts in the future.

Master Franchise

While not typically a low-cost option, a master franchise agreement involves the franchisor granting to a franchisee the limited right to recruit new franchisees and to provide specified field support services to franchisees in a given area. In exchange, the master franchisee receives a commission on franchise sales made and a percentage of the royalty revenues generated among the franchisees it serves. George's franchisor appoints him to serve as a master franchisee in Texas. He runs advertising to generate interested investors in Texas and meets with all prospects who respond. Serious, qualified investors are sent to the franchisor's headquarters, where the sale is closed. George has a regular schedule for visiting all 19 Texas franchises twice a year and runs three regional meetings each year. In return, George receives 35 percent of the initial franchise fees of sales made through his efforts and 25 percent of all royalties paid by Texas franchisees.

Subfranchising

Under a subfranchising arrangement, the franchisor grants to another entity (a subfranchisor) the right to enter into unit franchise agreements with subfranchisees in a specified area. The franchisor usually dictates the terms on which unit franchises are granted. As a subfranchisor, George has near complete autonomy in the franchise sales process. He actually grants franchises, provides training and field support and has the right to collect royalties and advertising contributions. George must pay to the franchisor 45 percent of all franchise revenue.

The most common of these types of multiple-unit programs is the area franchise. If an investor wants to secure the right to develop a large number of franchises in a favorite market, they should consider negotiating for a development agreement. A development agreement has the advantage of being relatively straightforward conceptually. It balances the aggression of the large developer with the franchisor's need to make sure that a designated market is fully developed in a timely manner.

The least common type of multiple-unit program is subfranchising. True subfranchising is relatively rare in the world of franchising.

PROTECTING YOUR DEVELOPMENT INVESTMENT

In order to balance these interests and risks financially, the developer usually pays upfront a substantial portion of the initial franchise fees of the units to be developed. Look at a quick example. Our ambitious George signs a development agreement and receives the right to develop six territories in Salt Lake City over 10 years. He pays a nonrefundable, upfront development fee of $60,000, which represents half of the $20,000 per-store initial franchise fee for the six units. The development agreement promises that George will have exclusive rights to develop Salt Lake City for the next decade. He signs six standard unit franchise agreements within his development period and achieves his financial ambition. If George defaults under the development agreement and slips off the development schedule agreed upon, he may forfeit the unallocated portion of the upfront $60,000.

Clearly, multiple franchise development occurs at the higher financial end of franchising. It can be extremely expensive to secure the rights to multiple franchises, and the legal rights granted can be quite complicated.

If you are presented with an opportunity to purchase the rights to multiple franchises, be sure to take the program to your attorney for a detailed review of your rights and obligations. Developers, especially those who are inexperienced in the business being franchised or who are not well capitalized, can put a significant investment at risk by signing onto an aggressive development schedule. When negotiating the terms of development, it is vital that the build-out schedule is reasonable and that the exchange of fees is properly weighted for the risks being taken by both sides.

SUMMARY NOTES
- ✓ There are several ways that multiple-franchise rights are granted.
- ✓ Development fees may be paid upfront, so it is important to protect the investment by carefully negotiating your legal rights.

Action **PLAN**

Read a development contract for a complete understanding of its dynamics. Sketch out a business plan and projection of the money that might be required to develop an entire market.

CHAPTER 5

How the Government Protects You

*J*IM THOUGHT HE WAS BEING HUSTLED. *The franchisor had not delivered any information about its program, and he was being pressured to sign a 40-page contract by the end of the week before it was offered to "the next person in line for the territory." It didn't feel right. Jim wondered, "Isn't there a body of franchise law that protects the little guy?"*

Given the early franchise success of companies like Holiday Inn and McDonald's and the sizzle that became associated with anything franchised ("Get in now—this is the next McDonald's!"), problems in the marketplace were perhaps inevitable.

In the 1970s, a number of fraudulent operators sold empty franchise opportunities that were all sizzle and no steak. Many people lost money investing in "can't lose" franchise propositions, and their shocking stories were told in the press. It wasn't long before state and federal regulators moved in. A dozen states and the FTC defined the franchise business concept in

statutes and imposed a strict set of rules for franchising, based in large part on state and federal securities regulation. The rules are designed to counter the tendency in franchising to over-hype the opportunity and to provide the prospective franchisee investor with key information on which to base a purchase decision. A number of states have also adopted regulations designed to protect franchise owners from the arbitrary termination of their rights.

The franchise laws require that the seller register the offering with state authorities and provide presale disclosure of material information to prospective investors.

Franchise regulation has a huge influence on how franchising is practiced. The following is a discussion of these rules of the franchise road.

HOW THE LAW DEFINES A FRANCHISE

How is a franchise defined under franchise laws? Ready for a little law school action? The law regulates a franchise transaction when three distinct elements are present:

1. The franchisor licenses the right to use its trademark in the operation of the business;
2. The franchisor prescribes in substantial part a marketing plan or provides significant assistance or control over the franchisee's business (some state definitions look for a "community of interest" between the franchisor and the franchisee); and
3. The franchisee is required to pay, directly or indirectly, a fee for the right to participate in the franchise program.

If one of these elements is missing, whatever the business transaction is, it is not regulated as a business franchise. In many circumstances the investment is then regulated as that close cousin, the "business opportunity."

 INsight

As a prospective franchisee, you should have little concern about complying with the franchise investment laws. They impose no obligations on you. But recognizing a franchise when you see one could be an important asset in protecting yourself. If you see a franchise but someone tells you it is not one, ask why not, and listen carefully! You may want to share your notes with your attorney or the enforcement authorities in your state.

It is quite possible to invest in a business program that enables you to start a business that is not a franchise. There are dozens and dozens of such programs available. You can spend a couple thousand dollars and receive a package of materials designed to teach you how to make money with a new business application of your computer. You are not granted the right to use a trademark, and you are expected to operate under your own name. It may be a business opportunity, but it is not a franchise.

THE CONSEQUENCES OF BEING A FRANCHISE

What if a transaction meets the franchise definition? Then there are three consequences:

1. ***Presale disclosure must be delivered.*** Under the FTC's Trade Regulation Rule on Franchising, if a franchise is offered anywhere in the U.S., a franchisor must deliver a disclosure document to a prospective franchisee, using either the FTC's format or the Uniform Franchise Offering Circular (UFOC) format. The franchisor does not have to register or file anything with the FTC; complying with the disclosure requirements satisfies the requirements of the federal rule.

   The UFOC is a gold mine of information for the franchise investor. Ask for one early; it will help you evaluate the offering.

   When must the UFOC be delivered to the prospective franchisee? Either 1) at the first face-to-face personal meeting for the purpose of discussing the franchise sale, or 2) at least 10 business days (14 calendar days in Illinois) before money is paid for the franchise or a binding franchise agreement is signed by the franchisee, whichever comes first. That means that the franchisor is not required by law to deliver a UFOC until fairly far along in the sales process. Talking to a franchisor representative at a trade show exhibitor's booth is not considered to be a "first personal meeting" that would trigger disclosure obligations, even though it is "face to face." The disclosure obligation will trigger if the meeting is a detailed, extended discussion about the franchise opportunity.

2. ***The offering must comply with state law.*** Fourteen states (California, Hawaii, Illinois, Indiana, Maryland, Michigan, Minnesota, New York, North Dakota, Rhode Island, South Dakota, Virginia, Washington and Wisconsin) require franchisors to file or register with the state officials prior to any offering activity taking place. The franchisor will submit its UFOC, adapted to meet the particular requirements of each state, along with an application form and the appropriate fees. State franchise examiners review the disclosure document to assure that it is complete. They do not determine if the offer is reasonable or exercise any judgment regarding whether it is a good deal, or fair. They only make sure that the franchisor has complied with the UFOC guidelines.

When approved, the franchisor is authorized to sell franchises and must renew the registration at the end of the registration period. Some states will grant a registration period of a full calendar year; others such as California and Hawaii will automatically end the registration period a certain number of days after the end of the franchisor's fiscal year. That means a company with a fiscal year ending on December 31 remains registered in Hawaii until March 31 and in California until April 20.

3. ***Relationship laws may apply.*** A transaction meeting the franchise definition may also fall under the protections of the various state franchise relationship laws. These generally prohibit termination and nonrenewal of a franchise in the absence of "good cause."

So what does this mean for investors? Franchise investors receive a generous amount of valuable information in the disclosure document. If the franchisee is in one of the 14 registration states, it means that the franchisor has gone through the process of document review by state examiners and achieved registration, clearing an important hurdle in the life of a franchisor. It is not easy to become registered in these states, although some are tougher than others.

Registration is no guarantee for the investor, of course. It does not tell you anything about the company, and it is not a qualifier in any sense. It simply means that the company has taken an important step to comply with the law. It has filed its offering on the public record in that state and will remain under the annual scrutiny of the state officials.

If you live in one of the registration states, you should plan to call the appropriate agency (see Appendix A) and confirm that the company is currently registered to offer and sell franchises.

SUMMARY NOTES

✓ If a business meets the legal definition of a franchise, it will be regulated as a franchise.

✓ The consequences of meeting the franchise definition include disclosure, registration in a number of states, and possible application of relationship laws.

✓ Registration under a state law is no guarantee of anything.

Action **PLAN**

Call the appropriate agencies to find out how franchising is regulated in your state. Keep addresses and phone numbers for key state officials on file so you can contact them later with specific questions.

Are You Suited to Be a Franchisee?

*B*ILL WAS EAGER TO GET INTO A GOOD BUSINESS *and happened to read about a franchise that was offering the opportunity to run an interesting tech-related business. But buying a franchise meant every aspect of the operation was dictated by the terms of an operating manual. He had always wanted to own a business in which he could express his own creativity and offbeat sense of humor. Looking at the detailed operational requirements, he now wondered whether he really was cut out to be a franchisee.*

IS A FRANCHISE FOR EVERYONE?

Clearly, owning a franchise is not for everyone. A capable person in the wrong program is not likely to stay happy for very long. Buying into a franchise is especially risky, since the investment can involve your life's savings and a long-term legal commitment.

Fiercely independent entrepreneurs are rarely happy in the franchise harness. If you are interested in running and designing every aspect of the operation, think twice before you buy that franchise. You might actually be better off with your own independent business. Most franchising programs impose a strict regimen on franchise owners, dictating everything from how to greet customers to how to prepare and present the product or service, and many people find the restrictions far too confining. They might be better off choosing a business opportunity program that offers more independence.

If you have been a secure employee of a large corporation for a long time, the jolt of making the transition to small-business ownership can be difficult. Franchise owners have to put themselves completely into the daily operation of the business; small-business owners do not delegate. They do whatever needs to be done. Remember the old line: You can always identify the owner of a small business—he or she is the one sweeping up after 6 p.m.

Nevertheless, there are many downsized middle managers bringing a wealth of business savvy to the franchise market. They are at that stage in their careers where they have some capital to invest, are not interested in inventing a new (and risky) business concept, and yet are attracted to the dream of self-employment. For them, franchising may be the ticket.

QUESTIONS TO CONSIDER

A careful approach to deciding whether or not owning a franchise is for you starts with a self-examination and a brief planning exercise. Consider the following key questions:

- *Are you motivated to invest the time and energy—not to mention money—necessary for small-business ownership?* The first year of business can be especially trying; the time required to get a business up and running—even a sophisticated franchise—is intimidating. Your days of punching and watching the clock will be long gone. Small-business ownership requires a sea change in your mental attitudes toward work, and a new level of dedication and perseverance.

- *Is your family behind you?* Many businesses are designed for total family involvement. Even if you invest in one that is not, you cannot commit the time and energy needed without the full support of every member of your family. Have you discussed it in detail with them? Your spouse may be supportive but skeptical (which is healthy). Involve them in the decision-making process, and listen to all their doubts or concerns. Try to help your kids understand that they are part of the whole family effort. You may also want to seek out experienced businesspeople you know who can help make sure you are thinking straight and not just daydreaming. Ask them to serve on your informal board of advisors so you can turn to them with questions.

- *Have you evaluated your resources?* Take out a pad of paper and jot down all possible sources of investment capital. Include not only cash, securities and other liquid assets, but also insurance policies, the equity in your home and retirement funds. Don't forget what the bankers refer to as NAR and NAF ("nail a relative" and "nail a friend"): Your well-heeled friends and relatives could make all the difference, especially if you need a cosignature or additional equity pledged as security when applying for financing. If your dear Aunt Edna once said she would back you in a business venture, now is the time to go see her.

Consider that you may need to maintain a revenue stream while the new business is being established. Your spouse may want to land a job to make ends meet until your franchise is kicking out a salary, which may take a while. Talk to a banker and an accountant. Discuss what you are planning, and ask about sources of capital, loans, investors and angels.

- *Have you evaluated your dreams?* Dreams provide the courage and drive that new entrepreneurs need to make the leap of faith into business ownership. But you must transform your dreams into an action plan. If you dream of being wealthy and living in a million-dollar home, turn your attention to the steps it will take to get there. If you start with owning a service business, research how much money such a business is likely to put in your pocket, and then determine how many of those businesses and how much time you will need to achieve your dream of a million-dollar house. Use dollars in your calculations, and add time frames. Anticipate milestones along the path, and work back to where you are today. Make notes about what you need to accomplish to make it successfully to the next milestone, and before you know it you will have created what looks to others like a business plan, but to you is nothing more than your dream path.

- ***Are you ready for the physical challenge?*** This question surprises a lot of people. Depending, of course, on the type of business you get involved in, business ownership can be physically demanding. Your sleep patterns may change, and you may be on your feet for 12 hours or more a day. Daily frustrations and the heightened stress of responding to unfamiliar challenges will draw on your deepest energy resources. You will need physical stamina

and a healthy, positive mental outlook. We strongly recommend that as part of your preparation for owning a business, you step up your exercise and stick to to a healthy diet. You will need every ounce of energy your personal fitness can deliver.

SUMMARY NOTES

✓ Owning a franchise is not for everyone. Strong-willed entrepreneurs who want to do things their own way may be unhappy owning a franchise.

✓ Before buying a franchise, consider the level of your motivation, how your family feels about the idea, your resources, how realistic your plans are and whether you are ready for the physical challenge.

Action **PLAN**

Write out complete responses to the questions in this chapter (be honest here; no one else will see your answers), and file them in your business planning folder.

CHAPTER 7

Attending a Franchise Trade Show

*J*ENNIFER HAD NEVER BEEN TO A FRANCHISE *trade show before, but she was told it is a great place to get started in business and learn a bit about franchising and other packaged business programs. She had no plan or goals for the show, but she wanted to cruise through. However, she was overwhelmed by the atmosphere. "I got so wrapped up in the games and cookies offered at one booth, I never saw most of the exhibitors. Maybe I'll go again when it comes through town next year."*

Attending a franchise trade show is the quickest, most enlightening way to search for the franchise program that best suits your needs. It can also be fun.

However, it helps to understand what you can expect at the show and to go with a plan. As many as 300 companies may be standing at their booths ready to talk to investors about their programs. Up to 10,000 people could pass through the convention center, each exploring the idea of buying a franchise as the ticket to business success. The effect can be dazzling: so

many concepts to evaluate and hardly enough time to see them all!

Of course, many of the investors attending the show, like Jennifer, are there out of curiosity and will have no focused plan. They may be lost in the crowd and have no clue as to how to get the most out of the show. We recommend that you be different.

PREPARE FOR THE SHOW

The first step in setting yourself apart from the crowd is to prepare and set goals for the session. Decide what types of businesses interest you. Are you fascinated by automobiles and interested in a business that is part of that industry? Do you want a high-end consumer products business that brings you into direct contact with your customers? What are your financial resources? Would a lower-level investment be better, perhaps a business you can operate from home? Giving some thought to these questions will allow you to focus your time at the show on programs that fit your needs.

It's a good idea to leave your usual funky weekend attire at home and dress conservatively. Your goal is to show franchisor representatives that you are there for business. A casual business look is fine; a suit is optional, but be sure you look sharp. If possible, leave the kids at home and take personal business cards if you have them. If you don't, consider having some printed up. They are inexpensive, project a business-like impression, and relieve you of having to dictate your name, address and telephone number over and over. Don't forget your briefcase for the papers you collect, and take paper and pen for taking notes. You are not there just to pass a few idle hours and eat the free cookies. Show the representatives you meet that you are a serious prospect and there to consider their business program.

HOW TO DEVELOP AN EFFECTIVE METHOD OF ATTENDING

Plan to arrive early in the morning on one of the first days of the show. The typical franchise show lasts for three days, from Friday to Sunday. By Sunday, everyone is tired and spent, so try to be there on Friday (typically the least crowded day) or early Saturday (the most crowded day). This is when everyone involved should be fresh, with anticipation running high.

When you arrive at the convention center to register, take a few minutes with the show brochure to understand the floor layout, and review the list of companies that are exhibiting. Find a quiet corner with a cup of coffee and read what the show offers. Mark those companies whose offerings appeal to you and seem to fit your needs and financial resources. As you stop by their booths during the day, you can check them off and make sure you are covering all the promising companies on your list.

It is important to understand why the exhibitors are there. They consider the show a success if they collect the names of several serious, qualified candidates and come away with a list of leads for follow-up calls. We are told by franchisors that if they sell one or two franchises as the result of a trade show, they can cover all their exhibiting costs and make a profit. To get that list of hot leads, they have to make about 1,000 contacts a day.

Many franchise shows schedule seminars for investors on subjects like "How to Buy a Franchise" and "Financing Your Franchise Purchase." Mark the ones that look interesting, and schedule time to attend them. This may be the most valuable part of your day at the trade show, especially if you actually purchase a business package.

Try to approach the exhibit floor methodically. The franchise investment possibilities are virtually endless, and you may feel overwhelmed if you do not remember the interests you identified before attending the show. Stick to your plan, and find as many of the exhibitors you marked off earlier in the day as you can.

It is easy to underestimate the time needed to meet with all the interesting exhibitors on your list. You might spend as much as five or 10 minutes with each exhibitor and discover in a couple of hours that you have met with only 10 or 15 companies, a mere fraction of those on your list.

THE RIGHT QUESTIONS

The secret is not to spend time with exhibitors whose programs are inappropriate for you or out of your financial reach. Prepare three "knock-out" questions that will allow you to eliminate those companies quickly and move on to more promising conversations. What are those questions? That depends on you and your circumstances. If you have limited resources (and who doesn't?), try "What are the minimum financial qualifications for your applicants?" or "What kind of business experience do you require?" and "Are you looking for franchisees in my town?" The franchisor's answers will tell you quickly whether their program is within your reach. If it seems to be, stay and find out more. If there is no fit, move on.

If you want to find out more about a particular franchisor, here are a few more good queries to generate useful conversation:

- *How would you describe the culture in your franchise/business opportunity system?* This wonderfully open-ended probe should draw a variety of responses. Every franchise system has a cultural character. Is it clubby, friendly, chilly, all business or distant? Listen carefully to the answer. You will pick up some good information that does not appear in any glossy brochures.
- *What are your plans for growth in this region over the next three years?* The answer to this question will give you an idea of the effort and energy that the organization has committed to your market. If you get a vague answer or a grandiose statement suggesting that the company expects to take over the retail world in that modest time period, well, you've been forewarned.
- *May I take a complete set of promotional materials?* Many exhibitors will have a limited supply of full brochures behind the table and less expensive fliers out front for the hundreds of casual visitors who stop by. Express serious interest in the investment, and ask if there are other materials

you can study at home. Request a copy of the company's Uniform Franchise Offering Circular. If it is not readily available, ask if the company can send you one, along with a set of promotional materials and an application package.

- *Tell me about your training program.* Find out how long it is (i.e., two weeks at the company headquarters and 10 days in the field), where it takes place and the general subjects covered. Look for a well-organized plan that combines classroom time with field orientation. A solid training program is the mark of a careful franchisor who is interested in the business success of its franchise owners.
- *Tell me about your franchisee support program.* Good support from a franchisor can spell the difference between failure and success. Look for support from the very beginning, as soon as you start to write a business plan. Will the company help you find financing? Will people be available when you are opening for business? Will someone be at the other end of the phone when things get crazy?

A question you might expect to be on this list, but that isn't, is "How much money can I expect to make with one of your businesses?" This is a difficult question for a franchisor to answer. Most would like to boast about the potential of their franchise, but it is a subject that is closely regulated under the franchise laws. In addition, no franchisor knows how much you can expect to make in a franchised business. The variables—including your business acumen and industry—make such estimates impossible.

Slinging numbers at a trade show would be a misleading and unfair inducement by the seller to get you to purchase the franchise. Franchisors generally do know how their existing franchise owners have performed, and some companies will make this information available in the disclosure document. Our best advice: Check it out for yourself. Go visit as many franchise owners as time and distances allow. Ask them how they have performed and whether, knowing what they now know, they would make the investment again. Their answers will be invaluable in your assessment of the franchise.

It is also important to understand that a franchise trade show event is designed to make an initial contact only. It is a meeting place that operates merely to introduce sellers to potential investors. The conversation on the floor of the trade show is preliminary and rarely delves deeply into the investment itself. The more in-depth discussion usually takes place in a follow-up meeting or sometimes in a nearby hospitality suite the seller has reserved. Leave behind one of your business cards so sellers may send you additional information. And make sure that you have contact information, either a contact listing in the program or the business card of the sales representative.

TRADE SHOW RED FLAGS

Risks abound in the search for a franchise. While at the trade show, keep alert to red flags that should tell you to avoid one company or another. Here are a few:

Shouting Performance Numbers

Dollar signs have no place at a franchise trade show. They can be the source of any number of legal problems for franchisors and should be avoided by well-disciplined companies. If per-

formance information is discussed, check out item 19 in the company's UFOC, which you will see sometime after the show. Any big talk about what you will earn should be a warning sign that this is not an experienced or well-disciplined representative. The talk may also be totally misleading.

The Hard Sell

A solid franchise investment should sell itself. If you find yourself at the receiving end of a hard sell, back slowly away.

The Startup Rookie

A franchising company with no track record presents risks that you should carefully evaluate. You may determine that the program is new enough and exciting enough that the potential for success outweighs the risks, but protect yourself as best you can. A new franchisor cannot offer the most attractive features of the franchise concept: a business that has been proven in the marketplace and experience that can help you handle the challenges of the business.

The Franchise Fad

Fads come and go in the franchise community. Remember that your investment needs to survive for the long term. Look out for concepts that are the flavor of the month but may have little staying power.

The Poorly Financed Franchisor

Most franchise financial advisors will tell you that one of the most common business mistakes made in this field is for the franchisor not to have enough capital to finance its rapid growth. The resulting under-financed company is weak and may not be in a position to deliver on its promises to new franchisees. The best measure of the franchisor's financial standing is its audited financial statements, which you will find as part of the UFOC.

THE FOLLOW-UP

Expect a follow-up call or visit after the show from any company where you showed serious interest. Remember, the companies that prepared and staffed a booth invested heavily in finding you—a qualified and interested investor. The follow-up is your opportunity to dig into the investment and explore every question that might occur to you. Be diligent and skeptical in your evaluation of the information you collect from the franchisor.

A franchise trade show may be your first step toward an exciting new business future. Increase the odds of your personal success by preparing carefully for the show and evaluating the opportunities presented with a detailed—and realistic—eye.

SUMMARY NOTES ———————

✓ A franchise trade show can be overwhelming if you are not prepared for it.

✓ Prepare for the show with a battle plan.

✓ Ask the right questions on the floor. If there is no fit with your plan, quickly move on down the aisle.

✓ Look for the red flags.

✓ Follow up with your show contacts to confirm you are serious about finding the right franchise program.

 IN*sight*

Your follow-up call may not come from the person you met at the show, but from a staff representative at the company's headquarters or a regional office. Find out who you are talking to, and get a good idea of where they fit into the company's organization.

Action **PLAN**

Find out when a good franchise trade show is coming to a city near you. Try searching the internet for trade show cities and dates. (See the next chapter for ideas on using the internet.)

CHAPTER 8

Research on the Internet

*M*ARCIE WAS DETERMINED TO FIND a franchise that would allow her to work part time at home around her young children and bring in more money for the family. Getting out of the house was difficult with the kids. She heard that a franchise show was coming to the downtown arena in a few weeks, and she wanted to find out a lot more about the whole concept of a home business. Marcie was a new internet user but thought it would be a good place to start.

Enter the word "franchise" into any of the competent search engines on the internet, and you may feel a bit like Alice falling down the rabbit hole.

A Google search kicks up 149 million franchise listings; on Yahoo! 74.8 million. Head down any of these pathways, and you will quickly find yourself browsing through dozens of sites extolling the virtues of various franchises, touting association membership benefits and describing individual franchise investment benefits.

WHAT TO LOOK FOR

The internet is an essential tool in the search for the right franchise. It has its strengths and weaknesses, of course, but you cannot afford to overlook it. Its greatest strength is that it gives you the ability to browse for ideas and prospects. If you have leads you want to check out or if you are curious about a particular franchise, a quick search will provide at least brochure-level information about the program.

The law has been slow to catch up to the franchise regulation implications of electronic commerce on the internet. The FTC has promised to address the rules surrounding electronic distribution of the UFOC and the posting of disclosure information on a website, but the rules are not yet final. Under current law, with rare exception, a franchisor may not comply with disclosure requirements by delivering a document in electronic form. This may change as early as 2005. Some states have issued regulations telling franchisors what disclaimers they must put on their sites, and you will find them in the small print of well-managed sites. In essence, the disclaimer says that the information on the site does not constitute an offer in franchise registration states. Seeing this disclaimer conveys to the experienced eye a subtle but important message: The company is receiving, and paying attention to, informed legal advice. You should wonder about franchise company sites that do not have this legal disclaimer.

INsight

The hype level tells you something about franchising sales. This is a market that enjoys a robust level of aggressive selling.

HANDLING THE HIGH HYPE-TO-FACT RATIO

The internet's weakness is the low quality and reliability of the information at its busy commercial locations. Lists of available "franchises" are littered with nonfranchised business opportunity offerings, and much of the information you see is essentially sponsored advertising. If you understand this inescapable feature of the internet and make allowances for it, you will not be misled.

THE IMPORTANCE OF FOCUS

The FTC has assembled a surprisingly useful site for franchise investors (www.ftc.gov). Here you will find general information about franchising, the federal laws that apply to a franchise sale, and current and recent investigations and legal actions taken by the FTC against offending franchisors.

Also, www.entrepreneur.com/franchise offers a site specifically for franchise seekers—it includes franchise listings and in-depth articles. Another information-packed site is www.franchise.org, the site of the International Franchise Association.

These are just a start. The problem with the internet, of course, is the sensation of trying to take a sip from a fire hose of information. The sites dedicated to franchising go on and on and may cause even an experienced internet researcher to suffer from MEGO (my eyes glaze over) in no time.

The secret to effective use of the internet for your franchise search is the same as with other kinds of franchise research: focus, focus, focus. Know your targets and general interest areas. Don't be distracted by the glitter, the pop-up ads, the eager virtual experts. Plan to use your computer connection for first-level contact and brochure-level information. Then roll up your sleeves and plan for person-to-person meetings and in-depth discussions about the franchise opportunity.

SUMMARY NOTES

✓ Use the internet judiciously. There is a high hype-to-fact ratio at most information sites.

✓ The internet is great for brochure-level information.

✓ Focus your search to your areas of interest.

Action PLAN

Spend some time on the internet and bookmark the sites that seem most helpful.

CHAPTER 9

Organizing the Information You Gather

ﾉL WAS NOT WELL-ORGANIZED IN HIS *work life, but then again he never had a job that required great organizational skills. However, now on the verge of quitting his job to find a franchise, he had started gathering information from a couple dozen companies. The amount of paper generated in his search surprised him, and it had formed a few messy piles on the floor of his bedroom. Now he was going to a trade show and dreaded the prospect of taking more paper home to his piles. Maybe this wasn't for him.*

The franchise search process can generate a lot of paper, and you will quickly become discouraged if you do not prepare to receive and keep it in an organized fashion. This is particularly true if you attend franchise trade shows, which are notorious for generating piles of promotional pieces of paper. (And you wondered why they handed you that big plastic bag with handles when you walked in!) You may also receive a stack of promotional materials when you write to franchisors for information.

 INsight

From the company's point of view, distributing glossy brochures is a cost of being a franchisor, and it can be quite expensive. More and more franchisors are putting their brochure money into website presentations. You may find that the quality of the brochures you receive will be modest, but the websites will be eye-popping.

SETTING UP A FILING SYSTEM

So get prepared before you go. Set up a few files, one for each seller with internal tabs or manila folders for different subjects. Take a quick trip to an office supply store, and buy a few packets of file folders, pocket files and tab labels.

Divide each seller's file into subsections, such as:

- **Promotional pieces.** Drop into this folder all the glossy brochures, fliers, handouts and form letters you pick up.

- *Letters, notes, contact information.* Take notes on each of the companies you visit at the trade show or elsewhere, and keep all the personalized letters they send you as well as copies of any letters you write. Staple into the file—or slide into a plastic sleeve—all the sales representatives' business cards you are handed.

- *UFOC.* After you read and mark up the UFOC with any questions or comments, drop it in the file for future use. If the franchisor is a serious prospect, you will want to take this document to your attorney and accountant. It is amazing how many people buy a franchise yet never read the UFOC. You must take the time to look through this important document. If you get serious about a program, take the documents to your attorney and your CPA for review.

- *Contracts.* Form contracts will be included in the UFOC, but other versions will be provided to you as you approach closing.

- *Site information, lease forms.* As you meet with landlords to review available sites for the business you have in mind, keep the information in its own section of your file.

With these files prepared ahead of time, you will be able to quickly file all the paperwork you bring home and have it easily accessible for follow-up reading.

Retain all your files until you have actually made a choice and invested in a franchise. Only then should you sort through them, keeping in your permanent records all of the documents relating to the business you purchase or remain interested in, and discarding the rest.

SUMMARY NOTES

✓ Prepare to organize informational materials before the franchise search begins.

✓ Set up labeled file folders so that you can file your papers when you get home from a trade show or other franchise or business opportunity

---

Action **PLAN**

Head to the supply store for the materials you will need to organize your franchise search files.

CHAPTER 10

Understanding the UFOC

ROBIN INQUIRED ABOUT A FRANCHISE *program and received a heavy spiral-bound book in the mail. It was at least an inch and a half thick! She did not know what it was or why they sent it. She flipped through it but did not expect to spend the time it would take to read it all.*

WHAT IS A UFOC?

Robin didn't know it yet, but what she had was the franchisee's bible: the Uniform Franchise Offering Circular, or UFOC.

Like Robin, all prospective franchisees receive detailed and extensive information about the franchisor, the franchise being offered and the franchise system. This gives you a distinct advantage over other investors. It contains sample forms of every contract you will be asked to sign as well as a set of audited financial statements for the franchisor. In franchise circles, the UFOC is also referred to as a "franchise disclosure document" or an "offering prospectus."

The UFOC format and presentation is prescribed by state and federal law and is designed to deliver key information about the franchise investment. In it you will find 23 different items of information that are all important to your investment decision. If there is one piece of advice you take, it should be to read the UFOC carefully. Sure, it may read like an insurance policy in places, but it is a treasure trove of details for the alert investor. The good news is, all UFOC documents must be written in "plain English"—no Latin phrases, no "hereinafters," no "wherein-befores" and no run-on sentences that only a lawyer could love. At least, that's the theory.

Does everyone get a UFOC? As a practical matter, franchisors do not deliver a UFOC to everyone who applies for a franchise. The typical UFOC runs from 75 to 350 pages in length and can be expensive to reproduce in large numbers. Expect to receive a copy as you progress through the evaluation process or if you visit the company's headquarters for a "first personal meeting," which will trigger the legal requirement that you receive a UFOC.

The best approach is to request a UFOC early in your discussions. If you are at all serious about a particular franchise, it makes no sense to spend time on it until you have a chance to read the UFOC.

INsight

Put yourself in the franchisor's shoes. You want to deliver a UFOC only to candidates who have been qualified and appear serious about the investment because each copy costs several dollars to reproduce. Let them know you are serious about their program and are genuinely interested in the information contained in their UFOC, and you increase your chances of receiving one early in the process.

THE SECTIONS OF THE UFOC

How do you read and comprehend a UFOC? Some sections are more important than others, but all are worth your attention.

Here is a short rundown of what to look for, section by section.

The Cover Page

This page shows the franchise logo. It also has a summary of the initial franchise fees and the total investment, followed by "Risk Factors" in all capitals. Most of the risk factors are boilerplate and address whether the franchise agreement requires the franchisee to litigate or arbitrate outside of the franchisee's home state. They also caution if the franchisor has little or no experience in business or in franchising. Make a note to discuss any such risk factor with your attorney.

Item 1: The Franchisor, Its Predecessors and Affiliates

This is a concise overview of the franchisor, its formal corporate name and state of incorporation, and its background, business experience, predecessors and affiliates. It tells you how long the company has been offering franchises and gives a general description of the franchisee's potential competition. Read the franchisor's business record carefully.

Item 2: Business Experience

This section gives you a bare-bones five-year outline of the business experience of the franchisor's key executives. It's just the facts: title, employer, dates of employment and city. Note if there are any gaps in the employment history (such as might be created by some time out of work).

Item 3: Litigation

This section requires the franchisor to reveal details about specific types of litigation that may be "material" (important) to prospective franchisees. If in the past 10 years the company itself or any of its directors or officers listed in Item 2 have been defendants in cases involving claims of franchise law, securities law, fraud, unfair or deceptive trade practices or comparable allegations, you will see it described here. You will also see arbitration actions listed in this section.

Don't be alarmed if there are one or two cases disclosed here. It is a rare franchisor, or one that has not been in the franchising business long, that has no litigation to disclose in Item 3. In this great country anyone can file a lawsuit alleging anything, so the cases disclosed may not convey the right impression of the company or its dispute resolution style. On the other hand, an Item 3 that discloses many cases may tell you a lot about the company. The best approach is to make a note to discuss with your own attorney and your franchisor representative any questions you have about disclosures in this item. You may also want to ask any existing franchisees you interview about the company's litigation history. They can probably shed light on what the company's litigation style means to franchisees.

Item 4: Bankruptcy

If there is a bankruptcy in the 10-year background of the franchisor, its predecessors, affiliates, partners or officers, you will see it briefly described in Item 4.

Item 5: Initial Franchise Fee

This section details all moneys paid to the franchisor prior to the time the franchisee opens for business. Typically, the franchisor imposes an initial franchise fee that is a lump sum payment—as much as $20,000, $30,000 or more— to be made at the time the franchise agreement is signed. Look for other fees, such as training fees, that may be included and the circumstances in which they might be refundable.

Item 6: Other Fees

The chart in Item 6 summarizes all the recurring or isolated fees that the franchisee must pay to the franchisor or its affiliates during the course of the franchise relationship. The royalty is listed, of course. The chart also includes any continuing advertising contributions to an advertising fund or otherwise, cooperative advertising organizations that charge advertising fees, transfer fees and audit costs.

Item 7: Initial Investment

This section of the UFOC is one of the most important for your planning purposes. In chart form, it summarizes the total initial expenses you can expect when opening the franchised business. It tells you what categories of expenses are typical, to whom payments are to be made, and when they are due. It also tells you whether payments are refundable under any circumstances. Use these figures when preparing your own business plan, but check with a good accountant and existing franchisees in the system to see if there are other expenses you should anticipate that are not included in Item 7. For instance, if you borrow a substantial portion of the investment, you will have debt service to anticipate that will not appear in this disclosure document. Consider this item as the starting point in your financial planning.

Item 8: Restrictions on Sources of Products and Services

The area of product sourcing is one of the most important aspects of franchise operations, but it is often well-hidden. Imagine that you are considering a franchise for an ice cream shop selling a premium ice cream manufactured especially for the franchise system. There is only one source of the product: the franchisor. You are required by the franchise agreement to purchase only from the designated source. Would you know whether $11.35 per tub is a reasonable price for ice cream inventory? What will you do if the franchisor raises its prices and cuts down your (already razor-thin) margins? Some franchisees feel trapped by a confining supply arrangement where they have no opportunity to seek out a competitive price. Supply arrangements are described in this item but may not paint the entire picture for you.

Item 9: Franchisee's Obligations

This item is nothing more than a cross-reference chart showing you where certain subjects are addressed in the franchise agreement.

Item 10: Financing

If the franchisor offers financing, either directly or indirectly, you will find it detailed here. It should lay out the terms of the financing in chart form and specify which portion of the purchase qualifies for the financing. Copies of any loan documents will be included as exhibits.

Item 11: Franchisor's Obligations

This provides a lengthy recital of the promises made by the franchisor, the services they will supply to you in the course of the franchise relationship, and details about some of the training and other programs offered. This is the longest section of the UFOC and it contains a wealth of information. Among the topics addressed are the pre-opening and post-opening services to be provided by the franchisor, the time that typically elapses between the date of signing the franchise agreement and opening the business, the specifications for any computerized cash registers or computers necessary in the business, and a detailed description of the training program.

Item 12: Territory

This is a description of any territorial rights granted as a part of the franchise agreement. It is fair to say that most, but not all, franchise systems include some form of territorial protection for the franchisee. The key point for the prospective franchisee is to read this section carefully and without the natural assumptions you may have of these intangible concepts. For instance, it may include a promise by the fran-chisor that says something like, "We will not develop ourselves or grant franchises to others to develop another franchise in your territory." Does this mean that you have absolute exclusivity in the territory? No. In fact, it is a rather narrow promise that prevents the establishment of competing units in your area but does not prevent the franchisor from selling product to customers in your territory. Ask your attorney to review the promises in this section so that you are clear on the nature of the rights you are receiving. They are important.

Item 13: Trademarks

It has been said that the trademark is the cornerstone of the franchise relationship. Item 13 provides some key details about the primary trademarks associated with the franchise package. First it tells you whether the trademark has been registered with the U.S. Patent and Trademark Office. While that registration is not necessary for a protectable trademark, it is an important step for the franchisor, and if it has not been done, it tells you and your attorney a lot. Having an unregistered mark may increase your risks that someone else with the same mark can claim superior legal rights and force you and the franchisor to find another trade name. If the franchisor has any litigation pending that pertains to the marks, it is described here, as are promises made by the franchisor to protect franchisees from claims of trademark infringement by third parties. Make sure that your attorney reviews Item 13 and advises you of any apparent problems.

Item 14: Patents, Copyrights and Proprietary Information

The majority of UFOCs contain boilerplate language in this section because so few franchise programs have patent rights that pertain to the franchise. The franchise operations manual and other printed advertising and operating materials are usually protected by copyright. There is also language in this section protecting the "trade secrets" and other "proprietary rights" of the franchisor in various aspects of the franchised business.

Item 15: Obligation to Participate in the Actual Operation of the Franchise Business

If the contract requires you to be present at the business for a certain number of hours each week, or to hire a trained manager who can supervise the operation at all times, that requirement should be disclosed here.

Item 16: Restrictions on What the Franchisee May Sell

If you will be required to sell only approved products, or only those supplied to you by approved suppliers, it will say so here.

Item 17: Renewal, Termination, Transfer and Dispute Resolution

This multipage chart provides the reader with a full cross-reference to the franchise agreement along with a summary of the key legal provisions relating to renewal (what happens at the end of the contract term), termination (the circumstances under which you and the franchisor may choose to end the contract before its expiration), transfer (the restrictions on your right to sell all or part of your franchised business) and dispute resolution (where and how legal disputes will be resolved). These topics are the most legally intense sections of the franchise agreement and deserve paerticularly careful review by your attorney.

Item 18: Public Figures

This section describes the terms of any endorsement or other involvement by a well-known figure who is promoting the franchise.

Item 19: Earnings Claims

This item may provide some of your most important clues to answering the question, "How much money does one of these babies make?" Franchisors are not required to supply any performance information about their program, but if they do, it must be disclosed here. Only about 20 percent of all UFOCs contain performance information. There could be a number of reasons for a company leaving this disclosure blank. It may be that they are concerned about potential misrepresentations and legal liability if they list performance figures for their existing franchisees. It may also be that the performance statistics do not tell a compelling story, and the company does not want to focus your attention on the low performance of its franchised businesses. If you do find performance information, be sure to use it when you prepare your business plan. Then supplement the bare statistics with franchisee interviews. If the company does not disclose anything, find out why, and press for performance information from other sources. Again, existing franchisees are the best place to start.

Item 20: List of Outlets

This section includes a series of charts about the growth or contraction of the franchise system for the prior three years as well as information about existing company-owned units and projected growth of the system during the coming year. There is an attached list of the names, addresses and telephone numbers of current franchisees, as well as a list of the names and the last-known addresses and telephone numbers of all franchisees who have left the system during the prior year or have not been in contact with the franchisor for at least 10 weeks. These lists are often attached as exhibits to the UFOC. Find out from these former franchise owners why they left and whether it was related to shortcomings in the program itself.

Item 21: Financial Statements

The law requires that a franchisor attach to the body of the UFOC as an exhibit a copy of its financial balance sheet and operating statements for the prior three years, all of which must be audited (or "certified") by a certified public accountant. If the franchisor has been in existence for less than three years or has only recently begun franchising, you may find fewer than three years of financial statements. However, the company is required to provide at least one certified statement, even if it is only an opening balance sheet. Make sure your accountant sees this information. You want to make sure the franchisor is on solid financial footing and in business for the long haul.

Item 22: Contracts

You will find a description of all the contracts you need to sign in order to purchase the franchise in this item. Copies of the contracts will also be attached to the UFOC as an exhibit. If the franchisor provides loan documents, equipment or real estate leases, they are also included in an exhibit, along with a sample franchise agreement form. Before you close on the transaction, make sure your attorney has a chance to review all these contracts.

Item 23: Receipt

The UFOC requires that two receipts be attached to it, one for the franchisee and the other for the franchisor. This is important for the franchisor in case they have to prove they delivered a disclosure document to you and that you received it. (Was it at least 10 business days before you signed the franchise agreement?) You must sign and date the receipt.

That's a lot of investment information in one document—and well worth reading through it.

SUMMARY NOTES

- ✓ The UFOC is a key document in your search for a franchise.
- ✓ READ the UFOC!
- ✓ Have professionals help you with parts of this document.
- ✓ Review the various sections of the UFOC. Some are more important than others.
- ✓ The UFOC does not contain *all* of the information you need to evaluate the franchise.

Action **PLAN**

Get a UFOC—any UFOC—and flip through it to see how it is organized and where to find key information.

CHAPTER 11

Five Great Questions *Not* Answered in the UFOC

*E*LLEN SLOGGED THROUGH THE UFOC for the franchise she was interested in and was proud of herself. She had every reason to be impressed by the program and wondered if there was anything else she needed to dig into. Surely, she thought, this huge tome told her everything she needed to know. Right?

THE UFOC DOES NOT DELIVER EVERYTHING

Ellen makes a mistake if she assumes that the UFOC will tell her everything she needs to know about the franchise investment. It is designed by regulators to deliver information that they consider "material" to the investment—that is, information that should be important to the investor. However, there are some gaping holes in the UFOC—key pieces of information it does not convey that are material to your purchase decision. Take a look at five of the most important areas. There may be more, depending on the type of business you are buying.

- *Pricing/product distribution.* Item 8 of the UFOC delivers some of the product and

pricing information you need, but the guidelines for franchisors to follow in preparing this section are complex and cumbersome, resulting in confusing disclosures that are not particularly helpful. After all, smooth product sourcing, the savings on prices available to franchisees based on large group purchases, and carefully considered product specifications are all fundamental business reasons for buying a franchise. If this part of the business is not working well, there may be little reason to go into the franchise.

Make a point of exploring product dynamics with the franchisees you meet. Press the franchisor representatives about purchasing arrangements, any buying cooperatives in your area and pricing strategies. Check the franchise agreement and any other paperwork from the franchisor describing product matters. In many franchises, this is the economic engine of the business. It never hurts to look under the hood and make sure it is running well.

IN*sight*

We talked to a franchisee of an ice cream concept who was beside himself. He has an MBA and thought his business looked great on paper. He liked the taste of the product, the well-designed brand name, the modern look of the stores, the sales figures he had seen, and the location in an enclosed mall without a food court. What he didn't count on was the price of the premium ice cream, which, under the terms of the franchise agreement, could be purchased only from the franchisor. The price was way too high, but he didn't realize it until he got into the business and learned about wholesale ice cream prices. The president of the company told him that there was no UFOC, because they were "not a public company." "How was I to know about that?" he says. Now he is saddled with an expensive business that is breaking even but not making much of a profit, and he is embarrassed to admit this could happen to an MBA.

- ***Franchisee associations.*** Nowhere in the UFOC is a franchisor required to disclose the existence of a franchisee association or advisory council. Yet this is an important aspect of the franchise program for a new investor. The presence of a strong association that is well-attended and governed by franchisees is an attractive asset of any franchise program.

I have long suspected that omitting any mention of a franchisee association in the UFOC is due to the swift internal political waters surrounding franchisee associations. Some associations are created by the franchisor and promoted by the company; others are "renegade associations" created by the franchisees and resented by the franchisor. Ask current franchisees about the role they play through an association or a franchisee council.

- ***Training.*** One of the keys to franchisee success is solid training. The UFOC will give you some of the basic facts, including a chart outlining the sections of the training, who teaches the sections, the experience of the trainers, how much time is devoted to each topic, and where the training takes place. However, you need assurances about the program that cannot be delivered in a disclosure document. Is the

IN*sight*

A franchisee association or council organizes and provides to the franchisor and all franchisees a valuable franchisee viewpoint of the business. Franchisee associations generally meet on a regular basis, and the prudent franchisor listens carefully to the advice and recommendations offered. They can provide new investors with a knowledgeable perspective independent of the franchisor and an in-depth evaluation of the whole franchise organization.

training effective? Do franchisees feel that they are well-prepared to run a successful business upon completing it? Is the training based on current thinking, and is it the best available in the field? Is it complete, and how much of it is hands-on, under supervision? Be sure you explore these ideas with franchisees and your franchisor representatives.

- *Market for product/service.* This is a basic but intangible question that is difficult to address in a disclosure document: Is the market for the product or service a strong one? Is the growth of the market for the business on the rise or decline?

- *Franchisor support.* The language in a franchise agreement that describes the level of the franchisor's continuing support may be surprising. You are likely to find something like: "The franchisor will provide such continuing advice and support as it deems appropriate in its absolute discretion."

How's that for reassurance?! Attorneys for franchisors learned decades ago that specific promises of support in the franchise agreement, such as quarterly meetings, monthly newsletters and regular telephone calls, would lead to legal trouble when the franchisor's business practices changed. And they always change. The result is the smallest, most flexible promise of support imaginable.

Even though the promises might be modest, the practice is important. Find out exactly—from franchisees and the franchisor's representatives—what the company does for its new franchisees when they are planning to locate the business, when they are hiring staff, and during the opening and start-up phase. Is help available? Is it responsive? Will the franchisor be there to help if and when things go wrong?

SUMMARY NOTES

✓ As lengthy as it is, the UFOC will not deliver all the information you need to know about a franchise program.

✓ Look to some key topics for more information: product distribution, franchisee associations, training, the market for the product and/or service, and franchisee support by the franchisor.

Action PLAN

Write a single-page list of questions and topics you want to discuss with any franchisor representative you meet. Ask your attorney and accountant if you should add other questions to your list.

CHAPTER 12

Key Sections of the Franchise Agreement

*B*ILL RECEIVED HIS FRANCHISE AGREEMENT *and figured he'd just look it over himself. Why hire an attorney? He knew attorneys could be expensive. After all, the contract was in English and looked straightforward to him. Sure it was long and the language was a little dense, but it was registered under Bill's state franchise law and seemed to be fully described in the UFOC. What could go wrong?*

UNDERSTANDING THE BASIC DYNAMIC OF THE FRANCHISE AGREEMENT

Bill is setting himself up for an expensive lesson. The agreement that grants a franchisee the right to operate a business in the franchisor's system is a complex commercial contract. It is designed to create a continuing business relationship that could span 20 years or more. It grants a panoply of intangible "intellectual property" rights, describes product and service standards, and sets the ground rules for the transfer, renewal and termination of the relationship.

This agreement is not an easy document to read or understand, and it makes sense to take it to an attorney who can help you understand it in detail. While the size, shape and style of franchise agreements are tailored to each system, many of their basic features are universal. You will be well ahead of the franchise game if you comprehend the basic legal dynamics of this complex contract.

KEY PROVISIONS CONSIDERED
Intellectual Property Rights

A franchise agreement has been described as a

IN*sight*

A franchise is, at its essence, the licensing of intellectual property. All the valuable information delivered to the franchisee, from the trademark, to the operating manuals, to the techniques taught in training, to the color designs of a retail franchise, is a form of intangible intellectual property.

trademark license with overdrive. It grants to the franchisee the limited right to use the trademarks, techniques, procedures, trade dress and know-how that comprise the franchise system. These rights are "limited" so that the franchisor can preserve its ownership rights of trademarks, copyrights and trade secrets.

Look closely at these terms:

- **Trademark.** This is a word, name, phrase, symbol, logo or, in some cases, a design that traditionally represents the source of a product or service. A leading example is McDonald's brand sandwiches, including the famous Big Mac® sandwich. A trademark owner has the legal right to license other people to use the trademark, and those licenses generally require correct display of the mark. If the colors of red and yellow in the McDonald's golden arches brand name are a bit off—if they turn out maroon and gold—you can expect the trademark owner to object. A "service mark" is the same thing as a trademark, but it specifically identifies a service, not a product.

- **Franchise system techniques and procedures.** In a franchise system, these terms denote the specifications, equipment and routines that are part of the franchise rights and obligations. They are usually found in an operating manual provided by the franchisor. In a restaurant franchise, for instance, the operating manual details the preparation of all menu items and their components, as well as things such as the timing of cooking and the temperature of cooking oil. Equipment specifications are included, as well as the uniform attire of employees. Many of these techniques that

are not obvious to the public may be claimed by the franchisor as trade secrets, which are confidential and not to be disclosed. All franchisees need to be aware of claimed trade secrets and take steps to keep them confidential.

- **Trade dress.** This is a legal term that describes the appearance of a product, product packaging or the distinctive style of a building or restaurant. Trade dress may be protected under the law in the same fashion as a trademark. What does this mean to a franchisee? If you operate a restaurant franchise in a building with a distinctive color design or roof line, those features may have to be changed if you leave the system, because they are owned by the franchisor.

- **Know-how.** This is often used to describe the knowledge and entire set of techniques that go into a franchise system. It includes the franchisor's experience in business and its knowledge of the bumps and bruises of the marketplace and how to avoid them, and it is imparted to the franchisee in a healthy franchise system.

- **Copyright.** This is the legal protection of an original work that is fixed in a tangible form, including books, songs, plays, software and all printed material. The legal copyright protects the author's exclusive right to use and exploit the value of the work. It cannot be published, copied or used without the author's permission. An author—and this is important—cannot protect an idea but can claim a copyright for the original expression of an idea (like a novel or a franchise operations manual). The franchise system's operations manual, advertising and other printed material may be copyright-protected by the franchisor. As a franchisee, you may be restricted in the ways you can use and exploit these materials for your own purposes.

- **Patent.** A patent is a property right, secured in the U.S. Constitution, protecting the rights to an invention, new device or innovation. As with a trademark, the owner has the right to license the use of his or her patented device to other people.
- **License rights.** The franchisee receives the right to use and display the trademark, or a family of trademarks, only as the franchisor authorizes, and only during the term of the franchise agreement. This means that all signs displaying the mark, and all printed materials, vehicles and even web locations used by the franchisee, must be approved in form, color and design by the franchisor.

Although this is a point of some contention in the franchise community, the "goodwill" of the franchised business represented by the trademark—which is to say much of the goodwill of the business itself—remains in the ownership of the franchisor, not the franchisee. In that sense, a franchise agreement is similar to a commercial lease: At the end of the lease term, the property that is granted reverts completely to the owner, not the tenant.

The same may be said of any of the other intellectual property of the franchise system. Its use is licensed only in the manner prescribed and only for the term of the franchise agreement. When the franchise agreement is expired or terminated, all rights to use the trademarks, copyrighted material, patents and/or trade secrets will also cease.

Contract Flexibility Over Time

How does the franchise relationship handle the marketplace changes that occur in the franchise system over a number of years? The changed appearance of American business establishments in the past 20 years, or even 10 years, is dramatic. Look at a picture of a McDonald's restaurant or a Holiday Inn from the 1980s. They've definitely changed!

Franchise relationships must allow for change over time, and they do it by incorporating a reference in the contract to a living, changing set of policies, standards, guidance and know-how contained in a confidential set of documents, usually called operating manuals. The operating manuals are typically updated as changes in the system occur or new policies are adopted.

The franchise agreement also usually describes a dynamic franchise system that changes over time. The parties stipulate that many aspects of the franchise will require alteration as the years go by.

Franchise agreements accommodate changes over time by expressly anticipating them, while assuring the franchisee that the fundamental rights of the contract will not change. While franchisees clearly want to receive their full contract rights and the undiluted benefit of their bargain, they also want the franchisor to take the lead in keeping their business concept fresh and competitive in the marketplace. Obviously, this creates something of a dynamic legal tension for the franchisee and franchisor. What is fundamental and what is allowed to change over time?

While there is no easy answer, the courts and franchise systems ask whether a particular change is "material" to the franchisee's business.

Is a proposed change so important (or fundamental) that it would have affected the franchisee's decision to purchase the franchise if they had known that such a change would be made to the program? If it is material or fundamental to the franchise, it may be in violation of the contract's promises to the franchisee.

Product Standards

The essential genius of franchising is the delivery of consistent products or services through independent businesses licensed to operate under a universal display mark. Isn't it remarkable that a Big Mac® sandwich purchased at a McDonald's in Bangor, Maine, tastes the same as one bought in Hawaii or Australia? What is more remarkable is that all the ingredients and sandwich components are provided by unaffiliated, third-party suppliers to the McDonald's system.

The franchise agreement addresses the requirements of product and service supply in one of several different ways, reflecting varying degrees of control that the company needs to exercise over the delivery of the products or services of the franchised business. In some systems, of course, the franchisor is the manufacturer of the product line carried by the franchisee, and the franchise is itself a "product franchise" through which independent franchisees distribute the line.

In most business format franchise programs, franchisees are required to purchase only from suppliers who have received the company's prior written approval. If the franchisee wants to buy product from a supplier who has not received approval, the franchise agreement requires that an application must be made to the franchisor. This way, the franchisor can assure that all suppliers to the system are capable of delivering specialized product and that system standards are not eroded through poor supply selections (which are often driven by price considerations) made by franchisees.

An even-handed supplier approval process also allows the franchisor to control quality without unreasonably restricting supplier access to its system of franchise buyers, which could have serious antitrust implications for the franchisor. An unreasonably restrictive supply arrangement might injure competition among suppliers to franchisees. Injury to competition is what antitrust laws were designed to combat.

Transfer

Can the franchisee build up the business and then sell it to another person? In most systems, the franchisee can sell the business only if the franchisor issues written permission, and permission is generally granted by a franchisor only after reviewing the qualifications of the prospective buyer. Most franchisors apply the same standards of qualification on the proposed transferee (the buyer) as they apply to new applicants.

If the transferee does not measure up, the franchisor has every right to deny consent to the transfer. The courts have made it clear that a franchisor has a legitimate interest in preventing its franchised businesses from being owned by businesspeople who are undercapitalized, lack necessary levels of business experience or fail to meet the company's objective qualifications.

The transfer, or assignment, sections of the typical franchise agreement are the most lengthy and dense legalese of the entire contract but are also the most important to the value of the franchisee's business. Your ability to sell your business and pull out your sweat equity is essential to the original decision to purchase the franchise.

It surprises many franchisees to learn that the transfer language of the contract may cover events that do not amount to the sale of the business, such as taking in a new partner, granting stock in an existing corporation that is the franchisee, the death of a minority owner of a franchise, and shifting ownership of the unit's assets to a newly formed corporation or limited liability company. All these events require the prior written consent of the franchisor, if the contract's transfer provisions are typical.

CORPORATE OWNERSHIP
Private Corporations, Limited Liability Companies (LLCs) and Personal Guarantees
Most franchisors allow an individual investor to create these legal entities to serve as the formal franchisee under the franchise agreement. It often makes sense: Create an LLC to hold the franchise rights, sign the franchise agreement, hold the assets of the operation, and accommodate multiple ownership and various positions and roles. However, there is usually one catch, and it's a significant one: Under the franchise agreement, you will be asked to personally guarantee to the franchisor the obligations of your new legal entity.

"Wait a minute," you say. "My lawyer told me that the main reason for creating an LLC was to shield my personal assets from the liabilities of the business!" That's right. The personal guarantee, if required by the franchisor, defeats that objective, at least insofar as you wanted to be shielded from the claims of the franchisor. If it is narrowly drafted, the guarantee should not defeat your objective relating to other aspects of the business.

What does this personal guarantee mean as a practical matter? Suppose your business falls on difficult times and you are unable to pay the royalties, and perhaps the franchisor terminates your franchise or you have to close the business. The franchisor will have legal claim for royalties and other damages against the LLC *and* you personally, as well as others who have guaranteed the obligations of your legal entity.

Right of First Refusal
Many franchise agreements reserve to the franchisor a "right of first refusal." This means that if you receive a formal offer to purchase your business, you must present the offer to the franchisor and allow them the opportunity to purchase your business on the same terms. This allows the franchisor to maintain control over the buying and selling of its franchises, but also draws criticism from franchisees who believe that it hampers their ability to attract a serious buyer. What buyer wants to go through the effort of putting together a detailed purchase offer, only to have the franchisor take it out from under them?

 **IN**sight

Most franchisors include a right of first refusal in their franchise agreements in order to control ownership of the franchised businesses and to buy out a franchisee if it fits with the company's business plans for that area. However, it is a right rarely exercised by a franchisor.

Termination

Oh, the dreaded termination section! It seems to rattle on ad nauseam, listing dozens of situations in which the franchisor may terminate the relationship, while rarely including even one circumstance in which the franchisee may terminate the relationship. Franchisors generally have only one enforcement tool, the threat of termination. They describe it at length, but use it gingerly.

Here are some of the typical termination grounds you will see in a franchise agreement, with notes on what to look out for:

- **Business abandonment.** Make sure you understand how abandonment is defined. You don't want a spring vacation to amount to abandonment of your business.
- **Criminal conviction.** How is a crime defined here? Is it a felony or any crime? The franchisor wants to protect its reputation if the franchisee commits a crime.
- **Lying on the application.** If you mislead the company during the application process, it wants to reserve the right to terminate the relationship.
- **Bankruptcy.** If your business does declare bankruptcy, the franchisor wants to be able to terminate the contractual relationship. This termination provision is often set to occur "automatically" if bankruptcy is declared, but in fact a whole body of federal bankruptcy law will take effect immediately. Bankruptcy legal specialists caution that the law may not allow the franchisor to terminate after a bankruptcy, regardless of what the contract says.
- **Termination after notice.** Most franchise agreements allow the franchisor to terminate the relationship if the franchisee

INsight

Many franchise agreements also include the broader termination grounds of the franchisee committing an act that injures the goodwill of the trademark. Plan to discuss this provision with your attorney.

receives notice of any default and does not correct the problem within a reasonable amount of time. The typical time to cure is 30 days, but it certainly could be a longer or shorter period, depending on the nature of the default.

Termination after notice is how most franchise terminations occur. If you receive a default notice that warns of the possible termination of your franchise rights, do not file it away. Respond to it immediately.

The franchise agreement, drafted by lawyers in the interests of franchisors, allows them to protect their trademarks, systems and other intellectual property if a franchisee abuses, misuses or misappropriates any portion of the franchised business. At the same time, exacting termination language allows the franchisor to protect other franchisees.

Look at it this way: If a franchisee on the other side of your small town is running a slovenly or dirty operation, your *own* business will suffer. That is the other sharp blade of the two-edged sword of franchising: You operate under the same trademark as many other operators; their businesses are indistinguishable from yours in the eye of the customer.

Most franchisees dislike the seemingly overbearing language of their own franchise agreement but are the first to insist that the franchisor use those rights to enforce system standards against another owner who is not doing the job.

The franchise laws of about 19 jurisdictions impose standards of termination that preempt conflicting language of a franchise agreement, allowing for termination or failure to renew only when the franchisor has good cause, as that term is defined in the statute. These statutes come into play if you get into a tangle with the franchisor and they notify you that your franchise is or will be canceled.

DISPUTE RESOLUTION PROVISIONS

The truth is, franchising tends to generate disputes. The interests of franchisor and franchisee are fundamentally at odds in a number of ways. Remember, the franchisor receives royalties based on a percentage of the gross sales of the business, *before* expenses are paid; franchisees take money home at the end of the day if they maximize profits, *after* expenses are paid. Franchisors therefore push for higher sales; franchisees for better profits.

One measure of excellence in franchising is the ability of the franchisor to avoid the courtroom when they must enforce the terms of its franchise agreements. The contract may contain a provision that requires the parties to submit all disputes to an arbitration process before any lawsuit may be filed. Where must that arbitration take place? Many franchise agreements specify that the process take place at the American Arbitration Association office closest to the franchisor headquarters. That means you have to travel to the franchisor's backyard in order to resolve a dispute.

INsight

Franchisors have additional motivation to avoid a courtroom or an arbitration procedure: disclosure. The UFOC requires that a franchisor disclose in Item 3 certain lawsuits and arbitration procedures during the prior 10 years as well as the terms of any settlement of those actions.

Even if there is no arbitration language in place, the franchise agreement may specify where a lawsuit must be filed if either party makes a legal claim under the contract. Franchisee attorneys generally resist accepting language mandating that legal actions must be filed in the home jurisdiction of the franchisor.

Remember, no prospective franchisee should attempt to fully comprehend a franchise agreement without the benefit of legal counsel. Your attorney is far more familiar with the complexities and limitations of contract law and can advise you about the obligations and rights it stipulates.

For all the attention the contract receives at the start of the relationship, it should not loom large in your daily business. When everything is going well, the franchised business is succeeding and your relationship with the franchisor is on solid footing, that carefully evaluated franchise agreement— the foundation of your business investment— will not even come out of the drawer. All solid foundations are supposed to work that way.

SUMMARY NOTES

✓ Take the proposed franchise agreement to an attorney. It's important.

✓ It is also important to understand some of the basic dynamics of a franchise agree-ment, such as intellectual property, license rights, product standards, transfer and termination.

✓ If the business works out well, the contract will not come out of the drawer. If problems

---

Action PLAN

Look immediately for a good attorney. Ask current franchisees or friends in business whom they use, or contact your state bar association.

CHAPTER 13

Franchisor Financial Information in the UFOC

(and How Do I Read This Gobbledegook?)

*E*RIC NEVER HAD A HEAD FOR NUMBERS *but thought he was pretty good at judging the financial status of a company by its balance sheets. Now the UFOC gave him an opportunity to do just that for the home health-care franchise he was evaluating. But he had never seen a franchisor balance sheet and operating statement before and was not sure what to make of them. So he decided to take them to his accountant. Something told him this was too important to be left to his amateur accounting skills.*

FRANCHISOR FINANCIAL DISCLOSURES

Eric's instincts are serving him well. Item 21 of the UFOC requires franchisors to supply two years of audited balance sheets and three years of audited operational statements. This is extremely important information for a prospective franchisee and should not be left to an amateur evaluation. It shows whether the franchisor is well-capitalized, how well they are managing their cash flow and whether the company is healthy and profitable. In short, it is a snapshot of the franchisor's finances, and it is invaluable to you.

You are considering entering into a five-, 10- or even 20-year relationship when you execute a franchise agreement. You want to know whether the franchisor has staying power and will be there for the duration.

AUDITS ACCORDING TO GAAP

What does it mean that a financial statement is "audited"? It means that a certified public accounting firm has independently reviewed the company's books and expressed its professional opinion in writing that the financial statements accurately reflect the company's financial position and have been prepared in accordance with Generally Accepted Accounting Principles (GAAP)—the standard financial statement rules.

This audit opinion is a big deal in the world of accountants. It is the highest level of review that a CPA conducts (the other two are a Compilation Report and a Review Report), and

IN*sight*

The auditors must consent to the inclusion of their report in the UFOC. They go through a rigorous process of inspecting the company's records for the period they are auditing, as required by the standards of the accounting profession. A Compilation Report or Review Report does not involve that level of accounting scrutiny.

it is as close as you're going to get to an independent third party approving the accuracy of a set of financials. You can usually rely on the accuracy of an audited statement.

So you peek at the exhibits in the back of your UFOC and there they are, the franchisor's financials. They are a sea of numbers. Now what do you do? Well, it goes without saying that most people have not made a study of how to read a financial statement. Now is not the time to start. Take the UFOC to an accountant, preferably a CPA, and have them conduct a review. You are going to need the services of a good accountant anyway when it comes time to plan the business, make some projections and create a business road map, so asking for a quick review of a set of financials is a good first step. Talk to the accountant about what it is you need and how much it will cost. Can't afford the full Cadillac review? Then ask how much half an hour of time costs. Present the financials, and ask the accountant to go over them slowly and explain what they mean to an experienced eye.

EVALUATING THE FRANCHISOR'S FINANCIAL STANDING

How do you evaluate the franchise company's financial standing in your investment decisions? Take a look at a common example. Say the franchisor is a subsidiary of a well-known corporation but is showing only a small net worth on an opening balance sheet with no operating history. What do you make of that?

First, understand why you are looking at a franchisor with a small net worth. When a well-established corporation considers franchising for the first time, the attorneys explain that it will need to provide a set of audited financial statements for the UFOC. If the company has never prepared an audited statement in the past, this can pose an extremely expensive problem. Auditors have to go over the corporation's old books in painful detail, and probably charge the corporation an arm and a leg. On top of that, the company is concerned about litigation arising out of the franchise program and figures that a subsidiary corporation will add an additional level of protection for the corporation. So the company decides it will be cheaper and smarter to create a new corporation to serve as the franchisor. A newly formed franchisor must provide only an audited opening balance sheet, which is a relatively simple matter for the auditor to complete. If the franchise program results in litigation, the assets of the established corporation are shielded.

This is perfectly legal, and quite common in franchising. When a thinly capitalized franchisor files in one of the registration states, however, it will probably be required to provide a surety bond to the state or make some other protective financial arrangement for investors as a condition of registration.

What does a surety bond do for franchisees? Imagine you have paid a $30,000 initial franchise fee, and the franchisor tells you that it cannot provide the promised training because it is low on funds and the training managers have quit. You request your money back, and the franchisor says it does not have that amount of cash in its accounts. In that situation, you would probably qualify to apply to be reimbursed under the surety bond on file with state authorities. It makes it relatively easy to be reimbursed for the investment of an initial fee if the franchisor goes out of business or is otherwise unable to perform basic obligations because it has no substantial assets. Without a protection like a surety bond, you may have no recourse at all, except filing a lawsuit against the franchisor and its principals.

Whether or not you are in a registration state, a low franchisor net worth increases the risks you are taking when you invest in a franchised business. If you are looking at a young program that has not been in operation very long, it may have an extremely low net worth. The profit potential of buying a franchise from a new concept may be high, but the concomitant risks should be part of your calculation when you evaluate any franchise investment.

The regulation of franchise sales is not designed to make all franchise investments safe. In order not to interfere unnecessarily in the marketplace, franchise regulation is designed to deliver all pertinent information into the hands of the investor, and then step back so that the investor can make an informed decision. That leaves a substantial burden on the prospective franchisee to consider all the relevant information.

SUMMARY NOTES

✓ The UFOC requires the inclusion of the franchisor's audited financial statements.

✓ Audits are generally presented by independent accountants, and they confirm that the numbers are prepared and presented according to the standards adopted in the business accounting industry known as Generally Accepted Accounting Principles (GAAP).

✓ Accountants conduct a ratio analysis and industry analysis and review the footnotes to the statements.

✓ A low net worth or otherwise shaky financial statement increases the risk that the company may not be there for the long term.

Action PLAN

Find a good accountant by asking current franchisees and friends or contacts already in business whom they use. Check the Yellow Pages, or search for a local CPA at the American Institute of Certified Public Accountants website (www.aicpa.org).

CHAPTER 14

Top 10 Warning Signs in Franchise Investments

*C*HRIS WAS HAVING TROUBLE EVALUATING *a restaurant franchise. The company would not give her a UFOC, its answers to her questions were confusing, and franchisees were giving a mixed review on some key issues. At what point, she wondered, should she back away from the program?*

DON'T GET SNAGGED

As exciting as it may be to purchase a franchise, this business requires all buyers to exercise caution. Regulations require franchisors to give you a UFOC, that's all. Once you have this document in hand, it is your responsibility to review it carefully and to ask more questions of the franchisor and as many franchisees as you can.

KEY WARNING SIGNS

Even if you follow this advice, how do you know if there are problems with a franchise you have your eye on? Although there is no way to be absolutely certain about a given investment, you can improve your odds of success if you keep an eye out for some of these key warning signs:

10. *Weak financial statements.* The UFOC contains three years of the franchisor's audited financial statements. Review them carefully, and take them to a knowledgeable CPA. If the franchisor is in a weak financial condition, it will raise the risk levels for your investment. You may find some terrific programs being offered by thinly capitalized franchisors or startup companies, but understand that your risks as a franchisee are magnified by the company's weak financial standing.

9. *No answers.* If you do not get all your questions answered by the franchisor, or if you start getting the feeling that the company is being evasive, move on.

8. *The hustle.* Buying a franchise is a substantial investment. It might wipe out your life savings and put you on a financial bubble. If the seller is hurrying you along, telling you that the window of opportunity is closing, or using any other tried and true closing techniques, be pre-

pared to walk away from the deal. This is too important to rush.

7. ***Product price squeeze.*** Product supply is the ticklish underbelly of franchise relationships. If you are buying a business that is designed to distribute the franchisor's product line, then you had better make sure the pricing of the product will allow you to be competitive in the marketplace. Ask other franchise owners how the pricing structure works for them. If you are going into a "business format" program where product is supplied by third parties, or some is supplied by the franchisor, make sure that it runs well. Have the franchisees established a buying cooperative? Do franchisees have input on the supply arrangements? Make sure this key aspect of your business will not frustrate you.

6. ***High turnover rates.*** Check Item 20 of the UFOC and confirm how many franchisees have left the system in the past three years. There is no rule of thumb to determine when the number is too high; this depends largely on the type of business. Lower-investment franchises generally have a higher turnover rate than more expensive businesses. If anything looks out of line, ask the franchisor what's going on.

5. ***Attorney avoidance.*** The franchisor discourages you from getting a lawyer involved, telling you it will unnecessarily complicate and slow the process.

4. ***Too many lawsuits.*** Ours has become a litigious society, of course, and most franchisors reflect that fact. Item 3 of the UFOC will reveal the 10-year history of "material" lawsuits and/or arbitration cases filed against the company. If you see a heavy litigation history, find out what has been going on. Ask your attorney's opinion. It could mean that franchisees are fundamentally unhappy in the business.

3. ***Earnings claims mumbo jumbo.*** Ask the seller's representative: "How much money can I make with this franchise?" If it is not in the UFOC, the company must decline to answer the question. If they say, "We are prohibited by federal law from answering the question," realize that although that may be true, it may also be because the earnings picture is not a pretty one.

2. ***No UFOC.*** All franchisors are required by federal law and many state laws to deliver a UFOC before you pay any money for the franchise or sign a franchise agreement. If you do not receive one, don't even think about buying the franchised business.

And the number-one warning sign in franchise investments:

1. ***Consistently bad reports from current franchisees.*** If you make the effort to visit with some current franchisees of the company, and each one tells you they are unhappy or would not make the investment in this franchise again, think long and hard about your own decision. There is no stronger or more trustworthy source of information about the company than those independents who are in the trenches. If they feel that the franchisor has let them down or has a flawed program, it will tell you to look more carefully before you take the plunge.

These warning signs should prompt you to ask more questions. If you don't like the answers you receive, and your gut (or your professional advisor) tells you to head for the door, this is probably not the program for you. Take the time to look around at other programs. For a decision as important as this one, you owe it to yourself and your family to be confident that it is the right business investment for you.

SUMMARY NOTES

✓ Look for red flags indicating problems in the franchise program.

✓ The decision about whether to invest in a particular franchise is yours, and no one knows better than you what will fit with your needs. Carefully consider anything else that appears to be a red flag in your own judgment.

Action **PLAN**

Move on if you encounter any serious problems regarding a franchise that are not cleared up to your satisfaction.

CHAPTER 15

Closing on Your Franchise Purchase

*N*OW IT WAS GETTING EXCITING FOR *Kevin. He had gone through all the steps with the franchisor, lined up the financing he needed to develop the new business, and was ready to close the transaction. In just a few days, he would launch a new chapter of personal success in his life. What did he need to know going into the closing meeting?*

Once the franchisor has thoroughly checked out the applicant's qualifications, and the applicant has reviewed all documents, seen an accountant and an attorney, scraped together the money necessary to buy the franchise, and completed all necessary discussions, it is time to close on the transaction.

Purchasing the franchise rights for a business that has not yet been built is not a complicated transaction, and the closing involves nothing more than signing a few contracts and sliding a check across the table for the initial franchise fee. Most "closings" for franchise sales do not take place in a room face to face with the franchisor. They take place through the mail. The company sends you a final package with tabs showing where your signature is needed and a cover letter stating the amount of the initial franchise fee. You sign and return, and it is done.

A CHECKLIST FOR CLOSING

However, you should pay attention to the following before you sign on the dotted line:

The Franchise Agreement

This contract should have been in your hands with all blanks filled in for at least five business days before you sign and date it. That is a requirement imposed on the franchisor by state and federal law; it is not the franchisee's responsibility to see that this is met. Make sure your attorney has reviewed the contract and signed off on it. If you have requested any changes to be made to accommodate you, make sure they appear in the final form of the contract.

Many companies ask you to sign two originals and return them to the company. The franchisor then executes them and returns one original to you for your records.

Always Date Your Signature

Begin the habit of adding a date to any legal document that contains your signature. If the signature form does not have a space to show the date, simply jot it immediately after your signature. Dates are important in the regulation of franchise sales, and you may be called upon to swear as to a series of dated events. The date of delivery of the UFOC, the date you first had a face-to-face meeting with the franchisor, the date on which you received a completed franchise agreement, and the date on which you signed the franchise agreement are all important.

Never backdate a document, even if asked to do so by the franchisor; it will only confuse your recollection of events. Make sure your document record is clear on the dates.

Other Contracts

You may be presented with other contracts to sign that are ancillary to the franchise agreement. All such documents should be included in the UFOC and should not come as a surprise at closing. If you do receive a surprise contract, check it with your attorney. Ancillary contracts may include a site selection agreement (if you do not have a site selected yet), an agreement regarding necessary lease terms and an acknowledgment of the training schedule.

UFOC

If you have not received the franchisor's UFOC at least 10 business days before you are asked to sign the franchise agreement, stop. Don't sign the contract, and don't send any money. This could indicate a mere oversight, or it could mean that you have a more serious problem. Contact your franchisor representative.

Bank Paperwork

If you have arranged a loan from a bank or other lending institution, it will want to receive a copy of the franchise agreement (and every other piece of paper related to the franchise) as soon as possible. Talk to your banker or lender about the steps necessary to provide the money you are borrowing and when the money will be available. Make sure all is in order before you close.

SUMMARY NOTES

- ✓ Prepare paperwork as you approach the closing.
- ✓ Prepare a checklist for the closing so that nothing is dropped. Confirm the list with your attorney.
- ✓ You should have checklist items for the contracts, the UFOC and financing paperwork

Action PLAN

Plan ahead so that you are sure of your costs and obligations before the closing. Meet with your attorney to consider all contingencies.

CHAPTER 16

Resolving Legal Disputes

A CCORDING TO JEFF, "IT SEEMED LIKE a good idea at the time." Jeff had carefully selected a franchise. He borrowed $50,000 and worked at the business 12 hours a day, seven days a week. He managed the buying, hiring and money. Six months after the opening, the business just wasn't cutting it, and Jeff was nearly out of operating cash. He stopped paying his royalties, telling the company that the program was not working in his town, and that he would pay the royalties as soon as the business made some money. Rather than come in to help, the franchisor sent a letter on lawyer's letterhead threatening termination for failure to pay royalties if the account was not brought up-to-date in 30 days.

"Now what do I do?" a bewildered Jeff asked.

The termination of a franchise agreement has been a legal flash point since the earliest days of franchising. Nowhere are the divergent interests of franchisors and franchisees brought into sharper focus, and no other feature of the franchise relationship has generated more disputes, arbitration and litigation. When you combine the complexities of the typical franchise agreement, the regulation of franchise sales, the perception that big corporations (franchisors) are against the little guy (franchisees), and the substantial amounts of money invested, it presents a ready-made formula for legal disputes.

Attorneys are building lucrative careers helping franchisors and franchisees resolve these disputes. There are almost 2,000 members of the Forum on Franchising of the American Bar Association, and the number is growing.

LINES OF DEFENSE: CONTRACT TERMS AND PROTECTIVE LAWS

Franchisees do have some tools, however. The first is the franchise agreement.

The Contract

The first line of defense for the franchisee, and the fundamental legal guideline for any termination for the franchisor, is the franchise agreement. The contract spells out the conditions under which either party may terminate the relationship. Typically the franchisor will reserve the right to terminate on a series of grounds, some based on the franchisee's failure to cure a default after a written notice is delivered, and others based on incurable violations that lead to immediate or automatic termination.

If a termination occurs in violation of the terms of the franchise agreement, the franchisee has the right to bring a lawsuit against the franchisor under state law, seeking either a court order that the termination be stopped, or damages, or both.

State Relationship Laws

The franchise relationship laws are state laws that regulate terminations, nonrenewals and some franchising practices. There are 19 U.S. jurisdictions that have adopted some form of franchise relationship law. The typical relationship law requires that a franchisor have "good cause" before it moves to terminate a franchisee. This protects a franchisee from arbitrary or baseless terminations and creates a right to sue the franchisor for damages if the standard is violated.

These laws were adopted in response to perceived widespread abuses in franchising. Unjust terminations and the absence of renewal rights seemed to be depriving franchisees of the value of the businesses they had built. Other abuses, such as no right of assignment, restricted right of association, unreasonable performance standards and encroachment (placing another unit too close to a franchised unit), also led to the legislative attempt to level the playing field.

If the franchisee has an argument that a state relationship law supersedes the contract, there may be an opportunity to seek court relief under that law. The state relationship laws allow termination where the franchisor has "good cause" to terminate the franchise. What is "good cause"?

GENERAL STANDARD. Where the state law does define the concept, "good cause" means "failure of the franchisee to comply substantially with the requirements imposed by the franchisor." In other words, it means a breach of the franchise agreement.

STATUTORY GROUNDS. Here are some of the additional statutory grounds where termination is lawful:

- Voluntary abandonment
- Criminal conviction of the franchisee on a charge related to the franchised business
- The franchisee's insolvency or declaration of bankruptcy
- Failure to pay the franchisor sums due
- Loss of the right to occupy the franchisee's business premises
- A material misrepresentation by the franchisee relating to the business
- Franchisee conduct that materially impairs the goodwill of the franchised business or the franchisor's trademark
- The franchisee's repeated noncompliance with the requirements of the franchise
- Imminent danger to public health or safety
- Failure to act in good faith and in a commercially reasonable manner
- A written agreement to terminate
- The franchisee's failure to comply with any law applicable to the operation of the franchise
- Government seizure of the franchised business or foreclosure by a creditor

DISPUTE RESOLUTION TOOLBOX

Obviously, there are lots of land mines on the path to franchise success. Given the strong interests and even stronger feelings among franchisors and franchisees over termination issues, resolving the inevitable disputes is something of an art form. As a franchisee, you need to understand the tools in your dispute resolution toolbox.

There are four distinct types of dispute resolution tools, and each of them can be used in the franchise context.

1. *Negotiation.* It has been said that negotiation and compromise are the oils that smooth the gears of business. Negotiation is the process of give and take that results in an acceptable solution for the parties involved. It takes a willingness to explore the possibilities with the other side and benefits from face-to-face discussions.

   What could our franchisee, Jeff, negotiate for in his situation? Perhaps he could seek a royalty concession until his business is on its feet, or propose to sign a promissory note for the amount of royalty owing with an installment repayment schedule. Or he could begin negotiations to either sell the business to a more aggressive owner or to the franchisor, or close the business with both parties working to minimize the financial impact on Jeff. The principal advantage of an effective negotiation is that it quickly embraces creative, business-oriented resolutions. With clever businesspeople working in good faith, a negotiated resolution of a difficult situation offers the greatest hope for a solution that is fair to all involved.

2. *Mediation.* Mediation is professionally assisted negotiation. Where franchisor and franchisee are unable to negotiate a satisfactory solution, they may choose to bring into the discussion a professional mediator. This is someone trained in the mediation process and possibly experienced in the franchised business, who can use their skills to help the parties fashion a creative resolution. Often the most effective mediators are retired civil court judges. Mediation is nonbinding unless and until the parties find an agreeable solution; then they may commit to binding terms. Disputing parties can turn to the American Arbitration Association or national private organizations like JAMS for mediation services. Of particular interest to franchisors is the fact that a franchisor/franchisee dispute that is taken through a mediation process need not be disclosed in Item 3 of the UFOC.

3. *Arbitration.* Arbitration is a more formal dispute resolution process that results in a final, nonappealable decision made by an

 **IN**sight

Franchise disputes can often be resolved if they are recognized and handled at an early moment in the dispute. Many franchisors express frustration that their contracts give them only one response to a serious problem—termination—and it is an atomic bomb. Mediation has become popular among franchisors and their lawyers as an effective technique for resolving business disputes without resorting to nuclear weaponry.

arbitrator or a panel of three arbitrators. Think of arbitration as litigation without the courtroom. The result is just as binding on the parties as a court decision, and it must be disclosed in Item 3 of the UFOC, just as with court cases.

If your franchise agreement contains a provision that commits all disputes to binding arbitration, then you will not have the right to sue in a court of law. Except in rather extreme cases of fraud in the formation of the contract, the arbitration provision is almost always enforced by a court if challenged by one of the parties. The Federal Arbitration Act and court decisions of the past 50 years have created an extremely strong policy in favor of enforcing arbitration agreements. The policy reduces the crushing case load in our public courts and allows private parties to resolve their disputes privately. It is not entirely private, however, because disputes submitted to arbitration must be disclosed in Item 3 of the franchisor's UFOC.

4. *Litigation.* A franchisee can always sue a franchisor in court to enforce the terms of the franchise agreement and try to stop a threatened termination. Of course, the franchisor can also sue to enforce the payment requirements or other terms of the franchise agreement. Of all the dispute resolution tools available to franchisors and franchisees, litigation is by far the most expensive and time-consuming.

One of your most important objectives once you're in business is to avoid litigation and, to a lesser degree, arbitration. Use these tools only as a last resort. It is a rare business owner who finds litigation satisfactory as a dispute resolution process.

SUMMARY NOTES

✓ In franchising, disputes happen.

✓ Your first line of defense as a franchisee is the franchise agreement. Look to the terms and conditions articulated in the contract, and ask your attorney for assistance.

✓ The second line of defense consists of specific standards adopted in the various franchise relationship laws.

✓ Dispute resolution techniques are important tools in your franchise business life. Familiarize yourself with the basic advantages and disadvantages of negotiation, mediation, arbitration and litigation.

Action **PLAN**

Talk to your attorney about alternate forms of dispute resolution, and ask how dispute resolution is addressed in the contract. Discuss with the franchisor how you both will handle a dispute if and when it arises.

CHAPTER 17

Renewing Your Franchise Rights

S AM REALIZED WITH A START ONE DAY THAT *his franchise agreement was due to expire in a year. "Where has the time gone?" he thought. The foreseeable arrival of the expiration date means that Sam has some decisions to make. "Do I want to sign on for another five years? If I don't re-up, what will happen to my business? If I have a buyer for my business walk in tomorrow, what do I have to sell? What hoops do I have to jump through to renew the franchise rights? Will the renewal contract be on the same terms as my current contract?"*

CONTRACT TERMS AND RENEWAL RIGHTS

The franchise agreement is a long-term arrangement that can last more than 20 years. Many of the earliest McDonald's franchise agreements from the 1960s and 1970s have completed their initial 20-year terms and have been renewed for another 20 years. We suspect some of those may even be coming around again.

Think of a franchise agreement as you would a lease for real estate. The lease/franchise agreement grants the tenant/franchisee the right to use the company's property (the building/franchise system) for a period of years and then, when the time is up, the relationship ends. The tenant/franchisee moves out and both parties go their separate ways.

As with many commercial leases, the franchise agreement often grants the franchisee the conditional right to renew the relationship for another term of years, and the renewal right usually depends on meeting a short list of preconditions.

Before looking at those preconditions, it is necessary to understand the overall structure of the franchise agreement term. Current practice and conventional wisdom among franchisors suggest that you are not likely to find a full 20-year term granted at the outset of the relationship. Why? Because things change too much over such a long period of time. When circumstances change, or when the franchise system itself changes, the franchisor does not want to be locked into contracts that cannot keep up with these changes.

For instance, say that in its first 15 franchise agreements, a franchisor designated that the franchisee had an exclusive territory covering a radius of 30 miles from the business location. But then things change: The franchise system expands at an astonishing rate so there are lots of new locations; the company develops smaller, mobile locations, for the service that can be flexible and nimble in following the market for the franchise product; the company develops a catalog to offer products directly to the customer; the company increases its standard royalty rate from 4 to 5 percent; the internet is invented; and so on. The franchisor wants to be able to respond to such changes, so it structures the franchise agreement to be for a five-year initial term with the option to renew for three additional terms of five years each.

The effect of such a multiterm structure is to allow the franchisor to present the franchisee with a new form of franchise agreement every five years, and each form can adapt the system to the current market circumstances. The franchisor wants to reduce the size of the exclusive territory and modify the concept of exclusivity. The franchisor can make those changes only if the terms of renewal allow the changes. The renewal also gives the franchisee a chance to evaluate the continuing value of participating in the franchise program. The franchisee can always walk away at the date of expiration. Today terms are shorter, and there are more renewals than in the past. That's why contract renewal is an important topic for any franchisee looking at a new franchise agreement.

RENEWAL CONDITIONS

Renewal by the franchisee is typically articulated as a "right" or "option," but it always comes with conditions to be met. As with any legal contract, read the fine print to understand the steps necessary to satisfy the conditions and enjoy the full rights under the agreement.

What sorts of conditions will you encounter at renewal time? Here are the most common:

Give Written Notice to the Franchisor

This provision usually requires a written notice no less than x months and no more than y months prior to the date of expiration. It is designed this way so that renewal paperwork can be prepared and the franchisor can comply with state laws that may require a franchisor to give a certain amount of notice before failing to renew a franchise.

No Defaults and In Full Compliance

Look for a provision that says something like "You must not currently be in default under the franchise agreement and must have remained in compliance during its term." What if you cured a minor default in your first year—are you in full compliance?

Sign a New Form of Franchise Agreement

This is the most sensitive of the renewal conditions. Does the contract allow the substitution of a new form of agreement and advise you that the terms of the renewal agreement may be substantially different from the current agreement? That allows the franchisor to increase your royalty rates, alter your grant of territorial protections and change other features that might directly affect the value of your business. Some franchise agreements specify that royalty rates and territories will not be changed but that other provisions may be changed on renewal. This is a step in the right direction. Be sure to go over this provision with your attorney.

Sign a Release of Claims

Why does the franchisor require you to release legal claims as a condition of renewal? It has everything to do with the company's opportunity to cut off problems that might have occurred during the expiring term. This way, the franchisor can begin the new term on a new slate without concern that it will renew the contract and then get hit with a lawsuit over something that occurred in the earlier term. One idea that is usually acceptable to the franchisor: Make the release mutual, so that the franchisor also releases any claims it may have against the franchisee under the expiring contract. Discuss this provision and any claims you may have under the current contract with your legal counsel.

Pay a Renewal Fee

A minority of franchise agreements require a renewal fee. Most don't, because franchisors generally want to impose no impediment to renewal. They want the franchisee to re-up. The franchisee represents an exceedingly valuable revenue stream for the franchisor, which would be expensive to replace if the franchisee did not renew.

Renewal is the strongest vote for the value of the franchise program that a franchisee can make. You will find that most franchisors generally want you to renew and will make renewal as easy and favorable as possible. A renewed franchise is far less expensive than finding, training and establishing a new franchisee.

The answers to most of the questions Sam was pondering at the beginning of this chapter should be answered in his franchise agreement and by the renewal policies of the particular franchise system. Many of the franchise relationship laws discussed in Chapter 16 apply the "good cause" standard to a franchisor's failure to renew a franchise agreement and may therefore preempt the renewal terms laid out in your franchise agreement. Check with your attorney to consider any applicable statutory renewal standards.

SUMMARY NOTES

- ✓ Like a commercial lease, a franchise agreement typically grants a term of years with conditional renewal rights.
- ✓ The duration of franchise agreement terms is getting shorter. This change in duration offers flexibility to franchisor and franchisee alike.
- ✓ The conditions imposed on renewal may include notice, contract compliance, a new form of franchise agreement, a release of claims and payment of a renewal fee.

Action PLAN

Keep these renewal concerns in mind when analyzing the initial franchise agreement. Ask the franchisor representative about renewal rights. Make sure your attorney is comfortable with the contract renewal language.

International Franchising

ENRIQUE FOUND THE FRANCHISE HE wanted to buy: a children's tutoring business. Everything about the franchise met with Enrique's approval, but he had one concern: the franchise was based in another country. Though the company boasted an active international franchising department, he wasn't sure whether the franchisor's overseas location would affect his ability to run the franchise in the U.S.

THE GLOBALIZATION OF FRANCHISING

The global expansion of U.S. franchisors is one of the most interesting business success stories of the past 30 years. The American franchise concept has dispersed its various familiar brand names in large and small countries around the world at an astonishing rate.

McDonald's has been a global franchise expansion leader. It has established over 30,000 restaurants worldwide with over 70 percent franchised. The InterContinental Hotels Group, a franchisor of Holiday Inn hotels and

INsight

The history of international franchise expansion has not been—as they say in the United Kingdom—all beer and skittles. In the 1980s, McDonald's restaurants reported enormous difficulties in establishing their food supply organization in foreign locations like Russia and Asia. Other franchisors have had their international expansion plans frustrated at huge expense by national laws restricting money transfer, trademark pirates and poorly enforced intellectual property laws, poor reception of their products because of cultural concerns, and communications problems.

other brands, has opened hotels in nearly 100 countries and territories.

Franchise regulation has been growing as well. The countries with a form of presale disclosure requirements for franchisors include Australia, Belgium, Brazil, Canada (Alberta, Prince Edward Island and Ontario), China, France, Indonesia, Italy, Japan, Malaysia, Mexico, South Korea, Spain, Sweden and the United States. Buy a franchise in one of these countries, and you will likely receive a presale disclosure statement presenting some of the key information you will need to evaluate the proposed franchise investment.

KEYS TO FOREIGN-BASED FRANCHISES

The international expansion of franchising has now come full circle as franchisors from other lands expand into the U.S. market. If you are interested in purchasing an international franchise, located in the U.S. market or another country, make sure you consider the following:

Find out if the company has taken steps to comply with all the laws on franchising in this country. Does the company have a UFOC or other disclosure statement? Is it complete? Has the company registered its offering in the U.S. registration states? If it has complied with these laws, that tells you the company has made a substantial investment in seeking successful franchisees in the U.S. market. If it has sidestepped these requirements, it is trying to cut some important corners, and you should be careful. You could be the next corner.

Is the program a regional offering or limited to one market? Will you receive rights for several markets or multiple states? Many companies new to the U.S. market divide up the country into separate, multistate regions so that penetrating such a huge commercial country is manageable.

How is the U.S. expansion going to be managed? Is there a regional manager or a master franchisee? Make sure you understand how the relationships are set up so that you know who will provide things like training and services. This may not be clear after you review the UFOC, so plan to discuss it with the sales representatives you meet.

One of the largest challenges of international franchising is effective communication. Will the company be communicating directly with the U.S. franchisees, or will it go through its regional managers/master franchisees? Find out if regular meetings will be held, and where. If they are overseas, be sure that you include these costs in your budgeting. Ask if the franchisor will assist with any meeting expenses.

Trademark protection can be a challenge for a franchisor from outside the U.S. Be sure to check Item 13 of the UFOC describing the U.S. registration status of the principal trademark. If it is not registered with the U.S. Patent and Trademark Office, exercise extreme caution and have your attorney check it out.

Is the cultural fit of the business a good one? Has the product/service been tested in the U.S. market, or are you the test? If you are the pioneer for this program, make sure you will not be too badly hurt if the product/service flops. It does happen. And it will happen regardless of the level of your enthusiasm and industry. Make sure your lawyer takes steps to protect you in the event the project goes south.

Don't shy away from an opportunity just because it is a franchisor from another country. The UFOC will tell you a lot about the company and how it is organized to service the U.S. market. Ask for the UFOC early on. If it does not exist, always proceed with extreme caution.

SUMMARY NOTES

✓ An international franchise can make an exciting investment, and more and more foreign-based franchisors tackle the U.S. market.

✓ Protect yourself by looking into the three key areas of an international relationship: control, communication and commitment.

✓ Find out how the market will be managed by the franchisor. Is there a regional manager or a U.S. master franchisee in charge, or will the company manage its franchisees directly?

✓ Make sure that the program will be successful in the U.S. market. Foreign success does not always translate to the U.S. market.

Action PLAN

Contact and meet with managers responsible for franchising an international brand in your area. Locate other franchisees of the system in your area.

CHAPTER 19

Negotiating Franchise Agreements

*M*ARIA DISLIKES BUYING CARS FOR *one reason: She hates having to negotiate aggressively on the price to get a fair deal. Now that she is buying a franchise, she has the same feeling as she gets closer to closing the transaction. Is it supposed to be like buying a car? Is she expected to negotiate? Maria wonders if she even has enough information effectively to negotiate on this purchase but remembers her dad always saying, "Everything is negotiable."*

The purchase of a franchise can be an intimidating process. Most Americans have never seen, let alone signed, a contract of such length and complexity as a typical business format franchise agreement. Signing one under any circumstances takes an act of courage and a leap of faith.

The lesson that Maria's dad taught her—that everything is negotiable—is always true in business, and it applies with equal force to franchises. Don't miss the opportunity to negotiate your purchase.

NEGOTIATING A FRANCHISE AGREEMENT

Signing a franchise agreement comes at the end of a lengthy process, highlighted by the delivery of a UFOC, promotional brochures, other system literature and personal interviews. Pressing for favorable contract terms may be the last thought on your mind. However, with some planning and understanding of the franchisor's position, you can cut a far better legal and financial deal.

WHY IS THE FRANCHISE AGREEMENT SO ONE-SIDED?

Franchise agreements have always been weighted in the franchisor's favor for one simple reason: The franchisor is not only your partner in this venture; it is the system-wide enforcer. It is in everyone's interests—the franchisor's, yours, and other franchisees'—that all franchisees operate in a manner that meets the highest system standards. If the business closest to you is dirty, slow or run-down, it affects your business directly and dramatically. Both units operate under the same trademark; if your neighbor is injuring the local reputation of the mark, you pay the price. To paraphrase the great Yogi Berra, "If people don't want to come to your store, how are you going to stop them?"

As the system standards enforcer, the franchisor must reserve draconian enforcement rights in the franchise agreement. These may strike you as overbearing, but they are designed to allow the franchisor to take action if a franchisee's operation is subpar. In a sense, the enforcement provisions are there to protect you as well. When your neighbor's careless operation starts to hurt your business, you will be the first one to request that the franchisor do something to correct the situation. The franchisor had better have tough enforcement provisions in the franchise agreement, or it will be powerless to do anything. Negotiating some of these provisions will be tough.

UNDERSTANDING THE SELLER'S POSITION

Powerful financial forces drive the franchisor to complete the franchise transaction. It is difficult, time-consuming and expensive for a franchisor to locate a qualified franchisee. Selling a franchise is the ultimate hard sell; the sales cycle is measured in months, not days. Most franchisors devote tens of thousands of dollars a year to recruiting franchisees, and once a qualified applicant shows an interest, the franchisor is highly motivated to complete the sale. A new franchisee in the system means a stream of revenue that will last for years and continued growth for the system.

Franchise sales representatives are often paid in whole or in part on commission. They are extremely motivated to see the transaction close; if you walk away, they lose money.

IN*sight*

The power of your position is expressed in your attitude: You are interested in buying but not overeager. You let the seller know that you are interested, but there are lots of other investments you are evaluating (even if in your heart you know this is the one). Negotiation expert Herb Cohen says the best negotiating attitude says to the other side: "I care about making this commitment, but not that much."

The point is that you are in a position of considerable power when it comes to negotiating a franchise agreement. Use that power to your advantage.

TAKE IT OR LEAVE IT?

How easy is it to negotiate the terms of a franchise agreement? While it complicates the life of franchisors, it is a well-known secret in the franchisor community that these contracts are negotiated all the time. You may hear from a franchisor that franchise law prohibits negotiation (it doesn't), or the company does not want to negotiate the terms that are offered to you, but you should not understand that to mean that the company *cannot* change its contract for you.

In fact, even the law of California—the toughest jurisdiction on negotiated changes in a franchise offering—allows franchisors to negotiate the terms of a franchise, but imposes a series of disclosure and registration obligations on a franchisor who changes the terms of its standard, registered offer. At the other end of the legal spectrum, the franchise law in the Commonwealth of Virginia states that a franchise agreement may be voided by the franchisee within a short time if it is not negotiated by the franchisor.

A franchisor can change the standard franchise contract terms for you if it chooses to make the changes.

FRANCHISORS' INFLEXIBLE POSITIONS

Many provisions of the franchise agreement can be negotiated, but there are a few areas where franchisors can be expected to dig in their heels:

Trademarks

As the owner of the trademarks, a franchisor will not be at all willing to water down their legal rights to control the display of the mark or protect the mark through enforcement actions. There is usually some wiggle room in the degree to which a franchisor is willing to stand behind the mark if the franchisee is attacked legally for its use of the mark. Look for language by which the company "indemnifies" (will pay) the franchisee for legal expenses incurred where the franchisee has properly used the marks and comes under legal attack by someone claiming infringement.

Royalty Rates

Conventional wisdom in the franchisor community suggests that all franchisees should pay the same rate of royalty whenever possible. This keeps everyone in the system on the same footing and avoids creating different classes of franchise citizens in the system. So if the standard royalty rate is set at 5 percent, don't expect the company to accept your suggestion that you pay a royalty rate of 4 percent.

INsight

Check Item 5 of the UFOC ("Initial Franchise Fee"). If the initial franchise fee is not uniform, the company is required to disclose a formula or actual initial fees paid in the prior fiscal year. If the company cut some deals on the initial franchise fee, they will be at least mentioned here.

There may be extenuating circumstances where you would be allowed to pay a lower rate for a period of time, but those are relatively rare. If you are taking over a store that has been poorly managed and the customer base is depleted, you may want to suggest a break in the royalty rate for your first year while you turn around the operation.

Assignment/Termination Controls

Franchisors will do their best to exercise control over the people who are allowed to own and operate their franchises. They have a direct interest; all those franchises are flying a flag owned by the company. If a weak operator is allowed to come in through a sale, or someone comes in who does not have the capital to run the business successfully, it creates a threat of business failure. That hurts the reputation of the system and, indirectly, all franchisees.

If an operator is not following the program or their operations are not clean or they are otherwise hurting the system's reputation, the company has little choice but to take corrective steps. For these reasons, franchisors are not likely to give on suggested changes to the assignment or termination provisions.

FRANCHISORS' FLEXIBLE POSITIONS

Franchisors tend to have more flexibility in other areas of the contract:

Initial Fee

The franchisor has great flexibility when it comes to the initial fee. If the initial fee is set at $30,000, you may be able to argue for a reduction of that amount or a plan by which you defer payment over time. Try suggesting that you pay $15,000 upfront and the balance over the first 18 months of your operation of the business.

There may be some resistance to this concept, of course. Perhaps the company needs the upfront fee to pay a commission to the broker or for its own operating expenses. Franchisors are also reluctant to make any changes that require additional disclosure. If there are variations in the initial fee, the company may have to disclose that fact in Item 5 of its UFOC. If the company offers financing, it may be required to disclose those terms as well as in Item 10. Go ahead and ask anyway; it's your money, after all.

Territorial Rights

This is ticklish in some systems, but well worth exploring in negotiations. What are the dimensions of the territory you are granted? Can you request an expansion of that area or ask for an option right on an adjoining territory? Perhaps you could request additional time and territorial protection during the first few years of your franchise. It may take a bit of creativity on your part, but it is well worth exploring if there are ways that you can structure the territorial rights to meet your own needs.

Marketing Contributions

This topic, and the franchisor's flexibility on it, will be determined by the type and the circumstances of the business.

Never forget the fundamental impulse of good negotiators: It never hurts to ask. Build a win-win franchise agreement going in, and your relationship will be that much stronger for the long term.

SUMMARY NOTES

- ✓ Get creative when buying a franchise or business opportunity. Propose price reductions and payment terms that fit your needs.
- ✓ When you first read a franchise agreement, it may strike you as one-sided. But there are reasons for that. There are other players here; this is not merely a two-party agreement.
- ✓ Position yourself for negotiation. Gather as much information as you can about deals the franchisor has granted to others.
- ✓ It's legal in all states to negotiate a franchise agreement.
- ✓ Remember some of the key rules of negotiation: do your homework, "start high," be willing to walk on the deal, and "it never hurts to ask."
- ✓ There are some areas (initial fees, territory, advertising contributions) where a franchisor is more likely to give than other areas (trademark, royalties and transfer rights).

Action PLAN

Become a good negotiator. Take a seminar on negotiation skills, or head to the library or the bookstore for a book on negotiation, such as the classic *You Can Negotiate Anything* by Herb Cohen (Bantam Books).

CHAPTER 20

Working with Lawyers and Accountants

*B*OBBY IS A PRO AT COACHING HIGH
*school kids but is lost when it comes to
reading a balance sheet or understanding dense legal language in a contract.
He had what he considered an excellent franchise
investment opportunity but knew he needed some
professional help. Could he afford it? Could he
afford not to get help?*

USING LEGAL SERVICES

Anyone buying a franchise today is well-
advised to retain the services of an experienced
attorney to review the franchise agreement and
any related contracts. Business opportunity
buyers, depending on the size of the investment, may need an attorney's help as well. The
objection is right on the tip of your tongue,
isn't it? "How can I afford a lawyer? I am putting this business together on a shoestring as it
is. A lawyer's going to cost me a fortune."

In the first place, using the services of an
attorney need not cost a fortune, and you can
work out in advance what fees are likely to be
involved. Most lawyers still charge for their

services by the hour, but many are willing to set
a quoted fee or agree to a cap on the fee for a
simple project like the review of a franchise
agreement and UFOC. If it takes a lawyer two
hours to review the document and another
hour to meet with you to discuss it, that suggests a legal fee—assuming a $150 hourly
rate—that does not exceed $500. Hiring an
attorney is like buying insurance. And as insurance goes, $500 is not expensive at all. You can
expect to purchase casualty insurance, health
coverage for your employees, and unemploy-
ment compensation insurance that will put the

INsight

Attorneys know their clients are concerned
about legal fees and generally encourage discussion of the subject at the first meeting.
Gone are the days when attorneys thought it
unprofessional to discuss money.

cost of your modest attorney fees to shame.

What can you expect to receive for your legal fees? At a minimum you want to hear from your learned counsel whether there are any provisions in the proposed contract that run distinctly against your interests. You also want to know about provisions that put your investment in a precarious position. For instance, what if the franchisor reserves the right to terminate the relationship with no advance notice if you fail to follow the standards in the operating manuals? Your lawyer should advise you that this is way too broad and threatens your business in an unacceptable manner. They may suggest that language be added that gives you the right to receive at least 30 days' written notice of the infraction and an opportunity to cure it without threatening your entire investment in the program.

You also want to hear from your lawyer if there are any other aspects of the franchise documents that cause concern or call for further investigation. If you live in one of the several states requiring a franchisor to register under a franchise law, your lawyer should make the phone call to check on the company's status. Ask your attorney to tell you if your state's law protects you from an arbitrary or groundless termination by the franchisor. They should be able to give you a copy of any such law.

DO YOU NEED A SPECIALIST?

In this age of professional specialization, how do you find a lawyer experienced enough to be of help reviewing a franchise agreement? Referrals are by far the most effective way to locate the right lawyer. As you meet franchise owners in the system you are investigating, ask them who they use. Every state has a lawyer referral system you can look up in your phone book. Ask your friends and business acquaintances for referrals. You don't want the name of a cousin's brother-in-law who just graduated from law school in another state, but you do want to hear about lawyers a person has used and knows are experienced. Get familiar with the *Martindale-Hubbell Law Directory*, available in every law library and most public libraries, and online (www.martindale.com). This directory lists lawyers by state and town, and many entries include a short description of their professional background. It even offers a rating system of lawyers.

USING ACCOUNTING SERVICES

The other professional assistance you should consider hiring is a competent accountant. Accountants are worth their weight in Big Mac® sandwiches if you are planning to go into business and are evaluating a franchise investment.

First and foremost, your accountant can put together a detailed projection for your business and help you consider how to finance the total investment. The projection will tell you a lot about the business. It should show where your break-even points will be, the number of customers you will need in order to generate your revenue, and the amount of your investment plus financing costs. It will also give you an idea of the return you can expect on your investment.

In short, your accountant can help you decide whether you would be better off financially buying the franchise or getting a job and putting your money in treasury bonds.

Your accountant can also look over the franchisor's three years of audited financial statements contained in the UFOC. These tell you a lot about the staying power of the company.

Will it be there for the long haul? Do the statements show healthy growth or stagnating losses? Your accountant should be able to provide a professional opinion about the standing of the franchisor.

A full review by a CPA can be expensive, running into a few thousand dollars rather quickly. Talk to your accountant about what you need and what it's going to cost. Then figure out a way to do it.

WHAT TO ASK YOUR ADVISORS

Some Great Questions for Your Attorney

Plan to explore these basic topics with your attorney, and add to the list whatever you think is appropriate for the franchise you are reviewing:

- How does this franchise agreement compare to others you have reviewed?
- Are there any provisions in this agreement that I should not agree to under any circumstances ("deal breakers")? Do you have any suggested changes for the agreement, and would they be accepted by the franchisor?
- Have you checked with state authorities to confirm that the company is registered to sell franchises or business opportunities in this state?
- How do the termination provisions stack up under this state's franchise laws or case law on termination? What exactly are my transfer rights under the agreement?
- Do any of the litigation or arbitration cases disclosed in Item 3 concern you?
- What protections do I need when buying this business opportunity? Should I defer payments or otherwise structure the transaction? Are there any surety bonds, escrow arrangements or trust accounts in place in this state to protect buyers of this program?

Some Great Questions for Your Accountant/CPA

- What is the seller's net worth? How does this amount relate to the size of my total investment in the franchise? Should I be concerned about it?
- Can you tell from the financial statement whether the seller's business is profitable? How would you describe the seller's financial health?
- Does the financial statement show the average annual royalty payment received from a franchisee? Can we extrapolate any average sales figures from that?
- Is there a surety bond, escrow account or deferred payment in place in this state? Is there another entity that guarantees the obligations of the seller for this franchise program?
- How do the Item 7 figures strike you compared to other small businesses you have advised? Do they look reasonable?
- What is the break-even point for this particular business? What type of revenues will I need to cover my expenses and make the franchise or business opportunity profitable?

SUMMARY NOTES

✓ Ask franchisees you meet who they use for legal services. Do your research and find a good lawyer with experience representing small businesses.

✓ Think of legal and accounting expenses as part of your insurance costs.

✓ Get organized in your use of legal and accounting services. Know what questions you want answered in the preliminary review process.

Action **PLAN**

Interview a few attorneys and accountants to determine their individual styles, experience and capabilities. Be sure to confirm in advance that you will not be billed for the interview.

CHAPTER 21

Questions for Franchisees

NANCY KNEW SHE NEEDED TO TALK TO *some franchisees in the business she was investigating but was a bit intimidated. Was she imposing on them? Would she offend these experienced businesspeople with her intrusive call? What would she say?*

THE KEY TO YOUR RESEARCH

Current franchisees are without a doubt the best source of information you will find on the benefits, drawbacks and strengths of the franchise business you are investigating. They can also generally provide some great insights and advice. It does take a bit of gumption to approach a business owner, but you should not hesitate.

The first step is to make arrangements to talk to the owner. Remember that business owners are extremely busy. It's best to call ahead and find a good time to visit. When the owner does meet with you, be sensitive to the time you spend. If you requested a 20-minute interview, stick to it.

FRANCHISE QUESTIONS

It also helps to have a set of questions prepared. Don't try to wing it. Here is a checklist of franchise questions to ask:

- Is the training program worthwhile? Did it leave you well-prepared to run this business?
- Has the franchisor's support been steady? Are they there when you need them?
- What is the culture of the franchise system? Are franchisees friendly with one another? Is it encouraging or discouraging to be with the franchisor?
- Is the business seasonal? What are the strongest and weakest times of the year?
- Does the franchisor provide continuing training?
- Is the market for this business a strong one? Is it growing or slowing?
- Is there a franchisee association or council? Do franchisees have a real role in the franchisor's decision-making process?
- Did you have a good year last year? Do you recall what your gross sales were? Will this year be stronger or weaker?

- How is product supply arranged for franchisees? Does it work well?
- What questions do you wish you had asked going into your franchise investment?
- Knowing what you now know, would you buy this franchise again?

INsight

Most franchise owners will discuss the performance of their business once you establish a rapport with them. They need to know you are not a competitor or a potential competitor but someone serious about making the same investment decision they made. Most want to help.

Don't hesitate to take notes during your conversations. It tells the franchisees you value their words and experience. And resist the urge to get too chatty or argumentative. Your objective is to gather information. If you hear comments that concern you, by all means follow up with the franchisor.

SUMMARY NOTES

✓ When approaching a franchisee, be respectful of his or her time and business demands.

✓ Visit the business as a customer to observe how it operates.

✓ Prepare a set of questions to discuss. Don't wing it.

✓ Take notes, and follow up with the franchisor if you hear answers that concern you.

Action PLAN

Create a list of owner questions for each franchise you investigate. Make full notes after each interview and drop them in your file.

CHAPTER 22

Skill Sets of the Successful Franchisee

*C*AROLYN PLANS TO BUY A RETAIL GIFT *business because she has always dreamed about pleasing customers with her scrumptious teas, cakes and other treats. She enjoys talking on the phone and looks forward to owning her own shop. She wonders what else she will need to know to be successful. Are there skills that she could learn that will help in her business?*

Carolyn is asking the right questions, because all successful small-business owners develop a distinct skill set. At the heart of any franchised business are some basic elements of business operation and business development that must be mastered. Falter on these basics, and your business may have some serious problems. The most successful business owners develop these skill sets and drill them into their employees.

THE ART OF THE SALE

Business is selling. All businesses boil down quickly to this realization; franchises are no exception. It does not matter whether you are a junior manager in the world's largest organization or the owner of your own small business; the engine of both businesses is driven primarily by sales activity.

Remember this basic truth of business: "Nothing happens in business until someone, somewhere makes a sale."

It follows that your key to success is to become a student of the sale; become an expert in the process and the techniques used by the best salespeople. Try to learn the basic rules for presenting features and benefits, overcoming objections and closing techniques. Park yourself in the business book section of your local library, and crawl through a few books on selling. There are dozens of titles available. Drink them in.

COUNTER MAGIC

One of the most fascinating aspects of retail business is the study of what happens at the counter, that magic place where the front-line representatives of your business meet your customers. When we say the "counter" of your business, we mean it literally and metaphorically. All businesses meet customers, whether it is on the telephone, over the internet or at the customer's residence or place of business. In a traditional retail business, it will literally be a countertop at your location. Successful franchise organizations have pioneered and perfected the techniques at the counter that can have enormous payoffs in business.

No one has taught us more than the great Ray Kroc of McDonald's restaurants. He insisted that counter workers greet all customers with a smile and a cheery "Welcome to McDonald's!" The company reinforced the message with advertising showing the warm smiles of perky counter people welcoming you to McDonald's. "We love to see you smile."

Kroc also drove billions of dollars in sales, and propelled his organization to prominence, by teaching all counter people to say six simple words to every customer: "Would you like fries with that?" The resulting sales figures changed the landscape of American business.

Whatever franchised business you manage, study what is happening at the counter. Put your training resources to work on the exchange. Make sure your employees follow your example and stick to your counter procedures. Study and watch their performance and try new ideas. Keep your counter fresh, enthusiastic and fun, and your customers will come back time and again for more.

YOUR PROFITS ARE IN THE DETAILS

One thundering lesson of business ownership is just how small is the portion of gross revenue that actually falls into your pocket as profit. These small "margins" can represent vast fortunes, of course, when a business is run on a modestly large scale. Even at a large scale, though, the details determine whether the business comes out on the profitable side of the small margins or on the loss side of the profit/loss measure.

You have no choice but to become a student of the details of your franchised business. A few cents break on the price of your wholesale inventory, the lower costs of office supplies when purchased in bulk, the small incremental costs of condiments, managing the costs of labor—these details make all the difference.

BECOME A BEAN COUNTER

Money is the language of business, and accountants are the interpreters of the language. As a business owner, you must master the language and become conversant in balance sheets and monthly operations statements. If problems are brewing in your business, they will show up first in the monthly numbers. You will get to know intimately your percentages of food costs, labor, administrative costs and gross profit. This takes some study, so cozy up to your favorite accountant and tell them that you think this is the beginning of a beautiful friendship.

BE A SKILLED NEGOTIATOR

It often surprises people coming from a job into business ownership just how much of small-business dealings are subject to a fluid marketplace, where prices and terms are determined by the give and take of negotiation. It takes a spot of courage to ask for a better price or payment terms or faster delivery, but it gives you the edge you need in your business. Your suppliers and business customers expect many aspects of the sale to be negotiated, so be prepared to jump in.

PEOPLE MANAGEMENT

Small-business ownership is little more than the management of employees. Keep them happy, well-paid and motivated, and your business will be on solid ground. Give no personal attention, underpay and discourage them with a punishing attitude, and you will experience high turnover and low productivity. Given typically low margins in small businesses, this can make the difference between a profitable business and a troubled one.

BUILD AN ORGANIZATION

It's been said that the owner does not build a business; they build an organization of people and the organization builds the business. Think about building a team of talented people, look for the best employees you can find, and try to stay out of their way as they build your business.

INsight

In all negotations, know beforehand how long you will go before you stop negotiating, and what you consider your target. When opening your discussion, "start high" and then be prepared to make concessions as the other side (starting low) pulls you down toward your target endpoint. Asking for more than you will settle for will not insult anyone. It will leave you some room to make concessions to the other side. That will put you in the give and take of business—right where you need to be.

BE AN A+ FRANCHISEE

If your business is a franchise, follow the rules of the system. Part of being a top-performing franchised business is full and careful compliance with all aspects of the franchise program. That means paying royalties on time, showing up for meetings and taking educational opportunities as they come along. Be a leader among franchise owners who do their best to promote the brand. Not only is this good business, but it will also add to the value of your business and may open opportunities down the road for expansion. The franchisor will naturally look to its A+ franchisees when new opportunities present themselves.

COLLECTING MONEY

The biggest challenge you face as a small-business owner is the collection of money owed to you. For all businesses, successful collection is a combination of smart routine business practice and persistence.

When do you know you have a collection problem? Here are the symptoms:

- An unacceptably high level of accounts receivable
- No office policy on collections
- Too many bad checks
- No information on the customer who pays on credit (including by check!)
- An inability to be decisive and move promptly against the deadbeat
- No way to recover the expenses associated with debt collection, such as attorney's fees, interest and late charges

No one likes collection problems. If you are new to business, the reluctance of your customers to pay their bills can be a surprise. After all, you have always paid your mortgage, utility bills, credit card statements and household expenses on time. Why can't your customers do the same?

Often the reason they do not pay in a timely fashion is *you*. Your routine credit extension practices, the information you gather on your customers and the way you respond to slow payment all dictate the success you have at getting paid.

The best advice is to create a written policy statement that details exactly how credit will be extended or how a new customer account will be set up. Give a copy of the policy to the customer. The policy should spell out all credit procedures and collection policies. For your internal use, develop form letters that you use when a customer is late, and prepare to respond immediately.

Use some form of credit application that gathers this basic information about the account: name, address, telephone number (work and residence), Social Security number (this is essential), place of employment, bank account information and property ownership information (automobiles and homes). If you are extending credit to a corporation, be sure to obtain the formal corporate name, the date and state of incorporation and the employer identification number. Without this basic information, collections can be a nightmare. The following are some tips for smart collection practices:

Don't Accept Bad Checks

Examine all checks carefully. A quick way to spot a forged check is to look for the perforations. Most forged checks are produced on plain paper stock with no perforated edges. Real check paper stock allows the check to be removed from a perforated edge. Bank tellers are trained to look for this distinctive feature.

Is the date correct? If the date is old (generally more than three or four weeks) or if it has been postdated, do not accept it.

Is the amount properly stated? Does the numerical figure agree with the written dollar amount? If the number, the written amount or the payee (you) is illegible, written over or hard to read in any way, do not take the check.

Be careful accepting a two-party check. A two-party check is made to one person, and that person offers to endorse the check to you. Unless you know both parties, you run a risk that the original maker will stop payment on the check.

Look out for checks that show a low sequence number. This indicates a recently opened account since most banks begin numbering a new checking account at #101. Just be more cautious when the number is low.

Do Not Put Off Collecting on the Debt

The longer you wait to take action, the more difficult it will be to collect on an overdue account. An account receivable that is more than 90 days old should be turned over for collection, either to a collection agency, which will handle the matter for a hefty percentage of the outstanding bill, or to your attorney.

Use a Credit Agreement

You cannot collect interest, late fees or attorney's fees without the written agreement of the customer. A credit agreement also spells out the terms of the credit being extended and shows you take this account, the credit and collections seriously.

SUMMARY NOTES ——————————

✓ Running your business is the ultimate challenge. Brush up on the skills that are essential to all business operations: master the art of the sale, manage details, count beans, negotiate, manage people effectively, build an organization, be an A+ franchisee and collect the money you are owed.

Action **PLAN**

Take a course at a local college, university or business school to learn more about areas of business that are mystifying to you.

CHAPTER 23

Make it Happen

*S*EAN HAS TOYED WITH THE IDEA STARTING OF *starting his own business for more than five years. He works up to a point of getting serious about an opportunity and then backs off and stays in the comfortable routine of his job. He's starting to wonder if he will ever make the commitment.*

Starting a business takes an enormous amount of initiative. If you have not done it before, it is easy not to start. There are mental obstacles at every turn. You can fall into a trap of indecision, where you constantly search for the exact business of your dreams but never seem to find it. People you love and respect can talk you out of it. You can be discouraged by the doom and gloom of the popular press. You can decide that your route to wealth is working your way up to middle management. There are a thousand reasons not to start.

But you know in your heart that the world rewards courage and persistence.

So start! Make that call. Contact your support team. Start lining up your money resources. Go to that trade show. Ask those questions, and present yourself in the finest light possible to your new business contacts.

You will be pleasantly surprised at how your hard work and persistence pays off, and the interesting places your initiative can lead you. If the words in this book help you take that first step, then you have made our day.

Good luck in your new business!

Action PLAN

There is no substitute for taking action. No amount of dreaming, planning or talking takes its place. If you want to be in business for yourself, you must make it happen. Take action today.

Ultimate Franchise Directory

Understanding the Directory

SECTION TWO OF OUR BOOK DETAILS THE basic startup information of 1,111 franchise opportunities. Use this information as a first step toward buying a franchise of your own.

This directory is not intended to endorse, advertise or recommend any particular franchise(s). It is solely a research tool you can use to compare franchise operations. You should always conduct your own independent investigation before you invest money in a franchise. If you haven't already, make sure you read Section One of this book.

KEY TO THE LISTINGS
Franchise 500® ranking

As an additional research tool, we've included the rankings of companies in *Entrepreneur* magazine's 2007 Franchise 500®. Rankings are based on objective factors, including financial stability of the system, growth rate and size of the system, years in business, length of time franchising, start-up costs, litigation, percentage of terminations and whether the company provides financing. For more information regarding the methodology used in these rankings, go to www.entrepreneur.com/franchise500.

Financial rating

$$$$: Exceeded our standards
$$$: Met all our standards
$$: Met most of our standards
$: Met our minimal standards
0: Did not meet our minimal standards

An important step in researching a franchise opportunity is determining the financial strength of the company. If a franchise company is in a weak financial condition, it could raise the risk levels for your investment.

For our financial ratings, based on a financial analysis of the 2007 Franchise 500®, we examined, among other things, liquidity ratios, debt to net worth, revenue or sales volume, and profitability. This information was taken from the financial information provided in the companies' Uniform Franchise Offering Circulars (UFOCs).

We strongly suggest that, when researching a franchise, you have your accountant read the financial statements included in the UFOC and ask for a more detailed opinion of the financial condition of the company.

Franchise units

Besides providing data on the number of units in a system, we tell you where the company wants to expand this year and the number of employees necessary to run a franchise unit.

Exclusive territories

The majority of franchise companies offer exclusive territories to their franchisees. Territory size typically is based on population size or by geographic area.

Absentee ownership

Many franchise companies require their franchisees to be hands-on owners. Here you can see whether absentee ownership is allowed.

Costs

Total cost: the initial investment necessary to open the franchise. This amount includes costs for equipment, initial supplies, business licenses, signage, working capital as well as the initial franchise fee.

Franchise fee: a lump sum payment made at the time the franchise agreement is signed. This fee generally covers the franchisor's cost of recruiting franchisees and of initial services like site location and training.

Royalty fee: typically a monthly fee paid by the franchisee to the franchisor, which is either calculated as a percentage of the franchisee's gross sales or on a flat-fee basis.

Term of agreement: the length of time the franchisee is granted the right to operate under the franchise system. When the time is up, most franchise companies offer a right to renew either for a fee or for free.

Franchisees required to buy multiple units? While many franchise companies encourage franchisees to buy more than one unit at a time, there are franchisors that require multiple franchise ownership.

Financing

Types of financing provided by the franchisor are listed under the "in-house" heading.

When the franchisor has developed a relationship with an outside lender to provide financing to its franchisees, the types of financing are listed under the "3rd party" heading.

Qualifications, Training, Business support, Marketing support

We provide additional information on these factors to help you make an informed decision.

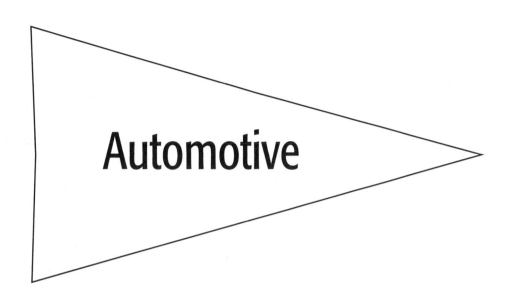

Automotive

AUTOMOTIVE ▸ *Appearance Services*

CLEARBRA FRANCHISE LLC

Financial rating: $$

452 E. 500 South
Salt Lake City, UT 84111
(801)359-0071
www.getclearbra.com
Automotive paint protection
Began: 1999, Franchising: 2005
Headquarters size: 8 employees

U.S. franchises: 2
Canadian franchises: 0
Other foreign franchises: 0
Company-owned: 1

Seeking: All U.S.
Seeking in Canada? Yes
Exclusive territories? Yes
Homebased option? No
Employees needed to run biz: 2
Absentee ownership? No

COSTS
Total cost: $102.8K-193K
Franchise fee: $20K-25K
Royalty fee: 5%
Term of agreement: 10 years renewable
for 25% of current franchise fee
Franchisees required to buy multiple
units? Outside the U.S. only

FINANCING
In-house: None
3rd-party: Accounts receivable,
equipment, franchise fee,
inventory, payroll, startup costs

QUALIFICATIONS
Net worth: $150K
Cash liquidity: $40K
Experience:
General business experience
Sales skills

TRAINING
At headquarters: 11 days

BUSINESS SUPPORT
Grand opening
Internet
Newsletter
Meetings
Toll-free phone line
Field operations/evaluations
Purchasing cooperatives
Security/safety procedures

MARKETING SUPPORT
Co-op advertising
Ad slicks

COLORS ON PARADE

Ranked #245 in Entrepreneur Magazine's 2007 Franchise 500   *Financial rating: $$$*

642 Century Cir.
Conway, SC 29526
(866)349-6786
www.colorsonparade.com
Mobile automotive appearance
    services
Began: 1989, Franchising: 1991
Headquarters size: 15 employees
Franchise department: 2 employees

U.S. franchises: 246
Canadian franchises: 0
Other foreign franchises: 0
Company-owned: 9

Seeking: All U.S.
Seeking in Canada? No
Exclusive territories? Yes
Homebased option? Yes
Employees needed to run biz: 0
Absentee ownership? No

COSTS
Total cost: $42.9K-597.2K
Franchise fee: $5K-15K
Royalty fee: 7-30%
Term of agreement: 10 years renewable
Franchisees required to buy multiple
    units? No

FINANCING
In-house: Franchise fee, startup costs
3rd-party: Equipment, franchise fee,
    inventory

QUALIFICATIONS
Net worth: $10K-500K
Cash liquidity: $10K-200K
Experience:
    General business experience
    Marketing skills
    Love of cars

TRAINING
At headquarters: 2 weeks
At franchisee's location: 3 months
Ongoing technical training

BUSINESS SUPPORT
Grand opening
Internet
Newsletter
Meetings
Toll-free phone line
Field operations/evaluations
Security/safety procedures

MARKETING SUPPORT
Co-op advertising
Ad slicks
National media campaign
Recruitment seminars

DENT DOCTOR

Financial rating: $$$

11301 W. Markham
Little Rock, AR 72211
(501)224-0500
www.dentdoctor.com
Paint-free dent repair & auto
    appearance services
Began: 1986, Franchising: 1990
Headquarters size: 6 employees
Franchise department: 3 employees

U.S. franchises: 27
Canadian franchises: 1
Other foreign franchises: 1
Company-owned: 3

Seeking: All U.S.
Seeking in Canada? Yes
Exclusive territories? Yes
Homebased option? No
Employees needed to run biz: 3
Absentee ownership? Yes

COSTS
Total cost: $49.9K-96.3K
Franchise fee: $9.9K-19.9K+
Royalty fee: 6%
Term of agreement: 10 years renewable
    at no charge
Franchisees required to buy multiple
    units? No

FINANCING
In-house: None
3rd-party: Equipment, franchise fee,
    inventory, startup costs

QUALIFICATIONS
Net worth: $75K
Cash liquidity: $10K
Experience:
    General business experience

TRAINING
At headquarters: 4 weeks
At franchisee's location: 4 weeks
Ongoing

BUSINESS SUPPORT
Grand opening
Internet
Newsletter
Meetings
Toll-free phone line
Field operations/evaluations
Lease negotiations
Purchasing cooperatives
Security/safety procedures

MARKETING SUPPORT
Co-op advertising
Ad slicks
Regional marketing

MAACO COLLISION REPAIR & AUTO PAINTING

Ranked #205 in Entrepreneur Magazine's 2007 Franchise 500　　　*Financial rating: $$$$*

381 Brooks Rd.
King of Prussia, PA 19406
(800)296-2226
www.franchise.maaco.com
Automotive painting & body repair
Began: 1972, Franchising: 1972
Headquarters size: 167 employees
Franchise department: 11 employees

U.S. franchises: 428
Canadian franchises: 35
Other foreign franchises: 0
Company-owned: 1

Seeking: All U.S.
Seeking in Canada? Yes
Exclusive territories? No
Homebased option? No
Employees needed to run biz: 7-8
Absentee ownership? No

COSTS
Total cost: $296.5K
Franchise fee: $40K
Royalty fee: 8%
Term of agreement: 15 years renewable
　　at no charge
Franchisees required to buy multiple
　　units? No

FINANCING
In-house: None
3rd-party: Equipment, franchise fee,
　　inventory, startup costs

QUALIFICATIONS
Net worth: $300K
Cash liquidity: $75K
Experience:
　　General business experience
　　Marketing skills

TRAINING
At headquarters: 4 weeks
At franchisee's location: 4 weeks
Ongoing support

BUSINESS SUPPORT
Grand opening
Internet
Newsletter
Meetings
Toll-free phone line
Field operations/evaluations
Purchasing cooperatives
Security/safety procedures

MARKETING SUPPORT
Ad slicks
National media campaign
Regional marketing

MARS INT'L. INC.

Ranked #174 in Entrepreneur Magazine's 2007 Franchise 500　　　*Financial rating: $$$$*

2001 E. Division St., #101
Arlington, TX 76006
(817)226-6277
www.marsinternational.com
Auto appearance reconditioning
　　services
Began: 1998, Franchising: 1998
Headquarters size: 22 employees
Franchise department: 6 employees

U.S. franchises: 306
Canadian franchises: 0
Other foreign franchises: 0
Company-owned: 0

Seeking: All U.S.
Seeking in Canada? Yes
Exclusive territories? No
Homebased option? Yes
Employees needed to run biz: 1
Absentee ownership? Yes

COSTS
Total cost: $500-49K
Franchise fee: $500-15K
Royalty fee: 10%
Term of agreement: 5 years renewable
　　for 50% of current franchise fee
Franchisees required to buy multiple
　　units? No

FINANCING
In-house: None
3rd-party: Accounts receivable,
　　equipment, franchise fee,
　　inventory, payroll, startup costs

QUALIFICATIONS
Experience:
　　General business experience

TRAINING
At headquarters: 2 weeks
At franchisee's location: 2 weeks

BUSINESS SUPPORT
Grand opening
Internet
Newsletter
Meetings
Toll-free phone line
Field operations/evaluations

MARKETING SUPPORT
Ad slicks
National media campaign
Online business development center

PATHETIC MEDIC FRANCHISING CORP.

Current financial data not available

88 Glocker Way, #125
Pottstown, PA 19465
(888)393-7262
www.patheticmedic.com
Mobile auto interior repairs/
    windshield repair
Began: 1984, Franchising: 2005
Headquarters size: 3 employees
Franchise department: 2 employees

U.S. franchises: 0
Canadian franchises: 0
Other foreign franchises: 0
Company-owned: 1

Seeking: All U.S.
Seeking in Canada? No
Exclusive territories? Yes
Homebased option? Yes
Employees needed to run biz: Info
    not provided
Absentee ownership? No

COSTS
Total cost: $44.8K-86.6K
Franchise fee: $25K
Royalty fee: 5%
Term of agreement: 10 years
Franchisees required to buy multiple
    units? No

FINANCING
In-house: None
3rd-party: Equipment, franchise fee,
    startup costs

QUALIFICATIONS
Net worth: $5K-15K
Cash liquidity: $5K

TRAINING
At headquarters: 2 weeks

BUSINESS SUPPORT
Internet
Toll-free phone line
Field operations/evaluations
Purchasing cooperatives
Security/safety procedures

MARKETING SUPPORT
Info not provided

SUPERGLASS WINDSHIELD REPAIR

Ranked #286 in Entrepreneur Magazine's 2007 Franchise 500

Financial rating: $$$

6101 Chancellor Dr., #200
Orlando, FL 32809
(407)240-1920
www.sgwr.com
Windshield repair
Began: 1992, Franchising: 1993
Headquarters size: 5 employees
Franchise department: 2 employees

U.S. franchises: 224
Canadian franchises: 0
Other foreign franchises: 10
Company-owned: 0

Seeking: All U.S.
Seeking in Canada? Yes
Exclusive territories? Yes
Homebased option? Yes
Employees needed to run biz: 1
Absentee ownership? Yes

COSTS
Total cost: $9.9K-31K
Franchise fee: $9.5K+
Royalty fee: 4%
Term of agreement: 10 years renewable
    for $1K
Franchisees required to buy multiple
    units? No

FINANCING
In-house: Equipment, franchise fee,
    inventory
3rd-party: None

QUALIFICATIONS
Net worth: $15K
Cash liquidity: $15K
Experience:
    Marketing skills
    People skills
    Must enjoy working outdoors

TRAINING
At headquarters: 5 days
At franchisee's location: 5 days
Ongoing

BUSINESS SUPPORT
Grand opening
Internet
Newsletter
Meetings
Toll-free phone line
Field operations/evaluations
Purchasing cooperatives
Security/safety procedures

MARKETING SUPPORT
Co-op advertising
Ad slicks
National media campaign
Regional marketing
Telephone marketing support
    w/B2B accounts

ZIEBART

Ranked #216 in Entrepreneur Magazine's 2007 Franchise 500　　　　*Financial rating: $$$$*

1290 E. Maple Rd.
Troy, MI 48007-1290
(800)877-1312/(248)588-4100
www.ziebart.com
Auto appearance services/products
Began: 1954, Franchising: 1963
Headquarters size: 40 employees
Franchise department: 4 employees

U.S. franchises: 114
Canadian franchises: 74
Other foreign franchises: 132
Company-owned: 20

Seeking: All U.S.
Seeking in Canada? Yes
Exclusive territories? No
Homebased option? No
Employees needed to run biz: 4
Absentee ownership? No

COSTS
Total cost: to $210K
Franchise fee: $25K
Royalty fee: 5%/8%
Term of agreement: 10 years renewable
　　for 15% of then-current fee
Franchisees required to buy multiple
　　units? No

FINANCING
No financing available

QUALIFICATIONS
Net worth: $300K
Cash liquidity: $75K-100K
Experience:
　　General business experience

TRAINING
At headquarters: 3-6 weeks
At franchisee's location: 3-6 weeks

BUSINESS SUPPORT
Grand opening
Internet
Newsletter
Meetings
Toll-free phone line
Field operations/evaluations
Security/safety procedures

MARKETING SUPPORT
Co-op advertising
Ad slicks
National media campaign
Regional marketing

AUTOMOTIVE ▸ *Maintenance & Repairs*

AMERICA'S FLEET SERVICE

Current financial data not available

402 E. Wapella St.
Minooka, IL 60447
(815)467-8828
www.americasfleetservice.com
On-site vehicle maintenance
Began: 1992, Franchising: 2004
Headquarters size: 6 employees
Franchise department: 2 employees

U.S. franchises: 1
Canadian franchises: 0
Other foreign franchises: 0
Company-owned: 4

Seeking: All U.S.
Seeking in Canada? No
Exclusive territories? Yes
Homebased option? Yes
Employees needed to run biz: 1
Absentee ownership? No

COSTS
Total cost: $32.8K-92.6K
Franchise fee: $12.5K
Royalty fee: 6%
Term of agreement: 20 years renewable
　　for 20% of then-current fee
Franchisees required to buy multiple
　　units? No

FINANCING
In-house: Franchise fee
3rd-party: None

QUALIFICATIONS
Net worth: $50K
Cash liquidity: $25K
Experience:
　　General business experience
　　Mechanical skills

TRAINING
At headquarters: 2 weeks

BUSINESS SUPPORT
Grand opening
Internet
Newsletter
Meetings
Toll-free phone line
Field operations/evaluations
Purchasing cooperatives
Security/safety procedures

MARKETING SUPPORT
Co-op advertising
Ad slicks
In-house sales team

BIG O TIRES INC.

Ranked #224 in Entrepreneur Magazine's 2007 Franchise 500　　　　*Financial rating: $$$$*

12650 E. Briarwood Ave., #2D
Englewood, CO 80112
(800)622-2446
www.bigotires.com
Tires, wheels, related under-car
　services
Began: 1962, Franchising: 1962
Headquarters size: 200 employees
Franchise department: 12 employees

U.S. franchises: 538
Canadian franchises: 1
Other foreign franchises: 0
Company-owned: 0

Seeking: Midwest, Northwest,
　Southwest, West
Seeking in Canada? No
Exclusive territories? Yes
Homebased option? No
Employees needed to run biz: 8
Absentee ownership? Yes

COSTS
Total cost: $284.8K-526.8K
Franchise fee: $30K
Royalty fee: 2%
Term of agreement: 10 years renewable
Franchisees required to buy multiple
　units? No

FINANCING
In-house: None
3rd-party: Accounts receivable,
　equipment, franchise fee,
　inventory, payroll, startup costs

QUALIFICATIONS
Net worth: $300K-600K
Cash liquidity: $100K-200K
Experience:
　General business experience
　Strong management skills

TRAINING
At headquarters: 4 weeks
At franchisee's location: 2 weeks at
　opening
Ongoing

BUSINESS SUPPORT
Grand opening
Internet
Newsletter
Meetings
Toll-free phone line
Field operations/evaluations
Lease negotiations
Purchasing cooperatives
Security/safety procedures

MARKETING SUPPORT
Co-op advertising
Ad slicks
National media campaign
Regional marketing

EXPRESS OIL CHANGE

Ranked #295 in Entrepreneur Magazine's 2007 Franchise 500　　　　*Financial rating: $$$$*

190 W. Valley Ave.
Birmingham, AL 35209
(205)945-1771
www.expressoil.com
Oil changes, transmission, brakes,
　tire services
Began: 1979, Franchising: 1983
Headquarters size: 30 employees
Franchise department: 10 employees

U.S. franchises: 108
Canadian franchises: 0
Other foreign franchises: 0
Company-owned: 50

Seeking: South, Southeast
Seeking in Canada? No
Exclusive territories? Yes
Homebased option? No
Employees needed to run biz: 6-8
Absentee ownership? Yes

COSTS
Total cost: $172.5K-1.2M
Franchise fee: $27.5K
Royalty fee: 5%
Term of agreement: 10 years renewable
　at no charge
Franchisees required to buy multiple
　units? No

FINANCING
In-house: None
3rd-party: Equipment, inventory

QUALIFICATIONS
Net worth: $450K
Cash liquidity: $200K
Experience:
　General business experience

TRAINING
At headquarters: 2 days
At franchisee's location: Varies
At training centers: 4-8 weeks

BUSINESS SUPPORT
Grand opening
Internet
Newsletter
Meetings
Toll-free phone line
Field operations/evaluations
Lease negotiations
Purchasing cooperatives
Security/safety procedures

MARKETING SUPPORT
Co-op advertising
Ad slicks
Regional marketing

GREASE MONKEY FRANCHISING LLC

Ranked #415 in Entrepreneur Magazine's 2007 Franchise 500   *Financial rating: $$$*

7100 E. Belleview Ave., #305
Greenwood Village, CO 80111
(800)364-0352/(303)308-1660
www.greasemonkeyintl.com
Preventive maintenance & quick
   lube
Began: 1978, Franchising: 1979
Headquarters size: 28 employees
Franchise department: 3 employees

U.S. franchises: 182
Canadian franchises: 0
Other foreign franchises: 46
Company-owned: 3

Seeking: All U.S.
Seeking in Canada? Yes
Exclusive territories? Yes
Homebased option? No
Employees needed to run biz: 8
Absentee ownership? Yes

COSTS
Total cost: $158K-259K+
Franchise fee: $18K-30K
Royalty fee: 5%
Term of agreement: 15 years renewable
   for $5K
Franchisees required to buy multiple
   units? No

FINANCING
In-house: None
3rd-party: Accounts receivable,
   equipment, franchise fee,
   inventory, payroll, startup costs

QUALIFICATIONS
Net worth: $500K
Cash liquidity: $200K-250K
Experience:
   General business experience
   Marketing skills

TRAINING
At headquarters: 5 days
At franchisee's location: As needed
Annual regional meetings

BUSINESS SUPPORT
Grand opening
Internet
Newsletter
Meetings
Toll-free phone line
Field operations/evaluations
Lease negotiations
Purchasing cooperatives
Security/safety procedures

MARKETING SUPPORT
Co-op advertising
Ad slicks
Regional marketing

LEE MYLES TRANSMISSIONS & AUTOCARE

Ranked #450 in Entrepreneur Magazine's 2007 Franchise 500   *Financial rating: $$$$*

650 From Rd., 4th Fl., S. Lobby
Paramus, NJ 07652
(800)533-6953/(201)262-0555
www.leemyles.com
Transmission & auto-care services
Began: 1947, Franchising: 1964
Headquarters size: 13 employees
Franchise department: 4 employees

U.S. franchises: 91
Canadian franchises: 0
Other foreign franchises: 0
Company-owned: 0

Seeking: All U.S.
Seeking in Canada? No
Exclusive territories? No
Homebased option? No
Employees needed to run biz: 4
Absentee ownership? No

COSTS
Total cost: $177.95K-205.8K
Franchise fee: $30K
Royalty fee: 7%
Term of agreement: 15 years renewable
   for 15% of current franchise fee
Franchisees required to buy multiple
   units? No

FINANCING
In-house: None
3rd-party: Equipment, franchise fee,
   inventory, startup costs

QUALIFICATIONS
Net worth: $250K-300K
Cash liquidity: $100K
Experience:
   Industry experience
   General business experience
   Marketing skills

TRAINING
At headquarters: 1-2 weeks
At franchisee's location: Ongoing

BUSINESS SUPPORT
Grand opening
Internet
Newsletter
Meetings
Toll-free phone line
Field operations/evaluations
Security/safety procedures

MARKETING SUPPORT
Co-op advertising
Ad slicks
National media campaign
Regional marketing

MEINEKE CAR CARE CENTERS

Ranked #89 in Entrepreneur Magazine's 2007 Franchise 500   *Financial rating: $$$$*

128 S. Tryon, #900
Charlotte, NC 28202
(800)275-5200
www.meinekefranchise.com
Exhaust systems, shocks, brakes,
    struts
Began: 1972, Franchising: 1972
Headquarters size: 110 employees
Franchise department: 17 employees

U.S. franchises: 833
Canadian franchises: 18
Other foreign franchises: 18
Company-owned: 2

Seeking: All U.S.
Seeking in Canada? Yes
Exclusive territories? Yes
Homebased option? No
Employees needed to run biz: 4-5
Absentee ownership? Yes

COSTS
Total cost: $190K-350K
Franchise fee: $30K
Royalty fee: 3-7%
Term of agreement: 15 years renewable
    for $2.5K
Franchisees required to buy multiple
    units? Outside the U.S. only

FINANCING
In-house: None
3rd-party: Equipment, franchise fee,
    inventory, startup costs, working
    capital

QUALIFICATIONS
Net worth: $150K
Cash liquidity: $60K
Experience:
    General business experience
    Management experience

TRAINING
At headquarters: 4 weeks
At franchisee's location: 4 days+
    per year
Online courses
Ongoing technical hotline

BUSINESS SUPPORT
Grand opening
Internet
Newsletter
Meetings
Toll-free phone line
Field operations/evaluations
Lease negotiations
Security/safety procedures

MARKETING SUPPORT
Co-op advertising
Ad slicks
National media campaign
Regional marketing
Yellow Pages

MERLIN 200,000 MILE SHOPS

Current financial data not available

1 N. River Ln., #206
Geneva, IL 60134
(800)652-9900/(630)208-9900
www.merlins.com
Brakes, exhaust, suspension,
    oil & lube
Began: 1975, Franchising: 1975
Headquarters size: 25 employees
Franchise department: 9 employees

U.S. franchises: 55
Canadian franchises: 0
Other foreign franchises: 0
Company-owned: 15

Seeking: Midwest, Southeast,
    Southwest
Seeking in Canada? No
Exclusive territories? Yes
Homebased option? No
Employees needed to run biz: 5
Absentee ownership? No

COSTS
Total cost: $193.6K-364K
Franchise fee: $26K-30K
Royalty fee: 4.9-6.9%
Term of agreement: 20 years renewable
    at no charge
Franchisees required to buy multiple
    units? No

FINANCING
In-house: None
3rd-party: Equipment, franchise fee,
    inventory, startup costs

QUALIFICATIONS
Net worth: $75K
Cash liquidity: $25K-60K
Experience:
    Industry experience
    General business experience
    Marketing skills
    Management experience
    Customer service skills

TRAINING
At headquarters: 6 weeks
At corporate training center: Varies

BUSINESS SUPPORT
Grand opening
Internet
Newsletter
Meetings
Toll-free phone line
Field operations/evaluations
Lease negotiations
Purchasing cooperatives
Security/safety procedures

MARKETING SUPPORT
Co-op advertising
Ad slicks
Regional marketing
Local marketing programs

MIDAS

Ranked #19 in Entrepreneur Magazine's 2007 Franchise 500   *Financial rating: $$$$*

1300 Arlington Heights Rd.
Itasca, IL 60143
(800)365-0007/(630)438-3000
www.midasfran.com
Auto repair & maintenance services
Began: 1956, Franchising: 1956
Headquarters size: 200 employees
Franchise department: 10 employees

U.S. franchises: 1,484
Canadian franchises: 209
Other foreign franchises: 823
Company-owned: 75

Seeking: All U.S.
Seeking in Canada? Yes
Exclusive territories? No
Homebased option? No
Employees needed to run biz: 9
Absentee ownership? No

COSTS
Total cost: $243K-329.7K
Franchise fee: $20K
Royalty fee: 10%
Term of agreement: 20 years renewable
    for 50% of franchise fee
Franchisees required to buy multiple
    units? No

FINANCING
In-house: None
3rd-party: Equipment, franchise fee,
    inventory, startup costs

QUALIFICATIONS
Net worth: $250K
Cash liquidity: $75K
Experience:
    General business experience
    Financial capability

TRAINING
At headquarters: 3 weeks
At franchisee's location: 1-2 weeks
    self-study
In-shop assignment: 1-2 weeks

BUSINESS SUPPORT
Grand opening
Internet
Newsletter
Meetings
Toll-free phone line
Field operations/evaluations
Security/safety procedures

MARKETING SUPPORT
Co-op advertising
Ad slicks
National media campaign
Regional marketing

MILEX TUNE-UP & BRAKES

Ranked #327 in Entrepreneur Magazine's 2007 Franchise 500   *Financial rating: $$$$*

4444 W. 147th St.
Midlothian, IL 60445
(800)581-8468/(708)389-5922
www.milextuneupbrake.com
Automotive tuneups & brakes
Began: 1978, Franchising: 1979
Headquarters size: 35 employees
Franchise department: 2 employees

U.S. franchises: 37
Canadian franchises: 0
Other foreign franchises: 0
Company-owned: 0

Seeking: All U.S.
Seeking in Canada? No
Exclusive territories? Yes
Homebased option? No
Employees needed to run biz: 3-4
Absentee ownership? Yes

COSTS
Total cost: $149K
Franchise fee: $27.5K
Royalty fee: 7%
Term of agreement: 20 years renewable
    for $2.5K
Franchisees required to buy multiple
    units? No

FINANCING
In-house: None
3rd-party: Equipment, franchise fee,
    inventory

QUALIFICATIONS
Net worth: $250K
Cash liquidity: $50K
Experience:
    General business experience
    Marketing skills

TRAINING
At headquarters: 1 week
At franchisee's location: 3 weeks

BUSINESS SUPPORT
Grand opening
Internet
Newsletter
Meetings
Toll-free phone line
Field operations/evaluations
Lease negotiations
Purchasing cooperatives
Security/safety procedures

MARKETING SUPPORT
Co-op advertising
Ad slicks
Regional marketing

MISTER TRANSMISSION INT'L. LTD.

Current financial data not available

9675 Yonge St., 2nd Fl.
Richmond Hill, ON L4C 1V7
 Canada
(905)884-1511
www.mistertransmission.com
Transmission repair & services
Began: 1963, Franchising: 1969
Headquarters size: 12 employees
Franchise department: 3 employees

U.S. franchises: 0
Canadian franchises: 85
Other foreign franchises: 0
Company-owned: 0

Seeking: Not available in the U.S.
Seeking in Canada? Yes
Exclusive territories? No
Homebased option? No
Employees needed to run biz: 4-5
Absentee ownership? No

COSTS
Total cost: $100K-125K
Franchise fee: $25K
Royalty fee: 7%
Term of agreement: 10 years renewable
 at no charge
Franchisees required to buy multiple
 units? No

FINANCING
In-house: None
3rd-party: Equipment

QUALIFICATIONS
Net worth: $300K
Cash liquidity: $75K
Experience:
 Industry experience
 General business experience

TRAINING
At headquarters: 1 week
At franchisee's location: Varies

BUSINESS SUPPORT
Internet
Newsletter
Meetings
Toll-free phone line
Field operations/evaluations

MARKETING SUPPORT
National media campaign
Regional marketing

OIL BUTLER INT'L. CORP.

Financial rating: $$$

1599 Rte. 22 W.
Union, NJ 07083
(908)687-3283
www.oilbutlerinternational.com
Mobile oil change, quick lube,
 windshield repair
Began: 1987, Franchising: 1991
Headquarters size: 6 employees
Franchise department: 4 employees

U.S. franchises: 72
Canadian franchises: 3
Other foreign franchises: 23
Company-owned: 1

Seeking: All U.S.
Seeking in Canada? Yes
Exclusive territories? Yes
Homebased option? Yes
Employees needed to run biz: 0
Absentee ownership? Yes

COSTS
Total cost: $28K-40.7K
Franchise fee: $15K
Royalty fee: 7%
Term of agreement: 10 years renewable
 for $1K
Franchisees required to buy multiple
 units? No

FINANCING
In-house: None
3rd-party: Accounts receivable,
 equipment, franchise fee,
 inventory, payroll, startup costs

QUALIFICATIONS
Cash liquidity: $15K

TRAINING
At headquarters: 4 days

BUSINESS SUPPORT
Grand opening
Internet
Newsletter
Toll-free phone line
Field operations/evaluations
Security/safety procedures

MARKETING SUPPORT
Co-op advertising
Ad slicks
National media campaign
Regional marketing
Weekly contact sheet evaluations

OIL CAN HENRY'S

Current financial data not available

1200 N.W. Naito Pkwy., #690
Portland, OR 97209
(800)765-6244/(503)243-6311
www.oilcanhenry.com
Automotive lubrication & filter
maintenance
Began: 1972, Franchising: 1988
Headquarters size: 17 employees

U.S. franchises: 59
Canadian franchises: 0
Other foreign franchises: 0
Company-owned: 8

Seeking: Northwest, Southeast,
Southwest, West
Seeking in Canada? No
Exclusive territories? Yes
Homebased option? No
Employees needed to run biz: 4-15
Absentee ownership? No

COSTS
Total cost: $201K-258K
Franchise fee: $25K
Royalty fee: 5.5%
Term of agreement: 15 years renewable
at no charge
Franchisees required to buy multiple
units? No

FINANCING
In-house: None
3rd-party: Equipment, inventory,
startup costs

QUALIFICATIONS
Net worth: $500K
Cash liquidity: $150K
Experience:
General business experience
Marketing skills

TRAINING
At headquarters: 5-6 weeks
At franchisee's location: 10 days+
Ongoing training available

BUSINESS SUPPORT
Grand opening
Internet
Newsletter
Meetings
Toll-free phone line
Field operations/evaluations
Lease negotiations
Security/safety procedures

MARKETING SUPPORT
Ad slicks
Regional marketing
TV & radio ads

PRECISION TUNE AUTO CARE

Ranked #167 in Entrepreneur Magazine's 2007 Franchise 500   *Financial rating: $$$$*

748 Miller Dr. S.E.
Leesburg, VA 20175
(800)438-8863/(703)669-2311
www.precisionac.com
Auto maintenance & engine
performance
Began: 1975, Franchising: 1978
Headquarters size: 32 employees
Franchise department: 3 employees

U.S. franchises: 316
Canadian franchises: 3
Other foreign franchises: 98
Company-owned: 0

Seeking: All U.S.
Seeking in Canada? Yes
Exclusive territories? Yes
Homebased option? No
Employees needed to run biz: 5-8
Absentee ownership? Yes

COSTS
Total cost: $123K-208.1K
Franchise fee: $25K
Royalty fee: 6-7.5%
Term of agreement: 10 years
Franchisees required to buy multiple
units? No

FINANCING
In-house: None
3rd-party: Accounts receivable,
equipment, franchise fee,
inventory, payroll, startup costs

QUALIFICATIONS
Net worth: $150K-200K
Cash liquidity: $70K
Experience:
General business experience

TRAINING
At headquarters: 2 weeks
At franchisee's location:
1 day-2 weeks+
Ongoing upon request

BUSINESS SUPPORT
Grand opening
Internet
Newsletter
Meetings
Toll-free phone line
Field operations/evaluations
Security/safety procedures

MARKETING SUPPORT
Co-op advertising
Ad slicks
National media campaign
Regional marketing
Radio & TV
National coupon advertising

SPEEDY TRANSMISSION CENTERS

Current financial data not available

235 N.E. 6th Ave., #H
Delray Beach, FL 33483
(800)336-0310/(561)274-0445
www.speedytransmission.com
Transmission repair
Began: 1983, Franchising: 1984
Headquarters size: 4 employees
Franchise department: 1 employee

U.S. franchises: 22
Canadian franchises: 0
Other foreign franchises: 0
Company-owned: 0

Seeking: South, Southeast
Seeking in Canada? No
Exclusive territories? Yes
Homebased option? No
Employees needed to run biz: 4
Absentee ownership? Yes

COSTS
Total cost: $58.5K-101.9K
Franchise fee: $24.5K
Royalty fee: 7%
Term of agreement: 20 years renewable
    for 50% of initial franchise fee
Franchisees required to buy multiple
    units? No

FINANCING
In-house: None
3rd-party: Equipment

QUALIFICATIONS
Net worth: $150K
Cash liquidity: $50K
Experience:
    General business experience
    Marketing skills

TRAINING
At headquarters: 3 weeks
At franchisee's location: Varies
Weekend training classes

BUSINESS SUPPORT
Grand opening
Internet
Newsletter
Meetings
Toll-free phone line
Field operations/evaluations

MARKETING SUPPORT
Ad slicks
Regional marketing
All-media production

TECHZONE AIRBAG SERVICE

Current financial data not available

13013 N.E. 20th St., #1
Bellevue, WA 98005-2039
(800)224-7224/(425)861-7939
www.techzoneairbagservice.com
Auto interior repairs & air bag
    services
Began: 1992, Franchising: 1994
Headquarters size: 11 employees
Franchise department: 4 employees

U.S. franchises: 31
Canadian franchises: 0
Other foreign franchises: 0
Company-owned: 1

Seeking: All U.S.
Seeking in Canada? Yes
Exclusive territories? Yes
Homebased option? Yes
Employees needed to run biz: 1
Absentee ownership? Yes

COSTS
Total cost: $36.5K-108.9K
Franchise fee: $15K-35K
Royalty fee: 8.5%
Term of agreement: 10 years renewable
    for $5K
Franchisees required to buy multiple
    units? No

FINANCING
In-house: None
3rd-party: Equipment, franchise fee,
    startup costs

QUALIFICATIONS
Net worth: $100K
Cash liquidity: $25K
Experience:
    Industry experience
    General business experience
    Marketing skills

TRAINING
At headquarters: 3 weeks
At franchisee's location: As needed
Ongoing

BUSINESS SUPPORT
Grand opening
Internet
Newsletter
Meetings
Toll-free phone line
Field operations/evaluations
Lease negotiations
Purchasing cooperatives
Security/safety procedures

MARKETING SUPPORT
Co-op advertising
Ad slicks
National media campaign
Regional marketing
Web media & online scheduling

TILDEN CAR CARE CENTERS

Ranked #344 in Entrepreneur Magazine's 2007 Franchise 500   *Financial rating: $$$$*

300 Hempstead Turnpike, #110
West Hempstead, NY 11552
(800)845-3367
www.tildencarcare.com
Full-service automotive repair
Began: 1923, Franchising: 1996
Headquarters size: 5 employees
Franchise department: 2 employees

U.S. franchises: 54
Canadian franchises: 0
Other foreign franchises: 0
Company-owned: 0

Seeking: All U.S.
Seeking in Canada? Yes
Exclusive territories? Yes
Homebased option? No
Employees needed to run biz: 4
Absentee ownership? Yes

COSTS
Total cost: $150K-200K
Franchise fee: $25K
Royalty fee: 6%
Term of agreement: 20 years renewable
    for 15% of franchise fee
Franchisees required to buy multiple
    units? No

FINANCING
In-house: None
3rd-party: Equipment, startup costs

QUALIFICATIONS
Net worth: $150K
Cash liquidity: $60K
Experience:
    General business experience
    Marketing skills

TRAINING
At headquarters: 2 weeks
At franchisee's location: 1 week
Ongoing

BUSINESS SUPPORT
Grand opening
Internet
Toll-free phone line
Field operations/evaluations
Lease negotiations
Purchasing cooperatives

MARKETING SUPPORT
Ad slicks

TUFFY ASSOCIATES CORP./CAR-X AUTO SERVICE

Ranked #126 in Entrepreneur Magazine's 2007 Franchise 500   *Financial rating: $$$$*

1414 Baronial Plaza Dr.
Toledo, OH 43615
(800)228-8339/(419)865-6900
www.tuffy.com
Complete automotive repair
Began: 1970, Franchising: 1971
Headquarters size: 39 employees
Franchise department: 39 employees

U.S. franchises: 392
Canadian franchises: 0
Other foreign franchises: 0
Company-owned: 34

Seeking: Midwest, Northeast, South,
    Southeast, Southwest
Seeking in Canada? No
Exclusive territories? Yes
Homebased option? No
Employees needed to run biz: 4-5
Absentee ownership? Yes

COSTS
Total cost: $239K-399.5K
Franchise fee: $25K
Royalty fee: 5%
Term of agreement: 15 years renewable
    at no charge
Franchisees required to buy multiple
    units? No

FINANCING
In-house: None
3rd-party: Equipment, franchise fee,
    inventory, startup costs

QUALIFICATIONS
Net worth: $200K
Cash liquidity: $100K
Experience:
    General business experience

TRAINING
At headquarters: 3 weeks
At franchisee's location: 2 weeks
At existing store: 1 week

BUSINESS SUPPORT
Grand opening
Internet
Newsletter
Meetings
Toll-free phone line
Field operations/evaluations
Purchasing cooperatives
Security/safety procedures

MARKETING SUPPORT
Co-op advertising
Ad slicks
National media campaign
Regional marketing

VICTORY LANE QUICK OIL CHANGE

Financial rating: $

405 Little Lake Dr.
Ann Arbor, MI 48103
(734)996-1196
www.victorylane.net
Oil changes & fluid maintenance
   services
Began: 1980, Franchising: 1986
Headquarters size: 10 employees
Franchise department: 4 employees

U.S. franchises: 35
Canadian franchises: 0
Other foreign franchises: 0
Company-owned: 5

Seeking: All U.S.
Seeking in Canada? Yes
Exclusive territories? Yes
Homebased option? No
Employees needed to run biz: 4-6
Absentee ownership? Yes

COSTS
Total cost: $229.5K-402K
Franchise fee: $30K
Royalty fee: 6%
Term of agreement: 20 years renewable
   for $5K
Franchisees required to buy multiple
   units? No

FINANCING
In-house: None
3rd-party: Equipment, startup costs

QUALIFICATIONS
Net worth: $500K
Cash liquidity: $100K
Experience:
   General business experience
   Marketing skills

TRAINING
At headquarters: 2 weeks
At franchisee's location: 1 week
Online support

BUSINESS SUPPORT
Grand opening
Internet
Newsletter
Meetings
Field operations/evaluations
Lease negotiations
Purchasing cooperatives
Security/safety procedures

MARKETING SUPPORT
Co-op advertising
Ad slicks
Regional marketing

AUTOMOTIVE *Rentals*

AFFILIATED CAR RENTAL LC

Ranked #211 in Entrepreneur Magazine's 2007 Franchise 500

Financial rating: $$$$

96 Freneau Ave., #2
Matawan, NJ 07747
(800)367-5159
www.sensiblecarrental.com
Car rentals
Began: 1987, Franchising: 1987
Headquarters size: 7 employees
Franchise department: 7 employees

U.S. franchises: 254
Canadian franchises: 0
Other foreign franchises: 0
Company-owned: 0

Seeking: All U.S.
Seeking in Canada? No
Exclusive territories? Yes
Homebased option? No
Employees needed to run biz: 2-3
Absentee ownership? Yes

COSTS
Total cost: $44.98K-71.8K
Franchise fee: $5K-11.6K
Royalty fee: Varies
Term of agreement: Perpetual
Franchisees required to buy multiple
   units? No

FINANCING
In-house: None
3rd-party: Equipment, inventory

QUALIFICATIONS
Experience:
   General business experience

TRAINING
At headquarters: 2 days
At franchisee's location: 2 days

BUSINESS SUPPORT
Internet
Newsletter
Meetings
Toll-free phone line
Field operations/evaluations
Purchasing cooperatives
Security/safety procedures

MARKETING SUPPORT
Co-op advertising
Ad slicks
National Yellow Pages ads

PRICELESS RENT-A-CAR

Current financial data not available

105 Main St.
Laurel, MD 20707
(240)581-1359
www.pricelesscar.com
Car rentals & leasing
Began: 1997, Franchising: 1997
Headquarters size: 10 employees
Franchise department: 4 employees

U.S. franchises: 77
Canadian franchises: 0
Other foreign franchises: 0
Company-owned: 0

Seeking: All U.S.
Seeking in Canada? No
Exclusive territories? No
Homebased option? No
Employees needed to run biz: 2
Absentee ownership? Yes

COSTS
Total cost: $37.2K-216K
Franchise fee: $7K
Royalty fee: $30/car/mo.
Term of agreement: Info not provided
Franchisees required to buy multiple
    units? No

FINANCING
In-house: None
3rd-party: Inventory

QUALIFICATIONS
Experience:
    General business experience
    Marketing skills

TRAINING
At headquarters: 1 week
At franchisee's location: Varies

BUSINESS SUPPORT
Grand opening
Internet
Newsletter
Meetings
Toll-free phone line
Field operations/evaluations
Purchasing cooperatives
Security/safety procedures

MARKETING SUPPORT
Co-op advertising
Ad slicks
National media campaign
Regional marketing

RENT-A-WRECK

Financial rating: $$$$

105 Main St.
Laurel, MD 20707
(240)581-1359
www.rentawreck.com
Auto rentals & leasing
Began: 1970, Franchising: 1977
Headquarters size: 35 employees
Franchise department: 7 employees

U.S. franchises: 281
Canadian franchises: 0
Other foreign franchises: 28
Company-owned: 0

Seeking: All U.S.
Seeking in Canada? Yes
Exclusive territories? No
Homebased option? No
Employees needed to run biz: 2
Absentee ownership? Yes

COSTS
Total cost: $100.1K-362K
Franchise fee: $8.5K
Royalty fee: $30/car/mo.
Term of agreement: 5 years renewable
    at no charge
Franchisees required to buy multiple
    units? Outside the U.S. only

FINANCING
In-house: None
3rd-party: Inventory

QUALIFICATIONS
Cash liquidity: $50K+
Experience:
    General business experience
    Marketing skills

TRAINING
At headquarters: 1 week
At franchisee's location: Varies
At counter classes
Marketing seminars
Via newsletter

BUSINESS SUPPORT
Grand opening
Internet
Newsletter
Meetings
Toll-free phone line
Field operations/evaluations
Purchasing cooperatives
Security/safety procedures

MARKETING SUPPORT
Co-op advertising
Ad slicks
National media campaign
Regional marketing

U-SAVE AUTO RENTAL OF AMERICA INC.

Current financial data not available

4780 I-55 N., #300
Jackson, MS 39211
(800)438-2300/(601)713-4333
www.usave.net
New & used auto rentals
Began: 1979, Franchising: 1979
Headquarters size: 31 employees
Franchise department: 5 employees

U.S. franchises: 225
Canadian franchises: 1
Other foreign franchises: 4
Company-owned: 0

Seeking: All U.S.
Seeking in Canada? No
Exclusive territories? Info not
provided
Homebased option? No
Employees needed to run biz: 5
Absentee ownership? No

COSTS
Total cost: $58K-700K
Franchise fee: $10K-250K
Royalty fee: 3-6%
Term of agreement: 10 years renewable
at no charge
Franchisees required to buy multiple
units? No

FINANCING
In-house: None
3rd-party: Fleet financing

QUALIFICATIONS
Net worth: $300K-500K
Cash liquidity: $60K-150K
Experience:
Industry experience

TRAINING
At headquarters: 5 days

BUSINESS SUPPORT
Grand opening
Internet
Newsletter
Meetings
Toll-free phone line
Field operations/evaluations

MARKETING SUPPORT
National media campaign
In-house marketing support

AUTOMOTIVE *Other Franchises*

AAMCO TRANSMISSIONS INC.
*Ranked #59 in Entrepreneur
Magazine's 2007 Franchise 500*
One Presidential Blvd.
Bala Cynwyd, PA 19004
(800)223-8887/(610)668-2900
www.aamcotransmissions.com
Transmission repair & services
Financial rating: $$$$

AERO COLOURS INC.
*Ranked #428 in Entrepreneur
Magazine's 2007 Franchise 500*
10824 Nesbitt Ave. S.
Bloomington, MN 55437
(800)696-2376
www.aerocolours.com
Mobile automotive paint repair
Financial rating: $$$$

ALL TUNE AND LUBE
*Ranked #421 in Entrepreneur
Magazine's 2007 Franchise 500*
8334 Veterans Hwy.
Millersville, MD 21108
(800)935-8863/(410)987-1011
www.alltuneandlube.com
Total car care
Financial rating: $$$

ALTA MERE INDUSTRIES
4444 W. 147th St.
Midlothian, IL 60445
(800)581-8468/(708)389-5922
www.altamere.com
Window tinting, auto alarms, auto
imaging
Financial rating: 0

ALTRACOLOR SYSTEMS
111 Phlox Ave.
Metairie, LA 70001
(800)727-6567
www.altracolor.com
Mobile auto painting & plastic
repair
Financial rating: Current financial
data not available

ATLANTIC WINDSHIELD REPAIR
107 C David Green Rd.
Birmingham, AL 35244
(877)230-4487
www.atlanticwindshieldrepair.com
Windshield repair
Financial rating: Current financial
data not available

JIFFY LUBE INT'L. INC.
Ranked #7 in Entrepreneur
Magazine's 2007 Franchise 500
P.O. Box 4427
Houston, TX 77210-4427
(800)327-9532
www.jiffylube.com
Fast oil change
Financial rating: $$$$

LINE-X CORP.
Ranked #80 in Entrepreneur
Magazine's 2007 Franchise 500
2400 S. Garnsey St.
Santa Ana, CA 92707
(800)831-3232
www.goline-x.com
Spray-on truck bed liners & indus-
    trial coatings
Financial rating: $$$$

MIRACLE AUTO PAINTING INC.
2343 Lincoln Ave.
Hayward, CA 94545
(877)647-2253/(510)887-2211
www.miracleautopainting.com
Automotive painting & body repair
Financial rating: $$$$

MR.TRANSMISSION/
TRANSMISSION USA
Ranked #284 in Entrepreneur
Magazine's 2007 Franchise 500
4444 W. 147th St.
Midlothian, IL 60445
(800)581-8468/(708)389-5922
www.mrtransmission.com
Transmission repair & services
Financial rating: $$$$

NOVUS AUTO GLASS
Ranked #65 in Entrepreneur
Magazine's 2007 Franchise 500
12800 Hwy. 13 S., #500
Savage, MN 55378
(800)944-6811
www.novusglass.com
Windshield repair & replacement
Financial rating: $$$$

1-800-RADIATOR
4401 Park Rd.
Benicia, CA 94510
(866)780-9392
www.1800radiator.com
Auto parts distribution
Financial rating: $$$

PAYLESS CAR RENTAL
SYSTEM INC.
2350-N 34th St. N.
St. Petersburg, FL 33713
(800)729-5255/(727)321-6352
www.paylesscarrental.com
Auto rentals & sales
Financial rating: Current financial
    data not available

RENT-N-ROLL
Ranked #426 in Entrepreneur
Magazine's 2007 Franchise 500
14620 N. Nebraska Ave.
Tampa, FL 33613
(813)977-9800
www.rentnroll.com
Custom wheels & tires
Financial rating: $$$$

SUPER WASH
Ranked #121 in Entrepreneur
Magazine's 2007 Franchise 500
707 W. Lincolnway
Morrison, IL 61270
(815)772-2111
www.superwash.com
Coin-operated self-serve/brushless
    automatic car washes
Financial rating: $$$$

TECHNA GLASS FRANCHISE INC.
460 W. 9000 South
Sandy, UT 84070
(801)676-3390/(801)562-2200
www.technaglass.com
Windshield repair & replacement
Financial rating: Current financial
    data not available

TIRE WAREHOUSE
492 Main St.
Keene, NH 03431
(603)352-4478
www.tirewarehouse.net
Tires, auto parts & accessories
Financial rating: Current financial
    data not available

BUSINESS ▸ *Advertising & Marketing*

ALLOVER MEDIA

Financial rating: $

7351 Kirkwood Ln. N., #100
Maple Grove, MN 55369
(763)488-4030
www.allovermedia.com
Indoor print, gas pump & electric
    LCD advertising
Began: 2002, Franchising: 2002
Headquarters size: 40 employees
Franchise department: 4 employees

U.S. franchises: 27
Canadian franchises: 0
Other foreign franchises: 0
Company-owned: 1

Seeking: All U.S.
Seeking in Canada? No
Exclusive territories? Yes
Homebased option? Yes
Employees needed to run biz: 1
Absentee ownership? No

COSTS
Total cost: $37.3K-124.8K
Franchise fee: $30K
Royalty fee: 6%
Term of agreement: 10 years renewable
    at no charge
Franchisees required to buy multiple
    units? No

FINANCING
In-house: Franchise fee
3rd-party: Accounts receivable,
    equipment, franchise fee,
    inventory, payroll, startup costs

QUALIFICATIONS
Net worth: $75K
Cash liquidity: $35K
Experience:
    Industry experience
    General business experience
    Marketing skills

TRAINING
At headquarters: 40 hours
At franchisee's location: 40 hours

BUSINESS SUPPORT
Internet
Newsletter
Meetings
Toll-free phone line
Field operations/evaluations
Lease negotiations
Security/safety procedures

MARKETING SUPPORT
National media campaign

BILLBOARD CONNECTION INC.

Ranked #416 in Entrepreneur Magazine's 2007 Franchise 500   *Financial rating: $$$*

2121 Vista Pkwy.
West Palm Beach, FL 33409
(866)257-6025/(561)868-1497
www.billboardconnection.com
Ad agency specializing in outdoor
  media
Began: 1997, Franchising: 2003
Headquarters size: 4 employees
Franchise department: 3 employees

U.S. franchises: 37
Canadian franchises: 2
Other foreign franchises: 3
Company-owned: 0

Seeking: All U.S.
Seeking in Canada? Yes
Exclusive territories? Yes
Homebased option? Yes
Employees needed to run biz: 1
Absentee ownership? Yes

COSTS
Total cost: $27K-35K
Franchise fee: $24.5K
Royalty fee: 3.5%
Term of agreement: 20 years renewable
  for $1K
Franchisees required to buy multiple
  units? No

FINANCING
In-house: Equipment
3rd-party: Equipment

QUALIFICATIONS
Net worth: $35K
Cash liquidity: $35K
Experience:
  Industry experience
  Marketing skills

TRAINING
At headquarters: 1 week
At franchisee's location: 1 week

BUSINESS SUPPORT
Grand opening
Internet
Newsletter
Meetings

MARKETING SUPPORT
Ad slicks
Regional marketing

BINGO BUGLE NEWSPAPER

Financial rating: $$$$

P.O. Box 527
Vashon, WA 98070
(800)327-6437/(206)463-5656
www.bingobugle.com
Specialty newspaper
Began: 1981, Franchising: 1983
Headquarters size: 3 employees
Franchise department: 2 employees

U.S. franchises: 57
Canadian franchises: 1
Other foreign franchises: 0
Company-owned: 0

Seeking: Midwest, South, Southeast,
  West
Seeking in Canada? No
Exclusive territories? Yes
Homebased option? Yes
Employees needed to run biz: 1
Absentee ownership? No

COSTS
Total cost: $5.1K-11.5K
Franchise fee: $1.5K
Royalty fee: 8%
Term of agreement: 5 years renewable
  at no charge
Franchisees required to buy multiple
  units? No

FINANCING
No financing available

QUALIFICATIONS
Cash liquidity: $7.5K
Experience:
  General business experience
  Outgoing personality required

TRAINING
At headquarters or regional location
At franchisee's location: 2 days

BUSINESS SUPPORT
Internet
Newsletter
Meetings
Toll-free phone line

MARKETING SUPPORT
Co-op advertising
Ad slicks

CITY PUBLICATIONS

Financial rating: 0

2018 Powers Ferry Rd., #535
Atlanta, GA 30339
(770)951-0441
www.citypublication.com
Publication for affluent
   homeowners
Began: 2002, Franchising: 2004
Headquarters size: 20 employees
Franchise department: 20 employees

U.S. franchises: 50
Canadian franchises: 0
Other foreign franchises: 0
Company-owned: 0

Seeking: All U.S.
Seeking in Canada? Yes
Exclusive territories? Yes
Homebased option? Yes
Employees needed to run biz: 1-2
Absentee ownership? No

COSTS
Total cost: $78.7K-267.9K
Franchise fee: $75K
Royalty fee: 6%
Term of agreement: 5 years/25 years
   renewable for $100
Franchisees required to buy multiple
   units? No

FINANCING
No financing available

QUALIFICATIONS
Net worth: $200K
Cash liquidity: $125K

TRAINING
At headquarters: 3 days
At franchisee's location: 3 days

BUSINESS SUPPORT
Grand opening
Internet
Newsletter
Meetings
Field operations/evaluations
Purchasing cooperatives

MARKETING SUPPORT
Ad slicks
National media campaign

COFFEE NEWS

Ranked #68 in Entrepreneur Magazine's 2007 Franchise 500   *Financial rating: $$$$*

P.O. Box 8444
Bangor, ME 04402-8444
(207)941-0860
www.coffeenewsusa.com
Weekly newspaper distributed at
   restaurants
Began: 1988, Franchising: 1994
Headquarters size: 7 employees
Franchise department: 2 employees

U.S. franchises: 549
Canadian franchises: 146
Other foreign franchises: 126
Company-owned: 0

Seeking: All U.S.
Seeking in Canada? Yes
Exclusive territories? Yes
Homebased option? Yes
Employees needed to run biz: 1
Absentee ownership? Yes

COSTS
Total cost: $7K
Franchise fee: $6K/4K
Royalty fee: $20-75/wk.
Term of agreement: 4 years renewable
   at no charge
Franchisees required to buy multiple
   units? No

FINANCING
No financing available

QUALIFICATIONS
Experience:
   General business experience
   Marketing skills
   Sales & advertising experience

TRAINING
At headquarters: 3 days
Mentor program

BUSINESS SUPPORT
Internet
Newsletter
Meetings
Purchasing cooperatives

MARKETING SUPPORT
Ad slicks

DISCOVERY MAP INT'L.

Financial rating: $

106 S. First St., #2A
La Conner, WA 98257
(877)820-7827/(360)588-0144
www.discoverymap.com
Specialty map advertising system
Began: 1987, Franchising: 1999
Headquarters size: 11 employees
Franchise department: 2 employees

U.S. franchises: 30
Canadian franchises: 0
Other foreign franchises: 0
Company-owned: 3

Seeking: All U.S.
Seeking in Canada? No
Exclusive territories? Yes
Homebased option? Yes
Employees needed to run biz: 1
Absentee ownership? Yes

COSTS
Total cost: $41.8K-60.8K
Franchise fee: $25K-40K
Royalty fee: 0
Term of agreement: 10 years renewable
    for 33% of franchise fee
Franchisees required to buy multiple
    units? No

FINANCING
No financing available

QUALIFICATIONS
Net worth: $150K
Cash liquidity: $30K
Experience:
    General business experience
    Marketing skills
    Sales experience

TRAINING
At headquarters: 8 days
At franchisee's location: 1-3 days

BUSINESS SUPPORT
Internet
Meetings
Toll-free phone line
Field operations/evaluations

MARKETING SUPPORT
Co-op advertising
Regional marketing

GOTCHA MOBILE MEDIA

Current financial data not available

455 Kern St., #E
Shafter, CA 93263
(661)746-0121
www.gotchamobilemedia.com
Mobile billboard advertising
Began: 2003, Franchising: 2004
Headquarters size: 4 employees
Franchise department: 2 employees

U.S. franchises: 11
Canadian franchises: 0
Other foreign franchises: 0
Company-owned: 1

Seeking: All U.S.
Seeking in Canada? Yes
Exclusive territories? Yes
Homebased option? Yes
Employees needed to run biz: Info
    not provided
Absentee ownership? Yes

COSTS
Total cost: $18.99K-134.99K
Franchise fee: $13.99K-49.99K
Royalty fee: $295-795/vehicle/mo.
Term of agreement: 5 years renewable
    for $5K
Franchisees required to buy multiple
    units? No

FINANCING
In-house: Franchise fee, startup
    costs
3rd-party: Equipment

QUALIFICATIONS
Net worth: $40K+
Cash liquidity: $25K
Experience:
    General business experience
    Marketing skills
    Sales experience

TRAINING
At headquarters: 2 days
At franchisee's location: Varies

BUSINESS SUPPORT
Internet
Newsletter
Toll-free phone line
Field operations/evaluations
Security/safety procedures

MARKETING SUPPORT
Co-op advertising
Ad slicks

HOMES & LAND MAGAZINE

Ranked #95 in Entrepreneur Magazine's 2007 Franchise 500   *Financial rating: $$$$*

1830 E. Park Ave.
Tallahassee, FL 32301
(800)458-9520
www.homesandland.com
Real estate advertising magazine
Began: 1973, Franchising: 1984
Headquarters size: 60 employees
Franchise department: 4 employees

U.S. franchises: 280
Canadian franchises: 12
Other foreign franchises: 0
Company-owned: 14

Seeking: All U.S.
Seeking in Canada? No
Exclusive territories? Yes
Homebased option? Yes
Employees needed to run biz: 2
Absentee ownership? Yes

COSTS
Total cost: $50K-125K
Franchise fee: $27K
Royalty fee: 10.5%
Term of agreement: 10 years renewable
    for $5K
Franchisees required to buy multiple
    units? No

FINANCING
In-house: None
3rd-party: Accounts receivable,
    equipment, inventory, payroll,
    startup costs

QUALIFICATIONS
Net worth: $150K
Cash liquidity: $50K
Experience:
    General business experience
    Marketing skills
    Sales experience

TRAINING
At headquarters: 2 weeks
In-field training

BUSINESS SUPPORT
Internet
Newsletter
Meetings
Toll-free phone line
Field operations/evaluations
Purchasing cooperatives

MARKETING SUPPORT
Co-op advertising
Ad slicks
National media campaign
Regional marketing

INDUSTRY MAGAZINE

Financial rating: $$

2500 N. Federal Hwy., #100
Fort Lauderdale, FL 32701
(954)566-7778
www.industrymagazine.com
Fashion publication
Began: 2001, Franchising: 2004
Headquarters size: 15 employees
Franchise department: 3 employees

U.S. franchises: 7
Canadian franchises: 0
Other foreign franchises: 0
Company-owned: 2

Seeking: All U.S.
Seeking in Canada? No
Exclusive territories? Yes
Homebased option? Yes
Employees needed to run biz: 3-5
Absentee ownership? Yes

COSTS
Total cost: $135.5K-145.2K
Franchise fee: $126.6K
Royalty fee: 0
Term of agreement: 3 years renewable
    for $500
Franchisees required to buy multiple
    units? Outside the U.S. only

FINANCING
No financing available

QUALIFICATIONS
Net worth: $200K
Cash liquidity: $50K
Experience:
    General business experience
    Marketing skills

TRAINING
At headquarters: 5 days

BUSINESS SUPPORT
Grand opening
Internet
Newsletter
Meetings
Field operations/evaluations

MARKETING SUPPORT
National media campaign

MAGNETSIGNS ADVERTISING INC.

Current financial data not available

4802 50th Ave.
Camrose, AB T4V 0R9 Canada
(780)672-8720
www.magnetsigns.com
Permanent & portable sign rentals
Began: 1995, Franchising: 1996
Headquarters size: 10 employees
Franchise department: 5 employees

U.S. franchises: 14
Canadian franchises: 97
Other foreign franchises: 0
Company-owned: 4

Seeking: All U.S.
Seeking in Canada? No
Exclusive territories? No
Homebased option? Yes
Employees needed to run biz: 1-2
Absentee ownership? Yes

COSTS
Total cost: $24K-80K
Franchise fee: $7.9K
Royalty fee: 10%
Term of agreement: 10 years renewable
    for $3K
Franchisees required to buy multiple
    units? No

FINANCING
In-house: Equipment
3rd-party: None

QUALIFICATIONS
Net worth: $50K
Cash liquidity: $10K
Experience:
    General business experience

TRAINING
At headquarters: 3 days
Annual visits by regional managers
Regional meetings
National convention

BUSINESS SUPPORT
Internet
Newsletter
Meetings
Toll-free phone line
Field operations/evaluations

MARKETING SUPPORT
Product brochures
Sales & presentation binders

MONEY MAILER LLC

Ranked #181 in Entrepreneur Magazine's 2007 Franchise 500

Financial rating: $$$$

14271 Corporate Dr.
Garden Grove, CA 92843
(888)446-4648
www.moneymailer.net
Direct-mail advertising
Began: 1979, Franchising: 1980
Headquarters size: 243 employees
Franchise department: 114 employees

U.S. franchises: 303
Canadian franchises: 0
Other foreign franchises: 0
Company-owned: 18

Seeking: All U.S.
Seeking in Canada? No
Exclusive territories? Yes
Homebased option? Yes
Employees needed to run biz: 0
Absentee ownership? No

COSTS
Total cost: $55.5K-80.5K
Franchise fee: $37.5K-52.5K
Royalty fee: Varies
Term of agreement: 10 years renewable
    for $2K
Franchisees required to buy multiple
    units? No

FINANCING
In-house: None
3rd-party: Accounts receivable,
    equipment, franchise fee,
    payroll, startup costs

QUALIFICATIONS
Cash liquidity: $55K
Experience:
    Sales experience
    Strong communication skills
    Good credit

TRAINING
At headquarters: 6 days
At franchisee's location: 13 days
Optional ongoing training
    throughout term

BUSINESS SUPPORT
Internet
Newsletter
Meetings
Toll-free phone line
Field operations/evaluations
Purchasing cooperatives

MARKETING SUPPORT
Co-op advertising
Ad slicks
Local advertising

OUR TOWN AMERICA

Financial rating: 0

3845 Gateway Centre Blvd., #300
Pinellas Park, FL 33782
(727)345-0811
www.ourtownamerica.com
Direct-mail new mover welcoming
service
Began: 1972, Franchising: 2004
Headquarters size: 40 employees
Franchise department: 3 employees

U.S. franchises: 35
Canadian franchises: 0
Other foreign franchises: 0
Company-owned: 1

Seeking: All U.S.
Seeking in Canada? No
Exclusive territories? Yes
Homebased option? Yes
Employees needed to run biz: 1
Absentee ownership? No

COSTS
Total cost: $43.7K-61.3K
Franchise fee: $29K
Royalty fee: 5%
Term of agreement: 10 years renewable
at no charge
Franchisees required to buy multiple
units? No

FINANCING
In-house: Franchise fee
3rd-party: None

QUALIFICATIONS
Cash liquidity: $40K-60K
Experience:
Industry experience
General business experience
Marketing skills

TRAINING
At headquarters: 3 weeks
At franchisee's location: 1 week
In franchisee's market during first
year: 2 weeks

BUSINESS SUPPORT
Newsletter
Meetings
Toll-free phone line

MARKETING SUPPORT
Co-op advertising

PROFIT-TELL INT'L.

Financial rating: $$$

201 E. Ogden Ave., #208
Hinsdale, IL 60521
(888)366-4653
www.profit-tell.com
Audio marketing/advertising
programs
Began: 1993, Franchising: 2001
Headquarters size: 7 employees
Franchise department: 7 employees

U.S. franchises: 16
Canadian franchises: 0
Other foreign franchises: 0
Company-owned: 1

Seeking: All U.S.
Seeking in Canada? Yes
Exclusive territories? No
Homebased option? Yes
Employees needed to run biz: 1
Absentee ownership? No

COSTS
Total cost: $30K-40.3K
Franchise fee: $24K
Royalty fee: 0
Term of agreement: 20 years renewable
for $1K
Franchisees required to buy multiple
units? No

FINANCING
In-house: None
3rd-party: Franchise fee

QUALIFICATIONS
Net worth: $125K
Cash liquidity: $23.7K
Experience:
General business experience
Sales experience

TRAINING
At headquarters: 1 week
At franchisee's location: As needed
Online training: 4 weeks

BUSINESS SUPPORT
Internet
Newsletter
Meetings
Toll-free phone line
Field operations/evaluations

MARKETING SUPPORT
Ad slicks
Regional marketing
FAF fund that allocates funds &
ad support to franchisees

PRSTORE LLC

Financial rating: $

15800 John J Delaney Dr., #400
Charlotte, NC 28277
(704)333-2200
www.prstore.com
B2B marketing services
Began: 2001, Franchising: 2002
Headquarters size: 10 employees
Franchise department: 3 employees

U.S. franchises: 13
Canadian franchises: 0
Other foreign franchises: 0
Company-owned: 0

Seeking: All U.S.
Seeking in Canada? No
Exclusive territories? No
Homebased option? No
Employees needed to run biz: 2
Absentee ownership? No

COSTS
Total cost: $121.9K-178.8K
Franchise fee: $59.5K
Royalty fee: 4.3%
Term of agreement: 5 years renewable
    at no charge
Franchisees required to buy multiple
    units? No

FINANCING
No financing available

QUALIFICATIONS
Net worth: $250K
Cash liquidity: $85K
Experience:
    Industry experience
    General business experience
    Marketing skills
    Sales experience

TRAINING
At headquarters: 10 days
At franchisee's location: Up to
    10 days
Periodic refresher training
New product training

BUSINESS SUPPORT
Grand opening
Internet
Newsletter
Meetings
Field operations/evaluations

MARKETING SUPPORT
Co-op advertising
Ad slicks
National media campaign
Regional marketing
Sales & marketing consulting
TV & radio scripting

RECOGNITION EXPRESS

Financial rating: $$$

6290 Harrison Dr., #7
Las Vegas, NV 89120
(866)838-5888/(702)795-4550
www.recognitionexpress.com
Badges, signs, awards, promotional
    products
Began: 1972, Franchising: 1974
Headquarters size: 5 employees
Franchise department: 5 employees

U.S. franchises: 10
Canadian franchises: 8
Other foreign franchises: 48
Company-owned: 0

Seeking: All U.S.
Seeking in Canada? Yes
Exclusive territories? Yes
Homebased option? Yes
Employees needed to run biz: 2
Absentee ownership? Yes

COSTS
Total cost: $82.1K-118.5K
Franchise fee: $29.5K
Royalty fee: 4-6%
Term of agreement: 10 years renewable
    at no charge
Franchisees required to buy multiple
    units? No

FINANCING
No financing available

QUALIFICATIONS
Net worth: $150K
Cash liquidity: $30K
Experience:
    Basic computer skills

TRAINING
At headquarters: 5 days
At franchisee's location: 2 days
Ongoing training

BUSINESS SUPPORT
Internet
Newsletter
Meetings
Toll-free phone line
Field operations/evaluations
Purchasing cooperatives
Security/safety procedures

MARKETING SUPPORT
Ad slicks
National media campaign
Direct mail w/telemarketing
    follow-up

SHOCK PR

Current financial data not available

34 Hayden Rowe St., #110
Hopkinton, MA 01748
(508)435-0900
www.shockpr.com
PR services
Began: 1992, Franchising: 2005
Headquarters size: 2 employees
Franchise department: 2 employees

U.S. franchises: 1
Canadian franchises: 0
Other foreign franchises: 0
Company-owned: 1

Seeking: All U.S.
Seeking in Canada? Yes
Exclusive territories? No
Homebased option? Yes
Employees needed to run biz: 1
Absentee ownership? Yes

COSTS
Total cost: $50.7K
Franchise fee: $25K
Royalty fee: 7.5%
Term of agreement: 5 years renewable
    for 50% of current fee
Franchisees required to buy multiple
    units? No

FINANCING
No financing available

QUALIFICATIONS
Experience:
    Industry experience
    Marketing skills

TRAINING
At headquarters: 1 week

BUSINESS SUPPORT
Grand opening
Internet
Newsletter
Meetings
Toll-free phone line
Field operations/evaluations
Purchasing cooperatives

MARKETING SUPPORT
National media campaign

SUN FRANCHISE GROUP INC.

Financial rating: 0

15851 Dallas Pkwy., #225
Addison, TX 75001
(972)392-1414
www.sunorganization.com
Sports & entertainment management/
    event planning
Began: 2005, Franchising: 2006
Headquarters size: 10 employees
Franchise department: 4 employees

U.S. franchises: 1
Canadian franchises: 0
Other foreign franchises: 0
Company-owned: 1

Seeking: All U.S.
Seeking in Canada? Yes
Exclusive territories? Yes
Homebased option? Yes
Employees needed to run biz: 3
Absentee ownership? Yes

COSTS
Total cost: $74.1K-237.8K
Franchise fee: $25K
Royalty fee: 0
Term of agreement: 5 years renewable
    for $5K
Franchisees required to buy multiple
    units? Yes

FINANCING
No financing available

QUALIFICATIONS
Net worth: $350K
Cash liquidity: $100K
Experience:
    General business experience
    Marketing skills

TRAINING
At headquarters: 5 days
At franchisee's location: 5 days
Monthly videoconferencing

BUSINESS SUPPORT
Grand opening
Newsletter
Meetings
Field operations/evaluations

MARKETING SUPPORT
Co-op advertising
Ad slicks
National media campaign

SUPERCOUPS

Ranked #382 in Entrepreneur Magazine's 2007 Franchise 500   *Financial rating: $$$$*

350 Revolutionary Dr.
East Taunton, MA 02718
(800)626-2620
www.supercoups.com
Co-op direct-mail advertising
Began: 1982, Franchising: 1983
Headquarters size: 100 employees
Franchise department: 10 employees

U.S. franchises: 283
Canadian franchises: 0
Other foreign franchises: 0
Company-owned: 4

Seeking: All U.S.
Seeking in Canada? No
Exclusive territories? Yes
Homebased option? Yes
Employees needed to run biz: 1
Absentee ownership? No

COSTS
Total cost: $46.8K-84.5K
Franchise fee: $26K
Royalty fee: Varies
Term of agreement: 10 years renewable
    for $2.5K
Franchisees required to buy multiple
    units? No

FINANCING
No financing available

QUALIFICATIONS
Net worth: $100K
Cash liquidity: $50K
Experience:
    General business experience
    Sales & sales-management
    experience

TRAINING
At headquarters: 1 week
At franchisee's location: 2 weeks

BUSINESS SUPPORT
Internet
Newsletter
Meetings
Toll-free phone line
Field operations/evaluations
Security/safety procedures

MARKETING SUPPORT
Ad slicks
Franchisee committee for marketing
    & business development

VALPAK DIRECT MARKETING SYSTEMS INC.

Ranked #392 in Entrepreneur Magazine's 2007 Franchise 500   *Financial rating: $$$$*

8605 Largo Lakes Dr.
Largo, FL 33773
(800)237-6266
www.valpak.com
Co-op direct-mail advertising
Began: 1968, Franchising: 1988
Headquarters size: 200 employees
Franchise department: 32 employees

U.S. franchises: 171
Canadian franchises: 13
Other foreign franchises: 0
Company-owned: 11

Seeking: All U.S.
Seeking in Canada? Yes
Exclusive territories? Yes
Homebased option? Yes
Employees needed to run biz: 2
Absentee ownership? No

COSTS
Total cost: $54.2K-94.8K
Franchise fee: $15K
Royalty fee: 0
Term of agreement: 10 years renewable
    at no charge
Franchisees required to buy multiple
    units? No

FINANCING
In-house: None
3rd-party: Franchise fee, startup
    costs
Other: Territory fee

QUALIFICATIONS
Net worth: $150K+
Cash liquidity: $75K+
Experience:
    General business experience
    Sales skills
    Management skills

TRAINING
At headquarters: 3 weeks & ongoing
At franchisee's location: 1 week

BUSINESS SUPPORT
Grand opening
Internet
Newsletter
Meetings
Toll-free phone line
Field operations/evaluations

MARKETING SUPPORT
Co-op advertising
Ad slicks
National media campaign

BUSINESS *Consulting & Brokerages*

ACTIONCOACH

Ranked #96 in Entrepreneur Magazine's 2007 Franchise 500   *Financial rating: $$$$*

5670 Wynn Rd., #A & C
Las Vegas, NV 89118
(702)795-3188
www.action-international.com
Business coaching, consulting,
   training
Began: 1993, Franchising: 1997
Headquarters size: 10 employees

U.S. franchises: 268
Canadian franchises: 38
Other foreign franchises: 521
Company-owned: 2

Seeking: All U.S.
Seeking in Canada? Yes
Exclusive territories? Yes
Homebased option? Yes
Employees needed to run biz: 1
Absentee ownership? Yes

COSTS
Total cost: $59.3K-1.6M
Franchise fee: $30K-1M
Royalty fee: $1.5K/mo.
Term of agreement: 5 years renewable
   for $2.5K
Franchisees required to buy multiple
   units? No

FINANCING
In-house: None
3rd-party: Franchise fee, startup
   costs

QUALIFICATIONS
Net worth: $100K
Cash liquidity: $20K
Experience:
   General business experience
   Marketing skills

TRAINING
At headquarters: 10 days
At various locations: 10 days

BUSINESS SUPPORT
Internet
Newsletter
Meetings
Toll-free phone line
Field operations/evaluations

MARKETING SUPPORT
Co-op advertising
Ad slicks
National media campaign
Regional marketing

THE ALTERNATIVE BOARD

Ranked #200 in Entrepreneur Magazine's 2007 Franchise 500   *Financial rating: $$$$*

1640 Grant St., #200
Denver, CO 80203
(800)727-0126/(303)839-1200
www.tabboards.com
Peer advisory boards & business
   coaching
Began: 1990, Franchising: 1996
Headquarters size: 27 employees
Franchise department: 6 employees

U.S. franchises: 134
Canadian franchises: 12
Other foreign franchises: 1
Company-owned: 8

Seeking: All U.S.
Seeking in Canada? Yes
Exclusive territories? Yes
Homebased option? Yes
Employees needed to run biz: 1
Absentee ownership? No

COSTS
Total cost: $44.4K-106.3K
Franchise fee: $25K-55K
Royalty fee: Varies
Term of agreement: 10 years renewable
   for $1.5K
Franchisees required to buy multiple
   units? No

FINANCING
In-house: None
3rd-party: Accounts receivable,
   equipment, franchise fee,
   inventory, payroll, startup costs

QUALIFICATIONS
Net worth: $200K+
Cash liquidity: $25K
Experience:
   Industry experience
   General business experience
   Marketing skills
   10 years+ senior-level executive
   experience

TRAINING
At headquarters: 6 days initially
At franchisee's location: 4 weeks
Monthly/quarterly conference calls

BUSINESS SUPPORT
Grand opening
Internet
Newsletter
Meetings
Toll-free phone line
Field operations/evaluations

MARKETING SUPPORT
Co-op advertising
Ad slicks
National media campaign
Regional marketing
Websites

BRIDGE BUSINESS & PROPERTY BROKERS INC.

Financial rating: 0

270 E. Main St.
Patchogue, NY 11727
(888)614-6592
www.bridgebrokers.com
Business/commercial brokerage,
    mergers & acquisitions, financing
Began: 2004, Franchising: 2005
Headquarters size: 30 employees
Franchise department: 8 employees

U.S. franchises: 2
Canadian franchises: 0
Other foreign franchises: 0
Company-owned: 10

Seeking: All U.S.
Seeking in Canada? Yes
Exclusive territories? Yes
Homebased option? Yes
Employees needed to run biz: 1-4
Absentee ownership? Yes

COSTS
Total cost: $38K-63K
Franchise fee: $25K
Royalty fee: 6%
Term of agreement: 5 years
    renewable
Franchisees required to buy multiple
    units? No

FINANCING
No financing available

QUALIFICATIONS
Cash liquidity: $25K

TRAINING
At headquarters: 1 week

BUSINESS SUPPORT
Internet
Newsletter
Meetings
Toll-free phone line
Field operations/evaluations
Purchasing cooperatives

MARKETING SUPPORT
Co-op advertising
Ad slicks
Regional marketing

BUSINESS ADVISERS INT'L

Ranked #398 in Entrepreneur Magazine's 2007 Franchise 500   *Financial rating: $$$*

900 Main St. S., Bldg. 2
Southbury, CT 06488
(800)892-1085
www.baiopportunity.com
Business advisory services
Began: 2002, Franchising: 2002
Headquarters size: 10 employees
Franchise department: 4 employees

U.S. franchises: 14
Canadian franchises: 0
Other foreign franchises: 4
Company-owned: 0

Seeking: All U.S.
Seeking in Canada? Yes
Exclusive territories? Yes
Homebased option? Yes
Employees needed to run biz: 0-1
Absentee ownership? No

COSTS
Total cost: $69K-82.3K
Franchise fee: $40K
Royalty fee: 20%
Term of agreement: 5 years renewable
    for 10% of franchise fee
Franchisees required to buy multiple
    units? No

FINANCING
In-house: None
3rd-party: Franchise fee, startup
    costs

QUALIFICATIONS
Net worth: $250K-350K
Cash liquidity: $50K-300K
Experience:
    General business experience
    Marketing skills

TRAINING
At headquarters: 14 days

BUSINESS SUPPORT
Grand opening
Internet
Newsletter
Meetings
Toll-free phone line
Field operations/evaluations
Security/safety procedures

MARKETING SUPPORT
Ad slicks
Customized marketing plan

BUSINESS ROUND TABLE

Current financial data not available

37 Chandler Crescent
Moncton, NB E1E 3W6 Canada
(506)857-8177
www.businessroundtable.ca
Mentoring groups for small businesses
Began: 1991, Franchising: 1998
Headquarters size: 2 employees
Franchise department: 1 employee

U.S. franchises: 0
Canadian franchises: 4
Other foreign franchises: 0
Company-owned: 1

Seeking: Not available in the U.S.
Seeking in Canada? Yes
Exclusive territories? Yes
Homebased option? Yes
Employees needed to run biz: 2
Absentee ownership? No

COSTS
Total cost: $20K
Franchise fee: $20K
Royalty fee: 5-10%
Term of agreement: 10 years renewable
    at no charge
Franchisees required to buy multiple
    units? No

FINANCING
No financing available

QUALIFICATIONS
Net worth: $100K
Cash liquidity: $25K
Experience:
    General business experience
    Marketing skills

TRAINING
At franchisee's location: 2 weeks

BUSINESS SUPPORT
Internet
Newsletter
Toll-free phone line
Field operations/evaluations

MARKETING SUPPORT
Ad slicks

THE ENTREPRENEUR'S SOURCE

Ranked #486 in Entrepreneur Magazine's 2007 Franchise 500   *Financial rating: $*

900 Main St. S., Bldg. 2
Southbury, CT 06488
(800)289-0086
www.topfranchises.com
Franchise consulting &
    development services
Began: 1984, Franchising: 1997
Headquarters size: 12 employees

U.S. franchises: 276
Canadian franchises: 3
Other foreign franchises: 1
Company-owned: 0

Seeking: All U.S.
Seeking in Canada? Yes
Exclusive territories? No
Homebased option? Yes
Employees needed to run biz: 0
Absentee ownership? No

COSTS
Total cost: $68.5K-76.5K
Franchise fee: $49K
Royalty fee: 0
Term of agreement: 10 years renewable
    for $5K
Franchisees required to buy multiple
    units? Outside the U.S. only

FINANCING
In-house: None
3rd-party: Equipment, franchise fee,
    startup costs

QUALIFICATIONS
Net worth: $150K
Cash liquidity: $50K

TRAINING
At headquarters: 8 days
Ongoing

BUSINESS SUPPORT
Internet
Newsletter
Meetings

MARKETING SUPPORT
Ad slicks
National media campaign
Regional marketing

EWF INT'L.

Financial rating: 0

4900 Richmond Sq., #105
Oklahoma City, OK 73118
(405)843-3934
www.ewfinternational.com
Peer advisory groups for women in
    business
Began: 1998, Franchising: 2002
Headquarters size: 3 employees
Franchise department: 1 employee

U.S. franchises: 3
Canadian franchises: 0
Other foreign franchises: 0
Company-owned: 1

Seeking: All U.S.
Seeking in Canada? No
Exclusive territories? Yes
Homebased option? Yes
Employees needed to run biz: 1
Absentee ownership? No

COSTS
Total cost: $30.5K-35K
Franchise fee: $25K
Royalty fee: 15%
Term of agreement: 3 years renewable
    at no charge
Franchisees required to buy multiple
    units? No

FINANCING
No financing available

QUALIFICATIONS
Experience:
    General business experience
    Marketing skills

TRAINING
At headquarters: 1 week
At franchisee's location: 4-6 days

BUSINESS SUPPORT
Internet
Newsletter
Meetings
Toll-free phone line

MARKETING SUPPORT
Ad slicks
Personalized electronic newsletter

THE GROWTH COACH

Ranked #198 in Entrepreneur Magazine's 2007 Franchise 500   *Financial rating: $$$$*

10700 Montgomery Rd., #300
Cincinnati, OH 45242
(888)292-7992
www.thegrowthcoach.com
Small-business coaching & mentoring
Began: 2002, Franchising: 2003
Headquarters size: 35 employees
Franchise department: 35 employees

U.S. franchises: 137
Canadian franchises: 2
Other foreign franchises: 0
Company-owned: 0

Seeking: All U.S.
Seeking in Canada? Yes
Exclusive territories? Yes
Homebased option? Yes
Employees needed to run biz: 0
Absentee ownership? No

COSTS
Total cost: $34.2K-54.4K
Franchise fee: $24.9K
Royalty fee: 6%
Term of agreement: 10 years renewable
    at no charge
Franchisees required to buy multiple
    units? No

FINANCING
In-house: Franchise fee
3rd-party: None

QUALIFICATIONS
Cash liquidity: $9K
Experience:
    General business experience

TRAINING
At headquarters: 5 days
Ongoing training & bootcamps

BUSINESS SUPPORT
Grand opening
Internet
Newsletter
Meetings
Toll-free phone line

MARKETING SUPPORT
Ad slicks
National media campaign
Regional marketing
Marketing plans & tools
Publicity assistance
National accounts

REFERRAL INSTITUTE LLC

Ranked #500 in Entrepreneur Magazine's 2007 Franchise 500   *Financial rating: $$$*

151 Virginia Ave.
Attleboro Falls, MA 02763
(508)809-9789
www.referralinstitute.com
Referral training, coaching, consulting
Began: 1999, Franchising: 2004
Headquarters size: 2 employees
Franchise department: 2 employees

U.S. franchises: 32
Canadian franchises: 0
Other foreign franchises: 3
Company-owned: 2

Seeking: All U.S.
Seeking in Canada? Yes
Exclusive territories? Yes
Homebased option? Yes
Employees needed to run biz: 6
Absentee ownership? No

COSTS
Total cost: $21.3K-25.8K
Franchise fee: $8.5K-10.5K
Royalty fee: 15%
Term of agreement: 5 years renewable
    for 25% of then-current fee
Franchisees required to buy multiple
    units? No

FINANCING
No financing available

QUALIFICATIONS
Experience:
    Industry experience
    General business experience
    Marketing skills

TRAINING
At headquarters: 128 hours

BUSINESS SUPPORT
Internet
Meetings
Purchasing cooperatives

MARKETING SUPPORT
Marketing plan

RENAISSANCE EXECUTIVE FORUMS INC.

Financial rating: $$$

7855 Ivanhoe Ave., #300
La Jolla, CA 92037
(858)551-6600
www.executiveforums.info
Business advisory boards & consulting
    services
Began: 1994, Franchising: 1994
Headquarters size: 12 employees
Franchise department: 2 employees

U.S. franchises: 36
Canadian franchises: 1
Other foreign franchises: 10
Company-owned: 0

Seeking: All U.S.
Seeking in Canada? Yes
Exclusive territories? Yes
Homebased option? Yes
Employees needed to run biz: 0
Absentee ownership? No

COSTS
Total cost: $55.4K-73.3K
Franchise fee: $39.5K
Royalty fee: 20%
Term of agreement: 10 years renewable
    for $3K
Franchisees required to buy multiple
    units? No

FINANCING
No financing available

QUALIFICATIONS
Net worth: $500K
Cash liquidity: $76K
Experience:
    General business experience
    Marketing skills
    Ability to deal with CEOs

TRAINING
At headquarters: 1 week
At franchisee's location: 2 days
Online training

BUSINESS SUPPORT
Grand opening
Internet
Newsletter
Meetings
Toll-free phone line
Field operations/evaluations
Purchasing cooperatives
Security/safety procedures

MARKETING SUPPORT
Ad slicks
Regional marketing
Intranet
Mentor program
PR

SIX DISCIPLINES LEADERSHIP CENTER

Current financial data not available

1000 E. Main Cross, #200
Findlay, OH 45840
(419)581-2821
www.sixdisciplines.com
Professional coaching & consulting
Began: 2001, Franchising: 2005
Headquarters size: 20 employees
Franchise department: 10 employees

U.S. franchises: 7
Canadian franchises: 0
Other foreign franchises: 0
Company-owned: 0

Seeking: Midwest
Seeking in Canada? No
Exclusive territories? Yes
Homebased option? No
Employees needed to run biz: 2-13
Absentee ownership? Yes

COSTS
Total cost: $408K
Franchise fee: $100K
Royalty fee: 20%
Term of agreement: 5 years renewable
    at no charge
Franchisees required to buy multiple
    units? No

FINANCING
In-house: Franchise fee, startup
    costs
3rd-party: None

QUALIFICATIONS
Net worth: $2M+
Cash liquidity: $500K
Experience:
    Industry experience
    General business experience
    Marketing skills
    15 years+ business-management
    experience

TRAINING
At headquarters: 2 weeks
At franchisee's location: Varies
Online: 2 weeks

BUSINESS SUPPORT
Grand opening
Internet
Newsletter
Meetings
Field operations/evaluations

MARKETING SUPPORT
Co-op advertising
Ad slicks
Regional marketing
Turnkey marketing programs

SUNBELT

Ranked #472 in Entrepreneur Magazine's 2007 Franchise 500

Financial rating: $$$$

7100 E. Pleasant Valley Rd., #260
Independence, OH 44131
(877)392-6278
www.sunbeltnetwork.com
Business brokerage
Began: 1979, Franchising: 1993
Headquarters size: 40 employees
Franchise department: 8 employees

U.S. franchises: 241
Canadian franchises: 14
Other foreign franchises: 40
Company-owned: 0

Seeking: All U.S.
Seeking in Canada? Yes
Exclusive territories? Yes
Homebased option? No
Employees needed to run biz: 2-5
Absentee ownership? No

COSTS
Total cost: $41.3K-105K
Franchise fee: $20K-30K
Royalty fee: $500-700/mo.
Term of agreement: 10 years renewable
    for $1K
Franchisees required to buy multiple
    units? No

FINANCING
In-house: Franchise fee
3rd-party: Franchise fee

QUALIFICATIONS
Net worth: $150K
Cash liquidity: $25K
Experience:
    General business experience

TRAINING
At headquarters: 1 week
Regional training

BUSINESS SUPPORT
Internet
Newsletter
Meetings
Toll-free phone line
Purchasing cooperatives

MARKETING SUPPORT
Co-op advertising
Ad slicks
National media campaign
Centralized PR services

BUSINESS ▸ *Shipping*

eSHIPPING

Financial rating: $$$

173 English Landing Dr., #210
Parkville, MD 64152
(888)313-6444
www.eshipping.biz
Freight & shipping services
Began: 2001, Franchising: 2006
Headquarters size: 6 employees

U.S. franchises: 7
Canadian franchises: 0
Other foreign franchises: 0
Company-owned: 2

Seeking: All U.S.
Seeking in Canada? No
Exclusive territories? Yes
Homebased option? Yes
Employees needed to run biz: Info
    not provided
Absentee ownership? Yes

COSTS
Total cost: $24.9K-52.5K
Franchise fee: $18.8K
Royalty fee: 0
Term of agreement: 5 years renewable
    for $2K
Franchisees required to buy multiple
    units? No

FINANCING
No financing available

QUALIFICATIONS
Experience:
    Marketing skills

TRAINING
At headquarters: 3-4 days

BUSINESS SUPPORT
Internet
Meetings
Toll-free phone line

MARKETING SUPPORT
Info not provided

UNITED SHIPPING SOLUTIONS

Ranked #130 in Entrepreneur Magazine's 2007 Franchise 500   *Financial rating: $$$$*

6985 Union Park Ctr., #565
Midvale, UT 84047
(866)744-7486/(801)352-0012
www.usshipit.com
Transportation services
Began: 2002, Franchising: 2002
Headquarters size: 12 employees
Franchise department: 2 employees

U.S. franchises: 227
Canadian franchises: 0
Other foreign franchises: 0
Company-owned: 0

Seeking: All U.S.
Seeking in Canada? No
Exclusive territories? Yes
Homebased option? Yes
Employees needed to run biz: 1
Absentee ownership? Yes

COSTS
Total cost: $53.7K-103.5K
Franchise fee: $50K-53K
Royalty fee: 6%
Term of agreement: 5 years renewable
    for $5K
Franchisees required to buy multiple
    units? No

FINANCING
No financing available

QUALIFICATIONS
Net worth: $150K
Cash liquidity: $70K
Experience:
    General business experience
    Marketing skills

TRAINING
At headquarters: 7 days
At franchisee's location: 7 days
Ongoing

BUSINESS SUPPORT
Internet
Newsletter
Meetings
Toll-free phone line
Field operations/evaluations
Purchasing cooperatives

MARKETING SUPPORT
Regional marketing
Face-to-face sales

WORLDWIDE EXPRESS

Ranked #247 in Entrepreneur Magazine's 2007 Franchise 500   *Financial rating: $$$$*

2828 Raith St., #400
Dallas, TX 75201
(214)720-2400
www.wwex.com
Discounted air express services
Began: 1991, Franchising: 1994
Headquarters size: 18 employees
Franchise department: 11 employees

U.S. franchises: 175
Canadian franchises: 0
Other foreign franchises: 0
Company-owned: 13

Seeking: All U.S.
Seeking in Canada? No
Exclusive territories? Yes
Homebased option? No
Employees needed to run biz: 1
Absentee ownership? No

COSTS
Total cost: $47.5K-348.8K
Franchise fee: $28.1K-315K
Royalty fee: 6%
Term of agreement: 5 years renewable
Franchisees required to buy multiple
    units? No

FINANCING
No financing available

QUALIFICATIONS
Net worth: $50K
Cash liquidity: $50K
Experience:
    General business experience
    Marketing skills

TRAINING
At headquarters
At franchisee's location

BUSINESS SUPPORT
Newsletter
Meetings
Toll-free phone line

MARKETING SUPPORT
Info not provided

BUSINESS ▸ *Shredding*

PROSHRED FRANCHISING CORP.

Current financial data not available

245 Yorkland Blvd., #100
Toronto, ON M4G 1N6 Canada
(416)490-8600
www.proshred.com
Mobile onsite document
    destruction/shredding
Began: 2004, Franchising: 2004
Headquarters size: 50 employees
Franchise department: 5 employees

U.S. franchises: 7
Canadian franchises: 0
Other foreign franchises: 0
Company-owned: 0

Seeking: All U.S.
Seeking in Canada? Yes
Exclusive territories? Yes
Homebased option? No
Employees needed to run biz: 2
Absentee ownership? Yes

COSTS
Total cost: $359.5K-464.5K
Franchise fee: $35K
Royalty fee: 6.5%
Term of agreement: 10 years
Franchisees required to buy multiple
    units? Outside the U.S. only

FINANCING
In-house: None
3rd-party: Equipment, franchise fee,
    inventory

QUALIFICATIONS
Net worth: $250K
Cash liquidity: $50K-100K
Experience:
    General business experience
    Marketing skills

TRAINING
At headquarters: 2 weeks
At franchisee's location: 1 week
Ongoing

BUSINESS SUPPORT
Grand opening
Internet
Newsletter
Meetings
Toll-free phone line
Field operations/evaluations
Lease negotiations
Purchasing cooperatives
Security/safety procedures

MARKETING SUPPORT
Co-op advertising
Ad slicks
National media campaign
Regional marketing

SECURE ECO SHRED AMERICA LLC

Financial rating: $$

33085 W. Nine Mile Rd.
Farmington, MI 48336
(248)476-6666
www.secureecoshred.com
Document shredding & recycling
Began: 2000, Franchising: 2005
Headquarters size: 30 employees
Franchise department: 12 employees

U.S. franchises: 3
Canadian franchises: 0
Other foreign franchises: 0
Company-owned: 1

Seeking: All U.S.
Seeking in Canada? No
Exclusive territories? Yes
Homebased option? No
Employees needed to run biz: 5
Absentee ownership? No

COSTS
Total cost: $299.1K-365.95K
Franchise fee: $25K
Royalty fee: 5%
Term of agreement: 10 years renewable
for $15K
Franchisees required to buy multiple
units? No

FINANCING
In-house: Franchise fee
3rd-party: None

QUALIFICATIONS
Net worth: $200K
Cash liquidity: $45K
Experience:
General business experience
Marketing skills

TRAINING
At headquarters: 2 weeks
At franchisee's location: 1 week

BUSINESS SUPPORT
Internet
Newsletter
Meetings
Toll-free phone line
Field operations/evaluations
Purchasing cooperatives
Security/safety procedures

MARKETING SUPPORT
Co-op advertising
Ad slicks
Regional marketing

BUSINESS ▶ *Signs*

FASTSIGNS INT'L. INC.

Ranked #100 in Entrepreneur Magazine's 2007 Franchise 500

Financial rating: $$$$

2542 Highlander Way
Carrollton, TX 75006
(800)827-7446/(214)346-5600
http://franchise.fastsigns.com
Signs & graphics solutions
Began: 1985, Franchising: 1986
Headquarters size: 95 employees
Franchise department: 7 employees

U.S. franchises: 420
Canadian franchises: 12
Other foreign franchises: 63
Company-owned: 0

Seeking: All U.S.
Seeking in Canada? Yes
Exclusive territories? Yes
Homebased option? No
Employees needed to run biz: 3-5
Absentee ownership? No

COSTS
Total cost: $208.1K-321.8K
Franchise fee: $25K
Royalty fee: 6%
Term of agreement: 20 years renewable
for 10% of current franchise fee
Franchisees required to buy multiple
units? No

FINANCING
In-house: None
3rd-party: Equipment, franchise fee,
inventory, payroll, startup costs

QUALIFICATIONS
Net worth: $250K
Cash liquidity: $75K
Experience:
General business experience
Marketing skills
Sales experience

TRAINING
At headquarters: 3 weeks
At franchisee's location: Up to 2 weeks
Ongoing visits
Regional & annual conventions
Ongoing web seminars

BUSINESS SUPPORT
Grand opening
Internet
Newsletter
Meetings
Toll-free phone line
Field operations/evaluations
Lease negotiations
Purchasing cooperatives
Security/safety procedures

MARKETING SUPPORT
Co-op advertising
Ad slicks
National media campaign
Regional marketing
R&D

SIGN-A-RAMA INC.

Ranked #74 in Entrepreneur Magazine's 2007 Franchise 500   *Financial rating: $$$$*

2121 Vista Pkwy.
West Palm Beach, FL 33411
(800)286-8671/(561)640-5570
www.signarama.com
Signs
Began: 1986, Franchising: 1987
Headquarters size: 100 employees
Franchise department: 5 employees

U.S. franchises: 563
Canadian franchises: 27
Other foreign franchises: 213
Company-owned: 0

Seeking: All U.S.
Seeking in Canada? Yes
Exclusive territories? Yes
Homebased option? No
Employees needed to run biz: 2-4
Absentee ownership? Yes

COSTS
Total cost: $50K-144.6K
Franchise fee: $39.5K
Royalty fee: 6% w/cap
Term of agreement: 35 years renewable
  for $1.5K
Franchisees required to buy multiple
  units? Outside the U.S. only

FINANCING
In-house: None
3rd-party: Equipment, franchise fee,
  inventory, startup costs

QUALIFICATIONS
Net worth: $75K
Cash liquidity: $50K-75K
Experience:
  General business experience
  Marketing skills

TRAINING
At headquarters: 2 weeks
At franchisee's location: 2 weeks
At mentor store: 1 week

BUSINESS SUPPORT
Grand opening
Internet
Newsletter
Meetings
Toll-free phone line
Field operations/evaluations
Lease negotiations
Purchasing cooperatives
Security/safety procedures

MARKETING SUPPORT
Co-op advertising
Ad slicks
National media campaign
Regional marketing
Phone support
Quarterly seminars

SIGNS BY TOMORROW

Ranked #263 in Entrepreneur Magazine's 2007 Franchise 500   *Financial rating: $$$$*

8681 Robert Fulton Dr.
Columbia, MD 21046
(800)765-7446/(410)312-3600
www.signsbytomorrow.com
One-day retail sign stores
Began: 1986, Franchising: 1987
Headquarters size: 27 employees
Franchise department: 3 employees

U.S. franchises: 178
Canadian franchises: 0
Other foreign franchises: 0
Company-owned: 1

Seeking: All U.S.
Seeking in Canada? No
Exclusive territories? Yes
Homebased option? No
Employees needed to run biz: 2
Absentee ownership? No

COSTS
Total cost: $201.9K-263K
Franchise fee: $34.5K
Royalty fee: 3-6%
Term of agreement: 20 years renewable
  at no charge
Franchisees required to buy multiple
  units? No

FINANCING
No financing available

QUALIFICATIONS
Net worth: $250K
Cash liquidity: $50K
Experience:
  General business experience
  Marketing skills

TRAINING
At headquarters: 3 weeks
At franchisee's location: 3 weeks
At various locations: 2-4 days

BUSINESS SUPPORT
Grand opening
Internet
Newsletter
Meetings
Toll-free phone line
Field operations/evaluations
Lease negotiations
Purchasing cooperatives
Security/safety procedures

MARKETING SUPPORT
Co-op advertising
Ad slicks
Sales training

SIGNS NOW

Ranked #361 in Entrepreneur Magazine's 2007 Franchise 500　　　　*Financial rating: $$$$*

6976 Professional Parkway E.
Sarasota, FL 34240
(800)356-3373/(941)373-1958
www.signsnow.com
Signs & graphics services
Began: 1983, Franchising: 1986
Headquarters size: 21 employees

U.S. franchises: 197
Canadian franchises: 10
Other foreign franchises: 5
Company-owned: 0

Seeking: All U.S.
Seeking in Canada? Yes
Exclusive territories? No
Homebased option? No
Employees needed to run biz: 3-5
Absentee ownership? No

COSTS
Total cost: $141.6K-293.7K
Franchise fee: $30K
Royalty fee: 6%
Term of agreement: 20 years renewable
　　for a percentage of current fee
Franchisees required to buy multiple
　　units? Outside the U.S. only

FINANCING
In-house: None
3rd-party: Equipment, franchise fee,
　　inventory, startup costs

QUALIFICATIONS
Net worth: $250K+
Cash liquidity: $50K-70K
Experience:
　　General business experience
　　Marketing skills
　　Management experience

TRAINING
At headquarters: 3 weeks
At franchisee's location: 2 weeks
At various locations: 2-5 days

BUSINESS SUPPORT
Grand opening
Internet
Newsletter
Meetings
Toll-free phone line
Field operations/evaluations
Purchasing cooperatives
Security/safety procedures

MARKETING SUPPORT
Ad slicks
Regional operations directors
R&D
Preferred vendors
Direct marketing
On-hold ads

BUSINESS ▶ *Staffing*

ATWORK MEDICAL SERVICES

Financial rating: $$$$

3215 John Sevier Hwy.
Knoxville, TN 37290
(800)383-0804
www.atworkmedical.com
Temporary & full-time medical
　　staffing services
Began: 1990, Franchising: 2003
Headquarters size: 20 employees
Franchise department: 20 employees

U.S. franchises: 22
Canadian franchises: 0
Other foreign franchises: 0
Company-owned: 0

Seeking: All U.S.
Seeking in Canada? No
Exclusive territories? Yes
Homebased option? No
Employees needed to run biz: 3
Absentee ownership? No

COSTS
Total cost: $65K-110.5K
Franchise fee: $17K
Royalty fee: 1.6-6.1%
Term of agreement: 10 years renewable
　　at no charge
Franchisees required to buy multiple
　　units? No

FINANCING
In-house: Accounts receivable, payroll
3rd-party: None

QUALIFICATIONS
Cash liquidity: $30K-35K
Experience:
　　Industry experience
　　General business experience
　　Marketing skills

TRAINING
At headquarters: 5 days+
At franchisee's location: 2-5 days

BUSINESS SUPPORT
Internet
Newsletter
Meetings
Toll-free phone line
Field operations/evaluations
Security/safety procedures

MARKETING SUPPORT
Ad slicks
Direct sales support

ATWORK PERSONNEL SERVICES

Ranked #374 in Entrepreneur Magazine's 2007 Franchise 500   *Financial rating: $$$$*

3215 John Sevier Hwy.
Knoxville, TN 37920
(800)383-0804
www.atworkpersonnel.com
Temporary & temp-to-hire staffing
    services
Began: 1990, Franchising: 1992
Headquarters size: 20 employees
Franchise department: 20 employees

U.S. franchises: 46
Canadian franchises: 0
Other foreign franchises: 0
Company-owned: 0

Seeking: All U.S.
Seeking in Canada? No
Exclusive territories? Yes
Homebased option? No
Employees needed to run biz: 2-4
Absentee ownership? No

COSTS
Total cost: $65K-110.5K
Franchise fee: $17K
Royalty fee: 1.6-6.1%
Term of agreement: 10 years renewable
    at no charge
Franchisees required to buy multiple
    units? No

FINANCING
In-house: Accounts receivable, payroll
3rd-party: None

QUALIFICATIONS
Cash liquidity: $30K-35K
Experience:
    Industry experience
    General business experience
    Marketing skills
    Sales experience
    Human resources experience
    Collections experience

TRAINING
At headquarters: 5 days+
At franchisee's location: 3-5 days+
Meetings: 2 days

BUSINESS SUPPORT
Internet
Newsletter
Meetings
Toll-free phone line
Field operations/evaluations
Security/safety procedures

MARKETING SUPPORT
Co-op advertising
Ad slicks
Regional marketing
Direct sales support

CAREERS USA

Financial rating: $$$$

6501 Congress Ave., #200
Boca Raton, FL 33487
(888)227-3375/(561)995-7000
www.careersusa.com
Staffing services
Began: 1981, Franchising: 1988
Headquarters size: 40 employees
Franchise department: 4 employees

U.S. franchises: 7
Canadian franchises: 0
Other foreign franchises: 0
Company-owned: 17

Seeking: All U.S.
Seeking in Canada? No
Exclusive territories? Yes
Homebased option? No
Employees needed to run biz: 3-4
Absentee ownership? Yes

COSTS
Total cost: $129.7K-170.6K
Franchise fee: $14.5K
Royalty fee: Varies
Term of agreement: 10 years renewable
    at no charge
Franchisees required to buy multiple
    units? No

FINANCING
In-house: Accounts receivable, payroll
3rd-party: None

QUALIFICATIONS
Net worth: $150K-250K
Cash liquidity: $100K-150K
Experience:
    General business experience
    Marketing skills

TRAINING
At headquarters: 2 weeks
At franchisee's location: 1 week
Ongoing sales support

BUSINESS SUPPORT
Grand opening
Internet
Newsletter
Meetings
Toll-free phone line
Field operations/evaluations
Lease negotiations
Purchasing cooperatives
Security/safety procedures

MARKETING SUPPORT
Co-op advertising
Ad slicks
National media campaign
Regional marketing
Internet & intranet marketing

EXPRESS PERSONNEL SERVICES

Ranked #69 in Entrepreneur Magazine's 2007 Franchise 500   *Financial rating: $$$$*

8516 Northwest Expwy.
Oklahoma City, OK 73162
(877)652-6400/(405)840-5000
www.expressfranchising.com
Staffing & HR solutions
Began: 1983, Franchising: 1985
Headquarters size: 190 employees
Franchise department: 8 employees

U.S. franchises: 489
Canadian franchises: 22
Other foreign franchises: 10
Company-owned: 0

Seeking: All U.S.
Seeking in Canada? Yes
Exclusive territories? Yes
Homebased option? No
Employees needed to run biz: 3
Absentee ownership? No

COSTS
Total cost: $116.9K-164.3K
Franchise fee: $27.5K
Royalty fee: 8-9%
Term of agreement: 5 years renewable
   at no charge
Franchisees required to buy multiple
   units? No

FINANCING
No financing available

QUALIFICATIONS
Net worth: $100K+
Cash liquidity: $50K
Experience:
   General business experience
   Marketing skills

TRAINING
At headquarters: 2 weeks
At franchisee's location: 2 weeks
At certified training office: 1 week

BUSINESS SUPPORT
Grand opening
Internet
Newsletter
Meetings
Toll-free phone line
Field operations/evaluations
Purchasing cooperatives
Security/safety procedures

MARKETING SUPPORT
Co-op advertising
Ad slicks
National media campaign
Regional marketing
Intranet & extranet support
Collateral sales materials

LABOR FINDERS

Ranked #104 in Entrepreneur Magazine's 2007 Franchise 500   *Financial rating: $$$$*

11426 N. Jog Rd.
Palm Beach Gardens, FL 33418
(561)627-6507
www.laborfinders.com
Industrial staffing services
Began: 1975, Franchising: 1975
Headquarters size: 26 employees
Franchise department: 23 employees

U.S. franchises: 240
Canadian franchises: 0
Other foreign franchises: 0
Company-owned: 22

Seeking: Midwest, Northeast, West
Seeking in Canada? Yes
Exclusive territories? Yes
Homebased option? No
Employees needed to run biz: 2-3
Absentee ownership? Yes

COSTS
Total cost: $96.2K-157.3K
Franchise fee: $10K
Royalty fee: 2.5%
Term of agreement: 10 years renewable
   at no charge
Franchisees required to buy multiple
   units? No

FINANCING
In-house: Accounts receivable,
   equipment, inventory, payroll
3rd-party: None

QUALIFICATIONS
Net worth: $500K+
Cash liquidity: $100K
Experience:
   General business experience
   Marketing skills

TRAINING
At headquarters: 1 week
At franchisee's location: Ongoing

BUSINESS SUPPORT
Grand opening
Internet
Newsletter
Meetings
Toll-free phone line
Field operations/evaluations
Lease negotiations
Purchasing cooperatives
Security/safety procedures

MARKETING SUPPORT
Co-op advertising
Ad slicks
National media campaign
Regional marketing

LINK STAFFING SERVICES
Ranked #355 in Entrepreneur Magazine's 2007 Franchise 500   *Financial rating: $$$*

1800 Bering, #800
Houston, TX 77057
(800)848-5465/(713)784-4400
www.linkstaffing.com
Temporary staffing services
Began: 1980, Franchising: 1994
Headquarters size: 45 employees
Franchise department: 5 employees

U.S. franchises: 45
Canadian franchises: 0
Other foreign franchises: 0
Company-owned: 10

Seeking: All U.S.
Seeking in Canada? No
Exclusive territories? Yes
Homebased option? No
Employees needed to run biz: 2
Absentee ownership? Yes

COSTS
Total cost: $85.5K-156K
Franchise fee: $17K
Royalty fee: Varies
Term of agreement: 10 years renewable
    at no charge
Franchisees required to buy multiple
    units? No

FINANCING
In-house: Accounts receivable, payroll
3rd-party: None

QUALIFICATIONS
Net worth: $200K+
Cash liquidity: $60K+
Experience:
    General business experience
    Marketing skills
    Management skills
    Sales skills
    Customer service skills

TRAINING
At headquarters: 2 weeks
At franchisee's location: 1 week
At field office: 5 days
At support center: 5 days

BUSINESS SUPPORT
Grand opening
Internet
Newsletter
Meetings
Toll-free phone line
Field operations/evaluations
Lease negotiations
Purchasing cooperatives
Security/safety procedures

MARKETING SUPPORT
Co-op advertising
Ad slicks
National media campaign
Regional marketing
Management, budgeting, billing &
    technical assistance

NEXTAFF
          Financial rating: $$$$

11660 W. 75th St.
Shawnee, KS 66214
(913)562-5605
www.nextaff.com
Staffing services
Began: 1998, Franchising: 2004
Headquarters size: Info not
    provided

U.S. franchises: 6
Canadian franchises: 0
Other foreign franchises: 0
Company-owned: 0

Seeking: All U.S.
Seeking in Canada? No
Exclusive territories? Yes
Homebased option? No
Employees needed to run biz: 2-5
Absentee ownership? Yes

COSTS
Total cost: $47.6K-154.5K
Franchise fee: $8.5K-45K
Royalty fee: 6%
Term of agreement: 10 years
Franchisees required to buy multiple
    units? No

FINANCING
In-house: Accounts receivable, payroll
3rd-party: Equipment, franchise fee,
    inventory, startup costs

QUALIFICATIONS
Net worth: $150K
Cash liquidity: $50K
Experience:
    General business experience
    Marketing skills

TRAINING
At headquarters: 1 week
At franchisee's location: 1 week
Additional training as needed

BUSINESS SUPPORT
Internet
Meetings
Toll-free phone line
Field operations/evaluations
Lease negotiations
Purchasing cooperatives

MARKETING SUPPORT
Ad slicks
Website & email marketing

PMA FRANCHISE SYSTEMS

Financial rating: 0

1950 Spectrum Cir., #B-310
Marietta, GA 30067
(800)466-7822
www.pmafranchise.com
Management recruiting services
Began: 1985, Franchising: 1999
Headquarters size: 5 employees
Franchise department: 4 employees

U.S. franchises: 6
Canadian franchises: 0
Other foreign franchises: 0
Company-owned: 1

Seeking: All U.S.
Seeking in Canada? No
Exclusive territories? Yes
Homebased option? Yes
Employees needed to run biz: 2
Absentee ownership? Yes

COSTS
Total cost: $43.3K-60K
Franchise fee: $30K
Royalty fee: 10-8%
Term of agreement: 10 years renewable
    for $5K
Franchisees required to buy multiple
    units? No

FINANCING
In-house: Franchise fee
3rd-party: None

QUALIFICATIONS
Net worth: $100K
Cash liquidity: $50K
Experience:
    General business experience

TRAINING
At headquarters: 4 weeks

BUSINESS SUPPORT
Internet
Newsletter
Meetings
Toll-free phone line
Field operations/evaluations

MARKETING SUPPORT
Internet

SANFORD ROSE ASSOCIATES

Financial rating: 0

3737 Embassy Pkwy., #200
Akron, OH 44333
(800)731-7724/(330)670-9797
www.sanfordrose.com
Executive search services
Began: 1959, Franchising: 1970
Headquarters size: 7 employees
Franchise department: 7 employees

U.S. franchises: 57
Canadian franchises: 0
Other foreign franchises: 5
Company-owned: 0

Seeking: All U.S.
Seeking in Canada? Yes
Exclusive territories? Yes
Homebased option? Yes
Employees needed to run biz: 2-5
Absentee ownership? No

COSTS
Total cost: $10.6K-100.3K
Franchise fee: to $41K
Royalty fee: 7-5%
Term of agreement: 10 years renewable
    at no charge
Franchisees required to buy multiple
    units? No

FINANCING
In-house: None
3rd-party: Franchise fee, startup
    costs

QUALIFICATIONS
Cash liquidity: $70.3K-98.1K
Experience:
    Industry experience
    General business experience
    Marketing skills

TRAINING
At headquarters: 13 days
At franchisee's location: 1-1/2 days
Entrepreneur Express: 1-1/2 days

BUSINESS SUPPORT
Internet
Newsletter
Meetings
Toll-free phone line
Field operations/evaluations
Lease negotiations
Purchasing cooperatives

MARKETING SUPPORT
Info not provided

SNELLING STAFFING SERVICES

Current financial data not available

12801 N. Central Expwy., #600
Dallas, TX 75243
(800)766-5556
www.snelling.com
Staffing services
Began: 1951, Franchising: 1956
Headquarters size: 147 employees
Franchise department: 10 employees

U.S. franchises: 150
Canadian franchises: 0
Other foreign franchises: 0
Company-owned: 52

Seeking: All U.S.
Seeking in Canada? No
Exclusive territories? Yes
Homebased option? No
Employees needed to run biz: 4
Absentee ownership? Yes

COSTS
Total cost: $89K-180K
Franchise fee: $25K
Royalty fee: Varies
Term of agreement: 7 years renewable
   at no charge
Franchisees required to buy multiple
   units? No

FINANCING
In-house: Accounts receivable, payroll
3rd-party: Equipment, franchise fee,
   startup costs

QUALIFICATIONS
Net worth: $300K
Cash liquidity: $100K
Experience:
   General business experience

TRAINING
At headquarters: 8 days
At franchisee's location: As needed
At field location

BUSINESS SUPPORT
Grand opening
Internet
Newsletter
Meetings
Toll-free phone line
Field operations/evaluations
Purchasing cooperatives
Security/safety procedures

MARKETING SUPPORT
Co-op advertising
Ad slicks
National media campaign

10 TIL 2

Financial rating: 0

13780 E. Rice Pl., #100
Aurora, CO 80015
(303)909-3868
www.tentiltwo.com
Parttime employment staffing
   services
Began: 2003, Franchising: 2006
Headquarters size: 14 employees
Franchise department: 6 employees

U.S. franchises: 4
Canadian franchises: 0
Other foreign franchises: 0
Company-owned: 1

Seeking: All U.S.
Seeking in Canada? No
Exclusive territories? Yes
Homebased option? Yes
Employees needed to run biz: 2
Absentee ownership? Yes

COSTS
Total cost: $31.2K-168.1K
Franchise fee: $15K-37.5K
Royalty fee: 5%
Term of agreement: 10 years renewable
   for a fee
Franchisees required to buy multiple
   units? No

FINANCING
No financing available

QUALIFICATIONS
Experience:
   General business experience

TRAINING
At headquarters: 1 week

BUSINESS SUPPORT
Grand opening
Internet
Newsletter
Meetings
Field operations/evaluations

MARKETING SUPPORT
Co-op advertising
Ad slicks
Regional marketing

BUSINESS — *Toner Replacements*

CARTRIDGE DEPOT

Financial rating: $$$

10324 S. Dolfield Rd.
Owings Mills, MD 21117
(800)914-5828
www.thecartridgedepot.com
Inkjet & laser toner cartridge refills
Began: 2004, Franchising: 2004
Headquarters size: 6 employees
Franchise department: 4 employees

U.S. franchises: 5
Canadian franchises: 1
Other foreign franchises: 4
Company-owned: 2

Seeking: All U.S.
Seeking in Canada? Yes
Exclusive territories? Yes
Homebased option? No
Employees needed to run biz: 2
Absentee ownership? Yes

COSTS
Total cost: $80.5K-170.3K
Franchise fee: $29K-74K
Royalty fee: $250-1K/mo.
Term of agreement: 10 years renewable
at no charge
Franchisees required to buy multiple
units? No

FINANCING
In-house: Franchise fee
3rd-party: None

QUALIFICATIONS
Net worth: $500K
Cash liquidity: $100K

TRAINING
At headquarters: 1 week
At franchisee's location: 1 week

BUSINESS SUPPORT
Internet
Newsletter
Meetings
Toll-free phone line

MARKETING SUPPORT
Ad slicks

CARTRIDGE WORLD

Ranked #33 in Entrepreneur Magazine's 2007 Franchise 500

Financial rating: $$$$

6460 Hollis St.
Emeryville, CA 94608
(510)594-9900
www.cartridgeworldusa.com
Printer/fax cartridge replacements
& sales
Began: 1997, Franchising: 1997
Headquarters size: 50 employees
Franchise department: 30 employees

U.S. franchises: 457
Canadian franchises: 17
Other foreign franchises: 795
Company-owned: 0

Seeking: All U.S.
Seeking in Canada? Yes
Exclusive territories? Yes
Homebased option? No
Employees needed to run biz: 3
Absentee ownership? No

COSTS
Total cost: $107.1K-175.1K
Franchise fee: $30K
Royalty fee: 6%
Term of agreement: 10 years renewable
for a percentage of franchise fee
Franchisees required to buy multiple
units? Yes

FINANCING
In-house: None
3rd-party: Accounts receivable,
equipment, franchise fee,
inventory, payroll, startup costs

QUALIFICATIONS
Net worth: $250K
Cash liquidity: $35K
Experience:
General business experience
Marketing skills
Management skills

TRAINING
At headquarters: 2 weeks
At franchisee's location: 2 weeks

BUSINESS SUPPORT
Grand opening
Internet
Newsletter
Meetings
Toll-free phone line
Field operations/evaluations
Lease negotiations
Purchasing cooperatives
Security/safety procedures

MARKETING SUPPORT
Ad slicks
National media campaign
Regional marketing

RAPID REFILL INK

Current financial data not available

919 International Wy.
Springfield, OR 97477
(541)431-4665
www.rapidrefillink.com
Inkjet & toner cartridge replacements
Began: 2002, Franchising: 2004
Headquarters size: 13 employees
Franchise department: 13 employees

U.S. franchises: 50
Canadian franchises: 0
Other foreign franchises: 0
Company-owned: 0

Seeking: All U.S.
Seeking in Canada? Yes
Exclusive territories? Yes
Homebased option? No
Employees needed to run biz: 3-5
Absentee ownership? Yes

COSTS
Total cost: $75K-220K
Franchise fee: $30K/20K
Royalty fee: 6%
Term of agreement: 10 years renewable
    for $7.5K
Franchisees required to buy multiple
    units? No

FINANCING
No financing available

QUALIFICATIONS
Experience:
    Industry experience
    General business experience
    Marketing skills

TRAINING
At headquarters: 2 weeks
Business training: 3 days

BUSINESS SUPPORT
Grand opening
Internet
Newsletter
Meetings
Toll-free phone line
Field operations/evaluations
Lease negotiations
Security/safety procedures

MARKETING SUPPORT
Co-op advertising
Ad slicks
National media campaign

BUSINESS ▶ *Training*

A.D. BANKER & COMPANY - TRAINING CENTERS

Current financial data not available

5000 College Blvd., #110
Overland Park, KS 66211
(800)255-0408
www.adbtc.com
Exam prep & continuing-education
    training
Began: 1979, Franchising: 2005
Headquarters size: 35 employees
Franchise department: 1 employee

U.S. franchises: 8
Canadian franchises: 0
Other foreign franchises: 0
Company-owned: 80

Seeking: All U.S.
Seeking in Canada? No
Exclusive territories? Yes
Homebased option? Yes
Employees needed to run biz: 0-1
Absentee ownership? No

COSTS
Total cost: $29K-97K
Franchise fee: $8.9K-36.4K
Royalty fee: 12%
Term of agreement: 15 years renewable
    for $5K
Franchisees required to buy multiple
    units? No

FINANCING
In-house: None
3rd-party: Accounts receivable,
    equipment, franchise fee,
    inventory, payroll, startup costs

QUALIFICATIONS
Experience:
    General business experience
    Marketing skills
    Sales or teaching experience

TRAINING
At headquarters: 5 days

BUSINESS SUPPORT
Internet
Newsletter
Meetings
Toll-free phone line
Field operations/evaluations

MARKETING SUPPORT
Ad slicks
National media campaign

CRESTCOM INT'L. LTD.

Ranked #441 in Entrepreneur Magazine's 2007 Franchise 500   *Financial rating: $$$$*

6900 E. Belleview Ave., 3rd Fl.
Greenwood Village, CO 80111
(303)267-8200
www.crestcom.com
Management, sales & office-personnel
   training
Began: 1987, Franchising: 1991
Headquarters size: 15 employees
Franchise department: 12 employees

U.S. franchises: 59
Canadian franchises: 16
Other foreign franchises: 82
Company-owned: 0

Seeking: All U.S.
Seeking in Canada? Yes
Exclusive territories? Yes
Homebased option? Yes
Employees needed to run biz: 1-5
Absentee ownership? Yes

COSTS
Total cost: $77.99K-94.2K
Franchise fee: $61.5K
Royalty fee: 1.5%
Term of agreement: 7 years renewable
   for $500
Franchisees required to buy multiple
   units? No

FINANCING
In-house: Franchise fee
3rd-party: Franchise fee

QUALIFICATIONS
Cash liquidity: $40K
Experience:
   General business experience
   Marketing skills

TRAINING
At headquarters: 7-10 days
At franchisee's location: As needed

BUSINESS SUPPORT
Internet
Newsletter
Meetings
Security/safety procedures

MARKETING SUPPORT
Local support

DEI SALES TRAINING SYSTEMS

Current financial data not available

250 W. 57th St., #2217
New York, NY 10107
(212)581-7390
www.dei-sales.com
Sales training programs
Began: 1979, Franchising: 2003
Headquarters size: Info not
   provided

U.S. franchises: 31
Canadian franchises: 3
Other foreign franchises: 3
Company-owned: 0

Seeking: All U.S.
Seeking in Canada? Yes
Exclusive territories? Yes
Homebased option? Yes
Employees needed to run biz: 1
Absentee ownership? Yes

COSTS
Total cost: $99.4K-153.7K
Franchise fee: $50K
Royalty fee: 7%
Term of agreement: 5 years renewable
   at no charge
Franchisees required to buy multiple
   units? No

FINANCING
In-house: Franchise fee, inventory,
   startup costs
3rd-party: None

QUALIFICATIONS
Net worth: $100K
Cash liquidity: $75K
Experience:
   Industry experience
   General business experience

TRAINING
At headquarters: 2 weeks

BUSINESS SUPPORT
Grand opening
Internet
Newsletter
Meetings
Toll-free phone line
Field operations/evaluations
Purchasing cooperatives

MARKETING SUPPORT
Ad slicks
National media campaign

LEADERSHIP MANAGEMENT INC.

Ranked #364 in Entrepreneur Magazine's 2007 Franchise 500   *Financial rating: $$$$*

4567 Lake Shore Dr.
Waco, TX 76710
(800)568-1241
www.lmi-bus.com
Executive/management training &
    development
Began: 1965, Franchising: 1965
Headquarters size: 25 employees
Franchise department: 2 employees

U.S. franchises: 219
Canadian franchises: 0
Other foreign franchises: 0
Company-owned: 1

Seeking: All U.S.
Seeking in Canada? No
Exclusive territories? No
Homebased option? Yes
Employees needed to run biz: 2-10
Absentee ownership? No

COSTS
Total cost: $35K-42.5K
Franchise fee: $30K
Royalty fee: 6%
Term of agreement: 10 years renewable
    for $2.5K
Franchisees required to buy multiple
    units? No

FINANCING
No financing available

QUALIFICATIONS
Experience:
    General business experience
    Marketing skills
    Enjoy helping people

TRAINING
At headquarters: 2 days
At franchisee's location: 2 days
Teleconferences

BUSINESS SUPPORT
Internet
Newsletter
Meetings
Toll-free phone line
Field operations/evaluations

MARKETING SUPPORT
Info not provided

SANDLER SALES INSTITUTE

Ranked #262 in Entrepreneur Magazine's 2007 Franchise 500   *Financial rating: $$$$*

10411 Stevenson Rd.
Stevenson, MD 21153
(800)669-3537/(410)653-1993
www.sandler.com
Sales & sales-management training
Began: 1967, Franchising: 1983
Headquarters size: 28 employees
Franchise department: 2 employees

U.S. franchises: 167
Canadian franchises: 17
Other foreign franchises: 15
Company-owned: 0

Seeking: All U.S.
Seeking in Canada? Yes
Exclusive territories? No
Homebased option? Yes
Employees needed to run biz: 1-2
Absentee ownership? No

COSTS
Total cost: $69.5K-86.3K
Franchise fee: $63K
Royalty fee: $1.2K/mo.
Term of agreement: 5 years renewable
    for $500
Franchisees required to buy multiple
    units? No

FINANCING
No financing available

QUALIFICATIONS
Net worth: $100K
Cash liquidity: $69.5K-86.3K
Experience:
    Sales experience

TRAINING
At headquarters: 8 days

BUSINESS SUPPORT
Grand opening
Internet
Newsletter
Meetings
Toll-free phone line
Field operations/evaluations

MARKETING SUPPORT
Ad slicks
Phone coaching
Radio ads

TURBO LEADERSHIP SYSTEMS

Current financial data not available

36280 N.E. Wilsonville Rd.
Newberg, OR 97132
(503)625-1867
www.turboleadershipsystems.com
Leadership development & training
Began: 1985, Franchising: 1995
Headquarters size: 6 employees
Franchise department: 6 employees

U.S. franchises: 1
Canadian franchises: 0
Other foreign franchises: 0
Company-owned: 1

Seeking: All U.S.
Seeking in Canada? Yes
Exclusive territories? Yes
Homebased option? Yes
Employees needed to run biz: 2
Absentee ownership? No

COSTS
Total cost: $33.3K-56.8K
Franchise fee: $29K
Royalty fee: 10%
Term of agreement: 10 years renewable
    at no charge
Franchisees required to buy multiple
    units? No

FINANCING
No financing available

QUALIFICATIONS
Net worth: $150K
Cash liquidity: $40K
Experience:
    Industry experience
    General business experience
    Marketing skills
    Speaking skills

TRAINING
At headquarters: 30 days

BUSINESS SUPPORT
Grand opening
Internet
Newsletter
Meetings
Toll-free phone line
Field operations/evaluations

MARKETING SUPPORT
Co-op advertising
Ad slicks

BUSINESS ► *Miscellaneous*

BEVINCO BAR SYSTEMS LTD.

Current financial data not available

510-505 Consumers Rd.
Toronto, ON M2J 4V8 Canada
(888)238-4626/(416)490-6266
www.bevinco.com
Liquor inventory-control service
Began: 1987, Franchising: 1990
Headquarters size: 14 employees
Franchise department: 5 employees

U.S. franchises: 220
Canadian franchises: 31
Other foreign franchises: 44
Company-owned: 1

Seeking: All U.S.
Seeking in Canada? Yes
Exclusive territories? Yes
Homebased option? Yes
Employees needed to run biz: 2
Absentee ownership? No

COSTS
Total cost: $42K-45K
Franchise fee: $34.9K
Royalty fee: $12/audit
Term of agreement: 20 years renewable
    for $1K every 5 years
Franchisees required to buy multiple
    units? Outside the U.S. only

FINANCING
No financing available

QUALIFICATIONS
Net worth: $50K
Cash liquidity: $30K
Experience:
    Industry experience
    General business experience
    Marketing skills
    Sales experience

TRAINING
At headquarters: 1 week
At franchisee's location: 2 weeks

BUSINESS SUPPORT
Grand opening
Internet
Newsletter
Meetings
Toll-free phone line
Field operations/evaluations

MARKETING SUPPORT
Co-op advertising
Ad slicks
National media campaign
Regional marketing

EXECUTIVE BUSINESS MAINTENANCE FRANCHISE

Financial rating: $$$

5931 Stanley Ave., #S-6
Carmichael, CA 95608
(877)326-8787
www.ebm-franchise.com
Janitorial-contract brokerage services
Began: 1996, Franchising: 2006
Headquarters size: 4 employees
Franchise department: 2 employees

U.S. franchises: 0
Canadian franchises: 0
Other foreign franchises: 0
Company-owned: 0

Seeking: West
Seeking in Canada? No
Exclusive territories? Yes
Homebased option? No
Employees needed to run biz: 2
Absentee ownership? No

COSTS
Total cost: $59K-89K
Franchise fee: $35K
Royalty fee: 8%
Term of agreement: 7 years renewable
    for $1.5K
Franchisees required to buy multiple
    units? No

FINANCING
No financing available

QUALIFICATIONS
Net worth: $150K
Cash liquidity: $80K
Experience:
    General business experience
    Marketing skills
    Sales skills

TRAINING
At headquarters: 5 days
At franchisee's location: 5 days

BUSINESS SUPPORT
Grand opening
Internet
Meetings
Toll-free phone line
Field operations/evaluations
Security/safety procedures

MARKETING SUPPORT
Co-op advertising
Ad slicks

HYDRO PHYSICS PIPE INSPECTION CORP.

Financial rating: $$$

1855 W. Union Ave., #N
Englewood, CO 80110
(800)781-3164/(303)783-8855
www.hydro-physics.com
Pipe inspection & locating services
Began: 1991, Franchising: 1996
Headquarters size: 6 employees
Franchise department: 5 employees

U.S. franchises: 9
Canadian franchises: 0
Other foreign franchises: 0
Company-owned: 0

Seeking: All U.S.
Seeking in Canada? No
Exclusive territories? Yes
Homebased option? Yes
Employees needed to run biz: 0
Absentee ownership? No

COSTS
Total cost: $70K-95K
Franchise fee: $25K
Royalty fee: 7.5%
Term of agreement: 10 years renewable
    at no charge
Franchisees required to buy multiple
    units? No

FINANCING
In-house: None
3rd-party: Equipment, franchise fee,
    inventory

QUALIFICATIONS
Net worth: $100K-150K
Cash liquidity: $50K
Experience:
    General business experience
    Marketing skills
    Mechanical aptitude

TRAINING
At headquarters: 2 weeks
At franchisee's location: 2-3 days+

BUSINESS SUPPORT
Grand opening
Internet
Newsletter
Meetings
Toll-free phone line
Field operations/evaluations
Purchasing cooperatives
Security/safety procedures

MARKETING SUPPORT
Co-op advertising
Ad slicks

PROFORMA
Ranked #134 in Entrepreneur Magazine's 2007 Franchise 500   *Financial rating: $$$$*

8800 E. Pleasant Valley Rd.
Cleveland, OH 44131
(800)825-1525/(216)520-8400
www.connectwithproforma.com
Printing & promotional products
Began: 1978, Franchising: 1985
Headquarters size: 100 employees
Franchise department: 10 employees

U.S. franchises: 567
Canadian franchises: 43
Other foreign franchises: 0
Company-owned: 0

Seeking: All U.S.
Seeking in Canada? Yes
Exclusive territories? No
Homebased option? Yes
Employees needed to run biz: 1
Absentee ownership? No

COSTS
Total cost: $7.2K-70.2K
Franchise fee: to $39.5K
Royalty fee: 6-8%
Term of agreement: 20 years renewable
    for $1K
Franchisees required to buy multiple
    units? No

FINANCING
In-house: Accounts receivable,
    equipment, franchise fee,
    inventory, startupcosts
3rd-party: Payroll

QUALIFICATIONS
Experience:
    General business experience
    Marketing skills
    Sales background

TRAINING
At headquarters: 1 week
At franchisee's location: Quarterly
At regional/annual convention:
    2-4 days

BUSINESS SUPPORT
Internet
Newsletter
Meetings
Toll-free phone line
Field operations/evaluations
Purchasing cooperatives

MARKETING SUPPORT
National media campaign
Regional marketing
Collateral
Product promotions
Direct-mail campaigns

BUSINESS ▸ *Other Franchises*

ADVENTURES IN ADVERTISING FRANCHISE INC.
Ranked #324 in Entrepreneur Magazine's 2007 Franchise 500
800 Winneconne Ave.
Neenah, WI 54956
(800)460-7836
www.exploreaia.com
Promotional products & advertising
    specialties
Financial rating: $$$

AROUND TOWN COMMUNITY MAGAZINE INC.
1025 Rose Creek Dr., #340
Woodstock, GA 30189
(770)516-7105
www.aroundtowncm.com
Direct-mail community magazine
Current financial data not available

CABOODLE CARTRIDGE
3233-F De La Cruz Blvd.
Santa Clara, CA 95054
(408)988-0064
www.caboodle.net
Inkjet & laser toner cartridge
    replacements/services
Current financial data not available

CYBERTARY
1217 Pleasant Grove Blvd.
Roseville, CA 95678
(888)292-8279
www.cybertaryfranchise.com
Virtual assistant services
Current financial data not available

EMQUEST BUSINESS BROKERS
111 N. Orange Ave., 20th Fl.
Orlando, FL 32801
(407)454-6699
www.emquestbb.com
Business & financial brokerage,
    franchise development & sales
Financial rating: $$$

FRANCHISEINC!
2148 Pelham Pkwy., Bldg. 300
Pelham, AL 35124
(800)961-0420
www.franchiseinc.com
Franchise consulting services
Current financial data not available

INNER CIRCLE INT'L. LTD.
3208 Lake St., #3
Minneapolis, MN 55416
(952)933-6629
www.theinnercircle.com
Peer advisory groups for business
    owners
Financial rating: 0

THE INTELLIGENT OFFICE

4450 Arapahoe Ave., #100
Boulder, CO 80303
(303)447-9000
www.intelligentoffice.com
Office suites & business services
Current financial data not available

ISLAND INK-JET SYSTEMS INC.

*Ranked #158 in Entrepreneur
Magazine's 2007 Franchise 500*
244 4th St.
Courtenay, BC V9N 1G6 Canada
(877)446-5538
www.islandinkjet.com
Inkjet cartridge refilling,
  replacements & sales
Financial rating: $$$

MRI NETWORK

*Ranked #57 in Entrepreneur
Magazine's 2007 Franchise 500*
1717 Arch St., 35th Fl.
Philadelphia, PA 19103
(215)569-2200
www.mrinetwork.com
Personnel placement, search &
  recruiting services
Financial rating: $$$$

PANACHE MAGAZINE

222 S. Church St., #204
Charlotte, NC 28202
(704)370-6999
www.panache.com
Luxury lifestyle magazine
Current financial data not available

PRIDESTAFF

7535 N. Palm Ave., #101
Fresno, CA 93711
(800)774-3316
www.pridestaff.com
Staffing services
Current financial data not available

RSVP PUBLICATIONS

*Ranked #345 in Entrepreneur
Magazine's 2007 Franchise 500*
6730 W. Linebaugh Ave., #201
Tampa, FL 33625
(800)360-7787/(813)960-7787
www.rsvppublications.com
Direct-mail advertising
Financial rating: $$$

SAVE IT NOW!

*Ranked #410 in Entrepreneur
Magazine's 2007 Franchise 500*
9100 Keystone Crossing, #750
Indianapolis, IN 46240
(317)208-4836
www.saveitnow.com
Group buying program for
  businesses
Financial rating: $$$

SPHERION CORP.

*Ranked #159 in Entrepreneur
Magazine's 2007 Franchise 500*
925 N. Point Pkwy.
Alpharetta, GA 30005
(678)867-3702
www.spherion.com
Staffing services
Financial rating: $$$$

VITAL DENT

17 Battery Pl., #205
New York, NY 10004
(212)967-2400
www.vitaldent.com
Dental-office management services
Current financial data not available

VITAL EXPRESS

433 N. Camden Dr., #600
Beverly Hills, CA 90210
(888)848-2591
www.vitalexpress.com
Transportation & logistics services
Current financial data not available

Children's Businesses

CHILDREN'S ▶ *Art Programs*

ABRAKADOODLE
Ranked #371 in Entrepreneur Magazine's 2007 Franchise 500   *Financial rating: $$$$*

1800 Robert Fulton Dr., #205
Reston, VA 20191
(703)860-6570
www.abrakadoodle.com
Art education classes for children
Began: 2002, Franchising: 2004
Headquarters size: 16 employees
Franchise department: 6 employees

U.S. franchises: 66
Canadian franchises: 0
Other foreign franchises: 0
Company-owned: 2

Seeking: All U.S.
Seeking in Canada? Yes
Exclusive territories? Yes
Homebased option? Yes
Employees needed to run biz: 5-10
Absentee ownership? No

COSTS
Total cost: $43.9K-77.97K
Franchise fee: $32.5K
Royalty fee: 8-6%
Term of agreement: 10 years renewable
    for 5% of current franchise fee
Franchisees required to buy multiple
    units? Outside the U.S. only

FINANCING
No financing available

QUALIFICATIONS
Net worth: $100K
Cash liquidity: $40K
Experience:
    General business experience
    Marketing skills
    Desire to teach children

TRAINING
At headquarters: 5 days
At franchisee's location: 20-60 hours
    pre-training

BUSINESS SUPPORT
Internet
Newsletter
Meetings
Field operations/evaluations
Purchasing cooperatives

MARKETING SUPPORT
Ad slicks
National media campaign
Intranet
Franchise Advisory Council

KIDS 'N' CLAY POTTERY STUDIO

Financial rating: $$$

1824 5th St.
Berkeley, CA 94710-1915
(866)543-2529
www.kidsnclay.com
Children's art studio
Began: 1988, Franchising: 2005
Headquarters size: 15 employees
Franchise department: 4 employees

U.S. franchises: 1
Canadian franchises: 0
Other foreign franchises: 0
Company-owned: 1

Seeking: All U.S.
Seeking in Canada? Yes
Exclusive territories? Yes
Homebased option? Yes
Employees needed to run biz: 3-15
Absentee ownership? Yes

COSTS
Total cost: $70.1K-117K
Franchise fee: $30K
Royalty fee: 7%
Term of agreement: 10 years renewable
at no charge
Franchisees required to buy multiple
units? Outside the U.S. only

FINANCING
No financing available

QUALIFICATIONS
Net worth: $100K
Cash liquidity: $40K
Experience:
General business experience
Marketing skills

TRAINING
At headquarters: 2 weeks
At franchisee's location: 1 week

BUSINESS SUPPORT
Grand opening
Internet
Newsletter
Meetings
Toll-free phone line
Field operations/evaluations
Lease negotiations
Purchasing cooperatives
Security/safety procedures

MARKETING SUPPORT
Ad slicks
Regional marketing

KIDZART

Ranked #461 in Entrepreneur Magazine's 2007 Franchise 500

Financial rating: 0

1902 E. Common St., #400
New Braunfels, TX 78130
(800)379-8302
www.kidzart.com
Drawing-based fine arts educational
programs
Began: 1997, Franchising: 2002
Headquarters size: 6 employees
Franchise department: 6 employees

U.S. franchises: 60
Canadian franchises: 0
Other foreign franchises: 0
Company-owned: 0

Seeking: All U.S.
Seeking in Canada? No
Exclusive territories? Yes
Homebased option? Yes
Employees needed to run biz: 2-4
Absentee ownership? No

COSTS
Total cost: $50K-75K
Franchise fee: $31.9K
Royalty fee: 8%
Term of agreement: 10 years renewable
at no charge
Franchisees required to buy multiple
units? No

FINANCING
In-house: None
3rd-party: Accounts receivable,
equipment, franchise fee,
inventory, payroll, startup costs

QUALIFICATIONS
Net worth: $150K-200K
Cash liquidity: $32.7K
Experience:
General business experience
Marketing skills
Sales skills
Management skills
HR skills

TRAINING
At headquarters: 5 days
Ongoing monthly training via
curriculum & conference calls

BUSINESS SUPPORT
Grand opening
Internet
Newsletter
Meetings
Toll-free phone line

MARKETING SUPPORT
Ad slicks
Regional marketing
PR

MONART SCHOOL OF THE ARTS

Financial rating: $$$

10736 Jefferson Blvd., #509
Culver City, CA 90230
(877)666-2781/(310)337-0107
www.monart.com
Art education
Began: 1979, Franchising: 2004
Headquarters size: 3 employees
Franchise department: 2 employees

U.S. franchises: 27
Canadian franchises: 0
Other foreign franchises: 0
Company-owned: 0

Seeking: Northeast, Northwest,
    South, Southeast, Southwest
Seeking in Canada? Yes
Exclusive territories? Yes
Homebased option? No
Employees needed to run biz: 1-2
Absentee ownership? Info not provided

COSTS
Total cost: $37.1K-49.7K
Franchise fee: $28K
Royalty fee: 8%
Term of agreement: 7 years renewable
    for $3K
Franchisees required to buy multiple
    units? No

FINANCING
No financing available

QUALIFICATIONS
Cash liquidity: $35K-45K
Experience:
    General business experience

TRAINING
At headquarters: 2 weeks
Ongoing follow-up training

BUSINESS SUPPORT
Grand opening
Internet
Newsletter
Meetings
Toll-free phone line
Field operations/evaluations

MARKETING SUPPORT
Monart Advisory Council
Annual franchise conference
Marketing materials

ODYSSEY ART CENTERS

Current financial data not available

Box 512
Tarrytown, NY 10591
(914)631-7148
www.odysseyart.com
Art classes
Began: 1974, Franchising: 1995
Headquarters size: Info not provided
Franchise department: 2 employees

U.S. franchises: 2
Canadian franchises: 0
Other foreign franchises: 0
Company-owned: 1

Seeking: All U.S.
Seeking in Canada? No
Exclusive territories? Yes
Homebased option? Yes
Employees needed to run biz: 1
Absentee ownership? No

COSTS
Total cost: $28.7K-56.2K
Franchise fee: $24K
Royalty fee: 6%
Term of agreement: 10 years renewable
    at no charge
Franchisees required to buy multiple
    units? No

FINANCING
No financing available

QUALIFICATIONS
Info not provided

TRAINING
At headquarters: 2 weeks
At franchisee's location: Periodic
    visits

BUSINESS SUPPORT
Grand opening
Internet
Newsletter
Meetings
Purchasing cooperatives

MARKETING SUPPORT
Info not provided

YOUNG REMBRANDTS FRANCHISE INC.

Ranked #479 in Entrepreneur Magazine's 2007 Franchise 500   *Financial rating: $*

23 N. Union St.
Elgin, IL 60123
(847)742-6966
www.youngrembrandts.com
Art classes for children ages 3 to 12
Began: 1988, Franchising: 1997
Headquarters size: 17 employees
Franchise department: 8 employees

U.S. franchises: 57
Canadian franchises: 0
Other foreign franchises: 0
Company-owned: 4

Seeking: All U.S.
Seeking in Canada? No
Exclusive territories? Yes
Homebased option? Yes
Employees needed to run biz: 2-20
Absentee ownership? No

COSTS
Total cost: $39.5K-48.8K
Franchise fee: $31.5K
Royalty fee: 10%/8%
Term of agreement: 15 years renewable
   at no charge
Franchisees required to buy multiple
   units? No

FINANCING
No financing available

QUALIFICATIONS
Cash liquidity: $75K
Experience:
   Industry experience
   General business experience
   Marketing skills
   Teaching skills
   Art skills
   Experience working with children

TRAINING
At headquarters: 5 days

BUSINESS SUPPORT
Internet
Meetings
Toll-free phone line
Field operations/evaluations

MARKETING SUPPORT
Co-op advertising
Ad slicks
Full marketing package

CHILDREN'S   *Child Care*

ABSOLUTE BEST CARE

Current financial data not available

220 Bridge Plaza Dr.
Manalapan, NJ 07726
(212)481-5705
www.absolutebestcare.com
Placement agency for nannies, baby
   nurses, housekeepers & sitters
Began: 2002, Franchising: 2006
Headquarters size: 8 employees
Franchise department: 2 employees

U.S. franchises: 3
Canadian franchises: 0
Other foreign franchises: 0
Company-owned: 2

Seeking: All U.S.
Seeking in Canada? No
Exclusive territories? Yes
Homebased option? No
Employees needed to run biz: 0-2
Absentee ownership? Info not provided

COSTS
Total cost: $42.99K-56.4K
Franchise fee: $29.9K
Royalty fee: 7.5-6%
Term of agreement: 5 years
Franchisees required to buy multiple
   units? No

FINANCING
No financing available

QUALIFICATIONS
Net worth: $200K
Cash liquidity: $75K
Experience:
   General business experience

TRAINING
At headquarters: 1 week
At franchisee's location: 1 site visit

BUSINESS SUPPORT
Grand opening
Internet
Toll-free phone line
Field operations/evaluations
Lease negotiations

MARKETING SUPPORT
Co-op advertising
Ad slicks
Regional marketing

CHILDRENS LIGHTHOUSE FRANCHISING CO.

Financial rating: $

101 S. Jennings, #209
Fort Worth, TX 76104
(888)338-4422/(817)338-1332
www.childrenslighthouse.com
Child-care services
Began: 1996, Franchising: 1999
Headquarters size: 10 employees
Franchise department: 10 employees

U.S. franchises: 6
Canadian franchises: 0
Other foreign franchises: 0
Company-owned: 9

Seeking: All U.S.
Seeking in Canada? Yes
Exclusive territories? Yes
Homebased option? No
Employees needed to run biz: 25
Absentee ownership? Yes

COSTS
Total cost: $1.8M-2.4M
Franchise fee: $50K
Royalty fee: 7%
Term of agreement: 20 years renewable
    at no charge
Franchisees required to buy multiple
    units? Yes

FINANCING
In-house: None
3rd-party: Accounts receivable,
    equipment, franchise fee,
    inventory, payroll, startup costs

QUALIFICATIONS
Net worth: $500K
Cash liquidity: $255K
Experience:
    Industry experience
    General business experience
    Marketing skills

TRAINING
At headquarters: 4 weeks
At franchisee's location: 4 weeks
Unlimited training for the first year

BUSINESS SUPPORT
Grand opening
Internet
Newsletter
Meetings
Toll-free phone line
Field operations/evaluations
Purchasing cooperatives
Security/safety procedures

MARKETING SUPPORT
Co-op advertising
Ad slicks
Regional marketing

GODDARD SYSTEMS INC.

Ranked #118 in Entrepreneur Magazine's 2007 Franchise 500   *Financial rating: $$$$*

1016 W. Ninth Ave.
King of Prussia, PA 19406
(800)272-4901
www.goddardschool.com
Preschool/child-care center
Began: 1986, Franchising: 1988
Headquarters size: 80 employees
Franchise department: 6 employees

U.S. franchises: 221
Canadian franchises: 0
Other foreign franchises: 0
Company-owned: 0

Seeking: All U.S.
Seeking in Canada? Yes
Exclusive territories? No
Homebased option? No
Employees needed to run biz: 25
Absentee ownership? No

COSTS
Total cost: $488.5K
Franchise fee: $75K
Royalty fee: 7%
Term of agreement: 15 years renewable
    at no charge
Franchisees required to buy multiple
    units? No

FINANCING
In-house: None
3rd-party: Equipment, franchise fee,
    startup costs

QUALIFICATIONS
Net worth: $450K
Cash liquidity: $100K
Experience:
    General business experience

TRAINING
At headquarters: 3 weeks
At franchisee's location: Ongoing
IACET training for teachers &
    directors

BUSINESS SUPPORT
Grand opening
Internet
Newsletter
Meetings
Toll-free phone line
Field operations/evaluations
Lease negotiations
Security/safety procedures

MARKETING SUPPORT
Co-op advertising
Ad slicks
National media campaign
Regional marketing
Full-service in-house ad agency

THE LEARNING EXPERIENCE

Current financial data not available

10 Sylvan Wy., #110
Parsippany, NJ 07054
(973)539-5392
www.thelearningexperience.com
Child-care services
Began: 1979, Franchising: 2003
Headquarters size: 150 employees
Franchise department: 3 employees

U.S. franchises: 14
Canadian franchises: 0
Other foreign franchises: 0
Company-owned: 7

Seeking: Midwest, Northeast
Seeking in Canada? Yes
Exclusive territories? Info not provided
Homebased option? No
Employees needed to run biz: 10-20
Absentee ownership? No

COSTS
Total cost: $275K-500K
Franchise fee: $50K
Royalty fee: 3-6%
Term of agreement: 15 years renewable
    at no charge
Franchisees required to buy multiple
    units? No

FINANCING
In-house: None
3rd-party: Equipment, franchise fee,
    inventory, payroll, startup costs

QUALIFICATIONS
Net worth: $500K
Cash liquidity: $125K

TRAINING
At headquarters: 2 weeks
At franchisee's location: 2 weeks

BUSINESS SUPPORT
Grand opening
Internet
Newsletter
Meetings
Field operations/evaluations
Lease negotiations
Security/safety procedures

MARKETING SUPPORT
Ad slicks
National media campaign
Regional marketing

LITTLE CITY KIDS

Financial rating: 0

10127 Northwestern Ave.
Franksville, WI 53597
(262)884-4226
www.littlecitykids.com
Child-care center
Began: 1998, Franchising: 2006
Headquarters size: 20 employees
Franchise department: 1 employee

U.S. franchises: 0
Canadian franchises: 0
Other foreign franchises: 0
Company-owned: 1

Seeking: Midwest
Seeking in Canada? No
Exclusive territories? Yes
Homebased option? No
Employees needed to run biz: 12-18
Absentee ownership? No

COSTS
Total cost: $118K-189K
Franchise fee: $35K
Royalty fee: 7%
Term of agreement: 5 years renewable
    at no charge
Franchisees required to buy multiple
    units? No

FINANCING
No financing available

QUALIFICATIONS
Net worth: $100K
Cash liquidity: $100K
Experience:
    General business experience

TRAINING
At headquarters: 30-60 days
At franchisee's location: 10 days

BUSINESS SUPPORT
Grand opening
Newsletter
Meetings
Field operations/evaluations

MARKETING SUPPORT
Co-op advertising

PRIMROSE SCHOOL FRANCHISING CO.

Current financial data not available

3660 S. Cedarcrest Rd.
Acworth, GA 30101
(800)774-6767/(770)529-4100
www.primroseschools.com
Educational child-care facility
Began: 1982, Franchising: 1988
Headquarters size: 33 employees
Franchise department: 3 employees

U.S. franchises: 156
Canadian franchises: 0
Other foreign franchises: 0
Company-owned: 1

Seeking: All U.S.
Seeking in Canada? No
Exclusive territories? Yes
Homebased option? No
Employees needed to run biz: 30
Absentee ownership? No

COSTS
Total cost: $2.6M-3.2M
Franchise fee: $60K
Royalty fee: 7%
Term of agreement: 11 years renewable
    at no charge
Franchisees required to buy multiple
    units? No

FINANCING
In-house: None
3rd-party: Equipment, franchise fee,
    inventory, startup costs

QUALIFICATIONS
Net worth: $500K
Cash liquidity: $280K-350K
Experience:
    General business experience
    Marketing skills
    People skills

TRAINING
At headquarters: 1 week
At franchisee's location: 1 week
At existing location: 1 week

BUSINESS SUPPORT
Grand opening
Internet
Newsletter
Meetings
Toll-free phone line
Field operations/evaluations
Purchasing cooperatives
Security/safety procedures

MARKETING SUPPORT
Co-op advertising
Ad slicks
National media campaign
Regional marketing
Radio

SUNBROOK ACADEMY

Current financial data not available

2933 Cherokee St.
Kennesaw, GA 30144
(770)426-0619
www.sunbrookacademy.com
Child-care center
Began: 1984, Franchising: 1999
Headquarters size: 8 employees
Franchise department: 8 employees

U.S. franchises: 5
Canadian franchises: 0
Other foreign franchises: 0
Company-owned: 4

Seeking: South, Southeast
Seeking in Canada? No
Exclusive territories? Yes
Homebased option? No
Employees needed to run biz: 30
Absentee ownership? No

COSTS
Total cost: $271.2K-2.1M
Franchise fee: $40K
Royalty fee: 6%
Term of agreement: 15 years renewable
    for $1K
Franchisees required to buy multiple
    units? No

FINANCING
In-house: None
3rd-party: Accounts receivable,
    equipment, franchise fee,
    inventory, payroll, startup costs

QUALIFICATIONS
Net worth: $300K
Cash liquidity: $200K-350K

TRAINING
At headquarters: 21 days
At franchisee's location: 30 days

BUSINESS SUPPORT
Grand opening
Internet
Newsletter
Meetings
Field operations/evaluations
Purchasing cooperatives
Security/safety procedures

MARKETING SUPPORT
Ad slicks

BATTER UP KIDS CULINARY CENTER

Financial rating: 0

4403 Canyonside Trail
Austin, TX 78731
(866)345-8682/(512)342-8682
www.batterupkids.com
Children's culinary program
Began: 1991, Franchising: 2006
Headquarters size: 8 employees
Franchise department: 3 employees

U.S. franchises: 0
Canadian franchises: 0
Other foreign franchises: 0
Company-owned: 1

Seeking: All U.S.
Seeking in Canada? No
Exclusive territories? No
Homebased option? No
Employees needed to run biz: 4-6
Absentee ownership? Yes

COSTS
Total cost: $178.1K-256K
Franchise fee: $25K
Royalty fee: 4%
Term of agreement: 10 years renewable
   at no charge
Franchisees required to buy multiple
   units? No

FINANCING
No financing available

QUALIFICATIONS
Net worth: $70K
Experience:
   General business experience
   Marketing skills
   Must love children
   Energetic personality

TRAINING
At headquarters: 4-5 days
At franchisee's location: 4-5 days

BUSINESS SUPPORT
Grand opening
Internet
Newsletter
Meetings
Toll-free phone line
Field operations/evaluations
Lease negotiations
Purchasing cooperatives
Security/safety procedures

MARKETING SUPPORT
Co-op advertising
Ad slicks
National media campaign

YOUNG CHEFS ACADEMY

Financial rating: $$

1404 S. New Rd.
Waco, TX 76708
(254)757-1554
www.youngchefsacademy.com
Children's cooking school
Began: 2004, Franchising: 2005
Headquarters size: 18 employees
Franchise department: 9 employees

U.S. franchises: 23
Canadian franchises: 0
Other foreign franchises: 0
Company-owned: 0

Seeking: All U.S.
Seeking in Canada? Yes
Exclusive territories? Yes
Homebased option? No
Employees needed to run biz: Info
   not provided
Absentee ownership? Info not provided

COSTS
Total cost: $57.3K-116.5K
Franchise fee: $29.5K
Royalty fee: $395/mo.
Term of agreement: 10 years renewable
   at no charge
Franchisees required to buy multiple
   units? No

FINANCING
In-house: None
3rd-party: Franchise fee, startup
   costs

QUALIFICATIONS
Experience:
   Industry experience
   General business experience
   Marketing skills

TRAINING
At headquarters: 3 days

BUSINESS SUPPORT
Grand opening
Internet
Newsletter
Toll-free phone line
Field operations/evaluations

MARKETING SUPPORT
Ad slicks
Regional marketing

CHILDREN'S **Drama Programs**

ACTOR'S GARAGE

Financial rating: $

152 Ryder Rd.
Manhasset, NY 11030
(866)627-7211
www.theactorsgarage.com
Children's acting schools
Began: 2004, Franchising: 2006
Headquarters size: 3 employees
Franchise department: 3 employees

U.S. franchises: 2
Canadian franchises: 0
Other foreign franchises: 0
Company-owned: 12

Seeking: All U.S.
Seeking in Canada? Yes
Exclusive territories? Yes
Homebased option? Yes
Employees needed to run biz: 2
Absentee ownership? Yes

COSTS
Total cost: $30K-33K
Franchise fee: $24K
Royalty fee: 9%
Term of agreement: 10 years renewable
    for up to $10K
Franchisees required to buy multiple
    units? No

FINANCING
No financing available

QUALIFICATIONS
Cash liquidity: $25K

TRAINING
At headquarters: 5 days

BUSINESS SUPPORT
Internet
Toll-free phone line
Field operations/evaluations

MARKETING SUPPORT
Regional marketing

DRAMA KIDS INT'L. INC.

Ranked #332 in Entrepreneur Magazine's 2007 Franchise 500

Financial rating: $$$$

3225-B Corporate Ct.
Ellicott City, MD 21042
(410)480-2015
www.dramakids.com
Children's after-school drama
    program
Began: 1979, Franchising: 1989
Headquarters size: 8 employees
Franchise department: 3 employees

U.S. franchises: 33
Canadian franchises: 0
Other foreign franchises: 122
Company-owned: 1

Seeking: All U.S.
Seeking in Canada? Yes
Exclusive territories? Yes
Homebased option? Yes
Employees needed to run biz: 4
Absentee ownership? No

COSTS
Total cost: $36.6K-39.4K
Franchise fee: $28.5K
Royalty fee: 10%
Term of agreement: 7 years renewable
    for $750
Franchisees required to buy multiple
    units? No

FINANCING
In-house: None
3rd-party: Accounts receivable,
    equipment, franchise fee,
    inventory, payroll, startup costs

QUALIFICATIONS
Net worth: $50K
Cash liquidity: $25K
Experience:
    General business experience
    Teaching or child-development
    experience

TRAINING
At headquarters: 5 days
At franchisee's location: 5 days
Regional training: 1 day
Annual conference

BUSINESS SUPPORT
Grand opening
Internet
Newsletter
Meetings
Toll-free phone line
Field operations/evaluations
Security/safety procedures

MARKETING SUPPORT
Co-op advertising
Ad slicks
National media campaign
Regional marketing

KIDSTAGE

Current financial data not available

P.O. Box 1072
Appleton, WI 54912
(877)415-5115
www.kidstage.net
Children's after-school drama
    program
Began: 1997, Franchising: 2003
Headquarters size: 2 employees

U.S. franchises: 12
Canadian franchises: 1
Other foreign franchises: 0
Company-owned: 1

Seeking: All U.S.
Seeking in Canada? Yes
Exclusive territories? Yes
Homebased option? Yes
Employees needed to run biz: 0-5
Absentee ownership? Yes

COSTS
Total cost: $13K-18.5K
Franchise fee: $12.5K
Royalty fee: 6%
Term of agreement: 5 years renewable
    at no charge
Franchisees required to buy multiple
    units? No

FINANCING
No financing available

QUALIFICATIONS
Cash liquidity: $13K
Experience:
    General business experience
    Desire to work with children

TRAINING
At headquarters: 4 days
At franchisee's location: 3 days

BUSINESS SUPPORT
Internet
Newsletter
Meetings
Toll-free phone line

MARKETING SUPPORT
Ad slicks
Regional marketing

CHILDREN'S *Fitness*

BABY POWER/FOREVER KIDS

Financial rating: 0

P.O. Box 526
Annandale, NJ 08801
(800)365-4847
www.babypower.com
Parent/child play program
Began: 1973, Franchising: 1998
Headquarters size: 3 employees
Franchise department: 3 employees

U.S. franchises: 7
Canadian franchises: 0
Other foreign franchises: 0
Company-owned: 0

Seeking: All U.S.
Seeking in Canada? No
Exclusive territories? Yes
Homebased option? No
Employees needed to run biz: 3
Absentee ownership? Yes

COSTS
Total cost: $85K-100K
Franchise fee: $30K
Royalty fee: 5%
Term of agreement: 10 years renewable
    for $5K
Franchisees required to buy multiple
    units? No

FINANCING
No financing available

QUALIFICATIONS
Net worth: $100K
Cash liquidity: $65K
Experience:
    General business experience

TRAINING
At headquarters: 5 days
At franchisee's location: 4 days

BUSINESS SUPPORT
Grand opening
Internet
Meetings
Toll-free phone line
Field operations/evaluations
Security/safety procedures

MARKETING SUPPORT
Co-op advertising
Regional marketing

FUN BUS

Ranked #475 in Entrepreneur Magazine's 2007 Franchise 500   *Financial rating: $$$*

32 Timothy Ln.
Tinton Falls, NJ 07724
(732)578-1287
www.funbuses.com
Mobile children's fitness program
Began: 2000, Franchising: 2003
Headquarters size: 2 employees
Franchise department: 2 employees

U.S. franchises: 16
Canadian franchises: 0
Other foreign franchises: 0
Company-owned: 0

Seeking: All U.S.
Seeking in Canada? No
Exclusive territories? Yes
Homebased option? Yes
Employees needed to run biz: 2
Absentee ownership? Yes

COSTS
Total cost: $67K-87K
Franchise fee: $30K
Royalty fee: 7%
Term of agreement: 7 years renewable
    for 25% of current franchise fee
Franchisees required to buy multiple
    units? No

FINANCING
In-house: None
3rd-party: Equipment, franchise fee,
    inventory, startup costs

QUALIFICATIONS
Net worth: $65K
Cash liquidity: $65K
Experience:
    General business experience

TRAINING
At headquarters: 1 day
At franchisee's location: 3 days
Bus driving school: 1 day

BUSINESS SUPPORT
Grand opening
Internet
Meetings
Toll-free phone line
Field operations/evaluations
Purchasing cooperatives
Security/safety procedures

MARKETING SUPPORT
Co-op advertising
Ad slicks
Ongoing marketing support

GYMBOREE

Ranked #175 in Entrepreneur Magazine's 2007 Franchise 500   *Financial rating: $$$$*

500 Howard
San Francisco, CA 94105
(800)520-7529/(415)278-7000
www.gymboree.com
Parent/child play program
Began: 1976, Franchising: 1978
Headquarters size: 320 employees
Franchise department: 20 employees

U.S. franchises: 284
Canadian franchises: 17
Other foreign franchises: 222
Company-owned: 3

Seeking: All U.S.
Seeking in Canada? Yes
Exclusive territories? Yes
Homebased option? No
Employees needed to run biz: 3-4
Absentee ownership? No

COSTS
Total cost: $142.6K-286.8K
Franchise fee: $45K
Royalty fee: 6%
Term of agreement: 10 years renewable
    for 10% of initial franchise fee
Franchisees required to buy multiple
    units? Outside the U.S. only

FINANCING
In-house: None
3rd-party: Equipment, inventory,
    startup costs

QUALIFICATIONS
Net worth: $250K
Cash liquidity: $70K
Experience:
    General business experience

TRAINING
At headquarters: 8 days
At regional location: 2 days biannually

BUSINESS SUPPORT
Grand opening
Internet
Newsletter
Meetings
Toll-free phone line
Field operations/evaluations
Purchasing cooperatives

MARKETING SUPPORT
Co-op advertising
Ad slicks
National media campaign
Regional marketing

JUMP 'N PLAY GYM

Financial rating: 0

1366 N. Leroy St.
Fenton, MI 48430
(810)714-4202
www.jumpnplaygym.com
Parent-child active learning
    program
Began: 2003, Franchising: 2005
Headquarters size: 3 employees
Franchise department: 2 employees

U.S. franchises: 0
Canadian franchises: 0
Other foreign franchises: 0
Company-owned: 1

Seeking: All U.S.
Seeking in Canada? No
Exclusive territories? Yes
Homebased option? No
Employees needed to run biz: 3-5
Absentee ownership? No

COSTS
Total cost: $90.5K-130.3K
Franchise fee: $26K
Royalty fee: 2-6%
Term of agreement: 10 years renewable
    for 15% of then-current fee
Franchisees required to buy multiple
    units? Yes

FINANCING
No financing available

QUALIFICATIONS
Net worth: $200K
Cash liquidity: $50K
Experience:
    General business experience

TRAINING
At headquarters: 3-4 days
At home: 4-6 hours+

BUSINESS SUPPORT
Grand opening
Internet
Newsletter
Meetings
Field operations/evaluations
Security/safety procedures

MARKETING SUPPORT
Ad slicks
Regional marketing
Commercials

JUMPBUNCH INC.

Ranked #403 in Entrepreneur Magazine's 2007 Franchise 500　　　*Financial rating: $$$*

1160 Spa Rd., #3B
Annapolis, MD 21403
(410)703-2300
www.jumpbunch.com
Preschool sports & fitness program
Began: 2002, Franchising: 2002
Headquarters size: 3 employees
Franchise department: 3 employees

U.S. franchises: 24
Canadian franchises: 0
Other foreign franchises: 0
Company-owned: 0

Seeking: All U.S.
Seeking in Canada? No
Exclusive territories? Yes
Homebased option? Yes
Employees needed to run biz: 1
Absentee ownership? No

COSTS
Total cost: $35.2K-77.2K
Franchise fee: $30K-50K
Royalty fee: 8%
Term of agreement: 10 years renewable
    for 25% of then-current fee
Franchisees required to buy multiple
    units? No

FINANCING
No financing available

QUALIFICATIONS
Net worth: $75K
Cash liquidity: $35.2K
Experience:
    General business experience

TRAINING
At headquarters: 2 days

BUSINESS SUPPORT
Internet
Newsletter
Meetings
Toll-free phone line
Field operations/evaluations
Security/safety procedures

MARKETING SUPPORT
Co-op advertising
Ad slicks
National media campaign
Regional marketing

J.W. TUMBLES, A CHILDREN'S GYM

Ranked #387 in Entrepreneur Magazine's 2007 Franchise 500   *Financial rating: $$$*

312 S. Cedros Ave., #329
Solana Beach, CA 92075
(858)794-0484
www.jwtumbles.com
Children's gym/parties
Began: 1985, Franchising: 1993
Headquarters size: 8 employees
Franchise department: 5 employees

U.S. franchises: 21
Canadian franchises: 0
Other foreign franchises: 4
Company-owned: 1

Seeking: All U.S.
Seeking in Canada? Yes
Exclusive territories? Yes
Homebased option? No
Employees needed to run biz: 3
Absentee ownership? Yes

COSTS
Total cost: $138.6K-215.6K
Franchise fee: $42.9K
Royalty fee: 5%
Term of agreement: 10 years renewable
    at no charge
Franchisees required to buy multiple
    units? Outside the U.S. only

FINANCING
In-house: None
3rd-party: Equipment, startup costs

QUALIFICATIONS
Net worth: $200K
Cash liquidity: $30K
Experience:
    General business experience
    Marketing skills

TRAINING
At headquarters: 4 weeks
At franchisee's location: 3 days

BUSINESS SUPPORT
Grand opening
Internet
Newsletter
Meetings
Toll-free phone line
Field operations/evaluations
Lease negotiations
Purchasing cooperatives
Security/safety procedures

MARKETING SUPPORT
Co-op advertising
Ad slicks
Regional marketing

KIDOKINETICS

Current financial data not available

318 Indian Trace, #121
Weston, FL 33326
(866)543-6546/(954)385-8511
www.kidokinetics.com
Sports fitness program for children
Began: 2000, Franchising: 2006
Headquarters size: 8 employees
Franchise department: 3 employees

U.S. franchises: 0
Canadian franchises: 0
Other foreign franchises: 0
Company-owned: 1

Seeking: Midwest, Southeast,
    Southwest
Seeking in Canada? No
Exclusive territories? No
Homebased option? Yes
Employees needed to run biz: Info
    not provided
Absentee ownership? No

COSTS
Total cost: $47.5K-60.9K
Franchise fee: $30K
Royalty fee: 7%
Term of agreement: 5 years renewable
    at no charge
Franchisees required to buy multiple
    units? No

FINANCING
No financing available

QUALIFICATIONS
Info not provided

TRAINING
At headquarters

BUSINESS SUPPORT
Meetings
Toll-free phone line
Field operations/evaluations

MARKETING SUPPORT
Info not provided

KINDERDANCE INT'L. INC.
Ranked #476 in Entrepreneur Magazine's 2007 Franchise 500
Financial rating: $$$$

1333 Gateway Dr., #1003
Melbourne, FL 32901
(800)554-2334/(321)984-4448
www.kinderdance.com
Children's movement/educational
    program
Began: 1979, Franchising: 1985
Headquarters size: 7 employees
Franchise department: 3 employees

U.S. franchises: 100
Canadian franchises: 1
Other foreign franchises: 3
Company-owned: 0

Seeking: All U.S.
Seeking in Canada? Yes
Exclusive territories? Yes
Homebased option? Yes
Employees needed to run biz: 1-2
Absentee ownership? No

COSTS
Total cost: $14.95K-39.1K
Franchise fee: $12K-33K
Royalty fee: 6-15%
Term of agreement: 10 years renewable
    for 10% of current fee
Franchisees required to buy multiple
    units? No

FINANCING
In-house: None
3rd-party: Franchise fee

QUALIFICATIONS
Net worth: $10K+
Cash liquidity: $6.4K+
Enjoys working with children
Energetic personality

TRAINING
At headquarters
Annual continuing education
    conference: 3 days

BUSINESS SUPPORT
Grand opening
Internet
Newsletter
Meetings
Toll-free phone line
Field operations/evaluations
Purchasing cooperatives
Security/safety procedures

MARKETING SUPPORT
Co-op advertising
Ad slicks
National media campaign
Regional marketing
Press releases

THE LITTLE GYM
Ranked #140 in Entrepreneur Magazine's 2007 Franchise 500
Financial rating: $$$

8970 E. Raintree Dr., #200
Scottsdale, AZ 85260
(888)228-2878/(480)948-2878
www.thelittlegym.com
Children's development/fitness
    program
Began: 1976, Franchising: 1992
Headquarters size: 39 employees
Franchise department: 6 employees

U.S. franchises: 212
Canadian franchises: 4
Other foreign franchises: 38
Company-owned: 0

Seeking: All U.S.
Seeking in Canada? Yes
Exclusive territories? Yes
Homebased option? No
Employees needed to run biz: 5-7
Absentee ownership? No

COSTS
Total cost: $155.7K-238K
Franchise fee: $64.5K
Royalty fee: 8%
Term of agreement: 10 years renewable
    at no charge
Franchisees required to buy multiple
    units? Outside the U.S. only

FINANCING
In-house: None
3rd-party: Equipment, franchise fee,
    inventory, payroll, startup costs

QUALIFICATIONS
Net worth: $200K
Cash liquidity: $50K
Experience:
    General business experience
    Marketing skills

TRAINING
At headquarters: 2 weeks
At franchisee's location: 5 days
At existing franchise location:
    1 week

BUSINESS SUPPORT
Grand opening
Internet
Newsletter
Meetings
Toll-free phone line
Field operations/evaluations
Lease negotiations
Purchasing cooperatives
Security/safety procedures

MARKETING SUPPORT
Ad slicks
National media campaign
Regional marketing
National & local PR support
Online marketing

MY GYM CHILDREN'S FITNESS CENTER

Ranked #221 in Entrepreneur Magazine's 2007 Franchise 500   *Financial rating: $$$$*

15300 Ventura Blvd., #423
Sherman Oaks, CA 91403
(800)469-4967
www.my-gym.com
Children's early learning/fitness
    program & facility
Began: 1983, Franchising: 1995
Headquarters size: 20 employees
Franchise department: 4 employees

U.S. franchises: 155
Canadian franchises: 0
Other foreign franchises: 8
Company-owned: 0

Seeking: All U.S.
Seeking in Canada? Yes
Exclusive territories? Yes
Homebased option? No
Employees needed to run biz: 6-10
Absentee ownership? Yes

COSTS
Total cost: $34.3K-223.3K
Franchise fee: $25K/49.5K
Royalty fee: 6%
Term of agreement: 12 years renewable
    at no charge
Franchisees required to buy multiple
    units? No

FINANCING
In-house: None
3rd-party: Equipment, franchise fee,
    inventory, startup costs

QUALIFICATIONS
Cash liquidity: $35K-50K
Experience:
    Industry experience
    General business experience
    Marketing skills

TRAINING
At headquarters: 21 days
At franchisee's location: Ongoing

BUSINESS SUPPORT
Grand opening
Internet
Newsletter
Meetings
Toll-free phone line
Field operations/evaluations
Security/safety procedures

MARKETING SUPPORT
Co-op advertising
Ad slicks
Regional marketing

SOCCER SHOTS

Current financial data not available

258 Calder St.
Harrisburg, PA 17102
(704)953-5868
www.soccershots.org
Soccer education for children ages 3-8
Began: 2002, Franchising: 2005
Headquarters size: Info not provided

U.S. franchises: 7
Canadian franchises: 0
Other foreign franchises: 0
Company-owned: 2

Seeking: All U.S.
Seeking in Canada? No
Exclusive territories? Yes
Homebased option? Yes
Employees needed to run biz:
    Info not provided
Absentee ownership? No

COSTS
Total cost: $8.5K-12K
Franchise fee: $7.5K
Royalty fee: 5-7%
Term of agreement: 10 years renewable
    for up to $1.2K
Franchisees required to buy multiple
    units? No

FINANCING
No financing available

QUALIFICATIONS
Cash liquidity: $5K
Experience:
    Industry experience
    General business experience

TRAINING
At headquarters or franchisee's
    location: 2 days

BUSINESS SUPPORT
Internet
Newsletter
Meetings
Purchasing cooperatives
Security/safety procedures

MARKETING SUPPORT
Info not provided

STRETCH-N-GROW INT'L. INC.

Ranked #217 in Entrepreneur Magazine's 2007 Franchise 500　　*Financial rating: $$*

P.O. Box 7599
Seminole, FL 33775
(727)596-7614
www.stretch-n-grow.com
On-site children's fitness program
Began: 1992, Franchising: 1993
Headquarters size: 4 employees
Franchise department: 4 employees

U.S. franchises: 206
Canadian franchises: 6
Other foreign franchises: 52
Company-owned: 0

Seeking: All U.S.
Seeking in Canada? Yes
Exclusive territories? Yes
Homebased option? Yes
Employees needed to run biz: 1
Absentee ownership? No

COSTS
Total cost: $23.6K
Franchise fee: $22.6K
Royalty fee: $150/mo.
Term of agreement: Info not provided
Franchisees required to buy multiple
    units? No

FINANCING
No financing available

QUALIFICATIONS
Cash liquidity: $20K-25K
Desire to work with children

TRAINING
At headquarters: 3 days
At Dallas location: 3 days

BUSINESS SUPPORT
Internet
Newsletter
Meetings
Toll-free phone line

MARKETING SUPPORT
National media campaign
Trade ads

STROLLERFIT INC.

Ranked #314 in Entrepreneur Magazine's 2007 Franchise 500　　*Financial rating: $$$*

100 E-Business Wy., #290
Cincinnati, OH 45241
(866)222-9348
www.strollerfit.com
Interactive fitness programs, classes
    & products for parents & babies
Began: 1997, Franchising: 2001
Headquarters size: 12 employees
Franchise department: 8 employees

U.S. franchises: 87
Canadian franchises: 0
Other foreign franchises: 0
Company-owned: 3

Seeking: All U.S.
Seeking in Canada? Yes
Exclusive territories? Yes
Homebased option? Yes
Employees needed to run biz:
    Info not provided
Absentee ownership? Yes

COSTS
Total cost: $4.9K-13.2K
Franchise fee: $3.8K
Royalty fee: 15%
Term of agreement: 2 years renewable
    at no charge
Franchisees required to buy multiple
    units? No

FINANCING
No financing available

QUALIFICATIONS
Cash liquidity: $5K
Experience:
    General business experience
    Marketing skills

TRAINING
At headquarters: 2 days

BUSINESS SUPPORT
Grand opening
Internet
Newsletter
Meetings
Toll-free phone line
Purchasing cooperatives
Security/safety procedures

MARKETING SUPPORT
Ad slicks

STROLLER STRIDES

Financial rating: 0

1531 Crescent Pl.
San Marcos, CA 92078
(866)348-4666
www.strollerstrides.com
Stroller fitness program
Began: 2001, Franchising: 2005
Headquarters size: 5 employees

U.S. franchises: 129
Canadian franchises: 0
Other foreign franchises: 0
Company-owned: 1

Seeking: All U.S.
Seeking in Canada? Yes
Exclusive territories? Yes
Homebased option? Yes
Employees needed to run biz: 2
Absentee ownership? Yes

COSTS
Total cost: $3.2K-16.98K
Franchise fee: $3K-5.5K
Royalty fee: $160-380/mo.
Term of agreement: 3 years renewable
    for 50% of then-current fee
Franchisees required to buy multiple
    units? Outside the U.S. only

FINANCING
No financing available

QUALIFICATIONS
Net worth: $100K
Cash liquidity: $20K
Experience:
    Marketing skills

TRAINING
At headquarters: 2 days
Virtual training via phone, web &
    DVD

BUSINESS SUPPORT
Grand opening
Internet
Newsletter
Meetings
Toll-free phone line

MARKETING SUPPORT
Ad slicks
National media campaign
PR firm for grand opening

CHILDREN'S ▶ *Identification Services*

CHIP - THE CHILD I.D. PROGRAM
Ranked #277 in Entrepreneur Magazine's 2007 Franchise 500   *Financial rating: $$$*

705 Lakefield Rd., Bldg. G
Westlake Village, CA 91361
(805)557-0577
www.chipfranchise.com
Children's ID & school safety
    program
Began: 2001, Franchising: 2002
Headquarters size: 10 employees
Franchise department: 3 employees

U.S. franchises: 152
Canadian franchises: 0
Other foreign franchises: 0
Company-owned: 1

Seeking: All U.S.
Seeking in Canada? Yes
Exclusive territories? Yes
Homebased option? Yes
Employees needed to run biz: 1-2
Absentee ownership? Yes

COSTS
Total cost: $23.5K-33.5K
Franchise fee: $23.5K-33.5K
Royalty fee: 0
Term of agreement: 5 years renewable
    at no charge
Franchisees required to buy multiple
    units? Outside the U.S. only

FINANCING
In-house: Franchise fee
3rd-party: None

QUALIFICATIONS
Info not provided

TRAINING
At headquarters: 3 days

BUSINESS SUPPORT
Internet
Newsletter
Meetings
Toll-free phone line
Security/safety procedures

MARKETING SUPPORT
Ad slicks

GUARD-A-KID

Ranked #458 in Entrepreneur Magazine's 2007 Franchise 500   *Financial rating: $$$$*

3785 N.W. 82nd Ave., #106
Miami, FL 33166
(800)679-4256/(305)477-3301
www.guardakid.com
Children's identification & safety
    services
Began: 2003, Franchising: 2005
Headquarters size: 6 employees
Franchise department: 2 employees

U.S. franchises: 60
Canadian franchises: 2
Other foreign franchises: 0
Company-owned: 1

Seeking: All U.S.
Seeking in Canada? Yes
Exclusive territories? Yes
Homebased option? Yes
Employees needed to run biz: 1
Absentee ownership? No

COSTS
Total cost: $20.9K
Franchise fee: $19.9K
Royalty fee: 0
Term of agreement: 10 years renewable
    for 20% of then-current fee
Franchisees required to buy multiple
    units? No

FINANCING
No financing available

QUALIFICATIONS
Net worth: $20.9K
Cash liquidity: $20.9K
Experience:
    General business experience

TRAINING
At headquarters: 1 day
At franchisee's location: 1 day

BUSINESS SUPPORT
Internet
Newsletter
Meetings
Toll-free phone line

MARKETING SUPPORT
National media campaign

IDENT-A-KID SERVICES OF AMERICA

Ranked #399 in Entrepreneur Magazine's 2007 Franchise 500   *Financial rating: $$$*

2810 Scherer Dr., #100
St. Petersburg, FL 33716
(727)577-4646
www.ident-a-kid.com
Children's identification products
    & services
Began: 1986, Franchising: 2000
Headquarters size: 5 employees

U.S. franchises: 224
Canadian franchises: 0
Other foreign franchises: 0
Company-owned: 0

Seeking: All U.S.
Seeking in Canada? Yes
Exclusive territories? Yes
Homebased option? Yes
Employees needed to run biz: 0-3
Absentee ownership? No

COSTS
Total cost: $33.6K-60.4K
Franchise fee: $24.5K
Royalty fee: 0
Term of agreement: 10 years renewable
    at no charge
Franchisees required to buy multiple
    units? Outside the U.S. only

FINANCING
In-house: None
3rd-party: Franchise fee

QUALIFICATIONS
Net worth: $100K
Cash liquidity: $25K
Experience:
    General business experience
    Marketing skills

TRAINING
At headquarters: 2-1/2 days
Via telephone/multimedia

BUSINESS SUPPORT
Internet
Newsletter
Meetings
Toll-free phone line

MARKETING SUPPORT
National media campaign

MCGRUFF SAFE KIDS TOTAL IDENTIFICATION SYSTEM

Financial rating: $

28059 US Highway 19 N., #317
Clearwater, FL 33761
(888)209-4218
www.mcgruff-tid.com
Children's ID products/services &
    safety education
Began: 2001, Franchising: 2002
Headquarters size: 3 employees
Franchise department: 5 employees

U.S. franchises: 28
Canadian franchises: 0
Other foreign franchises: 0
Company-owned: 0

Seeking: All U.S.
Seeking in Canada? No
Exclusive territories? Yes
Homebased option? Yes
Employees needed to run biz: 0
Absentee ownership? No

COSTS
Total cost: $33.3K-42.3K
Franchise fee: $30K
Royalty fee: $295/mo.
Term of agreement: 3 years renewable
    for $500
Franchisees required to buy multiple
    units? No

FINANCING
No financing available

QUALIFICATIONS
Net worth: $35K
Cash liquidity: $15K
Experience:
    General business experience

TRAINING
In Tampa Bay, FL: 24 hours

BUSINESS SUPPORT
Grand opening
Internet
Newsletter
Meetings
Toll-free phone line
Field operations/evaluations

MARKETING SUPPORT
Ad slicks
National media campaign

POSITIVE PROOF

Financial rating: $$$

1209 Oakwood Trail
Southlake, TX 76092
(888)631-7233
www.positive-proof.com
Child identification products
    & services
Began: 2000, Franchising: 2006
Headquarters size: 17 employees
Franchise department: 2 employees

U.S. franchises: 0
Canadian franchises: 0
Other foreign franchises: 0
Company-owned: 1

Seeking: All U.S.
Seeking in Canada? No
Exclusive territories? Yes
Homebased option? Yes
Employees needed to run biz: 1
Absentee ownership? No

COSTS
Total cost: $31.4K-44.7K
Franchise fee: $22K/27K
Royalty fee: 0
Term of agreement: 5 years
Franchisees required to buy multiple
    units? No

FINANCING
No financing available

QUALIFICATIONS
Net worth: Varies
Cash liquidity: Varies
Experience:
    Basic computer skills

TRAINING
At headquarters: 3 days
By phone: 1 day

BUSINESS SUPPORT
Internet
Meetings
Toll-free phone line
Field operations/evaluations

MARKETING SUPPORT
Internet

SAFE KIDS CARD

Current financial data not available

17100-B Bear Valley Rd., PMB #238
Victorville, CA 92392
(760)486-1506
www.myfamilycd.com
Child, adult & pet identification
system
Began: 2002, Franchising: 2003
Headquarters size: 2 employees
Franchise department: 1 employee

U.S. franchises: 58
Canadian franchises: 1
Other foreign franchises: 3
Company-owned: 0

Seeking: All U.S.
Seeking in Canada? Yes
Exclusive territories? Yes
Homebased option? Yes
Employees needed to run biz: 2
Absentee ownership? Yes

COSTS
Total cost: $20.4K-48.4K
Franchise fee: $18.9K
Royalty fee: $75/mo.
Term of agreement: 10 years renewable
for $1K
Franchisees required to buy multiple
units? Outside the U.S. only

FINANCING
No financing available

QUALIFICATIONS
Net worth: $20K
Cash liquidity: $7K+
Experience:
General business experience
Marketing skills
Must like children

TRAINING
At headquarters: 2 days
At franchisee's location: Optional

BUSINESS SUPPORT
Internet
Newsletter
Meetings
Purchasing cooperatives
Security/safety procedures

MARKETING SUPPORT
Co-op advertising

SAFETYNET4KIDS

Financial rating: 0

5540 Villa Lake Ct.
Suwanee, GA 30024
(877)729-2559
www.safetynet4kids.com
Digital children's ID services
Began: 2003, Franchising: 2006
Headquarters size: 3 employees
Franchise department: 3 employees

U.S. franchises: 4
Canadian franchises: 0
Other foreign franchises: 0
Company-owned: 0

Seeking: All U.S.
Seeking in Canada? No
Exclusive territories? Yes
Homebased option? Yes
Employees needed to run biz: 1-3
Absentee ownership? No

COSTS
Total cost: $36K-50K
Franchise fee: $19K
Royalty fee: 5%
Term of agreement: 10 years renewable
for 10% of current franchise fee
Franchisees required to buy multiple
units? No

FINANCING
In-house: None
3rd-party: Equipment

QUALIFICATIONS
Net worth: $50K
Cash liquidity: $19K
Experience:
General business experience
General computer knowledge

TRAINING
At headquarters: 4-5 days
At franchisee's location: 2-3 days

BUSINESS SUPPORT
Internet
Newsletter
Toll-free phone line
Purchasing cooperatives

MARKETING SUPPORT
Marketing/media kit

CHILDREN'S ▸ *Learning*

ABC TUTORS IN HOME TUTORING

Financial rating: $$$

7545 W. 150th St.
Overland Park, KS 66223
(913)961-7800
www.abctutors.com
Academic tutoring
Began: 2004, Franchising: 2005
Headquarters size: 3 employees
Franchise department: 3 employees

U.S. franchises: 1
Canadian franchises: 0
Other foreign franchises: 0
Company-owned: 1

Seeking: All U.S.
Seeking in Canada? No
Exclusive territories? Yes
Homebased option? Yes
Employees needed to run biz: 1-2
Absentee ownership? No

COSTS
Total cost: $29.5K-52.5K
Franchise fee: $19.5K
Royalty fee: 4-6%
Term of agreement: 10 years renewable
    for 10% of then-current fee
Franchisees required to buy multiple
    units? No

FINANCING
In-house: Franchise fee
3rd-party: None

QUALIFICATIONS
Experience:
    General business experience

TRAINING
At franchisee's location: 3 days

BUSINESS SUPPORT
Grand opening
Internet
Newsletter
Meetings
Toll-free phone line
Purchasing cooperatives

MARKETING SUPPORT
Co-op advertising
Ad slicks

CHILDREN'S TECHNOLOGY WORKSHOP

Ranked #496 in Entrepreneur Magazine's 2007 Franchise 500

Financial rating: $$$

109 Vanderhoof Ave., #101A
Toronto, ON M4G 2H7 Canada
(866)704-2267/(416)425-2289
www.ctworkshop.com
Children's enrichment programs in
    technology, engineering & science
Began: 1997, Franchising: 2004
Headquarters size: 10 employees
Franchise department: 10 employees

U.S. franchises: 24
Canadian franchises: 9
Other foreign franchises: 4
Company-owned: 1

Seeking: All U.S.
Seeking in Canada? Yes
Exclusive territories? Yes
Homebased option? Yes
Employees needed to run biz:
    Info not provided
Absentee ownership? No

COSTS
Total cost: $105K-150K
Franchise fee: $25K
Royalty fee: 6%
Term of agreement: 7 years renewable
    for $1K
Franchisees required to buy multiple
    units? No

FINANCING
In-house: None
3rd-party: Equipment, franchise fee,
    inventory, startup costs

QUALIFICATIONS
Net worth: $500K
Cash liquidity: $80K
Experience:
    Industry experience
    General business experience
    Marketing skills
    Enthusiasm for technology,
    engineering & science

TRAINING
At headquarters: 5 days
Ongoing web & teleconference
    training

BUSINESS SUPPORT
Internet
Newsletter
Meetings
Toll-free phone line
Field operations/evaluations
Security/safety procedures

MARKETING SUPPORT
Co-op advertising
Ad slicks
Regional marketing

CHYTEN EDUCATIONAL SERVICES

Current financial data not available

1723 Massachusetts Ave.
Lexington, MA 02420
(781)541-6279
www.chyten.com
Tutoring & test preparation
Began: 1983, Franchising: 2006
Headquarters size: 6 employees
Franchise department: 6 employees

U.S. franchises: 0
Canadian franchises: 0
Other foreign franchises: 0
Company-owned: 5

Seeking: Northeast, Southwest
Seeking in Canada? No
Exclusive territories? Yes
Homebased option? No
Employees needed to run biz: 1
Absentee ownership? Yes

COSTS
Total cost: $77.5K-204K
Franchise fee: $37.5K
Royalty fee: 10%
Term of agreement: 20 years renewable
at no charge
Franchisees required to buy multiple
units? No

FINANCING
No financing available

QUALIFICATIONS
Cash liquidity: $65K-150K
Experience:
General business experience
Education experience helpful

TRAINING
At headquarters: Up to 10 days
At franchisee's location: Up to
3 days

BUSINESS SUPPORT
Grand opening
Internet
Meetings
Toll-free phone line
Field operations/evaluations
Lease negotiations
Security/safety procedures

MARKETING SUPPORT
Co-op advertising
Ad slicks
Regional marketing

CLUB Z IN-HOME TUTORING SERVICES

Ranked #99 in Entrepreneur Magazine's 2007 Franchise 500   *Financial rating: $$$$*

15310 Amberly Dr., #185
Tampa, FL 33647
(800)434-2582
www.clubztutoring.com
In-home tutoring services
Began: 1995, Franchising: 1998
Headquarters size: 36 employees
Franchise department: 5 employees

U.S. franchises: 380
Canadian franchises: 2
Other foreign franchises: 0
Company-owned: 0

Seeking: All U.S.
Seeking in Canada? Yes
Exclusive territories? Yes
Homebased option? Yes
Employees needed to run biz: 1
Absentee ownership? Yes

COSTS
Total cost: $31.3K-63.95K
Franchise fee: $24.5K-54.5K
Royalty fee: 6%
Term of agreement: 7 years renewable
at no charge
Franchisees required to buy multiple
units? No

FINANCING
No financing available

QUALIFICATIONS
Cash liquidity: $25K
Experience:
General business experience

TRAINING
At headquarters: 2 days
At franchisee's location: 2 days

BUSINESS SUPPORT
Newsletter
Meetings
Toll-free phone line

MARKETING SUPPORT
Regional marketing

COLLEGE NANNIES & TUTORS

Financial rating: 0

109 Bushaway Rd., #100
Wayzata, MN 55391
(952)476-0262
www.collegenannies.com
Nanny & tutoring services
Began: 2001, Franchising: 2005
Headquarters size: 7 employees
Franchise department: 6 employees

U.S. franchises: 7
Canadian franchises: 0
Other foreign franchises: 0
Company-owned: 0

Seeking: All U.S.
Seeking in Canada? Yes
Exclusive territories? Yes
Homebased option? Yes
Employees needed to run biz: 2
Absentee ownership? No

COSTS
Total cost: $29K-113K
Franchise fee: $25K
Royalty fee: 5%
Term of agreement: 10 years renewable
    for $2K
Franchisees required to buy multiple
    units? Outside the U.S. only

FINANCING
In-house: Franchise fee
3rd-party: Equipment, startup costs

QUALIFICATIONS
Net worth: $200K
Cash liquidity: $25K
Experience:
    Industry experience
    General business experience
    Marketing skills

TRAINING
At headquarters: 1 week
At franchisee's location: 1 week

BUSINESS SUPPORT
Grand opening
Internet
Newsletter
Meetings
Toll-free phone line
Field operations/evaluations
Lease negotiations
Purchasing cooperatives
Security/safety procedures

MARKETING SUPPORT
Co-op advertising
Ad slicks
National media campaign
Regional marketing
Proprietary online resource center

ENOPI DAEKYO USA INC.

Ranked #170 in Entrepreneur Magazine's 2007 Franchise 500   *Financial rating: $$$$*

701 E. Palisades Ave., #201
Englewood Cliffs, NJ 07632
(888)835-1212/(201)894-1212
www.enopi.com
Tutoring services
Began: 1976, Franchising: 1976
Headquarters size: 30 employees
Franchise department: 10 employees

U.S. franchises: 99
Canadian franchises: 5
Other foreign franchises: 82
Company-owned: 481

Seeking: All U.S.
Seeking in Canada? Yes
Exclusive territories? No
Homebased option? No
Employees needed to run biz: 1-2
Absentee ownership? No

COSTS
Total cost: $9.5K-17K
Franchise fee: $2K
Royalty fee: Varies
Term of agreement: 2 years renewable
    at no charge
Franchisees required to buy multiple
    units? No

FINANCING
No financing available

QUALIFICATIONS
Net worth: $30K
Cash liquidity: $10K
Experience:
    Industry experience
    General business experience
    Marketing skills

TRAINING
At headquarters: 16 hours+
At franchisee's location: Ongoing
At regional office

BUSINESS SUPPORT
Grand opening
Internet
Newsletter
Meetings
Toll-free phone line

MARKETING SUPPORT
National media campaign
Statewide advertising

FASTRACKIDS INT'L. INC.

Ranked #274 in Entrepreneur Magazine's 2007 Franchise 500   *Financial rating: $$$$*

6900 E. Belleview Ave., 1st Fl.
Greenwood Village, CO 80111
(303)224-0200
www.fastrackids.com
Enrichment education for young
   children
Began: 1998, Franchising: 1998
Headquarters size: 14 employees
Franchise department: 4 employees

U.S. franchises: 88
Canadian franchises: 2
Other foreign franchises: 103
Company-owned: 0

Seeking: All U.S.
Seeking in Canada? Yes
Exclusive territories? Yes
Homebased option? No
Employees needed to run biz: 2-3
Absentee ownership? Yes

COSTS
Total cost: $79K-189K
Franchise fee: $22K
Royalty fee: 1.5%
Term of agreement: 5 years renewable
   for $1K
Franchisees required to buy multiple
   units? No

FINANCING
In-house: None
3rd-party: Accounts receivable,
   equipment, franchise fee,
   inventory, payroll, startup costs

QUALIFICATIONS
Experience:
   Industry experience
   General business experience
   Marketing skills

TRAINING
At headquarters: 10 days

BUSINESS SUPPORT
Internet
Newsletter
Meetings

MARKETING SUPPORT
Ad slicks

HALSTROM HIGH SCHOOL

Current financial data not available

2204 El Camino Real, #310
Oceanside, CA 92054
(888)425-7876/(760)721-2167
www.halstrom.org
High school diploma program
Began: 1985, Franchising: 2005
Headquarters size: 4 employees
Franchise department: 3 employees

U.S. franchises: 0
Canadian franchises: 0
Other foreign franchises: 0
Company-owned: 3

Seeking: Southeast, Southwest, West
Seeking in Canada? No
Exclusive territories? No
Homebased option? No
Employees needed to run biz: 7-20
Absentee ownership? Yes

COSTS
Total cost: $115.4K-216.5K
Franchise fee: $40K
Royalty fee: 8%
Term of agreement: 7 years
Franchisees required to buy multiple
   units? No

FINANCING
In-house: None
3rd-party: Equipment, franchise fee,
   inventory, startup costs

QUALIFICATIONS
Experience:
   Industry experience
   General business experience
   Marketing skills

TRAINING
At headquarters: 10 days
At franchisee's location: 2 days

BUSINESS SUPPORT
Grand opening
Newsletter
Meetings
Field operations/evaluations
Lease negotiations
Purchasing cooperatives
Security/safety procedures

MARKETING SUPPORT
Co-op advertising
Ad slicks
National media campaign
Regional marketing

HIGH TOUCH-HIGH TECH

Ranked #275 in Entrepreneur Magazine's 2007 Franchise 500   *Financial rating: $$$*

P.O. Box 8495
Asheville, NC 28814
(800)444-4968
www.hightouch-hightech.com
Science activities for schools/
    children's parties
Began: 1990, Franchising: 1993
Headquarters size: 9 employees
Franchise department: 3 employees

U.S. franchises: 128
Canadian franchises: 9
Other foreign franchises: 4
Company-owned: 6

Seeking: All U.S.
Seeking in Canada? Yes
Exclusive territories? Yes
Homebased option? Yes
Employees needed to run biz: 4
Absentee ownership? Yes

COSTS
Total cost: $40.1K
Franchise fee: $35K
Royalty fee: 7%
Term of agreement: 10 years renewable
    for $2.5K
Franchisees required to buy multiple
    units? No

FINANCING
In-house: Franchise fee
3rd-party: None

QUALIFICATIONS
Experience:
    General business experience
    Marketing skills
    Education or teaching experience

TRAINING
At headquarters: 5 days

BUSINESS SUPPORT
Internet
Newsletter
Meetings
Toll-free phone line
Field operations/evaluations
Security/safety procedures

MARKETING SUPPORT
Ad slicks

HO MATH & CHESS LEARNING CENTRE

Current financial data not available

#4, 2265 W. 41st
Vancouver, BC V6M 2A3 Canada
(604)266-4321
www.mathandchess.com
Math & chess learning
Began: 1995, Franchising: 2004
Headquarters size: 8 employees
Franchise department: 2 employees

U.S. franchises: 1
Canadian franchises: 3
Other foreign franchises: 3
Company-owned: 1

Seeking: Not available in the U.S.
Seeking in Canada? Yes
Exclusive territories? Yes
Homebased option? Yes
Employees needed to run biz: 1
Absentee ownership? No

COSTS
Total cost: $2K
Franchise fee: $2K
Royalty fee: 0
Term of agreement: 1 year
    renewable for less than $500
Franchisees required to buy multiple
    units? No

FINANCING
No financing available

QUALIFICATIONS
Net worth: $3K
Cash liquidity: $3K
Experience:
    Marketing skills
    Teaching experience

TRAINING
At headquarters: 1 week

BUSINESS SUPPORT
Internet
Newsletter
Purchasing cooperatives

MARKETING SUPPORT
Co-op advertising

THE HONORS LEARNING CENTER

Financial rating: $$$

P.O. Box 24055
Chattanooga, TN 37422-4055
(423)892-1803
www.honorslearningcenter.com
Supplemental educational services
& academic testing
Began: 1987, Franchising: 1991
Headquarters size: 2 employees
Franchise department: 2 employees

U.S. franchises: 1
Canadian franchises: 0
Other foreign franchises: 0
Company-owned: 0

Seeking: All U.S.
Seeking in Canada? No
Exclusive territories? Yes
Homebased option? No
Employees needed to run biz: 10
Absentee ownership? No

COSTS
Total cost: $64.5K-68.7K
Franchise fee: $25K
Royalty fee: $2.5K/mo.
Term of agreement: 10 years renewable
at no charge
Franchisees required to buy multiple
units? No

FINANCING
No financing available

QUALIFICATIONS
Net worth: $100K
Cash liquidity: $65K
Experience:
Marketing skills
Degree in education

TRAINING
At headquarters: 2 weeks
At franchisee's location: 1 week

BUSINESS SUPPORT
Grand opening
Internet
Newsletter
Meetings
Field operations/evaluations
Security/safety procedures

MARKETING SUPPORT
Ad slicks
Radio & TV dubs

HUNTINGTON LEARNING CENTERS INC.

Ranked #163 in Entrepreneur Magazine's 2007 Franchise 500

Financial rating: $$$$

496 Kinderkamack Rd.
Oradell, NJ 07649
(800)653-8400/(201)261-8400
www.huntingtonfranchise.com
Children's educational services
Began: 1977, Franchising: 1985
Headquarters size: 100 employees
Franchise department: 8 employees

U.S. franchises: 253
Canadian franchises: 0
Other foreign franchises: 0
Company-owned: 35

Seeking: All U.S.
Seeking in Canada? No
Exclusive territories? No
Homebased option? No
Employees needed to run biz: 3
Absentee ownership? No

COSTS
Total cost: $162K-283K
Franchise fee: $43K
Royalty fee: 8%
Term of agreement: 10 years renewable
for up to $20K
Franchisees required to buy multiple
units? Yes

FINANCING
In-house: None
3rd-party: Accounts receivable,
equipment, inventory, payroll,
startup costs

QUALIFICATIONS
Net worth: $250K
Cash liquidity: $60K
Experience:
General business experience

TRAINING
At headquarters: 4 weeks
Ongoing training 2-3 days, twice a
year

BUSINESS SUPPORT
Internet
Newsletter
Meetings
Toll-free phone line
Field operations/evaluations
Purchasing cooperatives

MARKETING SUPPORT
Co-op advertising
Ad slicks
National media campaign
National TV advertising

JEI SELF-LEARNING SYSTEMS INC.

Ranked #391 in Entrepreneur Magazine's 2007 Franchise 500　　　*Financial rating: $$$$*

4221 Wilshire Blvd., #224
Los Angeles, CA 90010
(323)936-3300
www.jeilearning.com
After-school learning center
Began: 1977, Franchising: 1992
Headquarters size: 322 employees
Franchise department: 14 employees

U.S. franchises: 66
Canadian franchises: 4
Other foreign franchises: 25
Company-owned: 284

Seeking: All U.S.
Seeking in Canada? Yes
Exclusive territories? No
Homebased option? No
Employees needed to run biz: 2
Absentee ownership? No

COSTS
Total cost: $57.6K-92K
Franchise fee: $25K
Royalty fee: Varies
Term of agreement: 5 years renewable
　　at no charge
Franchisees required to buy multiple
　　units? No

FINANCING
No financing available

QUALIFICATIONS
Net worth: $100K
Cash liquidity: $50K
Experience:
　　General business experience
　　Marketing skills
　　Education background

TRAINING
At headquarters: 1 week
At franchisee's location: 2 days

BUSINESS SUPPORT
Grand opening
Internet
Newsletter
Meetings
Toll-free phone line
Field operations/evaluations

MARKETING SUPPORT
Ad slicks
Regional marketing

KUMON MATH & READING CENTERS

Ranked #22 in Entrepreneur Magazine's 2007 Franchise 500　　　*Financial rating: $$$$*

300 Frank W. Burr Blvd., 5th Fl.
Teaneck, NJ 07666
(866)633-0740/(201)928-0444
www.kumon.com
Supplemental education
Began: 1958, Franchising: 1958
Headquarters size: 400 employees
Franchise department: 12 employees

U.S. franchises: 1,223
Canadian franchises: 332
Other foreign franchises: 24,094
Company-owned: 31

Seeking: All U.S.
Seeking in Canada? Yes
Exclusive territories? No
Homebased option? No
Employees needed to run biz: 2-3
Absentee ownership? No

COSTS
Total cost: $15.2K-37.8K
Franchise fee: $1K
Royalty fee: $30+/student/mo.
Term of agreement: 2 years renewable
　　at no charge
Franchisees required to buy multiple
　　units? No

FINANCING
No financing available

QUALIFICATIONS
Experience:
　　General business experience
　　Marketing skills
　　Good math, reading &
　　communications skills

TRAINING
At headquarters: 3 months+
At franchisee's location: Ongoing
At regional offices

BUSINESS SUPPORT
Grand opening
Internet
Newsletter
Meetings
Toll-free phone line

MARKETING SUPPORT
Co-op advertising
Regional marketing

LEARNINGRX

Financial rating: 0

5085 List Dr., #200
Colorado Springs, CO 80919
(719)264-8808
www.learningrx-franchise.com
Cognitive skills training
Began: 1986, Franchising: 2003
Headquarters size: 15 employees
Franchise department: 14 employees

U.S. franchises: 36
Canadian franchises: 0
Other foreign franchises: 0
Company-owned: 1

Seeking: All U.S.
Seeking in Canada? Yes
Exclusive territories? Yes
Homebased option? No
Employees needed to run biz: 3-30
Absentee ownership? Yes

COSTS
Total cost: $103K-190K
Franchise fee: $30K-45K
Royalty fee: 10%
Term of agreement: 10 years renewable
for $5K
Franchisees required to buy multiple
units? No

FINANCING
In-house: None
3rd-party: Accounts receivable,
equipment, franchise fee,
inventory, payroll, startup costs

QUALIFICATIONS
Net worth: $250K
Cash liquidity: $50K

TRAINING
At headquarters: 8 days
At franchisee's location: 4 days

BUSINESS SUPPORT
Grand opening
Internet
Newsletter
Meetings
Field operations/evaluations
Purchasing cooperatives
Security/safety procedures

MARKETING SUPPORT
Co-op advertising
Ad slicks

MATHNASIUM LEARNING CENTERS

Ranked #239 in Entrepreneur Magazine's 2007 Franchise 500 *Financial rating: $$$*

5120 W. Goldleaf Cir., #130
Los Angeles, CA 90056
(877)531-6284
www.mathnasium.com
Math learning center
Began: 2002, Franchising: 2003
Headquarters size: 20 employees
Franchise department: 12 employees

U.S. franchises: 110
Canadian franchises: 1
Other foreign franchises: 44
Company-owned: 2

Seeking: All U.S.
Seeking in Canada? Yes
Exclusive territories? No
Homebased option? No
Employees needed to run biz: 1
Absentee ownership? No

COSTS
Total cost: $50K-70K
Franchise fee: $15.5K
Royalty fee: Varies
Term of agreement: 5 years renewable
at no charge
Franchisees required to buy multiple
units? No

FINANCING
In-house: None
3rd-party: Franchise fee, payroll,
startup costs

QUALIFICATIONS
Net worth: $70K
Cash liquidity: $50K
Experience:
General business experience
Marketing skills
Must enjoy math & teaching
children

TRAINING
At headquarters: 6 days

BUSINESS SUPPORT
Internet
Newsletter
Meetings
Toll-free phone line
Field operations/evaluations

MARKETING SUPPORT
Ad slicks
Regional marketing

OXFORD LEARNING CENTERS INC.

Ranked #430 in Entrepreneur Magazine's 2007 Franchise 500

Financial rating: $

97B S. Livingston Ave.
Livingston, NJ 07039
(888)559-2212/(973)597-4300
www.oxfordlearning.com
Educational learning center
Began: 1984, Franchising: 1989
Headquarters size: 22 employees
Franchise department: 2 employees

U.S. franchises: 25
Canadian franchises: 77
Other foreign franchises: 2
Company-owned: 5

Seeking: All U.S.
Seeking in Canada? Yes
Exclusive territories? Yes
Homebased option? No
Employees needed to run biz: 3-10
Absentee ownership? Yes

COSTS
Total cost: $114.6K-243K
Franchise fee: $39.5K
Royalty fee: 10%
Term of agreement: 10 years renewable
for 50% of initial fee
Franchisees required to buy multiple
units? Outside the U.S. only

FINANCING
In-house: None
3rd-party: Accounts receivable,
equipment, franchise fee,
inventory, payroll, startup costs

QUALIFICATIONS
Net worth: $500K
Cash liquidity: $60K
Experience:
Industry experience
General business experience
Marketing skills

TRAINING
At headquarters: 12 days
At franchisee's location: Quarterly

BUSINESS SUPPORT
Newsletter
Meetings
Field operations/evaluations
Purchasing cooperatives

MARKETING SUPPORT
Ad slicks

SMART BRAIN AMERICA FRANCHISE CORP.

Financial rating: $

40 Hillside Ave.
Williston Park, NY 11596
(877)272-4647
www.smartbrainamerica.com
Children's abacus arithmetic &
enrichment program
Began: 2003, Franchising: 2005
Headquarters size: 5 employees
Franchise department: 3 employees

U.S. franchises: 3
Canadian franchises: 0
Other foreign franchises: 31
Company-owned: 3

Seeking: All U.S.
Seeking in Canada? Yes
Exclusive territories? Yes
Homebased option? No
Employees needed to run biz: 2-4
Absentee ownership? Yes

COSTS
Total cost: $60.2K-163.7K
Franchise fee: $25K
Royalty fee: $12-20/student/mo.
Term of agreement: 10 years renewable
for $3K
Franchisees required to buy multiple
units? Outside the U.S. only

FINANCING
No financing available

QUALIFICATIONS
Net worth: $150K
Cash liquidity: $20K
Experience:
General business experience
Marketing skills
Proven ability to work with
children

TRAINING
At headquarters: 7 days
At franchisee's location: 2-3 days

BUSINESS SUPPORT
Grand opening
Internet
Newsletter
Meetings
Toll-free phone line
Field operations/evaluations
Lease negotiations
Security/safety procedures

MARKETING SUPPORT
Co-op advertising
Ad slicks
Regional marketing

SPANISHFUN

Current financial data not available

2261 Tampa Rd., # 1
Tampa, FL 34685
(615)692-2290
www.spanishfun.net
Preschool Spanish language
    instruction
Began: 2005, Franchising: 2005
Headquarters size: 3 employees
Franchise department: 1 employee

U.S. franchises: 24
Canadian franchises: 0
Other foreign franchises: 0
Company-owned: 1

Seeking: All U.S.
Seeking in Canada? No
Exclusive territories? Yes
Homebased option? Yes
Employees needed to run biz: 0
Absentee ownership? Yes

COSTS
Total cost: $14.9K
Franchise fee: $14.9K
Royalty fee: $195/mo.
Term of agreement: 10 years renewable
    at no charge
Franchisees required to buy multiple
    units? No

FINANCING
No financing available

QUALIFICATIONS
Cash liquidity: $14.9K
Experience:
    General business experience

TRAINING
At franchisee's location: 3 days

BUSINESS SUPPORT
Internet
Newsletter
Meetings
Toll-free phone line

MARKETING SUPPORT
Internet

SYLVAN LEARNING CENTERS

Financial rating: $$$$

1001 Fleet St.
Baltimore, MD 21202
(800)284-8214/(410)843-8000
www.sylvanfranchise.com
Supplemental education
Began: 1979, Franchising: 1980
Headquarters size: 97 employees
Franchise department: 32 employees

U.S. franchises: 784
Canadian franchises: 70
Other foreign franchises: 5
Company-owned: 237

Seeking: All U.S.
Seeking in Canada? Yes
Exclusive territories? Yes
Homebased option? No
Employees needed to run biz: 2-4
Absentee ownership? No

COSTS
Total cost: $179.4K-297.4K
Franchise fee: $40K-48K
Royalty fee: 8-9%
Term of agreement: 10 years renewable
    for $1K
Franchisees required to buy multiple
    units? No

FINANCING
In-house: None
3rd-party: Equipment, franchise fee,
    inventory, startup costs

QUALIFICATIONS
Net worth: $150K
Cash liquidity: $75K
Experience:
    Industry experience
    General business experience
    Marketing skills
    Education background preferred

TRAINING
At headquarters: 1 week
At franchisee's location: During
    opening
At regional location: 5 days

BUSINESS SUPPORT
Grand opening
Internet
Newsletter
Meetings
Toll-free phone line
Field operations/evaluations

MARKETING SUPPORT
Co-op advertising
Ad slicks
National media campaign

THINKERTOTS

Current financial data not available

22214 Union Turnpike
Bayside, NY 11364
(718)740-1616
www.thinkertots.com
Early childhood education &
    development program
Began: 1998, Franchising: 2005
Headquarters size: 8 employees
Franchise department: 2 employees

U.S. franchises: 1
Canadian franchises: 0
Other foreign franchises: 0
Company-owned: 1

Seeking: Northeast
Seeking in Canada? No
Exclusive territories? Yes
Homebased option? No
Employees needed to run biz: 3
Absentee ownership? Yes

COSTS
Total cost: $83.1K-124.1K
Franchise fee: $35K
Royalty fee: 7%
Term of agreement: 5 years renewable
    at no charge
Franchisees required to buy multiple
    units? No

FINANCING
In-house: None
3rd-party: Accounts receivable,
    equipment, franchise fee,
    inventory, payroll, startup costs

QUALIFICATIONS
Net worth: $200K
Cash liquidity: $35K
Must love children

TRAINING
At headquarters: 2 weeks
At franchisee's location: 4 days

BUSINESS SUPPORT
Grand opening
Internet
Meetings
Toll-free phone line
Field operations/evaluations
Lease negotiations
Purchasing cooperatives
Security/safety procedures

MARKETING SUPPORT
Co-op advertising
Ad slicks
Regional marketing
Direct mail

TUTORING CLUB LLC

Ranked #146 in Entrepreneur Magazine's 2007 Franchise 500   *Financial rating: $$$$*

11241 Eastern Ave.
Henderson, NV 89052
(888)674-6425/(702)588-5288
www.tutoringclub.com
Individualized instruction for K-12
    students
Began: 1991, Franchising: 1999
Headquarters size: 10 employees
Franchise department: 7 employees

U.S. franchises: 177
Canadian franchises: 0
Other foreign franchises: 0
Company-owned: 8

Seeking: All U.S.
Seeking in Canada? Yes
Exclusive territories? Yes
Homebased option? No
Employees needed to run biz: 2
Absentee ownership? Yes

COSTS
Total cost: $83.2K-125.8K
Franchise fee: $34.5K
Royalty fee: 10%
Term of agreement: 20 years renewable
    for $1K
Franchisees required to buy multiple
    units? No

FINANCING
In-house: None
3rd-party: Accounts receivable,
    equipment, franchise fee,
    inventory, payroll, startup costs

QUALIFICATIONS
Net worth: $50K
Cash liquidity: $30K

TRAINING
At headquarters: 2 weeks
At franchisee's location: 1 day

BUSINESS SUPPORT
Grand opening
Internet
Newsletter
Meetings
Toll-free phone line
Field operations/evaluations
Lease negotiations
Purchasing cooperatives
Security/safety procedures

MARKETING SUPPORT
Co-op advertising
Ad slicks
National media campaign
Regional marketing

WHIZARD ACADEMY FOR MATHEMATICS & ENGLISH

Current financial data not available

30 Glen Cameron Rd., #200
Thornhill, ON L3T 1N7 Canada
(800)809-5555/(905)709-3233
www.whizardacademy.com
Tutorial/enrichment programs in
    mathematics & language arts
Began: 1993, Franchising: 1993
Headquarters size: 10 employees
Franchise department: 2 employees

U.S. franchises: 5
Canadian franchises: 50
Other foreign franchises: 0
Company-owned: 0

Seeking: All U.S.
Seeking in Canada? Yes
Exclusive territories? Yes
Homebased option? No
Employees needed to run biz:
    Info not provided
Absentee ownership? No

COSTS
Total cost: $125.8K-177.3K
Franchise fee: $38K
Royalty fee: 10%
Term of agreement: Info not provided
Franchisees required to buy multiple
    units? No

FINANCING
No financing available

QUALIFICATIONS
Net worth: $250K
Cash liquidity: $150K
Experience:
    General business experience
    Marketing skills

TRAINING
At headquarters: 3 weeks
At franchisee's location: 1 week

BUSINESS SUPPORT
Grand opening
Internet
Meetings
Toll-free phone line
Field operations/evaluations

MARKETING SUPPORT
Co-op advertising
Ad slicks
Regional marketing

THE WHOLE CHILD LEARNING CO.

Current financial data not available

2200 Kraft Dr., #1350
Blacksburg, VA 24060
(540)443-9252
www.wholechild.com
Children's enrichment programs
Began: 1996, Franchising: 1999
Headquarters size: 4 employees
Franchise department: 2 employees

U.S. franchises: 23
Canadian franchises: 0
Other foreign franchises: 0
Company-owned: 1

Seeking: All U.S.
Seeking in Canada? No
Exclusive territories? Yes
Homebased option? Yes
Employees needed to run biz: Info
    not provided
Absentee ownership? No

COSTS
Total cost: $24.5K
Franchise fee: $24.5K
Royalty fee: 7-8%
Term of agreement: 10 years renewable
    for 5% of franchise fee
Franchisees required to buy multiple
    units? No

FINANCING
In-house: Franchise fee
3rd-party: None

QUALIFICATIONS
Net worth: $25K
Cash liquidity: $14.5K
Experience:
    General business experience
    Marketing skills

TRAINING
At headquarters: 3 days
At franchisee's location: 3 days

BUSINESS SUPPORT
Grand opening
Internet
Meetings
Toll-free phone line
Field operations/evaluations

MARKETING SUPPORT
Info not provided

CHILDREN'S *Parties*

MONKEY JOE'S

Financial rating: $

1935 Peachtree Rd.
Atlanta, GA 30309
(404)844-3225
www.monkeyjoes.com
Children's entertainment facility
Began: 2004, Franchising: 2005
Headquarters size: 80 employees
Franchise department: 10 employees

U.S. franchises: 7
Canadian franchises: 0
Other foreign franchises: 0
Company-owned: 0

Seeking: All U.S.
Seeking in Canada? No
Exclusive territories? No
Homebased option? No
Employees needed to run biz:
    Info not provided
Absentee ownership? Info not
    provided

COSTS
Total cost: $256K-416K
Franchise fee: $25K
Royalty fee: 5%
Term of agreement: 10 years renewable
    for $25K
Franchisees required to buy multiple
    units? No

FINANCING
In-house: None
3rd-party: Accounts receivable,
    equipment, franchise fee,
    inventory, payroll, startup costs

QUALIFICATIONS
Net worth: $500K
Cash liquidity: $150K
Experience:
    General business experience

TRAINING
At headquarters: 8 days
At franchisee's location: 4 days

BUSINESS SUPPORT
Grand opening
Internet
Meetings
Field operations/evaluations
Security/safety procedures

MARKETING SUPPORT
Co-op advertising
Ad slicks

THE PARTY IMAGE

Current financial data not available

109 E. Main St.
Round Rock, TX 78664
(512)218-9390
www.thepartyimage.com
Pampering spa parties for girls 17
    & under
Began: 2005, Franchising: 2006
Headquarters size: 4 employees
Franchise department: 2 employees

U.S. franchises: 0
Canadian franchises: 0
Other foreign franchises: 0
Company-owned: 1

Seeking: All U.S.
Seeking in Canada? No
Exclusive territories? Yes
Homebased option? No
Employees needed to run biz: 8-10
Absentee ownership? No

COSTS
Total cost: $46K-80K
Franchise fee: $20K
Royalty fee: 6%
Term of agreement: 5 years renewable
    for $1K
Franchisees required to buy multiple
    units? No

FINANCING
In-house: None
3rd-party: Equipment, franchise fee,
    inventory, startup costs

QUALIFICATIONS
Net worth: $150K
Cash liquidity: $50K
Experience:
    General business experience
    Must love children

TRAINING
At headquarters: 4 days

BUSINESS SUPPORT
Grand opening
Internet
Newsletter
Meetings
Purchasing cooperatives

MARKETING SUPPORT
Co-op advertising
Ad slicks

PUMP IT UP

Ranked #395 in Entrepreneur Magazine's 2007 Franchise 500　　　　　*Financial rating: 0*

1249 Quarry Ln., #150
Pleasanton, CA 94566
(866)325-9663
www.pumpitupparty.com
Children's party facility
Began: 2000, Franchising: 2001
Headquarters size: 40 employees

U.S. franchises: 136
Canadian franchises: 0
Other foreign franchises: 0
Company-owned: 0

Seeking: Midwest, Northeast,
　　Southeast
Seeking in Canada? No
Exclusive territories? Yes
Homebased option? No
Employees needed to run biz: 20
Absentee ownership? Yes

COSTS
Total cost: $254K-708K
Franchise fee: $30K-35K
Royalty fee: 6%
Term of agreement: 10 years
Franchisees required to buy multiple
　　units? No

FINANCING
In-house: None
3rd-party: Equipment, startup costs

QUALIFICATIONS
Net worth: $500K
Cash liquidity: $80K

TRAINING
At headquarters: 3 days
At franchisee's location: 2-4 days

BUSINESS SUPPORT
Grand opening
Newsletter
Meetings
Toll-free phone line
Field operations/evaluations
Purchasing cooperatives
Security/safety procedures

MARKETING SUPPORT
Co-op advertising
Ad slicks
National marketing council
Multimedia advertising
Marketing collateral & guidance
PR
Franchisee intranet

CHILDREN'S　　　*Tech Learning*

BITS, BYTES & BOTS COMPUTER ADVENTURES

Current financial data not available

637-B S. Broadway, #248
Boulder, CO 80305
(888)494-2687
www.bitsbytesbots.com
Computer camps & enrichment
　　programs for kids
Began: 2002, Franchising: 2006
Headquarters size: 4 employees
Franchise department: 4 employees

U.S. franchises: 1
Canadian franchises: 0
Other foreign franchises: 0
Company-owned: 1

Seeking: All U.S.
Seeking in Canada? No
Exclusive territories? Yes
Homebased option? Yes
Employees needed to run biz: 1-5
Absentee ownership? No

COSTS
Total cost: $54K-113K
Franchise fee: $25K
Royalty fee: 6%
Term of agreement: 10 years renewable
　　for 25% of initial fee
Franchisees required to buy multiple
　　units? No

FINANCING
No financing available

QUALIFICATIONS
Net worth: $60K
Cash liquidity: $40K
Experience:
　　Computer background

TRAINING
At headquarters: 2 weeks

BUSINESS SUPPORT
Internet
Meetings
Toll-free phone line

MARKETING SUPPORT
Ad slicks
Franchisee web page

COMPUCHILD

Ranked #404 in Entrepreneur Magazine's 2007 Franchise 500　　　　*Financial rating: $$$*

405 Madison St.
Rochester, IN 46975
(800)619-5437
www.compuchild.com
Preschool computer education
Began: 1994, Franchising: 2001
Headquarters size: 2 employees
Franchise department: 2 employees

U.S. franchises: 56
Canadian franchises: 0
Other foreign franchises: 0
Company-owned: 1

Seeking: All U.S.
Seeking in Canada? Yes
Exclusive territories? Yes
Homebased option? Yes
Employees needed to run biz: 1
Absentee ownership? Yes

COSTS
Total cost: $16.3K-17.4K
Franchise fee: $14.9K
Royalty fee: $150/mo.
Term of agreement: 5 years renewable
　　at no charge
Franchisees required to buy multiple
　　units? No

FINANCING
No financing available

QUALIFICATIONS
Net worth: $50K
Cash liquidity: $16.3K-17.4K
Experience:
　　General business experience
　　Marketing skills

TRAINING
At headquarters: Varies
At franchisee's location: 3 days
Annual national meeting: 3 days

BUSINESS SUPPORT
Internet
Newsletter
Meetings
Toll-free phone line

MARKETING SUPPORT
National media campaign

COMPUTERTOTS/COMPUTER EXPLORERS

Ranked #315 in Entrepreneur Magazine's 2007 Franchise 500　　　　*Financial rating: $$$$*

12715 Telge Rd.
Cypress, TX 77429
(888)638-8722/(281)256-4100
www.computertots.com
Tech training for schools, kids &
　　adults
Began: 1983, Franchising: 1988
Headquarters size: Info not provided

U.S. franchises: 96
Canadian franchises: 1
Other foreign franchises: 7
Company-owned: 0

Seeking: All U.S.
Seeking in Canada? Yes
Exclusive territories? Yes
Homebased option? Yes
Employees needed to run biz: 6
Absentee ownership? No

COSTS
Total cost: $56.9K-65.3K
Franchise fee: $35K
Royalty fee: 8%
Term of agreement: 15 years renewable
　　for 5% of franchise fee
Franchisees required to buy multiple
　　units? Outside the U.S. only

FINANCING
No financing available

QUALIFICATIONS
Cash liquidity: $40K
Experience:
　　General business experience
　　Marketing skills

TRAINING
At headquarters: 10 days
At franchisee's location: 2 days

BUSINESS SUPPORT
Internet
Newsletter
Meetings
Toll-free phone line
Security/safety procedures

MARKETING SUPPORT
National media campaign
Regional marketing
Direct-mail campaign

PC KIDZ

Financial rating: $$$

P.O. Box 133002
Tyler, TX 75713
(888)311-5259
www.pckidzusa.com
Children's computer education
Began: 2001, Franchising: 2005
Headquarters size: 4 employees
Franchise department: 4 employees

U.S. franchises: 10
Canadian franchises: 0
Other foreign franchises: 0
Company-owned: 4

Seeking: All U.S.
Seeking in Canada? No
Exclusive territories? Yes
Homebased option? Yes
Employees needed to run biz: 1-30
Absentee ownership? No

COSTS
Total cost: $19.8K-91.3K
Franchise fee: $15K-45K
Royalty fee: 7%
Term of agreement: 10 years renewable
    at no charge
Franchisees required to buy multiple
    units? No

FINANCING
No financing available

QUALIFICATIONS
Net worth: $150K
Cash liquidity: $40K
Experience:
    General business experience
    Marketing skills

TRAINING
At headquarters: 4 days
At franchisee's location: 3 days

BUSINESS SUPPORT
Grand opening
Internet
Newsletter
Meetings
Toll-free phone line
Field operations/evaluations
Purchasing cooperatives
Security/safety procedures

MARKETING SUPPORT
Co-op advertising
Ad slicks
Regional marketing

CHILDREN'S ▶ *Miscellaneous*

CHILDREN'S ORCHARD

Current financial data not available

900 Victors Wy., #200
Ann Arbor, MI 48108
(800)999-5437
www.childrensorchard.com
Children's products resale stores
Began: 1980, Franchising: 1985
Headquarters size: 13 employees
Franchise department: 3 employees

U.S. franchises: 94
Canadian franchises: 0
Other foreign franchises: 0
Company-owned: 1

Seeking: All U.S.
Seeking in Canada? No
Exclusive territories? Yes
Homebased option? No
Employees needed to run biz: 3-6
Absentee ownership? No

COSTS
Total cost: $115.6K-197K
Franchise fee: $25K
Royalty fee: 5%
Term of agreement: 10 years renewable
Franchisees required to buy multiple
    units? No

FINANCING
No financing available

QUALIFICATIONS
Net worth: $225K
Cash liquidity: $40K
Experience:
    Customer service background

TRAINING
At headquarters: 12 days
At franchisee's location: 3 days

BUSINESS SUPPORT
Grand opening
Internet
Newsletter
Meetings
Toll-free phone line
Field operations/evaluations
Lease negotiations
Purchasing cooperatives
Security/safety procedures

MARKETING SUPPORT
Co-op advertising
Ad slicks
Regional marketing
Monthly promotions

EDUCATIONAL OUTFITTERS

Ranked #397 in Entrepreneur Magazine's 2007 Franchise 500   *Financial rating: $$$*

8002 E. Brainerd Rd.
Chattanooga, TN 37421
(877)814-1222/(423)499-5052
www.educationaloutfitters.com
School uniforms
Began: 1998, Franchising: 2001
Headquarters size: 7 employees
Franchise department: 2 employees

U.S. franchises: 27
Canadian franchises: 0
Other foreign franchises: 0
Company-owned: 0

Seeking: All U.S.
Seeking in Canada? No
Exclusive territories? Yes
Homebased option? No
Employees needed to run biz: 2
Absentee ownership? No

COSTS
Total cost: $90.6K-194.7K
Franchise fee: $29.5K
Royalty fee: 5%
Term of agreement: 10 years renewable
    at no charge
Franchisees required to buy multiple
    units? No

FINANCING
No financing available

QUALIFICATIONS
Net worth: $400K
Cash liquidity: $150K
Experience:
    General business experience
    Marketing skills

TRAINING
At headquarters: 1 week
At franchisee's location: 1 week

BUSINESS SUPPORT
Grand opening
Internet
Newsletter
Meetings
Toll-free phone line
Field operations/evaluations
Lease negotiations
Purchasing cooperatives
Security/safety procedures

MARKETING SUPPORT
Co-op advertising
Ad slicks
National media campaign
Regional marketing

KID TO KID

Ranked #342 in Entrepreneur Magazine's 2007 Franchise 500   *Financial rating: $$$$*

452 E. 500 South
Salt Lake City, UT 84111
(888)543-2543/(801)359-0071
www.kidtokid.com
New & used kid's/maternity
    clothing & products
Began: 1992, Franchising: 1994
Headquarters size: 8 employees
Franchise department: 2 employees

U.S. franchises: 48
Canadian franchises: 0
Other foreign franchises: 2
Company-owned: 2

Seeking: All U.S.
Seeking in Canada? Yes
Exclusive territories? Yes
Homebased option? No
Employees needed to run biz: 4
Absentee ownership? No

COSTS
Total cost: $126.8K-195.4K
Franchise fee: $25K
Royalty fee: 5%
Term of agreement: 10 years renewable
    for 25% of franchise fee
Franchisees required to buy multiple
    units? Outside the U.S. only

FINANCING
In-house: None
3rd-party: Accounts receivable,
    equipment, franchise fee,
    inventory, payroll, startup costs

QUALIFICATIONS
Net worth: $150K
Cash liquidity: $40K-50K
Experience:
    General business experience
    Knowledge of children's
    products helpful

TRAINING
At headquarters: 11 days
At franchisee's location: 3 days
At existing location: 5 days

BUSINESS SUPPORT
Grand opening
Internet
Newsletter
Meetings
Toll-free phone line
Field operations/evaluations
Lease negotiations
Purchasing cooperatives
Security/safety procedures

MARKETING SUPPORT
Co-op advertising
Ad slicks
Regional marketing
Customized marketing materials

LEARNING EXPRESS

Current financial data not available

29 Buena Vista St.
Ayer, MA 01432
(978)889-1000
www.learningexpress.com
Specialty toy store
Began: 1987, Franchising: 1987
Headquarters size: 21 employees
Franchise department: 17 employees

U.S. franchises: 119
Canadian franchises: 0
Other foreign franchises: 0
Company-owned: 0

Seeking: All U.S.
Seeking in Canada? No
Exclusive territories? Yes
Homebased option? No
Employees needed to run biz: 10
Absentee ownership? Yes

COSTS
Total cost: $170K-280K
Franchise fee: $30K
Royalty fee: 5%
Term of agreement: 10 years renewable
    at no charge
Franchisees required to buy multiple
    units? No

FINANCING
No financing available

QUALIFICATIONS
Net worth: 50% of investment
Cash liquidity: 50% of investment
Experience:
    General business experience
    Marketing skills
    People skills

TRAINING
At headquarters
At franchisee's location
At certified training center

BUSINESS SUPPORT
Grand opening
Internet
Newsletter
Meetings
Toll-free phone line
Field operations/evaluations
Lease negotiations

MARKETING SUPPORT
Ad slicks
Catalogs
Signage
Email campaigns

USA BABY

Financial rating: $$

793 Springer Dr.
Lombard, IL 60148
(630)652-0600
www.usababy.com
Baby/children's furniture &
    accessories
Began: 1975, Franchising: 1986
Headquarters size: 19 employees
Franchise department: 2 employees

U.S. franchises: 57
Canadian franchises: 0
Other foreign franchises: 1
Company-owned: 0

Seeking: All U.S.
Seeking in Canada? Yes
Exclusive territories? Yes
Homebased option? No
Employees needed to run biz: 8
Absentee ownership? No

COSTS
Total cost: $370.9K-688.7K
Franchise fee: $23.4K-60.2K
Royalty fee: 3%
Term of agreement: 10 years renewable
    at no charge
Franchisees required to buy multiple
    units? No

FINANCING
In-house: None
3rd-party: Equipment, franchise fee,
    inventory, startup costs

QUALIFICATIONS
Net worth: $175K
Cash liquidity: $145K
Experience:
    General business experience

TRAINING
At headquarters: 5 days
At franchisee's location: 14 days

BUSINESS SUPPORT
Grand opening
Internet
Newsletter
Meetings
Toll-free phone line
Field operations/evaluations
Lease negotiations
Purchasing cooperatives
Security/safety procedures

MARKETING SUPPORT
Ad slicks
Regional marketing
Direct mail

CHILDREN'S — *Other Franchises*

ANDY'S PARTIES
422 Main St., #100
Gaithersburg, MD 20878
(301)309-2386
www.andysparties.com
Children's parties & events
Current financial data not available

BABY BOOT CAMP
5053 Ocean Blvd.
Sarasota, FL 34242
(888)990-2229/(941)924-1000
www.babybootcamp.com
Pre & postnatal fitness
Financial rating: $$

KIDDIE ACADEMY CHILD CARE LEARNING CENTERS
Ranked #232 in Entrepreneur Magazine's 2007 Franchise 500
108 Wheel Rd.
Bel Air, MD 21015
(800)554-3343
www.kiddieacademy.com
Child-care learning center
Financial rating: $$$$

LITTLE SCOOPS
25 Smith St., #314
Nanuet, NY 10954
(877)572-6677
www.littlescoops.com
Retro '50s-style ice cream party
Financial rating: $

THE MAD SCIENCE GROUP
Ranked #272 in Entrepreneur Magazine's 2007 Franchise 500
8360 Bougainville St., #201
Montreal, PQ H4P 2G1 Canada
(800)586-5231
www.madscience.org
Science activities for children
Financial rating: $$$

ONCE UPON A CHILD
Ranked #362 in Entrepreneur Magazine's 2007 Franchise 500
4200 Dahlberg Dr., #100
Minneapolis, MN 55422-4837
(800)453-7750/(763)520-8490
www.ouac.com
New & used children's clothing,
    equipment, furniture, toys
Financial rating: $$$$

OOGLES N GOOGLES
9640 N. Augusta Dr., #435
Carmel, IN 46032
(317)228-9177
www.ooglesngoogles.com
Birthday parties & preschool
    enrichment programs
Current financial data not available

PARISI SPEED SCHOOL
291 Franklin Ave.
Wyckoff, NJ 07481
(201)847-1938
www.parisischool.com
Youth performance training
Current financial data not available

TUTOR TIME FRANCHISE LLC
21333 Haggerty Rd., #300
Novi, MI 48375
(800)275-1235
www.tutortimefranchise.com
Child-care learning center
Current financial data not available

UC MAS
130 Main Rd.
Huntsville, AL 35811
(888)826-2701
www.ucmasusa.com
Educational programs for children
Current financial data not available

WEBBY DANCE COMPANY
6975B Dixie Hwy.
Fairfield, OH 45014
(513)942-0100
www.webbydancecompany.com
Children's dance classes
Current financial data not available

FINANCIAL *Business Services*

ALLIANCE COST CONTAINMENT LLC

Financial rating: $$

222 S. First St., #301
Louisville, KY 40202
(502)635-3208
www.costcontain.com
Expense-reduction consulting
　　services
Began: 1992, Franchising: 2004
Headquarters size: Info not provided

U.S. franchises: 13
Canadian franchises: 0
Other foreign franchises: 0
Company-owned: 0

Seeking: All U.S.
Seeking in Canada? No
Exclusive territories? Yes
Homebased option? Yes
Employees needed to run biz: 0
Absentee ownership? Yes

COSTS
Total cost: $38.5K-54K
Franchise fee: $29.9K
Royalty fee: 9%
Term of agreement: 5 years renewable
　　for 10% of franchise fee
Franchisees required to buy multiple
　　units? No

FINANCING
No financing available

QUALIFICATIONS
Cash liquidity: $45K
Experience:
　　Industry experience
　　General business experience
　　Marketing skills
　　Executive presentation skills
　　Basic computer skills

TRAINING
At headquarters: 3-4 days
At annual conference: 3 days

BUSINESS SUPPORT
Internet
Newsletter
Meetings
Toll-free phone line
Purchasing cooperatives

MARKETING SUPPORT
Ad slicks

COMMISSION EXPRESS

Financial rating: 0

8306 Professional Hill Dr.
Fairfax, VA 22031
(703)560-5500
www.commissionexpress.com
Real estate commission factoring
Began: 1992, Franchising: 1996
Headquarters size: 4 employees
Franchise department: 3 employees

U.S. franchises: 69
Canadian franchises: 0
Other foreign franchises: 0
Company-owned: 1

Seeking: All U.S.
Seeking in Canada? Yes
Exclusive territories? Yes
Homebased option? No
Employees needed to run biz: 1
Absentee ownership? No

COSTS
Total cost: $89.3K-193.5K
Franchise fee: $15K-60K
Royalty fee: Varies
Term of agreement: 10 years renewable
    for $750-3K
Franchisees required to buy multiple
    units? No

FINANCING
No financing available

QUALIFICATIONS
Cash liquidity: $88.3K-182.5K
Experience:
    General business experience
    Real estate & law background

TRAINING
At headquarters: 1 week
At franchisee's location: 1 week
Annual conference: 3 days

BUSINESS SUPPORT
Internet
Newsletter
Meetings
Toll-free phone line
Field operations/evaluations
Purchasing cooperatives

MARKETING SUPPORT
Co-op advertising
Ad slicks
National media campaign
Regional marketing
Trade shows

EXPENSE REDUCTION ANALYSTS INC.

Financial rating: $$$

5050 Avenida Encinas, #200
Carlsbad, CA 92008
(760)712-3600
www.era-usa.com
Cost management consulting
Began: 1992, Franchising: 1992
Headquarters size: 12 employees
Franchise department: 12 employees

U.S. franchises: 50
Canadian franchises: 39
Other foreign franchises: 312
Company-owned: 0

Seeking: All U.S.
Seeking in Canada? Yes
Exclusive territories? No
Homebased option? Yes
Employees needed to run biz: Info
    not provided
Absentee ownership? No

COSTS
Total cost: $54.1K-69.3K
Franchise fee: $49.9K
Royalty fee: 15%
Term of agreement: 10 years renewable
    for $5K
Franchisees required to buy multiple
    units? No

FINANCING
No financing available

QUALIFICATIONS
Net worth: $150K
Cash liquidity: $54K-70K
Experience:
    General business experience

TRAINING
At headquarters
At franchisee's location

BUSINESS SUPPORT
Internet
Newsletter
Meetings
Toll-free phone line
Field operations/evaluations

MARKETING SUPPORT
Co-op advertising
Ad slicks
Regional marketing
Direct marketing

EXPENSE REDUCTION CONSULTING

Financial rating: $$$

6920 Annapolis Ct.
Parkland, FL 33067
(954)255-2511
www.ercfranchise.com
Corporate cost-reduction services
Began: 1993, Franchising: 2005
Headquarters size: 5 employees
Franchise department: 3 employees

U.S. franchises: 7
Canadian franchises: 0
Other foreign franchises: 0
Company-owned: 0

Seeking: All U.S.
Seeking in Canada? No
Exclusive territories? No
Homebased option? Yes
Employees needed to run biz: 1
Absentee ownership? Yes

COSTS
Total cost: $33K-45K
Franchise fee: $29.9K
Royalty fee: 7%
Term of agreement: 7 years
    renewable
Franchisees required to buy multiple
    units? No

FINANCING
No financing available

QUALIFICATIONS
Cash liquidity: $35K
Experience:
    General business experience
    Marketing skills
    Negotiation skills

TRAINING
At headquarters: 5 days
Sales training program: 1 year

BUSINESS SUPPORT
Internet
Newsletter
Meetings
Toll-free phone line
Purchasing cooperatives

MARKETING SUPPORT
Info not provided

INTERFACE FINANCIAL CORP.

Ranked #340 in Entrepreneur Magazine's 2007 Franchise 500   *Financial rating: $$$*

2182 Dupont Dr., #221
Irvine, CA 92612-1320
(800)387-0860
www.interfacefinancial.com
Invoice discounting
Began: 1971, Franchising: 1991
Headquarters size: 7 employees
Franchise department: 5 employees

U.S. franchises: 104
Canadian franchises: 25
Other foreign franchises: 8
Company-owned: 2

Seeking: All U.S.
Seeking in Canada? Yes
Exclusive territories? No
Homebased option? Yes
Employees needed to run biz: 0
Absentee ownership? No

COSTS
Total cost: $82.7K-133.8K
Franchise fee: $36K
Royalty fee: 8%
Term of agreement: 10 years renewable
    at no charge
Franchisees required to buy multiple
    units? Outside the U.S. only

FINANCING
No financing available

QUALIFICATIONS
Net worth: $250K
Cash liquidity: $75K
Experience:
    General business experience

TRAINING
At headquarters: 2 days
At franchisee's location: 3-5 days
Ongoing

BUSINESS SUPPORT
Internet
Newsletter
Meetings
Toll-free phone line
Field operations/evaluations

MARKETING SUPPORT
Co-op advertising
Ad slicks
National media campaign
Telemarketing

PADGETT BUSINESS SERVICES

Ranked #155 in Entrepreneur Magazine's 2007 Franchise 500   *Financial rating: $$$*

160 Hawthorne Pk.
Athens, GA 30606
(800)723-4388/(706)548-1040
www.smallbizpros.com
Financial, payroll, consulting &
    tax services
Began: 1965, Franchising: 1975
Headquarters size: 25 employees
Franchise department: 4 employees

U.S. franchises: 273
Canadian franchises: 106
Other foreign franchises: 0
Company-owned: 0

Seeking: All U.S.
Seeking in Canada? Yes
Exclusive territories? No
Homebased option? Yes
Employees needed to run biz: 1
Absentee ownership? No

COSTS
Total cost: $75K-80K
Franchise fee: $27.5K
Royalty fee: 4.5-9%
Term of agreement: 10 years renewable
    at no charge
Franchisees required to buy multiple
    units? No

FINANCING
In-house: None
3rd-party: Equipment, franchise fee,
    startup costs

QUALIFICATIONS
Net worth: $50K
Cash liquidity: $20K
Experience:
    Industry experience
    General business experience
    Marketing skills

TRAINING
At headquarters: 10 days
At franchisee's location: 6 days
Annual marketing convention &
    tax seminar

BUSINESS SUPPORT
Internet
Newsletter
Meetings
Toll-free phone line
Purchasing cooperatives

MARKETING SUPPORT
Ad slicks
Marketing materials

FINANCIAL ▶ *Check Cashing*

ACE AMERICA'S CASH EXPRESS

Ranked #66 in Entrepreneur Magazine's 2007 Franchise 500   *Financial rating: $$$$*

1231 Greenway Dr., #600
Irving, TX 75038
(800)713-3338
www.acecashexpress.com
Check cashing & related financial
    services
Began: 1968, Franchising: 1996
Headquarters size: 2,100 employees
Franchise department: 10 employees

U.S. franchises: 220
Canadian franchises: 0
Other foreign franchises: 0
Company-owned: 1,353

Seeking: All U.S.
Seeking in Canada? No
Exclusive territories? Yes
Homebased option? No
Employees needed to run biz: 2
Absentee ownership? Yes

COSTS
Total cost: $141.6K-282.95K
Franchise fee: $15K-30K
Royalty fee: 6%
Term of agreement: 10 years renewable
    for $500
Franchisees required to buy multiple
    units? No

FINANCING
In-house: None
3rd-party: Equipment, franchise fee,
    inventory, startup costs

QUALIFICATIONS
Net worth: $250K
Cash liquidity: $80K
Experience:
    General business experience

TRAINING
At headquarters: 2 weeks
At franchisee's location: 5 days

BUSINESS SUPPORT
Grand opening
Internet
Newsletter
Meetings
Toll-free phone line
Field operations/evaluations
Purchasing cooperatives
Security/safety procedures

MARKETING SUPPORT
Co-op advertising
Ad slicks

CASH PLUS INC.

Ranked #325 in Entrepreneur Magazine's 2007 Franchise 500   *Financial rating: $$$*

3002 Dow Ave., #120
Tustin, CA 92780
(888)707-2274/(714)731-2274
www.cashplusinc.com
Check cashing & related services
Began: 1985, Franchising: 1988
Headquarters size: 13 employees
Franchise department: 8 employees

U.S. franchises: 80
Canadian franchises: 1
Other foreign franchises: 0
Company-owned: 2

Seeking: Midwest, Southeast,
    Southwest, West
Seeking in Canada? No
Exclusive territories? Yes
Homebased option? No
Employees needed to run biz: 3
Absentee ownership? Yes

COSTS
Total cost: $160.2K-244.2K
Franchise fee: $35K
Royalty fee: 5-6%
Term of agreement: 10 years renewable
    for $5K
Franchisees required to buy multiple
    units? No

FINANCING
In-house: None
3rd-party: Accounts receivable,
    equipment, inventory, startup
    costs, working capital

QUALIFICATIONS
Net worth: $300K
Cash liquidity: $100K
Experience:
    General business experience
    People skills

TRAINING
At headquarters: 1 week
At franchisee's location: 1 week
Additional ongoing training:
    90 days

BUSINESS SUPPORT
Grand opening
Internet
Newsletter
Meetings
Toll-free phone line
Field operations/evaluations
Lease negotiations
Purchasing cooperatives
Security/safety procedures

MARKETING SUPPORT
Co-op advertising
Ad slicks
National media campaign
National sweepstakes

UNITED FINANCIAL SERVICES GROUP

Current financial data not available

325 Chestnut St., #3000
Philadelphia, PA 19106
(800)626-0787
www.unitedfsg.com
Financial services
Began: 1977, Franchising: 1991
Headquarters size: 20 employees
Franchise department: 4 employees

U.S. franchises: 152
Canadian franchises: 0
Other foreign franchises: 0
Company-owned: 0

Seeking: All U.S.
Seeking in Canada? No
Exclusive territories? Yes
Homebased option? No
Employees needed to run biz: 3
Absentee ownership? Yes

COSTS
Total cost: $203.5K-269.5K
Franchise fee: $30K
Royalty fee: 0.2%
Term of agreement: 15 years renewable
    for 25% of then-current fee
Franchisees required to buy multiple
    units? No

FINANCING
In-house: None
3rd-party: Accounts receivable,
    equipment, franchise fee,
    inventory, leasehold
    improvements, startup costs

QUALIFICATIONS
Net worth: $400K
Cash liquidity: $80K
Experience:
    General business experience
    Marketing skills

TRAINING
At headquarters: 2 weeks
At franchisee's location: 1 week

BUSINESS SUPPORT
Grand opening
Internet
Newsletter
Meetings
Toll-free phone line
Field operations/evaluations
Lease negotiations
Security/safety procedures

MARKETING SUPPORT
Co-op advertising
Ad slicks
Regional marketing

EXPRESSTAX

Ranked #318 in Entrepreneur Magazine's 2007 Franchise 500   *Financial rating: $$$$*

3030 Hartley Rd., #320
Jacksonville, FL 32257
(888)417-4461
www.expresstaxservice.com
Tax preparation & electronic filing
Began: 1997, Franchising: 2002
Headquarters size: 13 employees
Franchise department: 5 employees

U.S. franchises: 221
Canadian franchises: 0
Other foreign franchises: 0
Company-owned: 0

Seeking: All U.S.
Seeking in Canada? No
Exclusive territories? Yes
Homebased option? No
Employees needed to run biz: 2
Absentee ownership? No

COSTS
Total cost: $12.4K-19.1K
Franchise fee: $7.5K
Royalty fee: $12/return
Term of agreement: 10 years renewable
    for $1K
Franchisees required to buy multiple
    units? No

FINANCING
In-house: Franchise fee
3rd-party: None

QUALIFICATIONS
Cash liquidity: $9.9K-16.6K
Experience:
    General business experience
    Marketing skills

TRAINING
At headquarters: 3 days
Annual conference: 2 days

BUSINESS SUPPORT
Internet
Newsletter
Meetings
Toll-free phone line

MARKETING SUPPORT
Co-op advertising
Ad slicks
Regional marketing

INSTANT TAX SERVICE

Ranked #201 in Entrepreneur Magazine's 2007 Franchise 500   *Financial rating: $$$$*

1 S. Main St., #1430
Dayton, OH 45402
(937)425-6900
www.instanttaxservice.com
Retail tax preparation & electronic
    filing
Began: 2000, Franchising: 2004
Headquarters size: 30 employees
Franchise department: 30 employees

U.S. franchises: 527
Canadian franchises: 0
Other foreign franchises: 0
Company-owned: 66

Seeking: All U.S.
Seeking in Canada? No
Exclusive territories? Yes
Homebased option? No
Employees needed to run biz: 3
Absentee ownership? Yes

COSTS
Total cost: $41.6K-84.4K
Franchise fee: $25K-30K
Royalty fee: 14%
Term of agreement: 5 years renewable
    for 10% of franchise fee
Franchisees required to buy multiple
    units? No

FINANCING
In-house: Franchise fee
3rd-party: Accounts receivable,
    equipment, franchise fee,
    inventory, payroll, startup costs

QUALIFICATIONS
Net worth: $10K
Cash liquidity: $10K
Experience:
    General business experience

TRAINING
At headquarters: 5-1/2 days

BUSINESS SUPPORT
Grand opening
Internet
Newsletter
Meetings
Toll-free phone line
Field operations/evaluations
Purchasing cooperatives

MARKETING SUPPORT
Co-op advertising
Ad slicks
Regional marketing

JACKSON HEWITT TAX SERVICE

Ranked #3 in Entrepreneur Magazine's 2007 Franchise 500   *Financial rating: $$$$*

3 Sylvan Wy.
Parsippany, NJ 07054
(800)475-2904
www.jacksonhewitt.com
Tax preparation services
Began: 1960, Franchising: 1986
Headquarters size: 370 employees
Franchise department: 31 employees

U.S. franchises: 5,379
Canadian franchises: 0
Other foreign franchises: 0
Company-owned: 643

Seeking: All U.S.
Seeking in Canada? No
Exclusive territories? Yes
Homebased option? No
Employees needed to run biz: Info
   not provided
Absentee ownership? Yes

COSTS
Total cost: $48.6K-91.8K
Franchise fee: to $25K
Royalty fee: 15%
Term of agreement: 10 years renewable
   at no charge
Franchisees required to buy multiple
   units? No

FINANCING
In-house: Franchise fee
3rd-party: None

QUALIFICATIONS
Cash liquidity: $50K
Experience:
   General business experience

TRAINING
At headquarters: 5 days
Regional training: 2 days

BUSINESS SUPPORT
Grand opening
Internet
Newsletter
Meetings
Toll-free phone line
Field operations/evaluations
Purchasing cooperatives
Security/safety procedures

MARKETING SUPPORT
Co-op advertising
Ad slicks
National media campaign
Regional marketing
Website

LIBERTY TAX SERVICE

Ranked #17 in Entrepreneur Magazine's 2007 Franchise 500   *Financial rating: $$$$*

1716 Corporate Landing
Virginia Beach, VA 23454
(800)790-3863/(757)493-8855
www.libertytaxfranchise.com
Income-tax preparation services
Began: 1972, Franchising: 1973
Headquarters size: 250 employees
Franchise department: 15 employees

U.S. franchises: 1,727
Canadian franchises: 275
Other foreign franchises: 0
Company-owned: 42

Seeking: All U.S.
Seeking in Canada? Yes
Exclusive territories? Yes
Homebased option? No
Employees needed to run biz: 5-10
Absentee ownership? Yes

COSTS
Total cost: $33.4K-59.9K
Franchise fee: $15K-30K
Royalty fee: Varies
Term of agreement: Perpetual
Franchisees required to buy multiple
   units? No

FINANCING
In-house: Equipment, franchise fee,
   startupcosts, payroll
3rd-party: Equipment, payroll,
   startup costs

QUALIFICATIONS
Cash liquidity: $50K
Experience:
   General business experience
   Marketing skills
   Customer service experience

TRAINING
At headquarters: 1 week
At franchisee's location: 1 day
Additional 2-day training in various
   cities

BUSINESS SUPPORT
Grand opening
Internet
Newsletter
Meetings
Toll-free phone line
Field operations/evaluations
Purchasing cooperatives

MARKETING SUPPORT
Ad slicks
Regional marketing
Local marketing plans

TAX CENTERS OF AMERICA

Ranked #333 in Entrepreneur Magazine's 2007 Franchise 500   *Financial rating: $$$*

1611 E. Main
Russellville, AR 72801
(479)968-4796
www.tcoa.net
Tax preparation & electronic filing
Began: 1994, Franchising: 1997
Headquarters size: 15 employees
Franchise department: 3 employees

U.S. franchises: 104
Canadian franchises: 0
Other foreign franchises: 0
Company-owned: 2

Seeking: All U.S.
Seeking in Canada? No
Exclusive territories? Yes
Homebased option? No
Employees needed to run biz: 2
Absentee ownership? Yes

COSTS
Total cost: $29.99K-45.9K
Franchise fee: $20K
Royalty fee: Varies
Term of agreement: 10 years renewable
    for $1K
Franchisees required to buy multiple
    units? No

FINANCING
In-house: None
3rd-party: Equipment, franchise fee,
    payroll, startup costs

QUALIFICATIONS
Cash liquidity: $30K
Experience:
    General business experience

TRAINING
At headquarters: 4 days

BUSINESS SUPPORT
Internet
Newsletter
Meetings
Toll-free phone line

MARKETING SUPPORT
Ad slicks
Regional marketing
Commercial broadcast production

FINANCIAL   *Miscellaneous*

ACFN- THE ATM FRANCHISE BUSINESS

Financial rating: $

96 N. 3rd St., #600
San Jose, CA 95112
(888)794-2236
www.acfnfranchised.com
ATM machines
Began: 1986, Franchising: 2003
Headquarters size: 18 employees
Franchise department: 12 employees

U.S. franchises: 49
Canadian franchises: 0
Other foreign franchises: 0
Company-owned: 2

Seeking: All U.S.
Seeking in Canada? No
Exclusive territories? Yes
Homebased option? Yes
Employees needed to run biz: 1
Absentee ownership? Yes

COSTS
Total cost: $36K-78K
Franchise fee: $29K
Royalty fee: 0
Term of agreement: 10 years renewable
    for up to $5K
Franchisees required to buy multiple
    units? No

FINANCING
In-house: Franchise fee
3rd-party: None

QUALIFICATIONS
Cash liquidity: $29K

TRAINING
At headquarters: 3 days

BUSINESS SUPPORT
Internet
Newsletter
Meetings
Toll-free phone line
Field operations/evaluations
Lease negotiations

MARKETING SUPPORT
Co-op advertising
Ad slicks
Leads

AMERICAN PROSPERITY GROUP (APG)

Financial rating: 0

3 Sunny Knolls Ct.
Wayne, NJ 07470
(877)885-1274/(973)831-4424
www.apgfranchise.com
Retirement & estate planning
   products/services
Began: 1991, Franchising: 2006
Headquarters size: 4 employees
Franchise department: 4 employees

U.S. franchises: 3
Canadian franchises: 0
Other foreign franchises: 0
Company-owned: 1

Seeking: All U.S.
Seeking in Canada? No
Exclusive territories? No
Homebased option? No
Employees needed to run biz: Info
   not provided
Absentee ownership? Yes

COSTS
Total cost: $96K
Franchise fee: $50K
Royalty fee: Varies
Term of agreement: 15 years renewable
   at no charge
Franchisees required to buy multiple
   units? No

FINANCING
No financing available

QUALIFICATIONS
Net worth: $250K
Cash liquidity: $150K

TRAINING
At headquarters: 4 weeks
At franchisee's location: 1 week

BUSINESS SUPPORT
Grand opening
Internet
Newsletter
Meetings
Toll-free phone line
Field operations/evaluations
Security/safety procedures

MARKETING SUPPORT
Co-op advertising
Ad slicks
National media campaign

BLUE COLLAR FINANCIAL GROUP

Current financial data not available

P.O. Box 1654
Owasso, OK 74055-1654
(918)274-8260
www.bluecfg.com
Real estate buying/financing
   program
Began: 2005, Franchising: 2005
Headquarters size: 2 employees
Franchise department: 2 employees

U.S. franchises: 2
Canadian franchises: 0
Other foreign franchises: 0
Company-owned: 0

Seeking: All U.S.
Seeking in Canada? No
Exclusive territories? Yes
Homebased option? Yes
Employees needed to run biz: 1
Absentee ownership? Yes

COSTS
Total cost: $110K
Franchise fee: $50K
Royalty fee: $250/home
Term of agreement: 5 years renewable
   for $100K
Franchisees required to buy multiple
   units? No

FINANCING
No financing available

QUALIFICATIONS
Cash liquidity: $150K

TRAINING
At headquarters: Varies
At franchisee's location: Varies

BUSINESS SUPPORT
Info not provided

MARKETING SUPPORT
Info not provided

BROOKE FRANCHISE CORP.

Ranked #37 in Entrepreneur Magazine's 2007 Franchise 500   *Financial rating: $$$$*

10950 Grandview Dr., Bldg. 34, 5th Fl.
Overland Park, KS 66210
(800)642-1872
www.brookefranchise.com
Insurance & financial services
Began: 1986, Franchising: 1988
Headquarters size: 606 employees
Franchise department:
    509 employees

U.S. franchises: 639
Canadian franchises: 0
Other foreign franchises: 0
Company-owned: 5

Seeking: Midwest, South, Southeast,
    Southwest, West
Seeking in Canada? No
Exclusive territories? No
Homebased option? No
Employees needed to run biz: Info
    not provided
Absentee ownership? No

COSTS
Total cost: $165.7K-385.8K
Franchise fee: $165K
Royalty fee: 15%
Term of agreement: 5 years renewable
    at no charge
Franchisees required to buy multiple
    units? No

FINANCING
In-house: Accounts receivable,
    equipment, franchise fee,
    inventory, payroll, startup costs
3rd-party: None

QUALIFICATIONS
Experience:
    Industry experience
    General business experience

TRAINING
At headquarters: 24 hours
At franchisee's location: 30 hours

BUSINESS SUPPORT
Grand opening
Internet
Newsletter
Meetings
Toll-free phone line
Field operations/evaluations
Lease negotiations
Purchasing cooperatives
Security/safety procedures

MARKETING SUPPORT
Co-op advertising
Ad slicks
Regional marketing

NATIONAL HOME BUYERS ASSISTANCE

Current financial data not available

1 Manor House Rd.
Littleton, CO 80127
(888)888-6422/(303)703-6422
www.nhba.com
Lease-to-own home buying
    program
Began: 2001, Franchising: 2003
Headquarters size: 12 employees
Franchise department: 7 employees

U.S. franchises: 109
Canadian franchises: 0
Other foreign franchises: 0
Company-owned: 0

Seeking: All U.S.
Seeking in Canada? No
Exclusive territories? No
Homebased option? Yes
Employees needed to run biz: 1
Absentee ownership? Yes

COSTS
Total cost: $100K-200K
Franchise fee: $30K
Royalty fee: Varies
Term of agreement: 10 years renewable
    at no charge
Franchisees required to buy multiple
    units? No

FINANCING
No financing available

QUALIFICATIONS
Cash liquidity: $150K
Experience:
    General business experience
    Marketing skills

TRAINING
At headquarters: 5 days

BUSINESS SUPPORT
Internet
Newsletter
Meetings
Toll-free phone line
Field operations/evaluations
Purchasing cooperatives
Security/safety procedures

MARKETING SUPPORT
Ad slicks
National media campaign
Regional marketing

ONLINE TRADING ACADEMY

Financial rating: $$$

18004 Sky Park Cir., S., #140
Irvine, CA 92614
(949)608-6020
www.tradingacademy.com
Stock-trading instruction
Began: 1998, Franchising: 2004
Headquarters size: 11 employees
Franchise department: 3 employees

U.S. franchises: 5
Canadian franchises: 0
Other foreign franchises: 2
Company-owned: 0

Seeking: All U.S.
Seeking in Canada? Yes
Exclusive territories? Yes
Homebased option? No
Employees needed to run biz: 4
Absentee ownership? Yes

COSTS
Total cost: $200.4K-373K
Franchise fee: $65K-190K
Royalty fee: 10%
Term of agreement: 10 years renewable
for $7.5K or 10% of current fee
Franchisees required to buy multiple
units? No

FINANCING
In-house: None
3rd-party: Equipment, franchise fee,
inventory, startup costs

QUALIFICATIONS
Net worth: $250K
Cash liquidity: $100K
Experience:
General business experience
Marketing skills

TRAINING
At headquarters: 2 weeks
At franchisee's location: 1 week

BUSINESS SUPPORT
Grand opening
Internet
Newsletter
Meetings
Toll-free phone line
Field operations/evaluations
Lease negotiations

MARKETING SUPPORT
Co-op advertising
Ad slicks
National media campaign
Regional marketing

FINANCIAL ▸ *Other Franchises*

AFFIRMATIVE FRANCHISES INC.
8960 Taft St.
Pembroke Pines, FL 33024
(888)440-6875
www.fedusa.com
Insurance & financial services
Current financial data not available

CFO TODAY
401 St. Francis St.
Tallahassee, FL 32301
(888)643-1348/(850)681-1941
www.cfotoday.com
Accounting, tax & financial services
Current financial data not available

FAMILY FINANCIAL CENTERS
202 Farm Ln.
Doylestown, PA 18901
(215)230-5508
www.familyfinancialcenters.com
Check cashing & other financial
services
Financial rating: 0

MR. PAYROLL CHECK CASHING
1600 W. 7th St.
Fort Worth, TX 76102
(800)322-3250
www.cashamerica.com/mrpay.html
Check cashing & money orders
Current financial data not available

PROPERTY DAMAGE APPRAISERS
*Ranked #337 in Entrepreneur
Magazine's 2007 Franchise 500*
6100 Southwest Blvd., #200
Fort Worth, TX 76109-3964
(817)731-5555
www.pdahomeoffice.com
Auto & property appraisals for
insurance companies
Financial rating: $$$$

SAREEN & ASSOCIATES
10702 Vandor Ln.
Manassas, VA 20109
(703)366-3444
www.sareentax.com
Accounting, bookkeeping, taxes,
payroll
Financial rating: $$

WIRTH BUSINESS CREDIT
4200 Dahlberg Dr., #100
Minneapolis, MN 55422
(763)520-8500
www.wirthbusinesscredit.com
Equipment leasing & financing
Financial rating: $$$$

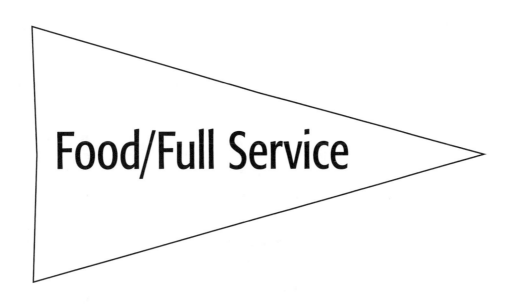

FULL SERVICE *Asian Restaurants*

BD'S MONGOLIAN BARBEQUE

Current financial data not available

642 E. Nine Mile Rd.
Ferndale, MI 48220
(248)398-2560
www.gomongo.com
Create-your-own stir fry restaurant
Began: 1992, Franchising: 1992
Headquarters size: 12 employees
Franchise department: 2 employees

U.S. franchises: 14
Canadian franchises: 0
Other foreign franchises: 1
Company-owned: 10

Seeking: Midwest
Seeking in Canada? No
Exclusive territories? Yes
Homebased option? No
Employees needed to run biz:
    75-100
Absentee ownership? Yes

COSTS
Total cost: $829K-2.9M
Franchise fee: $35K
Royalty fee: 5%
Term of agreement: 10 years renewable
    for 50% of then-current fee
Franchisees required to buy multiple
    units? Yes

FINANCING
In-house: None
3rd-party: Equipment

QUALIFICATIONS
Net worth: $2M
Cash liquidity: $500K
Experience:
    Industry experience
    General business experience
    Marketing skills

TRAINING
At headquarters: 1 week
At company-certified training
    restaurant

BUSINESS SUPPORT
Grand opening
Newsletter
Meetings
Toll-free phone line
Field operations/evaluations
Security/safety procedures

MARKETING SUPPORT
Co-op advertising
Ad slicks
National media campaign

GENGHIS GRILL

Financial rating: $$$$

4099 McEwen, #305
Dallas, TX 75244
(888)436-4447/(214)774-4240
www.genghisgrill.com
Mongolian stir-fry restaurant
Began: 1998, Franchising: 2001
Headquarters size: 7 employees
Franchise department: 2 employees

U.S. franchises: 6
Canadian franchises: 0
Other foreign franchises: 0
Company-owned: 5

Seeking: All U.S.
Seeking in Canada? No
Exclusive territories? Yes
Homebased option? No
Employees needed to run biz: 25
Absentee ownership? No

COSTS
Total cost: $289K-649K
Franchise fee: $30K
Royalty fee: 5%
Term of agreement: 10 years renewable
   at no charge
Franchisees required to buy multiple
   units? Yes

FINANCING
No financing available

QUALIFICATIONS
Net worth: $400K
Cash liquidity: $100K
Experience:
   Industry experience
   General business experience
   Marketing skills

TRAINING
At headquarters: 2 weeks
At franchisee's location: 1 week
Ongoing

BUSINESS SUPPORT
Grand opening
Internet
Newsletter
Meetings
Toll-free phone line
Field operations/evaluations
Lease negotiations
Purchasing cooperatives
Security/safety procedures

MARKETING SUPPORT
Co-op advertising
Ad slicks
National media campaign
Menu programs
Email database

ZYNG ASIAN GRILL

Current financial data not available

P.O. Box 72108 -RPO Atwater
Montreal, QC H3J 2Z6 Canada
(888)328-9964
www.zyng.com
Pan-Asian-style restaurant
Began: 1997, Franchising: 1999
Headquarters size: 4 employees
Franchise department: 4 employees

U.S. franchises: 8
Canadian franchises: 6
Other foreign franchises: 2
Company-owned: 0

Seeking: All U.S.
Seeking in Canada? Yes
Exclusive territories? Yes
Homebased option? No
Employees needed to run biz: 9
Absentee ownership? Yes

COSTS
Total cost: $212K-480K
Franchise fee: $25K
Royalty fee: 5%
Term of agreement: 10 years
Franchisees required to buy multiple
   units? Yes

FINANCING
In-house: None
3rd-party: Startup costs

QUALIFICATIONS
Net worth: $500K
Cash liquidity: $200K
Experience:
   Industry experience
   General business experience
   Marketing skills

TRAINING
At headquarters: 4 weeks
At franchisee's location: 2 weeks
Additional training available

BUSINESS SUPPORT
Grand opening
Internet
Newsletter
Meetings
Toll-free phone line
Field operations/evaluations
Purchasing cooperatives
Security/safety procedures

MARKETING SUPPORT
Co-op advertising
Ad slicks
National media campaign
Regional marketing

FULL SERVICE *Barbecue Restaurants*

BANDANA'S BAR-B-Q

Current financial data not available

15450 S. Outer Forty, #100
St. Louis, MO 63017
(636)537-8200
www.bandanasbbq.com
Barbecue restaurant
Began: 1996, Franchising: 2004
Headquarters size: 15 employees
Franchise department: 4 employees

U.S. franchises: 5
Canadian franchises: 0
Other foreign franchises: 0
Company-owned: 14

Seeking: All U.S.
Seeking in Canada? Yes
Exclusive territories? Yes
Homebased option? No
Employees needed to run biz: 40
Absentee ownership? Yes

COSTS
Total cost: $465K-1.1M
Franchise fee: $40K
Royalty fee: 5%
Term of agreement: 10 years renewable
   for 50% of current franchise fee
Franchisees required to buy multiple
   units? Yes

FINANCING
In-house: None
3rd-party: Equipment, startup costs

QUALIFICATIONS
Cash liquidity: $250K
Experience:
   Industry experience
   General business experience

TRAINING
At headquarters: 5 weeks
At franchisee's location: 10 days
Additional training as needed

BUSINESS SUPPORT
Grand opening
Internet
Newsletter
Meetings
Toll-free phone line
Field operations/evaluations
Purchasing cooperatives
Security/safety procedures

MARKETING SUPPORT
Ad slicks
Regional marketing

DICKEY'S BARBECUE PIT RESTAURANTS

Current financial data not available

4514 Cole Ave.
Dallas, TX 75205
(972)248-9899
www.dickeys.com
Texas-style barbecue restaurant
Began: 1941, Franchising: 1994
Headquarters size: 18 employees
Franchise department: 2 employees

U.S. franchises: 61
Canadian franchises: 0
Other foreign franchises: 0
Company-owned: 5

Seeking: All U.S.
Seeking in Canada? Yes
Exclusive territories? Yes
Homebased option? No
Employees needed to run biz: 15
Absentee ownership? Yes

COSTS
Total cost: $301.5K-1.5M
Franchise fee: $25K
Royalty fee: 4%
Term of agreement: 20 years renewable
   for $10K
Franchisees required to buy multiple
   units? No

FINANCING
In-house: None
3rd-party: Accounts receivable,
   equipment, franchise fee,
   inventory, payroll, startup costs

QUALIFICATIONS
Experience:
   General business experience

TRAINING
At headquarters: 3 weeks
At franchisee's location: 3 weeks

BUSINESS SUPPORT
Grand opening
Internet
Newsletter
Meetings
Toll-free phone line
Field operations/evaluations
Lease negotiations
Purchasing cooperatives
Security/safety procedures

MARKETING SUPPORT
Ad slicks
National media campaign
Regional marketing
Store marketing plan

FAMOUS DAVE'S

Ranked #177 in Entrepreneur Magazine's 2007 Franchise 500   *Financial rating: $$$$*

12701 Whitewater Dr., #200
Minnetonka, MN 55343
(952)294-1300
www.famousdaves.com
Barbecue-themed restaurant
Began: 1995, Franchising: 1998
Headquarters size: 75 employees
Franchise department: 2 employees

U.S. franchises: 97
Canadian franchises: 0
Other foreign franchises: 0
Company-owned: 41

Seeking: South, Southeast, West
Seeking in Canada? Yes
Exclusive territories? Yes
Homebased option? No
Employees needed to run biz: 65
Absentee ownership? No

COSTS
Total cost: $907K-3.6M
Franchise fee: $40K
Royalty fee: 5%
Term of agreement: 20 years renewable
for 50% of then-current fee
Franchisees required to buy multiple
units? Yes

FINANCING
In-house: None
3rd-party: Equipment, franchise fee,
inventory, startup costs

QUALIFICATIONS
Cash liquidity: $750K
Experience:
Industry experience
General business experience
Marketing skills

TRAINING
At headquarters: 35 days+
Executive/management training:
4 days

BUSINESS SUPPORT
Grand opening
Internet
Newsletter
Meetings
Toll-free phone line
Field operations/evaluations
Purchasing cooperatives
Security/safety procedures

MARKETING SUPPORT
Co-op advertising
Ad slicks
Regional marketing

MCGHIN'S SOUTHERN PIT BAR-B-QUE

Financial rating: 0

2964 N. Expressway
Griffin, GA 30223
(770)412-8222
www.southernpitbbq.com
Barbecue restaurant
Began: 1984, Franchising: 2006
Headquarters size: 25 employees
Franchise department: 4 employees

U.S. franchises: 1
Canadian franchises: 0
Other foreign franchises: 0
Company-owned: 1

Seeking: GA
Seeking in Canada? No
Exclusive territories? Yes
Homebased option? No
Employees needed to run biz: 8
Absentee ownership? No

COSTS
Total cost: $288K-800K
Franchise fee: $30K
Royalty fee: $500/wk.
Term of agreement: 15 years renewable
for 10% of then-current fee
Franchisees required to buy multiple
units? Info not provided

FINANCING
No financing available

QUALIFICATIONS
Net worth: $150K+
Cash liquidity: $280K
Experience:
General business experience
Restaurant management
experience

TRAINING
At headquarters: 3 weeks
At franchisee's location: 1 week

BUSINESS SUPPORT
Grand opening
Internet
Meetings
Toll-free phone line
Field operations/evaluations
Security/safety procedures

MARKETING SUPPORT
Ad slicks
Marketing portfolio

VIRGINIA BARBEQUE

Financial rating: $$$

1814 Country Rd.
Beaverdam, VA 23015-9567
(800)429-9965
www.virginiabbq.com
Barbecue restaurant
Began: 2000, Franchising: 2004
Headquarters size: 4 employees
Franchise department: 2 employees

U.S. franchises: 7
Canadian franchises: 0
Other foreign franchises: 0
Company-owned: 1

Seeking: Northeast, Southeast
Seeking in Canada? No
Exclusive territories? Yes
Homebased option? No
Employees needed to run biz: 6
Absentee ownership? Yes

COSTS
Total cost: $41.7K-207K
Franchise fee: $15K
Royalty fee: 6%
Term of agreement: 10 years renewable
    at no charge
Franchisees required to buy multiple
    units? No

FINANCING
In-house: None
3rd-party: Equipment, startup costs

QUALIFICATIONS
Net worth: $100K
Cash liquidity: $30K
Experience:
    Industry experience
    General business experience
    Marketing skills

TRAINING
At headquarters: 2 weeks
At franchisee's location: 1 week

BUSINESS SUPPORT
Grand opening
Internet
Meetings
Toll-free phone line
Field operations/evaluations
Security/safety procedures

MARKETING SUPPORT
Co-op advertising
National media campaign
Regional marketing

FULL SERVICE *Burger Restaurants*

JOHNNY ROCKETS GROUP INC.

Current financial data not available

25550 Commercentre Dr., #200
Lake Forest, CA 92630
(949)643-6100
www.johnnyrockets.com
1940s-style hamburger malt shop
Began: 1986, Franchising: 1987
Headquarters size: 40 employees
Franchise department: 2 employees

U.S. franchises: 123
Canadian franchises: 3
Other foreign franchises: 24
Company-owned: 51

Seeking: All U.S.
Seeking in Canada? Yes
Exclusive territories? Yes
Homebased option? No
Employees needed to run biz: Info
    not provided
Absentee ownership? No

COSTS
Total cost: $641K-920K
Franchise fee: $49K
Royalty fee: 5-7%
Term of agreement: 10 years w/two
    5-year options
Franchisees required to buy multiple
    units? Outside the U.S. only

FINANCING
No financing available

QUALIFICATIONS
Net worth: $1M+
Cash liquidity: $250K-500K
Experience:
    Industry experience

TRAINING
At headquarters

BUSINESS SUPPORT
Grand opening
Internet
Newsletter
Meetings
Toll-free phone line
Field operations/evaluations
Purchasing cooperatives
Security/safety procedures

MARKETING SUPPORT
Info not provided

STEAK N SHAKE

Ranked #298 in Entrepreneur Magazine's 2007 Franchise 500　　　*Financial rating: $$$*

36 S. Penn. St., #500
Indianapolis, IN 46204
(317)633-4100
www.steaknshake.com
Steakburgers, fries, milkshakes
Began: 1934, Franchising: 1945
Headquarters size: 160 employees
Franchise department: 6 employees

U.S. franchises: 46
Canadian franchises: 0
Other foreign franchises: 0
Company-owned: 424

Seeking: Midwest, Northeast, South,
　　Southeast, West
Seeking in Canada? No
Exclusive territories? Yes
Homebased option? No
Employees needed to run biz: 60-80
Absentee ownership? No

COSTS
Total cost: $1.3M-3.2M
Franchise fee: $40K
Royalty fee: 4%
Term of agreement: 20 years renewable
　　for 50% of initial franchise fee
Franchisees required to buy multiple
　　units? No

FINANCING
No financing available

QUALIFICATIONS
Net worth: $1.5M
Cash liquidity: $500K
Experience:
　　Industry experience

TRAINING
At franchisee's location: 1,152 hours
Manager training: 8 weeks &
　　24 weeks

BUSINESS SUPPORT
Grand opening
Meetings
Field operations/evaluations
Security/safety procedures

MARKETING SUPPORT
Ad slicks
Regional marketing

FULL SERVICE　　*Family-Style Restaurants*

DENNY'S INC.

Ranked #45 in Entrepreneur Magazine's 2007 Franchise 500　　　*Financial rating: $$$$*

203 E. Main St.
Spartanburg, SC 29319
(800)304-0222
www.dennys.com
Full-service family restaurant
Began: 1953, Franchising: 1984
Headquarters size: 350 employees
Franchise department: 12 employees

U.S. franchises: 947
Canadian franchises: 52
Other foreign franchises: 25
Company-owned: 538

Seeking: All U.S.
Seeking in Canada? Yes
Exclusive territories? No
Homebased option? No
Employees needed to run biz: 80
Absentee ownership? No

COSTS
Total cost: $1.3M-2M
Franchise fee: $40K
Royalty fee: 4%
Term of agreement: 20 years not
　　renewable
Franchisees required to buy multiple
　　units? No

FINANCING
No financing available

QUALIFICATIONS
Net worth: $1M
Cash liquidity: $350K
Experience:
　　Industry experience
　　General business experience
　　Restaurant operations experience

TRAINING
At franchisee's location: 19 days
At existing restaurants: Up to 10
　　weeks

BUSINESS SUPPORT
Newsletter
Meetings
Field operations/evaluations
Security/safety procedures

MARKETING SUPPORT
Co-op advertising
Ad slicks
National media campaign
Regional marketing

FRIENDLY'S RESTAURANTS FRANCHISE INC.

Ranked #109 in Entrepreneur Magazine's 2007 Franchise 500   *Financial rating: $$$$*

1855 Boston Rd.
Wilbraham, MA 01095
(413)731-4211
www.friendlys.com
Family-style restaurant/ice cream
Began: 1935, Franchising: 1996
Headquarters size: 263 employees
Franchise department: 12 employees

U.S. franchises: 211
Canadian franchises: 0
Other foreign franchises: 0
Company-owned: 310

Seeking: Northeast, South,
    Southeast
Seeking in Canada? No
Exclusive territories? Yes
Homebased option? No
Employees needed to run biz: Info
    not provided
Absentee ownership? No

COSTS
Total cost: $500.3K-2.1M
Franchise fee: $30K-35K
Royalty fee: 4%
Term of agreement: 20 years renewable
    for $5K
Franchisees required to buy multiple
    units? Yes

FINANCING
In-house: None
3rd-party: Equipment, inventory,
    startup costs

QUALIFICATIONS
Net worth: $1.5M
Cash liquidity: $650K
Experience:
    Industry experience

TRAINING
At headquarters: 12 weeks

BUSINESS SUPPORT
Grand opening
Internet
Newsletter
Meetings
Toll-free phone line
Field operations/evaluations
Lease negotiations
Security/safety procedures

MARKETING SUPPORT
Ad slicks
National media campaign
Grand opening campaign

GROUND ROUND I.O.C.

Financial rating: $$$

500 US Route One
Freeport, ME 04032
(207)865-4433
www.groundround.com
Casual-themed restaurant
Began: 1969, Franchising: 1970
Headquarters size: 9 employees
Franchise department: 3 employees

U.S. franchises: 57
Canadian franchises: 0
Other foreign franchises: 0
Company-owned: 0

Seeking: All U.S.
Seeking in Canada? No
Exclusive territories? Yes
Homebased option? No
Employees needed to run biz: Info
    not provided
Absentee ownership? Yes

COSTS
Total cost: $995K-1.8M
Franchise fee: $40K
Royalty fee: 3.5%
Term of agreement: 10 years renewable
Franchisees required to buy multiple
    units? No

FINANCING
No financing available

QUALIFICATIONS
Cash liquidity: $500K
Experience:
    Industry experience
    General business experience
    Marketing skills

TRAINING
At franchisee's location: Up to 14
    days

BUSINESS SUPPORT
Newsletter
Meetings
Field operations/evaluations

MARKETING SUPPORT
Co-op advertising
Ad slicks
National media campaign
Regional marketing

HUDDLE HOUSE

Ranked #369 in Entrepreneur Magazine's 2007 Franchise 500   Current financial data not available

5901-B Peachtree-Dunwoody Rd.
Atlanta, GA 30328
(800)868-5700
www.huddlehouse.com
Family-style diner
Began: 1964, Franchising: 1966
Headquarters size: 132 employees
Franchise department: 5 employees

U.S. franchises: 370
Canadian franchises: 0
Other foreign franchises: 0
Company-owned: 23

Seeking: Midwest, South, Southeast
Seeking in Canada? No
Exclusive territories? Yes
Homebased option? No
Employees needed to run biz: 24
Absentee ownership? Yes

COSTS
Total cost: $100K-850K
Franchise fee: $25K
Royalty fee: 4.8%
Term of agreement: 15 years renewable
    for 33% of then-current fee
Franchisees required to buy multiple
    units? No

FINANCING
No financing available

QUALIFICATIONS
Net worth: $250K
Cash liquidity: $150K
Experience:
    General business experience

TRAINING
At headquarters: 7 weeks

BUSINESS SUPPORT
Grand opening
Newsletter
Meetings
Toll-free phone line
Field operations/evaluations
Purchasing cooperatives
Security/safety procedures

MARKETING SUPPORT
Co-op advertising
Ad slicks
National media campaign

PERKINS RESTAURANT & BAKERY

Current financial data not available

6075 Poplar Ave., #800
Memphis, TN 38119
(800)877-7375/(901)766-6400
www.perkinsrestaurants.com
Full-service restaurant
Began: 1958, Franchising: 1958
Headquarters size: 136 employees
Franchise department: 6 employees

U.S. franchises: 306
Canadian franchises: 16
Other foreign franchises: 0
Company-owned: 155

Seeking: All U.S.
Seeking in Canada? Yes
Exclusive territories? No
Homebased option? No
Employees needed to run biz: Info
    not provided
Absentee ownership? No

COSTS
Total cost: $1.7M-3M
Franchise fee: $40K
Royalty fee: 4%
Term of agreement: 20 years renewable
    for $5K-7.5K
Franchisees required to buy multiple
    units? No

FINANCING
No financing available

QUALIFICATIONS
Net worth: $1.5M
Cash liquidity: $500K
Experience:
    Industry experience
    General business experience

TRAINING
At headquarters: 12 weeks

BUSINESS SUPPORT
Grand opening
Internet
Newsletter
Meetings
Toll-free phone line
Field operations/evaluations
Purchasing cooperatives
Security/safety procedures

MARKETING SUPPORT
Co-op advertising
Ad slicks
National media campaign
Regional marketing

FULL SERVICE *Italian Restaurants*

CICI'S PIZZA

Ranked #75 in Entrepreneur Magazine's 2007 Franchise 500   *Financial rating: $$$$*

1080 W. Bethel Rd.
Coppell, TX 75019
(972)745-4200
www.cicispizza.com
All-you-can-eat pizza buffet
Began: 1985, Franchising: 1987
Headquarters size: 76 employees
Franchise department: 2 employees

U.S. franchises: 574
Canadian franchises: 0
Other foreign franchises: 0
Company-owned: 17

Seeking: Midwest, South, Southeast,
    Southwest
Seeking in Canada? No
Exclusive territories? Yes
Homebased option? No
Employees needed to run biz: 20
Absentee ownership? No

COSTS
Total cost: $408.8K-650.8K
Franchise fee: $30K
Royalty fee: 4%
Term of agreement: 10 years
Franchisees required to buy multiple
    units? No

FINANCING
No financing available

QUALIFICATIONS
Cash liquidity: $81.8K-130.2K
Experience:
    General business experience

TRAINING
14 weeks+ training available

BUSINESS SUPPORT
Grand opening
Internet
Newsletter
Meetings
Field operations/evaluations
Security/safety procedures

MARKETING SUPPORT
Ad slicks
Regional marketing
Local media advertising

EATZA PIZZA

Current financial data not available

4800 N. Scottsdale Rd.
Scottsdale, AZ 85251
(800)596-8464
www.eatzapizza.com
Pizza restaurant
Began: 1996, Franchising: 1999
Headquarters size: 12 employees
Franchise department: 5 employees

U.S. franchises: 14
Canadian franchises: 0
Other foreign franchises: 0
Company-owned: 16

Seeking: Midwest, Northwest,
    South, Southeast, Southwest,
    West
Seeking in Canada? No
Exclusive territories? Yes
Homebased option? No
Employees needed to run biz: 20-25
Absentee ownership? Yes

COSTS
Total cost: $354.5K-552.5K
Franchise fee: $25K
Royalty fee: 5.5%
Term of agreement: 10 years renew-
    able for 33% of franchise fee
Franchisees required to buy multi-
    ple units? Outside the U.S. only

FINANCING
No financing available

QUALIFICATIONS
Net worth: $400K+
Cash liquidity: $50K+
Experience:
    Industry experience
    General business experience
    Marketing skills

TRAINING
At headquarters: 3 weeks
At franchisee's location: 1 week

BUSINESS SUPPORT
Grand opening
Internet
Newsletter
Meetings
Field operations/evaluations
Lease negotiations
Purchasing cooperatives
Security/safety procedures

MARKETING SUPPORT
Co-op advertising
Ad slicks
Regional marketing

ED & JOE'S RESTAURANT & PIZZERIA

Financial rating: 0

17332 S. Oak Park Ave.
Tinley Park, IL 60477
(708)532-3051
www.ednjoes.com
Pizzeria
Began: 1961, Franchising: 2004
Headquarters size: 50 employees
Franchise department: 6 employees

U.S. franchises: 0
Canadian franchises: 0
Other foreign franchises: 0
Company-owned: 1

Seeking: Midwest
Seeking in Canada? No
Exclusive territories? Info not
    provided
Homebased option? No
Employees needed to run biz: 50
Absentee ownership? No

COSTS
Total cost: $165K-540K
Franchise fee: $25K/45K
Royalty fee: 6%
Term of agreement: 10 years
Franchisees required to buy multiple
    units? No

FINANCING
No financing available

QUALIFICATIONS
Net worth: $150K-400K
Cash liquidity: $50K-100K

TRAINING
At headquarters: 6 weeks
At franchisee's location: 6 weeks

BUSINESS SUPPORT
Grand opening
Meetings
Field operations/evaluations
Lease negotiations
Purchasing cooperatives
Security/safety procedures

MARKETING SUPPORT
Co-op advertising

GREEN MILL RESTAURANTS

Ranked #487 in Entrepreneur Magazine's 2007 Franchise 500   *Financial rating: $$$$*

3900 Northwoods Dr., #215
Arden Hills, MN 55112
(651)203-3100
www.greenmill.com
Upscale pizza restaurant
Began: 1975, Franchising: 1991
Headquarters size: 13 employees
Franchise department: 13 employees

U.S. franchises: 33
Canadian franchises: 0
Other foreign franchises: 0
Company-owned: 0

Seeking: All U.S.
Seeking in Canada? No
Exclusive territories? Yes
Homebased option? No
Employees needed to run biz: 75
Absentee ownership? Yes

COSTS
Total cost: $1M-1.5M
Franchise fee: $45K
Royalty fee: 4%
Term of agreement: 20 years renewable
    at no charge
Franchisees required to buy multiple
    units? Yes

FINANCING
In-house: None
3rd-party: Equipment, startup costs

QUALIFICATIONS
Experience:
    Industry experience
    General business experience
    Marketing skills

TRAINING
At headquarters: 8 weeks
At franchisee's location: 2 weeks

BUSINESS SUPPORT
Grand opening
Internet
Meetings
Field operations/evaluations
Lease negotiations
Purchasing cooperatives
Security/safety procedures

MARKETING SUPPORT
Ad slicks
Regional marketing

THE ITALIAN PIE FRANCHISE LLC

Financial rating: $$

1923 Corporate Square Dr., #D
Slidell, LA 70458
(985)643-1113
www.italianpierestaurants.com
Casual Italian dining
Began: 1994, Franchising: 1995
Headquarters size: 8 employees
Franchise department: 2 employees

U.S. franchises: 24
Canadian franchises: 0
Other foreign franchises: 0
Company-owned: 1

Seeking: South, Southeast
Seeking in Canada? No
Exclusive territories? Yes
Homebased option? No
Employees needed to run biz: 30
Absentee ownership? No

COSTS
Total cost: $275.5K-416K
Franchise fee: $25K
Royalty fee: 4.5%
Term of agreement: 10 years renewable
　　at no charge
Franchisees required to buy multiple
　　units? Yes

FINANCING
No financing available

QUALIFICATIONS
Net worth: $500K+
Cash liquidity: $250K
Experience:
　　Industry experience
　　General business experience
　　Marketing skills

TRAINING
At headquarters: 4 weeks
At franchisee's location: 10 days
Additional programs available

BUSINESS SUPPORT
Grand opening
Internet
Newsletter
Meetings
Field operations/evaluations
Lease negotiations
Purchasing cooperatives
Security/safety procedures

MARKETING SUPPORT
Co-op advertising
Ad slicks
Regional marketing

LEDO PIZZA SYSTEM INC.

Ranked #282 in Entrepreneur Magazine's 2007 Franchise 500

Financial rating: $$$$

2001 Tidewater Colony Dr., #203
Annapolis, MD 21401
(410)721-6887
www.ledopizza.com
Pizza, subs, pasta
Began: 1986, Franchising: 1989
Headquarters size: 12 employees
Franchise department: 12 employees

U.S. franchises: 80
Canadian franchises: 0
Other foreign franchises: 0
Company-owned: 0

Seeking: All U.S.
Seeking in Canada? No
Exclusive territories? Yes
Homebased option? No
Employees needed to run biz: 40
Absentee ownership? No

COSTS
Total cost: $125.3K-429K
Franchise fee: $30K
Royalty fee: 5%
Term of agreement: 5 years renewable
　　at no charge
Franchisees required to buy multiple
　　units? No

FINANCING
No financing available

QUALIFICATIONS
Experience:
　　General business experience

TRAINING
At headquarters: 2-3 days
At franchisee's location: 30 days
Ongoing

BUSINESS SUPPORT
Internet
Newsletter
Meetings
Field operations/evaluations
Lease negotiations
Purchasing cooperatives
Security/safety procedures

MARKETING SUPPORT
Co-op advertising
Ad slicks
National media campaign
Regional marketing
Personal training

FULL SERVICE *Mexican Restaurants*

PEPE'S MEXICAN RESTAURANTS

Ranked #482 in Entrepreneur Magazine's 2007 Franchise 500　　　*Financial rating: $$$$*

1325 W. 15th St.
Chicago, IL 60608
(312)733-2500
www.pepes.com
Mexican restaurant
Began: 1967, Franchising: 1967
Headquarters size: 12 employees
Franchise department: 12 employees

U.S. franchises: 50
Canadian franchises: 0
Other foreign franchises: 0
Company-owned: 0

Seeking: Midwest, Northeast
Seeking in Canada? No
Exclusive territories? Yes
Homebased option? No
Employees needed to run biz: 10
Absentee ownership? No

COSTS
Total cost: $145.1K-316K
Franchise fee: $15K
Royalty fee: 4%
Term of agreement: 20 years renewable
　　at no charge
Franchisees required to buy multiple
　　units? Yes

FINANCING
No financing available

QUALIFICATIONS
Experience:
　　General business experience

TRAINING
At headquarters: 2 weeks
At franchisee's location: 2 weeks

BUSINESS SUPPORT
Grand opening
Newsletter
Meetings
Field operations/evaluations
Lease negotiations
Purchasing cooperatives

MARKETING SUPPORT
Co-op advertising
Ad slicks
National media campaign
Regional marketing

ROCKIN' BAJA LOBSTER

Current financial data not available

450 Newport Center Dr., #630
Newport Beach, CA 92660
(949)719-3800
www.rockinbaja.com
Baja-style Mexican seafood
　　restaurant
Began: 1992, Franchising: 2004
Headquarters size: 2 employees
Franchise department: 2 employees

U.S. franchises: 1
Canadian franchises: 0
Other foreign franchises: 0
Company-owned: 4

Seeking: All U.S.
Seeking in Canada? Yes
Exclusive territories? Yes
Homebased option? No
Employees needed to run biz: 30-40
Absentee ownership? Yes

COSTS
Total cost: $240.4K-1.2M
Franchise fee: $30K
Royalty fee: 5%
Term of agreement: 10 years renewable
　　at no charge
Franchisees required to buy multiple
　　units? Outside the U.S. only

FINANCING
In-house: None
3rd-party: Accounts receivable,
　　equipment, franchise fee,
　　inventory, payroll, startup costs

QUALIFICATIONS
Net worth: $750K-1M
Cash liquidity: $500K
Experience:
　　Industry experience
　　General business experience

TRAINING
At headquarters: 2 weeks

BUSINESS SUPPORT
Grand opening
Internet
Newsletter
Meetings
Toll-free phone line
Field operations/evaluations
Lease negotiations
Purchasing cooperatives
Security/safety procedures

MARKETING SUPPORT
Co-op advertising
Ad slicks
National media campaign
Regional marketing
International support

FULL SERVICE ▸ *Sports Bars*

BEEF `O'BRADY'S

Ranked #132 in Entrepreneur Magazine's 2007 Franchise 500 *Financial rating: $$$*

5510 LaSalle, #200
Tampa, FL 33607
(813)226-2333
www.beefobradys.com
Family sports pub
Began: 1985, Franchising: 1998
Headquarters size: 32 employees
Franchise department: 4 employees

U.S. franchises: 208
Canadian franchises: 0
Other foreign franchises: 0
Company-owned: 4

Seeking: Southeast
Seeking in Canada? No
Exclusive territories? Yes
Homebased option? No
Employees needed to run biz: 30
Absentee ownership? No

COSTS
Total cost: $256.5K-652.5K
Franchise fee: $35K
Royalty fee: 4%
Term of agreement: 10 years renewable
    at no charge
Franchisees required to buy multiple
    units? No

FINANCING
In-house: None
3rd-party: Accounts receivable,
    equipment, franchise fee,
    inventory, payroll, startup costs

QUALIFICATIONS
Net worth: $250K
Cash liquidity: $125K
Experience:
    General business experience
    Marketing skills

TRAINING
At headquarters: 8 weeks
At franchisee's location: 2 weeks
At Beef `O'Brady's University
Workshops

BUSINESS SUPPORT
Grand opening
Newsletter
Meetings
Toll-free phone line
Field operations/evaluations
Lease negotiations

MARKETING SUPPORT
Regional marketing

PO'BOYS CREOLE CAFE

Current financial data not available

224 E. College Ave.
Tallahassee, FL 32301
(850)224-5400
www.poboys.com
New Orleans-style sports bar
Began: 1992, Franchising: 2002
Headquarters size: 4 employees
Franchise department: 4 employees

U.S. franchises: 5
Canadian franchises: 0
Other foreign franchises: 0
Company-owned: 2

Seeking: Southeast
Seeking in Canada? No
Exclusive territories? Yes
Homebased option? No
Employees needed to run biz: 40
Absentee ownership? Yes

COSTS
Total cost: $500K-2M
Franchise fee: $25K
Royalty fee: $500/wk
Term of agreement: 10 years renewable
    for $15K
Franchisees required to buy multiple
    units? No

FINANCING
No financing available

QUALIFICATIONS
Net worth: $2M
Cash liquidity: $500K
Experience:
    Industry experience
    General business experience

TRAINING
At headquarters: 2 weeks
At franchisee's location: 3 weeks

BUSINESS SUPPORT
Grand opening
Toll-free phone line
Field operations/evaluations
Security/safety procedures

MARKETING SUPPORT
Ad slicks

FULL SERVICE ► *Miscellaneous*

5 & DINER FRANCHISE CORP.

Current financial data not available

1140 E. Greenway, #1
Mesa, AZ 85203
(480)962-7104
www.5anddiner.com
'50s-theme restaurant
Began: 1987, Franchising: 1993
Headquarters size: 9 employees
Franchise department: 4 employees

U.S. franchises: 18
Canadian franchises: 0
Other foreign franchises: 0
Company-owned: 1

Seeking: All U.S.
Seeking in Canada? Yes
Exclusive territories? Yes
Homebased option? No
Employees needed to run biz: 75
Absentee ownership? No

COSTS
Total cost: $300K-1M
Franchise fee: $35K
Royalty fee: 5%
Term of agreement: 20 years renewable
Franchisees required to buy multiple
 units? No

FINANCING
In-house: None
3rd-party: Equipment

QUALIFICATIONS
Net worth: $1M
Cash liquidity: $300K
Experience:
 Industry experience
 General business experience
 Marketing skills

TRAINING
At headquarters: 4 weeks
At franchisee's location: 5 weeks

BUSINESS SUPPORT
Grand opening
Internet
Newsletter
Field operations/evaluations

MARKETING SUPPORT
Co-op advertising
Ad slicks

THE GROUND PAT'I GRILLE & BAR

Current financial data not available

2727 Kaliste Saloom, #700
Lafayette, LA 70508
(337)984-7779
www.groundpati.com
Casual-dining restaurant
Began: 1971, Franchising: 1975
Headquarters size: 2 employees

U.S. franchises: 6
Canadian franchises: 0
Other foreign franchises: 0
Company-owned: 4

Seeking: All U.S.
Seeking in Canada? Yes
Exclusive territories? Yes
Homebased option? No
Employees needed to run biz:
 80-160
Absentee ownership? No

COSTS
Total cost: $359.8K-1.6M
Franchise fee: $22K-35K
Royalty fee: 4%
Term of agreement: 10 years renewable
 at no charge
Franchisees required to buy multiple
 units? No

FINANCING
No financing available

QUALIFICATIONS
Net worth: $1M
Cash liquidity: $300K
Experience:
 Industry experience
 General business experience

TRAINING
At headquarters: 3-5 days
At franchisee's location: 10 days

BUSINESS SUPPORT
Grand opening
Meetings
Field operations/evaluations
Purchasing cooperatives
Security/safety procedures

MARKETING SUPPORT
Co-op advertising

HOULIHAN'S

Ranked #266 in Entrepreneur Magazine's 2007 Franchise 500   *Financial rating: $$$*

8700 State Line Rd., #100
Leawood, KS 66206
(913)901-2500
www.houlihans.com
Full-service restaurant
Began: 1972, Franchising: 1994
Headquarters size: 44 employees
Franchise department: 2 employees

U.S. franchises: 59
Canadian franchises: 0
Other foreign franchises: 2
Company-owned: 43

Seeking: All U.S.
Seeking in Canada? No
Exclusive territories? Yes
Homebased option? No
Employees needed to run biz: 78
Absentee ownership? Yes

COSTS
Total cost: $1.6M-4.3M
Franchise fee: $40K
Royalty fee: 4%
Term of agreement: 20 years renewable
    for $5K
Franchisees required to buy multiple
    units? Yes

FINANCING
In-house: None
3rd-party: Equipment, inventory,
    startup costs

QUALIFICATIONS
Net worth: $2M+
Cash liquidity: 20-25% of total costs
Experience:
    Industry experience
    General business experience
    Must live in same market being
    developed

TRAINING
At franchisee's location: 40 days
At corporate training store: 40 days

BUSINESS SUPPORT
Grand opening
Internet
Meetings
Toll-free phone line
Field operations/evaluations
Purchasing cooperatives

MARKETING SUPPORT
Co-op advertising
Ad slicks
National media campaign
Regional marketing
Promo materials
Email promotions

JOEY'S ONLY SEAFOOD RESTAURANT

Current financial data not available

514-42nd Ave. S.E.
Calgary, AB T2G 1Y6 Canada
(800)661-2123/(403)243-4584
www.joeysonly.ca
Seafood, rotisserie chicken, ribs
Began: 1985, Franchising: 1985
Headquarters size: 20 employees
Franchise department: 2 employees

U.S. franchises: 17
Canadian franchises: 96
Other foreign franchises: 0
Company-owned: 2

Seeking: All U.S.
Seeking in Canada? Yes
Exclusive territories? Yes
Homebased option? No
Employees needed to run biz: 15
Absentee ownership? Yes

COSTS
Total cost: $330K-400K
Franchise fee: $25K
Royalty fee: 4.5%
Term of agreement: 10 years renewable
    for $5K
Franchisees required to buy multiple
    units? No

FINANCING
No financing available

QUALIFICATIONS
Net worth: $400K+
Cash liquidity: $150K+
Experience:
    General business experience
    Management experience
    Food-service background
    Computer skills

TRAINING
At headquarters: 5 weeks
At franchisee's location: 2 weeks

BUSINESS SUPPORT
Grand opening
Internet
Newsletter
Meetings
Toll-free phone line
Field operations/evaluations
Lease negotiations
Purchasing cooperatives
Security/safety procedures

MARKETING SUPPORT
Co-op advertising
Ad slicks
National media campaign
Regional marketing
POS materials

LOCOS GRILL & PUB

Ranked #405 in Entrepreneur Magazine's 2007 Franchise 500   *Financial rating: $$$*

290 Research Dr.
Athens, GA 30605
(706)548-7277
www.locosgrill.com
Sandwiches, salads, wings, burgers,
    entrees
Began: 1988, Franchising: 1997
Headquarters size: 11 employees
Franchise department: 3 employees

U.S. franchises: 23
Canadian franchises: 0
Other foreign franchises: 0
Company-owned: 3

Seeking: Southeast
Seeking in Canada? No
Exclusive territories? Yes
Homebased option? No
Employees needed to run biz: 40
Absentee ownership? Yes

COSTS

Total cost: $422K-878.2K
Franchise fee: $35K
Royalty fee: 4%
Term of agreement: 10 years renewable
    at no charge
Franchisees required to buy multiple
    units? No

FINANCING

No financing available

QUALIFICATIONS

Net worth: $380K
Cash liquidity: 50% of net worth
Experience:
    Customer service skills

TRAINING

At headquarters: 1 week
At franchisee's location: 9 weeks
Training seminars: 1-2 days

BUSINESS SUPPORT

Grand opening
Internet
Newsletter
Meetings
Toll-free phone line
Field operations/evaluations
Purchasing cooperatives
Security/safety procedures

MARKETING SUPPORT

Co-op advertising
Ad slicks
National media campaign
Regional marketing
Local publicity

THE MELTING POT RESTAURANTS INC.

Ranked #199 in Entrepreneur Magazine's 2007 Franchise 500   *Financial rating: $$$$*

8810 Twin Lakes Blvd.
Tampa, FL 33614
(813)881-0055
www.meltingpot.com
Fondue-specialty restaurant
Began: 1975, Franchising: 1984
Headquarters size: 22 employees
Franchise department: 15 employees

U.S. franchises: 100
Canadian franchises: 0
Other foreign franchises: 0
Company-owned: 6

Seeking: All U.S.
Seeking in Canada? No
Exclusive territories? Yes
Homebased option? No
Employees needed to run biz: Info
    not provided
Absentee ownership? No

COSTS

Total cost: $595.8K-1.2M
Franchise fee: $35K
Royalty fee: 4.5%
Term of agreement: 10 years renewable
    for 50% of current franchise fee
Franchisees required to buy multiple
    units? No

FINANCING

In-house: None
3rd-party: Equipment, franchise fee,
    inventory, startup costs

QUALIFICATIONS

Net worth: $500K
Cash liquidity: $200K-250K+
Experience:
    General business experience

TRAINING

At headquarters: 7 weeks
At franchisee's location

BUSINESS SUPPORT

Grand opening
Internet
Newsletter
Meetings
Toll-free phone line
Field operations/evaluations
Purchasing cooperatives
Security/safety procedures

MARKETING SUPPORT

Co-op advertising
Ad slicks
Local marketing & media planning

WINGER'S GRILL & BAR
Ranked #358 in Entrepreneur Magazine's 2007 Franchise 500   *Financial rating: $$$$*

404 E. 4500 South, #A12
Salt Lake City, UT 84107
(801)261-3700
www.wingers.info
Casual-themed restaurant & bar
Began: 1993, Franchising: 1997
Headquarters size: 18 employees
Franchise department: 8 employees

U.S. franchises: 25
Canadian franchises: 0
Other foreign franchises: 2
Company-owned: 9

Seeking: Midwest, Northeast,
    Southwest, West
Seeking in Canada? No
Exclusive territories? Yes
Homebased option? No
Employees needed to run biz: 35
Absentee ownership? Yes

COSTS
Total cost: $124.5K-1.1M
Franchise fee: $30K
Royalty fee: 4%
Term of agreement: 15 years renewable
    for 10% of current franchise fee
Franchisees required to buy multiple
    units? No

FINANCING
No financing available

QUALIFICATIONS
Net worth: $450K
Cash liquidity: $250K
Experience:
    General business experience

TRAINING
At franchisee's location: 2-3 weeks
    at opening
At company restaurant: 6 weeks

BUSINESS SUPPORT
Grand opening
Meetings
Field operations/evaluations
Purchasing cooperatives
Security/safety procedures

MARKETING SUPPORT
Co-op advertising
Ad slicks
Regional marketing
Advertising materials

FULL SERVICE — *Other Franchises*

BIG BOY RESTAURANTS INT'L.
4199 Marcy St.
Warren, MI 48091
(586)759-6000
www.bigboy.com
Family restaurant
Current financial data not available

BOSTON PIZZA
1501 LBJ Fwy., #450
Dallas, TX 75234
(866)277-8721
www.bostonsgourmet.com
Casual dining restaurant &
    sports bar
Current financial data not available

CHEEBURGER CHEEBURGER
15951 McGregor Blvd.
Fort Myers, FL 85303
(239)437-1611
www.cheeburger.com
Full-service restaurant
Current financial data not available

CITY WOK
73744 Hwy. 11, #3
Palm Desert, CA 92260
(760)346-7764
www.citywok.com
Contemporary Chinese restaurant
Financial rating: $$$

THE FIRKIN GROUP OF PUBS
*Ranked #499 in Entrepreneur
Magazine's 2007 Franchise 500*
20 Steelcase Rd., #1C
Markham, ON L3R 1B2 Canada
(905)305-9792
www.firkinpubs.com
English pub
Financial rating: $$$

GIMME SUM FRESH ASIAN GRILL
9850 S. Maryland Pkwy., #5-370
Las Vegas, NV 89123
(702)446-3786
www.gimmesum.com
Asian-style casual restaurant
Current financial data not available

GOLDEN CORRAL FRANCHISING SYSTEMS INC.
*Ranked #129 in Entrepreneur
Magazine's 2007 Franchise 500*
5151 Glenwood Ave.
Raleigh, NC 27612
(800)284-5673
www.goldencorralfranchise.com
Family steakhouse, buffet & bakery
Financial rating: $$$$

HUHOT MONGOLIAN GRILL
223 E. Main St.
Missoula, MT 59802
(406)251-4303
www.huhot.com
Mongolian grill restaurant
Current financial data not available

INDIGO JOE'S SPORTS PUB & RESTAURANT
23412 Moulton Pkwy., #131
Laguna Hills, CA 92653
(888)303-5637
www.indigojoes.com
Family sports pub restaurant
Current financial data not available

KRIEGER'S "YOUR HOMETOWN SPORTS GRILL"
744-F Spirit of St. Louis Blvd.
Chesterfield, MO 63005
(636)530-1395
www.kriegerspub.com
Family sports restaurant & bar
Current financial data not available

MAX & ERMA'S RESTAURANTS INC.
4849 Evanswood Dr.
Columbus, OH 43229
(614)431-5800
www.maxandermas.com
Casual dining restaurant
Financial rating: $$$

MR. GREEK RESTAURANTS
49 The Donway W., #402
Toronto, ON M3C 3M9 Canada
(416)444-3266
www.mrgreek.com
Greek & Mediterranean-style food
Financial rating: $$$

NATIVE NEW YORKER
4960 S. Alma School Rd., #B-24
Chandler, AZ 85225
(866)778-6283
www.nativenewyorker.com
Sports bar
Current financial data not available

R.J. GATOR'S FLORIDA SEA GRILL & BAR
609 N. Hepburn Ave.
Jupiter, FL 33458
(561)575-0326
www.rjgators.com
Casual dining restaurant
Current financial data not available

SHAKEY'S PIZZA RESTAURANT
2200 W. Valley Blvd.
Alhambra, CA 91803
(626)576-0737
www.shakeys.com
Pizza restaurant
Current financial data not available

SHONEY'S RESTAURANTS
1717 Elm Hill Pike, #B-1
Nashville, TN 37210
(877)377-2233
www.shoneys.com
Family dining restaurant
Current financial data not available

3 TOMATOES & A MOZZARELLA
7605 E. Pinnacle Peak Rd.
Scottsdale, AZ 85255
(480)585-6555
www.3tomatoes.com
Full-service pizza, panini & pasta
  restaurant
Current financial data not available

UNO CHICAGO GRILL
100 Charles Park Rd.
Boston, MA 02132
(617)218-5325
www.unos.com
Full-service restaurant
Current financial data not available

WESTERN SIZZLIN
Ranked #442 in Entrepreneur
Magazine's 2007 Franchise 500
P.O. Box 12167
Roanoke, VA 24023-2167
(540)345-3195
www.westernsizzlin.com
Family steakhouse
Financial rating: $$$$

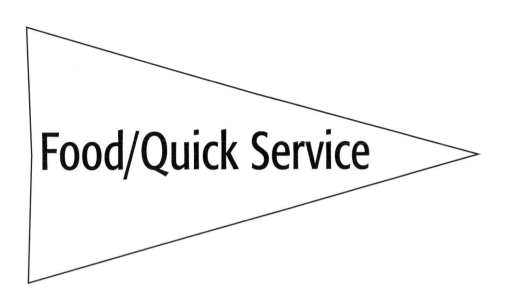

Food/Quick Service

QUICK SERVICE   *Asian*

ASIAN CHAO/MAKI OF JAPAN/CHAO CAJUN
Ranked #489 in Entrepreneur Magazine's 2007 Franchise 500   *Financial rating: $$$$*

385 Commerce Way
Longwood, FL 32750
(407)830-5338
www.asianchao.com
Asian fast food
Began: 1991, Franchising: 2001
Headquarters size: 20 employees
Franchise department: 3 employees

U.S. franchises: 21
Canadian franchises: 0
Other foreign franchises: 0
Company-owned: 42

Seeking: FL, GA, MA, NC, NY,
    OH, TN
Seeking in Canada? No
Exclusive territories? No
Homebased option? No
Employees needed to run biz: 5-6
Absentee ownership? No

COSTS
Total cost: $330K-475K
Franchise fee: $30K
Royalty fee: 6%
Term of agreement: 10 years renewable
    for $55K
Franchisees required to buy multiple
    units? No

FINANCING
In-house: None
3rd-party: Accounts receivable,
    equipment, franchise fee,
    inventory, payroll, startup costs

QUALIFICATIONS
Net worth: $250K-300K
Cash liquidity: $100K-250K
Experience:
    Industry experience
    General business experience
    Marketing skills

TRAINING
At headquarters: 2 weeks
At franchisee's location: 2 weeks

BUSINESS SUPPORT
Grand opening
Meetings
Toll-free phone line
Field operations/evaluations
Purchasing cooperatives
Security/safety procedures

MARKETING SUPPORT
Mall advertising

DOC CHEY'S ASIAN KITCHEN

Current financial data not available

1409 N. Highland Ave., #M
Atlanta, GA 30306
(404)541-1077
www.doccheys.com
Pan-Asian restaurant
Began: 1997, Franchising: 2004
Headquarters size: 7 employees
Franchise department: 7 employees

U.S. franchises: 5
Canadian franchises: 0
Other foreign franchises: 0
Company-owned: 3

Seeking: Midwest, Northeast, South,
    Southeast
Seeking in Canada? No
Exclusive territories? Yes
Homebased option? No
Employees needed to run biz: 25
Absentee ownership? No

COSTS
Total cost: $287.5K-462K
Franchise fee: $25K
Royalty fee: 5%
Term of agreement: 10 years renewable
    for 50% of then-current fee
Franchisees required to buy multiple
    units? No

FINANCING
No financing available

QUALIFICATIONS
Net worth: $500K
Cash liquidity: $100K
Experience:
    Industry experience
    3 years restaurant experience

TRAINING
At headquarters: 12 weeks
At franchisee's location: 1 week
Manager training: 4-6 weeks

BUSINESS SUPPORT
Grand opening
Internet
Newsletter
Meetings
Toll-free phone line
Field operations/evaluations

MARKETING SUPPORT
Info not provided

EDO JAPAN INC.

Current financial data not available

4838 32nd St. S.E.
Calgary, AB T2B 2S6 Canada
(403)215-8800
www.edojapan.com
Japanese fast food
Began: 1977, Franchising: 1986
Headquarters size: 10 employees
Franchise department: 6 employees

U.S. franchises: 21
Canadian franchises: 64
Other foreign franchises: 0
Company-owned: 2

Seeking: All U.S.
Seeking in Canada? No
Exclusive territories? No
Homebased option? No
Employees needed to run biz: 6
Absentee ownership? Yes

COSTS
Total cost: $180K-275K
Franchise fee: $25K
Royalty fee: 6%
Term of agreement: 10 years renewable
    for 25% of franchise fee
Franchisees required to buy multiple
    units? No

FINANCING
No financing available

QUALIFICATIONS
Net worth: $100K
Cash liquidity: $100K

TRAINING
At headquarters: 21 days
At franchisee's location: 14 days

BUSINESS SUPPORT
Grand opening
Newsletter
Meetings
Field operations/evaluations
Lease negotiations

MARKETING SUPPORT
Regional marketing

SAMURAI SAM'S TERIYAKI GRILL
Ranked #280 in Entrepreneur Magazine's 2007 Franchise 500

Financial rating: $$$$

7730 E. Greenway Rd., #104
Scottsdale, AZ 85260
(480)443-0200
www.kahalacorp.com
Quick-service Japanese restaurant
Began: 1994, Franchising: 1995
Headquarters size: 7 employees
Franchise department: 7 employees

U.S. franchises: 73
Canadian franchises: 0
Other foreign franchises: 0
Company-owned: 3

Seeking: All U.S.
Seeking in Canada? Yes
Exclusive territories? Yes
Homebased option? No
Employees needed to run biz: 10-25
Absentee ownership? Yes

COSTS
Total cost: $119.8K-483.5K
Franchise fee: $30K
Royalty fee: 6%
Term of agreement: 10 years renewable
    for $5K
Franchisees required to buy multiple
    units? No

FINANCING
In-house: None
3rd-party: Equipment, franchise fee,
    inventory, startup costs

QUALIFICATIONS
Cash liquidity: $30K
Experience:
    General business experience

TRAINING
At headquarters: 2 weeks
At franchisee's location: 1 week

BUSINESS SUPPORT
Grand opening
Newsletter
Meetings
Toll-free phone line
Field operations/evaluations
Purchasing cooperatives
Security/safety procedures

MARKETING SUPPORT
Co-op advertising
Ad slicks
Regional marketing

QUICK SERVICE ▶ *Bagels*

BETWEEN ROUNDS BAKERY SANDWICH CAFE

Financial rating: 0

19A John Fitch Blvd., Rte. 5
South Windsor, CT 06074
(860)291-0323
www.betweenroundsbagels.com
Bagels, baked goods, deli items,
    catering, sandwiches
Began: 1990, Franchising: 1992
Headquarters size: 4 employees
Franchise department: 3 employees

U.S. franchises: 1
Canadian franchises: 0
Other foreign franchises: 0
Company-owned: 3

Seeking: Northeast
Seeking in Canada? No
Exclusive territories? Yes
Homebased option? No
Employees needed to run biz: 8
Absentee ownership? No

COSTS
Total cost: $283K-381K
Franchise fee: $25K-30K
Royalty fee: 5%
Term of agreement: 10 years renewable
    for $3.6K
Franchisees required to buy multiple
    units? No

FINANCING
No financing available

QUALIFICATIONS
Net worth: $200K
Cash liquidity: $80K-100K
Experience:
    Industry experience
    General business experience
    Marketing skills

TRAINING
At headquarters: 2 weeks
At franchisee's location: 1 week
Additional training as needed

BUSINESS SUPPORT
Grand opening
Meetings
Field operations/evaluations
Lease negotiations
Purchasing cooperatives
Security/safety procedures

MARKETING SUPPORT
Co-op advertising
Ad slicks
Regional marketing

BIG APPLE BAGELS

Ranked #424 in Entrepreneur Magazine's 2007 Franchise 500   *Financial rating: $$$$*

500 Lake Cook Rd., #475
Deerfield, IL 60015
(800)251-6101/(847)948-7520
www.babcorp.com
Bagels, sandwiches, gourmet coffee,
    muffins
Began: 1993, Franchising: 1993
Headquarters size: 20 employees
Franchise department: 7 employees

U.S. franchises: 142
Canadian franchises: 0
Other foreign franchises: 1
Company-owned: 1

Seeking: All U.S.
Seeking in Canada? Yes
Exclusive territories? Yes
Homebased option? No
Employees needed to run biz: 15
Absentee ownership? Yes

COSTS
Total cost: $228.3K-367.5K
Franchise fee: $25K
Royalty fee: 5%
Term of agreement: 10 years renewable
    for $2.5K
Franchisees required to buy multiple
    units? Outside the U.S. only

FINANCING
In-house: None
3rd-party: Equipment, inventory,
    startup costs

QUALIFICATIONS
Net worth: $300K+
Cash liquidity: $60K
Experience:
    General business experience

TRAINING
At headquarters: 11 days
At franchisee's location: 5 days
Additional training as needed

BUSINESS SUPPORT
Grand opening
Internet
Newsletter
Meetings
Toll-free phone line
Field operations/evaluations
Security/safety procedures

MARKETING SUPPORT
Ad slicks
Regional marketing
In-store POP materials

BRUEGGER'S

Ranked #300 in Entrepreneur Magazine's 2007 Franchise 500   *Financial rating: $$$$*

159 Bank St.
Burlington, VT 05401-4420
(866)660-4104
www.brueggers.com
Bagels, breads, sandwiches, soups,
    salads
Began: 1983, Franchising: 1993
Headquarters size: 40 employees
Franchise department: 5 employees

U.S. franchises: 98
Canadian franchises: 0
Other foreign franchises: 0
Company-owned: 147

Seeking: All U.S.
Seeking in Canada? No
Exclusive territories? Yes
Homebased option? No
Employees needed to run biz: Info
    not provided
Absentee ownership? Yes

COSTS
Total cost: $230.1K-489.1K
Franchise fee: $30K
Royalty fee: 5%
Term of agreement: 10 years renewable
    for $5K
Franchisees required to buy multiple
    units? Yes

FINANCING
No financing available

QUALIFICATIONS
Net worth: $200K
Cash liquidity: $100K
Experience:
    Industry experience

TRAINING
At headquarters: 40 hours
On-the-job training: 4-8 weeks

BUSINESS SUPPORT
Grand opening
Field operations/evaluations

MARKETING SUPPORT
Co-op advertising
Ad slicks
Regional marketing

KETTLEMAN'S BAGEL CORP.

Current financial data not available

12 Inverary Dr.
Ottawa, ON K2K 2R9 Canada
(613)592-2211
www.kettlemansbagel.com
Bagels
Began: 1993, Franchising: 1996
Headquarters size: 27 employees
Franchise department: 1 employee

U.S. franchises: 0
Canadian franchises: 5
Other foreign franchises: 0
Company-owned: 1

Seeking: Not available in the U.S.
Seeking in Canada? Yes
Exclusive territories? Yes
Homebased option? No
Employees needed to run biz: 8-10
Absentee ownership? No

COSTS
Total cost: $300K-450K
Franchise fee: $25K
Royalty fee: 6%
Term of agreement: 10 years renewable
    for 25% of initial franchise fee
Franchisees required to buy multiple
    units? Yes

FINANCING
In-house: Franchise fee, inventory
3rd-party: Equipment, startup costs

QUALIFICATIONS
Net worth: $500K Cdn.
Cash liquidity: $150K Cdn.
Experience:
    Industry experience
    General business experience
    Marketing skills
    Customer service skills

TRAINING
At headquarters: 6 weeks
At franchisee's location: 4 weeks
At master franchisor's location:
    6 weeks

BUSINESS SUPPORT
Grand opening
Internet
Meetings
Toll-free phone line
Field operations/evaluations
Lease negotiations
Purchasing cooperatives
Security/safety procedures

MARKETING SUPPORT
Co-op advertising
Local marketing

QUICK SERVICE   *Baked Goods, Miscellaneous*

BEARD PAPA'S SWEETS CAFE

Current financial data not available

1040 Avenue of the Americas, #2415
New York, NY 10018
(646)418-3190
www.muginohousa.com
Cream puffs & baked goods
Began: 1998, Franchising: 1998
Headquarters size: 10 employees
Franchise department: 4 employees

U.S. franchises: 13
Canadian franchises: 0
Other foreign franchises: 300+
Company-owned: 1

Seeking: AZ, NV, WA, DC
Seeking in Canada? Yes
Exclusive territories? Yes
Homebased option? No
Employees needed to run biz: 4
Absentee ownership? Yes

COSTS
Total cost: $161K-326K
Franchise fee: $15K-40K
Royalty fee: 5%
Term of agreement: 5 years
    renewable
Franchisees required to buy multiple
    units? No

FINANCING
No financing available

QUALIFICATIONS
Net worth: $300K
Cash liquidity: $150K/unit
Experience:
    Industry experience
    General business experience

TRAINING
At headquarters: Varies
At franchisee's location: Varies

BUSINESS SUPPORT
Grand opening
Internet
Field operations/evaluations

MARKETING SUPPORT
Regional marketing

CINNABON INC.

Ranked #244 in Entrepreneur Magazine's 2007 Franchise 500   *Financial rating: $$*

200 Glenridge Point Pkwy., #200
Atlanta, GA 30342
(404)255-3250
www.cinnabon.com
Cinnamon rolls & baked goods
Began: 1985, Franchising: 1986
Headquarters size: 75 employees
Franchise department: 50 employees

U.S. franchises: 407
Canadian franchises: 26
Other foreign franchises: 218
Company-owned: 0

Seeking: All U.S.
Seeking in Canada? Yes
Exclusive territories? No
Homebased option? No
Employees needed to run biz: 8-10
Absentee ownership? Yes

COSTS
Total cost: $73K-338K
Franchise fee: $30K
Royalty fee: 6%
Term of agreement: 20 years renewable
for then-current fee
Franchisees required to buy multiple
units? Yes

FINANCING
In-house: None
3rd-party: Equipment, franchise fee,
inventory, startup costs

QUALIFICATIONS
Net worth: $300K+
Cash liquidity: $100K
Experience:
Industry experience
General business experience
Marketing skills

TRAINING
At headquarters: 5 days
At franchisee's location: 3-5 days
Additional training annually

BUSINESS SUPPORT
Grand opening
Internet
Newsletter
Meetings
Toll-free phone line
Field operations/evaluations
Purchasing cooperatives
Security/safety procedures

MARKETING SUPPORT
Co-op advertising
Ad slicks
Regional marketing

CINNAMON CITY

Current financial data not available

P.O. Box 490, 2265 W. Railway St.
Abbotsford, BC V2T 6Z7 Canada
(604)852-8771
www.shefield.com
Cinnamon rolls & baked goods
Began: 1992, Franchising: 1996
Headquarters size: 19 employees
Franchise department: 1 employee

U.S. franchises: 0
Canadian franchises: 6
Other foreign franchises: 0
Company-owned: 1

Seeking: Not available in the U.S.
Seeking in Canada? Yes
Exclusive territories? Yes
Homebased option? No
Employees needed to run biz: 4
Absentee ownership? Yes

COSTS
Total cost: $80K-200K
Franchise fee: $25K
Royalty fee: 6%
Term of agreement: 5 years renewable
at no charge
Franchisees required to buy multiple
units? No

FINANCING
No financing available

QUALIFICATIONS
Experience:
General business experience

TRAINING
At franchisee's location: 2 weeks

BUSINESS SUPPORT
Grand opening
Newsletter
Meetings
Toll-free phone line
Field operations/evaluations
Lease negotiations
Purchasing cooperatives

MARKETING SUPPORT
Co-op advertising
Ad slicks
National media campaign
Regional marketing

DUNKIN' DONUTS

Ranked #2 in Entrepreneur Magazine's 2007 Franchise 500   *Financial rating: $$$$*

130 Royall St.
Canton, MA 02021
(781)737-3000
www.dunkinfranchising.com
Donuts & baked goods
Began: 1950, Franchising: 1955
Headquarters size: 600 employees
Franchise department: 16 employees

U.S. franchises: 5,027
Canadian franchises: 0
Other foreign franchises: 1,865
Company-owned: 0

Seeking: All U.S.
Seeking in Canada? Yes
Exclusive territories? No
Homebased option? No
Employees needed to run biz: Info
  not provided
Absentee ownership? No

COSTS
Total cost: $179K-1.6M
Franchise fee: $40K-80K
Royalty fee: 5.9%
Term of agreement: Info not provided
Franchisees required to buy multiple
  units? Yes

FINANCING
In-house: None
3rd-party: Equipment

QUALIFICATIONS
Net worth: $1.5M
Cash liquidity: $750K
Experience:
  Industry experience
  General business experience
  Marketing skills
  QSR experience

TRAINING
At headquarters: Varies

BUSINESS SUPPORT
Grand opening
Newsletter
Meetings
Toll-free phone line
Field operations/evaluations
Security/safety procedures

MARKETING SUPPORT
Regional marketing

GREAT HARVEST FRANCHISING INC.

Ranked #260 in Entrepreneur Magazine's 2007 Franchise 500   *Financial rating: $$$*

28 S. Montana St.
Dillon, MT 59725
(800)442-0424/(406)683-6842
www.greatharvest.com
Bread bakery
Began: 1976, Franchising: 1978
Headquarters size: 28 employees
Franchise department: 5 employees

U.S. franchises: 197
Canadian franchises: 0
Other foreign franchises: 0
Company-owned: 1

Seeking: All U.S.
Seeking in Canada? Yes
Exclusive territories? Yes
Homebased option? No
Employees needed to run biz: 5-7
Absentee ownership? No

COSTS
Total cost: $107.6K-352.3K
Franchise fee: $3K-30K
Royalty fee: 4-7%
Term of agreement: 10 years renewable
  at no charge
Franchisees required to buy multiple
  units? No

FINANCING
No financing available

QUALIFICATIONS
Net worth: $250K
Cash liquidity: $65K-75K
Experience:
  General business experience

TRAINING
At headquarters: 1 week
At franchisee's location: 1 week
At existing locations: 2 weeks

BUSINESS SUPPORT
Grand opening
Internet
Newsletter
Meetings
Toll-free phone line
Field operations/evaluations
Lease negotiations
Purchasing cooperatives
Security/safety procedures

MARKETING SUPPORT
Co-op advertising
Ad slicks
Regional marketing
Opening PR campaign
Annual marketing plan
Monthly promotions

HOUSE OF BREAD

Financial rating: 0

858 Higuera St.
San Luis Obispo, CA 93401
(800)545-5146
www.houseofbread.com
Specialty breads, muffins, scones
Began: 1996, Franchising: 1998
Headquarters size: 18 employees
Franchise department: 4 employees

U.S. franchises: 8
Canadian franchises: 0
Other foreign franchises: 0
Company-owned: 1

Seeking: All U.S.
Seeking in Canada? Yes
Exclusive territories? Yes
Homebased option? No
Employees needed to run biz: 8
Absentee ownership? Yes

COSTS
Total cost: $153K-346K
Franchise fee: $28K
Royalty fee: 6%
Term of agreement: 10 years renewable
    for $5K
Franchisees required to buy multiple
    units? No

FINANCING
No financing available

QUALIFICATIONS
Net worth: $500K
Cash liquidity: $150K
Experience:
    General business experience

TRAINING
At headquarters: 14 days
At franchisee's location: 10 days

BUSINESS SUPPORT
Grand opening
Internet
Newsletter
Meetings
Toll-free phone line
Field operations/evaluations
Purchasing cooperatives
Security/safety procedures

MARKETING SUPPORT
Co-op advertising
Ad slicks
Regional marketing

KOLACHE FACTORY

Financial rating: $$$

15730 Park Row, #150
Houston, TX 77084
(281)829-6188
www.kolachefactory.com
Bakery cafe selling kolaches
Began: 1981, Franchising: 2000
Headquarters size: 8 employees
Franchise department: 4 employees

U.S. franchises: 14
Canadian franchises: 0
Other foreign franchises: 0
Company-owned: 15

Seeking: All U.S.
Seeking in Canada? No
Exclusive territories? Yes
Homebased option? No
Employees needed to run biz: 6
Absentee ownership? No

COSTS
Total cost: $295K-372K
Franchise fee: $25K
Royalty fee: 6%
Term of agreement: 10 years renewable
    for $10K
Franchisees required to buy multiple
    units? Outside the U.S. only

FINANCING
No financing available

QUALIFICATIONS
Net worth: $500K
Cash liquidity: $150K
Experience:
    Industry experience
    General business experience

TRAINING
At headquarters: 4 weeks
At franchisee's location: 1 week

BUSINESS SUPPORT
Grand opening
Internet
Newsletter
Toll-free phone line
Field operations/evaluations
Lease negotiations
Security/safety procedures

MARKETING SUPPORT
Co-op advertising
Ad slicks
Regional marketing

NESTLE TOLL HOUSE CAFE BY CHIP

Ranked #273 in Entrepreneur Magazine's 2007 Franchise 500   *Financial rating: $$$*

101 W. Renner Rd.
Richardson, TX 75082
(214)495-9533
www.nestlecafe.com/home
Cookies, baked goods, coffee,
    ice cream
Began: 2000, Franchising: 2000
Headquarters size: 11 employees

U.S. franchises: 69
Canadian franchises: 0
Other foreign franchises: 0
Company-owned: 0

Seeking: All U.S.
Seeking in Canada? Yes
Exclusive territories? Yes
Homebased option? No
Employees needed to run biz: 6-10
Absentee ownership? Yes

COSTS
Total cost: $165K-620K
Franchise fee: $30K
Royalty fee: 6%
Term of agreement: Info not provided
Franchisees required to buy multiple
    units? No

FINANCING
In-house: None
3rd-party: Accounts receivable,
    equipment, franchise fee,
    inventory, payroll, startup costs

QUALIFICATIONS
Net worth: $250K
Cash liquidity: $100K/location

TRAINING
At headquarters: 12 days

BUSINESS SUPPORT
Grand opening
Internet
Newsletter
Meetings
Field operations/evaluations
Security/safety procedures

MARKETING SUPPORT
Ad slicks
Regional marketing

SAINT CINNAMON BAKERY LTD.

Current financial data not available

350 Esna Park Dr.
Markham, ON L3R 1H5 Canada
(905)470-1517
www.saintcinnamon.com
Cinnamon rolls & baked goods
Began: 1986, Franchising: 1986
Headquarters size: 8 employees

U.S. franchises: 3
Canadian franchises: 60
Other foreign franchises: 31
Company-owned: 1

Seeking: Midwest, Southeast
Seeking in Canada? Yes
Exclusive territories? Yes
Homebased option? No
Employees needed to run biz: Info
    not provided
Absentee ownership? No

COSTS
Total cost: $144.1K-264.7K
Franchise fee: $25K
Royalty fee: 6%
Term of agreement: 10 years
    maximum
Franchisees required to buy multiple
    units? No

FINANCING
No financing available

QUALIFICATIONS
Experience:
    Business experience

TRAINING
At headquarters: 10 days
At franchisee's location: 4 days

BUSINESS SUPPORT
Grand opening
Internet
Newsletter
Meetings
Toll-free phone line
Field operations/evaluations
Lease negotiations
Security/safety procedures

MARKETING SUPPORT
Co-op advertising
Ad slicks
Regional marketing

SAN FRANCISCO BREAD CO.

Current financial data not available

101 Main St.
Little Rock, AR 72116
(501)240-8110
www.sfbreadco.com
Bakery cafe
Began: 2001, Franchising: 2003
Headquarters size: 3 employees
Franchise department: 1 employee

U.S. franchises: 11
Canadian franchises: 0
Other foreign franchises: 0
Company-owned: 1

Seeking: All U.S.
Seeking in Canada? No
Exclusive territories? Yes
Homebased option? No
Employees needed to run biz: 25-35
Absentee ownership? No

COSTS
Total cost: $370K-450K
Franchise fee: $35K
Royalty fee: 5%
Term of agreement: 5 years renewable
    for $10K
Franchisees required to buy multiple
    units? No

FINANCING
No financing available

QUALIFICATIONS
Net worth: $1M
Cash liquidity: $300K
Experience:
    Industry experience
    General business experience
    Marketing skills

TRAINING
At headquarters: 2 months
At franchisee's location: 1 week

BUSINESS SUPPORT
Grand opening
Internet
Newsletter
Meetings
Field operations/evaluations
Lease negotiations
Purchasing cooperatives

MARKETING SUPPORT
Co-op advertising
Regional marketing

QUICK SERVICE ▶ *Chicken*

CHESTER'S INT'L. LLC

Ranked #378 in Entrepreneur Magazine's 2007 Franchise 500

Financial rating: 0

3500 Colonnade Pkwy., #325
Birmingham, AL 35243
(800)288-1555
www.chestersinternational.com
Quick-service chicken restaurant
Began: 1952, Franchising: 2004
Headquarters size: 160 employees
Franchise department: 18 employees

U.S. franchises: 31
Canadian franchises: 0
Other foreign franchises: 5
Company-owned: 1

Seeking: All U.S.
Seeking in Canada? Yes
Exclusive territories? Yes
Homebased option? No
Employees needed to run biz: 5-15
Absentee ownership? Yes

COSTS
Total cost: $105.9K-407K
Franchise fee: $15K-20K
Royalty fee: 4%
Term of agreement: 10 years renewable
    for $2.5K
Franchisees required to buy multiple
    units? Outside the U.S. only

FINANCING
In-house: None
3rd-party: Accounts receivable,
    equipment, franchise fee,
    inventory, payroll, startup costs

QUALIFICATIONS
Net worth: $250K
Cash liquidity: $75K
Experience:
    General business experience

TRAINING
At headquarters: 1 week
At franchisee's location: 4 days
Ongoing

BUSINESS SUPPORT
Grand opening
Internet
Newsletter
Meetings
Toll-free phone line
Field operations/evaluations
Security/safety procedures

MARKETING SUPPORT
Co-op advertising
Ad slicks
Regional marketing
In-store promotional support
Local marketing & PR

EAST COAST WINGS CORP.

Financial rating: $$$$

1365 Westgate Center Dr., #B
Winston-Salem, NC 27103
(336)760-4985
www.eastcoastwings.net
Buffalo-style wings & deli foods
Began: 1995, Franchising: 2004
Headquarters size: 7 employees
Franchise department: 3 employees

U.S. franchises: 9
Canadian franchises: 0
Other foreign franchises: 0
Company-owned: 1

Seeking: Southeast
Seeking in Canada? No
Exclusive territories? Yes
Homebased option? No
Employees needed to run biz: 14-26
Absentee ownership? No

COSTS
Total cost: $152.8K-525.9K
Franchise fee: $25K/20K
Royalty fee: 5%/4%
Term of agreement: 10 years renewable
  for 25% of then-current fee
Franchisees required to buy multiple
  units? No

FINANCING
No financing available

QUALIFICATIONS
Net worth: $300K
Cash liquidity: $70K+
Experience:
  Industry experience
  General business experience
  Marketing skills

TRAINING
At headquarters: 1 week
At franchisee's location: 3 weeks
Commissary: 1 week

BUSINESS SUPPORT
Grand opening
Internet
Newsletter
Meetings
Toll-free phone line
Field operations/evaluations
Purchasing cooperatives
Security/safety procedures

MARKETING SUPPORT
Co-op advertising
Ad slicks
National media campaign
Regional marketing

EL POLLO LOCO

Current financial data not available

3333 Michelson Dr., #550
Irvine, CA 92612-0680
(949)399-2000
www.elpolloloco.com
Flame-grilled chicken meals &
  Mexican entrees
Began: 1975, Franchising: 1980
Headquarters size: 100 employees
Franchise department: 15 employees

U.S. franchises: 194
Canadian franchises: 0
Other foreign franchises: 0
Company-owned: 145

Seeking: Southwest, West
Seeking in Canada? Yes
Exclusive territories? Yes
Homebased option? No
Employees needed to run biz: 25
Absentee ownership? No

COSTS
Total cost: $465K-670K
Franchise fee: $40K
Royalty fee: 4%
Term of agreement: 20 years
Franchisees required to buy multiple
  units? Yes

FINANCING
In-house: None
3rd-party: Equipment

QUALIFICATIONS
Net worth: $1.5M
Cash liquidity: $750K
Experience:
  Industry experience
  General business experience
  Marketing skills
  Food-service franchise
  background

TRAINING
At headquarters: 6 weeks
At franchisee's location: 2 weeks
At certified training stores: 6 weeks

BUSINESS SUPPORT
Grand opening
Internet
Meetings
Toll-free phone line
Field operations/evaluations
Purchasing cooperatives
Security/safety procedures

MARKETING SUPPORT
Ad slicks
Regional marketing

RANCH 1

Financial rating: $$$$

7730 E. Greenway Rd., #104
Scottsdale, AZ 85260
(480)443-0200
www.kahalacorp.com
Grilled & fried chicken sandwiches
Began: 1991, Franchising: 1993
Headquarters size: 30 employees
Franchise department: 30 employees

U.S. franchises: 29
Canadian franchises: 0
Other foreign franchises: 2
Company-owned: 3

Seeking: All U.S.
Seeking in Canada? Yes
Exclusive territories? Yes
Homebased option? No
Employees needed to run biz: 8
Absentee ownership? Yes

COSTS
Total cost: $142.8K-495.5K
Franchise fee: $30K
Royalty fee: 6%
Term of agreement: 10 years renewable
    for 75% of then-current fee
Franchisees required to buy multiple
    units? No

FINANCING
In-house: None
3rd-party: Equipment, franchise fee,
    inventory, startup costs

QUALIFICATIONS
Cash liquidity: $30K
Experience:
    Industry experience
    General business experience

TRAINING
At headquarters: 1 week
At franchisee's location: 2 weeks

BUSINESS SUPPORT
Grand opening
Internet
Newsletter
Meetings
Toll-free phone line
Field operations/evaluations
Purchasing cooperatives
Security/safety procedures

MARKETING SUPPORT
Co-op advertising
Ad slicks
National media campaign
Regional marketing

WING ZONE FRANCHISE CORP.

Ranked #240 in Entrepreneur Magazine's 2007 Franchise 500   *Financial rating: $$$$*

900 Circle 75 Pkwy., #930
Atlanta, GA 30339
(877)333-9464/(404)875-5045
www.wingzone.com
Buffalo wings
Began: 1991, Franchising: 1999
Headquarters size: 12 employees
Franchise department: 12 employees

U.S. franchises: 77
Canadian franchises: 0
Other foreign franchises: 0
Company-owned: 3

Seeking: Northeast, South,
    Southeast
Seeking in Canada? No
Exclusive territories? Yes
Homebased option? No
Employees needed to run biz: 12
Absentee ownership? No

COSTS
Total cost: $189K-249K
Franchise fee: $25K
Royalty fee: 5%
Term of agreement: 10 years renewable
    for $10K
Franchisees required to buy multiple
    units? No

FINANCING
In-house: None
3rd-party: Accounts receivable,
    equipment, franchise fee,
    inventory, payroll, startup costs

QUALIFICATIONS
Net worth: $200K
Cash liquidity: $60K-75K
Experience:
    Industry experience
    General business experience
    Marketing skills

TRAINING
At headquarters: 12 days
At franchisee's location: 10 days

BUSINESS SUPPORT
Grand opening
Internet
Newsletter
Meetings
Toll-free phone line
Field operations/evaluations
Purchasing cooperatives
Security/safety procedures

MARKETING SUPPORT
Ad slicks
National media campaign
Regional marketing

WINGS OVER...

Ranked #492 in Entrepreneur Magazine's 2007 Franchise 500   *Financial rating: $$*

67 Hunt St., #7
Agawam, MA 01001
(413)789-8632
www.wingsover.com
Chicken wings
Began: 2000, Franchising: 2002
Headquarters size: 6 employees
Franchise department: 6 employees

U.S. franchises: 11
Canadian franchises: 0
Other foreign franchises: 0
Company-owned: 1

Seeking: Northeast, South,
   Southeast
Seeking in Canada? No
Exclusive territories? Yes
Homebased option? No
Employees needed to run biz: 20
Absentee ownership? Yes

COSTS
Total cost: $152.7K-334.5K
Franchise fee: $20K
Royalty fee: 4%
Term of agreement: 5 years renewable
   for $7.5K
Franchisees required to buy multiple
   units? No

FINANCING
No financing available

QUALIFICATIONS
Net worth: $275K
Cash liquidity: $50K
Experience:
   Industry experience
   General business experience

TRAINING
At headquarters: 32 days
At franchisee's location: 2 weeks

BUSINESS SUPPORT
Grand opening
Internet
Newsletter
Meetings
Toll-free phone line
Field operations/evaluations
Lease negotiations
Purchasing cooperatives
Security/safety procedures

MARKETING SUPPORT
Info not provided

WINGS TO GO

                            Current financial data not available

846 Ritchie Hwy., #1B
Severna Park, MD 21146
(800)552-9464
www.wingstogo.com
Buffalo-style chicken wings, shrimp,
   sandwiches
Began: 1985, Franchising: 1989
Headquarters size: 9 employees
Franchise department: 5 employees

U.S. franchises: 90
Canadian franchises: 0
Other foreign franchises: 0
Company-owned: 0

Seeking: All U.S.
Seeking in Canada? No
Exclusive territories? Yes
Homebased option? No
Employees needed to run biz: 2
Absentee ownership? No

COSTS
Total cost: $219.5K-354.5K
Franchise fee: $20K
Royalty fee: 4%
Term of agreement: 10 years
Franchisees required to buy multiple
   units? No

FINANCING
No financing available

QUALIFICATIONS
Net worth: $250K
Cash liquidity: $100K
Experience:
   General business experience
   Marketing skills

TRAINING
At headquarters: 1 week
At franchisee's location: 2 days

BUSINESS SUPPORT
Grand opening
Internet
Newsletter
Meetings
Toll-free phone line
Field operations/evaluations

MARKETING SUPPORT
Ad slicks
National media campaign

WINGSTOP RESTAURANTS INC.

Ranked #137 in Entrepreneur Magazine's 2007 Franchise 500   *Financial rating: $$*

1101 E. Arapaho Rd., #150
Richardson, TX 75081
(972)686-6500
www.wingstop.com
Chicken wings
Began: 1994, Franchising: 1998
Headquarters size: 40 employees
Franchise department: 5 employees

U.S. franchises: 263
Canadian franchises: 0
Other foreign franchises: 0
Company-owned: 7

Seeking: All U.S.
Seeking in Canada? Yes
Exclusive territories? Yes
Homebased option? No
Employees needed to run biz: 8-10
Absentee ownership? Yes

COSTS
Total cost: $210.9K-366.9K
Franchise fee: $25K
Royalty fee: 5%
Term of agreement: 10 years renewable
    at no charge
Franchisees required to buy multiple
    units? No

FINANCING
No financing available

QUALIFICATIONS
Net worth: $250K
Cash liquidity: $100K
Experience:
    General business experience

TRAINING
At headquarters: 3 weeks
At franchisee's location: 1 week &
    as needed

BUSINESS SUPPORT
Grand opening
Internet
Meetings
Field operations/evaluations
Purchasing cooperatives
Security/safety procedures

MARKETING SUPPORT
Co-op advertising
Ad slicks
Regional marketing

WOW CAFE & WINGERY

Current financial data not available

109 New Camellia Blvd., #200
Covington, LA 70433
(985)792-5776
www.wingery.com
Wings, wraps, sandwiches, salads
Began: 2001, Franchising: 2002
Headquarters size: 10 employees
Franchise department: 2 employees

U.S. franchises: 19
Canadian franchises: 0
Other foreign franchises: 0
Company-owned: 2

Seeking: All U.S.
Seeking in Canada? Yes
Exclusive territories? Yes
Homebased option? No
Employees needed to run biz: 35-40
Absentee ownership? Yes

COSTS
Total cost: $195.4K-439.7K
Franchise fee: $25K
Royalty fee: 5%
Term of agreement: 10 years renewable
    at no charge
Franchisees required to buy multiple
    units? Info not provided

FINANCING
In-house: None
3rd-party: Accounts receivable,
    equipment, franchise fee,
    inventory, payroll, startup costs

QUALIFICATIONS
Net worth: $300K
Cash liquidity: $75K-100K
Experience:
    Industry experience
    General business experience

TRAINING
At headquarters: 15 days
At franchisee's location: 14 days

BUSINESS SUPPORT
Internet
Meetings
Field operations/evaluations
Purchasing cooperatives
Security/safety procedures

MARKETING SUPPORT
Co-op advertising
Ad slicks
Regional marketing
TV & radio ads
National promotions

QUICK SERVICE ▸ *Coffee*

BAD ASS COFFEE CO.

Ranked #256 in Entrepreneur Magazine's 2007 Franchise 500　　　　*Financial rating: $$$$*

166 W. 2700 South
Salt Lake City, UT 84115
(888)422-3277/(801)463-1966
www.badasscoffee.com
Coffee & logo wear
Began: 1991, Franchising: 1998
Headquarters size: 10 employees
Franchise department: 2 employees

U.S. franchises: 52
Canadian franchises: 0
Other foreign franchises: 1
Company-owned: 0

Seeking: All U.S.
Seeking in Canada? Yes
Exclusive territories? Yes
Homebased option? No
Employees needed to run biz: 10
Absentee ownership? Yes

COSTS
Total cost: $225K
Franchise fee: $25K
Royalty fee: 6%
Term of agreement: 5 years renewable
　　for $2.5K
Franchisees required to buy multiple
　　units? Outside the U.S. only

FINANCING
In-house: None
3rd-party: Accounts receivable,
　　equipment, franchise fee,
　　inventory, payroll, startup costs

QUALIFICATIONS
Cash liquidity: $100K

TRAINING
At headquarters: 2 week
At franchisee's location: Upon
　　request

BUSINESS SUPPORT
Grand opening
Internet
Newsletter
Toll-free phone line
Field operations/evaluations
Purchasing cooperatives
Security/safety procedures

MARKETING SUPPORT
Co-op advertising
Ad slicks
Regional marketing

BEANER'S COFFEE

Financial rating: $$

P.O. Box 710
East Lansing, MI 48826
(517)482-8145
www.beaners.com
Espresso bar, sandwiches, salads,
　　baked goods
Began: 1994, Franchising: 1999
Headquarters size: 50 employees
Franchise department: 16 employees

U.S. franchises: 63
Canadian franchises: 0
Other foreign franchises: 0
Company-owned: 0

Seeking: All U.S.
Seeking in Canada? No
Exclusive territories? Yes
Homebased option? No
Employees needed to run biz: 15
Absentee ownership? Yes

COSTS
Total cost: $240K-300K
Franchise fee: $25K
Royalty fee: 5%
Term of agreement: 10 years renewable
　　for 10% of current franchise fee
Franchisees required to buy multiple
　　units? No

FINANCING
No financing available

QUALIFICATIONS
Net worth: $400K
Cash liquidity: $100K

TRAINING
At headquarters: 4 weeks
At franchisee's location: 3 weeks
Ongoing

BUSINESS SUPPORT
Grand opening
Internet
Meetings
Toll-free phone line
Field operations/evaluations
Purchasing cooperatives
Security/safety procedures

MARKETING SUPPORT
Co-op advertising
Ad slicks
National media campaign
Regional marketing

THE BEARCLAW COFFEE COMPANY

Financial rating: 0

780 Taylor St.
Chelsea, MI 48118
(734)395-3864
www.bearclawcoffee.com
Coffee & espresso-based drinks
Began: 2002, Franchising: 2002
Headquarters size: 4 employees
Franchise department: 2 employees

U.S. franchises: 14
Canadian franchises: 0
Other foreign franchises: 0
Company-owned: 2

Seeking: All U.S.
Seeking in Canada? No
Exclusive territories? Yes
Homebased option? No
Employees needed to run biz: 6-8
Absentee ownership? Info not
    provided

COSTS
Total cost: $52.7K-223.9K
Franchise fee: $15K
Royalty fee: 6%
Term of agreement: Info not provided
Franchisees required to buy multiple
    units? No

FINANCING
No financing available

QUALIFICATIONS
Info not provided

TRAINING
At headquarters: 1 week
At franchisee's location

BUSINESS SUPPORT
Grand opening
Internet
Newsletter
Meetings
Field operations/evaluations
Purchasing cooperatives
Security/safety procedures

MARKETING SUPPORT
Co-op advertising
Regional marketing

CAFFINO

Current financial data not available

4070 Nelson Ave., #G
Concord, CA 94520
(925)363-3200
www.caffino.com
Coffee
Began: 1993, Franchising: 2002
Headquarters size: 7 employees

U.S. franchises: 19
Canadian franchises: 0
Other foreign franchises: 0
Company-owned: 8

Seeking: West
Seeking in Canada? Yes
Exclusive territories? Info not
    provided
Homebased option? No
Employees needed to run biz: 6-8
Absentee ownership? Info not
    provided

COSTS
Total cost: $212.9K-373K
Franchise fee: $10K
Royalty fee: 8%
Term of agreement: 15 years
Franchisees required to buy multiple
    units? No

FINANCING
No financing available

QUALIFICATIONS
Net worth: $1M
Cash liquidity: $200K
Experience:
    Industry experience

TRAINING
At headquarters: 3 weeks

BUSINESS SUPPORT
Info not provided

MARKETING SUPPORT
Info not provided

DAILY GRIND COFFEE HOUSE & CAFE

Ranked #234 in Entrepreneur Magazine's 2007 Franchise 500   *Financial rating: $$$$*

307 S. Loudoun St.
Winchester, VA 22601
(540)450-2701
www.dailygrindunwind.com
Coffeehouse & cafe
Began: 1995, Franchising: 2000
Headquarters size: 12 employees
Franchise department: 2 employees

U.S. franchises: 50
Canadian franchises: 0
Other foreign franchises: 0
Company-owned: 2

Seeking: All U.S.
Seeking in Canada? Yes
Exclusive territories? No
Homebased option? No
Employees needed to run biz: 15
Absentee ownership? Yes

COSTS
Total cost: $152.7K-329K
Franchise fee: $30K
Royalty fee: 5%
Term of agreement: 5 years renewable
   for $5K
Franchisees required to buy multiple
   units? No

FINANCING
In-house: None
3rd-party: Accounts receivable,
   equipment, franchise fee,
   inventory, payroll, startup costs

QUALIFICATIONS
Net worth: $250K
Cash liquidity: $75K

TRAINING
At headquarters: 5 days
At franchisee's location: 7 days
Training facility/store: 5 days

BUSINESS SUPPORT
Grand opening
Internet
Newsletter
Meetings
Field operations/evaluations
Security/safety procedures

MARKETING SUPPORT
Co-op advertising
Ad slicks
Regional marketing

ELLIANOS COFFEE CO.

Current financial data not available

426 S.W. Commerce Dr., #130
Lake City, FL 32025
(386)755-5828
www.ellianos.com
Drive-thru coffee shop
Began: 2002, Franchising: 2003
Headquarters size: 6 employees
Franchise department: 6 employees

U.S. franchises: 8
Canadian franchises: 0
Other foreign franchises: 0
Company-owned: 0

Seeking: All U.S.
Seeking in Canada? No
Exclusive territories? Yes
Homebased option? No
Employees needed to run biz: 10
Absentee ownership? Yes

COSTS
Total cost: $133.3K-256K
Franchise fee: $20K
Royalty fee: 5%
Term of agreement: 5 years renewable
   at no charge
Franchisees required to buy multiple
   units? No

FINANCING
In-house: None
3rd-party: Accounts receivable,
   equipment, franchise fee,
   inventory, payroll, startup costs

QUALIFICATIONS
Net worth: $150K
Cash liquidity: $50K
Experience:
   General business experience

TRAINING
At headquarters: 1-2 weeks
At franchisee's location: 3 days
Additional training as needed

BUSINESS SUPPORT
Grand opening
Internet
Newsletter
Meetings
Field operations/evaluations
Lease negotiations
Purchasing cooperatives
Security/safety procedures

MARKETING SUPPORT
Co-op advertising
Ad slicks
Regional marketing
Marketing manual
Promotions
Media buying
Marketing consulting

GLORIA JEAN'S GOURMET COFFEES FRANCHISING CORP.

Current financial data not available

28 Executive Park, #200
Irvine, CA 92614
(949)260-1600
www.gloriajeans.com
Gourmet coffee, teas, accessories
Began: 1979, Franchising: 1986
Headquarters size: 40 employees
Franchise department: 4 employees

U.S. franchises: 142
Canadian franchises: 0
Other foreign franchises: 0
Company-owned: 6

Seeking: All U.S.
Seeking in Canada? No
Exclusive territories? No
Homebased option? No
Employees needed to run biz: Info
   not provided
Absentee ownership? No

COSTS
Total cost: $183.5K-484.4K
Franchise fee: $16.3K-32.5K
Royalty fee: 6%
Term of agreement: 15 years
   maximum
Franchisees required to buy multiple
   units? No

FINANCING
No financing available

QUALIFICATIONS
Net worth: $350K+
Cash liquidity: $125K
Experience:
   Retail or restaurant-management
   experience

TRAINING
Info not provided

BUSINESS SUPPORT
Info not provided

MARKETING SUPPORT
Info not provided

GOURMET CUP

Current financial data not available

2265 W. Railway St., P.O. Box 490
Abbotsford, BC V2T 6Z7 Canada
(604)852-8771
www.shefield.com
Coffees, teas, accessories
Began: 1985, Franchising: 1986
Headquarters size: 19 employees
Franchise department: 1 employee

U.S. franchises: 0
Canadian franchises: 17
Other foreign franchises: 0
Company-owned: 0

Seeking: Not available in the U.S.
Seeking in Canada? Yes
Exclusive territories? No
Homebased option? No
Employees needed to run biz: 4
Absentee ownership? Yes

COSTS
Total cost: $120K-200K
Franchise fee: $25K
Royalty fee: 8%
Term of agreement: 5 years renewable
   for $5K
Franchisees required to buy multiple
   units? No

FINANCING
No financing available

QUALIFICATIONS
Experience:
   General business experience

TRAINING
At franchisee's location: 2 weeks

BUSINESS SUPPORT
Grand opening
Internet
Newsletter
Toll-free phone line
Field operations/evaluations
Lease negotiations
Purchasing cooperatives
Security/safety procedures

MARKETING SUPPORT
Co-op advertising
Ad slicks
National media campaign

IT'S A GRIND COFFEE HOUSE

Ranked #427 in Entrepreneur Magazine's 2007 Franchise 500   *Financial rating: $*

6272 E. Pacific Coast Hwy., #E
Long Beach, CA 90803
(562)594-5600
www.itsagrind.com
Coffeehouse
Began: 1995, Franchising: 2000
Headquarters size: 31 employees
Franchise department: 4 employees

U.S. franchises: 86
Canadian franchises: 0
Other foreign franchises: 0
Company-owned: 4

Seeking: All U.S.
Seeking in Canada? No
Exclusive territories? Yes
Homebased option? No
Employees needed to run biz: 14-16
Absentee ownership? No

COSTS
Total cost: $279K-492K
Franchise fee: $36K
Royalty fee: 6%
Term of agreement: 10 years
Franchisees required to buy multiple
     units? No

FINANCING
In-house: None
3rd-party: Equipment, franchise fee,
     inventory, startup costs,
     leasehold improvements

QUALIFICATIONS
Net worth: $500K
Cash liquidity: $175K
Experience:
     General business experience
     Strong people skills

TRAINING
At headquarters: 2 weeks
At franchisee's location: 10 days
Additional training as needed

BUSINESS SUPPORT
Grand opening
Internet
Newsletter
Meetings
Toll-free phone line
Field operations/evaluations
Lease negotiations
Purchasing cooperatives
Security/safety procedures

MARKETING SUPPORT
Co-op advertising
Ad slicks
Regional marketing
Franchisee Advertising Council

JO TO GO COFFEE

Financial rating: $$$

1263 Main St.
Green Bay, WI 54302
(866)568-6461
www.jotogo.com
Coffee, tea, smoothies, baked goods
Began: 1998, Franchising: 2001
Headquarters size: 30 employees
Franchise department: 6 employees

U.S. franchises: 7
Canadian franchises: 0
Other foreign franchises: 0
Company-owned: 6

Seeking: All U.S.
Seeking in Canada? Yes
Exclusive territories? Yes
Homebased option? No
Employees needed to run biz: 7
Absentee ownership? Yes

COSTS
Total cost: $84.9K-779.6K
Franchise fee: $25K
Royalty fee: 7%
Term of agreement: 5 years renewable
     at no charge
Franchisees required to buy multiple
     units? No

FINANCING
In-house: None
3rd-party: Accounts receivable,
     equipment, franchise fee,
     inventory, payroll, startup costs

QUALIFICATIONS
Net worth: $1M
Cash liquidity: $250K
Experience:
     General business experience

TRAINING
At headquarters: 1 week
At franchisee's location: 1 week
At a corporate store: 1 week

BUSINESS SUPPORT
Grand opening
Internet
Newsletter
Meetings
Toll-free phone line
Field operations/evaluations
Lease negotiations
Purchasing cooperatives
Security/safety procedures

MARKETING SUPPORT
Co-op advertising
Ad slicks
National media campaign
Regional marketing

PORT CITY JAVA

Ranked #420 in Entrepreneur Magazine's 2007 Franchise 500   *Financial rating: $$*

2101 Market St.
Wilmington, NC 28403
(910)796-6646
www.portcityjava.com
Gourmet coffees, smoothies,
    sandwiches
Began: 1995, Franchising: 2003
Headquarters size: 125 employees
Franchise department: 4 employees

U.S. franchises: 38
Canadian franchises: 0
Other foreign franchises: 3
Company-owned: 11

Seeking: All U.S.
Seeking in Canada? No
Exclusive territories? Yes
Homebased option? No
Employees needed to run biz: 8-12
Absentee ownership? No

COSTS
Total cost: $213.3K-399.3K
Franchise fee: $27.5K
Royalty fee: 5%
Term of agreement: 10 years renewable
    for 25% of current fee
Franchisees required to buy multiple
    units? No

FINANCING
In-house: None
3rd-party: Equipment, franchise fee,
    inventory, startup costs

QUALIFICATIONS
Net worth: $500K
Cash liquidity: $300K
Experience:
    Industry experience
    General business experience
    Marketing skills
    Food-service unit operating
    experience

TRAINING
At headquarters: 18 days
At franchisee's location: 14 days

BUSINESS SUPPORT
Grand opening
Internet
Newsletter
Meetings
Field operations/evaluations
Purchasing cooperatives
Security/safety procedures

MARKETING SUPPORT
Co-op advertising
Ad slicks
Regional marketing

ROCKN' JOE COFFEEHOUSE & BISTRO

Current financial data not available

5 Eastman St.
Cranford, NJ 07016
(908)276-4983
www.rocknjoe.net
Coffee, sandwiches, salads, desserts
Began: 1993, Franchising: 2005
Headquarters size: 4 employees
Franchise department: 4 employees

U.S. franchises: 2
Canadian franchises: 0
Other foreign franchises: 0
Company-owned: 1

Seeking: Midwest, Northeast,
    Southeast
Seeking in Canada? No
Exclusive territories? No
Homebased option? No
Employees needed to run biz: 16
Absentee ownership? Yes

COSTS
Total cost: $170K-225K
Franchise fee: $35K
Royalty fee: 6%
Term of agreement: 5 years renewable
    at no charge
Franchisees required to buy multiple
    units? No

FINANCING
No financing available

QUALIFICATIONS
Cash liquidity: $60K
Experience:
    General business experience

TRAINING
At headquarters: 4 weeks
At franchisee's location: 10 days

BUSINESS SUPPORT
Grand opening
Internet
Newsletter
Meetings
Toll-free phone line
Field operations/evaluations
Lease negotiations
Purchasing cooperatives
Security/safety procedures

MARKETING SUPPORT
Co-op advertising
Ad slicks
Regional marketing
PR

SCOOTER'S COFFEEHOUSE

Ranked #379 in Entrepreneur Magazine's 2007 Franchise 500   *Financial rating: $$$*

10665 Bedford Ave., #201
Omaha, NE 68134
(866)863-7266
www.scooterscoffee.com
Coffee, teas, smoothies, pastries
Began: 1998, Franchising: 2002
Headquarters size: 6 employees
Franchise department: 6 employees

U.S. franchises: 48
Canadian franchises: 0
Other foreign franchises: 0
Company-owned: 2

Seeking: All U.S.
Seeking in Canada? Yes
Exclusive territories? Yes
Homebased option? No
Employees needed to run biz: 3-20
Absentee ownership? Yes

COSTS
Total cost: $60K-410K
Franchise fee: $25K
Royalty fee: 6%
Term of agreement: 10 years
    renewable for $5K
Franchisees required to buy
    multiple units? No

FINANCING
No financing available

QUALIFICATIONS
Net worth: $100K-250K
Cash liquidity: $25K-70K
Experience:
    General business experience

TRAINING
At headquarters: 2-4 weeks
At franchisee's location: 1-2 weeks
At existing stores

BUSINESS SUPPORT
Grand opening
Internet
Newsletter
Meetings
Toll-free phone line
Field operations/evaluations
Lease negotiations
Purchasing cooperatives
Security/safety procedures

MARKETING SUPPORT
Co-op advertising
Ad slicks
National media campaign
Regional marketing
Ad & PR support

QUICK SERVICE ▶ *Hamburgers*

BACK YARD BURGERS INC.

Ranked #178 in Entrepreneur Magazine's 2007 Franchise 500   *Financial rating: $$$$*

1657 N. Shelby Oaks Dr., #105
Memphis, TN 38134
(901)367-0888
www.backyardburgers.com
Hamburgers & chicken sandwiches
Began: 1986, Franchising: 1988
Headquarters size: 30 employees
Franchise department: 3 employees

U.S. franchises: 133
Canadian franchises: 0
Other foreign franchises: 0
Company-owned: 42

Seeking: Midwest, Northeast, South,
    Southeast, Southwest
Seeking in Canada? No
Exclusive territories? Yes
Homebased option? No
Employees needed to run biz: 35
Absentee ownership? No

COSTS
Total cost: $445K-1.9M
Franchise fee: $25K
Royalty fee: 4%
Term of agreement: 10 years renewable
    for $1K
Franchisees required to buy multiple
    units? No

FINANCING
No financing available

QUALIFICATIONS
Net worth: $750K
Cash liquidity: $500K
Experience:
    Industry experience
    General business experience
    Marketing skills

TRAINING
At headquarters: 6 weeks
At franchisee's location: 2 weeks

BUSINESS SUPPORT
Grand opening
Internet
Newsletter
Meetings
Toll-free phone line
Field operations/evaluations
Purchasing cooperatives
Security/safety procedures

MARKETING SUPPORT
Co-op advertising
Ad slicks
National media campaign
Regional marketing

THE COUNTER GOURMET BURGERS

Current financial data not available

950 S. Flower St., #105
Los Angeles, CA 90015
(213)236-0950
www.flavorfirm.com
Build-your-own-burger restaurant
Began: 2003, Franchising: 2005
Headquarters size: 10 employees
Franchise department: 3 employees

U.S. franchises: 1
Canadian franchises: 0
Other foreign franchises: 0
Company-owned: 1

Seeking: All U.S.
Seeking in Canada? Yes
Exclusive territories? Yes
Homebased option? No
Employees needed to run biz: 15
Absentee ownership? Yes

COSTS
Total cost: $300K-650K
Franchise fee: $40K
Royalty fee: 6%
Term of agreement: 10 years
    renewable for $12.5K
Franchisees required to buy
    multiple units? Yes

FINANCING
In-house: None
3rd-party: Accounts receivable,
    equipment, franchise fee,
    inventory, payroll, startup costs

QUALIFICATIONS
Net worth: $750K
Cash liquidity: $250K
Experience:
    Industry experience
    General business experience
    Marketing skills

TRAINING
At headquarters: 2 weeks
At franchisee's location: 2 weeks

BUSINESS SUPPORT
Grand opening
Internet
Newsletter
Meetings
Toll-free phone line
Field operations/evaluations
Security/safety procedures

MARKETING SUPPORT
Co-op advertising
Ad slicks
Regional marketing

FARMER BOYS

Financial rating: $$$

3452 University Ave.
Riverside, CA 92501
(888)930-3276/(951)275-9900
www.farmerboys.com
Hamburgers
Began: 1981, Franchising: 1997
Headquarters size: 22 employees
Franchise department: 2 employees

U.S. franchises: 40
Canadian franchises: 0
Other foreign franchises: 0
Company-owned: 15

Seeking: Southwest
Seeking in Canada? No
Exclusive territories? Yes
Homebased option? No
Employees needed to run biz: 30
Absentee ownership? No

COSTS
Total cost: $1.2M-2.2M
Franchise fee: $45K
Royalty fee: 5%
Term of agreement: 20 years renewable
    at no charge
Franchisees required to buy multiple
    units? No

FINANCING
In-house: None
3rd-party: Accounts receivable,
    equipment, franchise fee,
    inventory, payroll, startup costs

QUALIFICATIONS
Net worth: $750K
Cash liquidity: $350K
Experience:
    Industry experience
    General business experience

TRAINING
At headquarters: 13 weeks
At franchisee's location: 4 weeks

BUSINESS SUPPORT
Grand opening
Internet
Newsletter
Meetings
Toll-free phone line
Field operations/evaluations
Purchasing cooperatives
Security/safety procedures

MARKETING SUPPORT
Co-op advertising
Ad slicks
Regional marketing

MCDONALD'S

Ranked #9 in Entrepreneur Magazine's 2007 Franchise 500　　　*Financial rating: $$$$*

Kroc Dr.
Oak Brook, IL 60523
(630)623-6196
www.mcdonalds.com
Hamburgers, chicken, salads
Began: 1955, Franchising: 1955
Headquarters size: 885 employees
Franchise department: 20 employees

U.S. franchises: 11,608
Canadian franchises: 890
Other foreign franchises: 10,056
Company-owned: 8,269

Seeking: All U.S.
Seeking in Canada? Yes
Exclusive territories? No
Homebased option? No
Employees needed to run biz: Info
    not provided
Absentee ownership? No

COSTS
Total cost: $506K-1.6M
Franchise fee: $45K
Royalty fee: 12.5%+
Term of agreement: 20 years renewable
    for $45K
Franchisees required to buy multiple
    units? No

FINANCING
No financing available

QUALIFICATIONS
Cash liquidity: $100K
Experience:
    Industry experience
    General business experience
    Marketing skills

TRAINING
At headquarters: 1 week
At local existing restaurant: 12-24
    months full time

BUSINESS SUPPORT
Grand opening
Internet
Newsletter
Meetings
Toll-free phone line
Field operations/evaluations
Lease negotiations
Purchasing cooperatives
Security/safety procedures

MARKETING SUPPORT
Co-op advertising
Ad slicks
National media campaign
Regional marketing
Restaurant-specific support

QUICK SERVICE　　*Hot Dogs & Sausages*

MANDLER'S THE ORIGINAL SAUSAGE CO.

Financial rating: $$$

38 W. 32nd St., #1601
New York, NY 10001
(212)730-2267
www.mandlers.com
European-style sausages, salads,
    mustard bar
Began: 2003, Franchising: 2005
Headquarters size: 11 employees
Franchise department: 4 employees

U.S. franchises: 0
Canadian franchises: 0
Other foreign franchises: 0
Company-owned: 1

Seeking: Northeast, Southeast
Seeking in Canada? No
Exclusive territories? Yes
Homebased option? No
Employees needed to run biz: 5
Absentee ownership? No

COSTS
Total cost: $230K-430K
Franchise fee: $25K
Royalty fee: 6%
Term of agreement: 7 years
Franchisees required to buy multi-
    ple units? Info not provided

FINANCING
In-house: None
3rd-party: Equipment, franchise fee,
    inventory, startup costs

QUALIFICATIONS
Net worth: $450K
Cash liquidity: $50K-100K

TRAINING
At headquarters: 2 weeks
At franchisee's location: 2 weeks

BUSINESS SUPPORT
Newsletter
Meetings
Field operations/evaluations
Purchasing cooperatives
Security/safety procedures

MARKETING SUPPORT
Info not provided

NEW ENGLAND HOT DOG COMPANY

Current financial data not available

100 Cummings Center, #231G
Beverly, MA 01915
(978)922-5105
www.nehotdog.com
Hot dogs & ice cream
Began: 2004, Franchising: 2005
Headquarters size: 4 employees
Franchise department: 3 employees

U.S. franchises: 3
Canadian franchises: 0
Other foreign franchises: 0
Company-owned: 1

Seeking: Northeast
Seeking in Canada? No
Exclusive territories? Yes
Homebased option? No
Employees needed to run biz: 3-5
Absentee ownership? No

COSTS
Total cost: $135K-250K
Franchise fee: $30K
Royalty fee: 6%
Term of agreement: 5 years renewable
    at no charge
Franchisees required to buy multiple
    units? No

FINANCING
In-house: None
3rd-party: Equipment

QUALIFICATIONS
Net worth: $250K
Cash liquidity: $100K
Experience:
    General business experience
    Marketing skills

TRAINING
At headquarters: 2 weeks
At franchisee's location: 4 weeks

BUSINESS SUPPORT
Grand opening
Internet
Toll-free phone line
Field operations/evaluations
Lease negotiations
Security/safety procedures

MARKETING SUPPORT
Co-op advertising
Ad slicks
Regional marketing

WIENERSCHNITZEL

Current financial data not available

4440 Von Karman
Newport Beach, CA 92660
(800)764-9353
www.wienerschnitzel.com
Hot dogs & hamburgers
Began: 1961, Franchising: 1965
Headquarters size: 45 employees
Franchise department: 5 employees

U.S. franchises: 353
Canadian franchises: 0
Other foreign franchises: 0
Company-owned: 0

Seeking: Southwest, West
Seeking in Canada? No
Exclusive territories? No
Homebased option? No
Employees needed to run biz: Info
    not provided
Absentee ownership? Yes

COSTS
Total cost: $136K-1M
Franchise fee: $32K
Royalty fee: 5%
Term of agreement: 20 years renewable
    for $1.6K per year
Franchisees required to buy multiple
    units? Yes

FINANCING
In-house: None
3rd-party: Accounts receivable,
    equipment, franchise fee,
    inventory, payroll, startup costs

QUALIFICATIONS
Net worth: $1M
Cash liquidity: $100K
Experience:
    Industry experience
    General business experience

TRAINING
At headquarters: 1 week
At franchisee's location: 5 weeks

BUSINESS SUPPORT
Grand opening
Internet
Newsletter
Meetings
Toll-free phone line
Field operations/evaluations
Purchasing cooperatives
Security/safety procedures

MARKETING SUPPORT
Co-op advertising
Ad slicks
Radio & TV spots

WOODY'S CHICAGO STYLE

Financial rating: $

19423 N. Turkey Creek Rd.
Morrison, CO 80465
(877)469-6639/(303)697-3962
www.woodyshotdogs.com
Hot dog, beverage & coffee carts/
in-line outlets
Began: 1987, Franchising: 1991
Headquarters size: 10 employees
Franchise department: 10 employees

U.S. franchises: 98
Canadian franchises: 0
Other foreign franchises: 0
Company-owned: 1

Seeking: All U.S.
Seeking in Canada? No
Exclusive territories? Yes
Homebased option? No
Employees needed to run biz: 1-3
Absentee ownership? No

COSTS
Total cost: $54.1K-464K
Franchise fee: Varies
Royalty fee: 6%
Term of agreement: 5 years renewable
for $2K
Franchisees required to buy multiple
units? No

FINANCING
In-house: Equipment, franchise fee
3rd-party: Equipment, franchise fee,
startup costs

QUALIFICATIONS
Net worth: $70K
Cash liquidity: $10K
Experience:
General business experience

TRAINING
At franchisee's location: 1 week
3-day follow-up within 30 days of
opening

BUSINESS SUPPORT
Grand opening
Internet
Newsletter
Meetings
Toll-free phone line
Field operations/evaluations
Security/safety procedures

MARKETING SUPPORT
Regional marketing
Grass-roots marketing program

QUICK SERVICE ▶ *Ice Cream & Frozen Desserts*

APPLEGATE INC.

Financial rating: 0

616 Grove St.
Upper Montclair, NJ 07043
(973)744-7000
www.applegatefarm.com
Ice cream
Began: 1848, Franchising: 2002
Headquarters size: Info not provided
Franchise department: 4 employees

U.S. franchises: 7
Canadian franchises: 0
Other foreign franchises: 0
Company-owned: 1

Seeking: Northeast
Seeking in Canada? No
Exclusive territories? No
Homebased option? No
Employees needed to run biz:
Info not provided
Absentee ownership? No

COSTS
Total cost: $137.7K-322K
Franchise fee: $25K
Royalty fee: 5%
Term of agreement: 5 years renewable
at no charge
Franchisees required to buy multiple
units? No

FINANCING
In-house: None
3rd-party: Accounts receivable,
equipment, franchise fee,
inventory, payroll, startup costs

QUALIFICATIONS
Experience:
General business experience
Marketing skills

TRAINING
At headquarters: 2 weeks
At franchisee's location: 1 week

BUSINESS SUPPORT
Grand opening
Meetings
Field operations/evaluations
Security/safety procedures

MARKETING SUPPORT
Regional marketing
Local advertising

BEN & JERRY'S

Ranked #82 in Entrepreneur Magazine's 2007 Franchise 500   *Financial rating: $$$$*

30 Community Dr.
South Burlington, VT 05403
(802)846-1500
www.benjerry.com
Ice cream parlor
Began: 1978, Franchising: 1981
Headquarters size: 120 employees
Franchise department: 27 employees

U.S. franchises: 420
Canadian franchises: 18
Other foreign franchises: 204
Company-owned: 11

Seeking: All U.S.
Seeking in Canada? No
Exclusive territories? Yes
Homebased option? No
Employees needed to run biz: Info
    not provided
Absentee ownership? No

COSTS
Total cost: $127K-396K
Franchise fee: $7.5K-30K
Royalty fee: 3%
Term of agreement: 10 years renewable
    for 50% of then-current fee
Franchisees required to buy multiple
    units? No

FINANCING
In-house: None
3rd-party: Accounts receivable,
    equipment, franchise fee,
    inventory, startup costs

QUALIFICATIONS
Net worth: $200K+
Cash liquidity: $80K+
Experience:
    Industry experience
    General business experience
    Marketing skills

TRAINING
At headquarters: 11 days
At franchisee's location: 3-5 days

BUSINESS SUPPORT
Grand opening
Internet
Newsletter
Meetings
Toll-free phone line
Field operations/evaluations
Security/safety procedures

MARKETING SUPPORT
Co-op advertising
Ad slicks
National media campaign
Regional marketing

BLUE SKY CREAMERY

Financial rating: $$

1323 XB Pl.
Boone, IA 50036
(515)268-4336
www.blueskycreamery.com
Ice cream, gourmet coffees, desserts
Began: 2000, Franchising: 2004
Headquarters size: 9 employees
Franchise department: 5 employees

U.S. franchises: 5
Canadian franchises: 0
Other foreign franchises: 0
Company-owned: 2

Seeking: All U.S.
Seeking in Canada? No
Exclusive territories? Yes
Homebased option? No
Employees needed to run biz: 5-15
Absentee ownership? Yes

COSTS
Total cost: $138.8K-373.9K
Franchise fee: $25K-35K
Royalty fee: 6%
Term of agreement: 6 years renewable
    for $1K
Franchisees required to buy multiple
    units? No

FINANCING
In-house: None
3rd-party: Accounts receivable,
    equipment, franchise fee,
    inventory, payroll, startup costs

QUALIFICATIONS
Net worth: $150K-400K
Cash liquidity: $35K-95K
Experience:
    General business experience
    Marketing skills

TRAINING
At headquarters: 1-2 weeks
At franchisee's location: 3-5 days

BUSINESS SUPPORT
Internet
Toll-free phone line
Field operations/evaluations

MARKETING SUPPORT
Ad slicks
Local store marketing
Promotional plans

BRUSTER'S REAL ICE CREAM

Ranked #124 in Entrepreneur Magazine's 2007 Franchise 500   *Financial rating: $$$*

730 Mulberry St.
Bridgewater, PA 15009
(724)774-4250
www.brusters.com
Homemade ice cream
Began: 1989, Franchising: 1993
Headquarters size: 34 employees
Franchise department: 2 employees

U.S. franchises: 249
Canadian franchises: 0
Other foreign franchises: 0
Company-owned: 5

Seeking: Northeast, South,
    Southeast
Seeking in Canada? No
Exclusive territories? Yes
Homebased option? No
Employees needed to run biz: 15-30
Absentee ownership? Yes

COSTS
Total cost: $172K-1.2M
Franchise fee: $35K
Royalty fee: 5%
Term of agreement: 10 years renewable
    at no charge
Franchisees required to buy multiple
    units? No

FINANCING
In-house: None
3rd-party: Accounts receivable,
    equipment, inventory, payroll,
    startup costs

QUALIFICATIONS
Cash liquidity: $200K
Experience:
    General business experience

TRAINING
At headquarters: 13 days

BUSINESS SUPPORT
Grand opening
Internet
Newsletter
Meetings
Field operations/evaluations
Purchasing cooperatives
Security/safety procedures

MARKETING SUPPORT
Co-op advertising
Ad slicks
National media campaign
Regional marketing

CARVEL

Ranked #165 in Entrepreneur Magazine's 2007 Franchise 500   *Financial rating: $$*

200 Glenridge Point Pkwy., #200
Atlanta, GA 30342
(404)255-3250
www.carvel.com
Ice cream & ice cream cakes
Began: 1934, Franchising: 1947
Headquarters size: 75 employees
Franchise department: 50 employees

U.S. franchises: 576
Canadian franchises: 2
Other foreign franchises: 0
Company-owned: 23

Seeking: All U.S.
Seeking in Canada? Yes
Exclusive territories? No
Homebased option? No
Employees needed to run biz: 6
Absentee ownership? Yes

COSTS
Total cost: $46.9K-388.7K
Franchise fee: $30K
Royalty fee: 6%
Term of agreement: 20 years renewable
    for then current fee
Franchisees required to buy multiple
    units? Outside the U.S. only

FINANCING
In-house: None
3rd-party: Equipment, franchise fee,
    inventory, startup costs

QUALIFICATIONS
Net worth: $300K+
Cash liquidity: $100K+
Experience:
    General business experience

TRAINING
At headquarters: 10 days
At franchisee's location: 5 days
Additional training annually

BUSINESS SUPPORT
Grand opening
Internet
Newsletter
Meetings
Toll-free phone line
Field operations/evaluations
Purchasing cooperatives
Security/safety procedures

MARKETING SUPPORT
Co-op advertising
Ad slicks
Regional marketing
Broadcast media

COLD STONE CREAMERY

Ranked #14 in Entrepreneur Magazine's 2007 Franchise 500　　　　*Financial rating: $$$*

9311 E. Via De Ventura
Scottsdale, AZ 85258
(480)362-4800
www.coldstonecreamery.com
Ice cream, Italian sorbet
Began: 1988, Franchising: 1994
Headquarters size: 190 employees
Franchise department: 11 employees

U.S. franchises: 1,328
Canadian franchises: 0
Other foreign franchises: 6
Company-owned: 18

Seeking: All U.S.
Seeking in Canada? Yes
Exclusive territories? No
Homebased option? No
Employees needed to run biz: 15
Absentee ownership? No

COSTS

Total cost: $294.3K-438.9K
Franchise fee: $42K
Royalty fee: 6%
Term of agreement: 10 years renewable
　　for 50% of then-current fee
Franchisees required to buy multiple
　　units? No

FINANCING

In-house: None
3rd-party: Accounts receivable,
　　equipment, inventory, payroll,
　　startup costs

QUALIFICATIONS

Cash liquidity: $125K
Experience:
　　General business experience
　　Marketing skills

TRAINING

At headquarters: 11 days
At franchisee's location: 3 days

BUSINESS SUPPORT

Grand opening
Internet
Newsletter
Meetings
Toll-free phone line
Field operations/evaluations
Lease negotiations
Purchasing cooperatives
Security/safety procedures

MARKETING SUPPORT

Co-op advertising
Ad slicks
National media campaign
Regional marketing
In-house creative services group
Local store marketing support

CULVER FRANCHISING SYSTEM INC.

Ranked #90 in Entrepreneur Magazine's 2007 Franchise 500　　　　*Financial rating: $$$$*

540 Water St.
Prairie du Sac, WI 53578
(608)643-7980
www.culvers.com
Frozen custard & specialty burgers
Began: 1984, Franchising: 1988
Headquarters size: 98 employees
Franchise department: 4 employees

U.S. franchises: 326
Canadian franchises: 0
Other foreign franchises: 0
Company-owned: 6

Seeking: Midwest, South, Southwest,
　　West
Seeking in Canada? No
Exclusive territories? No
Homebased option? No
Employees needed to run biz: 40-50
Absentee ownership? No

COSTS

Total cost: $340.4K-2.9M
Franchise fee: $55K
Royalty fee: 4%
Term of agreement: 15 years renewable
　　for $30K
Franchisees required to buy multiple
　　units? No

FINANCING

In-house: None
3rd-party: Accounts receivable,
　　equipment, franchise fee,
　　inventory, payroll, startup costs

QUALIFICATIONS

Net worth: $500K
Cash liquidity: $200K

TRAINING

At headquarters: 16 weeks

BUSINESS SUPPORT

Grand opening
Internet
Newsletter
Meetings
Field operations/evaluations
Purchasing cooperatives
Security/safety procedures

MARKETING SUPPORT

Ad slicks
National media campaign
Regional marketing

DAIRY QUEEN

Financial rating: $$$$

P.O. Box 39286
Minneapolis, MN 55439-0286
(800)679-6556/(952)830-0200
www.dairyqueen.com
Soft-serve dairy products &
    sandwiches
Began: 1940, Franchising: 1944
Headquarters size: 320 employees
Franchise department: 33 employees

U.S. franchises: 4,743
Canadian franchises: 575
Other foreign franchises: 352
Company-owned: 69

Seeking: All U.S.
Seeking in Canada? Yes
Exclusive territories? No
Homebased option? No
Employees needed to run biz: 20-40
Absentee ownership? Yes

COSTS
Total cost: $655K-1.3M
Franchise fee: $20K/35K
Royalty fee: 4-5%
Term of agreement: Varies
Franchisees required to buy multiple
    units? Outside the U.S. only

FINANCING
No financing available

QUALIFICATIONS
Net worth: $750K
Cash liquidity: $400K
Experience:
    Industry experience
    General business experience

TRAINING
At headquarters: 3 weeks
At franchisee's location: Pre- &
    post-opening
At existing store: 2 weeks

BUSINESS SUPPORT
Grand opening
Newsletter
Meetings
Toll-free phone line
Field operations/evaluations
Purchasing cooperatives

MARKETING SUPPORT
Co-op advertising
Ad slicks
National media campaign
Regional marketing
Local promotions program

DIPPIN' DOTS FRANCHISING INC.

Financial rating: $$$$

1640 McCracken Blvd., #100
Paducah, KY 42001
(270)575-6990
www.dippindots.com
Specialty ice cream, frozen yogurt,
    ices
Began: 1988, Franchising: 2000
Headquarters size: 22 employees
Franchise department: 12 employees

U.S. franchises: 448
Canadian franchises: 1
Other foreign franchises: 0
Company-owned: 2

Seeking: All U.S.
Seeking in Canada? No
Exclusive territories? No
Homebased option? No
Employees needed to run biz: 3
Absentee ownership? Yes

COSTS
Total cost: $70.2K-215.95K
Franchise fee: $12.5K
Royalty fee: 4%
Term of agreement: 5 years renewable
Franchisees required to buy multiple
    units? No

FINANCING
No financing available

QUALIFICATIONS
Net worth: $250K
Cash liquidity: $75K
Experience:
    General business experience

TRAINING
At headquarters: 3 days
At franchisee's location: 2 days

BUSINESS SUPPORT
Grand opening
Internet
Newsletter
Meetings
Field operations/evaluations
Lease negotiations
Purchasing cooperatives

MARKETING SUPPORT
Ad slicks
POP customization

THE HAAGEN-DAZS SHOPPE CO. INC.

Ranked #401 in Entrepreneur Magazine's 2007 Franchise 500　　　*Financial rating: $$$$*

500 Washington Ave. S., #2040
Minneapolis, MN 55415
(800)793-6872
www.haagendazs.com
Ice cream & frozen yogurt
Began: 1961, Franchising: 1977
Headquarters size: 22 employees
Franchise department: 4 employees

U.S. franchises: 220
Canadian franchises: 0
Other foreign franchises: 0
Company-owned: 0

Seeking: All U.S.
Seeking in Canada? No
Exclusive territories? No
Homebased option? No
Employees needed to run biz: 8
Absentee ownership? Yes

COSTS
Total cost: $86.8K-397.1K
Franchise fee: $30K
Royalty fee: 4%
Term of agreement: 10 years renewable
　for $10K
Franchisees required to buy multiple
　units? No

FINANCING
No financing available

QUALIFICATIONS
Net worth: $200K
Cash liquidity: $80K
Experience:
　General business experience

TRAINING
At headquarters: 2 weeks
Regional training sessions

BUSINESS SUPPORT
Grand opening
Newsletter
Meetings
Field operations/evaluations

MARKETING SUPPORT
National media campaign
Local store marketing

MAGGIEMOO'S INT'L. LLC

Ranked #408 in Entrepreneur Magazine's 2007 Franchise 500　　　*Financial rating: $*

10025 Governor Warfield Pkwy.,
　#301
Columbia, MD 21044
(800)949-8114
www.maggiemoos.com
Ice cream, smoothies, cakes
Began: 1996, Franchising: 1997
Headquarters size: 25 employees
Franchise department: 5 employees

U.S. franchises: 174
Canadian franchises: 0
Other foreign franchises: 0
Company-owned: 8

Seeking: All U.S.
Seeking in Canada? Yes
Exclusive territories? Yes
Homebased option? No
Employees needed to run biz: 12
Absentee ownership? Yes

COSTS
Total cost: $237K-336.7K
Franchise fee: $30K
Royalty fee: 6%
Term of agreement: 10 years
Franchisees required to buy multiple
　units? Outside the U.S. only

FINANCING
In-house: None
3rd-party: Equipment, inventory,
　startup costs

QUALIFICATIONS
Net worth: $275K
Cash liquidity: $75K

TRAINING
At headquarters: 14 days

BUSINESS SUPPORT
Grand opening
Internet
Newsletter
Meetings
Field operations/evaluations
Lease negotiations
Security/safety procedures

MARKETING SUPPORT
Co-op advertising
Ad slicks

MARBLE SLAB CREAMERY INC.

Ranked #93 in Entrepreneur Magazine's 2007 Franchise 500　　　　*Financial rating: $$$$*

3100 S. Gessner, #305
Houston, TX 77063
(713)780-3601
www.marbleslab.com
Ice cream, frozen yogurt, baked
    goods
Began: 1983, Franchising: 1984
Headquarters size: 25 employees
Franchise department: 8 employees

U.S. franchises: 347
Canadian franchises: 20
Other foreign franchises: 10
Company-owned: 1

Seeking: All U.S.
Seeking in Canada? Yes
Exclusive territories? No
Homebased option? No
Employees needed to run biz: 8-10
Absentee ownership? Yes

COSTS
Total cost: $205.2K-313.3K
Franchise fee: $32K
Royalty fee: 6%
Term of agreement: 10 years renewable
    for 20% of current fee
Franchisees required to buy multiple
    units? No

FINANCING
In-house: None
3rd-party: Equipment, franchise fee,
    inventory, startup costs

QUALIFICATIONS
Net worth: $250K
Cash liquidity: $60K
Experience:
    General business experience

TRAINING
At headquarters: 10 days
At franchisee's location: 6 days

BUSINESS SUPPORT
Grand opening
Internet
Newsletter
Meetings
Toll-free phone line
Field operations/evaluations
Security/safety procedures

MARKETING SUPPORT
Co-op advertising
Ad slicks
Regional marketing
Market-specific advertising

MELT INC.

Financial rating: $$$

22912 Mill Creek Dr., #D
Laguna Hills, CA 92653
(949)707-0456
www.meltgelato.com
Gelato, Italian coffee, crepes
Began: 2003, Franchising: 2005
Headquarters size: 6 employees
Franchise department: 4 employees

U.S. franchises: 8
Canadian franchises: 0
Other foreign franchises: 0
Company-owned: 2

Seeking: All U.S.
Seeking in Canada? Yes
Exclusive territories? No
Homebased option? No
Employees needed to run biz: Info
    not provided
Absentee ownership? Yes

COSTS
Total cost: $200K-400K
Franchise fee: $25K
Royalty fee: 6%
Term of agreement: 7 years renewable
    at no charge
Franchisees required to buy multiple
    units? Outside the U.S. only

FINANCING
In-house: None
3rd-party: Equipment, franchise fee,
    inventory, startup costs

QUALIFICATIONS
Net worth: $300K
Cash liquidity: $75K

TRAINING
At headquarters: 6 days
At franchisee's location: 4 days

BUSINESS SUPPORT
Grand opening
Internet
Meetings
Field operations/evaluations
Lease negotiations
Purchasing cooperatives
Security/safety procedures

MARKETING SUPPORT
Co-op advertising
National media campaign

PACIUGO ITALIAN GELATO

Financial rating: $$$

9761 Clifford Dr., #170
Dallas, TX 75220-5330
(214)654-9501
www.paciugo.com
Gelato
Began: 2000, Franchising: 2004
Headquarters size: 12 employees
Franchise department: 5 employees

U.S. franchises: 10
Canadian franchises: 0
Other foreign franchises: 1
Company-owned: 9

Seeking: All U.S.
Seeking in Canada? Yes
Exclusive territories? Yes
Homebased option? No
Employees needed to run biz: 5
Absentee ownership? No

COSTS
Total cost: $78.5K-377.6K
Franchise fee: $30K
Royalty fee: 4.5%
Term of agreement: 10 years renewable
    for $15K
Franchisees required to buy multiple
    units? No

FINANCING
In-house: None
3rd-party: Equipment, franchise fee,
    inventory, startup costs

QUALIFICATIONS
Cash liquidity: $150K
Compatibility with franchisor's
    system

TRAINING
At headquarters: 2 weeks
At franchisee's location: 1 week
DVD

BUSINESS SUPPORT
Grand opening
Internet
Newsletter
Meetings
Toll-free phone line
Field operations/evaluations
Purchasing cooperatives
Security/safety procedures

MARKETING SUPPORT
Ad slicks
Regional marketing
Grass-roots marketing

RITA'S FRANCHISE CO. LLC

Ranked #88 in Entrepreneur Magazine's 2007 Franchise 500

Financial rating: $$$$

1525 Ford Rd.
Bensalem, PA 19020
(800)677-7482
www.ritasice.com
Italian ices, frozen custard, gelati,
    soft pretzels
Began: 1984, Franchising: 1989
Headquarters size: 60 employees
Franchise department: 9 employees

U.S. franchises: 384
Canadian franchises: 0
Other foreign franchises: 0
Company-owned: 2

Seeking: Northeast, South,
    Southeast
Seeking in Canada? No
Exclusive territories? Yes
Homebased option? No
Employees needed to run biz: 10-15
Absentee ownership? No

COSTS
Total cost: $166.3K-347K
Franchise fee: $30K
Royalty fee: 6.5%
Term of agreement: 10 years renewable
    for 50% of current franchise fee
Franchisees required to buy multiple
    units? No

FINANCING
In-house: None
3rd-party: Equipment, startup costs

QUALIFICATIONS
Net worth: $250K
Cash liquidity: $75K
Experience:
    General business experience
    Marketing skills

TRAINING
At headquarters: 6 days
At franchisee's location: 2-4 days

BUSINESS SUPPORT
Grand opening
Internet
Newsletter
Meetings
Toll-free phone line
Field operations/evaluations
Lease negotiations
Purchasing cooperatives
Security/safety procedures

MARKETING SUPPORT
Co-op advertising
Ad slicks
National media campaign
Regional marketing
PR

STRICKLAND'S

Financial rating: $

388 S. Main St., #400
Akron, OH 44311
(330)564-1601
www.mystricklands.com
Homemade ice cream & related
    products
Began: 1936, Franchising: 2002
Headquarters size: 3 employees
Franchise department: 1 employee

U.S. franchises: 14
Canadian franchises: 0
Other foreign franchises: 0
Company-owned: 0

Seeking: All U.S.
Seeking in Canada? No
Exclusive territories? Yes
Homebased option? No
Employees needed to run biz: 10
Absentee ownership? Yes

COSTS
Total cost: $224.5K-337K
Franchise fee: $25K
Royalty fee: 6%
Term of agreement: 15 years renewable
    for $500
Franchisees required to buy multiple
    units? No

FINANCING
No financing available

QUALIFICATIONS
Net worth: $1M
Cash liquidity: $250K
Experience:
    General business experience

TRAINING
At headquarters: 2 weeks
At franchisee's location: 50 hours
Additional training as needed

BUSINESS SUPPORT
Grand opening
Internet
Newsletter
Meetings
Toll-free phone line
Field operations/evaluations
Purchasing cooperatives
Security/safety procedures

MARKETING SUPPORT
Ad slicks
Regional marketing

2 SCOOPS CAFE

Current financial data not available

2431 Aloma Ave., #124
Winter Park, FL 32792
(407)657-0363
www.2scoopscafe.com
Ice cream parlor/cafe
Began: 2002, Franchising: 2002
Headquarters size: 3 employees
Franchise department: 2 employees

U.S. franchises: 1
Canadian franchises: 0
Other foreign franchises: 0
Company-owned: 0

Seeking: Southeast
Seeking in Canada? No
Exclusive territories? Yes
Homebased option? No
Employees needed to run biz: 5-7
Absentee ownership? No

COSTS
Total cost: $99K-175K
Franchise fee: $35K
Royalty fee: 6%
Term of agreement: 5 years renewable
    for 25% of current franchise fee
Franchisees required to buy multiple
    units? No

FINANCING
No financing available

QUALIFICATIONS
Net worth: $150K
Cash liquidity: $40K-50K
Experience:
    General business experience
    People skills

TRAINING
At headquarters: 1 week
At franchisee's location: 1 week
Business coaching
Accounting & POS training

BUSINESS SUPPORT
Grand opening
Internet
Newsletter
Meetings
Toll-free phone line
Field operations/evaluations
Lease negotiations
Purchasing cooperatives
Security/safety procedures

MARKETING SUPPORT
Co-op advertising
Ad slicks
Regional marketing

YOGEN FRUZ WORLDWIDE

Current financial data not available

8300 Woodbine Ave., 5th Fl.
Markham, ON L3R 9Y7 Canada
(905)479-8762
www.yogenfruz.com
Frozen yogurt & ice cream
Began: 1986, Franchising: 1987
Headquarters size: 20 employees
Franchise department: 14 employees

U.S. franchises: 1,706
Canadian franchises: 805
Other foreign franchises: 2,806
Company-owned: 10

Seeking: All U.S.
Seeking in Canada? Yes
Exclusive territories? Yes
Homebased option? No
Employees needed to run biz: 4-7
Absentee ownership? No

COSTS
Total cost: $100K-200K
Franchise fee: $25K
Royalty fee: 6%
Term of agreement: 7-10 years
    renewable for 50% of current fee
Franchisees required to buy multiple
    units? Outside the U.S. only

FINANCING
No financing available

QUALIFICATIONS
Net worth: $150K+
Cash liquidity: $75K+
Experience:
    General business experience

TRAINING
At headquarters: 1 week
At franchisee's location: 1 week

BUSINESS SUPPORT
Grand opening
Internet
Meetings
Field operations/evaluations
Lease negotiations
Purchasing cooperatives
Security/safety procedures

MARKETING SUPPORT
Co-op advertising
Ad slicks
National media campaign
Regional marketing

QUICK SERVICE   *Italian*

AMATO'S

Current financial data not available

312 Saint John St.
Portland, ME 04107
(207)828-5981
www.amatos.com
Pizza, pasta, sandwiches
Began: 1902, Franchising: 2002
Headquarters size: 12 employees
Franchise department: 3 employees

U.S. franchises: 13
Canadian franchises: 0
Other foreign franchises: 0
Company-owned: 13

Seeking: Northeast
Seeking in Canada? No
Exclusive territories? Info not provided
Homebased option? No
Employees needed to run biz: 20
Absentee ownership? Info not provided

COSTS
Total cost: $395K-530K
Franchise fee: $25K
Royalty fee: 6%
Term of agreement: 20 years renewable
    at no charge
Franchisees required to buy multiple
    units? No

FINANCING
No financing available

QUALIFICATIONS
Net worth: $400K
Cash liquidity: $80K
Experience:
    General business experience

TRAINING
At headquarters: 4 weeks
At franchisee's location: 3 weeks

BUSINESS SUPPORT
Grand opening
Internet
Field operations/evaluations
Purchasing cooperatives

MARKETING SUPPORT
Regional marketing

ARTUZZI'S ITALIAN KITCHEN

Financial rating: 0

10779 Alpharetta Hwy.
Roswell, GA 30076
(404)630-3505
www.artuzzis.com
Fast-casual Italian restaurant
Began: 2005, Franchising: 2005
Headquarters size: 5 employees
Franchise department: 2 employees

U.S. franchises: 2
Canadian franchises: 0
Other foreign franchises: 0
Company-owned: 2

Seeking: All U.S.
Seeking in Canada? No
Exclusive territories? Yes
Homebased option? No
Employees needed to run biz: 20
Absentee ownership? No

COSTS
Total cost: $307.5K-367K
Franchise fee: $25K
Royalty fee: 5%
Term of agreement: 10 years renewable
    for 50% of then-current fee
Franchisees required to buy multiple
    units? No

FINANCING
No financing available

QUALIFICATIONS
Net worth: $500K
Cash liquidity: 30% of initial
    investment
Experience:
    Industry experience
    General business experience
    Marketing skills

TRAINING
At headquarters: 4 weeks
At franchisee's location: 1 week

BUSINESS SUPPORT
Grand opening
Internet
Newsletter
Meetings
Field operations/evaluations
Lease negotiations
Security/safety procedures

MARKETING SUPPORT
Ad slicks

SAVOIA T'GO FRANCHISE LLC

Current financial data not available

85 Independence Wy.
Chicago Heights, IL 60411
(800)867-2782
www.savoiatgo.com
Italian food
Began: 1974, Franchising: 2000
Headquarters size: 4 employees
Franchise department: 4 employees

U.S. franchises: 1
Canadian franchises: 0
Other foreign franchises: 0
Company-owned: 2

Seeking: Midwest
Seeking in Canada? No
Exclusive territories? Yes
Homebased option? No
Employees needed to run biz: 10
Absentee ownership? No

COSTS
Total cost: $287K-377K
Franchise fee: $25K
Royalty fee: 4%
Term of agreement: 10 years renewable
    at no charge
Franchisees required to buy multiple
    units? No

FINANCING
No financing available

QUALIFICATIONS
Cash liquidity: $75K
Experience:
    Industry experience
    General business experience
    Marketing skills

TRAINING
At headquarters: 8 weeks
At franchisee's location: 10 days

BUSINESS SUPPORT
Grand opening
Toll-free phone line
Field operations/evaluations
Lease negotiations
Purchasing cooperatives

MARKETING SUPPORT
Info not provided

AMAZON CAFE

Current financial data not available

127 S. State St.
Newtown, PA 18940
(800)945-1998
www.amazoncafes.com
Smoothies, sandwiches, soups,
  salads, wraps
Began: 1998, Franchising: 2002
Headquarters size: 7 employees
Franchise department: 3 employees

U.S. franchises: 47
Canadian franchises: 0
Other foreign franchises: 0
Company-owned: 4

Seeking: Northeast, Southeast
Seeking in Canada? No
Exclusive territories? Yes
Homebased option? No
Employees needed to run biz: 8-12
Absentee ownership? Yes

COSTS
Total cost: $269K-368K
Franchise fee: $29.5K
Royalty fee: 5%
Term of agreement: 10 years renewable
  for $15K
Franchisees required to buy multiple
  units? No

FINANCING
In-house: None
3rd-party: Accounts receivable,
  equipment, franchise fee,
  inventory, payroll, startup costs

QUALIFICATIONS
Net worth: $300K
Cash liquidity: $50K
Experience:
  General business experience

TRAINING
At headquarters: 5 days
At franchisee's location: 7 days
At approved store: 7-10 days

BUSINESS SUPPORT
Grand opening
Internet
Newsletter
Meetings
Toll-free phone line
Field operations/evaluations
Lease negotiations
Purchasing cooperatives
Security/safety procedures

MARKETING SUPPORT
Co-op advertising
Ad slicks
Regional marketing

INDIGOS FRUIT SMOOTHIES

Financial rating: $$

6810 Lyons Technology Cir., #180
Coconut Creek, FL 33073
(866)332-7482/(954)834-0691
www.indigossmoothies.com
Fruit smoothies, fresh-squeezed
  juices, salads, pitas
Began: 2000, Franchising: 2004
Headquarters size: 4 employees
Franchise department: 4 employees

U.S. franchises: 8
Canadian franchises: 1
Other foreign franchises: 1
Company-owned: 1

Seeking: All U.S.
Seeking in Canada? Yes
Exclusive territories? Yes
Homebased option? No
Employees needed to run biz: 5-10
Absentee ownership? No

COSTS
Total cost: $155.6K-270K
Franchise fee: $25K
Royalty fee: 6%
Term of agreement: 5 years renewable
  for $5K
Franchisees required to buy multiple
  units? Yes

FINANCING
No financing available

QUALIFICATIONS
Net worth: $250K
Cash liquidity: $100K
Experience:
  General business experience

TRAINING
At headquarters: 1 week
At franchisee's location: 1 week
Ongoing

BUSINESS SUPPORT
Grand opening
Internet
Newsletter
Meetings
Toll-free phone line
Field operations/evaluations
Lease negotiations
Purchasing cooperatives
Security/safety procedures

MARKETING SUPPORT
Co-op advertising
Ad slicks
Regional marketing

JUGO JUICE

Current financial data not available

A8-416 Meridian Rd. S.E.
Calgary, AB T2A 1X2 Canada
(877)377-5846
www.jugojuice.com
Juice bar
Began: 1998, Franchising: 2002
Headquarters size: 12 employees
Franchise department: 3 employees

U.S. franchises: 4
Canadian franchises: 64
Other foreign franchises: 0
Company-owned: 0

Seeking: All U.S.
Seeking in Canada? Yes
Exclusive territories? Yes
Homebased option? No
Employees needed to run biz: 10
Absentee ownership? Yes

COSTS
Total cost: $225K
Franchise fee: $25K
Royalty fee: 6%
Term of agreement: 20 years renewable
    at no charge
Franchisees required to buy multiple
    units? No

FINANCING
In-house: None
3rd-party: Accounts receivable,
    equipment, franchise fee,
    inventory, payroll, startup costs

QUALIFICATIONS
Cash liquidity: $50K

TRAINING
At headquarters: 7 days
At franchisee's location: 5 days

BUSINESS SUPPORT
Internet
Newsletter
Toll-free phone line
Field operations/evaluations
Lease negotiations
Security/safety procedures

MARKETING SUPPORT
Co-op advertising

JUICE IT UP!

Ranked #189 in Entrepreneur Magazine's 2007 Franchise 500   *Financial rating: $$$$*

17915 Sky Park Cir., #J
Irvine, CA 92614
(949)475-0146
www.juiceitup.com
Juice bar
Began: 1995, Franchising: 1998
Headquarters size: 13 employees
Franchise department: 13 employees

U.S. franchises: 114
Canadian franchises: 0
Other foreign franchises: 0
Company-owned: 5

Seeking: All U.S.
Seeking in Canada? No
Exclusive territories? Yes
Homebased option? No
Employees needed to run biz: 10
Absentee ownership? No

COSTS
Total cost: $173.8K-277.7K
Franchise fee: $25K
Royalty fee: 6%
Term of agreement: 10 years renewable
    at no charge
Franchisees required to buy multiple
    units? No

FINANCING
In-house: None
3rd-party: Financing available

QUALIFICATIONS
Net worth: $250K
Cash liquidity: $50K
Experience:
    General business experience
    Marketing skills

TRAINING
At headquarters: 2 weeks
At franchisee's location: 1 week

BUSINESS SUPPORT
Grand opening
Internet
Newsletter
Meetings
Toll-free phone line
Field operations/evaluations
Lease negotiations
Purchasing cooperatives
Security/safety procedures

MARKETING SUPPORT
Co-op advertising
Ad slicks
Regional marketing

JUICEBLENDZ INT'L. INC.

Current financial data not available

4533 Weston Rd
Weston, FL 33331
(866)525-3639
www.juiceblendz.com
Smoothies, juices, dietary
  supplements
Began: 2004, Franchising: 2005
Headquarters size: 10 employees
Franchise department: 4 employees

U.S. franchises: 3
Canadian franchises: 0
Other foreign franchises: 0
Company-owned: 0

Seeking: All U.S.
Seeking in Canada? Yes
Exclusive territories? Yes
Homebased option? No
Employees needed to run biz: 10-20
Absentee ownership? Yes

COSTS
Total cost: $219K-350K
Franchise fee: $50K
Royalty fee: 6%
Term of agreement: 5 years renewable
  for $15K
Franchisees required to buy multiple
  units? No

FINANCING
In-house: None
3rd-party: Equipment, franchise fee,
  startup costs

QUALIFICATIONS
Net worth: $375K
Cash liquidity: $125K
Experience:
  Industry experience
  General business experience

TRAINING
At franchisee's location: 1-6 months

BUSINESS SUPPORT
Grand opening
Internet
Newsletter
Meetings
Toll-free phone line
Field operations/evaluations
Security/safety procedures

MARKETING SUPPORT
Co-op advertising
Ad slicks
Regional marketing

MAUI WOWI HAWAIIAN COFFEES & SMOOTHIES

Ranked #417 in Entrepreneur Magazine's 2007 Franchise 500

Financial rating: $$

5445 DTC Pkwy., #1050
Greenwood Village, CO 80111
(877)849-6992
www.mauiwowi.com
Hawaiian coffees & smoothies
Began: 1983, Franchising: 1997
Headquarters size: 30 employees
Franchise department: 9 employees

U.S. franchises: 345
Canadian franchises: 0
Other foreign franchises: 0
Company-owned: 0

Seeking: All U.S.
Seeking in Canada? Yes
Exclusive territories? Yes
Homebased option? No
Employees needed to run biz: 2-3
Absentee ownership? Yes

COSTS
Total cost: $75K-550K
Franchise fee: $27.5K/34.5K/59.5K
Royalty fee: 0
Term of agreement: 10 years renewable
  for 20% of current fee
Franchisees required to buy multiple
  units? No

FINANCING
In-house: None
3rd-party: Accounts receivable,
  equipment, franchise fee,
  inventory, payroll, startup costs

QUALIFICATIONS
Net worth: $250K
Cash liquidity: $50K
Experience:
  General business experience
  Sales & marketing experience

TRAINING
At headquarters: 4 days
At franchisee's location: 1-2 days+
Ongoing support

BUSINESS SUPPORT
Grand opening
Internet
Newsletter
Meetings
Toll-free phone line
Field operations/evaluations
Lease negotiations
Security/safety procedures

MARKETING SUPPORT
Co-op advertising
National media campaign
Regional marketing
PR

ROBEKS FRUIT SMOOTHIES & HEALTHY EATS

Ranked #222 in Entrepreneur Magazine's 2007 Franchise 500　　　*Financial rating: $$$*

1230 E. Rosecrans Ave., #400
Manhattan Beach, CA 90266
(866)476-2357
www.robeks.com
Fruit smoothies & healthy foods
Began: 1996, Franchising: 2001
Headquarters size: 25 employees
Franchise department: 3 employees

U.S. franchises: 96
Canadian franchises: 0
Other foreign franchises: 0
Company-owned: 0

Seeking: All U.S.
Seeking in Canada? No
Exclusive territories? No
Homebased option? No
Employees needed to run biz: 12-20
Absentee ownership? No

COSTS
Total cost: $228.7K-335.9K
Franchise fee: $25K
Royalty fee: 7%
Term of agreement: 10 years renewable
　　for 25% of then-current fee
Franchisees required to buy multiple
　　units? No

FINANCING
In-house: Accounts receivable, payroll
3rd-party: Equipment, franchise fee,
　　inventory, startup costs

QUALIFICATIONS
Net worth: $250K
Cash liquidity: $100K
Experience:
　　General business experience
　　Marketing skills
　　Customer-service skills
　　Outgoing & energetic

TRAINING
At headquarters/regional training
　　store: 2 weeks
At franchisee's location: 1 week

BUSINESS SUPPORT
Grand opening
Internet
Newsletter
Meetings
Toll-free phone line
Field operations/evaluations
Lease negotiations
Purchasing cooperatives
Security/safety procedures

MARKETING SUPPORT
Co-op advertising
Ad slicks
Regional marketing
Local store marketing program

SMOOTHIE KING

Ranked #91 in Entrepreneur Magazine's 2007 Franchise 500　　　*Financial rating: $$$$*

121 Park Pl.
Covington, LA 70433
(800)577-4200/(504)467-4006
www.smoothieking.com
Smoothies & healthy products
Began: 1987, Franchising: 1988
Headquarters size: 60 employees
Franchise department: 4 employees

U.S. franchises: 419
Canadian franchises: 0
Other foreign franchises: 18
Company-owned: 1

Seeking: All U.S.
Seeking in Canada? Yes
Exclusive territories? No
Homebased option? No
Employees needed to run biz: 6-9
Absentee ownership? Yes

COSTS
Total cost: $121K-251K
Franchise fee: $25K
Royalty fee: 6%
Term of agreement: 10 years renewable
　　for $5K
Franchisees required to buy multiple
　　units? No

FINANCING
In-house: None
3rd-party: Accounts receivable,
　　equipment, franchise fee,
　　inventory, payroll, startup costs

QUALIFICATIONS
Net worth: $100K+
Cash liquidity: $50K
Experience:
　　General business experience
　　Marketing skills

TRAINING
At headquarters: 1 day
At franchisee's location: 1 week
Managment training at corporate
　　store: 14 days

BUSINESS SUPPORT
Grand opening
Internet
Newsletter
Meetings
Toll-free phone line
Field operations/evaluations
Lease negotiations
Purchasing cooperatives
Security/safety procedures

MARKETING SUPPORT
Co-op advertising
Ad slicks
National media campaign

SQUEEZE FRESH SMOOTHIES

Financial rating: $$$

5445 DTC Pkwy., #1110
Greenwood Village, CO 80111
(303)350-1886
www.squeezeusa.com
Smoothies
Began: 2004, Franchising: 2004
Headquarters size: 11 employees
Franchise department: 7 employees

U.S. franchises: 8
Canadian franchises: 0
Other foreign franchises: 0
Company-owned: 3

Seeking: All U.S.
Seeking in Canada? No
Exclusive territories? Yes
Homebased option? No
Employees needed to run biz: Info
    not provided
Absentee ownership? Yes

COSTS
Total cost: $160K-244K
Franchise fee: $25K
Royalty fee: 6.3%
Term of agreement: 7 years
    renewable at no charge
Franchisees required to buy
    multiple units? No

FINANCING
No financing available

QUALIFICATIONS
Net worth: $250K
Cash liquidity: $75K
Experience:
    General business experience

TRAINING
At headquarters
At franchisee's location

BUSINESS SUPPORT
Grand opening
Internet
Newsletter
Meetings
Toll-free phone line
Field operations/evaluations
Purchasing cooperatives
Security/safety procedures

MARKETING SUPPORT
Ad slicks
Regional marketing

SURF CITY SQUEEZE

Ranked #162 in Entrepreneur Magazine's 2007 Franchise 500

Financial rating: $$$$

7730 E. Greenway Rd., 104
Scottsdale, AZ 85260
(480)443-0200
www.kahalacorp.com
Smoothies, fruit drinks, nutritional
    supplements
Began: 1988, Franchising: 1994
Headquarters size: 30 employees
Franchise department: 30 employees

U.S. franchises: 133
Canadian franchises: 9
Other foreign franchises: 6
Company-owned: 2

Seeking: All U.S.
Seeking in Canada? Yes
Exclusive territories? Yes
Homebased option? No
Employees needed to run biz: 5
Absentee ownership? Yes

COSTS
Total cost: $77.4K-360.5K
Franchise fee: $30K
Royalty fee: 6%
Term of agreement: 10 years renewable
    for 75% of then-current fee
Franchisees required to buy multiple
    units? No

FINANCING
In-house: None
3rd-party: Equipment, franchise fee,
    inventory, startup costs

QUALIFICATIONS
Cash liquidity: $30K
Experience:
    Industry experience
    General business experience

TRAINING
At headquarters: 1 week
At franchisee's location: 2 weeks

BUSINESS SUPPORT
Grand opening
Internet
Newsletter
Meetings
Toll-free phone line
Field operations/evaluations
Purchasing cooperatives
Security/safety procedures

MARKETING SUPPORT
Co-op advertising
Ad slicks
Regional marketing

TROPICAL SMOOTHIE CAFE
Ranked #127 in Entrepreneur Magazine's 2007 Franchise 500   *Financial rating: $$$*

4100 Legendary Dr., #250
Destin, FL 32541
(888)292-2522
www.tropicalsmoothie.com
Smoothies, sandwiches, wraps,
    coffee
Began: 1997, Franchising: 1997
Headquarters size: 15 employees
Franchise department: 2 employees

U.S. franchises: 204
Canadian franchises: 0
Other foreign franchises: 6
Company-owned: 1

Seeking: All U.S.
Seeking in Canada? Yes
Exclusive territories? No
Homebased option? No
Employees needed to run biz: 10-20
Absentee ownership? Yes

COSTS
Total cost: $200K-300K
Franchise fee: $20K
Royalty fee: 6%
Term of agreement: 20 years
    renewable at no charge
Franchisees required to buy
    multiple units? No

FINANCING
In-house: None
3rd-party: Accounts receivable,
    equipment, franchise fee,
    inventory, payroll, startup costs

QUALIFICATIONS
Net worth: $150K
Cash liquidity: $80K
Experience:
    General business experience

TRAINING
At headquarters: 1 week
At franchisee's location: 1 week
At existing store: 80 hours

BUSINESS SUPPORT
Grand opening
Internet
Newsletter
Meetings
Toll-free phone line
Field operations/evaluations
Purchasing cooperatives
Security/safety procedures

MARKETING SUPPORT
Co-op advertising
Ad slicks
National media campaign
Regional marketing

VITALITY JUICE, JAVA & SMOOTHIE BAR
Current financial data not available

790 Florida St., #1
Mandeville, LA 70448
(985)674-6898
www.vitalityjuice.com
Smoothies, juices, coffee, vitamins
Began: 2004, Franchising: 2005
Headquarters size: 12 employees
Franchise department: 12 employees

U.S. franchises: 1
Canadian franchises: 0
Other foreign franchises: 0
Company-owned: 2

Seeking: All U.S.
Seeking in Canada? No
Exclusive territories? Yes
Homebased option? No
Employees needed to run biz: 10-12
Absentee ownership? No

COSTS
Total cost: $86K-300.5K
Franchise fee: $15K/25K/35K
Royalty fee: 5%
Term of agreement: 15 years renewable
    for $10K
Franchisees required to buy multiple
    units? No

FINANCING
In-house: None
3rd-party: Accounts receivable,
    equipment, franchise fee,
    inventory, payroll, startup costs

QUALIFICATIONS
Experience:
    Industry experience
    General business experience
    Interest in health & wellness

TRAINING
At headquarters: 2 weeks
At franchisee's location: 1 week
Ongoing

BUSINESS SUPPORT
Grand opening
Internet
Newsletter
Toll-free phone line
Field operations/evaluations
Lease negotiations
Purchasing cooperatives
Security/safety procedures

MARKETING SUPPORT
Co-op advertising
Ad slicks
Regional marketing

BAJA SOL TORTILLA GRILL

Current financial data not available

7173 Oak Pointe Curve
Bloomington, MN 55438
(612)280-1467
www.baja-sol.com
Fresh-Mex food
Began: 1995, Franchising: 1995
Headquarters size: 3 employees
Franchise department: 1 employee

U.S. franchises: 7
Canadian franchises: 0
Other foreign franchises: 0
Company-owned: 4

Seeking: Midwest, Northeast
Seeking in Canada? No
Exclusive territories? Yes
Homebased option? No
Employees needed to run biz: 12
Absentee ownership? No

COSTS
Total cost: $186K-400K
Franchise fee: $25K
Royalty fee: 4.5%
Term of agreement: 10 years renewable
at no charge
Franchisees required to buy multiple
units? No

FINANCING
No financing available

QUALIFICATIONS
Net worth: $500K
Cash liquidity: $100K
Experience:
General business experience

TRAINING
At headquarters: 4 weeks

BUSINESS SUPPORT
Grand opening
Internet
Field operations/evaluations
Lease negotiations
Purchasing cooperatives

MARKETING SUPPORT
Co-op advertising

IZZO'S ILLEGAL BURRITO

Financial rating: $

422 Pinewold Dr.
Houston, TX 77056
(713)552-8118
www.izzos.com
Fast-casual Mexican food
Began: 2001, Franchising: 2006
Headquarters size: 5 employees

U.S. franchises: 0
Canadian franchises: 0
Other foreign franchises: 0
Company-owned: 2

Seeking: All U.S.
Seeking in Canada? No
Exclusive territories? Yes
Homebased option? No
Employees needed to run biz: Info
not provided
Absentee ownership? No

COSTS
Total cost: $380.5K-744.9K
Franchise fee: $40K
Royalty fee: 5%
Term of agreement: 10 years renewable
for $4K
Franchisees required to buy multiple
units? Yes

FINANCING
No financing available

QUALIFICATIONS
Experience:
Industry experience
General business experience
Marketing skills

TRAINING
At headquarters: 12 days
At franchisee's location: 7 days

BUSINESS SUPPORT
Grand opening
Toll-free phone line
Purchasing cooperatives
Security/safety procedures

MARKETING SUPPORT
Co-op advertising
Ad slicks
In-store promotions

MOE'S SOUTHWEST GRILL

Ranked #73 in Entrepreneur Magazine's 2007 Franchise 500

Financial rating: $$$$

2915 Peachtree Rd.
Atlanta, GA 30305
(404)844-3225
www.moes.com
Quick-service fresh-Mex restaurant
Began: 2000, Franchising: 2001
Headquarters size: 40 employees
Franchise department: 4 employees

U.S. franchises: 335
Canadian franchises: 0
Other foreign franchises: 0
Company-owned: 1

Seeking: All U.S.
Seeking in Canada? Yes
Exclusive territories? No
Homebased option? No
Employees needed to run biz: 15
Absentee ownership? Yes

COSTS
Total cost: $252K-634K
Franchise fee: $25K
Royalty fee: 5%
Term of agreement: 10 years renewable
    for then-current franchise fee
Franchisees required to buy multiple
    units? No

FINANCING
In-house: None
3rd-party: Accounts receivable,
    equipment, franchise fee,
    inventory, payroll, startup costs

QUALIFICATIONS
Net worth: $500K
Cash liquidity: $150K
Experience:
    Industry experience
    General business experience
    Marketing skills
    Excellent attention to detail

TRAINING
At headquarters: 2 weeks
At franchisee's location: 1 week

BUSINESS SUPPORT
Grand opening
Internet
Newsletter
Meetings
Field operations/evaluations
Purchasing cooperatives
Security/safety procedures

MARKETING SUPPORT
Co-op advertising
Ad slicks
National media campaign
Regional marketing
Website
Promo tools

PANCHERO'S MEXICAN GRILL

Current financial data not available

2475 Coral Ct., #B
Coralville, IA 52241
(888)639-2378
www.pancheros.com
Fresh-Mex quick-service restaurant
Began: 1992, Franchising: 1995
Headquarters size: 12 employees

U.S. franchises: 20
Canadian franchises: 0
Other foreign franchises: 0
Company-owned: 15

Seeking: All U.S.
Seeking in Canada? Yes
Exclusive territories? Yes
Homebased option? No
Employees needed to run biz: Info
    not provided
Absentee ownership? Yes

COSTS
Total cost: $250K-380K
Franchise fee: $20K-30K
Royalty fee: 5%
Term of agreement: 5 years renewable
    at no charge
Franchisees required to buy multiple
    units? No

FINANCING
In-house: None
3rd-party: Equipment, franchise fee,
    inventory, startup costs

QUALIFICATIONS
Net worth: $250K
Cash liquidity: $70K
Experience:
    General business experience
    Marketing skills

TRAINING
At headquarters
At franchisee's location

BUSINESS SUPPORT
Grand opening
Newsletter
Toll-free phone line

MARKETING SUPPORT
Regional marketing
Radio & TV

QDOBA MEXICAN GRILL

Ranked #87 in Entrepreneur Magazine's 2007 Franchise 500   *Financial rating: $$$$*

4865 Ward Rd., #500
Wheat Ridge, CO 80033
(720)898-2300
www.qdoba.com
Fast-casual Mexican food
Began: 1995, Franchising: 1997
Headquarters size: 50 employees
Franchise department: 3 employees

U.S. franchises: 235
Canadian franchises: 0
Other foreign franchises: 0
Company-owned: 66

Seeking: All U.S.
Seeking in Canada? No
Exclusive territories? Yes
Homebased option? No
Employees needed to run biz: 15
Absentee ownership? Yes

COSTS
Total cost: $395K-605K
Franchise fee: $25K
Royalty fee: 5%
Term of agreement: 10 years renewable
    for $5K
Franchisees required to buy multiple
    units? Yes

FINANCING
In-house: None
3rd-party: Accounts receivable,
    equipment, franchise fee,
    inventory, payroll, startup costs

QUALIFICATIONS
Net worth: $3M
Cash liquidity: $750K
Experience:
    Industry experience
    General business experience
    Marketing skills

TRAINING
At headquarters: 4 weeks

BUSINESS SUPPORT
Grand opening
Internet
Newsletter
Meetings
Toll-free phone line
Field operations/evaluations
Purchasing cooperatives
Security/safety procedures

MARKETING SUPPORT
Co-op advertising
Ad slicks
Local marketing

SALSARITA'S FRESH CANTINA

Ranked #243 in Entrepreneur Magazine's 2007 Franchise 500   *Financial rating: $$$*

7301 Carmel Executive Park Dr.,
    #101-A
Charlotte, NC 28226
(704)540-9447
www.salsaritas.com
Fresh-Mex-style cantina
Began: 1999, Franchising: 2000
Headquarters size: 18 employees
Franchise department: 1 employee

U.S. franchises: 51
Canadian franchises: 0
Other foreign franchises: 0
Company-owned: 2

Seeking: All U.S.
Seeking in Canada? Yes
Exclusive territories? Yes
Homebased option? No
Employees needed to run biz: 10
Absentee ownership? Yes

COSTS
Total cost: $217.9K-360.7K
Franchise fee: $20K
Royalty fee: 5-6%
Term of agreement: 10 years renewable
    for 15% of then-current fee
Franchisees required to buy multiple
    units? Outside the U.S. only

FINANCING
In-house: None
3rd-party: Equipment, franchise fee,
    inventory, startup costs

QUALIFICATIONS
Net worth: $500K
Cash liquidity: $100K
Experience:
    General business experience
    Restaurant experience helpful

TRAINING
At headquarters: 3 weeks
At franchisee's location: 2 weeks

BUSINESS SUPPORT
Grand opening
Internet
Newsletter
Field operations/evaluations
Purchasing cooperatives
Security/safety procedures

MARKETING SUPPORT
Co-op advertising
Ad slicks
Regional marketing

TACO BELL CORP.

Current financial data not available

1900 Colonel Sanders Ln.
Louisville, KY 40213
(502)874-8300
www.yumfranchises.com
Quick-service Mexican restaurant
Began: 1962, Franchising: 1964
Headquarters size: 500 employees

U.S. franchises: 4,577
Canadian franchises: 86
Other foreign franchises: 149
Company-owned: 1,275

Seeking: All U.S.
Seeking in Canada? Yes
Exclusive territories? No
Homebased option? No
Employees needed to run biz: 25
Absentee ownership? Yes

COSTS
Total cost: $1.1M-1.7M
Franchise fee: $45K
Royalty fee: 5.5%
Term of agreement: 20 years not
    renewable
Franchisees required to buy multiple
    units? Yes

FINANCING
No financing available

QUALIFICATIONS
Net worth: $1M
Cash liquidity: $360K
Experience:
    Industry experience
    General business experience
    Marketing skills

TRAINING
At headquarters
Additional training available

BUSINESS SUPPORT
Grand opening
Internet
Newsletter
Meetings
Field operations/evaluations
Security/safety procedures

MARKETING SUPPORT
Co-op advertising
National media campaign
Regional marketing

TACO JOHN'S INT'L. INC.

Financial rating: $$$$

808 W. 20th St.
Cheyenne, WY 82003
(800)854-0819
www.tacojohns.com
Mexican food
Began: 1968, Franchising: 1969
Headquarters size: 60 employees
Franchise department: 2 employees

U.S. franchises: 410
Canadian franchises: 0
Other foreign franchises: 0
Company-owned: 10

Seeking: Midwest, Northwest,
    South, West
Seeking in Canada? No
Exclusive territories? Yes
Homebased option? No
Employees needed to run biz: 15
Absentee ownership? Yes

COSTS
Total cost: $495K-709.5K
Franchise fee: $25K
Royalty fee: 4%
Term of agreement: 20 years renewable
    at no charge
Franchisees required to buy multiple
    units? No

FINANCING
In-house: None
3rd-party: Equipment, franchise fee,
    inventory, startup costs

QUALIFICATIONS
Net worth: $400K
Cash liquidity: $150K
Experience:
    Industry experience
    General business experience

TRAINING
At headquarters: 4-5 weeks
At franchisee's location: 1 week

BUSINESS SUPPORT
Grand opening
Internet
Newsletter
Meetings
Toll-free phone line
Field operations/evaluations
Purchasing cooperatives
Security/safety procedures

MARKETING SUPPORT
Co-op advertising
Ad slicks

TACOTIME

Ranked #145 in Entrepreneur Magazine's 2007 Franchise 500　　　*Financial rating: $$$$*

7730 E. Greenway Rd., #104
Scottsdale, AZ 85260
(480)443-0200
www.kahalacorp.com
Quick-service Mexican restaurant
Began: 1958, Franchising: 1961
Headquarters size: Info not provided

U.S. franchises: 179
Canadian franchises: 108
Other foreign franchises: 1
Company-owned: 2

Seeking: All U.S.
Seeking in Canada? Yes
Exclusive territories? Yes
Homebased option? No
Employees needed to run biz: 15
Absentee ownership? Yes

COSTS
Total cost: $139.8K-698.5K
Franchise fee: $30K
Royalty fee: 6%
Term of agreement: 10 years renewable
　at no charge
Franchisees required to buy multiple
　units? No

FINANCING
In-house: None
3rd-party: Equipment, franchise fee,
　inventory, startup costs

QUALIFICATIONS
Cash liquidity: $30K
Experience:
　General business experience

TRAINING
At headquarters: 2-4 weeks

BUSINESS SUPPORT
Grand opening
Newsletter
Meetings
Toll-free phone line
Field operations/evaluations
Security/safety procedures

MARKETING SUPPORT
Co-op advertising
National media campaign
Regional marketing

QUICK SERVICE　　*Pizza*

BREADEAUX PIZZA

Current financial data not available

P.O. Box 6158, Fairleigh Sta.
St. Joseph, MO 64506
(816)364-1088
www.breadeauxpizza.com
French-crust pizza & cookies
Began: 1985, Franchising: 1985
Headquarters size: 15 employees
Franchise department: 1 employee

U.S. franchises: 92
Canadian franchises: 4
Other foreign franchises: 0
Company-owned: 2

Seeking: Midwest
Seeking in Canada? No
Exclusive territories? Yes
Homebased option? No
Employees needed to run biz: 12
Absentee ownership? Yes

COSTS
Total cost: $69.5K-310K
Franchise fee: $15K
Royalty fee: 5%
Term of agreement: 15 years renewable
　for 25% of then-current fee
Franchisees required to buy multiple
　units? No

FINANCING
In-house: None
3rd-party: Equipment

QUALIFICATIONS
Cash liquidity: $100K

TRAINING
At headquarters: 2 weeks
At franchisee's location: During
　first week

BUSINESS SUPPORT
Grand opening
Internet
Newsletter
Meetings
Toll-free phone line
Field operations/evaluations
Purchasing cooperatives

MARKETING SUPPORT
Co-op advertising
Ad slicks
National media campaign
Individualized support

BUCK'S PIZZA

Financial rating: $$$$

P.O. Box 405
DuBois, PA 15801
(800)310-8848
www.buckspizza.com
Pizza
Began: 1994, Franchising: 1994
Headquarters size: 10 employees
Franchise department: 6 employees

U.S. franchises: 80
Canadian franchises: 0
Other foreign franchises: 0
Company-owned: 0

Seeking: All U.S.
Seeking in Canada? Yes
Exclusive territories? Yes
Homebased option? No
Employees needed to run biz: 12
Absentee ownership? Yes

COSTS
Total cost: $111.3K-196.9K
Franchise fee: $20K
Royalty fee: 5%
Term of agreement: 10 years renewable
    at no charge
Franchisees required to buy multiple
    units? No

FINANCING
In-house: None
3rd-party: Equipment, franchise fee,
    inventory, startup costs

QUALIFICATIONS
Cash liquidity: $50K-80K
Experience:
    General business experience
    Marketing skills

TRAINING
At headquarters: 1-2 days
At franchisee's location: 10-14 days

BUSINESS SUPPORT
Grand opening
Internet
Newsletter
Meetings
Toll-free phone line
Field operations/evaluations
Purchasing cooperatives

MARKETING SUPPORT
Co-op advertising
Ad slicks

CHICAGO'S PIZZA FRANCHISES

Financial rating: $$$

1111 N. Broadway
Greenfield, IN 46140
(317)462-9878
Pizza, salad, sandwiches
Began: 1979, Franchising: 1981
Headquarters size: 2 employees
Franchise department: 2 employees

U.S. franchises: 12
Canadian franchises: 0
Other foreign franchises: 0
Company-owned: 0

Seeking: Midwest
Seeking in Canada? No
Exclusive territories? Yes
Homebased option? No
Employees needed to run biz: 15
Absentee ownership? No

COSTS
Total cost: $89.3K-175.5K
Franchise fee: $10K
Royalty fee: 4%
Term of agreement: 5 years renewable
    at no charge
Franchisees required to buy multiple
    units? No

FINANCING
No financing available

QUALIFICATIONS
Net worth: $100K-200K
Cash liquidity: $43.5K-86.5K
Experience:
    Industry experience
    General business experience
    Marketing skills
    People skills

TRAINING
At headquarters: 2 weeks
At franchisee's location: 4 weeks
At existing stores: 2 weeks

BUSINESS SUPPORT
Grand opening
Field operations/evaluations
Lease negotiations
Purchasing cooperatives

MARKETING SUPPORT
Co-op advertising
Ad slicks
Additional support available

DOMINO'S PIZZA LLC

Ranked #6 in Entrepreneur Magazine's 2007 Franchise 500   *Financial rating: $$$$*

30 Frank Lloyd Wright Dr.,
    P.O. Box 997
Ann Arbor, MI 48106
(734)930-3030
www.dominos.com
Pizza, breadsticks, buffalo wings
Began: 1960, Franchising: 1967
Headquarters size: 350 employees
Franchise department: 75 employees

U.S. franchises: 4,553
Canadian franchises: 0
Other foreign franchises: 3,099
Company-owned: 576

Seeking: All U.S.
Seeking in Canada? Yes
Exclusive territories? No
Homebased option? No
Employees needed to run biz: 15-20
Absentee ownership? No

COSTS
Total cost: $141.4K-415.1K
Franchise fee: $15K
Royalty fee: 5.5%
Term of agreement: 10 years renewable
    at no charge
Franchisees required to buy multiple
    units? No

FINANCING
In-house: None
3rd-party: Equipment, franchise fee,
    inventory, startup costs

QUALIFICATIONS
Cash liquidity: $75K
Experience:
    Industry experience
    Entrepreneurial experience
    Successful experience in
    food-service/retail management

TRAINING
At headquarters
At certified training store: 6-8 weeks

BUSINESS SUPPORT
Grand opening
Internet
Newsletter
Meetings
Field operations/evaluations
Security/safety procedures

MARKETING SUPPORT
Co-op advertising
Ad slicks
National media campaign

DOUGHBOYS FRANCHISING LLC

Current financial data not available

251 Market St. W.
Gaithersburg, MD 20878
(301)330-3212
www.doughboyscafe.com
Wood-fired pizza, panini, salads,
    catering
Began: 2004, Franchising: 2006
Headquarters size: 15 employees
Franchise department: 3 employees

U.S. franchises: 0
Canadian franchises: 0
Other foreign franchises: 0
Company-owned: 1

Seeking: MD, VA
Seeking in Canada? No
Exclusive territories? Info not
    provided
Homebased option? No
Employees needed to run biz: 12-15
Absentee ownership? No

COSTS
Total cost: $143K-477K
Franchise fee: $20K/25K/30K
Royalty fee: 5%
Term of agreement: 10 years renewable
    for $2K
Franchisees required to buy multiple
    units? No

FINANCING
No financing available

QUALIFICATIONS
Net worth: $200K
Cash liquidity: $50K
Experience:
    General business experience
    Marketing skills

TRAINING
At headquarters: 2-4 weeks
At franchisee's location: 2-4 weeks

BUSINESS SUPPORT
Grand opening
Internet
Newsletter
Meetings
Toll-free phone line
Field operations/evaluations
Purchasing cooperatives
Security/safety procedures

MARKETING SUPPORT
Co-op advertising
Ad slicks
Regional marketing

EXTREME PIZZA

Current financial data not available

1052 Folsom St.
San Francisco, CA 94103
(866)695-5595
www.extremepizza.com
Gourmet pizzas, take-&-bake pizza,
  subs, salads
Began: 1994, Franchising: 2000
Headquarters size: 11 employees
Franchise department: 6 employees

U.S. franchises: 22
Canadian franchises: 0
Other foreign franchises: 0
Company-owned: 8

Seeking: All U.S.
Seeking in Canada? No
Exclusive territories? Yes
Homebased option? No
Employees needed to run biz: 10
Absentee ownership? Yes

COSTS
Total cost: $202K-406K
Franchise fee: $30K
Royalty fee: 4%
Term of agreement: 15 years renewable
  for $5K
Franchisees required to buy multiple
  units? No

FINANCING
In-house: None
3rd-party: Equipment, inventory,
  startup costs

QUALIFICATIONS
Net worth: $400K
Cash liquidity: $150K
Experience:
  Industry experience
  General business experience
  Marketing skills

TRAINING
At headquarters: 4 weeks
At franchisee's location: 2 weeks

BUSINESS SUPPORT
Grand opening
Internet
Newsletter
Meetings
Toll-free phone line
Field operations/evaluations
Lease negotiations
Security/safety procedures

MARKETING SUPPORT
Co-op advertising
Ad slicks

FOX'S PIZZA DEN

Ranked #136 in Entrepreneur Magazine's 2007 Franchise 500   *Financial rating: $$$*

3243 Old Frankstown Rd.
Pittsburgh, PA 15239
(724)733-7888
www.foxspizza.com
Pizza & sandwiches
Began: 1971, Franchising: 1974
Headquarters size: 12 employees
Franchise department: 3 employees

U.S. franchises: 284
Canadian franchises: 0
Other foreign franchises: 0
Company-owned: 0

Seeking: All U.S.
Seeking in Canada? No
Exclusive territories? Yes
Homebased option? No
Employees needed to run biz: 10
Absentee ownership? No

COSTS
Total cost: $80K-100K
Franchise fee: $8K
Royalty fee: $200/mo.
Term of agreement: 5 years renewable
  at no charge
Franchisees required to buy multiple
  units? No

FINANCING
No financing available

QUALIFICATIONS
Info not provided

TRAINING
At headquarters: Varies
At franchisee's location: 7 days

BUSINESS SUPPORT
Internet
Newsletter
Toll-free phone line
Purchasing cooperatives

MARKETING SUPPORT
Co-op advertising
Ad slicks
Regional marketing
Direct-mail marketing

GARLIC JIM'S FAMOUS GOURMET PIZZA

Financial rating: 0

802 134th St. S.W., #130
Everett, WA 98204
(425)918-1900
www.garlicjims.com
Gourmet pizza
Began: 2004, Franchising: 2004
Headquarters size: 20 employees
Franchise department: 5 employees

U.S. franchises: 28
Canadian franchises: 0
Other foreign franchises: 0
Company-owned: 3

Seeking: All U.S.
Seeking in Canada? Yes
Exclusive territories? Yes
Homebased option? No
Employees needed to run biz: 15-25
Absentee ownership? Yes

COSTS
Total cost: $175.6K-347.3K
Franchise fee: $15K-20K
Royalty fee: 5.5%
Term of agreement: 10 years renewable
for $3K
Franchisees required to buy multiple
units? No

FINANCING
In-house: None
3rd-party: Accounts receivable,
equipment, franchise fee,
inventory, payroll, startup costs

QUALIFICATIONS
Net worth: $275K
Cash liquidity: $100K

TRAINING
At headquarters: 1 week
At franchisee's location: 1 week
At regional training store: 4 weeks

BUSINESS SUPPORT
Grand opening
Internet
Newsletter
Meetings
Field operations/evaluations
Purchasing cooperatives
Security/safety procedures

MARKETING SUPPORT
Co-op advertising
Ad slicks
National media campaign
Regional marketing

HUNGRY HOWIE'S PIZZA & SUBS

Ranked #84 in Entrepreneur Magazine's 2007 Franchise 500

Financial rating: $$$$

30300 Stephenson Hwy.
Madison Heights, MI 48071
(800)624-8122
www.hungryhowies.com
Pizza, subs, salads
Began: 1973, Franchising: 1982
Headquarters size: 50 employees
Franchise department: 10 employees

U.S. franchises: 540
Canadian franchises: 0
Other foreign franchises: 0
Company-owned: 0

Seeking: All U.S.
Seeking in Canada? No
Exclusive territories? Yes
Homebased option? No
Employees needed to run biz: 10
Absentee ownership? No

COSTS
Total cost: $91.1K-282K
Franchise fee: $15K/9.5K
Royalty fee: 5%
Term of agreement: 20 years renewable
at no charge
Franchisees required to buy multiple
units? No

FINANCING
In-house: None
3rd-party: Equipment, franchise fee,
startup costs

QUALIFICATIONS
Net worth: $150K
Cash liquidity: $50K
Experience:
Industry experience
General business experience
Marketing skills

TRAINING
At headquarters: 4 weeks
Regional seminars

BUSINESS SUPPORT
Grand opening
Internet
Newsletter
Meetings
Field operations/evaluations
Lease negotiations
Security/safety procedures

MARKETING SUPPORT
Co-op advertising
Ad slicks
National media campaign
Regional marketing

JET'S PIZZA

Ranked #285 in Entrepreneur Magazine's 2007 Franchise 500

Financial rating: $$$$

37177 Mound Rd.
Sterling Heights, MI 48310
(586)268-5870
Pizza, subs, salads
Began: 1978, Franchising: 1990
Headquarters size: 8 employees
Franchise department: 5 employees

U.S. franchises: 115
Canadian franchises: 0
Other foreign franchises: 0
Company-owned: 11

Seeking: All U.S.
Seeking in Canada? No
Exclusive territories? Yes
Homebased option? No
Employees needed to run biz: 15
Absentee ownership? No

COSTS

Total cost: $225K+
Franchise fee: $20K
Royalty fee: 4-10%
Term of agreement: 10 years renewable
    for $2K
Franchisees required to buy multiple
    units? Outside the U.S. only

FINANCING

No financing available

QUALIFICATIONS

Net worth: $240K
Cash liquidity: $100K
Experience:
    Industry experience
    General business experience
    Management skills
    Customer-service skills

TRAINING

At headquarters: 4 weeks
At franchisee's location: 7 days

BUSINESS SUPPORT

Grand opening
Newsletter
Field operations/evaluations
Purchasing cooperatives

MARKETING SUPPORT

Co-op advertising
Ad slicks

JOHNNIE'S PIZZA

Financial rating: $$$$

7730 E. Greenway Rd., #104
Scottsdale, AZ 85260
(480)443-0200
www.kahalacorp.com
Pizza & Italian cuisine
Began: 1984, Franchising: 2005
Headquarters size: Info not
    provided

U.S. franchises: 1
Canadian franchises: 0
Other foreign franchises: 0
Company-owned: 8

Seeking: All U.S.
Seeking in Canada? Yes
Exclusive territories? Yes
Homebased option? No
Employees needed to run biz: Info
    not provided
Absentee ownership? No

COSTS

Total cost: $112.2K-537.5K
Franchise fee: $30K
Royalty fee: 6%
Term of agreement: 10 years
Franchisees required to buy multiple
    units? No

FINANCING

No financing available

QUALIFICATIONS

Experience:
    Industry experience
    General business experience

TRAINING

At headquarters: 1 week
At franchisee's location: 2 weeks

BUSINESS SUPPORT

Grand opening
Newsletter
Meetings
Toll-free phone line
Field operations/evaluations
Security/safety procedures

MARKETING SUPPORT

Co-op advertising
National media campaign

MARCO'S FRANCHISING LLC

Ranked #185 in Entrepreneur Magazine's 2007 Franchise 500   *Financial rating: $$$*

5252 Monroe St.
Toledo, OH 43623
(800)262-7267/(419)885-7000
www.marcos.com
Pizza & submarine sandwiches
Began: 1978, Franchising: 1979
Headquarters size: 34 employees
Franchise department: 6 employees

U.S. franchises: 155
Canadian franchises: 0
Other foreign franchises: 0
Company-owned: 0

Seeking: All U.S.
Seeking in Canada? No
Exclusive territories? Yes
Homebased option? No
Employees needed to run biz: 20
Absentee ownership? No

COSTS

Total cost: $184K-338K
Franchise fee: $17.5K
Royalty fee: 4-5.5%
Term of agreement: 10 years renewable
    for $3K or 25% of franchise fee
Franchisees required to buy multiple
    units? No

FINANCING

In-house: None
3rd-party: Equipment, inventory,
    startup costs

QUALIFICATIONS

Net worth: $100K
Cash liquidity: $70K
Experience:
    Industry experience
    General business experience
    Marketing skills

TRAINING

At headquarters: 6-8 weeks
At franchisee's location: 1-2 weeks

BUSINESS SUPPORT

Grand opening
Internet
Newsletter
Meetings
Toll-free phone line
Field operations/evaluations
Purchasing cooperatives
Security/safety procedures

MARKETING SUPPORT

Co-op advertising
Ad slicks
Regional marketing

N.Y.P.D. PIZZA

Financial rating: 0

127 W. Church St., #350
Orlando, FL 32801
(407)872-6973
www.nypdpizza.net
Pizzeria
Began: 1996, Franchising: 2004
Headquarters size: 30 employees
Franchise department: 15 employees

U.S. franchises: 7
Canadian franchises: 0
Other foreign franchises: 0
Company-owned: 1

Seeking: All U.S.
Seeking in Canada? Yes
Exclusive territories? Yes
Homebased option? No
Employees needed to run biz: 3-15
Absentee ownership? Yes

COSTS

Total cost: $278K-1.1M
Franchise fee: $25K-35K
Royalty fee: 6%
Term of agreement: 10 years
Franchisees required to buy multiple
    units? No

FINANCING

In-house: None
3rd-party: Accounts receivable,
    equipment, inventory, payroll,
    startup costs

QUALIFICATIONS

Cash liquidity: $75K+
Experience:
    Industry experience
    General business experience
    Marketing skills
    Restaurant experience

TRAINING

At headquarters: 4 weeks
At franchisee's location: 2 weeks
New-management training at
    corporate stores

BUSINESS SUPPORT

Grand opening
Internet
Newsletter
Meetings
Toll-free phone line
Field operations/evaluations
Lease negotiations
Purchasing cooperatives
Security/safety procedures

MARKETING SUPPORT

Ad slicks
National media campaign
Regional marketing

THE ORIGINAL PIZZA PAN

Current financial data not available

11621 Lorain Ave.
Cleveland, OH 44111
(216)299-5020
www.pizzapanonline.com
Pizza, subs, wings
Began: 1984, Franchising: 1992
Headquarters size: 10 employees
Franchise department: 8 employees

U.S. franchises: 98
Canadian franchises: 0
Other foreign franchises: 0
Company-owned: 0

Seeking: All U.S.
Seeking in Canada? No
Exclusive territories? Yes
Homebased option? No
Employees needed to run biz: 12
Absentee ownership? No

COSTS
Total cost: $150K
Franchise fee: $25K
Royalty fee: $1K/mo.
Term of agreement: 10 years renewable
  at no charge
Franchisees required to buy multiple
  units? No

FINANCING
In-house: None
3rd-party: Equipment, franchise fee,
  startup costs

QUALIFICATIONS
Net worth: $50K
Cash liquidity: $25K
Experience:
  Industry experience
  General business experience

TRAINING
At headquarters
At franchisee's location: Ongoing

BUSINESS SUPPORT
Grand opening
Newsletter
Meetings
Toll-free phone line
Field operations/evaluations
Purchasing cooperatives
Security/safety procedures

MARKETING SUPPORT
Co-op advertising
Ad slicks
National media campaign
Regional marketing
Direct mail

PAPA JOHN'S INT'L. INC.

Ranked #10 in Entrepreneur Magazine's 2007 Franchise 500   *Financial rating: $$$$*

P.O. Box 99900
Louisville, KY 40299
(502)261-7272
www.papajohns.com
Pizza
Began: 1985, Franchising: 1986
Headquarters size: 500 employees
Franchise department: 10 employees

U.S. franchises: 2,091
Canadian franchises: 15
Other foreign franchises: 299
Company-owned: 557

Seeking: All U.S.
Seeking in Canada? Yes
Exclusive territories? Yes
Homebased option? No
Employees needed to run biz: 20
Absentee ownership? Yes

COSTS
Total cost: $250K
Franchise fee: $25K
Royalty fee: 4%
Term of agreement: 10 years renewable
  for $3K
Franchisees required to buy multiple
  units? No

FINANCING
In-house: None
3rd-party: Equipment, franchise fee,
  startup costs

QUALIFICATIONS
Net worth: $185K
Cash liquidity: $100K
Experience:
  General business experience
  Marketing skills
  Multi-unit QSR management
  experience

TRAINING
At headquarters: 3 weeks
At existing location: 3-4 weeks

BUSINESS SUPPORT
Grand opening
Internet
Newsletter
Meetings
Toll-free phone line
Field operations/evaluations
Lease negotiations
Purchasing cooperatives
Security/safety procedures

MARKETING SUPPORT
Ad slicks
National media campaign
Regional marketing
Marketing planning & support

PARROT PIZZA

Financial rating: 0

3801 Knights Bridge Close
Worcester, MA 01609
(508)829-9111
www.parrotpizza.com
Pizza, pasta, subs, sandwiches
Began: 1993, Franchising: 2003
Headquarters size: 5 employees
Franchise department: 3 employees

U.S. franchises: 1
Canadian franchises: 0
Other foreign franchises: 0
Company-owned: 1

Seeking: All U.S.
Seeking in Canada? Yes
Exclusive territories? Yes
Homebased option? No
Employees needed to run biz: 5
Absentee ownership? No

COSTS

Total cost: $178K
Franchise fee: $25K
Royalty fee: 5%
Term of agreement: 10 years renewable
    at no charge
Franchisees required to buy multiple
    units? No

FINANCING

In-house: None
3rd-party: Financing available

QUALIFICATIONS

Net worth: $60K
Cash liquidity: $60K

TRAINING

At headquarters: 20 days
At franchisee's location

BUSINESS SUPPORT

Grand opening
Internet
Newsletter
Field operations/evaluations
Lease negotiations
Purchasing cooperatives
Security/safety procedures

MARKETING SUPPORT

Ad slicks

PETER PIPER

Ranked #491 in Entrepreneur Magazine's 2007 Franchise 500   *Financial rating: $$$*

14635 N. Kierland Blvd., #160
Scottsdale, AZ 85254
(480)609-6400
www.peterpiperpizza.com
Pizza
Began: 1973, Franchising: 1977
Headquarters size: 55 employees
Franchise department: 3 employees

U.S. franchises: 68
Canadian franchises: 0
Other foreign franchises: 31
Company-owned: 39

Seeking: Midwest, Southwest, West
Seeking in Canada? No
Exclusive territories? Yes
Homebased option? No
Employees needed to run biz: 35
Absentee ownership? No

COSTS

Total cost: $1.3M
Franchise fee: $25K
Royalty fee: 5%
Term of agreement: 10 years renewable
    for $5K
Franchisees required to buy multiple
    units? Yes

FINANCING

No financing available

QUALIFICATIONS

Net worth: $900K
Cash liquidity: $300K
Experience:
    Industry experience
    General business experience

TRAINING

At headquarters: 4 weeks
At franchisee's location: 1-2 weeks

BUSINESS SUPPORT

Grand opening
Newsletter
Meetings
Field operations/evaluations
Security/safety procedures

MARKETING SUPPORT

Co-op advertising
Regional marketing
Local marketing programs for
    schools & community-service
    organizations

PIZZA FACTORY INC.

Ranked #226 in Entrepreneur Magazine's 2007 Franchise 500   *Financial rating: $$$$*

49430 Rd. 426, P.O. Box 989
Oakhurst, CA 93644
(800)654-4840/(559)683-3377
www.pizzafactory.com
Pizza, pasta, sandwiches
Began: 1979, Franchising: 1985
Headquarters size: 9 employees
Franchise department: 9 employees

U.S. franchises: 133
Canadian franchises: 0
Other foreign franchises: 1
Company-owned: 0

Seeking: All U.S.
Seeking in Canada? Yes
Exclusive territories? No
Homebased option? No
Employees needed to run biz: 8-10
Absentee ownership? Yes

COSTS
Total cost: $129.2K-425K
Franchise fee: $5K-20K
Royalty fee: 5%
Term of agreement: 20 years renewable
    for $5K
Franchisees required to buy multiple
    units? No

FINANCING
In-house: None
3rd-party: Equipment, startup costs

QUALIFICATIONS
Net worth: $250K
Cash liquidity: $125K-150K
Experience:
    General business experience

TRAINING
At training store: 325 hours

BUSINESS SUPPORT
Grand opening
Internet
Newsletter
Meetings
Toll-free phone line
Field operations/evaluations
Security/safety procedures

MARKETING SUPPORT
Ad slicks
National media campaign
Regional marketing

PIZZA INN INC.

Ranked #411 in Entrepreneur Magazine's 2007 Franchise 500   *Financial rating: $$$*

3551 Plano Pkwy.
The Colony, TX 75056
(469)384-5000
www.pizzainn.com
Pizza, pasta, salads
Began: 1960, Franchising: 1963
Headquarters size: 48 employees
Franchise department: 4 employees

U.S. franchises: 290
Canadian franchises: 0
Other foreign franchises: 72
Company-owned: 3

Seeking: South, Southeast,
    Southwest
Seeking in Canada? Yes
Exclusive territories? Yes
Homebased option? No
Employees needed to run biz: Info
    not provided
Absentee ownership? Yes

COSTS
Total cost: $34.8K-751.9K
Franchise fee: $5K-25K
Royalty fee: 4-5%
Term of agreement: 10 years
    renewable
Franchisees required to buy multiple
    units? Outside the U.S. only

FINANCING
No financing available

QUALIFICATIONS
Net worth: $80K-300K
Cash liquidity: $30K-150K
Experience:
    Industry experience
    General business experience

TRAINING
At headquarters: 24 days

BUSINESS SUPPORT
Grand opening
Internet
Newsletter
Meetings
Toll-free phone line
Field operations/evaluations

MARKETING SUPPORT
Co-op advertising
Ad slicks
Regional marketing

PIZZA MAN - HE DELIVERS

Current financial data not available

6930 1/2 Tujunga Ave.
North Hollywood, CA 91605
(818)766-4395
Pizza, chicken, ribs
Began: 1964, Franchising: 1971
Headquarters size: 8 employees
Franchise department: 3 employees

U.S. franchises: 45
Canadian franchises: 0
Other foreign franchises: 0
Company-owned: 0

Seeking: All U.S.
Seeking in Canada? Yes
Exclusive territories? Yes
Homebased option? No
Employees needed to run biz: 0-3
Absentee ownership? Yes

COSTS
Total cost: $162.9K-178.5K
Franchise fee: $25K
Royalty fee: 4%
Term of agreement: 1 year renewable
    at no charge
Franchisees required to buy multiple
    units? No

FINANCING
In-house: Franchise fee, inventory
3rd-party: Accounts receivable,
    equipment, payroll, startup costs

QUALIFICATIONS
Net worth: $160K
Cash liquidity: $20K
Experience:
    Industry experience
    General business experience
    Marketing skills

TRAINING
At headquarters: 2 weeks
At franchisee's location: 2 weeks

BUSINESS SUPPORT
Grand opening
Internet
Meetings
Field operations/evaluations
Lease negotiations
Purchasing cooperatives

MARKETING SUPPORT
Co-op advertising
Regional marketing

THE PIZZA PIPELINE

Financial rating: $$$

418 W. Sharp
Spokane, WA 99201
(509)326-1977
www.pizzapipeline.com
Pizza delivery
Began: 1988, Franchising: 1988
Headquarters size: 10 employees
Franchise department: 4 employees

U.S. franchises: 9
Canadian franchises: 0
Other foreign franchises: 0
Company-owned: 6

Seeking: All U.S.
Seeking in Canada? No
Exclusive territories? Yes
Homebased option? No
Employees needed to run biz: 20
Absentee ownership? Yes

COSTS
Total cost: $138K-341.8K
Franchise fee: $20K
Royalty fee: 5%
Term of agreement: 10 years renewable
    for $1K
Franchisees required to buy multiple
    units? No

FINANCING
No financing available

QUALIFICATIONS
Net worth: $500K
Cash liquidity: $50K
Experience:
    General business experience

TRAINING
At headquarters: 4-6 weeks
At franchisee's location: 2 weeks

BUSINESS SUPPORT
Grand opening
Internet
Meetings
Toll-free phone line
Field operations/evaluations
Lease negotiations
Purchasing cooperatives
Security/safety procedures

MARKETING SUPPORT
Co-op advertising
Ad slicks
National media campaign
Regional marketing

REDBRICK PIZZA

Current financial data not available

40320 Nido Ct., #2-B1
Palmdale, CA 93551
(661)722-5895
www.redbrickpizza.com
Pizza
Began: 2001, Franchising: 2001
Headquarters size: 20 employees

U.S. franchises: 55
Canadian franchises: 0
Other foreign franchises: 0
Company-owned: 0

Seeking: All U.S.
Seeking in Canada? Yes
Exclusive territories? Yes
Homebased option? No
Employees needed to run biz: 15-20
Absentee ownership? No

COSTS
Total cost: $175K-499K
Franchise fee: $25K
Royalty fee: 6%
Term of agreement: 10 years renewable
    at no charge
Franchisees required to buy multiple
    units? Yes

FINANCING
In-house: None
3rd-party: Accounts receivable,
    equipment, franchise fee,
    inventory, payroll, startup costs

QUALIFICATIONS
Experience:
    General business experience

TRAINING
Info not available

BUSINESS SUPPORT
Grand opening
Internet
Meetings
Field operations/evaluations
Lease negotiations
Purchasing cooperatives
Security/safety procedures

MARKETING SUPPORT
Ad slicks
National media campaign
Regional marketing

RONZIO PIZZA

Financial rating: $$$

111 John St.
Lincoln, RI 02865
(401)334-9750
www.ronziopizza.com
Pizza & subs
Began: 1986, Franchising: 1992
Headquarters size: 3 employees
Franchise department: 2 employees

U.S. franchises: 19
Canadian franchises: 0
Other foreign franchises: 0
Company-owned: 1

Seeking: Northeast
Seeking in Canada? No
Exclusive territories? Yes
Homebased option? No
Employees needed to run biz: 12-15
Absentee ownership? Yes

COSTS
Total cost: $134K-183K
Franchise fee: $15K
Royalty fee: 4%
Term of agreement: 10 years renewable
    at no charge
Franchisees required to buy multiple
    units? No

FINANCING
No financing available

QUALIFICATIONS
Net worth: $100K
Cash liquidity: $40K
Experience:
    General business experience

TRAINING
At headquarters: 2 weeks
At franchisee's location: 2 weeks

BUSINESS SUPPORT
Grand opening
Internet
Newsletter
Meetings
Field operations/evaluations
Purchasing cooperatives
Security/safety procedures

MARKETING SUPPORT
Co-op advertising
Ad slicks
Regional marketing

SAN FRANCISCO OVEN

Financial rating: $

9150 S. Hills Blvd., #225
Cleveland, OH 44147
(440)717-9450
www.sanfranciscooven.com
Brick-oven pizza, soups, salads,
    sandwiches
Began: 2001, Franchising: 2003
Headquarters size: 5 employees
Franchise department: 4 employees

U.S. franchises: 12
Canadian franchises: 0
Other foreign franchises: 0
Company-owned: 1

Seeking: All U.S.
Seeking in Canada? No
Exclusive territories? Yes
Homebased option? No
Employees needed to run biz: 20-30
Absentee ownership? No

COSTS
Total cost: $474.1K-807.3K
Franchise fee: $25K
Royalty fee: 5%
Term of agreement: 10 years renewable
    at no charge
Franchisees required to buy multiple
    units? Yes

FINANCING
No financing available

QUALIFICATIONS
Net worth: $1M
Cash liquidity: $500K
Experience:
    Industry experience
    General business experience
    Marketing skills

TRAINING
At headquarters: 3 weeks
At franchisee's location: 2 weeks

BUSINESS SUPPORT
Grand opening
Internet
Newsletter
Meetings
Toll-free phone line
Field operations/evaluations
Purchasing cooperatives
Security/safety procedures

MARKETING SUPPORT
Co-op advertising
Ad slicks
Regional marketing
Local & neighborhood marketing

STRAW HAT PIZZA

Current financial data not available

18 Crow Canyon Ct., #150
San Ramon, CA 94583
(925)837-3400
www.strawhatpizza.com
Pizza
Began: 1959, Franchising: 1969
Headquarters size: 6 employees
Franchise department: 6 employees

U.S. franchises: 45
Canadian franchises: 0
Other foreign franchises: 0
Company-owned: 0

Seeking: All U.S.
Seeking in Canada? No
Exclusive territories? No
Homebased option? No
Employees needed to run biz: 20
Absentee ownership? Yes

COSTS
Total cost: Varies
Franchise fee: $25K
Royalty fee: 2%
Term of agreement: 10 years renewable
    at no charge
Franchisees required to buy multiple
    units? No

FINANCING
In-house: None
3rd-party: Equipment, franchise fee,
    inventory, startup costs

QUALIFICATIONS
Net worth: $300K
Cash liquidity: $100K
Experience:
    Industry experience
    General business experience
    Marketing skills

TRAINING
At franchisee's location: 4 weeks

BUSINESS SUPPORT
Grand opening
Internet
Newsletter
Meetings
Toll-free phone line
Field operations/evaluations
Purchasing cooperatives
Security/safety procedures

MARKETING SUPPORT
Co-op advertising
Ad slicks
Regional marketing

TOPPER'S PIZZA

Financial rating: $

261 S. Fourth St.
Whitewater, WI 53190
(262)473-6666
www.toppers.com
Pizza
Began: 1991, Franchising: 2000
Headquarters size: 8 employees
Franchise department: 1 employee

U.S. franchises: 14
Canadian franchises: 0
Other foreign franchises: 0
Company-owned: 0

Seeking: Midwest, Southeast
Seeking in Canada? No
Exclusive territories? Yes
Homebased option? No
Employees needed to run biz: Info
    not provided
Absentee ownership? No

COSTS
Total cost: $213.2K-379K
Franchise fee: $20K
Royalty fee: 5%
Term of agreement: 5 years renewable
    at no charge
Franchisees required to buy multiple
    units? Yes

FINANCING
In-house: None
3rd-party: Accounts receivable,
    equipment, inventory, startup
    costs

QUALIFICATIONS
Net worth: $150K
Cash liquidity: $100K

TRAINING
At headquarters: 30 days

BUSINESS SUPPORT
Grand opening
Internet
Newsletter
Meetings
Toll-free phone line
Field operations/evaluations
Lease negotiations
Purchasing cooperatives
Security/safety procedures

MARKETING SUPPORT
National media campaign
Direct mail

Z PIZZA

Current financial data not available

450 Newport Center Dr., #630
Newport Beach, CA 92660
(800)230-5761
www.zpizza.com
Pizza, salads, sandwiches, calzones
Began: 1986, Franchising: 1999
Headquarters size: 8 employees
Franchise department: 6 employees

U.S. franchises: 28
Canadian franchises: 0
Other foreign franchises: 0
Company-owned: 8

Seeking: All U.S.
Seeking in Canada? No
Exclusive territories? Yes
Homebased option? No
Employees needed to run biz: 15
Absentee ownership? No

COSTS
Total cost: $190.5K-261.5K
Franchise fee: $25K
Royalty fee: 5%
Term of agreement: 10 years renewable
    at no charge
Franchisees required to buy multiple
    units? Yes

FINANCING
In-house: None
3rd-party: Accounts receivable,
    equipment, franchise fee,
    inventory, payroll, startup costs

QUALIFICATIONS
Net worth: $500K
Cash liquidity: $75K-100K
Experience:
    General business experience

TRAINING
At headquarters: 4 weeks
At franchisee's location: 2 weeks
Additional training available

BUSINESS SUPPORT
Grand opening
Internet
Newsletter
Meetings
Field operations/evaluations
Lease negotiations
Purchasing cooperatives
Security/safety procedures

MARKETING SUPPORT
Co-op advertising
Ad slicks
National media campaign
Regional marketing

AUNTIE ANNE'S HAND-ROLLED SOFT PRETZELS

Current financial data not available

160-A Rte. 41
Gap, PA 17527
(717)442-4766
www.auntieannes.com
Hand-rolled soft pretzels
Began: 1988, Franchising: 1989
Headquarters size: 150 employees
Franchise department: 8 employees

U.S. franchises: 751
Canadian franchises: 0
Other foreign franchises: 175
Company-owned: 8

Seeking: All U.S.
Seeking in Canada? Yes
Exclusive territories? No
Homebased option? No
Employees needed to run biz: 9-12
Absentee ownership? No

COSTS
Total cost: $192.6K-373.6K
Franchise fee: $30K
Royalty fee: 7%
Term of agreement: 20 years renewable
    for $15K or 50% of franchise fee
Franchisees required to buy multiple
    units? No

FINANCING
No financing available

QUALIFICATIONS
Net worth: $300K
Experience:
    Industry experience
    General business experience

TRAINING
At headquarters: Up to 2 weeks
At franchisee's location:
    Up to 5 days

BUSINESS SUPPORT
Grand opening
Internet
Newsletter
Meetings
Toll-free phone line
Field operations/evaluations
Lease negotiations
Purchasing cooperatives
Security/safety procedures

MARKETING SUPPORT
Ad slicks
Regional marketing
Online toolbox

PRETZELS PLUS INC.

Current financial data not available

639 Frederick St.
Hanover, PA 17331
(800)559-7927
www.pretzelsplus.com
Hand-rolled soft pretzels,
    sandwiches, ice cream
Began: 1991, Franchising: 1991
Headquarters size: 10 employees
Franchise department: 5 employees

U.S. franchises: 20
Canadian franchises: 0
Other foreign franchises: 3
Company-owned: 0

Seeking: All U.S.
Seeking in Canada? Yes
Exclusive territories? Yes
Homebased option? No
Employees needed to run biz: 5-15
Absentee ownership? Yes

COSTS
Total cost: $103.1K
Franchise fee: $12K
Royalty fee: 4%
Term of agreement: 5 years renewable
    for 50% of franchise fee
Franchisees required to buy multiple
    units? No

FINANCING
No financing available

QUALIFICATIONS
Net worth: $100K
Cash liquidity: $25K
Experience:
    General business experience

TRAINING
At headquarters
At franchisee's location: 3 days+ &
    after opening

BUSINESS SUPPORT
Grand opening
Internet
Newsletter
Toll-free phone line
Field operations/evaluations
Lease negotiations

MARKETING SUPPORT
Photography

WE'RE ROLLING PRETZEL CO.

Financial rating: $

2500 W. State St.
Alliance, OH 44601
(888)549-7655/(330)823-0575
www.wererolling.com
Homemade soft pretzels & pretzel
 sandwiches
Began: 1996, Franchising: 2000
Headquarters size: 10 employees
Franchise department: 2 employees

U.S. franchises: 48
Canadian franchises: 0
Other foreign franchises: 0
Company-owned: 6

Seeking: Midwest
Seeking in Canada? No
Exclusive territories? No
Homebased option? No
Employees needed to run biz: 6-8
Absentee ownership? Yes

COSTS
Total cost: $65K-149K
Franchise fee: $15K
Royalty fee: 5%
Term of agreement: 5 years renewable
 for $1K
Franchisees required to buy multiple
 units? No

FINANCING
In-house: None
3rd-party: Accounts receivable,
 equipment, franchise fee,
 inventory, payroll, startup costs

QUALIFICATIONS
Net worth: $100K
Cash liquidity: $30K
Experience:
 General business experience

TRAINING
At headquarters: 7 days
At franchisee's location: 7 days

BUSINESS SUPPORT
Grand opening
Internet
Newsletter
Meetings
Toll-free phone line
Field operations/evaluations
Lease negotiations
Security/safety procedures

MARKETING SUPPORT
Ad slicks
Regional marketing

WETZEL'S PRETZELS

Ranked #202 in Entrepreneur Magazine's 2007 Franchise 500

Financial rating: $$$$

35 Hugus Alley., #300
Pasadena, CA 91103
(626)432-6900
www.wetzels.com
Soft pretzels, lemonade, hot dogs
Began: 1994, Franchising: 1996
Headquarters size: 12 employees
Franchise department: 3 employees

U.S. franchises: 176
Canadian franchises: 30
Other foreign franchises: 22
Company-owned: 6

Seeking: All U.S.
Seeking in Canada? Yes
Exclusive territories? Yes
Homebased option? No
Employees needed to run biz: 5
Absentee ownership? No

COSTS
Total cost: $128.9K-352.5K
Franchise fee: $30K
Royalty fee: 6%
Term of agreement: 10 years
Franchisees required to buy multiple
 units? No

FINANCING
In-house: None
3rd-party: Equipment, franchise fee,
 inventory, startup costs

QUALIFICATIONS
Net worth: $200K
Cash liquidity: $50K
Experience:
 General business experience

TRAINING
At headquarters: 2 weeks
At franchisee's location: 4 days

BUSINESS SUPPORT
Grand opening
Internet
Newsletter
Meetings
Field operations/evaluations
Purchasing cooperatives
Security/safety procedures

MARKETING SUPPORT
Co-op advertising
Ad slicks

 QUICK SERVICE — *Salad-Only Restaurants*

DOC GREEN'S GOURMET SALADS

Financial rating: $

782 Ponce de Leon Ave.
Atlanta, GA 30306
(404)844-3225
www.docgreens.com
Salads, flatbread sandwiches,
bistro fare
Began: 2003, Franchising: 2004
Headquarters size: 80 employees
Franchise department: 10 employees

U.S. franchises: 12
Canadian franchises: 0
Other foreign franchises: 0
Company-owned: 1

Seeking: All U.S.
Seeking in Canada? No
Exclusive territories? No
Homebased option? No
Employees needed to run biz: 25
Absentee ownership? No

COSTS
Total cost: $367K-655K
Franchise fee: $25K
Royalty fee: 5%
Term of agreement: 10 years renewable
for $25K
Franchisees required to buy multiple
units? No

FINANCING
In-house: None
3rd-party: Accounts receivable,
equipment, franchise fee,
inventory, payroll, startup costs

QUALIFICATIONS
Net worth: $500K
Cash liquidity: $150K
Experience:
General business experience

TRAINING
At headquarters: 2-1/2 weeks
At franchisee's location: 1 week

BUSINESS SUPPORT
Grand opening
Internet
Meetings
Toll-free phone line
Field operations/evaluations
Security/safety procedures

MARKETING SUPPORT
Co-op advertising
Ad slicks

SALAD CREATIONS INC.

Financial rating: $$

5100 W. Copans Rd., #410
Margate, FL 33063
(954)590-2467
www.saladcreations.net
Salads
Began: 2002, Franchising: 2004
Headquarters size: 10 employees
Franchise department: 4 employees

U.S. franchises: 8
Canadian franchises: 0
Other foreign franchises: 0
Company-owned: 1

Seeking: All U.S.
Seeking in Canada? Yes
Exclusive territories? Yes
Homebased option? No
Employees needed to run biz: 8-10
Absentee ownership? No

COSTS
Total cost: $122K-298.5K
Franchise fee: $25K
Royalty fee: 6%
Term of agreement: 10 years renewable
for $5K
Franchisees required to buy multiple
units? No

FINANCING
In-house: None
3rd-party: Accounts receivable,
equipment, franchise fee,
inventory, payroll, startup costs

QUALIFICATIONS
Net worth: $250K
Cash liquidity: $100K
Experience:
General business experience

TRAINING
At headquarters: 12 days
At franchisee's location: 3 days

BUSINESS SUPPORT
Grand opening
Internet
Meetings
Field operations/evaluations
Lease negotiations
Purchasing cooperatives
Security/safety procedures

MARKETING SUPPORT
Ad slicks
Regional marketing

QUICK SERVICE ▶ *Sandwiches*

ARBY'S

Ranked #70 in Entrepreneur Magazine's 2007 Franchise 500　　　　*Financial rating: $$$*

1155 Perimeter Center West
Atlanta, GA 30338
(678)514-4100
www.arbys.com
Roast beef sandwiches, chicken,
　wraps, salads
Began: 1964, Franchising: 1965
Headquarters size: 300 employees
Franchise department: 60 employees

U.S. franchises: 2,339
Canadian franchises: 121
Other foreign franchises: 9
Company-owned: 1,037

Seeking: All U.S.
Seeking in Canada? Yes
Exclusive territories? Yes
Homebased option? No
Employees needed to run biz: Info
　not provided
Absentee ownership? Yes

COSTS
Total cost: $336.5K-2.4M
Franchise fee: $25K/37.5K
Royalty fee: 4%
Term of agreement: 20 years renewable
　for 10% of current franchise fee
Franchisees required to buy multiple
　units? No

FINANCING
In-house: None
3rd-party: Accounts receivable,
　equipment, inventory, payroll,
　startup costs

QUALIFICATIONS
Experience:
　Industry experience
　General business experience
　Marketing skills

TRAINING
At franchisee's location: Ongoing
At certified training restaurant:
　5 weeks

BUSINESS SUPPORT
Grand opening
Newsletter
Meetings
Toll-free phone line
Field operations/evaluations
Purchasing cooperatives
Security/safety procedures

MARKETING SUPPORT
National media campaign
Regional marketing
All marketing supplied by
　franchisee association

ATLANTIC CITY SUB SHOPS

Current financial data not available

124 Wharf Rd.
Egg Harbor Township, NJ 08234
(609)926-4560
www.atlanticcitysubs.com
Submarine sandwiches & salads
Began: 1986, Franchising: 1995
Headquarters size: 17 employees
Franchise department: 2 employees

U.S. franchises: 2
Canadian franchises: 0
Other foreign franchises: 0
Company-owned: 1

Seeking: Northeast, South,
　Southeast
Seeking in Canada? No
Exclusive territories? Yes
Homebased option? No
Employees needed to run biz: 13-15
Absentee ownership? No

COSTS
Total cost: $100K-275K
Franchise fee: $15K
Royalty fee: 5%
Term of agreement: 3 years
　renewable for $1K
Franchisees required to buy
　multiple units? No

FINANCING
No financing available

QUALIFICATIONS
Net worth: $300K
Cash liquidity: $120K
Experience:
　General business experience

TRAINING
At headquarters: 4-6 weeks
At franchisee's location: 2 weeks

BUSINESS SUPPORT
Grand opening
Internet
Field operations/evaluations

MARKETING SUPPORT
Ad slicks
Regional marketing

BELLACINO'S PIZZA & GRINDERS INC.

Ranked #267 in Entrepreneur Magazine's 2007 Franchise 500   *Financial rating: $$$$*

10096 Shaver Rd.
Portage, MI 49024
(877)379-0700
www.bellacinos.com
Oven-baked grinders & pizza
Began: 1993, Franchising: 1995
Headquarters size: 9 employees
Franchise department: 1 employee

U.S. franchises: 93
Canadian franchises: 0
Other foreign franchises: 0
Company-owned: 0

Seeking: All U.S.
Seeking in Canada? No
Exclusive territories? Yes
Homebased option? No
Employees needed to run biz: 22
Absentee ownership? No

COSTS
Total cost: $330K
Franchise fee: $30K
Royalty fee: 3%
Term of agreement: 10 years renewable
  for $10K
Franchisees required to buy multiple
  units? No

FINANCING
No financing available

QUALIFICATIONS
Cash liquidity: $80K

TRAINING
At headquarters: 14 days
At franchisee's location: 10 days
Ongoing

BUSINESS SUPPORT
Grand opening
Internet
Newsletter
Meetings
Toll-free phone line
Field operations/evaluations
Lease negotiations
Purchasing cooperatives
Security/safety procedures

MARKETING SUPPORT
Co-op advertising
Ad slicks
National media campaign
Regional marketing

BLIMPIE INT'L. INC.

Ranked #54 in Entrepreneur Magazine's 2007 Franchise 500   *Financial rating: $$$$*

7730 E. Greenway Rd., #104
Scottsdale, AZ 85260
(480)443-0200
www.kahalacorp.com
Sandwiches & salads
Began: 1964, Franchising: 1970
Headquarters size: Info not provided

U.S. franchises: 1,170
Canadian franchises: 0
Other foreign franchises: 12
Company-owned: 10

Seeking: All U.S.
Seeking in Canada? Yes
Exclusive territories? Yes
Homebased option? No
Employees needed to run biz: 6
Absentee ownership? Yes

COSTS
Total cost: $133K-377.1K
Franchise fee: $18K
Royalty fee: 6%
Term of agreement: 10 years renewable
  for 75% of then-current fee
Franchisees required to buy multiple
  units? Yes

FINANCING
In-house: None
3rd-party: Equipment, franchise fee,
  inventory, startup costs

QUALIFICATIONS
Cash liquidity: $75K
Experience:
  Industry experience
  General business experience

TRAINING
At headquarters: 1 week
At franchisee's location: 2 weeks

BUSINESS SUPPORT
Grand opening
Internet
Newsletter
Meetings
Toll-free phone line
Field operations/evaluations
Purchasing cooperatives
Security/safety procedures

MARKETING SUPPORT
Co-op advertising
Ad slicks
Regional marketing

BOLOCO INSPIRED BURRITOS

Financial rating: $$$

188 N. Brookwood Ave., #100
Hamilton, OH 45013
(513)896-9695
www.boloco.com
Wraps & smoothies
Began: 1997, Franchising: 2004
Headquarters size: Info not provided

U.S. franchises: 15
Canadian franchises: 0
Other foreign franchises: 0
Company-owned: 0

Seeking: All U.S.
Seeking in Canada? Yes
Exclusive territories? Yes
Homebased option? No
Employees needed to run biz: 15
Absentee ownership? Yes

COSTS
Total cost: $190K-400K
Franchise fee: $25K
Royalty fee: 6%
Term of agreement: 10 years renewable
    for $10K
Franchisees required to buy multiple
    units? No

FINANCING
No financing available

QUALIFICATIONS
Net worth: $500K
Cash liquidity: $100K
Experience:
    General business experience

TRAINING
At headquarters: 2-3 weeks
At franchisee's location: 2-3 weeks

BUSINESS SUPPORT
Grand opening
Internet
Field operations/evaluations
Security/safety procedures

MARKETING SUPPORT
Regional marketing

CAMILLE'S SIDEWALK CAFE

Ranked #209 in Entrepreneur Magazine's 2007 Franchise 500

Financial rating: $$$$

8801 S. Yale, #400
Tulsa, OK 74137
(918)488-9727
www.camillescafe.com
Sandwiches, soups, salads, desserts
Began: 1996, Franchising: 1999
Headquarters size: 20 employees
Franchise department: 20 employees

U.S. franchises: 84
Canadian franchises: 0
Other foreign franchises: 0
Company-owned: 1

Seeking: All U.S.
Seeking in Canada? Yes
Exclusive territories? Yes
Homebased option? No
Employees needed to run biz: 30
Absentee ownership? Yes

COSTS
Total cost: $210K-586K
Franchise fee: $30K
Royalty fee: 6%
Term of agreement: 20 years renewable
    for 50% of current franchise fee
Franchisees required to buy multiple
    units? Yes

FINANCING
In-house: None
3rd-party: Equipment, franchise fee,
    inventory, startup costs

QUALIFICATIONS
Experience:
    Industry experience
    General business experience
    Marketing skills

TRAINING
At headquarters: 2-3 weeks
At franchisee's location: 2-3 days

BUSINESS SUPPORT
Grand opening
Internet
Newsletter
Toll-free phone line
Field operations/evaluations
Purchasing cooperatives

MARKETING SUPPORT
Co-op advertising
Ad slicks

CHARLEY'S GRILLED SUBS

Ranked #122 in Entrepreneur Magazine's 2007 Franchise 500   *Financial rating: $$$$*

2500 Farmers Dr., #140
Columbus, OH 43235
(800)437-8325/(614)923-4700
www.charleys.com
Grilled subs, fries, salads
Began: 1986, Franchising: 1991
Headquarters size: 35 employees
Franchise department: 8 employees

U.S. franchises: 241
Canadian franchises: 4
Other foreign franchises: 18
Company-owned: 27

Seeking: All U.S.
Seeking in Canada? No
Exclusive territories? No
Homebased option? No
Employees needed to run biz: 20
Absentee ownership? No

COSTS
Total cost: $138K-400K
Franchise fee: $19.5K
Royalty fee: 5%
Term of agreement: 10 years renewable
    for $5K
Franchisees required to buy multiple
    units? No

FINANCING
In-house: None
3rd-party: Accounts receivable,
    equipment, inventory, payroll,
    startup costs

QUALIFICATIONS
Net worth: $300K
Cash liquidity: $100K
Experience:
    General business experience

TRAINING
At headquarters: 5 weeks
At franchisee's location: 7 days

BUSINESS SUPPORT
Grand opening
Internet
Newsletter
Meetings
Toll-free phone line
Field operations/evaluations
Lease negotiations
Purchasing cooperatives
Security/safety procedures

MARKETING SUPPORT
Ad slicks

COUSINS SUBS

Current financial data not available

N83 W13400 Leon Rd.
Menomonee Falls, WI 53051
(800)238-9736/(262)253-7700
www.cousinssubs.com
Subs, salads, soups, desserts
Began: 1972, Franchising: 1985
Headquarters size: 50 employees
Franchise department: 5 employees

U.S. franchises: 139
Canadian franchises: 0
Other foreign franchises: 0
Company-owned: 16

Seeking: Midwest, Southwest, West
Seeking in Canada? No
Exclusive territories? Yes
Homebased option? No
Employees needed to run biz: 20
Absentee ownership? No

COSTS
Total cost: $198.2K-284.3K
Franchise fee: $25K
Royalty fee: 6%
Term of agreement: 10 years renewable
    for then-current franchise fee
Franchisees required to buy multiple
    units? No

FINANCING
No financing available

QUALIFICATIONS
Net worth: $300K
Cash liquidity: $60K-100K

TRAINING
At headquarters
At franchisee's location: 5 days

BUSINESS SUPPORT
Grand opening
Internet
Newsletter
Meetings
Toll-free phone line
Field operations/evaluations
Lease negotiations
Purchasing cooperatives

MARKETING SUPPORT
Co-op advertising
Ad slicks
National media campaign
Regional marketing

D'ANGELO GRILLED SANDWICHES

Ranked #444 in Entrepreneur Magazine's 2007 Franchise 500　　　*Financial rating: $$*

600 Providence Hwy.
Dedham, MA 02026
(781)467-1668
www.dangelos.com
Sandwiches, soups, salads
Began: 1967, Franchising: 1988
Headquarters size: 200 employees
Franchise department: 5 employees

U.S. franchises: 51
Canadian franchises: 0
Other foreign franchises: 0
Company-owned: 139

Seeking: Northeast, Southeast
Seeking in Canada? No
Exclusive territories? Yes
Homebased option? No
Employees needed to run biz: 12
Absentee ownership? No

COSTS
Total cost: $399.3K-589.7K
Franchise fee: $20K
Royalty fee: 6%
Term of agreement: 20 years renewable
　for $10K
Franchisees required to buy multiple
　units? Yes

FINANCING
In-house: None
3rd-party: Accounts receivable,
　equipment, franchise fee,
　inventory, payroll, startup costs

QUALIFICATIONS
Net worth: $400K-1M
Cash liquidity: $127K-157K
Experience:
　General business experience

TRAINING
At headquarters: 5 weeks
In-shop training: 2 weeks

BUSINESS SUPPORT
Grand opening
Internet
Newsletter
Meetings
Toll-free phone line
Field operations/evaluations
Purchasing cooperatives
Security/safety procedures

MARKETING SUPPORT
Co-op advertising
Ad slicks
Regional marketing

DAGWOOD'S SANDWICH SHOPPES

　　　Current financial data not available

17757 U.S. Hwy 19 N., Bldg. 2, #500
Clearwater, FL 33764
(727)507-7300
www.dagwoods.us.com
Sandwiches, salads, soups
Began: 2005, Franchising: 2006
Headquarters size: 24 employees
Franchise department: 20 employees

U.S. franchises: 0
Canadian franchises: 0
Other foreign franchises: 0
Company-owned: 0

Seeking: All U.S.
Seeking in Canada? Yes
Exclusive territories? No
Homebased option? No
Employees needed to run biz: 12-14
Absentee ownership? Yes

COSTS
Total cost: $220K-256K
Franchise fee: $20K
Royalty fee: 6.5%
Term of agreement: 15 years renewable
　for 25% of current fee
Franchisees required to buy multiple
　units? No

FINANCING
In-house: None
3rd-party: Accounts receivable,
　equipment, franchise fee,
　inventory, payroll, startup costs

QUALIFICATIONS
Net worth: $125K
Cash liquidity: $75K

TRAINING
At headquarters: 2 weeks
At regional training store: 4 weeks

BUSINESS SUPPORT
Grand opening
Internet
Newsletter
Meetings
Toll-free phone line
Field operations/evaluations
Lease negotiations
Purchasing cooperatives
Security/safety procedures

MARKETING SUPPORT
Co-op advertising
Ad slicks
National media campaign
Regional marketing

DOMINIC'S OF NEW YORK/JOHNNYBOY'S

Financial rating: $$

4101 Cox Rd., #120
Glen Allen, VA 23060-3320
(804)273-0600
www.dominicsofnewyork.com
Italian sausages, hot dogs,
    sandwiches
Began: 1995, Franchising: 1996
Headquarters size: 10 employees
Franchise department: 10 employees

U.S. franchises: 50
Canadian franchises: 0
Other foreign franchises: 0
Company-owned: 0

Seeking: All U.S.
Seeking in Canada? No
Exclusive territories? Yes
Homebased option? No
Employees needed to run biz: 4
Absentee ownership? Yes

COSTS
Total cost: $31.2K-211.6K
Franchise fee: $15K
Royalty fee: 4%
Term of agreement: Varies
Franchisees required to buy
    multiple units? No

FINANCING
No financing available

QUALIFICATIONS
Net worth: $100K
Cash liquidity: $20K
Experience:
    Industry experience
    General business experience
    Marketing skills

TRAINING
At headquarters: 2 days
At franchisee's location: 120 hours

BUSINESS SUPPORT
Internet
Newsletter
Meetings
Field operations/evaluations

MARKETING SUPPORT
Regional marketing

FIREHOUSE SUBS

Ranked #111 in Entrepreneur Magazine's 2007 Franchise 500

Financial rating: $$$$

3410 Kori Rd.
Jacksonville, FL 32257
(904)886-8300
www.firehousesubs.com
Hot & cold sandwiches
Began: 1994, Franchising: 1995
Headquarters size: 45 employees
Franchise department: 11 employees

U.S. franchises: 199
Canadian franchises: 0
Other foreign franchises: 0
Company-owned: 36

Seeking: All U.S.
Seeking in Canada? No
Exclusive territories? Yes
Homebased option? No
Employees needed to run biz: 18
Absentee ownership? No

COSTS
Total cost: $191.2K-355.5K
Franchise fee: $20K
Royalty fee: 6%
Term of agreement: 10 years renewable
    for 50% of current franchise fee
Franchisees required to buy multiple
    units? No

FINANCING
In-house: Equipment
3rd-party: None

QUALIFICATIONS
Experience:
    General business experience

TRAINING
At headquarters: 2 weeks
Training restaurant: 6 weeks

BUSINESS SUPPORT
Grand opening
Internet
Newsletter
Meetings
Field operations/evaluations
Lease negotiations
Security/safety procedures

MARKETING SUPPORT
Ad slicks
National media campaign
Regional marketing
Agency field support

FRULLATI CAFE & BAKERY

Ranked #456 in Entrepreneur Magazine's 2007 Franchise 500   *Financial rating: $$$$*

7730 E. Greenway Rd., #104
Scottsdale, AZ 85260
(480)443-0200
www.kahalacorp.com
Salads, sandwiches, soups, fresh
    baked goods
Began: 1985, Franchising: 1994
Headquarters size: 30 employees
Franchise department: 30 employees

U.S. franchises: 87
Canadian franchises: 0
Other foreign franchises: 0
Company-owned: 1

Seeking: All U.S.
Seeking in Canada? Yes
Exclusive territories? Yes
Homebased option? No
Employees needed to run biz: 6
Absentee ownership? Yes

COSTS
Total cost: $145.3K-488.5K
Franchise fee: $30K
Royalty fee: 6%
Term of agreement: 10 years renewable
    for 75% of then-current fee
Franchisees required to buy multiple
    units? Yes

FINANCING
In-house: None
3rd-party: Equipment, franchise fee,
    inventory, startup costs

QUALIFICATIONS
Cash liquidity: $30K
Experience:
    Industry experience
    General business experience

TRAINING
At headquarters: 1 week
At franchisee's location: 2 weeks

BUSINESS SUPPORT
Grand opening
Internet
Newsletter
Meetings
Toll-free phone line
Field operations/evaluations
Purchasing cooperatives
Security/safety procedures

MARKETING SUPPORT
Co-op advertising
Ad slicks
Regional marketing

THE GREAT STEAK & POTATO CO.

Ranked #363 in Entrepreneur Magazine's 2007 Franchise 500   *Financial rating: $$$$*

7730 E. Greenway Rd., #104
Scottsdale, AZ 85260
(480)443-0200
www.kahalacorp.com
Philadelphia cheesesteak sandwiches
    & fries
Began: 1985, Franchising: 1986
Headquarters size: 18 employees
Franchise department: 11 employees

U.S. franchises: 214
Canadian franchises: 8
Other foreign franchises: 6
Company-owned: 2

Seeking: All U.S.
Seeking in Canada? Yes
Exclusive territories? Yes
Homebased option? No
Employees needed to run biz: 10
Absentee ownership? Yes

COSTS
Total cost: $147.8K-433.5K
Franchise fee: $30K
Royalty fee: 6%
Term of agreement: 10 years renewable
    for $5K
Franchisees required to buy multiple
    units? Outside the U.S. only

FINANCING
In-house: None
3rd-party: Equipment, franchise fee,
    inventory, startup costs

QUALIFICATIONS
Cash liquidity: $30K
Experience:
    Industry experience
    General business experience

TRAINING
At headquarters: 2 weeks
At franchisee's location: 2 weeks
At existing locations

BUSINESS SUPPORT
Grand opening
Internet
Newsletter
Meetings
Field operations/evaluations
Purchasing cooperatives
Security/safety procedures

MARKETING SUPPORT
Ad slicks
National media campaign
Regional marketing

GREAT WRAPS INC.

Ranked #219 in Entrepreneur Magazine's 2007 Franchise 500   *Financial rating: $$$$*

4 Executive Pk. E., #315
Atlanta, GA 30329
(404)248-9900
www.greatwraps.com
Hot wrapped sandwiches & grilled
    subs
Began: 1974, Franchising: 1983
Headquarters size: 15 employees
Franchise department: 15 employees

U.S. franchises: 86
Canadian franchises: 0
Other foreign franchises: 0
Company-owned: 1

Seeking: All U.S.
Seeking in Canada? No
Exclusive territories? Yes
Homebased option? No
Employees needed to run biz: 8-10
Absentee ownership? No

COSTS
Total cost: $212.6K-316.2K
Franchise fee: $19.5K
Royalty fee: 5.5%
Term of agreement: 15 years renewable
    for $5K
Franchisees required to buy multiple
    units? No

FINANCING
In-house: None
3rd-party: Accounts receivable,
    equipment, franchise fee,
    inventory, payroll, startup costs

QUALIFICATIONS
Net worth: $250K
Cash liquidity: $85K
Experience:
    General business experience

TRAINING
At headquarters: 3 weeks
At franchisee's location: 10 days

BUSINESS SUPPORT
Grand opening
Internet
Newsletter
Meetings
Toll-free phone line
Field operations/evaluations
Lease negotiations
Purchasing cooperatives
Security/safety procedures

MARKETING SUPPORT
Ad slicks
National media campaign
Regional marketing

GROUCHO'S DELI

Current financial data not available

611 Harden St.
Columbia, SC 29205
(803)799-5708
www.grouchos.com
Subs & salads
Began: 1941, Franchising: 2001
Headquarters size: 4 employees
Franchise department: 4 employees

U.S. franchises: 14
Canadian franchises: 0
Other foreign franchises: 0
Company-owned: 1

Seeking: South, Southeast
Seeking in Canada? No
Exclusive territories? Yes
Homebased option? No
Employees needed to run biz: 13
Absentee ownership? Yes

COSTS
Total cost: $115.7K-163.2K
Franchise fee: $20K
Royalty fee: 5%
Term of agreement: 10 years renewable
    at no charge
Franchisees required to buy multiple
    units? No

FINANCING
In-house: None
3rd-party: Accounts receivable,
    equipment, franchise fee,
    inventory, payroll, startup costs

QUALIFICATIONS
Net worth: $150K
Cash liquidity: $60K
Experience:
    Industry experience
    General business experience

TRAINING
At headquarters: 7 days
At franchisee's location: 10 days
Additional training: 30 days

BUSINESS SUPPORT
Grand opening
Internet
Newsletter
Meetings
Toll-free phone line
Field operations/evaluations
Lease negotiations
Purchasing cooperatives
Security/safety procedures

MARKETING SUPPORT
Co-op advertising
Regional marketing

HEIDI'S BROOKLYN DELI

Current financial data not available

195 S. Union Blvd.
Lakewood, CO 80228
(303)458-0997
www.heidisbrooklyndeli.com
Deli sandwiches, salads, wraps,
smoothies, ice cream
Began: 1994, Franchising: 2004
Headquarters size: 12 employees
Franchise department: 1 employee

U.S. franchises: 25
Canadian franchises: 0
Other foreign franchises: 0
Company-owned: 4

Seeking: All U.S.
Seeking in Canada? Yes
Exclusive territories? Yes
Homebased option? No
Employees needed to run biz: 12-15
Absentee ownership? No

COSTS
Total cost: $307.7K-428.9K
Franchise fee: $35K
Royalty fee: 6%
Term of agreement: 15 years renewable
at no charge
Franchisees required to buy multiple
units? No

FINANCING
In-house: None
3rd-party: Accounts receivable,
equipment, franchise fee,
inventory, payroll, startup costs

QUALIFICATIONS
Net worth: $120K
Cash liquidity: $80K

TRAINING
At headquarters: 1 week
At existing franchise locations:
3 weeks

BUSINESS SUPPORT
Grand opening
Meetings
Toll-free phone line
Field operations/evaluations
Lease negotiations
Purchasing cooperatives
Security/safety procedures

MARKETING SUPPORT
Co-op advertising
Ad slicks
Regional marketing
Billboards

JIMMY JOHN'S GOURMET SANDWICH SHOPS

Ranked #58 in Entrepreneur Magazine's 2007 Franchise 500   *Financial rating: $$$$*

2212 Fox Dr.
Champaign, IL 61820
(800)546-6904
www.jimmyjohns.com
Gourmet sandwiches
Began: 1983, Franchising: 1993
Headquarters size: 90 employees
Franchise department: 25 employees

U.S. franchises: 460
Canadian franchises: 0
Other foreign franchises: 0
Company-owned: 19

Seeking: All U.S.
Seeking in Canada? No
Exclusive territories? Yes
Homebased option? No
Employees needed to run biz: 20
Absentee ownership? Info not
provided

COSTS
Total cost: $287.4K-373K
Franchise fee: $35K
Royalty fee: 6%
Term of agreement: 10 years renewable
for $2.5K
Franchisees required to buy multiple
units? No

FINANCING
In-house: None
3rd-party: Accounts receivable,
equipment, franchise fee,
inventory, payroll, startup costs

QUALIFICATIONS
Net worth: $300K
Cash liquidity: $80K
Experience:
General business experience

TRAINING
7-week training for general
managers
3-week training for assistant
managers

BUSINESS SUPPORT
Grand opening
Internet
Newsletter
Meetings
Toll-free phone line
Field operations/evaluations

MARKETING SUPPORT
Co-op advertising
Ad slicks
Regional marketing

LARRY'S GIANT SUBS

Current financial data not available

4479 Deerwood Lake Pkwy., #1
Jacksonville, FL 32216
(904)739-9069
www.larryssubs.com
New York-style subs, sandwiches,
    salads
Began: 1982, Franchising: 1986
Headquarters size: 10 employees
Franchise department: 4 employees

U.S. franchises: 100
Canadian franchises: 0
Other foreign franchises: 0
Company-owned: 4

Seeking: All U.S.
Seeking in Canada? Yes
Exclusive territories? Info not provided
Homebased option? No
Employees needed to run biz: 5-10
Absentee ownership? Yes

COSTS
Total cost: $136.8K-201.9K
Franchise fee: $20K
Royalty fee: 6%
Term of agreement: 10 years renewable
    for $6.7K
Franchisees required to buy multiple
    units? No

FINANCING
No financing available

QUALIFICATIONS
Net worth: $100K
Cash liquidity: $60K
Experience:
    Industry experience
    General business experience
    Marketing skills

TRAINING
At headquarters: 3 weeks
At franchisee's location: 1-2 weeks

BUSINESS SUPPORT
Grand opening
Internet
Newsletter
Meetings
Field operations/evaluations

MARKETING SUPPORT
Co-op advertising
Regional marketing

MCALISTER'S DELI

Ranked #142 in Entrepreneur Magazine's 2007 Franchise 500   *Financial rating: $$$$*

731 S. Pear Orchard Rd., #51
Ridgeland, MS 39157
(888)855-3354
www.mcalistersdeli.com
Southern-style upscale deli
Began: 1989, Franchising: 1994
Headquarters size: 45 employees
Franchise department: 10 employees

U.S. franchises: 184
Canadian franchises: 0
Other foreign franchises: 0
Company-owned: 22

Seeking: All U.S.
Seeking in Canada? No
Exclusive territories? Yes
Homebased option? No
Employees needed to run biz: 40
Absentee ownership? Yes

COSTS
Total cost: $397.5K-1.5M
Franchise fee: $20K-35K
Royalty fee: 5%
Term of agreement: 10 years renewable
    at no charge
Franchisees required to buy multiple
    units? Yes

FINANCING
In-house: None
3rd-party: Equipment, franchise fee,
    inventory, startup costs

QUALIFICATIONS
Net worth: $1M
Cash liquidity: $500K
Experience:
    General business experience

TRAINING
At headquarters: 10 weeks
At franchisee's location: 10 days

BUSINESS SUPPORT
Grand opening
Internet
Newsletter
Meetings
Toll-free phone line
Field operations/evaluations
Purchasing cooperatives
Security/safety procedures

MARKETING SUPPORT
Ad slicks
Regional marketing

MR. GOODCENTS FRANCHISE SYSTEMS INC.

Ranked #446 in Entrepreneur Magazine's 2007 Franchise 500   *Financial rating: $$$$*

8997 Commerce Dr.
De Soto, KS 66018
(800)648-2368/(913)583-8400
www.mrgoodcents.com
Submarine sandwiches & pastas
Began: 1988, Franchising: 1990
Headquarters size: 28 employees
Franchise department: 7 employees

U.S. franchises: 110
Canadian franchises: 0
Other foreign franchises: 0
Company-owned: 2

Seeking: All U.S.
Seeking in Canada? No
Exclusive territories? Yes
Homebased option? No
Employees needed to run biz: 10
Absentee ownership? Yes

COSTS
Total cost: $126K-259K
Franchise fee: $15K
Royalty fee: 5%
Term of agreement: 10 years renewable
    for 60% of current fee
Franchisees required to buy multiple
    units? No

FINANCING
In-house: None
3rd-party: Equipment, franchise fee,
    inventory, payroll, startup costs

QUALIFICATIONS
Net worth: $150K+
Cash liquidity: $35K-50K
Experience:
    Industry experience
    General business experience
    Marketing skills

TRAINING
At headquarters: 5 days
At franchisee's location: 20 days

BUSINESS SUPPORT
Grand opening
Internet
Newsletter
Meetings
Toll-free phone line
Field operations/evaluations
Purchasing cooperatives
Security/safety procedures

MARKETING SUPPORT
Co-op advertising
Ad slicks
National media campaign

MR. PICKLE'S SANDWICH SHOP

Current financial data not available

5098 Foothills Blvd., #3-346
Roseville, CA 95747
(916)746-7727
www.mrpicklesinc.com
Sandwiches, soups, salads
Began: 1996, Franchising: 2006
Headquarters size: 4 employees
Franchise department: 4 employees

U.S. franchises: 15
Canadian franchises: 0
Other foreign franchises: 0
Company-owned: 0

Seeking: All U.S.
Seeking in Canada? No
Exclusive territories? Yes
Homebased option? No
Employees needed to run biz: 9
Absentee ownership? No

COSTS
Total cost: $249K
Franchise fee: $25K
Royalty fee: 0
Term of agreement: 5 years renewable
    for $5K
Franchisees required to buy multiple
    units? No

FINANCING
In-house: None
3rd-party: Available

QUALIFICATIONS
Net worth: $250K
Cash liquidity: $80K
Experience:
    Industry experience
    General business experience

TRAINING
At franchisee's location: 2 weeks

BUSINESS SUPPORT
Grand opening
Newsletter
Field operations/evaluations
Lease negotiations
Purchasing cooperatives
Security/safety procedures

MARKETING SUPPORT
Local advertising support

MUSTARD CAFE

Financial rating: $

2 Venture Plaza, #460
Irvine, CA 92618
(949)753-0753
www.mustardfranchise.com
Sandwiches, soups, salads
Began: 2002, Franchising: 2004
Headquarters size: 6 employees
Franchise department: 6 employees

U.S. franchises: 3
Canadian franchises: 0
Other foreign franchises: 0
Company-owned: 0

Seeking: All U.S.
Seeking in Canada? No
Exclusive territories? Yes
Homebased option? No
Employees needed to run biz: 14
Absentee ownership? Yes

COSTS
Total cost: $304.6K-426K
Franchise fee: $25K
Royalty fee: 5%
Term of agreement: 10 years renewable
    for $5K
Franchisees required to buy multiple
    units? No

FINANCING
In-house: None
3rd-party: Equipment, startup costs

QUALIFICATIONS
Net worth: $350K
Cash liquidity: $70K
Experience:
    Industry experience
    General business experience
    Management experience

TRAINING
At headquarters: 2 weeks
At franchisee's location: 4 weeks

BUSINESS SUPPORT
Grand opening
Internet
Meetings
Toll-free phone line
Field operations/evaluations
Lease negotiations
Purchasing cooperatives
Security/safety procedures

MARKETING SUPPORT
Co-op advertising
Catering support
Order-taking center

NEW YORK NY FRESH DELI

Ranked #394 in Entrepreneur Magazine's 2007 Franchise 500   *Financial rating: $$$*

100 W. Hoover Ave., #12-14
Mesa, AZ 85210
(480)632-9884
www.nynyfreshdeli.com
New York-style deli subs & gourmet
    sandwiches
Began: 2001, Franchising: 2002
Headquarters size: 20 employees
Franchise department: 5 employees

U.S. franchises: 34
Canadian franchises: 0
Other foreign franchises: 0
Company-owned: 0

Seeking: All U.S.
Seeking in Canada? No
Exclusive territories? Yes
Homebased option? No
Employees needed to run biz: 6-15
Absentee ownership? Yes

COSTS
Total cost: $49K-210.4K
Franchise fee: $12.5K/17.5K
Royalty fee: 6%
Term of agreement: 10 years renewable
    at no charge
Franchisees required to buy multiple
    units? No

FINANCING
In-house: None
3rd-party: Equipment, franchise fee,
    payroll, startup costs

QUALIFICATIONS
Net worth: $250K+
Cash liquidity: $40K-60K
Experience:
    General business experience

TRAINING
At headquarters: 1 week
At franchisee's location: 5 days
Operations visits

BUSINESS SUPPORT
Grand opening
Internet
Newsletter
Meetings
Toll-free phone line
Field operations/evaluations
Lease negotiations
Purchasing cooperatives
Security/safety procedures

MARKETING SUPPORT
Co-op advertising
Ad slicks

PENN STATION EAST COAST SUBS

Ranked #196 in Entrepreneur Magazine's 2007 Franchise 500   *Financial rating: $$$$*

8276 Beechmont Ave.
Cincinnati, OH 45255
(513)474-5957
www.penn-station.com
Specialty sandwiches
Began: 1985, Franchising: 1988
Headquarters size: 11 employees
Franchise department: 1 employee

U.S. franchises: 159
Canadian franchises: 0
Other foreign franchises: 0
Company-owned: 3

Seeking: Midwest, South, Southeast
Seeking in Canada? No
Exclusive territories? Yes
Homebased option? No
Employees needed to run biz: 15
Absentee ownership? Yes

COSTS
Total cost: $229.6K-434.7K
Franchise fee: $25K
Royalty fee: 4-8%
Term of agreement: 5 years renewable
    for $2.5K
Franchisees required to buy multiple
    units? No

FINANCING
In-house: None
3rd-party: Equipment, franchise fee,
    inventory, startup costs

QUALIFICATIONS
Cash liquidity: $100K+
Experience:
    Industry experience
    General business experience
    3 years+ restaurant-management
    experience

TRAINING
At headquarters: 3 weeks
At franchisee's location: 1 week

BUSINESS SUPPORT
Grand opening
Internet
Newsletter
Meetings
Field operations/evaluations
Lease negotiations

MARKETING SUPPORT
Ad slicks
National media campaign
Regional marketing

PITA PIT INC.

Ranked #212 in Entrepreneur Magazine's 2007 Franchise 500   *Financial rating: $$$$*

801 S. 11th St.
Coeur d'Alene, ID 83814
(208)765-3326
www.pitapitusa.com
Pita sandwiches
Began: 1995, Franchising: 1997
Headquarters size: 15 employees
Franchise department: 4 employees

U.S. franchises: 102
Canadian franchises: 0
Other foreign franchises: 0
Company-owned: 1

Seeking: All U.S.
Seeking in Canada? No
Exclusive territories? Yes
Homebased option? No
Employees needed to run biz: 25
Absentee ownership? Yes

COSTS
Total cost: $219K-326K
Franchise fee: $25K/20K/15K
Royalty fee: 5-6%
Term of agreement: 10 years renewable
    for $10K
Franchisees required to buy multiple
    units? No

FINANCING
In-house: None
3rd-party: Equipment, franchise fee,
    inventory, startup costs

QUALIFICATIONS
Cash liquidity: $50K
People skills
Good work ethic

TRAINING
At headquarters: 10 days
At franchisee's location: 5-7 days

BUSINESS SUPPORT
Grand opening
Internet
Newsletter
Meetings
Toll-free phone line
Field operations/evaluations
Lease negotiations
Purchasing cooperatives

MARKETING SUPPORT
National media campaign

PORT OF SUBS

Current financial data not available

5365 Mae Anne Ave., #A29
Reno, NV 89523
(800)245-0245/(775)747-0555
www.portofsubs.com
Submarine sandwiches & salads
Began: 1972, Franchising: 1985
Headquarters size: 25 employees
Franchise department: 3 employees

U.S. franchises: 121
Canadian franchises: 0
Other foreign franchises: 0
Company-owned: 24

Seeking: Northwest, West
Seeking in Canada? No
Exclusive territories? Yes
Homebased option? No
Employees needed to run biz: 6
Absentee ownership? Yes

COSTS
Total cost: $181.8K-279.5K
Franchise fee: $5K-16K
Royalty fee: 5.5%
Term of agreement: 10 years renewable
  at no charge
Franchisees required to buy multiple
  units? No

FINANCING
In-house: None
3rd-party: Accounts receivable,
  equipment, franchise fee,
  inventory, payroll, startup costs

QUALIFICATIONS
Net worth: $250K
Cash liquidity: $75K-80K
Experience:
  Industry experience
  General business experience
  Marketing skills
  People skills
  Good credit history

TRAINING
At headquarters: 1 week
At corporate training store: 2 weeks

BUSINESS SUPPORT
Grand opening
Internet
Newsletter
Meetings
Toll-free phone line
Field operations/evaluations
Purchasing cooperatives
Security/safety procedures

MARKETING SUPPORT
Co-op advertising
Ad slicks
National media campaign
Regional marketing

ROLLERZ

Financial rating: $$$$

7730 E. Greenway Rd., #104
Scottsdale, AZ 85260
(480)443-0200
www.kahalacorp.com
Rolled sandwiches, salads, soups,
  baked goods
Began: 2000, Franchising: 2000
Headquarters size: Info not
  provided

U.S. franchises: 11
Canadian franchises: 0
Other foreign franchises: 0
Company-owned: 1

Seeking: All U.S.
Seeking in Canada? Yes
Exclusive territories? Yes
Homebased option? No
Employees needed to run biz: 6
Absentee ownership? Yes

COSTS
Total cost: $137.8K-418.5K
Franchise fee: $30K
Royalty fee: 6%
Term of agreement: 10 years renewable
  for 75% of then-current fee
Franchisees required to buy multiple
  units? No

FINANCING
In-house: None
3rd-party: Equipment, franchise fee,
  inventory, startup costs

QUALIFICATIONS
Cash liquidity: $30K
Experience:
  Industry experience
  General business experience

TRAINING
At headquarters: 1 week
At franchisee's location: 2 weeks

BUSINESS SUPPORT
Grand opening
Internet
Newsletter
Meetings
Toll-free phone line
Field operations/evaluations
Purchasing cooperatives
Security/safety procedures

MARKETING SUPPORT
Co-op advertising
Ad slicks
Regional marketing

SPICY PICKLE

Financial rating: 0

90 Madison St., #700
Denver, CO 80206
(303)297-1902
www.spicypickle.com
Panini, salads, subs, soups
Began: 1999, Franchising: 2003
Headquarters size: 18 employees
Franchise department: 2 employees

U.S. franchises: 12
Canadian franchises: 0
Other foreign franchises: 0
Company-owned: 1

Seeking: All U.S.
Seeking in Canada? No
Exclusive territories? Yes
Homebased option? No
Employees needed to run biz: 12-15
Absentee ownership? Yes

COSTS
Total cost: $300K
Franchise fee: $30K
Royalty fee: 5%
Term of agreement: 10 years renewable
    for 20% of then-current fee
Franchisees required to buy multiple
    units? No

FINANCING
In-house: None
3rd-party: Accounts receivable,
    equipment, franchise fee,
    inventory, payroll, startup costs

QUALIFICATIONS
Net worth: $500K
Cash liquidity: $150K
Experience:
    Industry experience
    General business experience
    People skills

TRAINING
At headquarters: 4 weeks
At franchisee's location: 10 days

BUSINESS SUPPORT
Grand opening
Internet
Meetings
Field operations/evaluations
Lease negotiations
Security/safety procedures

MARKETING SUPPORT
Co-op advertising
Ad slicks
National media campaign
Regional marketing
Marketing program

THE STEAK ESCAPE

Ranked #468 in Entrepreneur Magazine's 2007 Franchise 500   *Financial rating: $$$$*

222 Neilston St.
Columbus, OH 43215
(614)224-0300
www.steakescape.com
Grilled sandwiches, baked potatoes,
    salads
Began: 1982, Franchising: 1983
Headquarters size: 35 employees
Franchise department: 3 employees

U.S. franchises: 132
Canadian franchises: 0
Other foreign franchises: 0
Company-owned: 0

Seeking: All U.S.
Seeking in Canada? Yes
Exclusive territories? Yes
Homebased option? No
Employees needed to run biz: 20-25
Absentee ownership? Yes

COSTS
Total cost: $190.2K-1.3M
Franchise fee: $25K
Royalty fee: 6%
Term of agreement: 20 years
Franchisees required to buy multiple
    units? Outside the U.S. only

FINANCING
No financing available

QUALIFICATIONS
Net worth: $350K
Cash liquidity: $100K
Experience:
    General business experience

TRAINING
At headquarters: 3 weeks
At franchisee's location: 1 week

BUSINESS SUPPORT
Grand opening
Internet
Newsletter
Toll-free phone line
Field operations/evaluations

MARKETING SUPPORT
National media campaign

SUBWAY

Ranked #1 in Entrepreneur Magazine's 2007 Franchise 500   *Financial rating: $$$$*

325 Bic Dr.
Milford, CT 06460
(800)888-4848/(203)877-4281
www.subway.com
Submarine sandwiches & salads
Began: 1965, Franchising: 1974
Headquarters size: 650 employees
Franchise department: 20 employees

U.S. franchises: 20,265
Canadian franchises: 2,165
Other foreign franchises: 3,767
Company-owned: 0

Seeking: All U.S.
Seeking in Canada? Yes
Exclusive territories? No
Homebased option? No
Employees needed to run biz: 6-10
Absentee ownership? No

COSTS
Total cost: $74.9K-222.8K
Franchise fee: $15K
Royalty fee: 8%
Term of agreement: 20 years renewable
    at no charge
Franchisees required to buy multiple
    units? No

FINANCING
In-house: Equipment, franchise fee
3rd-party: Equipment, franchise fee,
    startup costs

QUALIFICATIONS
Net worth: $30K-90K
Cash liquidity: $30K-90K
Experience:
    General business experience

TRAINING
At headquarters: 2 weeks
Training available in Miami, FL;
    Montreal, Canada; China,
    Germany & India

BUSINESS SUPPORT
Grand opening
Internet
Newsletter
Meetings
Toll-free phone line
Field operations/evaluations
Lease negotiations
Purchasing cooperatives
Security/safety procedures

MARKETING SUPPORT
Co-op advertising
Ad slicks
National media campaign
Regional marketing
Local store marketing

TUBBY'S SUB SHOPS

Current financial data not available

35807 Moravian
Clinton Township, MI 48035
(586)792-2369
www.tubby.com
Subs, salads, soups, pita sandwiches,
    desserts
Began: 1968, Franchising: 1978
Headquarters size: 15 employees
Franchise department: 2 employees

U.S. franchises: 86
Canadian franchises: 0
Other foreign franchises: 0
Company-owned: 1

Seeking: Midwest, Northeast
Seeking in Canada? No
Exclusive territories? Yes
Homebased option? No
Employees needed to run biz: 3-4
Absentee ownership? Yes

COSTS
Total cost: $72.9K-243.5K
Franchise fee: $12.5K/15K
Royalty fee: 6%
Term of agreement: 10 years
Franchisees required to buy multiple
    units? No

FINANCING
In-house: None
3rd-party: Accounts receivable,
    equipment, franchise fee,
    inventory, payroll, startup costs

QUALIFICATIONS
Net worth: $350K-500K
Cash liquidity: $75K

TRAINING
At company store: 120 hours+

BUSINESS SUPPORT
Grand opening
Newsletter
Field operations/evaluations
Purchasing cooperatives

MARKETING SUPPORT
Co-op advertising
Ad slicks

WHICH WICH? SUPERIOR SANDWICHES

Financial rating: 0

1310 Elm St., #180LL
Dallas, TX 75202
(214)747-9424
www.whichwich.com
Sandwiches, milkshakes, cookies
Began: 2003, Franchising: 2004
Headquarters size: 8 employees
Franchise department: 8 employees

U.S. franchises: 10
Canadian franchises: 0
Other foreign franchises: 0
Company-owned: 2

Seeking: All U.S.
Seeking in Canada? No
Exclusive territories? Yes
Homebased option? No
Employees needed to run biz: 10
Absentee ownership? No

COSTS
Total cost: $185K-305.6K
Franchise fee: $25K
Royalty fee: 6%
Term of agreement: 10 years renewable
  for $5K
Franchisees required to buy multiple
  units? Yes

FINANCING
In-house: None
3rd-party: Equipment, franchise fee,
  startup costs

QUALIFICATIONS
Net worth: $150K/unit
Cash liquidity: $50K
Experience:
    General business experience
    Marketing skills

TRAINING
At headquarters: 3 weeks
At franchisee's location: 1-2 weeks

BUSINESS SUPPORT
Internet
Meetings
Field operations/evaluations
Security/safety procedures

MARKETING SUPPORT
Online marketing manual

QUICK SERVICE ▶ *Miscellaneous*

BANNASTROW'S

Current financial data not available

20871 Johnson St., #102
Pembroke Pines, FL 33029
(954)602-1001
www.bannastrows.com
Crepes & coffee
Began: 2001, Franchising: 2003
Headquarters size: 4 employees
Franchise department: 3 employees

U.S. franchises: 2
Canadian franchises: 0
Other foreign franchises: 4
Company-owned: 3

Seeking: All U.S.
Seeking in Canada? Yes
Exclusive territories? Yes
Homebased option? No
Employees needed to run biz: 3
Absentee ownership? Yes

COSTS
Total cost: $110.9K-171K
Franchise fee: $25K
Royalty fee: 5%
Term of agreement: 5 years renewable
  at no charge
Franchisees required to buy multiple
  units? No

FINANCING
No financing available

QUALIFICATIONS
Net worth: $150K
Cash liquidity: $30K

TRAINING
At headquarters: 80 hours
At franchisee's location: 10 days
Ongoing support

BUSINESS SUPPORT
Grand opening
Internet
Meetings
Toll-free phone line
Field operations/evaluations
Lease negotiations
Security/safety procedures

MARKETING SUPPORT
Ad slicks

BAR-B-CUTIE

Financial rating: $$$

5120 Virginia Wy., #B-23
Brentwood, TN 37027
(615)372-0707
www.bar-b-cutie.com
Barbecue restaurant
Began: 1950, Franchising: 2003
Headquarters size: 48 employees
Franchise department: 5 employees

U.S. franchises: 5
Canadian franchises: 0
Other foreign franchises: 0
Company-owned: 2

Seeking: Southeast
Seeking in Canada? No
Exclusive territories? Yes
Homebased option? No
Employees needed to run biz: 20
Absentee ownership? No

COSTS
Total cost: $265K-393K
Franchise fee: $35K
Royalty fee: 5%
Term of agreement: 10 years renewable
for $5K
Franchisees required to buy multiple
units? No

FINANCING
In-house: None
3rd-party: Equipment, startup costs

QUALIFICATIONS
Net worth: $500K
Cash liquidity: $200K
Experience:
General business experience

TRAINING
At headquarters: 3 weeks
At franchisee's location: 1 week

BUSINESS SUPPORT
Grand opening
Internet
Newsletter
Meetings
Field operations/evaluations
Lease negotiations

MARKETING SUPPORT
Co-op advertising

BLENDZ FRANCHISE SYSTEM INC.

Financial rating: 0

267 E. Campbell Ave., #200
Campbell, CA 95008
(866)425-3639
www.blendz.com
Salads, panini, smoothies, soups
Began: 2002, Franchising: 2005
Headquarters size: 25 employees
Franchise department: 5 employees

U.S. franchises: 1
Canadian franchises: 0
Other foreign franchises: 0
Company-owned: 4

Seeking: AZ, CA, CO, NV
Seeking in Canada? No
Exclusive territories? Yes
Homebased option? No
Employees needed to run biz: 12
Absentee ownership? Yes

COSTS
Total cost: $227.8K-295.3K
Franchise fee: $25K
Royalty fee: 6%
Term of agreement: 10 years renewable
for $2.5K
Franchisees required to buy multiple
units? No

FINANCING
In-house: None
3rd-party: Equipment, inventory,
startup costs

QUALIFICATIONS
Net worth: $150K
Cash liquidity: $70K
Experience:
General business experience
Marketing skills

TRAINING
At headquarters: 4 weeks
At franchisee's location: 1 week
Home study: 1 week

BUSINESS SUPPORT
Grand opening
Internet
Newsletter
Meetings
Toll-free phone line
Field operations/evaluations
Security/safety procedures

MARKETING SUPPORT
Co-op advertising
Ad slicks
Regional marketing

BONEHEADS GRILLED FISH & PIRI PIRI CHICKEN

Financial rating: $$

2349 Peachtree Rd.
Atlanta, GA 30305
(404)844-3225
www.eatboneheads.com
Fire-grilled fish & chicken
Began: 2004, Franchising: 2005
Headquarters size: 80 employees
Franchise department: 10 employees

U.S. franchises: 5
Canadian franchises: 0
Other foreign franchises: 0
Company-owned: 1

Seeking: All U.S.
Seeking in Canada? Yes
Exclusive territories? No
Homebased option? No
Employees needed to run biz: 25
Absentee ownership? No

COSTS
Total cost: $387K-668K
Franchise fee: $25K
Royalty fee: 5%
Term of agreement: 10 years renewable
    for $25K
Franchisees required to buy multiple
    units? No

FINANCING
In-house: None
3rd-party: Accounts receivable,
    equipment, franchise fee,
    inventory, payroll, startup costs

QUALIFICATIONS
Net worth: $500K
Cash liquidity: $150K
Experience:
    General business experience

TRAINING
At headquartaers: 2-1/2 weeks
At franchisee's location: 1 week

BUSINESS SUPPORT
Grand opening
Internet
Toll-free phone line
Field operations/evaluations
Security/safety procedures

MARKETING SUPPORT
Ad slicks

CALIFORNIA QUIVERS

Financial rating: 0

5284 Eastgate Mall
San Diego, CA 92121
(858)558-1300
www.californiaquivers.com
Carts serving fruit ices, hot dogs
    & coffee
Began: 1997, Franchising: 2004
Headquarters size: 45 employees
Franchise department: 4 employees

U.S. franchises: 2
Canadian franchises: 0
Other foreign franchises: 0
Company-owned: 10

Seeking: All U.S.
Seeking in Canada? Yes
Exclusive territories? Yes
Homebased option? No
Employees needed to run biz: 3-5
Absentee ownership? Yes

COSTS
Total cost: $45K-149.3K
Franchise fee: $22.5K-27.5K
Royalty fee: 6%
Term of agreement: 10 years renewable
    for 50% of then-current fee
Franchisees required to buy multiple
    units? No

FINANCING
No financing available

QUALIFICATIONS
Cash liquidity: $35K
Experience:
    General business experience

TRAINING
At headquarters: 1 week
At franchisee's location: Varies

BUSINESS SUPPORT
Grand opening
Internet
Newsletter
Meetings
Field operations/evaluations
Security/safety procedures

MARKETING SUPPORT
Web-based marketing

CEREALITY FRANCHISING CORP.

Financial rating: $$$

54 W. Hubbard St., #100
Chicago, IL 60610
(312)893-1234
www.cereality.com
Cereal restaurant
Began: 2001, Franchising: 2006
Headquarters size: 15 employees
Franchise department: 4 employees

U.S. franchises: 0
Canadian franchises: 0
Other foreign franchises: 0
Company-owned: 3

Seeking: All U.S.
Seeking in Canada? Yes
Exclusive territories? Yes
Homebased option? No
Employees needed to run biz: 12-20
Absentee ownership? Yes

COSTS
Total cost: $212K-375K
Franchise fee: $25K
Royalty fee: 6%
Term of agreement: 15 years renewable
    for $1.5K/yr.
Franchisees required to buy multiple
    units? Yes

FINANCING
No financing available

QUALIFICATIONS
Net worth: $1M
Cash liquidity: $500K
Experience:
    Industry experience
    General business experience
    Marketing skills
    Customer service experience

TRAINING
At headquarters: 3 weeks
At franchisee's location: 3 days
At existing franchise locations:
    Varies

BUSINESS SUPPORT
Grand opening
Field operations/evaluations
Security/safety procedures

MARKETING SUPPORT
Ad slicks
PR

CREPEMAKER

Financial rating: $$$

8925 S.W. 148th St., #200
Village of Palmetto Bay, FL 33176
(888)427-3737/(305)233-1113
www.crepemaker.com
Crepes
Began: 1992, Franchising: 2001
Headquarters size: 30 employees
Franchise department: 3 employees

U.S. franchises: 5
Canadian franchises: 0
Other foreign franchises: 0
Company-owned: 5

Seeking: All U.S.
Seeking in Canada? No
Exclusive territories? Yes
Homebased option? No
Employees needed to run biz: 5-30
Absentee ownership? Yes

COSTS
Total cost: $106.6K-375.3K
Franchise fee: $25K
Royalty fee: 6%
Term of agreement: 7 years
    renewable
Franchisees required to buy multiple
    units? Yes

FINANCING
In-house: None
3rd-party: Accounts receivable,
    equipment, franchise fee,
    inventory, payroll, startup costs

QUALIFICATIONS
Net worth: $100K
Cash liquidity: $50K
Experience:
    Industry experience
    General business experience

TRAINING
At headquarters: 4 weeks
At franchisee's location: 1 week
Additional training as needed

BUSINESS SUPPORT
Grand opening
Newsletter
Toll-free phone line
Field operations/evaluations
Lease negotiations
Purchasing cooperatives

MARKETING SUPPORT
Ad slicks

ENERGY KITCHEN

Current financial data not available

1089 Second Ave.
New York, NY 10022
(917)733-7600
www.energykitchen.com
Quick-service restaurant serving
    high-protein/low-fat meals
Began: 1998, Franchising: 2005
Headquarters size: 4 employees
Franchise department: 3 employees

U.S. franchises: 0
Canadian franchises: 0
Other foreign franchises: 0
Company-owned: 3

Seeking: Northeast
Seeking in Canada? No
Exclusive territories? No
Homebased option? No
Employees needed to run biz: 10
Absentee ownership? No

COSTS
Total cost: $223.5K-491K
Franchise fee: $25K
Royalty fee: 5%
Term of agreement: 10 years
Franchisees required to buy multiple
    units? No

FINANCING
No financing available

QUALIFICATIONS
Net worth: $250K
Cash liquidity: $250K-400K
Experience:
    General business experience

TRAINING
At headquarters: 1 month
At franchisee's location: 2 weeks

BUSINESS SUPPORT
Grand opening
Internet
Newsletter
Meetings
Field operations/evaluations
Security/safety procedures

MARKETING SUPPORT
Ad slicks
Regional marketing

GOLDEN KRUST FRANCHISING INC.

Ranked #241 in Entrepreneur Magazine's 2007 Franchise 500   *Financial rating: $$$*

3958 Park Ave.
Bronx, NY 10457
(718)655-7878
www.goldenkrustbakery.com
Caribbean-style restaurant
Began: 1989, Franchising: 1996
Headquarters size: 120 employees
Franchise department: 10 employees

U.S. franchises: 105
Canadian franchises: 0
Other foreign franchises: 0
Company-owned: 1

Seeking: All U.S.
Seeking in Canada? Yes
Exclusive territories? No
Homebased option? No
Employees needed to run biz: 8
Absentee ownership? Yes

COSTS
Total cost: $91.8K-395K
Franchise fee: $25K
Royalty fee: 3%
Term of agreement: 10 years
    renewable
Franchisees required to buy multiple
    units? No

FINANCING
In-house: None
3rd-party: Equipment, franchise fee,
    startup costs

QUALIFICATIONS
Net worth: $444K
Cash liquidity: $90K
Experience:
    Industry experience
    General business experience
    Marketing skills
    Organizational skills

TRAINING
At headquarters: 1 week+
At franchisee's location: 1 week+
At existing store: 1 week

BUSINESS SUPPORT
Grand opening
Internet
Newsletter
Meetings
Field operations/evaluations
Purchasing cooperatives
Security/safety procedures

MARKETING SUPPORT
Co-op advertising
Ad slicks
National media campaign
Regional marketing
Radio, TV, newspapers, magazines,
    billboards

HAPPY JOE'S

Current financial data not available

2705 Happy Joe Dr.
Bettendorf, IA 52722
(563)332-8811
www.happyjoes.com
Pizza, pasta, ice cream
Began: 1972, Franchising: 1973
Headquarters size: 20 employees
Franchise department: 2 employees

U.S. franchises: 56
Canadian franchises: 0
Other foreign franchises: 0
Company-owned: 7

Seeking: All U.S.
Seeking in Canada? Yes
Exclusive territories? Yes
Homebased option? No
Employees needed to run biz: 45
Absentee ownership? Yes

COSTS
Total cost: $98.2K-1.1M
Franchise fee: $20K-25K
Royalty fee: 4.5%
Term of agreement: 15 years renewable
    for 10% of current fee
Franchisees required to buy multiple
    units? No

FINANCING
No financing available

QUALIFICATIONS
Cash liquidity: $300K
Experience:
    General business experience

TRAINING
At headquarters: 6 weeks

BUSINESS SUPPORT
Grand opening
Internet
Newsletter
Meetings
Toll-free phone line
Field operations/evaluations
Lease negotiations
Purchasing cooperatives
Security/safety procedures

MARKETING SUPPORT
Co-op advertising
Ad slicks
National media campaign
Regional marketing
Market research firm

HOT STUFF FOODS LLC

Ranked #52 in Entrepreneur Magazine's 2007 Franchise 500   *Financial rating: $$$*

2930 W. Maple, P.O. Box 85210
Sioux Falls, SD 57118
(605)336-6961
www.hotstufffoods.com
Fast-food systems for nontraditional
    markets
Began: 1982, Franchising: 1993
Headquarters size: 300 employees
Franchise department: 20 employees

U.S. franchises: 1,190
Canadian franchises: 25
Other foreign franchises: 0
Company-owned: 0

Seeking: All U.S.
Seeking in Canada? Yes
Exclusive territories? Yes
Homebased option? No
Employees needed to run biz: 4-6
Absentee ownership? Yes

COSTS
Total cost: $15K-175K
Franchise fee: $1.99K
Royalty fee: 0
Term of agreement: 10 years renewable
    for $1K
Franchisees required to buy multiple
    units? No

FINANCING
In-house: Equipment
3rd-party: Equipment, franchise fee,
    inventory, startup costs

QUALIFICATIONS
Net worth: $100K
Experience:
    Industry experience
    General business experience
    Marketing skills

TRAINING
At franchisee's location: 5 days

BUSINESS SUPPORT
Grand opening
Internet
Newsletter
Meetings
Toll-free phone line
Field operations/evaluations
Security/safety procedures

MARKETING SUPPORT
Ad slicks
National media campaign
Regional marketing

MIAMI RICE PUDDING CO.

Financial rating: $$$

4 Mulberry Ln.
Denville, NJ 07834
(866)632-8742
www.miamiricepuddingco.com
Gourmet rice puddings
Began: 2006, Franchising: 2006
Headquarters size: 6 employees
Franchise department: 3 employees

U.S. franchises: 0
Canadian franchises: 0
Other foreign franchises: 0
Company-owned: 1

Seeking: All U.S.
Seeking in Canada? No
Exclusive territories? Yes
Homebased option? No
Employees needed to run biz: 3
Absentee ownership? Yes

COSTS
Total cost: $75K-140K
Franchise fee: $24.5K
Royalty fee: 6%
Term of agreement: 10 years
Franchisees required to buy multiple
    units? No

FINANCING
No financing available

QUALIFICATIONS
Net worth: $190K
Cash liquidity: $25K

TRAINING
At headquarters: 1 week
At franchisee's location: 1 week

BUSINESS SUPPORT
Grand opening
Internet
Newsletter
Meetings
Toll-free phone line
Field operations/evaluations
Purchasing cooperatives
Security/safety procedures

MARKETING SUPPORT
Co-op advertising
Ad slicks

NATURE'S WAY CAFE

Ranked #384 in Entrepreneur Magazine's 2007 Franchise 500

Financial rating: $$$$

720 Sandpiper Wy.
North Palm Beach, FL 33408
(561)714-4500
www.natureswaycafe.com
Healthy foods, salads, wraps, soups,
    smoothies
Began: 1978, Franchising: 1992
Headquarters size: 4 employees
Franchise department: 4 employees

U.S. franchises: 13
Canadian franchises: 0
Other foreign franchises: 0
Company-owned: 0

Seeking: All U.S.
Seeking in Canada? No
Exclusive territories? Yes
Homebased option? No
Employees needed to run biz: 5
Absentee ownership? No

COSTS
Total cost: $103.3K-201.5K
Franchise fee: $20K
Royalty fee: 4%
Term of agreement: 15 years renewable
    at no charge
Franchisees required to buy multiple
    units? No

FINANCING
No financing available

QUALIFICATIONS
Net worth: $200K
Cash liquidity: $75K
Experience:
    General business experience
    Marketing skills

TRAINING
At headquarters: 2 weeks
At franchisee's location: 1 week

BUSINESS SUPPORT
Grand opening
Internet
Meetings
Field operations/evaluations
Lease negotiations
Purchasing cooperatives
Security/safety procedures

MARKETING SUPPORT
Co-op advertising

O'NATURALS

Financial rating: $$$

44 Exchange St., #305
Portland, ME 04101
(207)874-4911
www.onaturals.com
Fast-casual cafe serving natural &
organic foods
Began: 1998, Franchising: 2005
Headquarters size: 5 employees
Franchise department: 4 employees

U.S. franchises: 0
Canadian franchises: 0
Other foreign franchises: 0
Company-owned: 4

Seeking: All U.S.
Seeking in Canada? No
Exclusive territories? Yes
Homebased option? No
Employees needed to run biz: 10-25
Absentee ownership? Yes

COSTS
Total cost: $764K-1M
Franchise fee: $25K
Royalty fee: 5%
Term of agreement: 15 years renewable
for 50% of current franchise fee
Franchisees required to buy multiple
units? No

FINANCING
No financing available

QUALIFICATIONS
Net worth: $375K
Cash liquidity: $150K
Experience:
Industry experience
General business experience
Marketing skills

TRAINING
At headquarters: 6 weeks
At franchisee's location: Up to
5 days

BUSINESS SUPPORT
Grand opening
Internet
Newsletter
Field operations/evaluations
Purchasing cooperatives
Security/safety procedures

MARKETING SUPPORT
Ad slicks
Regional marketing
Community-based marketing
program

OFF THE GRILL FRANCHISING INC.

Current financial data not available

325 Seaboard Ln., #110
Franklin, TN 37067
(615)771-8020
www.offthegrill.com
Fast-casual restaurant with takeout
& delivery
Began: 1999, Franchising: 1999
Headquarters size: 8 employees
Franchise department: 8 employees

U.S. franchises: 10
Canadian franchises: 0
Other foreign franchises: 0
Company-owned: 3

Seeking: All U.S.
Seeking in Canada? No
Exclusive territories? Yes
Homebased option? No
Employees needed to run biz: 20
Absentee ownership? Yes

COSTS
Total cost: $375K-425K
Franchise fee: $25K
Royalty fee: 4%
Term of agreement: 10 years renewable
for $12.5K
Franchisees required to buy multiple
units? No

FINANCING
In-house: None
3rd-party: Equipment, franchise fee,
inventory, startup costs

QUALIFICATIONS
Net worth: $500K
Cash liquidity: $150K/unit
Experience:
General business experience
Marketing skills

TRAINING
At headquarters: 6 weeks
At franchisee's location: 2 weeks
Additional training available

BUSINESS SUPPORT
Grand opening
Internet
Newsletter
Meetings
Toll-free phone line
Field operations/evaluations
Purchasing cooperatives
Security/safety procedures

MARKETING SUPPORT
Co-op advertising
National media campaign

ORANGE JULIUS OF AMERICA

Financial rating: $$$$

P.O. Box 39286
Minneapolis, MN 55439-0286
(952)830-0200
www.orangejulius.com
Fast food
Began: 1926, Franchising: 1948
Headquarters size: 320 employees
Franchise department: 33 employees

U.S. franchises: 133
Canadian franchises: 9
Other foreign franchises: 70
Company-owned: 0

Seeking: All U.S.
Seeking in Canada? Yes
Exclusive territories? No
Homebased option? No
Employees needed to run biz: 10-20
Absentee ownership? Yes

COSTS
Total cost: $194.2K-380.6K
Franchise fee: $20K-35K
Royalty fee: 6%
Term of agreement: 15 years
    (co-terminus w/lease) renewable
    for $2.5K
Franchisees required to buy multiple
    units? No

FINANCING
No financing available

QUALIFICATIONS
Net worth: $200K
Cash liquidity: $175K
Experience:
    Industry experience
    General business experience

TRAINING
At headquarters: 1-1/2 weeks
At franchisee's location: Pre- &
    post-opening
At existing location: 4 days+

BUSINESS SUPPORT
Grand opening
Internet
Newsletter
Meetings
Toll-free phone line
Field operations/evaluations
Purchasing cooperatives

MARKETING SUPPORT
Co-op advertising
Ad slicks
Local promotions

P.B.LOCO PEANUTBUTTERLICIOUS CAFES

Financial rating: 0

2124 University Ave. W.
Saint Paul, MN 55114
(651)641-1422
www.pbloco.com
Peanut butter restaurant
Began: 2003, Franchising: 2004
Headquarters size: 15 employees
Franchise department: 5 employees

U.S. franchises: 2
Canadian franchises: 0
Other foreign franchises: 0
Company-owned: 1

Seeking: All U.S.
Seeking in Canada? Yes
Exclusive territories? Yes
Homebased option? No
Employees needed to run biz: 5-10
Absentee ownership? Yes

COSTS
Total cost: $179.7K-338.2K
Franchise fee: $24K
Royalty fee: 5%
Term of agreement: 10 years renewable
    at no charge
Franchisees required to buy multiple
    units? No

FINANCING
In-house: None
3rd-party: Equipment, franchise fee,
    inventory, startup costs

QUALIFICATIONS
Info not provided

TRAINING
At headquarters: 7-10 days
At franchisee's location: 2-4 days

BUSINESS SUPPORT
Grand opening
Internet
Field operations/evaluations

MARKETING SUPPORT
Co-op advertising
Ad slicks

SANTORINI ISLAND GRILL

Current financial data not available

10545 Scripps Poway Pkwy., #D
San Diego, CA 92131
(858)675-7455
www.santoriniislandgrill.co/dev
Greek restaurant
Began: 1999, Franchising: 2006
Headquarters size: 14 employees
Franchise department: 6 employees

U.S. franchises: 0
Canadian franchises: 0
Other foreign franchises: 0
Company-owned: 2

Seeking: All U.S.
Seeking in Canada? Yes
Exclusive territories? Yes
Homebased option? No
Employees needed to run biz: 6
Absentee ownership? Yes

COSTS
Total cost: $154.5K-273K
Franchise fee: $39.5K
Royalty fee: 6%
Term of agreement: 10 years renewable
   for 25% of then-current fee
Franchisees required to buy multiple
   units? Outside the U.S. only

FINANCING
In-house: Franchise fee
3rd-party: Equipment, inventory

QUALIFICATIONS
Net worth: $750K
Cash liquidity: $150K
Experience:
   General business experience
   Customer-service skills

TRAINING
At headquarters: 3 weeks
At franchisee's location: 3-4 weeks

BUSINESS SUPPORT
Grand opening
Internet
Newsletter
Meetings
Toll-free phone line
Field operations/evaluations
Purchasing cooperatives
Security/safety procedures

MARKETING SUPPORT
Ad slicks
National media campaign
Regional marketing

STEAK-OUT FRANCHISING INC.

Ranked #465 in Entrepreneur Magazine's 2007 Franchise 500   *Financial rating: $$$$*

3091 Governors Lake Dr., #500
Norcross, GA 30071-1130
(678)533-6000
www.steakout.com
Charbroiled steaks, burgers &
   chicken delivery
Began: 1986, Franchising: 1988
Headquarters size: 18 employees
Franchise department: 9 employees

U.S. franchises: 68
Canadian franchises: 0
Other foreign franchises: 0
Company-owned: 3

Seeking: Midwest, South, Southeast
Seeking in Canada? No
Exclusive territories? Yes
Homebased option? No
Employees needed to run biz: 30
Absentee ownership? Yes

COSTS
Total cost: $249.5K-429.4K
Franchise fee: $25K
Royalty fee: 5%
Term of agreement: 10 years renewable
   for $12.5K
Franchisees required to buy multiple
   units? No

FINANCING
In-house: None
3rd-party: Equipment, leasehold
   improvements

QUALIFICATIONS
Net worth: $300K+
Cash liquidity: $75K-100K
Experience:
   General business experience
   Marketing skills
   Industry experience for multi-unit
   operations

TRAINING
At headquarters: 4 weeks
At franchisee's location: 1-2 weeks

BUSINESS SUPPORT
Grand opening
Internet
Newsletter
Meetings
Toll-free phone line
Field operations/evaluations
Purchasing cooperatives
Security/safety procedures

MARKETING SUPPORT
Ad slicks
National media campaign
Local store marketing

QUICK SERVICE ▶ *Other Franchises*

A & W RESTAURANTS INC.
1441 Gardiner Ln.
Louisville, KY 40213
(866)298-6986
www.yumfranchises.com
Burgers, hot dogs, root beer
Current financial data not available

BAHAMA BUCK'S ORIGINAL SHAVED ICE CO.
5123 69th St.
Lubbock, TX 79424
(806)771-2189
www.bahamabucks.com
Shaved ice & fruit smoothies
Current financial data not available

BARNIE'S COFFEE & TEA CO.
Ranked #346 in Entrepreneur Magazine's 2007 Franchise 500
2126 W. Landstreet Rd., #300
Orlando, FL 32809
(407)854-6600
www.barniescoffee.com
Specialty gourmet coffee, teas, related accessories
Financial rating: $$$$

BASKIN-ROBBINS USA CO.
130 Royall St.
Canton, MA 02021
(781)737-3000
www.dunkin-baskin.com
Ice cream, frozen yogurt, frozen beverages
Financial rating: $$$$

BOJANGLES' FAMOUS CHICKEN 'N BISCUITS
Ranked #138 in Entrepreneur Magazine's 2007 Franchise 500
P.O. Box 240239
Charlotte, NC 28224
(800)366-9921
www.bojangles.com
Chicken & biscuits
Financial rating: $$$$

BREADSMITH
409 E. Silver Spring Dr.
Whitefish Bay, WI 53217
(414)962-1965
www.breadsmith.com
Hearth-baked breads
Financial rating: $$$$

BUFFALO PHILLY'S
1954 Opitz Blvd.
Woodbridge, VA 22191
(703)490-3428
www.buffalophillys.com
Buffalo-style wings & cheesesteaks
Financial rating: $$

BUFFALO WILD WINGS
Ranked #85 in Entrepreneur Magazine's 2007 Franchise 500
1600 Utica Ave. S., #700
Minneapolis, MN 55416
(800)499-9586
www.buffalowildwings.com
Buffalo wings & sandwiches
Financial rating: $$$$

BURGER KING CORP.
5505 Blue Lagoon Dr.
Miami, FL 33126
(866)546-4252
www.burgerking.com
Hamburgers, fries, breakfast, other items
Current financial data not available

CAPTAIN D'S SEAFOOD
Ranked #128 in Entrepreneur Magazine's 2007 Franchise 500
1717 Elm Hill Pike, #A-1
Nashville, TN 37210
(949)462-7320
www.captainds.com
Quick-service seafood restaurant & drive-thru
Financial rating: $$$$

CARL'S JR. RESTAURANTS
6307 Carpinteria Ave., #A
Carpinteria, CA 93013
(866)253-7655/(805)745-7842
www.ckr.com
Hamburgers & chicken sandwiches
Current financial data not available

CASINO TONY GOES RESTAURANT
15 Anderson St.
Trenton, NJ 08611
(609)213-2984
www.casinotonygoes.com
Quick-service Italian restaurant specializing in Italian hot dogs
Current financial data not available

CHECKERS DRIVE-IN RESTAURANTS INC.
4300 W. Cypress St., #600
Tampa, FL 33607
(813)283-7000
www.checkers.com
Burgers & fries
Current financial data not available

CHURCH'S CHICKEN
980 Hammond Dr., #1100
Atlanta, GA 30328
(770)350-3800
www.churchs.com
Quick-service chicken restaurant
Current financial data not available

CIANCI EUROPEAN EATERY
331 Newman Springs Rd., Bldg. 1, 4th Fl., #143
Red Bank, NJ 07701
(732)784-2882
www.ciancifranchise.com
Crepes, sandwiches, salads, soups, smoothies, coffee
Current financial data not available

THE COFFEE BEANERY

Ranked #452 in Entrepreneur Magazine's 2007 Franchise 500
3429 Pierson Pl.
Flushing, MI 48433
(888)385-2326
www.coffeebeanery.com
Gourmet coffees, desserts, accessories
Financial rating: $$$

CUPPY'S COFFEE, SMOOTHIES & MORE

348 Miracle Strip Pkwy., #10C
Fort Walton Beach, FL 32548
(888)241-4324
www.cuppys.com
Coffee carts, kiosks & full-service cafes
Current financial data not available

DESERT MOON-FRESH MEXICAN GRILLE

612 Corporate Way, #1M
Valley Cottage, NY 10989
(845)267-3300
www.desertmooncafe.com
Fresh Mexican/Southwestern food
Current financial data not available

DUNN BROS COFFEE

Ranked #218 in Entrepreneur Magazine's 2007 Franchise 500
111 3rd Ave. S., #220
Minneapolis, MN 55401-2552
(612)334-9746
www.dunnbros.com
Coffeehouse
Financial rating: $$$$

EARL OF SANDWICH (USA) LLC

7598 W. Sand Lake Rd.
Orlando, FL 32819
(407)992-2989
www.earlofsandwichusa.com
Sandwiches, wraps, salads, desserts
Financial rating: $$$

EAST OF CHICAGO PIZZA COMPANY

512 E. Tiffin St.
Willard, OH 44890
(419)935-3033
www.eastofchicago.com
Pizza buffet restaurant
Current financial data not available

THE EXTREME PITA

Ranked #172 in Entrepreneur Magazine's 2007 Franchise 500
2187 Dunwin Dr.
Mississauga, ON L5L 1X2 Canada
(888)729-7482/(905)820-7887
www.extremepita.com
Pita wrap sandwiches
Financial rating: $$$$

FAMOUS FAMIGLIA

Ranked #370 in Entrepreneur Magazine's 2007 Franchise 500
199 Main St., 8th Fl.
White Plains, NY 10601
(914)328-4444
www.famousfamiglia.com
Pizza
Financial rating: $$$$

FIGARO'S PIZZA

Ranked #310 in Entrepreneur Magazine's 2007 Franchise 500
1500 Liberty St. S.E., #160
Salem, OR 97302
(503)371-9318
www.figaros.com
Baked pizza & bake-at-home pizza
Financial rating: $$$$

GOLDEN CHICK

11488 Luna Rd., #100B
Dallas, TX 75234-9430
(972)831-0911
www.goldenchick.com
Quick-service chicken restaurant
Current financial data not available

HARDEE'S

6307 Carpinteria Ave., #A
Carpinteria, CA 93013
(866)253-7655/(805)745-7842
www.ckr.com
Burgers, chicken, biscuits
Current financial data not available

JERK Q'ZINE

117 Rte. 303
Tappan, NY 10983
(845)398-3000
www.jerkqzine.com
Caribbean food
Current financial data not available

JERRY'S CURB SERVICE

730 Mulberry St.
Bridgewater, PA 15009
(724)774-4250
www.jerryscurbservice.com
Burgers, fries, shakes
Current financial data not available

JODY MARONI'S SAUSAGE KINGDOM

2011 Ocean Front Walk
Venice, CA 90291
(310)348-1500
www.jodymaroni.com
Gourmet sausages & hot dogs
Financial rating: $$$$

JUST FRESH FRANCHISE SYSTEMS

12125 Herbert Wayne Ct., #180
Huntersville, NC 28078
(866)468-3935/(704)992-1818
www.justfresh.com
Sandwiches, baked goods, salads, soups, pizza
Current financial data not available

KFC CORP.

1441 Gardiner Ln.
Louisville, KY 40213
(866)298-6986
www.yumfranchises.com
Chicken
Current financial data not available

KRYSTAL RESTAURANTS

1 Union Sq.
Chattanooga, TN 37402
(800)458-5912
www.krystal.com
Hamburgers
Current financial data not available

L&L FRANCHISE INC.
*Ranked #179 in Entrepreneur
Magazine's 2007 Franchise 500*
931 University Ave., #202
Honolulu, HI 96826
(808)951-9888
www.hawaiianbarbecue.com
Quick-service Hawaiian restaurant
Financial rating: $$$$

LA PALETERA
3000 Weslayan, #108
Houston, TX 77027
(866)621-6200/(713)621-6200
www.lapaletera.com
Paletas, fruit cups, smoothies,
  ice cream
Current financial data not available

LA SALSA FRESH MEXICAN GRILL
6307 Carpinteria Ave., #A
Carpinteria, CA 93013
(866)253-7655/(805)745-7843
www.lasalsa.com
Fresh Mexican grill
Current financial data not available

LONG JOHN SILVER'S RESTAURANTS INC.
1441 Gardiner Ln.
Louisville, KY 40213
(866)298-6986
www.yumfranchises.com
Fish & chicken
Current financial data not available

MADE IN JAPAN TERIYAKI EXPERIENCE
*Ranked #347 in Entrepreneur
Magazine's 2007 Franchise 500*
700 Kerr St., #100
Oakville, ON L6K 3W5 Canada
(905)337-7777
www.teriyakiexperience.com
Quick-service Japanese restaurant
Financial rating: $$$

MAMA FU'S NOODLE HOUSE INC.
1935 Peachtree Rd.
Atlanta, GA 30309
(404)367-5443
www.mamafus.com
Pan-Asian food
Current financial data not available

MANCHU WOK
*Ranked #281 in Entrepreneur
Magazine's 2007 Franchise 500*
85 Citizen Ct., #9
Markham, ON L6G 1A8 Canada
(800)361-8864
www.manchuwok.com
Chinese fast food
Financial rating: $$$

MR. SUB
4576 Yonge St., #600
Toronto, ON M2N 6P1 Canada
(416)225-5545
www.mrsub.ca
Subs, wraps, salads
Current financial data not available

NOTHING BUT NOODLES
14500 N. Northsight, #216
Scottsdale, AZ 85255
(480)513-7008
www.nothingbutnoodles.com
Noodles, pasta, salads
Current financial data not available

THE ORIGINAL SOUPMAN
28 W. 44th St.
New York, NY 10036
(877)768-7626
www.originalsoupman.com
Soups
Financial rating: $$$

PAPA MURPHY'S
*Ranked #50 in Entrepreneur
Magazine's 2007 Franchise 500*
8000 N.E. Parkway Dr., #350
Vancouver, WA 98662
(360)260-7272
www.papamurphys.com
Take-&-bake pizza
Financial rating: $$$$

PHILLY CONNECTION
120 Interstate N. Pkwy. East, #112
Atlanta, GA 30339-2103
(800)886-8826/(770)952-6152
www.phillyconnection.com
Cheesesteak sandwiches, hoagies,
  salads, ice cream
Current financial data not available

PIZZA HUT INC.
14841 Dallas Pkwy.
Dallas, TX 75254
(866)298-6986
www.yumfranchises.com
Pizza
Current financial data not available

THE PIZZA RANCH
1121 Main, Box 823
Hull, IA 51239
(800)321-3401/(712)439-1150
www.pizzaranch.com
Pizza, chicken, wraps
Current financial data not available

POPEYES CHICKEN & BISCUITS
5555 Glenridge Connector N.E., #300
Atlanta, GA 30342
(800)639-3780
www.popeyesfranchising.com
New Orleans-style fried chicken,
  seafood & biscuits
Current financial data not available

THE PRETZEL TWISTER
3705 Mason Rd.
New Hill, NC 27562
(888)638-8806/(919)387-8929
www.pretzeltwister.com
Hand-twisted soft pretzels & fruit
  shakes
Financial rating: $

QUIZNOS SUB
1475 Lawrence St., #400
Denver, CO 80202
(720)359-3300
www.quiznos.com
Submarine sandwiches, soups, salads
Current financial data not available

RITTER'S FROZEN CUSTARD
12400 N. Meridian St., #190
Carmel, IN 46032
(866)748-8374
www.ritters.com
Frozen custard
Current financial data not available

ROY ROGERS FRANCHISE CO. LLC
Ranked #455 in Entrepreneur Magazine's 2007 Franchise 500
321 Ballenger Center Dr., #201
Frederick, MD 21703
(301)695-8563
www.royrogersrestaurants.com
Quick-service restaurant
Financial rating: $$$

SALADWORKS
Ranked #474 in Entrepreneur Magazine's 2007 Franchise 500
Eight Tower Bridge, 161 Washington St., #225
Conshohocken, PA 19428
(610)825-3080
www.saladworks.com
Salads, pastas, sandwiches
Financial rating: 0

SBARRO THE ITALIAN EATERY
401 Broadhollow Rd.
Melville, NY 11787
(631)715-4150
www.sbarro.com
Quick-service Italian restaurant
Financial rating: $$$$

SEEKERS COFFEE HOUSE & CAFE
13365 Smith Rd.
Middleburg Heights, OH 44130
(440)884-4888
www.seekerscoffeehouse.com
Coffeehouse
Current financial data not available

SHAKE'S FROZEN CUSTARD
P.O. Box 8700
Fayetteville, AR 72703
(479)587-9115
www.shakesfrozencustard.com
Frozen custard
Financial rating: $

SONIC DRIVE IN RESTAURANTS
Ranked #8 in Entrepreneur Magazine's 2007 Franchise 500
300 Johnny Bench Dr.
Oklahoma City, OK 73104
(800)569-6656/(405)225-5000
www.sonicdrivein.com
Drive-in restaurant
Financial rating: $$$$

SOUL FIXINS' RESTAURANT
200 Highpoint Dr., #215
Chalfont, PA 18914
(215)882-1550
www.soulfixinsfranchise.com
Soul food/comfort food
Current financial data not available

TACO BUENO
Ranked #485 in Entrepreneur Magazine's 2007 Franchise 500
3033 Kellway Dr., #122
Carrollton, TX 75006
(972)417-4843
www.tacobueno.com
Quick-service Mexican restaurant
Financial rating: $$$

THE TACO MAKER/JAKE'S OVER THE TOP
P.O. Box 150650
Ogden, UT 84415
(801)476-9780
www.tacomaker.com
Mexican fast food/50's-style burgers, shakes & fries
Current financial data not available

TACONE
950 S. Flower St., #105
Los Angeles, CA 90015
(213)236-0950
www.tacone.com
Sandwiches, soups, salads, smoothies
Current financial data not available

TIJUANA FLATS BURRITO CO.
1390 Hope Rd., #400
Maitland, FL 32751
(407)339-2222
www.tijuanaflats.com
Quick-service Tex-Mex restaurant
Current financial data not available

VOCELLI PIZZA
2101 Greentree Rd., #A-202
Pittsburgh, PA 15220
(412)279-9100
www.vocellipizza.com
Pizza, subs, wings
Current financial data not available

ZERO'S SUBS
Ranked #278 in Entrepreneur Magazine's 2007 Franchise 500
2859 Virginia Beach Blvd., #105
Virginia Beach, VA 23452
(757)486-8338
www.zeros.com
Subs, pizza, wraps
Financial rating: $$$

FOOD/RETAIL　　*Candy*

CHOCOLATE CHOCOLATE CHOCOLATE COMPANY

Ranked #413 in Entrepreneur Magazine's 2007 Franchise 500　　　　　*Financial rating: $$$*

112 N. Kirkwood Rd.
St. Louis, MO 63122
(314)832-2639
www.chocolatechocolate.com
Chocolates & candies
Began: 1981, Franchising: 2002
Headquarters size: 13 employees
Franchise department: 4 employees

U.S. franchises: 13
Canadian franchises: 0
Other foreign franchises: 0
Company-owned: 0

Seeking: All U.S.
Seeking in Canada? No
Exclusive territories? Yes
Homebased option? No
Employees needed to run biz: 4
Absentee ownership? Yes

COSTS
Total cost: $185K
Franchise fee: $20K
Royalty fee: 5%
Term of agreement: 5 years renewable
　for $2K
Franchisees required to buy multiple
　units? No

FINANCING
No financing available

QUALIFICATIONS
Net worth: $300K
Cash liquidity: $100K
Experience:
　　General business experience

TRAINING
At headquarters: 3 weeks & as needed
At franchisee's location: 1 week & as
　needed
Additional training as needed

BUSINESS SUPPORT
Grand opening
Internet
Newsletter
Meetings
Field operations/evaluations
Purchasing cooperatives
Security/safety procedures

MARKETING SUPPORT
Ad slicks
Regional marketing

FUZZIWIG'S CANDY FACTORY INC.

Ranked #412 in Entrepreneur Magazine's 2007 Franchise 500   *Financial rating: $*

10 Town Plaza, P.O. Box 222
Durango, CO 81301
(970)247-2770
www.fuzziwigscandyfactory.com
Self-serve bulk candy
Began: 1996, Franchising: 2002
Headquarters size: 6 employees
Franchise department: 6 employees

U.S. franchises: 50
Canadian franchises: 0
Other foreign franchises: 0
Company-owned: 9

Seeking: All U.S.
Seeking in Canada? Yes
Exclusive territories? Yes
Homebased option? No
Employees needed to run biz: 4
Absentee ownership? Yes

COSTS
Total cost: $194.8K-315.1K
Franchise fee: $20K-30K
Royalty fee: 6%
Term of agreement: 10 years renewable
    for $100
Franchisees required to buy multiple
    units? No

FINANCING
No financing available

QUALIFICATIONS
Net worth: $400K
Cash liquidity: $75K
Experience:
    General business experience
    Marketing skills

TRAINING
At headquarters: 7 days
At franchisee's location: 5 days

BUSINESS SUPPORT
Grand opening
Internet
Newsletter
Meetings
Toll-free phone line
Field operations/evaluations
Lease negotiations
Purchasing cooperatives

MARKETING SUPPORT
Info not provided

KILWIN'S CHOCOLATES FRANCHISE

Ranked #497 in Entrepreneur Magazine's 2007 Franchise 500   *Financial rating: $$$*

355 N. Division Rd.
Petoskey, MI 49770
(231)347-3800/(231)439-0972
www.kilwins.com
Chocolate, fudge, ice cream
Began: 1946, Franchising: 1982
Headquarters size: 8 employees
Franchise department: 8 employees

U.S. franchises: 50
Canadian franchises: 0
Other foreign franchises: 0
Company-owned: 2

Seeking: Northeast, Southeast
Seeking in Canada? No
Exclusive territories? Yes
Homebased option? No
Employees needed to run biz: 6
Absentee ownership? Yes

COSTS
Total cost: $303.7K-579K
Franchise fee: $40K
Royalty fee: 5%
Term of agreement: 10 years renewable
    at no charge
Franchisees required to buy multiple
    units? No

FINANCING
No financing available

QUALIFICATIONS
Net worth: $500K
Cash liquidity: $60K-70K
Experience:
    General business experience

TRAINING
At headquarters: 1 week
At franchisee's location: 1 week

BUSINESS SUPPORT
Grand opening
Internet
Newsletter
Field operations/evaluations
Lease negotiations
Security/safety procedures

MARKETING SUPPORT
Promotions & marketing assistance

RICKY'S CANDY, CONES & CHAOS

Current financial data not available

140 Nassau St.
Princeton, NJ 08542
(609)430-9096
www.candyconesandchaos.com
Candy, ice cream, parties
Began: 2003, Franchising: 2004
Headquarters size: 5 employees

U.S. franchises: 8
Canadian franchises: 0
Other foreign franchises: 0
Company-owned: 1

Seeking: All U.S.
Seeking in Canada? No
Exclusive territories? No
Homebased option? No
Employees needed to run biz: 10-12
Absentee ownership? Yes

COSTS
Total cost: $378.5K-563.8K
Franchise fee: $30K
Royalty fee: 5%
Term of agreement: 10 years renewable
    at no charge
Franchisees required to buy multiple
    units? No

FINANCING
In-house: None
3rd-party: Accounts receivable,
    equipment, franchise fee,
    inventory, startup costs

QUALIFICATIONS
Net worth: $250K-500K
Cash liquidity: $100K
Experience:
    General business experience
    Must work well with children

TRAINING
At headquarters: 2 weeks
At franchisee's location: 1 week

BUSINESS SUPPORT
Grand opening
Internet
Newsletter
Meetings
Field operations/evaluations
Purchasing cooperatives

MARKETING SUPPORT
Co-op advertising
National media campaign
Regional marketing

SCHAKOLAD CHOCOLATE FACTORY

Ranked #373 in Entrepreneur Magazine's 2007 Franchise 500   *Financial rating: $$$*

5966 Lake Hurst Dr.
Orlando, FL 32819
(407)248-6400
www.schakolad.com
Freshly made European-style
    chocolates
Began: 1995, Franchising: 1999
Headquarters size: 4 employees
Franchise department: 10 employees

U.S. franchises: 33
Canadian franchises: 0
Other foreign franchises: 2
Company-owned: 0

Seeking: Midwest, Northeast, South,
    Southeast, Southwest
Seeking in Canada? No
Exclusive territories? No
Homebased option? No
Employees needed to run biz: 2-5
Absentee ownership? No

COSTS
Total cost: $110K-150K
Franchise fee: $30K
Royalty fee: 4%
Term of agreement: 5 years renewable
    for 20% of current franchise fee
Franchisees required to buy multiple
    units? No

FINANCING
In-house: None
3rd-party: Equipment, inventory,
    startup costs

QUALIFICATIONS
Net worth: $250K
Cash liquidity: $75K
Experience:
    General business experience
    Marketing skills

TRAINING
At headquarters: 1-2 weeks
At franchisee's location: 1-2 weeks

BUSINESS SUPPORT
Grand opening
Internet
Newsletter
Field operations/evaluations
Purchasing cooperatives

MARKETING SUPPORT
Co-op advertising
Regional marketing

TROPIK SUN FRUIT & NUT

Ranked #478 in Entrepreneur Magazine's 2007 Franchise 500　　　*Financial rating: $$$$*

14052 Petronella Dr., #102
Libertyville, IL 60048
(847)968-4415
www.tropiksun.com
Candy, nuts, popcorn, chocolates,
　gifts
Began: 1980, Franchising: 1980
Headquarters size: 8 employees
Franchise department: 3 employees

U.S. franchises: 58
Canadian franchises: 0
Other foreign franchises: 0
Company-owned: 0

Seeking: All U.S.
Seeking in Canada? Yes
Exclusive territories? No
Homebased option? No
Employees needed to run biz: 6-8
Absentee ownership? Yes

COSTS
Total cost: $93K-218K
Franchise fee: $20K
Royalty fee: 6%
Term of agreement: Varies based on
　lease term
Franchisees required to buy multiple
　units? No

FINANCING
In-house: None
3rd-party: Equipment, franchise fee,
　inventory, startup costs

QUALIFICATIONS
Net worth: $150K
Cash liquidity: $35K
Experience:
　General business experience

TRAINING
At headquarters: As needed
At franchisee's location: During
　opening

BUSINESS SUPPORT
Grand opening
Newsletter
Meetings
Field operations/evaluations
Purchasing cooperatives

MARKETING SUPPORT
Info not provided

FOOD/RETAIL ▶ *Food-Design Services*

CANDY BOUQUET

Ranked #71 in Entrepreneur Magazine's 2007 Franchise 500　　　*Financial rating: $$$$*

423 E. Third St.
Little Rock, AR 72201
(877)226-3901
www.candybouquet.com
Floral-like designer gifts & gourmet
　confections
Began: 1989, Franchising: 1993
Headquarters size: 30 employees
Franchise department: 30 employees

U.S. franchises: 731
Canadian franchises: 47
Other foreign franchises: 50
Company-owned: 0

Seeking: All U.S.
Seeking in Canada? Yes
Exclusive territories? Yes
Homebased option? Yes
Employees needed to run biz: 1
Absentee ownership? Yes

COSTS
Total cost: $7.7K-50K
Franchise fee: $3.9K-31K
Royalty fee: 0
Term of agreement: 5 years renewable
　for 25% of original fee
Franchisees required to buy multiple
　units? No

FINANCING
No financing available

QUALIFICATIONS
Experience:
　Industry experience
　General business experience
　Marketing skills

TRAINING
At headquarters: 5 days

BUSINESS SUPPORT
Internet
Newsletter
Meetings
Toll-free phone line

MARKETING SUPPORT
Co-op advertising
Ad slicks

COOKIES BY DESIGN/COOKIE BOUQUET
Ranked #406 in Entrepreneur Magazine's 2007 Franchise 500   *Financial rating: $$$$*

1865 Summit Ave., #605
Plano, TX 75074
(800)945-2665/(972)398-9536
www.cookiesbydesign.com
Cookies & cookie arrangements
Began: 1983, Franchising: 1987
Headquarters size: 25 employees
Franchise department: 2 employees

U.S. franchises: 207
Canadian franchises: 0
Other foreign franchises: 0
Company-owned: 0

Seeking: All U.S.
Seeking in Canada? No
Exclusive territories? Yes
Homebased option? No
Employees needed to run biz: 5
Absentee ownership? No

COSTS
Total cost: $90K-180K
Franchise fee: $12.5K-35K
Royalty fee: 6%
Term of agreement: 5 years renewable
    for 25% of initial fee
Franchisees required to buy multiple
    units? No

FINANCING
No financing available

QUALIFICATIONS
Cash liquidity: $30K
Experience:
    General business experience
    Marketing skills

TRAINING
At headquarters: 2 weeks
At franchisee's location: 2 days

BUSINESS SUPPORT
Internet
Newsletter
Meetings
Toll-free phone line
Field operations/evaluations

MARKETING SUPPORT
Ad slicks
National media campaign

COOKIES IN BLOOM
Current financial data not available

7208 La Cosa Dr.
Dallas, TX 75248
(800)222-3104/(972)490-8644
www.cookiesinbloom.com
Cookie gift baskets
Began: 1988, Franchising: 1992
Headquarters size: 5 employees
Franchise department: 2 employees

U.S. franchises: 19
Canadian franchises: 0
Other foreign franchises: 0
Company-owned: 0

Seeking: All U.S.
Seeking in Canada? Yes
Exclusive territories? Yes
Homebased option? No
Employees needed to run biz: 4
Absentee ownership? Yes

COSTS
Total cost: $60K-114K
Franchise fee: $19.5K
Royalty fee: 5%
Term of agreement: 5 years renewable
    for $1K
Franchisees required to buy multiple
    units? Outside the U.S. only

FINANCING
No financing available

QUALIFICATIONS
Net worth: $200K
Cash liquidity: $50K
Experience:
    General business experience
    Marketing skills
    Customer service skills
    Creativity

TRAINING
At headquarters: 10 days
At franchisee's location: 5 days
On-the-job training at corporate-
    approved store

BUSINESS SUPPORT
Grand opening
Internet
Newsletter
Meetings
Toll-free phone line
Field operations/evaluations
Purchasing cooperatives
Security/safety procedures

MARKETING SUPPORT
Co-op advertising
Ad slicks
Regional marketing

EDIBLE ARRANGEMENTS

Ranked #56 in Entrepreneur Magazine's 2007 Franchise 500   *Financial rating: $$$*

1952 Whitney Ave.
Hamden, CT 06517
(888)727-4258
www.ediblearrangements.com
Floral-like designs from sculpted
    fresh fruit
Began: 1998, Franchising: 2000
Headquarters size: 50 employees
Franchise department: 7 employees

U.S. franchises: 280
Canadian franchises: 11
Other foreign franchises: 0
Company-owned: 1

Seeking: All U.S.
Seeking in Canada? Yes
Exclusive territories? Yes
Homebased option? No
Employees needed to run biz: 4
Absentee ownership? No

COSTS
Total cost: $150.95K-291.2K
Franchise fee: $25K
Royalty fee: 5%
Term of agreement: 10 years
    renewable for $2K
Franchisees required to buy
    multiple units? No

FINANCING
In-house: None
3rd-party: Equipment, franchise fee,
    inventory, startup costs

QUALIFICATIONS
Experience:
    General business experience

TRAINING
At headquarters: 1 week
At franchisee's location: 1 week
On-the-job training: 1 week

BUSINESS SUPPORT
Internet
Toll-free phone line
Field operations/evaluations
Lease negotiations
Purchasing cooperatives

MARKETING SUPPORT
Co-op advertising
Ad slicks
National media campaign
Regional marketing

FRUITFLOWERS/INCREDIBLY EDIBLE DELITES

Ranked #366 in Entrepreneur Magazine's 2007 Franchise 500   *Financial rating: $$$*

One Summit Ave.
Broomall, PA 19008
(610)353-8702
www.fruitflowers.com
Floral-like fruit & vegetable
    bouquets
Began: 1985, Franchising: 1993
Headquarters size: 8 employees
Franchise department: 5 employees

U.S. franchises: 34
Canadian franchises: 0
Other foreign franchises: 0
Company-owned: 2

Seeking: All U.S.
Seeking in Canada? Yes
Exclusive territories? Yes
Homebased option? No
Employees needed to run biz: 6-8
Absentee ownership? No

COSTS
Total cost: $127.2K-185.5K
Franchise fee: $35K
Royalty fee: 4.5%
Term of agreement: 10 years renewable
    for $5K
Franchisees required to buy multiple
    units? No

FINANCING
In-house: None
3rd-party: Accounts receivable,
    equipment, franchise fee,
    inventory, payroll, startup costs

QUALIFICATIONS
Net worth: $500K
Cash liquidity: $50K
Experience:
    Marketing skills

TRAINING
At headquarters: 2 weeks
At franchisee's location: Up to 1
    week during startup
Additional on-site training

BUSINESS SUPPORT
Grand opening
Internet
Newsletter
Meetings
Toll-free phone line
Field operations/evaluations
Purchasing cooperatives
Security/safety procedures

MARKETING SUPPORT
Co-op advertising
Ad slicks
National media campaign
Regional marketing

FOOD/RETAIL *Meal-Preparation Services*

THE DINNER A'FARE

Financial rating: $

5417 Landsdowne Ct.
Cumming, GA 30041
(770)887-4059
www.thedinnerafare.com
Do-it-yourself home meal preparation
Began: 2004, Franchising: 2005
Headquarters size: 4 employees
Franchise department: 3 employees

U.S. franchises: 4
Canadian franchises: 0
Other foreign franchises: 0
Company-owned: 2

Seeking: All U.S.
Seeking in Canada? Yes
Exclusive territories? Yes
Homebased option? No
Employees needed to run biz: 3-4
Absentee ownership? No

COSTS
Total cost: $114.2K-213.5K
Franchise fee: $30K
Royalty fee: 5%
Term of agreement: 15 years renewable
    for 10% of fee
Franchisees required to buy multiple
    units? No

FINANCING
In-house: None
3rd-party: Equipment, franchise fee,
    inventory, startup costs

QUALIFICATIONS
Net worth: $100K
Cash liquidity: $30K
Experience:
    Marketing skills

TRAINING
At headquarters: 15 days
At franchisee's location: 3-4 days

BUSINESS SUPPORT
Grand opening
Internet
Newsletter
Field operations/evaluations
Purchasing cooperatives
Security/safety procedures

MARKETING SUPPORT
Co-op advertising
Ad slicks
National media campaign

DINNER BY DESIGN

Financial rating: $$

10 N. Lake St.
Grayslake, IL 60030
(847)986-3565
www.dinnerbydesignkitchen.com
Do-it-yourself home meal
    preparation
Began: 2003, Franchising: 2004
Headquarters size: 12 employees
Franchise department: 12 employees

U.S. franchises: 55
Canadian franchises: 0
Other foreign franchises: 0
Company-owned: 1

Seeking: Midwest, Northeast
Seeking in Canada? Yes
Exclusive territories? Yes
Homebased option? No
Employees needed to run biz: 8-10
Absentee ownership? No

COSTS
Total cost: $115.3K-170.5K
Franchise fee: $40K
Royalty fee: 6%
Term of agreement: 10 years renewable
    for 50% of current franchise fee
Franchisees required to buy multiple
    units? No

FINANCING
No financing available

QUALIFICATIONS
Net worth: $150K
Cash liquidity: $100K
Experience:
    General business experience

TRAINING
At headquarters: 4 days+
At franchisee's location: 6 days

BUSINESS SUPPORT
Grand opening
Internet
Newsletter
Meetings
Field operations/evaluations
Lease negotiations
Purchasing cooperatives
Security/safety procedures

MARKETING SUPPORT
Co-op advertising
Ad slicks
National media campaign

DREAM DINNERS INC.

Ranked #154 in Entrepreneur Magazine's 2007 Franchise 500　　　*Financial rating: $$$$*

P.O. Box 889
Snohomish, WA 98291
(425)397-3511
www.dreamdinners.com
Do-it-yourself home meal preparation
Began: 2002, Franchising: 2003
Headquarters size: 50 employees
Franchise department: 4 employees

U.S. franchises: 178
Canadian franchises: 0
Other foreign franchises: 0
Company-owned: 2

Seeking: All U.S.
Seeking in Canada? Yes
Exclusive territories? No
Homebased option? No
Employees needed to run biz: 5
Absentee ownership? No

COSTS
Total cost: $230K-340K
Franchise fee: $35K
Royalty fee: 6%
Term of agreement: 10 years renewable
　　for 50% of original franchise fee
Franchisees required to buy multiple
　　units? No

FINANCING
No financing available

QUALIFICATIONS
Experience:
　　Industry experience
　　General business experience
　　Marketing skills

TRAINING
At headquarters: 1 week
At franchisee's location: 2 days

BUSINESS SUPPORT
Grand opening
Internet
Newsletter
Meetings
Field operations/evaluations
Purchasing cooperatives
Security/safety procedures

MARKETING SUPPORT
Ad slicks
National media campaign
Regional marketing

ENTREES MADE EASY

Financial rating: $$

4858 E. Baseline Rd., #104
Mesa, AZ 85206
(480)985-7900
www.entreesmadeeasy.com
Meal preparation service
Began: 2004, Franchising: 2006
Headquarters size: 15 employees
Franchise department: 15 employees

U.S. franchises: 2
Canadian franchises: 0
Other foreign franchises: 0
Company-owned: 2

Seeking: All U.S.
Seeking in Canada? Yes
Exclusive territories? Yes
Homebased option? No
Employees needed to run biz: 8-10
Absentee ownership? Yes

COSTS
Total cost: $152.8K-271.7K
Franchise fee: $30K
Royalty fee: 5%
Term of agreement: 10 years renewable
　　at no charge
Franchisees required to buy multiple
　　units? No

FINANCING
No financing available

QUALIFICATIONS
Net worth: $150K
Cash liquidity: $50K
Experience:
　　General business experience

TRAINING
At headquarters: 1 week
At franchisee's location: 1 week

BUSINESS SUPPORT
Grand opening
Internet
Newsletter
Meetings
Field operations/evaluations
Purchasing cooperatives
Security/safety procedures

MARKETING SUPPORT
Co-op advertising
Ad slicks
National media campaign
Regional marketing

LET'S DISH

Financial Rating: $$

12204 Nicollet Ave. S.
Burnsville, MN 55337
(952)767-3474
www.letsdish.com
Meal preparation service
Began: 2003, Franchising: 2005
Headquarters size: 15 employees
Franchise department: 3 employees

U.S. franchises: 15
Canadian franchises: 0
Other foreign franchises: 0
Company-owned: 4

Seeking: All U.S.
Seeking in Canada? No
Exclusive territories? Info not
    provided
Homebased option? No
Employees needed to run biz:
    Info not provided
Absentee ownership? Yes

COSTS
Total cost: $214.5K-340.5K
Franchise fee: $35K
Royalty fee: 6%
Term of agreement: 15 years renewable
    for $5K
Franchisees required to buy multiple
    units?No

FINANCING
No financing available

QUALIFICATIONS
Net worth: $500K
Cash liquidity: $150K
Experience:
    General business experience
    Marketing skills
    Community involvement

TRAINING
At headquarters: 8 days
At franchisee's location: 5 days

BUSINESS SUPPORT
Grand opening
Internet
Meetings
Field operations/evaluations
Security/safety procedures

MARKETING SUPPORT
Ad slicks

MY GIRLFRIEND'S KITCHEN

Financial rating: $

5107 S. 900 East, #250
Salt Lake City, UT 84117
(801)747-2201
www.mgfk.com
Ready-to-cook entrees & side dishes
Began: 2003, Franchising: 2004
Headquarters size: 15 employees
Franchise department: 9 employees

U.S. franchises: 18
Canadian franchises: 0
Other foreign franchises: 0
Company-owned: 1

Seeking: All U.S.
Seeking in Canada? Yes
Exclusive territories? Yes
Homebased option? No
Employees needed to run biz: 6
Absentee ownership? Yes

COSTS
Total cost: $179K-374K
Franchise fee: $35K
Royalty fee: 5%
Term of agreement: 10 years renewable
    for $2.5K
Franchisees required to buy multiple
    units? No

FINANCING
In-house: None
3rd-party: Accounts receivable,
    equipment, inventory, payroll,
    startup costs

QUALIFICATIONS
Net worth: $400K
Cash liquidity: $55K
Experience:
    General business experience
    Customer service skills

TRAINING
At headquarters: 9 days
At franchisee's location: 3-5 days
Additional training as needed

BUSINESS SUPPORT
Grand opening
Internet
Newsletter
Meetings
Field operations/evaluations
Security/safety procedures

MARKETING SUPPORT
Co-op advertising
Ad slicks
Affiliate agency
Radio spots

SOCIALE MAKE & TAKE GOURMET

Financial rating: $$$

5001 Penn Ave. S.
Minneapolis, MN 55419
(651)994-9000
www.socialegourmet.com
Meal preparation service
Began: 2004, Franchising: 2005
Headquarters size: 10 employees
Franchise department: 5 employees

U.S. franchises: 0
Canadian franchises: 0
Other foreign franchises: 0
Company-owned: 3

Seeking: All U.S.
Seeking in Canada? No
Exclusive territories? Yes
Homebased option? No
Employees needed to run biz: 5
Absentee ownership? Yes

COSTS
Total cost: $140K-250K
Franchise fee: $30K
Royalty fee: 5%
Term of agreement: 10 years renewable
  for $1K
Franchisees required to buy multiple
  units? No

FINANCING
In-house: None
3rd-party: Accounts receivable,
  equipment, franchise fee,
  inventory, payroll, startup costs

QUALIFICATIONS
Net worth: $300K
Cash liquidity: $75K
Experience:
  General business experience

TRAINING
At headquarters: 6 days
At franchisee's location: 3 days+

BUSINESS SUPPORT
Grand opening
Internet
Newsletter
Meetings
Field operations/evaluations
Security/safety procedures

MARKETING SUPPORT
Co-op advertising
Ad slicks
Regional marketing
PR

SUPER SUPPERS

Ranked #151 in Entrepreneur Magazine's 2007 Franchise 500

Financial rating: $$$

6100 Camp Bowie Blvd.
Fort Worth, TX 76132
(817)732-6100
www.supersuppers.com
Do-it-yourself home meal preparation
Began: 1986, Franchising: 2004
Headquarters size: 15 employees
Franchise department: 12 employees

U.S. franchises: 152
Canadian franchises: 0
Other foreign franchises: 0
Company-owned: 0

Seeking: All U.S.
Seeking in Canada? No
Exclusive territories? Yes
Homebased option? No
Employees needed to run biz: 5
Absentee ownership? No

COSTS
Total cost: $175.4K-263.2K
Franchise fee: $35K
Royalty fee: 4%
Term of agreement: 10 years renewable
  for $5K
Franchisees required to buy multiple
  units? No

FINANCING
No financing available

QUALIFICATIONS
Net worth: $150K
Cash liquidity: $100K
Experience:
  General business experience

TRAINING
At headquarters: 1 week
At franchisee's location: 3 days
Regional seminars

BUSINESS SUPPORT
Grand opening
Internet
Newsletter
Meetings
Toll-free phone line
Field operations/evaluations
Purchasing cooperatives
Security/safety procedures

MARKETING SUPPORT
Ad slicks
National media campaign

SUPPER THYME USA

Current financial data not available

2536 S. 156th Cir.
Omaha, NE 68130
(866)867-5001
www.supperthymeusa.com
Do-it-yourself meal preparation
Began: 2003, Franchising: 2004
Headquarters size: 6 employees
Franchise department: 6 employees

U.S. franchises: 13
Canadian franchises: 0
Other foreign franchises: 0
Company-owned: 1

Seeking: All U.S.
Seeking in Canada? No
Exclusive territories? Yes
Homebased option? No
Employees needed to run biz: 5
Absentee ownership? No

COSTS
Total cost: $114K-184K
Franchise fee: $35K
Royalty fee: 6%
Term of agreement: 5 years renewable
   at no charge
Franchisees required to buy multiple
   units? No

FINANCING
In-house: None
3rd-party: Franchise fee, startup
   costs

QUALIFICATIONS
Net worth: $200K
Cash liquidity: $60K
Experience:
   Marketing skills

TRAINING
At headquarters: 4 days
At franchisee's location: 2 weeks

BUSINESS SUPPORT
Grand opening
Internet
Newsletter
Meetings
Toll-free phone line
Field operations/evaluations
Purchasing cooperatives
Security/safety procedures

MARKETING SUPPORT
Co-op advertising
Ad slicks
National media campaign
Regional marketing

FOOD/RETAIL ▶ *Parties & Catering*

CAFE ALA CARTE

Current financial data not available

19512 S. Coquina Way
Weston, FL 33332
(954)349-1030
www.cafealacarte.com
Cappucino catering service
Began: 1996, Franchising: 2000
Headquarters size: 11 employees
Franchise department: 2 employees

U.S. franchises: 2
Canadian franchises: 0
Other foreign franchises: 0
Company-owned: 13

Seeking: All U.S.
Seeking in Canada? Yes
Exclusive territories? Yes
Homebased option? Yes
Employees needed to run biz: 2
Absentee ownership? No

COSTS
Total cost: $56.2K-80.8K
Franchise fee: $25K
Royalty fee: 8-5%
Term of agreement: 10 years renewable
   for then-current franchise fee
Franchisees required to buy multiple
   units? Outside the U.S. only

FINANCING
No financing available

QUALIFICATIONS
Experience:
   Industry experience
   General business experience
   Marketing skills

TRAINING
At headquarters: 1 week
In Fort Lauderdale, FL: 1 week

BUSINESS SUPPORT
Grand opening
Internet
Toll-free phone line

MARKETING SUPPORT
Ad slicks
Internet

COOL DADDY'S

Current financial data not available

1456 Chattahoochee Ave.
Atlanta, GA 30318
(404)352-9996
www.cooldaddys.com
Frozen drink party rentals &
    entertainment
Began: 2000, Franchising: 2005
Headquarters size: 5 employees
Franchise department: 2 employees

U.S. franchises: 1
Canadian franchises: 0
Other foreign franchises: 0
Company-owned: 1

Seeking: All U.S.
Seeking in Canada? No
Exclusive territories? Yes
Homebased option? No
Employees needed to run biz: 2-3
Absentee ownership? No

COSTS
Total cost: $105K-187.5K
Franchise fee: $25K
Royalty fee: 6%
Term of agreement: 10 years renewable
    for 50% of current franchise fee
Franchisees required to buy multiple
    units? No

FINANCING
In-house: None
3rd-party: Accounts receivable,
    equipment, inventory, startup
    costs

QUALIFICATIONS
Experience:
    General business experience

TRAINING
At headquarters: 2 weeks
At franchisee's location: 1 week

BUSINESS SUPPORT
Grand opening
Internet
Newsletter
Meetings
Toll-free phone line
Field operations/evaluations

MARKETING SUPPORT
Co-op advertising
Ad slicks
National media campaign
Regional marketing

CORPORATE CATERERS

Current financial data not available

4155 S.W. 130th Ave., #208
Miami, FL 33175
(305)223-1230
www.corpcaterers.com
Catering for professional offices &
    business events
Began: 1997, Franchising: 2006
Headquarters size: 12 employees
Franchise department: 5 employees

U.S. franchises: 0
Canadian franchises: 0
Other foreign franchises: 0
Company-owned: 2

Seeking: Southeast
Seeking in Canada? No
Exclusive territories? Yes
Homebased option? No
Employees needed to run biz: 5-25
Absentee ownership? Yes

COSTS
Total cost: $142K-188K
Franchise fee: $30K
Royalty fee: 4%
Term of agreement: 10 years
Franchisees required to buy multiple
    units? No

FINANCING
No financing available

QUALIFICATIONS
Net worth: $200K
Cash liquidity: $60K
Experience:
    Industry experience
    General business experience

TRAINING
At headquarters: 4 weeks
At franchisee's location: 10 days

BUSINESS SUPPORT
Internet
Newsletter
Meetings
Toll-free phone line
Field operations/evaluations
Lease negotiations
Purchasing cooperatives
Security/safety procedures

MARKETING SUPPORT
Ad slicks
National media campaign
Regional marketing
Marketing programs

IAF BEVERAGE

Current financial data not available

9761 Clifford Dr.
Dallas, TX 75220
(214)366-2219
www.iafbeverage.com
Frozen beverage equipment
  distribution
Began: 2002, Franchising: 2004
Headquarters size: 15 employees
Franchise department: 10 employees

U.S. franchises: 79
Canadian franchises: 0
Other foreign franchises: 0
Company-owned: 0

Seeking: All U.S.
Seeking in Canada? Yes
Exclusive territories? No
Homebased option? Yes
Employees needed to run biz: 1
Absentee ownership? Yes

COSTS
Total cost: $44.8K
Franchise fee: 0
Royalty fee: 0
Term of agreement: 10 years renewable
  at no charge
Franchisees required to buy multiple
  units? Yes

FINANCING
In-house: None
3rd-party: Equipment, startup costs

QUALIFICATIONS
Experience:
  General business experience
  Marketing skills

TRAINING
At headquarters: 2 days
At franchisee's location: 5 days

BUSINESS SUPPORT
Internet
Newsletter
Field operations/evaluations

MARKETING SUPPORT
Ad slicks
On-site promotional materials

SHOWCOLATE FONDUE EXPRESS

Financial rating: $$$

1404 S. New Rd.
Waco, TX 76711
(254)757-0944
www.showcolate.com
Express chocolate fondue &
  chocolate-dipped fruit
Began: 2003, Franchising: 2003
Headquarters size: 14 employees
Franchise department: 10 employees

U.S. franchises: 2
Canadian franchises: 0
Other foreign franchises: 73
Company-owned: 0

Seeking: All U.S.
Seeking in Canada? Yes
Exclusive territories? Yes
Homebased option? No
Employees needed to run biz: 4
Absentee ownership? Yes

COSTS
Total cost: $99.5K-155K
Franchise fee: $27.5K
Royalty fee: 6%
Term of agreement: 10 years renewable
  at no charge
Franchisees required to buy multiple
  units? No

FINANCING
No financing available

QUALIFICATIONS
Net worth: $200K
Cash liquidity: $100K
Experience:
  General business experience
  Marketing skills

TRAINING
At headquarters: 2-3 days

BUSINESS SUPPORT
Grand opening
Internet
Newsletter
Meetings
Toll-free phone line
Field operations/evaluations
Security/safety procedures

MARKETING SUPPORT
Ad slicks

SIR CHOCOLATE

Financial rating: $$

13900 E. Florida Ave., #F
Aurora, CO 80012
(303)671-7150
www.sirchocolate.com
Chocolate fountain catering &
   kiosks
Began: 2003, Franchising: 2004
Headquarters size: 25 employees
Franchise department: 3 employees

U.S. franchises: 2
Canadian franchises: 0
Other foreign franchises: 0
Company-owned: 1

Seeking: All U.S.
Seeking in Canada? No
Exclusive territories? Yes
Homebased option? Yes
Employees needed to run biz: 2
Absentee ownership? No

COSTS
Total cost: $41.3K-136.5K
Franchise fee: $25K
Royalty fee: 5%
Term of agreement: 7 years renewable
   for $5K/$10K
Franchisees required to buy multiple
   units? No

FINANCING
No financing available

QUALIFICATIONS
Outgoing personality

TRAINING
At headquarters: 3 days
At franchisee's location: 3-5 days

BUSINESS SUPPORT
Internet
Toll-free phone line
Field operations/evaluations

MARKETING SUPPORT
Co-op advertising

FOOD/RETAIL   *Miscellaneous*

BERRYBROOK FARM FRANCHISING INC.

Financial rating: 0

1257 East Blvd.
Charlotte, NC 28203
(704)334-6528
www.berrybrookfarm.com
Natural foods, supplements, health
   & beauty aids, juice bar/deli
Began: 1972, Franchising: 2005
Headquarters size: 12 employees
Franchise department: 2 employees

U.S. franchises: 1
Canadian franchises: 0
Other foreign franchises: 0
Company-owned: 0

Seeking: Southeast
Seeking in Canada? No
Exclusive territories? Yes
Homebased option? No
Employees needed to run biz: 3-6
Absentee ownership? No

COSTS
Total cost: $95K-175K
Franchise fee: $25K
Royalty fee: 5%
Term of agreement: 15 years renewable
   for 10% of new fee
Franchisees required to buy multiple
   units? No

FINANCING
No financing available

QUALIFICATIONS
Cash liquidity: $25K

TRAINING
At headquarters: 16 days
At franchisee's location: 14 days

BUSINESS SUPPORT
Grand opening
Internet
Newsletter
Meetings
Toll-free phone line
Field operations/evaluations
Purchasing cooperatives
Security/safety procedures

MARKETING SUPPORT
Co-op advertising
Ad slicks
Regional marketing

BREEZE FREEZE

Financial rating: $$

41303 Concept Dr.
Plymouth, MI 48170
(866)472-6482
www.breezefreeze.com
Frozen fruit drinks
Began: 2001, Franchising: 2004
Headquarters size: 20 employees
Franchise department: 3 employees

U.S. franchises: 31
Canadian franchises: 0
Other foreign franchises: 0
Company-owned: 303

Seeking: All U.S.
Seeking in Canada? Yes
Exclusive territories? Yes
Homebased option? Yes
Employees needed to run biz: 1
Absentee ownership? Yes

COSTS
Total cost: $9.2K-94.3K
Franchise fee: $5K/40K
Royalty fee: 0
Term of agreement: 5 years renewable
    at no charge
Franchisees required to buy multiple
    units? No

FINANCING
In-house: Franchise fee
3rd-party: Equipment

QUALIFICATIONS
Net worth: $10K+
Cash liquidity: $7K+
Experience:
    Marketing skills
    Strong work ethic

TRAINING
At headquarters: 1-3 days
At franchisee's location: 1-2 days

BUSINESS SUPPORT
Internet
Meetings
Field operations/evaluations

MARKETING SUPPORT
Co-op advertising
Ad slicks
Regional marketing

COFFEE PERKS

Current financial data not available

2985 Mercury Rd.
Jacksonville, FL 32207
(866)473-7571
www.coffeeperks.com
Office coffee & food-service
    distribution
Began: 1993, Franchising: 2004
Headquarters size: 30 employees
Franchise department: 4 employees

U.S. franchises: 3
Canadian franchises: 0
Other foreign franchises: 0
Company-owned: 1

Seeking: All U.S.
Seeking in Canada? Yes
Exclusive territories? Yes
Homebased option? No
Employees needed to run biz: 5-30
Absentee ownership? Yes

COSTS
Total cost: $116.1K+
Franchise fee: $18K+
Royalty fee: 6%
Term of agreement: 10 years renewable
    for $5K
Franchisees required to buy multiple
    units? No

FINANCING
In-house: Franchise fee
3rd-party: Equipment

QUALIFICATIONS
Net worth: $250K+
Cash liquidity: $50K+
Experience:
    Industry experience
    General business experience
    Marketing skills

TRAINING
At headquarters: 2 weeks
At franchisee's location: 1 week

BUSINESS SUPPORT
Grand opening
Internet
Newsletter
Meetings
Toll-free phone line
Field operations/evaluations
Purchasing cooperatives
Security/safety procedures

MARKETING SUPPORT
Co-op advertising
Ad slicks
National media campaign
Regional marketing

HAPPY & HEALTHY PRODUCTS INC.

Ranked #466 in Entrepreneur Magazine's 2007 Franchise 500

Financial rating: $$$$

1600 S. Dixie Hwy., #200
Boca Raton, FL 33432
(800)764-6114
www.fruitfull.com
Frozen fruit bars & smoothies
Began: 1991, Franchising: 1993
Headquarters size: 10 employees
Franchise department: 4 employees

U.S. franchises: 83
Canadian franchises: 0
Other foreign franchises: 0
Company-owned: 0

Seeking: All U.S.
Seeking in Canada? No
Exclusive territories? No
Homebased option? Yes
Employees needed to run biz: 0
Absentee ownership? No

COSTS
Total cost: $29K-65K
Franchise fee: $21K
Royalty fee: 0
Term of agreement: 10 years renewable
   for $500
Franchisees required to buy multiple
   units? No

FINANCING
In-house: None
3rd-party: Equipment, franchise fee,
   inventory, startup costs

QUALIFICATIONS
Net worth: $28K+
Cash liquidity: $28K+
Experience:
   General business experience
   Marketing skills

TRAINING
At franchisee's location: 1-2 weeks
Additional training: 1 week

BUSINESS SUPPORT
Internet
Newsletter
Meetings
Toll-free phone line
Field operations/evaluations

MARKETING SUPPORT
Ad slicks
National media campaign

THE HONEYBAKED HAM CO. & CAFE

Current financial data not available

5445 Triangle Pkwy., #400
Norcross, GA 30092
(678)966-3100
www.honeybakedfranchising.com
Specialty hams & turkeys/cafe
Began: 1957, Franchising: 1998
Headquarters size: 125 employees
Franchise department: 12 employees

U.S. franchises: 100
Canadian franchises: 0
Other foreign franchises: 0
Company-owned: 280

Seeking: All U.S.
Seeking in Canada? No
Exclusive territories? Yes
Homebased option? No
Employees needed to run biz: 7-10
Absentee ownership? Yes

COSTS
Total cost: $266.5K-389.1K
Franchise fee: $30K
Royalty fee: 5-6%
Term of agreement: 7 years
Franchisees required to buy multiple
   units? No

FINANCING
In-house: None
3rd-party: Equipment, franchise fee,
   inventory, payroll, startup costs

QUALIFICATIONS
Net worth: $350K
Cash liquidity: $125K
Experience:
   Industry experience
   General business experience
   Marketing skills

TRAINING
At headquarters: 2 weeks
At franchisee's location: 1 week

BUSINESS SUPPORT
Grand opening
Internet
Newsletter
Meetings
Toll-free phone line
Field operations/evaluations
Purchasing cooperatives
Security/safety procedures

MARKETING SUPPORT
Co-op advertising
Ad slicks
National media campaign
Regional marketing

THE NEW YORK BUTCHER SHOPPE

Financial rating: $$$

2131 Woodruff Rd., #2100-128
Greenville, SC 29607
(864)234-5684
www.nybutcher.net
Full-service butcher shop, prepared
    foods, grocery store
Began: 1999, Franchising: 2003
Headquarters size: 2 employees
Franchise department: 2 employees

U.S. franchises: 6
Canadian franchises: 0
Other foreign franchises: 0
Company-owned: 0

Seeking: Southeast
Seeking in Canada? No
Exclusive territories? Yes
Homebased option? No
Employees needed to run biz: 3
Absentee ownership? No

COSTS
Total cost: $206.5K-370.3K
Franchise fee: $25K
Royalty fee: 6%
Term of agreement: 10 years renewable
    for 25% of current fee
Franchisees required to buy multiple
    units? No

FINANCING
No financing available

QUALIFICATIONS
Net worth: $300K
Cash liquidity: $125K
Experience:
    General business experience
    Retail experience helpful

TRAINING
At headquarters: 4-6 weeks
At franchisee's location: 2 weeks

BUSINESS SUPPORT
Grand opening
Internet
Newsletter
Meetings
Field operations/evaluations
Purchasing cooperatives
Security/safety procedures

MARKETING SUPPORT
Co-op advertising
Ad slicks
Regional marketing

WINESTYLES INC.

Ranked #183 in Entrepreneur Magazine's 2007 Franchise 500

Financial rating: $$$$

5100 Copans Rd., #310
Margate, FL 33063
(954)984-0070
www.winestyles.net
Wine store
Began: 2002, Franchising: 2002
Headquarters size: 12 employees
Franchise department: 4 employees

U.S. franchises: 80
Canadian franchises: 0
Other foreign franchises: 1
Company-owned: 0

Seeking: All U.S.
Seeking in Canada? Yes
Exclusive territories? Yes
Homebased option? No
Employees needed to run biz: 3
Absentee ownership? No

COSTS
Total cost: $151.3K-238K
Franchise fee: $25K
Royalty fee: 6%
Term of agreement: Info not provided
Franchisees required to buy multiple
    units? No

FINANCING
In-house: None
3rd-party: Accounts receivable,
    equipment, franchise fee,
    inventory, payroll, startup costs

QUALIFICATIONS
Net worth: $200K
Cash liquidity: $75K
Experience:
    General business experience

TRAINING
At headquarters: 5 days
At franchisee's location: 3 days

BUSINESS SUPPORT
Grand opening
Internet
Newsletter
Meetings
Field operations/evaluations
Lease negotiations
Purchasing cooperatives
Security/safety procedures

MARKETING SUPPORT
Ad slicks
National media campaign
Regional marketing

FOOD/RETAIL *Other Franchises*

GOURMADE FRANCHISE
7060 Koll Center Pkwy., #320
Pleasanton, CA 94566
(925)846-4774
www.gourmadecookery.com
Meal assembly & meals-to-go
Current financial data not available

LET'S EAT
1221 Bricknell Ave., #1590
Tampa, FL 33131
(813)258-0555
www.letseatdinner.com
Meal preparation service
Current financial data not available

ROCKY MOUNTAIN CHOCOLATE FACTORY
Ranked #135 in Entrepreneur Magazine's 2007 Franchise 500
265 Turner Dr.
Durango, CO 81303
(800)438-7623/(970)259-0554
www.sweetfranchise.com
Chocolates & confections
Financial rating: $$$$

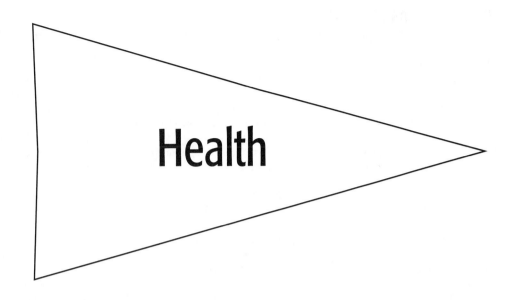

HEALTH | *Dental Handpiece Repairs*

THE DENTIST'S CHOICE
Ranked #469 in Entrepreneur Magazine's 2007 Franchise 500   *Financial rating: $$$*

774 Mays Blvd., #10-297
Incline Village, NV 89451
(800)757-1333
www.thedentistschoice.com
Dental handpiece repairs
Began: 1992, Franchising: 1994
Headquarters size: 5 employees
Franchise department: 1 employee

U.S. franchises: 113
Canadian franchises: 6
Other foreign franchises: 0
Company-owned: 3

Seeking: All U.S.
Seeking in Canada? Yes
Exclusive territories? Yes
Homebased option? Yes
Employees needed to run biz: 0
Absentee ownership? No

COSTS
Total cost: $33.4K-37.6K
Franchise fee: $25K
Royalty fee: 1-5%
Term of agreement: 10 years renewable
    for $2.5K
Franchisees required to buy multiple
    units? No

FINANCING
In-house: Franchise fee
3rd-party: None

QUALIFICATIONS
Cash liquidity: $32.5K
Experience:
    Marketing skills

TRAINING
At headquarters: 1 week

BUSINESS SUPPORT
Newsletter
Meetings
Toll-free phone line
Field operations/evaluations
Purchasing cooperatives

MARKETING SUPPORT
Ad slicks

HAYES HANDPIECE FRANCHISES INC.

Ranked #471 in Entrepreneur Magazine's 2007 Franchise 500

Financial rating: $$$$

5375 Avenida Encinas
Carlsbad, CA 92008
(760)602-0521
www.hayeshandpiece.com
Dental handpiece repairs
Began: 1989, Franchising: 1995
Headquarters size: 30 employees
Franchise department: 3 employees

U.S. franchises: 68
Canadian franchises: 3
Other foreign franchises: 2
Company-owned: 5

Seeking: Northeast
Seeking in Canada? Yes
Exclusive territories? Yes
Homebased option? Yes
Employees needed to run biz: 1
Absentee ownership? No

COSTS
Total cost: $33K-44.5K
Franchise fee: $29K
Royalty fee: 3.5-5%
Term of agreement: 10 years renewable
    at no charge
Franchisees required to buy multiple
    units? No

FINANCING
No financing available

QUALIFICATIONS
Experience:
    General business experience
    Marketing skills
    Sales experience

TRAINING
At headquarters: 2 weeks
At franchisee's location: 3 days
Annual free training: 1 week

BUSINESS SUPPORT
Grand opening
Internet
Newsletter
Meetings
Toll-free phone line
Field operations/evaluations
Purchasing cooperatives
Security/safety procedures

MARKETING SUPPORT
Co-op advertising
Ad slicks
National media campaign
Regional marketing
Call center

HEALTH *Vitamins*

DISCOUNT SPORT NUTRITION

Financial rating: $$$

1920 Abrams Pkwy., #422
Dallas, TX 75214
(972)489-7925
www.sportsupplements.com
Sports supplements, vitamins, herbs
Began: 1996, Franchising: 2000
Headquarters size: 8 employees
Franchise department: 2 employees

U.S. franchises: 4
Canadian franchises: 0
Other foreign franchises: 0
Company-owned: 0

Seeking: All U.S.
Seeking in Canada? Yes
Exclusive territories? Yes
Homebased option? No
Employees needed to run biz: 2-3
Absentee ownership? Yes

COSTS
Total cost: $87.7K-175.3K
Franchise fee: $25K
Royalty fee: 5%
Term of agreement: 10 years renewable
    for $25K
Franchisees required to buy multiple
    units? No

FINANCING
In-house: None
3rd-party: Accounts receivable,
    equipment, franchise fee,
    inventory, payroll, startup costs

QUALIFICATIONS
Net worth: $50K
Cash liquidity: $25K
Experience:
    General business experience

TRAINING
At headquarters: 2-3 days
At franchisee's location: 3-5 days

BUSINESS SUPPORT
Grand opening
Internet
Newsletter
Toll-free phone line
Field operations/evaluations
Purchasing cooperatives
Security/safety procedures

MARKETING SUPPORT
Co-op advertising
Ad slicks
National media campaign
Regional marketing

MAX MUSCLE

Ranked #437 in Entrepreneur Magazine's 2007 Franchise 500   *Financial rating: $$*

1641 S. Sinclair
Anaheim, CA 92806
(714)456-0700
www.maxmusclefranchise.com
Sports nutrition products & athletic
   apparel
Began: 1991, Franchising: 2001
Headquarters size: 50 employees
Franchise department: 5 employees

U.S. franchises: 90
Canadian franchises: 0
Other foreign franchises: 0
Company-owned: 0

Seeking: All U.S.
Seeking in Canada? No
Exclusive territories? Yes
Homebased option? No
Employees needed to run biz: 2-5
Absentee ownership? Yes

COSTS
Total cost: $175K
Franchise fee: $30K
Royalty fee: 3%
Term of agreement: 10 years renewable
   for $1.5K
Franchisees required to buy multiple
   units? No

FINANCING
In-house: None
3rd-party: Equipment, inventory,
   startup costs

QUALIFICATIONS
Net worth: $250K
Cash liquidity: $150K
Experience:
   General business experience
   Marketing skills

TRAINING
At headquarters: 2 weeks

BUSINESS SUPPORT
Grand opening
Internet
Newsletter
Meetings
Toll-free phone line
Field operations/evaluations
Lease negotiations
Purchasing cooperatives
Security/safety procedures

MARKETING SUPPORT
Co-op advertising
Ad slicks
National media campaign
Regional marketing

SANGSTER'S HEALTH CENTRES

Current financial data not available

2218 Hanselman Ave.
Saskatoon, SK S7L 6A4 Canada
(306)653-4481
www.sangsters.com
Vitamins, cosmetics, food
Began: 1971, Franchising: 1978
Headquarters size: 14 employees
Franchise department: 14 employees

U.S. franchises: 0
Canadian franchises: 48
Other foreign franchises: 1
Company-owned: 5

Seeking: Not available in the U.S.
Seeking in Canada? Yes
Exclusive territories? Yes
Homebased option? No
Employees needed to run biz: 4
Absentee ownership? Yes

COSTS
Total cost: $50K-150K
Franchise fee: $25K
Royalty fee: 5%
Term of agreement: 2-5 years
   renewable for $5K
Franchisees required to buy multiple
   units? No

FINANCING
In-house: Equipment, inventory
3rd-party: None

QUALIFICATIONS
Net worth: $75K
Cash liquidity: $30K
Experience:
   General business experience
   Marketing skills

TRAINING
At headquarters: 2 weeks
At franchisee's location: 1 week

BUSINESS SUPPORT
Grand opening
Internet
Newsletter
Meetings
Field operations/evaluations
Lease negotiations
Purchasing cooperatives

MARKETING SUPPORT
Co-op advertising
Ad slicks
National media campaign
Regional marketing

HEALTH   *Weight-Loss Programs*

HYTECH WEIGHT LOSS

Current financial data not available

16909 Lakeside Hills, #112
Omaha, NE 68130
(402)330-9100
www.hytechweightloss.com
Weight-loss center
Began: 2004, Franchising: 2005
Headquarters size: 10 employees
Franchise department: 5 employees

U.S. franchises: 3
Canadian franchises: 0
Other foreign franchises: 0
Company-owned: 2

Seeking: All U.S.
Seeking in Canada? No
Exclusive territories? Yes
Homebased option? No
Employees needed to run biz: 3
Absentee ownership? Yes

COSTS
Total cost: $46.5K-118K
Franchise fee: $19.5K
Royalty fee: 5%
Term of agreement: 10 years renewable
   for 50% of then-current fee
Franchisees required to buy multiple
   units? No

FINANCING
In-house: None
3rd-party: Equipment, franchise fee,
   inventory, startup costs

QUALIFICATIONS
Net worth: $100K
Cash liquidity: $50K
Experience:
   General business experience
   Marketing skills

TRAINING
At headquarters: 1 week
At franchisee's location: 1 week

BUSINESS SUPPORT
Grand opening
Internet
Toll-free phone line
Field operations/evaluations
Security/safety procedures

MARKETING SUPPORT
Ad slicks
TV & radio ads

INTRIVAH HEALTH & WELLNESS

Financial rating: 0

2012 8th Ave.
Altoona, PA 16602
(800)941-9251
www.intrivah.com
Health & wellness center
Began: 2002, Franchising: 2004
Headquarters size: 3 employees
Franchise department: 3 employees

U.S. franchises: 1
Canadian franchises: 0
Other foreign franchises: 0
Company-owned: 1

Seeking: All U.S.
Seeking in Canada? No
Exclusive territories? Yes
Homebased option? No
Employees needed to run biz: 3
Absentee ownership? No

COSTS
Total cost: $112K
Franchise fee: $30K
Royalty fee: 5%
Term of agreement: 5 years renewable
   at no charge
Franchisees required to buy multiple
   units? No

FINANCING
In-house: None
3rd-party: Equipment, franchise fee,
   inventory, payroll, startup costs

QUALIFICATIONS
Net worth: $150K
Cash liquidity: $30K
Experience:
   Industry experience
   General business experience

TRAINING
At headquarters: 2 weeks
At franchisee's location: 5 days

BUSINESS SUPPORT
Grand opening
Internet
Newsletter
Meetings
Toll-free phone line
Field operations/evaluations

MARKETING SUPPORT
Co-op advertising
Ad slicks
National media campaign
Regional marketing

JENNY CRAIG

Ranked #125 in Entrepreneur Magazine's 2007 Franchise 500

Financial rating: $$$$

5770 Fleet St.
Carlsbad, CA 92008
(888)848-8885/(760)696-4000
www.jennycraig.com/franchise
Weight-loss program
Began: 1983, Franchising: 1987
Headquarters size: 3,000 employees

U.S. franchises: 89
Canadian franchises: 9
Other foreign franchises: 114
Company-owned: 432

Seeking: All U.S.
Seeking in Canada? No
Exclusive territories? Yes
Homebased option? No
Employees needed to run biz: 4
Absentee ownership? No

COSTS
Total cost: $165.6K-350.5K
Franchise fee: $25K
Royalty fee: to 7%
Term of agreement: 10 years renewable
   for 50% of then-current fee
Franchisees required to buy multiple
   units? No

FINANCING
No financing available

QUALIFICATIONS
Net worth: $300K
Cash liquidity: $150K
Experience:
   General business experience
   Marketing skills

TRAINING
At headquarters: 7 days
At franchisee's location: 7 days
At local/regional training center:
   6-10 days
Business consultant follow-up at
   location: 8-10 days

BUSINESS SUPPORT
Grand opening
Internet
Newsletter
Meetings
Toll-free phone line
Field operations/evaluations
Lease negotiations
Security/safety procedures

MARKETING SUPPORT
National & local media campaigns
PR

LA WEIGHT LOSS CENTERS

Ranked #60 in Entrepreneur Magazine's 2007 Franchise 500

Financial rating: $$$$

747 Dresher Rd., #150
Horsham, PA 19044
(888)258-7099
www.laweightloss.com
Health services & weight-loss
   counseling
Began: 1989, Franchising: 1998
Headquarters size: 100 employees
Franchise department: 100 employees

U.S. franchises: 356
Canadian franchises: 60
Other foreign franchises: 12
Company-owned: 392

Seeking: All U.S.
Seeking in Canada? No
Exclusive territories? Yes
Homebased option? No
Employees needed to run biz: 5
Absentee ownership? No

COSTS
Total cost: $84.6K-139.9K
Franchise fee: $20K
Royalty fee: 7%
Term of agreement: 10 years renewable
   at no charge
Franchisees required to buy multiple
   units? Yes

FINANCING
In-house: Franchise fee
3rd-party: Equipment, inventory,
   startup costs

QUALIFICATIONS
Net worth: $100K
Cash liquidity: $70K-100K
Experience:
   Industry experience
   General business experience
   Marketing skills

TRAINING
At headquarters: 4 weeks
At franchisee's location: 3 weeks

BUSINESS SUPPORT
Grand opening
Internet
Newsletter
Meetings
Toll-free phone line
Field operations/evaluations
Lease negotiations
Purchasing cooperatives

MARKETING SUPPORT
Ad slicks
National media campaign
Regional marketing

PERSONAL TRAINING INSTITUTE FRANCHISE LLC

Financial rating: 0

500 N. Broadway
Jericho, NY 11753
(516)342-9064
www.ptifranchise.com
Weight loss & personal training
Began: 1987, Franchising: 2005
Headquarters size: 6 employees
Franchise department: 6 employees

U.S. franchises: 5
Canadian franchises: 0
Other foreign franchises: 0
Company-owned: 7

Seeking: All U.S.
Seeking in Canada? No
Exclusive territories? Yes
Homebased option? No
Employees needed to run biz: 10
Absentee ownership? Yes

COSTS
Total cost: $99.4K-188K
Franchise fee: $19.5K
Royalty fee: 5%
Term of agreement: 10 years renewable
    for 25% of current franchise fee
Franchisees required to buy multiple
    units? No

FINANCING
No financing available

QUALIFICATIONS
Cash liquidity: $50K+
Experience:
    Marketing skills

TRAINING
At headquarters: 2 weeks
At franchisee's location: 1 week

BUSINESS SUPPORT
Grand opening
Internet
Meetings
Field operations/evaluations
Lease negotiations
Security/safety procedures

MARKETING SUPPORT
Ad slicks
National media campaign
Regional marketing

HEALTH ◀ *Miscellaneous*

AMERICAN RAMP SYSTEMS

Ranked #383 in Entrepreneur Magazine's 2007 Franchise 500

Financial rating: $$

202 W. First St.
South Boston, MA 02127-1110
(800)649-5215
www.americanramp.com
Wheelchair ramps
Began: 1970, Franchising: 2002
Headquarters size: 25 employees
Franchise department: 3 employees

U.S. franchises: 30
Canadian franchises: 0
Other foreign franchises: 0
Company-owned: 1

Seeking: All U.S.
Seeking in Canada? No
Exclusive territories? Yes
Homebased option? Yes
Employees needed to run biz: 2
Absentee ownership? Yes

COSTS
Total cost: $81.9K-189.5K
Franchise fee: $39.3K
Royalty fee: 3-12%
Term of agreement: 10 years renewable
    for $5K
Franchisees required to buy multiple
    units? No

FINANCING
In-house: None
3rd-party: Equipment, franchise fee,
    inventory, startup costs

QUALIFICATIONS
Net worth: $200K
Cash liquidity: $75K
Experience:
    Marketing skills
    Understanding of clients' needs

TRAINING
At headquarters: 1 week

BUSINESS SUPPORT
Internet
Newsletter
Meetings
Toll-free phone line
Field operations/evaluations
Purchasing cooperatives

MARKETING SUPPORT
Co-op advertising
Ad slicks
National media campaign
Regional marketing

FOOT SOLUTIONS INC.

Ranked #112 in Entrepreneur Magazine's 2007 Franchise 500   *Financial rating: $$$$*

2359 Windy Hill Rd., #400
Marietta, GA 30067
(866)338-2597/(770)955-0099
www.footsolutions.com
Custom insoles & comfort shoes
Began: 2000, Franchising: 2000
Headquarters size: 50 employees
Franchise department: 10 employees

U.S. franchises: 188
Canadian franchises: 16
Other foreign franchises: 6
Company-owned: 1

Seeking: All U.S.
Seeking in Canada? Yes
Exclusive territories? Yes
Homebased option? No
Employees needed to run biz: 3
Absentee ownership? No

COSTS
Total cost: $195.7K-236.3K
Franchise fee: $27.5K
Royalty fee: 5%
Term of agreement: 20 years renewable
    for 10% of current franchise fee
Franchisees required to buy multiple
    units? No

FINANCING
No financing available

QUALIFICATIONS
Net worth: $200K+
Cash liquidity: $50K-70K
Experience:
    General business experience

TRAINING
At headquarters: 14 days
At franchisee's location: 4-6 days
Ongoing

BUSINESS SUPPORT
Grand opening
Internet
Newsletter
Meetings
Toll-free phone line
Field operations/evaluations
Lease negotiations
Purchasing cooperatives
Security/safety procedures

MARKETING SUPPORT
Co-op advertising
Ad slicks
National media campaign
Regional marketing
Website
Professional associations

MEDSONIX INC.

Current financial data not available

2626 S. Rainbow Blvd.
Las Vegas, NV 89146
(800)631-2272/(702)873-3700
www.medsonix.com
Pain therapy
Began: 2003, Franchising: 2003
Headquarters size: 3 employees
Franchise department: 1 employee

U.S. franchises: 1
Canadian franchises: 0
Other foreign franchises: 0
Company-owned: 1

Seeking: All U.S.
Seeking in Canada? No
Exclusive territories? Yes
Homebased option? No
Employees needed to run biz: 4
Absentee ownership? Yes

COSTS
Total cost: $79.9K
Franchise fee: $19.9K
Royalty fee: Varies
Term of agreement: 10 years
    renewable for $2.5K
Franchisees required to buy
    multiple units? No

FINANCING
No financing available

QUALIFICATIONS
Net worth: $100K
Cash liquidity: $30K
Experience:
    General business experience

TRAINING
At headquarters

BUSINESS SUPPORT
Grand opening

MARKETING SUPPORT
Info not provided

PASSPORT HEALTH INC.

Ranked #331 in Entrepreneur Magazine's 2007 Franchise 500

Financial rating: $$$$

921 E. Fort Ave., #102
Baltimore, MD 21230
(410)727-0556
www.passporthealthusa.com
Immunization/vaccination service
   for international travelers
Began: 1995, Franchising: 1997
Headquarters size: 5 employees
Franchise department: 3 employees

U.S. franchises: 56
Canadian franchises: 0
Other foreign franchises: 0
Company-owned: 2

Seeking: All U.S.
Seeking in Canada? Yes
Exclusive territories? Yes
Homebased option? No
Employees needed to run biz: 3
Absentee ownership? No

COSTS
Total cost: $63.6K-166.5K
Franchise fee: $25K-100K
Royalty fee: 7-5%
Term of agreement: 10 years renewable
   for $3K
Franchisees required to buy multiple
   units? No

FINANCING
No financing available

QUALIFICATIONS
Net worth: $76K-150K
Cash liquidity: $50K
Experience:
   General business experience

TRAINING
At headquarters: 1 week
At franchisee's location: 3 days
On-location marketing assistance:
   2 days-1 week

BUSINESS SUPPORT
Internet
Newsletter
Meetings
Toll-free phone line
Field operations/evaluations

MARKETING SUPPORT
Website
National contract negotiations

RELAX THE BACK CORP.

Ranked #436 in Entrepreneur Magazine's 2007 Franchise 500

Financial rating: $

6 Centerpointe Dr., #350
La Palma, CA 90623
(800)290-2225
www.relaxtheback.com
Products for relief/prevention of
   back & neck pain
Began: 1984, Franchising: 1989
Headquarters size: 24 employees
Franchise department: 3 employees

U.S. franchises: 105
Canadian franchises: 2
Other foreign franchises: 0
Company-owned: 0

Seeking: All U.S.
Seeking in Canada? Yes
Exclusive territories? Yes
Homebased option? No
Employees needed to run biz: 2-5
Absentee ownership? No

COSTS
Total cost: $235.7K-380K
Franchise fee: $49.5K
Royalty fee: 5%
Term of agreement: 10 years renewable
   at no charge
Franchisees required to buy multiple
   units? No

FINANCING
In-house: None
3rd-party: Equipment, franchise fee,
   inventory, startup costs

QUALIFICATIONS
Net worth: $500K+
Cash liquidity: $100K
Experience:
   General business experience
   Marketing skills

TRAINING
At headquarters: 14 days
At franchisee's location: 4 days
Regional training: 2 days

BUSINESS SUPPORT
Grand opening
Internet
Newsletter
Meetings
Field operations/evaluations

MARKETING SUPPORT
Ad slicks
National media campaign
Regional marketing
Regional PR
CDs

SHOES-N-FEET

Current financial data not available

15015 Main St., #211
Bellevue, WA 98007
(425)830-1605
www.shoesnfeet.com
Retail comfort shoes, arch supports,
    accessories
Began: 1998, Franchising: 2002
Headquarters size: 8 employees
Franchise department: 3 employees

U.S. franchises: 8
Canadian franchises: 0
Other foreign franchises: 0
Company-owned: 1

Seeking: Midwest, Northwest, West
Seeking in Canada? No
Exclusive territories? Yes
Homebased option? No
Employees needed to run biz: 3
Absentee ownership? Yes

COSTS
Total cost: $185K-226.5K
Franchise fee: $25K
Royalty fee: 5%
Term of agreement: 10 years renewable
    for $5K
Franchisees required to buy multiple
    units? No

FINANCING
No financing available

QUALIFICATIONS
Net worth: $250K
Cash liquidity: $25K-30K
Experience:
    General business experience

TRAINING
At headquarters: 160 hours
At franchisee's location: 160 hours
    & as needed

BUSINESS SUPPORT
Grand opening
Internet
Newsletter
Meetings
Toll-free phone line
Field operations/evaluations
Lease negotiations
Purchasing cooperatives
Security/safety procedures

MARKETING SUPPORT
Co-op advertising
Ad slicks
Regional marketing
Marketing to the medical community

SILVER CROSS

Financial rating: $

1005 Skyview Dr., #200
Burlington, ON L7P 5B1 Canada
(800)572-9310
www.silvercross.com/franchise
Home accessibility & mobility
    equipment
Began: 1993, Franchising: 1994
Headquarters size: 3 employees
Franchise department: 3 employees

U.S. franchises: 4
Canadian franchises: 10
Other foreign franchises: 0
Company-owned: 0

Seeking: All U.S.
Seeking in Canada? Yes
Exclusive territories? Yes
Homebased option? No
Employees needed to run biz: 1
Absentee ownership? No

COSTS
Total cost: $99K-150K
Franchise fee: $25K
Royalty fee: 5%
Term of agreement: 5 years renewable
    for $5K
Franchisees required to buy multiple
    units? No

FINANCING
No financing available

QUALIFICATIONS
Net worth: $350K
Cash liquidity: $99.6K-151.6K
Experience:
    General business experience
    Marketing skills

TRAINING
At headquarters: 6 days
At franchisee's location: 3-4 days
Ongoing support

BUSINESS SUPPORT
Internet
Meetings
Field operations/evaluations
Purchasing cooperatives

MARKETING SUPPORT
Ad slicks

WHEELCHAIR GETAWAYS INC.

Financial rating: $$$$

P.O. Box 605
Versailles, KY 40383
(800)536-5518/(859)873-4973
www.wheelchairgetaways.com
Wheelchair-accessible van rentals
Began: 1988, Franchising: 1989
Headquarters size: 5 employees
Franchise department: 2 employees

U.S. franchises: 44
Canadian franchises: 0
Other foreign franchises: 0
Company-owned: 2

Seeking: All U.S.
Seeking in Canada? Yes
Exclusive territories? Yes
Homebased option? Yes
Employees needed to run biz: 3
Absentee ownership? Yes

COSTS
Total cost: $40K-112K
Franchise fee: $17.5K
Royalty fee: $550/van/yr.
Term of agreement: 10 years renewable
    for $5K
Franchisees required to buy multiple
    units? No

FINANCING
No financing available

QUALIFICATIONS
Experience:
    Industry experience
    General business experience
    Marketing skills

TRAINING
At existing franchise location: 2 days

BUSINESS SUPPORT
Internet
Newsletter
Meetings
Toll-free phone line
Field operations/evaluations
Purchasing cooperatives

MARKETING SUPPORT
Co-op advertising
Ad slicks
National media campaign
Regional marketing

HEALTH ◄ *Other Franchises*

GNC FRANCHISING INC.
*Ranked #32 in Entrepreneur
Magazine's 2007 Franchise 500*
300 6th Ave., 4th Fl.
Pittsburgh, PA 15222
(800)766-7099/(412)338-2503
www.gncfranchising.com
Vitamin & nutrition store
Financial rating: $$$$

PEARLE VISION INC.
*Ranked #94 in Entrepreneur
Magazine's 2007 Franchise 500*
4000 Luxottica Pl.
Mason, OH 45040
(800)732-7531/(513)765-3327
www.pearlevision.com/franchise
Eye-care center
Financial rating: $$$$

PURIFIED WATER TO GO
5160 S. Valley View Blvd., #100
Las Vegas, NV 89118-1778
(800)976-9283/(702)895-9350
www.watertogo.com
Retail water & nutrition store
Current financial data not available

HOME ▸ *Building & Remodeling*

A-1 CONCRETE LEVELING INC.

Financial rating: $$$

388 S. Main St., #402
Akron, OH 44311
(888)675-3835
www.a1concrete.com
Concrete leveling & repairs
Began: 1992, Franchising: 1993
Headquarters size: 1 employee
Franchise department: 1 employee

U.S. franchises: 51
Canadian franchises: 0
Other foreign franchises: 0
Company-owned: 0

Seeking: All U.S.
Seeking in Canada? No
Exclusive territories? Yes
Homebased option? Yes
Employees needed to run biz: 2
Absentee ownership? Yes

COSTS
Total cost: $115.9K-140.9K
Franchise fee: $80K
Royalty fee: 6%
Term of agreement: 15 years
Franchisees required to buy multiple
   units? No

FINANCING
In-house: Accounts receivable,
   franchise fee, payroll
3rd-party: Equipment, inventory,
   startup costs

QUALIFICATIONS
Cash liquidity: $5K
Experience:
   General business experience

TRAINING
At headquarters: 1 week
At franchisee's location: 2 weeks
Ongoing

BUSINESS SUPPORT
Internet
Newsletter
Meetings
Toll-free phone line
Field operations/evaluations
Security/safety procedures

MARKETING SUPPORT
Ad slicks

ABC INC.

Ranked #419 in Entrepreneur Magazine's 2007 Franchise 500   *Financial rating: $$$$*

3001 Fiechtner Dr.
Fargo, ND 58103
(800)732-6577/(701)293-5952
www.abcseamless.com
Seamless siding & gutters
Began: 1973, Franchising: 1978
Headquarters size: 92 employees
Franchise department: 12 employees

U.S. franchises: 120
Canadian franchises: 0
Other foreign franchises: 0
Company-owned: 4

Seeking: All U.S.
Seeking in Canada? No
Exclusive territories? Yes
Homebased option? Yes
Employees needed to run biz: 10
Absentee ownership? No

COSTS
Total cost: $100.5K-219.5K
Franchise fee: $18K-24K
Royalty fee: Varies
Term of agreement: 10 years renewable
    at no charge
Franchisees required to buy multiple
    units? No

FINANCING
In-house: None
3rd-party: Equipment

QUALIFICATIONS
Experience:
    Industry experience
    General business experience

TRAINING
At headquarters: Monthly sales class
    & ongoing
At franchisee's location: 3 weeks
Annual & regional meetings:
    2-4 days

BUSINESS SUPPORT
Internet
Newsletter
Meetings
Toll-free phone line
Field operations/evaluations
Security/safety procedures

MARKETING SUPPORT
Ad slicks
Advertising materials

ARCHADECK

Financial rating: 0

2112 W. Laburnum Ave., #100
Richmond, VA 23227
(800)789-3325/(804)353-6999
www.archadeck.com
Wooden decks, screened porches,
    gazebos
Began: 1980, Franchising: 1984
Headquarters size: 20 employees
Franchise department: 2 employees

U.S. franchises: 75
Canadian franchises: 5
Other foreign franchises: 1
Company-owned: 1

Seeking: All U.S.
Seeking in Canada? No
Exclusive territories? Yes
Homebased option? Yes
Employees needed to run biz: 1
Absentee ownership? No

COSTS
Total cost: $80K-150K
Franchise fee: $39.5K
Royalty fee: 3.5-5.5%+
Term of agreement: 5 years renewable
    for $2.5K
Franchisees required to buy multiple
    units? Outside the U.S. only

FINANCING
In-house: Franchise fee
3rd-party: Equipment, franchise fee,
    startup costs

QUALIFICATIONS
Net worth: $150K
Cash liquidity: $65K-110K
Experience:
    General business experience

TRAINING
At headquarters: 20 days
At franchisee's location: 9 days

BUSINESS SUPPORT
Internet
Newsletter
Meetings
Toll-free phone line
Field operations/evaluations

MARKETING SUPPORT
Ad slicks
National media campaign

B-DRY SYSTEM INC.

Financial rating: 0

1341 Copley Rd.
Akron, OH 44320
(330)867-2576
www.bdry.com
Basement waterproofing
Began: 1958, Franchising: 1978
Headquarters size: 7 employees
Franchise department: 5 employees

U.S. franchises: 39
Canadian franchises: 0
Other foreign franchises: 0
Company-owned: 0

Seeking: Northeast, Midwest
Seeking in Canada? Yes
Exclusive territories? Yes
Homebased option? Yes
Employees needed to run biz: 3
Absentee ownership? No

COSTS

Total cost: $95K-105K
Franchise fee: $35K-60K
Royalty fee: 8%
Term of agreement: 5 years renewable
    at no charge
Franchisees required to buy multiple
    units? No

FINANCING

In-house: Franchise fee
3rd-party: None

QUALIFICATIONS

Experience:
    General business experience
    Sales background helpful

TRAINING

At headquarters: 1 week
At franchisee's location: At opening
    & as needed
In existing market: Up to 1 week

BUSINESS SUPPORT

Internet
Newsletter
Meetings
Toll-free phone line
Field operations/evaluations
Security/safety procedures

MARKETING SUPPORT

Ad slicks
National media campaign

BORDER MAGIC LLC

Ranked #434 in Entrepreneur Magazine's 2007 Franchise 500

Financial rating: $$$

1503 CR 2700 N.
Rantoul, IL 61866
(217)892-2954
www.bordermagic.com
Concrete landscape edging
Began: 1987, Franchising: 2003
Headquarters size: 12 employees
Franchise department: 7 employees

U.S. franchises: 71
Canadian franchises: 0
Other foreign franchises: 0
Company-owned: 0

Seeking: All U.S.
Seeking in Canada? No
Exclusive territories? Yes
Homebased option? Yes
Employees needed to run biz: 3
Absentee ownership? Yes

COSTS

Total cost: $79.9K
Franchise fee: $25K
Royalty fee: $250-400/mo.
Term of agreement: 5 years renewable
    for $12.5K
Franchisees required to buy multiple
    units? No

FINANCING

In-house: None
3rd-party: Equipment, franchise fee

QUALIFICATIONS

Experience:
    General business experience
    Entrepreneurial spirit

TRAINING

At headquarters: 3 days
At franchisee's location: Ongoing

BUSINESS SUPPORT

Internet
Newsletter
Meetings
Toll-free phone line
Field operations/evaluations
Purchasing cooperatives
Security/safety procedures

MARKETING SUPPORT

Co-op advertising
Ad slicks
National media campaign
Regional marketing
Direct mail

CONCRETE RAISING OF AMERICA INC.

Financial rating: $$$

2855 S. 166th St.
New Berlin, WI 53151
(800)270-0011/(262)827-5000
www.crc1.com
Concrete/foundation raising, stabilizing & repairs
Began: 1947, Franchising: 1993
Headquarters size: 26 employees
Franchise department: 6 employees

U.S. franchises: 14
Canadian franchises: 0
Other foreign franchises: 0
Company-owned: 3

Seeking: All U.S.
Seeking in Canada? Yes
Exclusive territories? Yes
Homebased option? Yes
Employees needed to run biz: 3-4
Absentee ownership? Yes

COSTS
Total cost: $16.9K-200K
Franchise fee: $16.9K-25K
Royalty fee: 4-8%
Term of agreement: 20 years renewable at no charge
Franchisees required to buy multiple units? No

FINANCING
In-house: Franchise fee
3rd-party: Equipment, franchise fee, startup costs

QUALIFICATIONS
Cash liquidity: $35K
Experience:
    Industry experience
    General business skills
    Marketing skills

TRAINING
At headquarters: 5-10 days
At franchisee's location: 10 days & as needed
Biannual operator certification

BUSINESS SUPPORT
Internet
Newsletter
Meetings
Toll-free phone line
Field operations/evaluations
Lease negotiations
Purchasing cooperatives
Security/safety procedures

MARKETING SUPPORT
Co-op advertising
Ad slicks
National media campaign
Marketing planning & research

THE CRACK TEAM

Financial rating: 0

11694 Lackland Rd.
St. Louis, MO 63146
(866)905-5200/(314)426-0900
www.thecrackteam.com
Foundation crack repairs
Began: 1985, Franchising: 2000
Headquarters size: 10 employees
Franchise department: 10 employees

U.S. franchises: 19
Canadian franchises: 0
Other foreign franchises: 0
Company-owned: 0

Seeking: All U.S.
Seeking in Canada? No
Exclusive territories? Yes
Homebased option? Yes
Employees needed to run biz: 1-4
Absentee ownership? No

COSTS
Total cost: $72K-103K
Franchise fee: $35K/20K
Royalty fee: 6%
Term of agreement: 10 years renewable at no charge
Franchisees required to buy multiple units? No

FINANCING
No financing available

QUALIFICATIONS
Net worth: $150K
Cash liquidity: $100K
Experience:
    General business experience
    Marketing skills

TRAINING
At headquarters: 2 weeks

BUSINESS SUPPORT
Internet
Newsletter
Meetings
Toll-free phone line
Field operations/evaluations

MARKETING SUPPORT
In-house PR/marketing

DECKARE SERVICES

Current financial data not available

P.O. Box 2483
Goose Creek, SC 29445
(843)824-6090
www.deckare.com
Deck maintenance & outdoor wood
 preservation
Began: 1995, Franchising: 1997
Headquarters size: 4 employees
Franchise department: 3 employees

U.S. franchises: 12
Canadian franchises: 0
Other foreign franchises: 0
Company-owned: 0

Seeking: All U.S.
Seeking in Canada? No
Exclusive territories? Yes
Homebased option? Yes
Employees needed to run biz: 2
Absentee ownership? Yes

COSTS
Total cost: $25K
Franchise fee: $14.5K
Royalty fee: 5%
Term of agreement: 5 years renewable
 at no charge
Franchisees required to buy multiple
 units? No

FINANCING
In-house: None
3rd-party: Equipment, franchise fee,
 startup costs

QUALIFICATIONS
Net worth: $35K
Cash liquidity: $10K
Experience:
 General business experience
 Marketing skills

TRAINING
At headquarters: 4 days
At franchisee's location: 4 days
Ongoing

BUSINESS SUPPORT
Grand opening
Internet
Newsletter
Toll-free phone line
Security/safety procedures

MARKETING SUPPORT
Ad slicks
National media campaign

DREAMMAKER BATH & KITCHEN BY WORLDWIDE

Ranked #323 in Entrepreneur Magazine's 2007 Franchise 500   *Financial rating: $$$*

1020 N. University Parks Dr.
Waco, TX 76707
(800)583-9099
www.dreammaker-remodel.com
Bath & kitchen remodeling
Began: 1971, Franchising: 1972
Headquarters size: 17 employees
Franchise department: 4 employees

U.S. franchises: 104
Canadian franchises: 0
Other foreign franchises: 76
Company-owned: 0

Seeking: All U.S.
Seeking in Canada? Yes
Exclusive territories? Yes
Homebased option? No
Employees needed to run biz: 4
Absentee ownership? Yes

COSTS
Total cost: $88K-291K
Franchise fee: $35K
Royalty fee: 6-3%
Term of agreement: 10 years renewable
 for $2.5K
Franchisees required to buy multiple
 units? Outside the U.S. only

FINANCING
In-house: Franchise fee
3rd-party: Equipment, inventory,
 startup costs

QUALIFICATIONS
Net worth: $100K
Cash liquidity: $63K-266K
Experience:
 Industry experience
 General business experience
 Marketing skills
 Remodeling & construction
 experience

TRAINING
At headquarters: 8 days

BUSINESS SUPPORT
Internet
Newsletter
Meetings
Toll-free phone line
Field operations/evaluations
Security/safety procedures

MARKETING SUPPORT
Ad slicks
National media campaign

ENTRYPOINT

Financial rating: $$$

8010 Sunport Dr., #114
Orlando, FL 32809
(407)926-1870
www.entrypointglass.com
Decorative door-glass installation &
    showrooms
Began: 2003, Franchising: 2005
Headquarters size: 6 employees
Franchise department: 2 employees

U.S. franchises: 15
Canadian franchises: 0
Other foreign franchises: 0
Company-owned: 2

Seeking: All U.S.
Seeking in Canada? No
Exclusive territories? Yes
Homebased option? No
Employees needed to run biz: 2
Absentee ownership? No

COSTS
Total cost: $101.2K-122.8K
Franchise fee: $15K
Royalty fee: 5%
Term of agreement: 10 years renewable
    for 50% of current franchise fee
Franchisees required to buy multiple
    units? No

FINANCING
In-house: None
3rd-party: Equipment, franchise fee,
    inventory, startup costs

QUALIFICATIONS
Net worth: $110K
Cash liquidity: $45K
Experience:
    General business experience
    Marketing skills

TRAINING
At headquarters: 1 week
At franchisee's location: 1 week

BUSINESS SUPPORT
Internet
Newsletter
Meetings
Toll-free phone line
Field operations/evaluations
Purchasing cooperatives
Security/safety procedures

MARKETING SUPPORT
Co-op advertising
Ad slicks
Catalogs & brochures

EXOVATIONS

Current financial data not available

1550-A Oak Industrial Ln.
Cumming, GA 30041
(770)205-2995
www.exovations.com
Exterior home remodeling
Began: 1996, Franchising: 2006
Headquarters size: 24 employees
Franchise department: 2 employees

U.S. franchises: 1
Canadian franchises: 0
Other foreign franchises: 0
Company-owned: 1

Seeking: All U.S.
Seeking in Canada? No
Exclusive territories? Info not
    provided
Homebased option? No
Employees needed to run biz: 4-20
Absentee ownership? Info not
    provided

COSTS
Total cost: $150K+
Franchise fee: $30K-60K
Royalty fee: 5%
Term of agreement: 5 years
Franchisees required to buy multiple
    units? No

FINANCING
In-house: None
3rd-party: Accounts receivable,
    equipment, franchise fee,
    inventory, payroll, startup costs

QUALIFICATIONS
Net worth: $150K+
Experience:
    Industry experience
    General business experience
    Sales skills

TRAINING
At headquarters: 2 weeks
At franchisee's location: 2 weeks

BUSINESS SUPPORT
Grand opening
Internet
Meetings
Toll-free phone line
Field operations/evaluations
Purchasing cooperatives
Security/safety procedures

MARKETING SUPPORT
Co-op advertising
Ad slicks
Regional marketing

INTERIOR DOOR REPLACEMENT COMPANY FRANCHISING

Financial rating: $$$

231 S. Whisman Rd., #C
Mountain View, CA 94041
(866)315-4372
www.idrcfranchising.com
Interior door replacement services
Began: 1997, Franchising: 2001
Headquarters size: 15 employees
Franchise department: 3 employees

U.S. franchises: 17
Canadian franchises: 0
Other foreign franchises: 0
Company-owned: 1

Seeking: AZ, CA, CO, NV, OR, TX,
WA
Seeking in Canada? No
Exclusive territories? Yes
Homebased option? No
Employees needed to run biz: 4-6
Absentee ownership? No

COSTS
Total cost: $144K-194.5K
Franchise fee: $20K-40K
Royalty fee: 6%
Term of agreement: 10 years renewable
at no charge
Franchisees required to buy multiple
units? No

FINANCING
No financing available

QUALIFICATIONS
Cash liquidity: $150K
Experience:
General business experience
Marketing skills

TRAINING
At headquarters: Up to 10 days
At franchisee's location: 5 days

BUSINESS SUPPORT
Grand opening
Internet
Newsletter
Meetings
Field operations/evaluations
Purchasing cooperatives

MARKETING SUPPORT
Co-op advertising
Regional marketing

KITCHEN SOLVERS INC.

Ranked #304 in Entrepreneur Magazine's 2007 Franchise 500

Financial rating: $$$$

401 Jay St.
LaCrosse, WI 54601
(800)845-6779/(608)791-5516
www.kitchensolvers.com
Kitchen/bath remodeling & design
services, cabinet refacing,
flooring, closets
Began: 1982, Franchising: 1984
Headquarters size: 11 employees
Franchise department: 11 employees

U.S. franchises: 121
Canadian franchises: 3
Other foreign franchises: 0
Company-owned: 0

Seeking: All U.S.
Seeking in Canada? No
Exclusive territories? Yes
Homebased option? Yes
Employees needed to run biz: 1-2
Absentee ownership? No

COSTS
Total cost: $57.3K-114K
Franchise fee: $28K-31.8K
Royalty fee: 5%
Term of agreement: 10 years renewable
at no charge
Franchisees required to buy multiple
units? No

FINANCING
In-house: Franchise fee
3rd-party: Equipment, startup costs

QUALIFICATIONS
Net worth: $200K
Cash liquidity: $50K
Experience:
General business experience

TRAINING
At headquarters: 10 days

BUSINESS SUPPORT
Internet
Newsletter
Meetings
Toll-free phone line
Field operations/evaluations
Purchasing cooperatives

MARKETING SUPPORT
Co-op advertising
Ad slicks
National media campaign
Regional marketing

KITCHEN TUNE-UP

Ranked #302 in Entrepreneur Magazine's 2007 Franchise 500　　　*Financial rating: $$$$*

813 Circle Dr.
Aberdeen, SD 57401
(800)333-6385/(605)225-4049
www.kitchentuneup.com
Residential & commercial remodeling
Began: 1986, Franchising: 1988
Headquarters size: 14 employees
Franchise department: 12 employees

U.S. franchises: 292
Canadian franchises: 3
Other foreign franchises: 0
Company-owned: 0

Seeking: All U.S.
Seeking in Canada? Yes
Exclusive territories? Yes
Homebased option? Yes
Employees needed to run biz: 3
Absentee ownership? Yes

COSTS
Total cost: $79.5K-86.1K
Franchise fee: $25K
Royalty fee: 4.5-7%
Term of agreement: 10 years renewable
at no charge
Franchisees required to buy multiple
units? Outside the U.S. only

FINANCING
In-house: Equipment, inventory
3rd-party: Franchise fee, startup
costs

QUALIFICATIONS
Net worth: $150K
Cash liquidity: $45K-50K
Experience:
General business experience

TRAINING
At headquarters: 10 days
At franchisee's location: Varies
In-field training: 4 days
Acrylic tub training: 3 days

BUSINESS SUPPORT
Grand opening
Internet
Newsletter
Meetings
Toll-free phone line
Field operations/evaluations
Purchasing cooperatives

MARKETING SUPPORT
Co-op advertising
Ad slicks
National media campaign
Regional marketing
Internet advertising

OWENS CORNING BASEMENT FINISHING SYSTEM

Current financial data not available

One Owens Corning Pkwy.
Toledo, OH 43659
(419)248-5826
www.owenscorning.com
Basement finishing system
Began: 2000, Franchising: 2000
Headquarters size: 1,000 employees
Franchise department: 15 employees

U.S. franchises: 94
Canadian franchises: 0
Other foreign franchises: 0
Company-owned: 0

Seeking: All U.S.
Seeking in Canada? Yes
Exclusive territories? Yes
Homebased option? No
Employees needed to run biz: 20
Absentee ownership? No

COSTS
Total cost: $55.4K-156.7K
Franchise fee: $15K+
Royalty fee: 5%
Term of agreement: 5 years renewable
for $9K
Franchisees required to buy multiple
units? No

FINANCING
No financing available

QUALIFICATIONS
Cash liquidity: $150K
Experience:
Industry experience
General business experience
Marketing skills
General contracting license

TRAINING
At headquarters: 1 week
At franchisee's location: 1-3 days

BUSINESS SUPPORT
Internet
Meetings
Field operations/evaluations
Purchasing cooperatives

MARKETING SUPPORT
Co-op advertising
Ad slicks
National media campaign

THE OWNER/BUILDER NETWORK

Current financial data not available

1809 Goff Cove
Beebe, AR 72012
(281)798-5911
www.ownerbuildernetwork.com
Residential construction consulting
    services
Began: 1997, Franchising: 2005
Headquarters size: 20 employees
Franchise department: 4 employees

U.S. franchises: 10
Canadian franchises: 0
Other foreign franchises: 0
Company-owned: 4

Seeking: All U.S.
Seeking in Canada? No
Exclusive territories? Yes
Homebased option? No
Employees needed to run biz: 3
Absentee ownership? Yes

COSTS
Total cost: $51.4K-218.3K
Franchise fee: $5K-35K
Royalty fee: $400/mo.
Term of agreement: 5 years renewable
    for 50% of current fee
Franchisees required to buy multiple
    units? No

FINANCING
In-house: Franchise fee
3rd-party: Accounts receivable,
    equipment, franchise fee,
    inventory, payroll, startup costs

QUALIFICATIONS
Net worth: $100K
Cash liquidity: $50K
Experience:
    General business experience
    Marketing skills
    Sales skills

TRAINING
At headquarters: 1 week
At franchisee's location: 1 week
Field training: 2 weeks

BUSINESS SUPPORT
Grand opening
Internet
Newsletter
Meetings
Toll-free phone line
Field operations/evaluations
Lease negotiations
Purchasing cooperatives
Security/safety procedures

MARKETING SUPPORT
Ad slicks
National media campaign
Regional marketing

PRECISION CONCRETE CUTTING

Ranked #376 in Entrepreneur Magazine's 2007 Franchise 500   *Financial rating: $$$$*

3191 N. Canyon Rd.
Provo, UT 84604
(801)373-3990
www.pccfranchise.com
Trip-hazard removal
Began: 1991, Franchising: 2002
Headquarters size: 15 employees
Franchise department: 4 employees

U.S. franchises: 14
Canadian franchises: 0
Other foreign franchises: 0
Company-owned: 1

Seeking: All U.S.
Seeking in Canada? No
Exclusive territories? Yes
Homebased option? Yes
Employees needed to run biz: 3
Absentee ownership? Yes

COSTS
Total cost: $110K
Franchise fee: $45K
Royalty fee: 4%
Term of agreement: 10 years renewable
    for $1K
Franchisees required to buy multiple
    units? No

FINANCING
No financing available

QUALIFICATIONS
Net worth: $70K
Cash liquidity: $40K
Experience:
    General business experience
    Marketing skills

TRAINING
At headquarters: 1 week
At franchisee's location: 1 week

BUSINESS SUPPORT
Internet
Meetings
Toll-free phone line
Purchasing cooperatives
Security/safety procedures

MARKETING SUPPORT
Ad slicks
Regional marketing
Sales leads

READY DECKS FRANCHISE SYSTEMS INC.

Current financial data not available

1250 New Natchitoches Rd.
West Monroe, LA 71292
(318)362-9990
www.readydecks.com
Decking services
Began: 2001, Franchising: 2005
Headquarters size: 6 employees
Franchise department: 3 employees

U.S. franchises: 0
Canadian franchises: 0
Other foreign franchises: 0
Company-owned: 2

Seeking: All U.S.
Seeking in Canada? No
Exclusive territories? Yes
Homebased option? Yes
Employees needed to run biz: 2
Absentee ownership? No

COSTS
Total cost: $84K-168K
Franchise fee: $29K
Royalty fee: 5%
Term of agreement: 10 years renewable
    for $14.5K
Franchisees required to buy multiple
    units? Outside the U.S. only

FINANCING
In-house: None
3rd-party: Equipment, inventory,
    startup costs

QUALIFICATIONS
Net worth: $150K
Cash liquidity: $30K
Experience:
    General business experience

TRAINING
At headquarters: 2 weeks
At franchisee's location: 1 week

BUSINESS SUPPORT
Grand opening
Internet
Newsletter
Meetings
Toll-free phone line
Field operations/evaluations
Lease negotiations
Purchasing cooperatives
Security/safety procedures

MARKETING SUPPORT
Ad slicks
Regional marketing

SYSTEMS PAVING FRANCHISING INC.

Current financial data not available

1600 Dove St., #250
Newport Beach, CA 92660
(949)263-8300
www.systemspavingfranchise.com
Interlocking stone paving system
Began: 1992, Franchising: 2001
Headquarters size: 30 employees
Franchise department: 6 employees

U.S. franchises: 6
Canadian franchises: 0
Other foreign franchises: 0
Company-owned: 9

Seeking: All U.S.
Seeking in Canada? No
Exclusive territories? Yes
Homebased option? Yes
Employees needed to run biz: 1-5
Absentee ownership? No

COSTS
Total cost: $39.95K-120.8K
Franchise fee: $14.8K-17.8K
Royalty fee: 6%
Term of agreement: 10 years renewable
    for $500
Franchisees required to buy multiple
    units? No

FINANCING
No financing available

QUALIFICATIONS
Cash liquidity: $40K-100K
Experience:
    General business experience
    Sales & sales-management
    experience

TRAINING
At headquarters: 10-12 days
At franchisee's location: 10 days
Training available for new employees

BUSINESS SUPPORT
Internet
Newsletter
Meetings
Toll-free phone line

MARKETING SUPPORT
Co-op advertising
National media campaign
Regional marketing
Leads

UBUILDIT

Ranked #279 in Entrepreneur Magazine's 2007 Franchise 500   *Financial rating: $$$*

12006 98th Ave. N.E., #200
Kirkland, WA 98034
(800)992-4357/(425)821-6200
www.ubuildit.com
Construction consulting services
Began: 1988, Franchising: 1998
Headquarters size: 25 employees
Franchise department: 5 employees

U.S. franchises: 117
Canadian franchises: 0
Other foreign franchises: 0
Company-owned: 0

Seeking: All U.S.
Seeking in Canada? No
Exclusive territories? No
Homebased option? No
Employees needed to run biz: 3
Absentee ownership? No

COSTS
Total cost: $175K-275K
Franchise fee: $29.5K
Royalty fee: 5-8%
Term of agreement: 10 years renewable
   for $2K
Franchisees required to buy multiple
   units? No

FINANCING
In-house: None
3rd-party: Equipment, inventory,
   payroll, startup costs

QUALIFICATIONS
Net worth: $100K
Cash liquidity: $125K-250K
Experience:
   General business experience
   Marketing skills
   Sales skills

TRAINING
At headquarters: 2 weeks
Annual convention/training: 3 days

BUSINESS SUPPORT
Grand opening
Internet
Newsletter
Meetings
Toll-free phone line
Field operations/evaluations
Purchasing cooperatives

MARKETING SUPPORT
Co-op advertising
Ad slicks
Regional marketing

UNITED STATES SEAMLESS INC.

Ranked #438 in Entrepreneur Magazine's 2007 Franchise 500   *Financial rating: $$$$*

474 45th St. S., P.O. Box 2426
Fargo, ND 58103-2426
(701)241-8888
www.usseamless.com
Seamless steel siding, gutters, doors
Began: 1992, Franchising: 1992
Headquarters size: 6 employees
Franchise department: 6 employees

U.S. franchises: 82
Canadian franchises: 0
Other foreign franchises: 0
Company-owned: 0

Seeking: All U.S.
Seeking in Canada? No
Exclusive territories? Yes
Homebased option? Yes
Employees needed to run biz: 4
Absentee ownership? Yes

COSTS
Total cost: $44.5K-147K
Franchise fee: $8.5K
Royalty fee: Varies
Term of agreement: 15 years renewable
   at no charge
Franchisees required to buy multiple
   units? No

FINANCING
In-house: Equipment, franchise fee,
   startup costs
3rd-party: Accounts receivable,
   equipment, inventory, payroll,
   startup costs

QUALIFICATIONS
Cash liquidity: $4.5K-18.5K
Experience:
   Industry experience
   General business experience

TRAINING
At headquarters: Unlimited
Annual training

BUSINESS SUPPORT
Internet
Newsletter
Meetings
Toll-free phone line
Field operations/evaluations
Security/safety procedures

MARKETING SUPPORT
Ad slicks
Pitch books
Marketing literature
Promotional apparel

WOOD RE NEW

Financial rating: 0

220 S. Dysart
Springfield, MO 65802
(417)833-3303
www.woodrenew.com
Exterior wood restoration
Began: 1993, Franchising: 2001
Headquarters size: 11 employees
Franchise department: 4 employees

U.S. franchises: 21
Canadian franchises: 0
Other foreign franchises: 0
Company-owned: 1

Seeking: Midwest, South, Southeast
Seeking in Canada? No
Exclusive territories? Yes
Homebased option? Yes
Employees needed to run biz: 1
Absentee ownership? Yes

COSTS
Total cost: $50K
Franchise fee: $25K
Royalty fee: 4%
Term of agreement: 10 years renewable
   for $2.5K
Franchisees required to buy multiple
   units? No

FINANCING
No financing available

QUALIFICATIONS
Info not provided

TRAINING
At headquarters: 1 week
At franchisee's location: 1 week
Ongoing

BUSINESS SUPPORT
Internet
Newsletter
Meetings
Toll-free phone line
Field operations/evaluations

MARKETING SUPPORT
Info not provided

HOME　　　　*Decorating*

CHRISTMAS DECOR INC.

Ranked #291 in Entrepreneur Magazine's 2007 Franchise 500　　　*Financial rating: $$$$*

P.O. Box 5946
Lubbock, TX 79408-5946
(800)687-9551
www.christmasdecor.net
Holiday & event decorating services
Began: 1984, Franchising: 1996
Headquarters size: 24 employees
Franchise department: 20 employees

U.S. franchises: 345
Canadian franchises: 18
Other foreign franchises: 1
Company-owned: 0

Seeking: All U.S.
Seeking in Canada? Yes
Exclusive territories? Yes
Homebased option? Yes
Employees needed to run biz: 3-10
Absentee ownership? No

COSTS
Total cost: $16.95K-59.4K
Franchise fee: $8.5K-28.5K
Royalty fee: 5%
Term of agreement: 5 years renewable
   for $2K
Franchisees required to buy multiple
   units? No

FINANCING
In-house: Franchise fee
3rd-party: None

QUALIFICATIONS
Experience:
   General business experience

TRAINING
At headquarters: 4 days
At regional location: 4 days

BUSINESS SUPPORT
Internet
Newsletter
Meetings
Toll-free phone line
Purchasing cooperatives
Security/safety procedures

MARKETING SUPPORT
Co-op advertising
Ad slicks
National media campaign

DECOR & YOU INC.

Ranked #431 in Entrepreneur Magazine's 2007 Franchise 500   *Financial rating: 0*

900 Main St. S., Bldg. 2
Southbury, CT 06488
(203)264-3500
www.decorandyou.com
Interior decorating services &
    products
Began: 1994, Franchising: 1998
Headquarters size: 5 employees
Franchise department: 4 employees

U.S. franchises: 103
Canadian franchises: 0
Other foreign franchises: 0
Company-owned: 0

Seeking: All U.S.
Seeking in Canada? No
Exclusive territories? Yes
Homebased option? Yes
Employees needed to run biz: 0
Absentee ownership? No

COSTS
Total cost: $48K/132.2K
Franchise fee: $17K/75K
Royalty fee: 10%
Term of agreement: 10 years renewable
    for 10% of franchise fee
Franchisees required to buy multiple
    units? No

FINANCING
No financing available

QUALIFICATIONS
Net worth: $50K
Cash liquidity: $50K+
Experience:
    General business skills
    Marketing skills
    Interest in decorating

TRAINING
At headquarters: 12 days
At franchisee's location: As needed
By phone
Seminars & conferences
Virtual classes

BUSINESS SUPPORT
Grand opening
Meetings
Field operations/evaluations
Purchasing cooperatives

MARKETING SUPPORT
Ad slicks
Regional marketing

INTERIORS BY DECORATING DEN

Ranked #98 in Entrepreneur Magazine's 2007 Franchise 500   *Financial rating: $$$$*

8659 Commerce Dr.
Easton, MD 21601
(410)822-9001
www.decoratingden.com
Interior decorating services &
    products
Began: 1969, Franchising: 1970
Headquarters size: 38 employees
Franchise department: 6 employees

U.S. franchises: 471
Canadian franchises: 31
Other foreign franchises: 0
Company-owned: 0

Seeking: All U.S.
Seeking in Canada? Yes
Exclusive territories? Yes
Homebased option? Yes
Employees needed to run biz: 0
Absentee ownership? No

COSTS
Total cost: $49.9K
Franchise fee: $29.9K
Royalty fee: 7-9%
Term of agreement: 10 years renewable
    at no charge
Franchisees required to buy multiple
    units? No

FINANCING
No financing available

QUALIFICATIONS
Net worth: $50K
Cash liquidity: $40K
Experience:
    General business experience
    Decorating skills
    People skills

TRAINING
At headquarters: 2 weeks
At franchisee's location: Ongoing

BUSINESS SUPPORT
Grand opening
Internet
Newsletter
Meetings
Toll-free phone line
Purchasing cooperatives

MARKETING SUPPORT
Co-op advertising
Ad slicks
National media campaign
Regional marketing

GROUT DOCTOR GLOBAL FRANCHISE CORP.

Financial rating: $$$

7923 E. Palm Ln.
Mesa, AZ 85207
(877)476-8800
www.groutdoctor.com
Ceramic tile grout repair &
    maintenance
Began: 1994, Franchising: 2001
Headquarters size: 8 employees
Franchise department: 6 employees

U.S. franchises: 49
Canadian franchises: 0
Other foreign franchises: 0
Company-owned: 0

Seeking: All U.S.
Seeking in Canada? No
Exclusive territories? Yes
Homebased option? Yes
Employees needed to run biz: 0
Absentee ownership? Yes

COSTS
Total cost: $16K-29.9K
Franchise fee: $13K-19K
Royalty fee: Varies
Term of agreement: 7 years
    renewable for $500
Franchisees required to buy
    multiple units? No

FINANCING
No financing available

QUALIFICATIONS
Cash liquidity: $16K-29.9K

TRAINING
In Phoenix & Chicago: 50 hours

BUSINESS SUPPORT
Grand opening
Internet
Newsletter
Meetings
Toll-free phone line
Field operations/evaluations
Purchasing cooperatives
Security/safety procedures

MARKETING SUPPORT
Co-op advertising
Ad slicks
Regional marketing
Teleconferences
Intranet support
Marketing materials & plans
Vendor discounts
R&D
Trade show signage

THE GROUT MEDIC

Financial rating: $$$

1585 Beverly Court, #111
Aurora, IL 60502
(800)700-1411
www.thegroutmedic.com
Tile/grout maintenance, repair &
    restoration
Began: 1997, Franchising: 2001
Headquarters size: 4 employees
Franchise department: 4 employees

U.S. franchises: 45
Canadian franchises: 0
Other foreign franchises: 0
Company-owned: 0

Seeking: All U.S.
Seeking in Canada? Yes
Exclusive territories? Yes
Homebased option? Yes
Employees needed to run biz: 2-3
Absentee ownership? Yes

COSTS
Total cost: $23.3K-34.7K
Franchise fee: $17.2K
Royalty fee: $220-970/mo.
Term of agreement: 12 years renewable
    at no charge
Franchisees required to buy multiple
    units? No

FINANCING
No financing available

QUALIFICATIONS
Net worth: $20K
Cash liquidity: $20K
Experience:
    General business experience

TRAINING
At headquarters: 5 days

BUSINESS SUPPORT
Grand opening
Internet
Newsletter
Meetings
Toll-free phone line
Field operations/evaluations
Purchasing cooperatives
Security/safety procedures

MARKETING SUPPORT
Co-op advertising
Ad slicks
Trade show materials & banners

GROUT WIZARD

Current financial data not available

1056 El Capitan Dr.
Danville, CA 94526
(925)866-5000/(925)314-0369
www.groutwizard.com
Grout cleaning & restoration
Began: 1997, Franchising: 2001
Headquarters size: 2 employees
Franchise department: 1 employee

U.S. franchises: 6
Canadian franchises: 0
Other foreign franchises: 0
Company-owned: 1

Seeking: All U.S.
Seeking in Canada? No
Exclusive territories? Yes
Homebased option? Yes
Employees needed to run biz: 2-4
Absentee ownership? No

COSTS
Total cost: $15.6K-25.2K
Franchise fee: $12.5K
Royalty fee: 5%
Term of agreement: 5 years
    renewable at no charge
Franchisees required to buy
    multiple units? No

FINANCING
In-house: Franchise fee
3rd-party: None

QUALIFICATIONS
Experience:
    General business experience
    Marketing skills

TRAINING
At headquarters: 1 week+

BUSINESS SUPPORT
Internet
Meetings
Field operations/evaluations
Security/safety procedures

MARKETING SUPPORT
Ad slicks

HOME ▶ *Organizing*

CLOSET & STORAGE CONCEPTS

Ranked #388 in Entrepreneur Magazine's 2007 Franchise 500   *Financial rating: $$$*

1000 Laurel Oak Corp. Ctr., #208
Voorhees, NJ 08043
(856)627-5700
www.closetandstorageconcepts.com
Residential/commercial closet &
    storage systems
Began: 1987, Franchising: 2000
Headquarters size: 22 employees
Franchise department: 7 employees

U.S. franchises: 25
Canadian franchises: 0
Other foreign franchises: 0
Company-owned: 1

Seeking: All U.S.
Seeking in Canada? Yes
Exclusive territories? Yes
Homebased option? No
Employees needed to run biz: 10-12
Absentee ownership? No

COSTS
Total cost: $155K
Franchise fee: $40K
Royalty fee: 5%
Term of agreement: 10 years renewable
    for lesser of inital or current fee
Franchisees required to buy multiple
    units? No

FINANCING
In-house: None
3rd-party: Accounts receivable,
    equipment, franchise fee,
    inventory, payroll, startup costs

QUALIFICATIONS
Net worth: $100K
Cash liquidity: $50K
Experience:
    General business experience
    Marketing skills
    Strong sales background

TRAINING
At headquarters: 2 weeks
At franchisee's location: 2 weeks

BUSINESS SUPPORT
Grand opening
Internet
Newsletter
Meetings
Toll-free phone line
Field operations/evaluations
Lease negotiations
Purchasing cooperatives
Security/safety procedures

MARKETING SUPPORT
Co-op advertising
Ad slicks
National media campaign
Regional marketing
In-house graphics department

CLOSETS BY DESIGN FRANCHISING
Ranked #481 in Entrepreneur Magazine's 2007 Franchise 500   *Financial rating: $$$$*

11145 Knott Ave., #A
Cypress, CA 90630
(800)377-5737/(714)890-5860
www.closets-by-design.com
Custom closet & home/office
    organization systems
Began: 1982, Franchising: 1998
Headquarters size: 120 employees
Franchise department: 12 employees

U.S. franchises: 34
Canadian franchises: 0
Other foreign franchises: 0
Company-owned: 4

Seeking: All U.S.
Seeking in Canada? Yes
Exclusive territories? Yes
Homebased option? No
Employees needed to run biz: 5
Absentee ownership? No

COSTS
Total cost: $98.5K-340.9K
Franchise fee: $24.5K-39.9K
Royalty fee: 6%
Term of agreement: 5 years renewable
    for up to $5K
Franchisees required to buy multiple
    units? No

FINANCING
In-house: Franchise fee
3rd-party: Accounts receivable,
    equipment, inventory, payroll,
    startup costs

QUALIFICATIONS
Cash liquidity: $50K-80K
Experience:
    General business experience
    Marketing skills

TRAINING
At headquarters: 3 weeks
At franchisee's location: 3 weeks

BUSINESS SUPPORT
Grand opening
Internet
Newsletter
Meetings
Toll-free phone line
Field operations/evaluations
Purchasing cooperatives
Security/safety procedures

MARKETING SUPPORT
Co-op advertising
Ad slicks
National media campaign
Regional marketing
In-house art department

CLUTTERBUSTERS

Financial rating: $$$

15521 Grinnell Terrace
Derwood, MD 20855
(301)309-9614
www.clutterbusters.com
Professional organizing
Began: 2002, Franchising: 2005
Headquarters size: 3 employees
Franchise department: 3 employees

U.S. franchises: 0
Canadian franchises: 0
Other foreign franchises: 0
Company-owned: 1

Seeking: All U.S.
Seeking in Canada? No
Exclusive territories? Yes
Homebased option? Yes
Employees needed to run biz: 1
Absentee ownership? No

COSTS
Total cost: $45.7K-73.5K
Franchise fee: $25K
Royalty fee: 8%
Term of agreement: 5 years renewable
    at no charge
Franchisees required to buy multiple
    units? No

FINANCING
In-house: None
3rd-party: Accounts receivable,
    equipment, franchise fee,
    inventory, payroll, startup costs

QUALIFICATIONS
Net worth: $100K
Cash liquidity: $100K
Experience:
    General business experience
    Marketing skills

TRAINING
At headquarters: 5 days+
At franchisee's location: 2 days+

BUSINESS SUPPORT
Grand opening
Internet
Newsletter
Meetings
Toll-free phone line
Field operations/evaluations

MARKETING SUPPORT
Co-op advertising
Ad slicks
Regional marketing
Proprietary software
Web lead generation
Individual web pages

THE COMPLETE GARAGE

Financial rating: $$$

2814 Hedberg Dr.
Minnetonka, MN 55305
(952)931-0416
www.completegarage.com
Garage flooring & organization
   systems
Began: 2002, Franchising: 2003
Headquarters size: 12 employees
Franchise department: 4 employees

U.S. franchises: 12
Canadian franchises: 0
Other foreign franchises: 1
Company-owned: 2

Seeking: All U.S.
Seeking in Canada? Yes
Exclusive territories? Yes
Homebased option? No
Employees needed to run biz: 3
Absentee ownership? Yes

COSTS
Total cost: $186.8K-265.6K
Franchise fee: $50K
Royalty fee: 6%
Term of agreement: 10 years
   renewable for $5K
Franchisees required to buy
   multiple units? No

FINANCING
No financing available

QUALIFICATIONS
Net worth: $800K
Cash liquidity: $400K
Experience:
   General business experience
   Marketing skills

TRAINING
At headquarters: 1 week
At franchisee's location: 1 week

BUSINESS SUPPORT
Grand opening
Internet
Meetings
Toll-free phone line
Field operations/evaluations
Purchasing cooperatives
Security/safety procedures

MARKETING SUPPORT
Co-op advertising
Ad slicks
National media campaign
Regional marketing

HOUSEWALL GARAGE SYSTEM

Financial rating: 0

8100 W. 30th Ct.
Hialeah, FL 33018
(305)817-9881
www.housewall.com
Garage organization systems
Began: 2002, Franchising: 2006
Headquarters size: 35 employees
Franchise department: 2 employees

U.S. franchises: 7
Canadian franchises: 0
Other foreign franchises: 0
Company-owned: 1

Seeking: Midwest, Northeast, South,
   Southeast, Southwest
Seeking in Canada? No
Exclusive territories? Yes
Homebased option? No
Employees needed to run biz: 4
Absentee ownership? No

COSTS
Total cost: $136K-168K
Franchise fee: $15K+
Royalty fee: 6-5.5%
Term of agreement: 10 years renewable
   for then current franchise fee
Franchisees required to buy multiple
   units? No

FINANCING
In-house: Franchise fee
3rd-party: Equipment, franchise fee,
   inventory, startup costs

QUALIFICATIONS
Net worth: $250K
Cash liquidity: $65K
Experience:
   General business experience
   Marketing skills

TRAINING
At headquarters: 1 week

BUSINESS SUPPORT
Internet
Meetings
Toll-free phone line
Field operations/evaluations
Security/safety procedures

MARKETING SUPPORT
Co-op advertising
Advertising & marketing programs

PREMIERGARAGE

Ranked #208 in Entrepreneur Magazine's 2007 Franchise 500

Financial rating: $$$$

1616 W. Williams Dr.
Phoenix, AZ 85027
(866)483-4272/(480)483-3030
www.premiergarage.com
Garage cabinetry, floor coatings,
    organizers
Began: 1999, Franchising: 2002
Headquarters size: 45 employees
Franchise department: 13 employees

U.S. franchises: 77
Canadian franchises: 6
Other foreign franchises: 0
Company-owned: 1

Seeking: All U.S.
Seeking in Canada? Yes
Exclusive territories? Yes
Homebased option? No
Employees needed to run biz: Info
    not provided
Absentee ownership? No

COSTS

Total cost: $133K-408K
Franchise fee: $35K-75K
Royalty fee: $3.5K-7.5K/yr.
Term of agreement: 5 years renewable
    at no charge
Franchisees required to buy multiple
    units? No

FINANCING

In-house: None
3rd-party: Accounts receivable,
    equipment, franchise fee,
    inventory, payroll, startup costs

QUALIFICATIONS

Net worth: $250K
Cash liquidity: $100K
Experience:
    General business experience

TRAINING

At headquarters: 2 weeks

BUSINESS SUPPORT

Internet
Meetings
Toll-free phone line
Field operations/evaluations
Security/safety procedures

MARKETING SUPPORT

Ad slicks
Brochures & all printed materials

HOME ◄ *Painting*

CERTAPRO PAINTERS LTD.

Ranked #86 in Entrepreneur Magazine's 2007 Franchise 500

Financial rating: $$$$

P.O. Box 836
Oaks, PA 19456
(800)462-3782
www.certapro-franchise.com
Residential & commercial painting
Began: 1992, Franchising: 1992
Headquarters size: 40 employees
Franchise department: 15 employees

U.S. franchises: 317
Canadian franchises: 24
Other foreign franchises: 5
Company-owned: 0

Seeking: All U.S.
Seeking in Canada? No
Exclusive territories? Yes
Homebased option? Yes
Employees needed to run biz: Info
    not provided
Absentee ownership? No

COSTS

Total cost: $113K-123K
Franchise fee: $40K
Royalty fee: 5%
Term of agreement: 10 years renewable
    for 10% of current franchise fee
Franchisees required to buy multiple
    units? No

FINANCING

In-house: None
3rd-party: Equipment, franchise fee,
    startup costs

QUALIFICATIONS

Experience:
    General business experience

TRAINING

At headquarters: 2 weeks
At franchisee's location: 1 week
Additional training available

BUSINESS SUPPORT

Grand opening
Internet
Newsletter
Meetings
Toll-free phone line
Field operations/evaluations
Purchasing cooperatives
Security/safety procedures

MARKETING SUPPORT

Co-op advertising
Ad slicks
National media campaign
Regional marketing
Local marketing materials & support
National & local PR

COLORCHEF CUSTOM PAINTERS

Financial rating: $$$

1035 Virginia Dr., #202
Fort Washington, PA 19034
(888)945-4350
www.colorchef.com
Residential & commercial painting
Began: 1980, Franchising: 2006
Headquarters size: 6 employees

U.S. franchises: 0
Canadian franchises: 0
Other foreign franchises: 0
Company-owned: 1

Seeking: Northeast, Southeast
Seeking in Canada? No
Exclusive territories? Yes
Homebased option? Yes
Employees needed to run biz: 5
Absentee ownership? Yes

COSTS
Total cost: $121.3K-162.5K
Franchise fee: $25K
Royalty fee: 8%
Term of agreement: 5 years
Franchisees required to buy multiple
    units? No

FINANCING
In-house: None
3rd-party: Equipment, franchise fee,
    inventory, startup costs

QUALIFICATIONS
Net worth: $80K
Cash liquidity: $25K

TRAINING
At headquarters: 3 weeks

BUSINESS SUPPORT
Grand opening
Internet
Newsletter
Meetings
Toll-free phone line
Field operations/evaluations
Purchasing cooperatives
Security/safety procedures

MARKETING SUPPORT
Co-op advertising
Ad slicks
Regional marketing

FRESH COAT

Financial rating: $$$

10700 Montgomery Rd., #300
Cincinnati, OH 45242
(800)317-7089
www.freshcoatpainters.com
Interior painting
Began: 2005, Franchising: 2005
Headquarters size: 35 employees
Franchise department: 35 employees

U.S. franchises: 35
Canadian franchises: 1
Other foreign franchises: 0
Company-owned: 0

Seeking: All U.S.
Seeking in Canada? Yes
Exclusive territories? Yes
Homebased option? Yes
Employees needed to run biz: 2
Absentee ownership? Yes

COSTS
Total cost: $26.4K-47.9K
Franchise fee: $18.9K
Royalty fee: 6%
Term of agreement: 10 years renewable
    at no charge
Franchisees required to buy multiple
    units? Outside the U.S. only

FINANCING
In-house: Franchise fee
3rd-party: None

QUALIFICATIONS
Net worth: $26K
Cash liquidity: $9.5K

TRAINING
At headquarters: 5 days
Meetings
Sales boot camps

BUSINESS SUPPORT
Grand opening
Internet
Newsletter
Meetings
Toll-free phone line
Purchasing cooperatives
Security/safety procedures

MARKETING SUPPORT
Co-op advertising
Ad slicks
National media campaign

360 PAINTING INC.

Financial rating: $$

1940 Duke St., #200
Alexandria, VA 22314
(866)997-2468
www.360painting.com
Residential & commercial painting
Began: 2005, Franchising: 2006
Headquarters size: 3 employees
Franchise department: 3 employees

U.S. franchises: 0
Canadian franchises: 0
Other foreign franchises: 0
Company-owned: 1

Seeking: All U.S.
Seeking in Canada? Yes
Exclusive territories? Yes
Homebased option? Yes
Employees needed to run biz: 6
Absentee ownership? Yes

COSTS
Total cost: $60.4K-109.5K
Franchise fee: $35K
Royalty fee: 3-5%
Term of agreement: 5 years renewable
    for 10% of current franchise fee
Franchisees required to buy multiple
    units? No

FINANCING
In-house: None
3rd-party: Accounts receivable,
    equipment, franchise fee,
    inventory, payroll, startup costs

QUALIFICATIONS
Experience:
    General business experience

TRAINING
At headquarters: 5 days
At franchisee's location: 5 days
Additional training as needed

BUSINESS SUPPORT
Grand opening
Internet
Newsletter
Meetings
Toll-free phone line
Field operations/evaluations
Purchasing cooperatives
Security/safety procedures

MARKETING SUPPORT
Ad slicks
National media campaign
Regional marketing
Website
Lawn signs

HOME ◀ *Surface Refinishing & Restoration*

MIRACLE METHOD SURFACE RESTORATION
Ranked #297 in Entrepreneur Magazine's 2007 Franchise 500

Financial rating: $$$$

4239 N. Nevada, #115
Colorado Springs, CO 80907
(800)444-8827/(719)594-9196
www.miraclemethod.com
Bathtub, sink, countertop & tile
    repair/refinishing
Began: 1977, Franchising: 1980
Headquarters size: 4 employees
Franchise department: 4 employees

U.S. franchises: 95
Canadian franchises: 0
Other foreign franchises: 22
Company-owned: 0

Seeking: All U.S.
Seeking in Canada? Yes
Exclusive territories? Yes
Homebased option? Yes
Employees needed to run biz: 1-6
Absentee ownership? Yes

COSTS
Total cost: $45K
Franchise fee: $24K
Royalty fee: 5%
Term of agreement: 5 years
    renewable
Franchisees required to buy multiple
    units? Outside the U.S. only

FINANCING
In-house: Franchise fee
3rd-party: None

QUALIFICATIONS
Net worth: $50K
Cash liquidity: $30K
Experience:
    General business experience
    Marketing skills

TRAINING
At headquarters: 2 weeks

BUSINESS SUPPORT
Internet
Newsletter
Meetings
Toll-free phone line
Field operations/evaluations
Purchasing cooperatives
Security/safety procedures

MARKETING SUPPORT
Co-op advertising
Ad slicks
National media campaign
Regional marketing

MR. SANDLESS INC.

Financial rating: 0

2970 Concord Rd.
Aston, PA 19014
(610)364-2080
www.mrsandless.com
Sandless wood floor refinishing
Began: 2004, Franchising: 2005
Headquarters size: 12 employees
Franchise department: 2 employees

U.S. franchises: 1
Canadian franchises: 1
Other foreign franchises: 0
Company-owned: 15

Seeking: All U.S.
Seeking in Canada? Yes
Exclusive territories? Yes
Homebased option? Yes
Employees needed to run biz: 2
Absentee ownership? Yes

COSTS
Total cost: $25K-45K
Franchise fee: $10K
Royalty fee: 5%
Term of agreement: 10 years renewable
  for $3K
Franchisees required to buy multiple
  units? No

FINANCING
In-house: Equipment, franchise fee,
  inventory, startup costs
3rd-party: None

QUALIFICATIONS
Experience:
  General business experience

TRAINING
At headquarters: 1 week

BUSINESS SUPPORT
Grand opening
Internet
Newsletter
Meetings

MARKETING SUPPORT
Info not provided

N-HANCE

Ranked #194 in Entrepreneur Magazine's 2007 Franchise 500

Financial rating: $$$$

1530 N. 1000 West
Logan, UT 84321
(435)755-0099
www.nhancefranchise.com
Wood floor & cabinet renewal
  systems
Began: 2001, Franchising: 2003
Headquarters size: 70 employees
Franchise department: 7 employees

U.S. franchises: 129
Canadian franchises: 0
Other foreign franchises: 0
Company-owned: 0

Seeking: All U.S.
Seeking in Canada? No
Exclusive territories? Yes
Homebased option? Yes
Employees needed to run biz: 2
Absentee ownership? No

COSTS
Total cost: $31K-94.2K
Franchise fee: Varies
Royalty fee: $220-660/mo.
Term of agreement: 5 years renewable
Franchisees required to buy multiple
  units? No

FINANCING
In-house: Equipment, franchise fee
3rd-party: None

QUALIFICATIONS
Net worth: $27.5K-90.7K
Cash liquidity: $10K

TRAINING
At headquarters: 1 week
At franchisee's location: As needed

BUSINESS SUPPORT
Internet
Newsletter
Meetings
Toll-free phone line

MARKETING SUPPORT
Ad slicks

RE-BATH LLC
Ranked #259 in Entrepreneur Magazine's 2007 Franchise 500

Financial rating: $$$$

1055 S. Country Club Dr., Bldg. 2
Mesa, AZ 85210-4613
(800)426-4573/(480)844-1575
www.re-bath.com
Acrylic liners for bathtubs, showers
   & walls
Began: 1979, Franchising: 1991
Headquarters size: 13 employees
Franchise department: 3 employees

U.S. franchises: 157
Canadian franchises: 7
Other foreign franchises: 2
Company-owned: 0

Seeking: All U.S.
Seeking in Canada? Yes
Exclusive territories? Yes
Homebased option? No
Employees needed to run biz: 3-5
Absentee ownership? No

COSTS
Total cost: $35.6K-256K
Franchise fee: $3.5K-40K
Royalty fee: $25/liner
Term of agreement: 5 years renewable
   for $1K
Franchisees required to buy multiple
   units? No

FINANCING
In-house: None
3rd-party: Equipment, franchise fee,
   startup costs

QUALIFICATIONS
Net worth: $250K
Cash liquidity: $100K
Experience:
   Industry experience
   General business experience
   Marketing skills

TRAINING
At headquarters: 9 days
At franchisee's location: As needed
Sales training: 3 days

BUSINESS SUPPORT
Grand opening
Internet
Newsletter
Meetings
Toll-free phone line
Field operations/evaluations
Lease negotiations
Purchasing cooperatives

MARKETING SUPPORT
Co-op advertising
Ad slicks
National media campaign
Regional marketing

SANDFREE INC.

Current financial data not available

116 Cricket Ave.
Ardmore, PA 19003
(888)202-3794
www.sandfree.com
Wood floor refinishing
Began: 2001, Franchising: 2002
Headquarters size: 14 employees
Franchise department: 2 employees

U.S. franchises: 2
Canadian franchises: 1
Other foreign franchises: 0
Company-owned: 1

Seeking: All U.S.
Seeking in Canada? No
Exclusive territories? Info not
   provided
Homebased option? Yes
Employees needed to run biz: 3
Absentee ownership? Yes

COSTS
Total cost: $48.5K
Franchise fee: $20K
Royalty fee: 5%
Term of agreement: 10 years renewable
   at no charge
Franchisees required to buy multiple
   units? No

FINANCING
In-house: Franchise fee
3rd-party: Accounts receivable,
   equipment, inventory, payroll,
   startup costs

QUALIFICATIONS
Experience:
   General business experience

TRAINING
At headquarters: 3 days+

BUSINESS SUPPORT
Internet
Newsletter
Toll-free phone line
Field operations/evaluations
Purchasing cooperatives

MARKETING SUPPORT
Co-op advertising
Ad slicks
National media campaign
Regional marketing
Trade show supplies

SURFACE SPECIALISTS SYSTEMS INC.

Financial rating: $

621-B Stallings Rd.
Matthews, NC 28105
(866)239-8707
www.surfacespecialists.com
Kitchen/bath repair, refinishing &
    resurfacing, acrylic tub liners
Began: 1981, Franchising: 1982
Headquarters size: 3 employees
Franchise department: 1 employee

U.S. franchises: 44
Canadian franchises: 1
Other foreign franchises: 0
Company-owned: 0

Seeking: All U.S.
Seeking in Canada? Yes
Exclusive territories? Yes
Homebased option? Yes
Employees needed to run biz: 2-3
Absentee ownership? No

COSTS
Total cost: $26.8K-37.5K
Franchise fee: $21K
Royalty fee: 5%
Term of agreement: 10 years renewable
    at no charge
Franchisees required to buy multiple
    units? No

FINANCING
In-house: Franchise fee
3rd-party: None

QUALIFICATIONS
Net worth: $75K
Cash liquidity: $25K
Experience:
    Industry experience
    General business experience
    Marketing skills

TRAINING
At headquarters: 3 weeks
At franchisee's location: Follow-up
    training

BUSINESS SUPPORT
Internet
Newsletter
Meetings
Toll-free phone line
Purchasing cooperatives
Security/safety procedures

MARKETING SUPPORT
Ad slicks
Manual

HOME *Tech*

AUDIO/VIDEO HANDYMAN

Current financial data not available

9548-D Mt. Holly/Huntersville Rd.
Huntersville, NC 28078
(888)812-5085
www.audiovideohandyman.com
Audio/video & home theater
    equipment sales & installation
Began: 2003, Franchising: 2005
Headquarters size: 4 employees
Franchise department: 4 employees

U.S. franchises: 1
Canadian franchises: 0
Other foreign franchises: 0
Company-owned: 2

Seeking: All U.S.
Seeking in Canada? Yes
Exclusive territories? Yes
Homebased option? Yes
Employees needed to run biz: 2-3
Absentee ownership? Yes

COSTS
Total cost: $11K-31.9K
Franchise fee: $6K-8K
Royalty fee: $300/mo.
Term of agreement: 5 years renewable
    for $1.5K
Franchisees required to buy multiple
    units? No

FINANCING
In-house: Franchise fee
3rd-party: None

QUALIFICATIONS
Cash liquidity: $10K-25K
Experience:
    General business experience
    Marketing skills

TRAINING
At headquarters: 5 days
Regional training: 5 days

BUSINESS SUPPORT
Internet
Newsletter
Meetings
Toll-free phone line
Purchasing cooperatives
Security/safety procedures

MARKETING SUPPORT
Ad slicks
National media campaign
Regional marketing

THEATER XTREME

Financial rating: $$

250 Corporate Blvd., #E
Newark, DE 19702
(302)455-1334
www.theaterxtreme.com
Home theaters & furnishings
Began: 2003, Franchising: 2004
Headquarters size: 15 employees
Franchise department: 5 employees

U.S. franchises: 6
Canadian franchises: 0
Other foreign franchises: 0
Company-owned: 5

Seeking: Northeast
Seeking in Canada? Yes
Exclusive territories? Yes
Homebased option? No
Employees needed to run biz: 5
Absentee ownership? Yes

COSTS
Total cost: $400K-700K
Franchise fee: $40K
Royalty fee: 4%
Term of agreement: 10 years renewable
    for 50% of original franchise fee
Franchisees required to buy multiple
    units? No

FINANCING
In-house: None
3rd-party: Accounts receivable,
    equipment, franchise fee,
    inventory, payroll, startup costs

QUALIFICATIONS
Net worth: $500K
Cash liquidity: $200K
Experience:
    General business experience
    Marketing skills

TRAINING
At headquarters: 2 weeks
At franchisee's location
Ongoing

BUSINESS SUPPORT
Grand opening
Internet
Newsletter
Meetings
Field operations/evaluations
Lease negotiations
Purchasing cooperatives
Security/safety procedures

MARKETING SUPPORT
Co-op advertising
Ad slicks

HOME   *Windows & Floors*

BLIND BROKERS NETWORK

Current financial data not available

9 Orchard, #103
Lake Forest, CA 92630
(949)768-6695
www.myblindbiz.com
Discount blinds, shades, shutters
Began: 1986, Franchising: 2006
Headquarters size: 3 employees
Franchise department: 3 employees

U.S. franchises: 26
Canadian franchises: 0
Other foreign franchises: 0
Company-owned: 0

Seeking: All U.S.
Seeking in Canada? No
Exclusive territories? No
Homebased option? Yes
Employees needed to run biz: 1
Absentee ownership? Yes

COSTS
Total cost: $9.4K-24.3K
Franchise fee: $5.99K
Royalty fee: 0
Term of agreement: Info not provided
Franchisees required to buy multiple
    units? No

FINANCING
No financing available

QUALIFICATIONS
Net worth: $10K
Cash liquidity: $10K

TRAINING
At headquarters: 3 days
By phone
Vendor training

BUSINESS SUPPORT
Grand opening
Internet
Newsletter
Toll-free phone line
Field operations/evaluations
Purchasing cooperatives
Security/safety procedures

MARKETING SUPPORT
Ad slicks

BUDGET BLINDS INC.

Ranked #29 in Entrepreneur Magazine's 2007 Franchise 500   *Financial rating: $$$$*

1927 N. Glassell St.
Orange, CA 92865
(800)420-5374
www.budgetblinds.com
Window coverings
Began: 1992, Franchising: 1994
Headquarters size: 86 employees
Franchise department: 7 employees

U.S. franchises: 1,062
Canadian franchises: 25
Other foreign franchises: 3
Company-owned: 3

Seeking: All U.S.
Seeking in Canada? Yes
Exclusive territories? Yes
Homebased option? Yes
Employees needed to run biz: 1-3
Absentee ownership? No

COSTS
Total cost: $79.7K-111.1K
Franchise fee: $24.9K
Royalty fee: Varies
Term of agreement: 10 years renewable
    for $5K
Franchisees required to buy multiple
    units? No

FINANCING
In-house: Franchise fee
3rd-party: None

QUALIFICATIONS
Cash liquidity: $54.7K-86.1K
Experience:
    Industry experience
    Marketing skills

TRAINING
At headquarters: 2 weeks
At franchisee's location: Optional
Ongoing

BUSINESS SUPPORT
Internet
Newsletter
Meetings
Toll-free phone line
Field operations/evaluations

MARKETING SUPPORT
Co-op advertising
Ad slicks
National media campaign
Regional marketing

CARPET NETWORK

Financial rating: 0

109 Gaither Dr., #302
Mt. Laurel, NJ 08054
(800)428-1067/(856)273-9393
www.carpetnetwork.com
Mobile floor coverings & window
    treatments
Began: 1991, Franchising: 1992
Headquarters size: 5 employees
Franchise department: 2 employees

U.S. franchises: 35
Canadian franchises: 0
Other foreign franchises: 0
Company-owned: 0

Seeking: All U.S.
Seeking in Canada? No
Exclusive territories? Yes
Homebased option? Yes
Employees needed to run biz: 0
Absentee ownership? No

COSTS
Total cost: $42.6K-63.7K
Franchise fee: $24.5K
Royalty fee: 7-2%
Term of agreement: 15 years renewable
    at no charge
Franchisees required to buy multiple
    units? No

FINANCING
In-house: Franchise fee
3rd-party: None

QUALIFICATIONS
Net worth: $100K
Experience:
    General business experience
    Must enjoy working with people

TRAINING
At headquarters: 6 days
At franchisee's location: Ongoing

BUSINESS SUPPORT
Internet
Newsletter
Meetings
Toll-free phone line
Purchasing cooperatives

MARKETING SUPPORT
Ad slicks
National media campaign

GOTCHA COVERED

Ranked #425 in Entrepreneur Magazine's 2007 Franchise 500   *Financial rating: $$*

1611 N. Stemmons Fwy., #318
Carrollton, TX 75006
(972)466-2544
www.gotchacoveredfranchise.com
Blinds, shades, shutters, draperies
Began: 1995, Franchising: 1999
Headquarters size: 14 employees
Franchise department: 8 employees

U.S. franchises: 128
Canadian franchises: 0
Other foreign franchises: 0
Company-owned: 0

Seeking: All U.S.
Seeking in Canada? No
Exclusive territories? Yes
Homebased option? Yes
Employees needed to run biz: 1-5
Absentee ownership? Yes

COSTS
Total cost: $98.3K-146.2K
Franchise fee: $24.95K
Royalty fee: $300-1.1K/mo.
Term of agreement: 10 years renewable
    for $1K
Franchisees required to buy multiple
    units? No

FINANCING
In-house: Franchise fee
3rd-party: Accounts receivable,
    equipment, franchise fee,
    inventory, payroll, startup costs

QUALIFICATIONS
Net worth: $150K
Cash liquidity: $30K
Experience:
    General business experience
    Marketing skills
    People skills

TRAINING
At headquarters: 2 weeks
At franchisee's location: 19 weeks
Annual seminar
Trimester business development
    review

BUSINESS SUPPORT
Grand opening
Internet
Newsletter
Meetings
Toll-free phone line
Field operations/evaluations
Lease negotiations
Purchasing cooperatives
Security/safety procedures

MARKETING SUPPORT
Co-op advertising
Ad slicks
National media campaign
Regional marketing

NATIONWIDE FLOOR & WINDOW COVERINGS

Financial rating: $$$

111 E. Kilbourn Ave., #2400
Milwaukee, WI 53202
(800)366-8088
www.floorsandwindows.com
Mobile floor & window coverings
Began: 1992, Franchising: 1992
Headquarters size: 14 employees
Franchise department: 3 employees

U.S. franchises: 68
Canadian franchises: 4
Other foreign franchises: 0
Company-owned: 0

Seeking: All U.S.
Seeking in Canada? Yes
Exclusive territories? Yes
Homebased option? Yes
Employees needed to run biz: 1-2
Absentee ownership? No

COSTS
Total cost: $59.9K-129.8K
Franchise fee: $25K-55K
Royalty fee: 5-1%
Term of agreement: 10 years renewable
    at no charge
Franchisees required to buy multiple
    units? No

FINANCING
In-house: None
3rd-party: Accounts receivable,
    equipment, franchise fee,
    inventory, payroll, startup costs

QUALIFICATIONS
Net worth: $100K
Cash liquidity: $50K
Experience:
    General business experience
    Marketing skills

TRAINING
At headquarters: 2 weeks
At franchisee's location: 6 weeks

BUSINESS SUPPORT
Grand opening
Internet
Newsletter
Meetings
Toll-free phone line
Field operations/evaluations
Purchasing cooperatives
Security/safety procedures

MARKETING SUPPORT
Co-op advertising
Ad slicks
National media campaign
Regional marketing

TODAY'S WINDOW FASHIONS

Current financial data not available

5256 S. Mission Rd., #809
Bonsall, CA 92003
(877)998-6329/(760)630-8119
www.todaysblinds.com
Custom blinds, shades, shutters
Began: 1993, Franchising: 1997
Headquarters size: 6 employees
Franchise department: 3 employees

U.S. franchises: 31
Canadian franchises: 0
Other foreign franchises: 0
Company-owned: 0

Seeking: All U.S.
Seeking in Canada? No
Exclusive territories? Yes
Homebased option? Yes
Employees needed to run biz: 0
Absentee ownership? Yes

COSTS
Total cost: $52K-59K
Franchise fee: $49K
Royalty fee: 4%
Term of agreement: 5 years renewable
  for $500
Franchisees required to buy multiple
  units? No

FINANCING
In-house: None
3rd-party: Equipment, franchise fee,
  inventory, startup costs

QUALIFICATIONS
Net worth: $100K
Cash liquidity: $50K

TRAINING
At headquarters: 5 days
At franchisee's location: 5 days

BUSINESS SUPPORT
Internet
Newsletter
Toll-free phone line
Field operations/evaluations

MARKETING SUPPORT
Co-op advertising
Ad slicks

V2K WINDOW DECOR & MORE

Ranked #176 in Entrepreneur Magazine's 2007 Franchise 500   *Financial rating: $$$*

1127 Auraria Pkwy., #204
Denver, CO 80204
(800)200-0835
www.v2k.com
Blinds, shades, shutters
Began: 1996, Franchising: 1997
Headquarters size: 34 employees
Franchise department: 23 employees

U.S. franchises: 177
Canadian franchises: 2
Other foreign franchises: 0
Company-owned: 0

Seeking: All U.S.
Seeking in Canada? Yes
Exclusive territories? Yes
Homebased option? Yes
Employees needed to run biz: 1
Absentee ownership? Yes

COSTS
Total cost: $69.7K-87.3K
Franchise fee: $59.9K
Royalty fee: 4-8%
Term of agreement: 10 years renewable
  at no charge
Franchisees required to buy multiple
  units? No

FINANCING
In-house: None
3rd-party: Equipment, franchise fee,
  inventory, startup costs

QUALIFICATIONS
Cash liquidity: $65K
Experience:
    Sales & marketing skills

TRAINING
At headquarters: 2 weeks
Additional week of training at
  headquarters
Ongoing field training & support

BUSINESS SUPPORT
Internet
Meetings
Toll-free phone line
Field operations/evaluations
Purchasing cooperatives

MARKETING SUPPORT
Co-op advertising
Ad slicks
Regional marketing
TV & radio ads
Direct-mail advertising

HOME ▶ *Miscellaneous*

NATIONWIDE LIFTS INC.

Financial rating: 0

11 Broad St.
Glen Falls, NY 12801
(888)323-8755
www.nwlifts.com
Residential elevators & dumbwaiters
Began: 1998, Franchising: 2004
Headquarters size: 10 employees
Franchise department: 3 employees

U.S. franchises: 8
Canadian franchises: 0
Other foreign franchises: 0
Company-owned: 2

Seeking: All U.S.
Seeking in Canada? No
Exclusive territories? Yes
Homebased option? Yes
Employees needed to run biz: 3-5
Absentee ownership? No

COSTS
Total cost: $39.8K-69.5K
Franchise fee: $25K
Royalty fee: 5%
Term of agreement: 10 years renewable
for 10% of then-current fee
Franchisees required to buy multiple
units? No

FINANCING
No financing available

QUALIFICATIONS
Experience:
General business experience
Sales skills

TRAINING
At headquarters: 3 days
At manufacturing plant: 5-10 days

BUSINESS SUPPORT
Internet
Newsletter
Meetings
Toll-free phone line
Field operations/evaluations

MARKETING SUPPORT
Ad slicks
Regional marketing

NITE TIME DECOR INC.

Financial rating: $$

P.O. Box 5183
Lubbock, TX 79408-5183
(877)552-4242
www.nitetimedecor.com
Landscape & architectural lighting
Began: 1989, Franchising: 1999
Headquarters size: 20 employees
Franchise department: 6 employees

U.S. franchises: 28
Canadian franchises: 0
Other foreign franchises: 0
Company-owned: 0

Seeking: All U.S.
Seeking in Canada? No
Exclusive territories? No
Homebased option? Yes
Employees needed to run biz: 3-4
Absentee ownership? No

COSTS
Total cost: $31K-59K
Franchise fee: $5.5K
Royalty fee: $2K/yr.
Term of agreement: 5 years renewable
for $2K
Franchisees required to buy multiple
units? No

FINANCING
No financing available

QUALIFICATIONS
Experience:
General business experience

TRAINING
At headquarters: 4 days

BUSINESS SUPPORT
Internet
Newsletter
Meetings
Toll-free phone line
Field operations/evaluations
Purchasing cooperatives
Security/safety procedures

MARKETING SUPPORT
Ad slicks
National media campaign

TILE OUTLET ALWAYS IN STOCK

Ranked #316 in Entrepreneur Magazine's 2007 Franchise 500   *Financial rating: $$$$*

3329 Fitzgerald Rd., #1
Rancho Cordova, CA 95742
(916)861-0855
www.tileoutlet.net
Discount tile store
Began: 2001, Franchising: 2002
Headquarters size: 15 employees
Franchise department: 7 employees

U.S. franchises: 58
Canadian franchises: 0
Other foreign franchises: 0
Company-owned: 4

Seeking: Southwest, West
Seeking in Canada? No
Exclusive territories? Yes
Homebased option? No
Employees needed to run biz: 1-3
Absentee ownership? Yes

COSTS
Total cost: $64.4K-117.8K
Franchise fee: $20K
Royalty fee: 5-3%
Term of agreement: 15 years renewable
  at no charge
Franchisees required to buy multiple
  units? No

FINANCING
In-house: None
3rd-party: Equipment, inventory

QUALIFICATIONS
Net worth: $250K
Cash liquidity: $60K
Experience:
  General business experience
  Sales experience

TRAINING
At headquarters: 3 days
At franchisee's location: 5 days
Ongoing

BUSINESS SUPPORT
Grand opening
Internet
Newsletter
Meetings
Toll-free phone line
Field operations/evaluations
Purchasing cooperatives

MARKETING SUPPORT
Ad slicks
Regional marketing

TUFF TURF INC.

Current financial data not available

6822 W. Grovers Ave.
Glendale, AZ 85308
(866)431-2468/(602)290-0499
www.tuffturfinc.com
Synthetic turf
Began: 1998, Franchising: 2002
Headquarters size: Info not provided

U.S. franchises: 7
Canadian franchises: 0
Other foreign franchises: 0
Company-owned: 0

Seeking: All U.S.
Seeking in Canada? Yes
Exclusive territories? Yes
Homebased option? Yes
Employees needed to run biz: 3
Absentee ownership? No

COSTS
Total cost: $35.9K-65.1K
Franchise fee: $19.5K
Royalty fee: 0
Term of agreement: 10 years renewable
  at no charge
Franchisees required to buy multiple
  units? No

FINANCING
No financing available

QUALIFICATIONS
Net worth: $100K
Cash liquidity: $40K
Experience:
  General business experience
  Marketing skills

TRAINING
At headquarters: 3 days
At franchisee's location: 3 days
Ongoing

BUSINESS SUPPORT
Internet
Newsletter
Field operations/evaluations
Purchasing cooperatives

MARKETING SUPPORT
Ad slicks

A DESIGNER'S EYE
6303 Owensmouth Ave., 10th Fl.
Woodland Hills, CA 91367
(818)936-3333
www.adefranchising.com
Home & garden design services
Current financial data not available

THE CLOSET FACTORY
Ranked #453 in Entrepreneur Magazine's 2007 Franchise 500
12800 S. Broadway
Los Angeles, CA 90061
(800)318-8800
www.closetfactory.com
Custom closet & storage systems
Financial rating: $$$$

DECK RENEWAL SYSTEMS USA
623 Congress Park Dr.
Dayton, OH 45459
(937)434-3256
www.deckrenewalsystems.com
Wood restoration
Current financial data not available

FLOOR COVERINGS INTERNATIONAL
Ranked #473 in Entrepreneur Magazine's 2007 Franchise 500
200 Technology Ct., S.E. #1200
Smyrna, GA 30082
(800)955-4324/(770)874-7600
www.floorcoveringsinternational.com
Mobile floor coverings & window blinds
Financial rating: $$$$

FOLIAGE DESIGN SYSTEMS
7048 Narcoossee Rd.
Orlando, FL 32822
(800)933-7351/(407)245-7776
www.foliagedesign.com
Interior foliage & plant maintenance
Financial rating: $$$$

GARAGE FLOOR COATING.COM
3801 E. Roeser Rd., #1
Phoenix, AZ 85040
(602)579-2628
www.garagefloorcoating.com
Epoxy coating for garage floors & concrete surfaces
Current financial data not available

GARAGETEK INC.
5 Aerial Wy., #200
Syosset, NY 11791
(516)621-4300
www.garagetek.com
Garage organization systems
Current financial data not available

GRANITE TRANSFORMATIONS
Ranked #210 in Entrepreneur Magazine's 2007 Franchise 500
10360 USA Today Wy.
Miramar, FL 33025
(954)435-5538
www.granitetransformations.com
Granite resurfacing
Financial rating: $$$$

GREEN LIFE INTERIORS
1404 S. New Rd.
Waco, TX 76708
(254)757-1445
www.findleygroup.com
Interiorscape design & plant maintenance
Financial rating: $$$

NITELITES OUTDOOR LIGHTING
6107 Market Ave.
Franklin, OH 45005
(513)424-5510
www.nitelites.com
Landscape & architectural lighting
Financial rating: 0

OUTDOOR LIGHTING PERSPECTIVES
1238 Mann Dr., #100
Matthews, NC 28105
(704)841-2666
www.olpfranchise.com
Landscape & architectural lighting, home lighting automation
Current financial data not available

PERMA-GLAZE
1638 S. Research Loop Rd., #160
Tucson, AZ 85710
(520)722-9718
www.permaglaze.com
Bathroom/kitchen fixture restoration & refinishing
Financial rating: $$$

STAINED GLASS OVERLAY
1827 N. Case St.
Orange, CA 92865
(800)944-4746/(714)974-6124
www.stainedglassoverlay.com
Patented overlay process for creating art glass
Current financial data not available

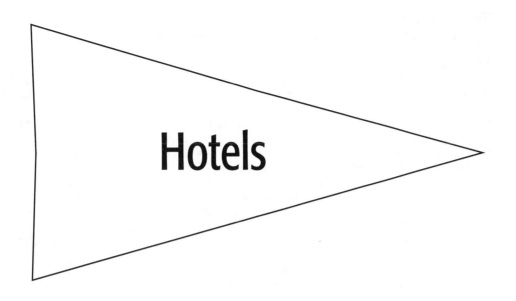

HOTELS

BAYMONT INNS & SUITES
Ranked #184 in Entrepreneur Magazine's 2007 Franchise 500   *Financial rating: $$$$*

1 Sylvan Wy.
Parsippany, NJ 07054
(800)758-8999
www.baymontinns.com
Hotels
Began: 1974, Franchising: 1987
Headquarters size: 17 employees

U.S. franchises: 129
Canadian franchises: 0
Other foreign franchises: 0
Company-owned: 0

Seeking: All U.S.
Seeking in Canada? No
Exclusive territories? Yes
Homebased option? No
Employees needed to run biz: Info
    not provided
Absentee ownership? Yes

COSTS
Total cost: $3.7M-4.9M
Franchise fee: $25K
Royalty fee: 4-4.5%
Term of agreement: 20 years not
    renewable
Franchisees required to buy multiple
    units? Outside the U.S. only

FINANCING
In-house: Accounts receivable,
    equipment, inventory, payroll,
    startup costs
3rd-party: Accounts receivable,
    equipment, franchise fee,
    inventory, payroll, startup costs

QUALIFICATIONS
Experience:
    General business experience

TRAINING
At headquarters: 5 days
At franchisee's location: 2 days
Regional workshops: 1-3 days
Customized property training

BUSINESS SUPPORT
Grand opening
Internet
Newsletter
Meetings
Toll-free phone line
Field operations/evaluations
Purchasing cooperatives

MARKETING SUPPORT
Ad slicks
National media campaign

CHOICE HOTELS INT'L.

Ranked #41 in Entrepreneur Magazine's 2007 Franchise 500   *Financial rating: $*

10750 Columbia Pike
Silver Spring, MD 20901
(866)560-9871
www.choicehotelsfranchise.com
Hotels, inns, suites, resorts
Began: 1939, Franchising: 1962
Headquarters size: 400 employees
Franchise department: 90 employees

U.S. franchises: 4,113
Canadian franchises: 262
Other foreign franchises: 906
Company-owned: 3

Seeking: All U.S.
Seeking in Canada? Yes
Exclusive territories? Yes
Homebased option? No
Employees needed to run biz: Info
    not provided
Absentee ownership? Yes

COSTS
Total cost: $1.9M-11.8M
Franchise fee: $7.5K-60K
Royalty fee: Varies
Term of agreement: 20 years not
    renewable
Franchisees required to buy multiple
    units? No

FINANCING
In-house: Franchise fee, startup
    costs
3rd-party: None

QUALIFICATIONS
Net worth: $750K
Cash liquidity: $200K
Experience:
    Industry experience
    General business experience

TRAINING
At headquarters: 1 week
Ongoing regional training

BUSINESS SUPPORT
Grand opening
Internet
Newsletter
Meetings
Toll-free phone line
Field operations/evaluations

MARKETING SUPPORT
Co-op advertising
Ad slicks
National media campaign
Regional marketing
PR

COUNTRY INNS & SUITES BY CARLSON

Ranked #107 in Entrepreneur Magazine's 2007 Franchise 500   *Financial rating: $$$$*

P.O. Box 59159
Minneapolis, MN 55459-8203
(763)212-1000
www.countryinns.com
Hotels
Began: 1986, Franchising: 1987
Headquarters size: 250 employees
Franchise department: 25 employees

U.S. franchises: 357
Canadian franchises: 13
Other foreign franchises: 16
Company-owned: 9

Seeking: All U.S.
Seeking in Canada? Yes
Exclusive territories? Yes
Homebased option? No
Employees needed to run biz: 25
Absentee ownership? Yes

COSTS
Total cost: $3.2M-5.5M
Franchise fee: Varies
Royalty fee: 4.5%
Term of agreement: 15 years not
    renewable
Franchisees required to buy multiple
    units? No

FINANCING
No financing available

QUALIFICATIONS
Experience:
    Industry experience
    General business experience
    Marketing skills

TRAINING
At headquarters: 1 day
At franchisee's location: 20 hours
Additional training available

BUSINESS SUPPORT
Grand opening
Internet
Newsletter
Meetings
Toll-free phone line
Field operations/evaluations
Purchasing cooperatives
Security/safety procedures

MARKETING SUPPORT
Co-op advertising
Ad slicks
National media campaign
Regional marketing

DAYS INNS WORLDWIDE

Ranked #28 in Entrepreneur Magazine's 2007 Franchise 500   *Financial rating: $$$$*

1 Sylvan Wy.
Parsippany, NJ 07054
(800)758-8999
www.daysinn.com
Hotels & inns
Began: 1970, Franchising: 1972
Headquarters size: 33 employees

U.S. franchises: 1,704
Canadian franchises: 83
Other foreign franchises: 63
Company-owned: 0

Seeking: All U.S.
Seeking in Canada? Yes
Exclusive territories? Yes
Homebased option? No
Employees needed to run biz: Info
    not provided
Absentee ownership? Yes

COSTS
Total cost: $391K-5.7M
Franchise fee: Varies
Royalty fee: 5%
Term of agreement: 15-20 years not
    renewable
Franchisees required to buy multiple
    units? Outside the U.S. only

FINANCING
In-house: Accounts receivable,
    equipment, inventory, payroll,
    startup costs
3rd-party: Accounts receivable,
    equipment, franchise fee,
    inventory, payroll, startup costs

QUALIFICATIONS
Experience:
    General business experience

TRAINING
At headquarters: 5 days
At franchisee's location: 2 days
Regional workshops: 1-3 days

BUSINESS SUPPORT
Grand opening
Internet
Newsletter
Meetings
Toll-free phone line
Field operations/evaluations
Lease negotiations
Purchasing cooperatives

MARKETING SUPPORT
Co-op advertising
Ad slicks
National media campaign
Regional marketing

DOUBLETREE HOTELS, SUITES, RESORTS

Ranked #160 in Entrepreneur Magazine's 2007 Franchise 500   *Financial rating: $$$$*

9336 Civic Center Dr.
Beverly Hills, CA 90210
(800)286-0645/(310)278-4321
www.doubletreefranchise.com
Upscale full-service hotels, resorts,
    guest suites
Began: 1969, Franchising: 1989
Headquarters size: 2,332 employees
Franchise department: 67 employees

U.S. franchises: 117
Canadian franchises: 3
Other foreign franchises: 1
Company-owned: 48

Seeking: All U.S.
Seeking in Canada? Yes
Exclusive territories? Yes
Homebased option? No
Employees needed to run biz: 100
Absentee ownership? Yes

COSTS
Total cost: $24.8M-39.2M
Franchise fee: $75K+
Royalty fee: 4%
Term of agreement: 22 years
    renewable
Franchisees required to buy multiple
    units? No

FINANCING
In-house: None
3rd-party: Financing available

QUALIFICATIONS
Experience:
    Industry experience
    General business experience

TRAINING
General manager training prior to
    certification for opening

BUSINESS SUPPORT
Grand opening
Internet
Newsletter
Meetings
Toll-free phone line
Field operations/evaluations
Purchasing cooperatives
Security/safety procedures

MARKETING SUPPORT
Co-op advertising
Ad slicks
National media campaign
Regional marketing

EMBASSY SUITES HOTELS

Ranked #293 in Entrepreneur Magazine's 2007 Franchise 500   *Financial rating: $$$$*

9336 Civic Center Dr.
Beverly Hills, CA 90210
(800)286-0645/(310)278-4321
www.embassyfranchise.com
Upscale all-suite hotels
Began: 1983, Franchising: 1984
Headquarters size: 2,332 employees
Franchise department: 67 employees

U.S. franchises: 97
Canadian franchises: 1
Other foreign franchises: 3
Company-owned: 84

Seeking: All U.S.
Seeking in Canada? Yes
Exclusive territories? No
Homebased option? No
Employees needed to run biz: 75
Absentee ownership? Yes

COSTS
Total cost: $18.1M-42.7M
Franchise fee: $75K+
Royalty fee: 5%
Term of agreement: 22 years
   renewable
Franchisees required to buy multiple
   units? No

FINANCING
In-house: None
3rd-party: Financing available

QUALIFICATIONS
Experience:
   Industry experience
   General business experience

TRAINING
At Memphis, TN, corporate office:
   2 weeks

BUSINESS SUPPORT
Grand opening
Internet
Newsletter
Meetings
Toll-free phone line
Field operations/evaluations
Lease negotiations
Purchasing cooperatives
Security/safety procedures

MARKETING SUPPORT
Co-op advertising
Ad slicks
National media campaign
Regional marketing

HAMPTON INN/HAMPTON INN & SUITES

Ranked #26 in Entrepreneur Magazine's 2007 Franchise 500   *Financial rating: $$$$*

9336 Civic Center Dr.
Beverly Hills, CA 90210
(800)286-0645/(310)278-4321
www.hamptonfranchise.com
Midpriced hotels
Began: 1983, Franchising: 1984
Headquarters size: 2,332 employees
Franchise department: 67 employees

U.S. franchises: 1,304
Canadian franchises: 18
Other foreign franchises: 11
Company-owned: 36

Seeking: All U.S.
Seeking in Canada? Yes
Exclusive territories? No
Homebased option? No
Employees needed to run biz: 25
Absentee ownership? Yes

COSTS
Total cost: $3M-10.5M
Franchise fee: $50K+
Royalty fee: 5%
Term of agreement: 22 years
   renewable
Franchisees required to buy multiple
   units? No

FINANCING
In-house: None
3rd-party: Financing available

QUALIFICATIONS
Experience:
   Industry experience
   General business experience

TRAINING
At Memphis, TN corporate office:
   2 weeks
Training for new owner & GM:
   3 days

BUSINESS SUPPORT
Grand opening
Internet
Newsletter
Meetings
Toll-free phone line
Field operations/evaluations
Purchasing cooperatives
Security/safety procedures

MARKETING SUPPORT
Co-op advertising
Ad slicks
National media campaign
Regional marketing

HAWTHORN SUITES

Ranked #448 in Entrepreneur Magazine's 2007 Franchise 500

Financial rating: $$$$

13 Corporate Sq., #250
Atlanta, GA 30329
(404)321-4045
www.hawthorn.com
Extended-stay suite hotels
Began: 1986, Franchising: 1986
Headquarters size: 93 employees
Franchise department: 93 employees

U.S. franchises: 92
Canadian franchises: 0
Other foreign franchises: 3
Company-owned: 0

Seeking: All U.S.
Seeking in Canada? Yes
Exclusive territories? Yes
Homebased option? No
Employees needed to run biz: 20-30
Absentee ownership? Yes

COSTS
Total cost: $4.4M-7.4M
Franchise fee: $40K
Royalty fee: 5%
Term of agreement: 20 years renewable
    for 50% of current franchise fee
Franchisees required to buy multiple
    units? No

FINANCING
In-house: None
3rd-party: Accounts receivable,
    construction, equipment,
    inventory, startup costs

QUALIFICATIONS
Net worth: $3M+
Cash liquidity: $750K
Experience:
    Industry experience
    General business experience
    Marketing skills

TRAINING
At headquarters: Varies
At franchisee's location: Varies
At regional location: 2-3 days

BUSINESS SUPPORT
Grand opening
Internet
Newsletter
Meetings
Toll-free phone line
Field operations/evaluations
Purchasing cooperatives
Security/safety procedures

MARKETING SUPPORT
Co-op advertising
Ad slicks
National media campaign

HILTON GARDEN INN

Ranked #102 in Entrepreneur Magazine's 2007 Franchise 500

Financial rating: $$$$

9336 Civic Center Dr.
Beverly Hills, CA 90210
(800)286-0645/(310)278-4321
www.hiltongardeninnfranchise.com
Upscale midpriced hotels
Began: 1996, Franchising: 1996
Headquarters size: 2,332 employees
Franchise department: 67 employees

U.S. franchises: 253
Canadian franchises: 13
Other foreign franchises: 4
Company-owned: 9

Seeking: All U.S.
Seeking in Canada? Yes
Exclusive territories? No
Homebased option? No
Employees needed to run biz: 35-50
Absentee ownership? Yes

COSTS
Total cost: $9.7M-16.3M
Franchise fee: $60K+
Royalty fee: 5%
Term of agreement: 22 years
    renewable
Franchisees required to buy multiple
    units? No

FINANCING
In-house: None
3rd-party: Financing available

QUALIFICATIONS
Experience:
    Industry experience
    General business experience

TRAINING
At headquarters: 3 days
Owner orientation in
    Beverly Hills, CA: 3 days

BUSINESS SUPPORT
Grand opening
Internet
Newsletter
Meetings
Toll-free phone line
Field operations/evaluations
Purchasing cooperatives
Security/safety procedures

MARKETING SUPPORT
Co-op advertising
Ad slicks
National media campaign
Regional marketing

HILTON HOTELS & RESORTS

Ranked #117 in Entrepreneur Magazine's 2007 Franchise 500   *Financial rating: $$$$*

9336 Civic Center Dr.
Beverly Hills, CA 90210
(800)286-0645/(310)278-4321
www.hiltonfranchise.com
Upscale hotels & resorts
Began: 1919, Franchising: 1965
Headquarters size: 2,332 employees
Franchise department: 67 employees

U.S. franchises: 167
Canadian franchises: 11
Other foreign franchises: 30
Company-owned: 400

Seeking: All U.S.
Seeking in Canada? Yes
Exclusive territories? No
Homebased option? No
Employees needed to run biz: 150
Absentee ownership? Yes

COSTS

Total cost: $33M-57M
Franchise fee: $85K+
Royalty fee: 5%
Term of agreement: 22 years
    renewable
Franchisees required to buy
    multiple units? No

FINANCING

In-house: None
3rd-party: Financing available

QUALIFICATIONS

Experience:
    Industry experience
    General business experience

TRAINING

At headquarters: 3 days
At existing hotels: 3 days
At regional office: 4 days

BUSINESS SUPPORT

Grand opening
Internet
Newsletter
Meetings
Toll-free phone line
Field operations/evaluations
Purchasing cooperatives
Security/safety procedures

MARKETING SUPPORT

Co-op advertising
Ad slicks
National media campaign
Regional marketing

HOMEWOOD SUITES BY HILTON

Ranked #156 in Entrepreneur Magazine's 2007 Franchise 500   *Financial rating: $$$$*

9336 Civic Center Dr.
Beverly Hills, CA 90210
(800)286-0645/(310)278-4321
www.homewoodfranchise.com
Upscale extended-stay hotels
Began: 1988, Franchising: 1988
Headquarters size: 2,332 employees
Franchise department: 67 employees

U.S. franchises: 132
Canadian franchises: 4
Other foreign franchises: 0
Company-owned: 42

Seeking: All U.S.
Seeking in Canada? Yes
Exclusive territories? No
Homebased option? No
Employees needed to run biz: 25
Absentee ownership? Yes

COSTS

Total cost: $9.3M-14.5M
Franchise fee: $60K+
Royalty fee: 4%
Term of agreement: 22 years
    renewable for initial fee
Franchisees required to buy multiple
    units? No

FINANCING

In-house: None
3rd-party: Financing available

QUALIFICATIONS

Experience:
    Industry experience
    General business experience

TRAINING

At Memphis, TN, corporate office:
    2 weeks

BUSINESS SUPPORT

Grand opening
Internet
Newsletter
Meetings
Toll-free phone line
Field operations/evaluations
Lease negotiations
Purchasing cooperatives
Security/safety procedures

MARKETING SUPPORT

Co-op advertising
Ad slicks
National media campaign
Regional marketing

HOSPITALITY INT'L. INC.

Ranked #147 in Entrepreneur Magazine's 2007 Franchise 500　　*Financial rating: $$$$*

1726 Montreal Cir.
Tucker, GA 30084
(770)270-1180
www.hifranchise.com
Hotels & motels
Began: 1971, Franchising: 1977
Headquarters size: 20 employees
Franchise department: 8 employees

U.S. franchises: 294
Canadian franchises: 3
Other foreign franchises: 1
Company-owned: 0

Seeking: All U.S.
Seeking in Canada? Yes
Exclusive territories? No
Homebased option? No
Employees needed to run biz: Info
　　not provided
Absentee ownership? Yes

COSTS
Total cost: Varies
Franchise fee: $3.3K-6K
Royalty fee: 3-4%
Term of agreement: 5 years renewable
　　at no charge
Franchisees required to buy multiple
　　units? No

FINANCING
No financing available

QUALIFICATIONS
Net worth: 20% of total costs
Cash liquidity: 15% of total costs
Experience:
　　General business experience

TRAINING
At headquarters: 2 days
At franchisee's location: 1-2 days
At regional training seminars:
　　2 days

BUSINESS SUPPORT
Internet
Newsletter
Meetings
Toll-free phone line
Field operations/evaluations
Security/safety procedures

MARKETING SUPPORT
Ad slicks
National media campaign
Regional marketing

HOWARD JOHNSON INT'L.

Ranked #242 in Entrepreneur Magazine's 2007 Franchise 500　　*Financial rating: $$$$*

1 Sylvan Wy.
Parsippany, NJ 07054
(800)758-8999
www.howardjohnson.com
Hotels
Began: 1925, Franchising: 1954
Headquarters size: 19 employees

U.S. franchises: 362
Canadian franchises: 47
Other foreign franchises: 50
Company-owned: 0

Seeking: All U.S.
Seeking in Canada? Yes
Exclusive territories? Yes
Homebased option? No
Employees needed to run biz: 25
Absentee ownership? Yes

COSTS
Total cost: $372K-6.7M
Franchise fee: Varies
Royalty fee: 4%
Term of agreement: 15-20 years not
　　renewable
Franchisees required to buy multiple
　　units? Outside the U.S. only

FINANCING
In-house: Accounts receivable,
　　equipment, inventory, payroll,
　　startup costs
3rd-party: Accounts receivable,
　　equipment, franchise fee,
　　inventory, payroll, startup costs

QUALIFICATIONS
Experience:
　　General business experience

TRAINING
At headquarters: 5 days
At franchisee's location: 2 days
Regional workshops
Customized property training

BUSINESS SUPPORT
Grand opening
Internet
Newsletter
Meetings
Toll-free phone line
Field operations/evaluations
Purchasing cooperatives
Security/safety procedures

MARKETING SUPPORT
Co-op advertising
Ad slicks
National media campaign
Regional marketing

INTERCONTINENTAL HOTELS GROUP

Ranked #12 in Entrepreneur Magazine's 2007 Franchise 500   *Financial rating: $$$$*

3 Ravinia Dr., #1000
Atlanta, GA 30346
(770)604-2000
www.ichotelsgroup.com
Hotels
Began: 1952, Franchising: 1954
Headquarters size: 1,800 employees
Franchise department: 100 employees

U.S. franchises: 2,398
Canadian franchises: 112
Other foreign franchises: 598
Company-owned: 544

Seeking: All U.S.
Seeking in Canada? Yes
Exclusive territories? Yes
Homebased option? No
Employees needed to run biz: Info
    not provided
Absentee ownership? Yes

COSTS
Total cost: Varies
Franchise fee: Varies
Royalty fee: 5%
Term of agreement: 10 years (average)
    renewable
Franchisees required to buy multiple
    units? No

FINANCING
In-house: None
3rd-party: Accounts receivable,
    equipment, franchise fee,
    inventory, payroll, startup costs

QUALIFICATIONS
Experience:
    Industry experience
    General business experience
    Marketing skills

TRAINING
At headquarters: Varies
At franchisee's location: Varies

BUSINESS SUPPORT
Grand opening
Internet
Newsletter
Meetings
Toll-free phone line
Field operations/evaluations
Security/safety procedures

MARKETING SUPPORT
Co-op advertising
Ad slicks
National media campaign
Regional marketing

KNIGHTS FRANCHISE SYSTEMS

Ranked #193 in Entrepreneur Magazine's 2007 Franchise 500   *Financial rating: $$$$*

1 Sylvan Wy.
Parsippany, NJ 07054
(800)758-8999
www.knightsinn.com
Hotels
Began: 1972, Franchising: 1991
Headquarters size: 5 employees

U.S. franchises: 211
Canadian franchises: 10
Other foreign franchises: 0
Company-owned: 0

Seeking: All U.S.
Seeking in Canada? No
Exclusive territories? Yes
Homebased option? No
Employees needed to run biz: Info
    not provided
Absentee ownership? Yes

COSTS
Total cost: $183K-4.4M
Franchise fee: $5K
Royalty fee: Varies
Term of agreement: 3 years renewable
    at no charge
Franchisees required to buy multiple
    units? Outside the U.S. only

FINANCING
In-house: None
3rd-party: Accounts receivable,
    equipment, franchise fee,
    inventory, payroll, startup costs

QUALIFICATIONS
Experience:
    General business experience

TRAINING
At headquarters: 5 days
At franchisee's location: 2 days
Regional workshops: 1-3 days
Property training

BUSINESS SUPPORT
Internet
Newsletter
Meetings
Toll-free phone line
Field operations/evaluations
Purchasing cooperatives

MARKETING SUPPORT
National media campaign

MICROTEL INNS & SUITES

Ranked #195 in Entrepreneur Magazine's 2007 Franchise 500   *Financial rating: $$$$*

13 Corporate Sq., #250
Atlanta, GA 30329
(404)321-4045
www.microtelinn.com
Economy hotels
Began: 1987, Franchising: 1988
Headquarters size: 93 employees
Franchise department: 93 employees

U.S. franchises: 252
Canadian franchises: 1
Other foreign franchises: 10
Company-owned: 0

Seeking: All U.S.
Seeking in Canada? Yes
Exclusive territories? Yes
Homebased option? No
Employees needed to run biz: 12-20
Absentee ownership? Yes

COSTS
Total cost: $2.8M-5.6M
Franchise fee: $35K
Royalty fee: 4-6%
Term of agreement: 20 years renewable
    for 50% of current franchise fee
Franchisees required to buy multiple
    units? No

FINANCING
In-house: None
3rd-party: Accounts receivable,
    equipment, inventory, payroll,
    startup costs

QUALIFICATIONS
Cash liquidity: $500K-1.5M
Experience:
    General business experience

TRAINING
At headquarters: Varies
At franchisee's location: Varies
At regional location: 2-3 days

BUSINESS SUPPORT
Grand opening
Internet
Newsletter
Meetings
Toll-free phone line
Field operations/evaluations
Purchasing cooperatives
Security/safety procedures

MARKETING SUPPORT
Co-op advertising
Ad slicks
National media campaign
Regional marketing

MOTEL 6

Current financial data not available

4001 International Pkwy.
Carrollton, TX 75007
(888)842-2942
www.motel6.com
Economy lodging
Began: 1962, Franchising: 1996
Headquarters size: 500 employees
Franchise department: 29 employees

U.S. franchises: 189
Canadian franchises: 0
Other foreign franchises: 5
Company-owned: 675

Seeking: All U.S.
Seeking in Canada? Yes
Exclusive territories? Yes
Homebased option? No
Employees needed to run biz: 2-10
Absentee ownership? Yes

COSTS
Total cost: $2.2M-2.6M
Franchise fee: $25K
Royalty fee: 4%
Term of agreement: 10-15 years
    renewable for 50% of current
    franchise fee
Franchisees required to buy multiple
    units? No

FINANCING
In-house: None
3rd-party: Equipment, franchise fee,
    inventory, startup costs

QUALIFICATIONS
Net worth: $1.5M
Cash liquidity: $300K
Experience:
    General business experience

TRAINING
At headquarters: 1 week
At franchisee's location
Annual convention

BUSINESS SUPPORT
Internet
Newsletter
Meetings
Field operations/evaluations
Purchasing cooperatives
Security/safety procedures

MARKETING SUPPORT
Ad slicks
National media campaign

PARK INN

Financial rating: $$$$

P.O. Box 59159
Minneapolis, MN 55459-8204
(763)212-1000
www.parkinns.com
Hotels
Began: 1986, Franchising: 1993
Headquarters size: 250 employees
Franchise department: 25 employees

U.S. franchises: 10
Canadian franchises: 0
Other foreign franchises: 72
Company-owned: 0

Seeking: All U.S.
Seeking in Canada? Yes
Exclusive territories? Yes
Homebased option? No
Employees needed to run biz: 20-25
Absentee ownership? Yes

COSTS

Total cost: $56.4K-4.98M
Franchise fee: Varies
Royalty fee: 4.5%
Term of agreement: 15 years
Franchisees required to buy multiple
   units? No

FINANCING

No financing available

QUALIFICATIONS

Experience:
   Industry experience
   General business experience
   Marketing skills

TRAINING

At headquarters: 1 day
At franchisee's location: 1 day
At Omaha, NE reservation center:
   2 days

BUSINESS SUPPORT

Grand opening
Internet
Newsletter
Meetings
Toll-free phone line
Field operations/evaluations
Purchasing cooperatives
Security/safety procedures

MARKETING SUPPORT

Co-op advertising
Ad slicks
National media campaign
Regional marketing

PARK PLAZA HOTELS AND RESORTS

Financial rating: $$$$

P.O. Box 59159
Minneapolis, MN 55459-8204
(763)212-1000
www.parkplaza.com
Hotels
Began: 1986, Franchising: 1993
Headquarters size: 250 employees
Franchise department: 25 employees

U.S. franchises: 6
Canadian franchises: 3
Other foreign franchises: 29
Company-owned: 4

Seeking: All U.S.
Seeking in Canada? Yes
Exclusive territories? Yes
Homebased option? No
Employees needed to run biz: 40
Absentee ownership? Yes

COSTS

Total cost: $193.99K-1.2M
Franchise fee: Varies
Royalty fee: 5%
Term of agreement: 15 years not
   renewable
Franchisees required to buy multiple
   units? No

FINANCING

No financing available

QUALIFICATIONS

Experience:
   Industry experience
   General business experience
   Marketing skills

TRAINING

At headquarters: 1 day
At franchisee's location: 1 day
At Omaha, NE reservation center:
   2 days

BUSINESS SUPPORT

Grand opening
Internet
Newsletter
Meetings
Toll-free phone line
Field operations/evaluations
Purchasing cooperatives
Security/safety procedures

MARKETING SUPPORT

Co-op advertising
Ad slicks
National media campaign
Regional marketing

RADISSON HOTELS & RESORTS WORLDWIDE

Ranked #402 in Entrepreneur Magazine's 2007 Franchise 500   *Financial rating: $$$$*

P.O. Box 59159
Minneapolis, MN 55459-8204
(763)212-1000
www.radisson.com
Hotels & resorts
Began: 1962, Franchising: 1983
Headquarters size: 250 employees
Franchise department: 25 employees

U.S. franchises: 152
Canadian franchises: 19
Other foreign franchises: 211
Company-owned: 5

Seeking: All U.S.
Seeking in Canada? Yes
Exclusive territories? Yes
Homebased option? No
Employees needed to run biz: Info
    not provided
Absentee ownership? Yes

COSTS
Total cost: $2.2M-2.8M
Franchise fee: Varies
Royalty fee: Varies
Term of agreement: 20 years not
    renewable
Franchisees required to buy multiple
    units? No

FINANCING
No financing available

QUALIFICATIONS
Experience:
    Industry experience
    General business experience
    Marketing skills

TRAINING
At headquarters: 1 day
At franchisee's location: 3 days
At Omaha, NE reservation center:
    2 days

BUSINESS SUPPORT
Grand opening
Internet
Newsletter
Meetings
Toll-free phone line
Field operations/evaluations
Purchasing cooperatives
Security/safety procedures

MARKETING SUPPORT
Co-op advertising
Ad slicks
National media campaign
Regional marketing

RAMADA WORLDWIDE

Ranked #139 in Entrepreneur Magazine's 2007 Franchise 500   *Financial rating: $$$$*

1 Sylvan Wy.
Parsippany, NJ 07054
(800)758-8999
www.ramada.com
Limiteds, inns, plaza hotels
Began: 1954, Franchising: 1990
Headquarters size: 33 employees

U.S. franchises: 634
Canadian franchises: 62
Other foreign franchises: 190
Company-owned: 0

Seeking: All U.S.
Seeking in Canada? Yes
Exclusive territories? Yes
Homebased option? No
Employees needed to run biz: 10-15
Absentee ownership? Yes

COSTS
Total cost: $382K-10.1M
Franchise fee: Varies
Royalty fee: 4%
Term of agreement: 15-20 years not
    renewable
Franchisees required to buy multiple
    units? No

FINANCING
In-house: Accounts receivable,
    equipment, inventory, payroll,
    startup costs
3rd-party: Accounts receivable,
    equipment, franchise fee,
    inventory, payroll, startup costs

QUALIFICATIONS
Experience:
    General business experience

TRAINING
At headquarters: 5 days
At franchisee's location: 2 days
Regional workshops
Property training

BUSINESS SUPPORT
Grand opening
Internet
Newsletter
Meetings
Toll-free phone line
Field operations/evaluations
Lease negotiations
Purchasing cooperatives
Security/safety procedures

MARKETING SUPPORT
Co-op advertising
Ad slicks
National media campaign
Regional marketing
Online support
Trade shows

RED ROOF INNS INC.

Current financial data not available

4001 International Pkwy.
Carrollton, TX 75007
(888)842-2942
www.redroof.com
Economy business lodging
Began: 1967, Franchising: 1996
Headquarters size: 500 employees
Franchise department: 29 employees

U.S. franchises: 100
Canadian franchises: 0
Other foreign franchises: 0
Company-owned: 238

Seeking: All U.S.
Seeking in Canada? Yes
Exclusive territories? Yes
Homebased option? No
Employees needed to run biz: Info
    not provided
Absentee ownership? Yes

COSTS
Total cost: $2.7M-3.1M
Franchise fee: $30K
Royalty fee: 4.5%
Term of agreement: 20 years renewable
    for 50% of current franchise fee
Franchisees required to buy multiple
    units? No

FINANCING
In-house: None
3rd-party: Equipment, franchise fee,
    inventory, startup costs

QUALIFICATIONS
Net worth: $1.5M
Cash liquidity: $300K
Experience:
    General business experience

TRAINING
At headquarters: 2 weeks
At franchisee's location: 1 week
Annual convention: 3 days

BUSINESS SUPPORT
Grand opening
Internet
Newsletter
Meetings
Field operations/evaluations
Purchasing cooperatives
Security/safety procedures

MARKETING SUPPORT
Ad slicks
National media campaign

STUDIO 6

Current financial data not available

4001 International Pkwy.
Carrollton, TX 75007
(888)842-2942
www.staystudio6.com
Extended-stay lodging
Began: 1998, Franchising: 1999
Headquarters size: 500 employees
Franchise department: 29 employees

U.S. franchises: 8
Canadian franchises: 0
Other foreign franchises: 1
Company-owned: 37

Seeking: All U.S.
Seeking in Canada? Yes
Exclusive territories? Yes
Homebased option? No
Employees needed to run biz: Info
    not provided
Absentee ownership? Yes

COSTS
Total cost: $3M-3.5M
Franchise fee: $30K
Royalty fee: 5%
Term of agreement: 10-15 years
    renewable for 50% of current
    franchise fee
Franchisees required to buy multiple
    units? No

FINANCING
In-house: None
3rd-party: Equipment, franchise fee,
    inventory, startup costs

QUALIFICATIONS
Net worth: $1.5M
Cash liquidity: $300K
Experience:
    General business experience

TRAINING
At headquarters: 1 week
At franchisee's location
Annual convention

BUSINESS SUPPORT
Internet
Newsletter
Meetings
Field operations/evaluations
Purchasing cooperatives

MARKETING SUPPORT
Ad slicks

SUPER 8 MOTELS

Ranked #20 in Entrepreneur Magazine's 2007 Franchise 500   *Financial rating: $$$$*

1 Sylvan Wy.
Parsippany, NJ 07054
(800)758-8999
www.super8.com
Economy motels
Began: 1974, Franchising: 1976
Headquarters size: 38 employees

U.S. franchises: 1,901
Canadian franchises: 110
Other foreign franchises: 23
Company-owned: 0

Seeking: All U.S.
Seeking in Canada? Yes
Exclusive territories? Yes
Homebased option? No
Employees needed to run biz: Info
    not provided
Absentee ownership? Yes

COSTS
Total cost: $285K-2.8M
Franchise fee: Varies
Royalty fee: 5%
Term of agreement: 20 years not
    renewable
Franchisees required to buy multiple
    units? Outside the U.S. only

FINANCING
In-house: Accounts receivable,
    equipment, inventory, payroll,
    startup costs
3rd-party: Accounts receivable,
    equipment, franchise fee,
    inventory, payroll, startup costs

QUALIFICATIONS
Experience:
    General business experience

TRAINING
At headquarters: 5 days
At franchisee's location: 2 days
Regional workshops
Customized property training

BUSINESS SUPPORT
Internet
Newsletter
Meetings
Toll-free phone line
Field operations/evaluations
Purchasing cooperatives

MARKETING SUPPORT
National media campaign

TRAVELODGE HOTELS

Ranked #197 in Entrepreneur Magazine's 2007 Franchise 500   *Financial rating: $$$$*

1 Sylvan Wy.
Parsippany, NJ 07054
(800)758-8999
www.travelodge.com
Hotels & motels
Began: 1939, Franchising: 1966
Headquarters size: 19 employees

U.S. franchises: 384
Canadian franchises: 113
Other foreign franchises: 1
Company-owned: 0

Seeking: All U.S.
Seeking in Canada? No
Exclusive territories? Yes
Homebased option? No
Employees needed to run biz: 25
Absentee ownership? Yes

COSTS
Total cost: $366K-5.7M
Franchise fee: Varies
Royalty fee: 4.5%
Term of agreement: 15 years not
    renewable
Franchisees required to buy multiple
    units? Outside the U.S. only

FINANCING
In-house: None
3rd-party: Accounts receivable,
    equipment, franchise fee,
    inventory, payroll, startup costs

QUALIFICATIONS
Experience:
    General business experience

TRAINING
At headquarters: 5 days
At franchisee's location: 2 days
Regional workshops
Customized property training

BUSINESS SUPPORT
Grand opening
Internet
Newsletter
Meetings
Toll-free phone line
Field operations/evaluations
Purchasing cooperatives

MARKETING SUPPORT
Co-op advertising
Ad slicks
National media campaign
Regional marketing
Race car sponsorship

VAGABOND INNS

Ranked #407 in Entrepreneur Magazine's 2007 Franchise 500   *Financial rating: $$$*

5933 W. Century Blvd., #200
Los Angeles, CA 90045
(310)410-5739
www.vagabondinn.com
Hotels
Began: 1958, Franchising: 2000
Headquarters size: 30 employees

U.S. franchises: 33
Canadian franchises: 0
Other foreign franchises: 0
Company-owned: 9

Seeking: All U.S.
Seeking in Canada? No
Exclusive territories? Yes
Homebased option? No
Employees needed to run biz: 10
Absentee ownership? Yes

COSTS
Total cost: $2.8M-5.8M
Franchise fee: $20K
Royalty fee: 2.5%
Term of agreement: 20 years
Franchisees required to buy multiple
    units? No

FINANCING
No financing available

QUALIFICATIONS
Experience:
    Industry experience

TRAINING
At headquarters: As needed
At franchisee's location: As needed

BUSINESS SUPPORT
Grand opening
Internet
Newsletter
Meetings
Toll-free phone line
Field operations/evaluations

MARKETING SUPPORT
Ad slicks
Internet

VALUE PLACE

Financial rating: $

8621 E. 21st St. N., #250
Wichita, KS 67206
(316)630-5505
www.valueplace.com
Short-term residential properties
Began: 2003, Franchising: 2004
Headquarters size: 50 employees
Franchise department: 10 employees

U.S. franchises: 11
Canadian franchises: 0
Other foreign franchises: 0
Company-owned: 12

Seeking: All U.S.
Seeking in Canada? No
Exclusive territories? Yes
Homebased option? No
Employees needed to run biz: 4-5
Absentee ownership? Yes

COSTS
Total cost: $3.1M-6.1M
Franchise fee: Varies
Royalty fee: 5%
Term of agreement: 20 years renewable
    for 50% of current franchise fee
Franchisees required to buy multiple
    units? No

FINANCING
No financing available

QUALIFICATIONS
Net worth: $1M
Cash liquidity: $560K-840K
Experience:
    Industry experience
    General business experience

TRAINING
At headquarters: Varies
At franchisee's location: Upon
    request

BUSINESS SUPPORT
Grand opening
Internet
Meetings
Field operations/evaluations
Purchasing cooperatives
Security/safety procedures

MARKETING SUPPORT
Promotional items

WINGATE INNS INT'L.

Ranked #238 in Entrepreneur Magazine's 2007 Franchise 500   *Financial rating: $$$$*

1 Sylvan Wy.
Parsippany, NJ 07054
(800)758-8999
www.wingateinns.com
Hotels
Began: 1995, Franchising: 1995
Headquarters size: 33 employees

U.S. franchises: 146
Canadian franchises: 2
Other foreign franchises: 0
Company-owned: 0

Seeking: All U.S.
Seeking in Canada? No
Exclusive territories? Yes
Homebased option? No
Employees needed to run biz: Info
  not provided
Absentee ownership? Yes

COSTS
Total cost: $5.9M-6.5M
Franchise fee: Varies
Royalty fee: 4.5%
Term of agreement: 20 years not
  renewable
Franchisees required to buy multiple
  units? Outside the U.S. only

FINANCING
In-house: Accounts receivable,
  equipment, inventory, payroll,
  startup costs
3rd-party: Accounts receivable,
  equipment, franchise fee,
  inventory, payroll, startup costs

QUALIFICATIONS
Experience:
  General business experience

TRAINING
At headquarters: 5 days
At franchisee's location: 2 days
Regional workshops: 1-3 days
Customized property training

BUSINESS SUPPORT
Grand opening
Meetings
Toll-free phone line
Field operations/evaluations
Purchasing cooperatives

MARKETING SUPPORT
Co-op advertising
Ad slicks
National media campaign
Regional marketing
Online
Trade shows

WYNDHAM HOTEL & RESORTS

Ranked #351 in Entrepreneur Magazine's 2007 Franchise 500   *Financial rating: $$$$*

1 Sylvan Way
Parsippany, NJ 07054
(800)758-8999
www.wyndham.com
Hotels
Began: 1981, Franchising: 1996
Headquarters size: 115 employees

U.S. franchises: 58
Canadian franchises: 2
Other foreign franchises: 10
Company-owned: 17

Seeking: All U.S.
Seeking in Canada? Yes
Exclusive territories? No
Homebased option? No
Employees needed to run biz: 10-15
Absentee ownership? Yes

COSTS
Total cost: $28M-49M
Franchise fee: $35K-225K
Royalty fee: 5%
Term of agreement: 15-20 years
  renewable for 50% of initial fee
Franchisees required to buy multiple
  units? Outside the U.S. only

FINANCING
No financing available

QUALIFICATIONS
Experience:
  General business experience

TRAINING
At headquarters: 5 days
At franchisee's location: 2 days
Regional workshops: 1-3 days

BUSINESS SUPPORT
Grand opening
Internet
Newsletter
Meetings
Toll-free phone line
Field operations/evaluations
Security/safety procedures

MARKETING SUPPORT
National media campaign
B2B
Print advertising & marketing

KAMPGROUNDS OF AMERICA INC.
550 N. 31st St., 4th Fl.
Billings, MT 59101
(406)248-7444
www.koa.com
Campgrounds
Current financial data not available

LA QUINTA INN/
LA QUINTA INN & SUITES
909 Hidden Ridge, #600
Irving, TX 75038
(866)832-6574
www.laquintafranchise.com
Limited-sevice hotels
Current financial data not available

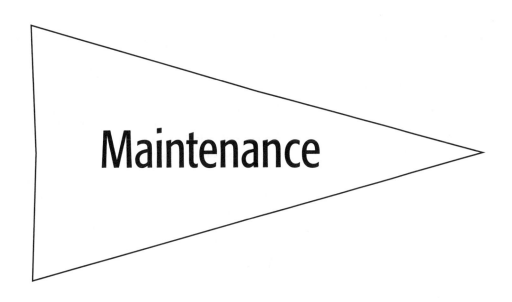

Maintenance

MAINTENANCE ▸ *Air Duct Cleaning*

DUCT DOCTOR USA INC.

Ranked #377 in Entrepreneur Magazine's 2007 Franchise 500   *Financial rating: $$$$*

5555 Oakbrook Pkwy., #660
Atlanta, GA 30093
(770)446-1764
www.ductdoctorusa.com
Residential & commercial air-duct
   cleaning
Began: 1985, Franchising: 2000
Headquarters size: 12 employees
Franchise department: 3 employees

U.S. franchises: 15
Canadian franchises: 0
Other foreign franchises: 1
Company-owned: 8

Seeking: All U.S.
Seeking in Canada? Yes
Exclusive territories? Yes
Homebased option? Yes
Employees needed to run biz: 2
Absentee ownership? No

COSTS
Total cost: $41K-64K
Franchise fee: $25K
Royalty fee: 5-8%
Term of agreement: 10 years renewable
   for 10% of initial franchise fee
Franchisees required to buy multiple
   units? No

FINANCING
In-house: None
3rd-party: Equipment

QUALIFICATIONS
Net worth: $100K
Cash liquidity: $50K
Experience:
   General business experience
   Mechanical or HVAC skills

TRAINING
At headquarters: 3 weeks
At franchisee's location: 1 week
Ongoing

BUSINESS SUPPORT
Grand opening
Internet
Newsletter
Meetings
Toll-free phone line
Field operations/evaluations
Purchasing cooperatives
Security/safety procedures

MARKETING SUPPORT
Ad slicks
Regional marketing
In-market business development

DUCTZ INT'L. INC.

Ranked #418 in Entrepreneur Magazine's 2007 Franchise 500　　　　*Financial rating: $$$*

3948 Ranchero Dr.
Ann Arbor, MI 48108
(888)313-8289
www.ductz.com
Duct & vent cleaning
Began: 2001, Franchising: 2003
Headquarters size: 10 employees
Franchise department: 2 employees

U.S. franchises: 36
Canadian franchises: 0
Other foreign franchises: 2
Company-owned: 1

Seeking: All U.S.
Seeking in Canada? Yes
Exclusive territories? Yes
Homebased option? Yes
Employees needed to run biz: 2
Absentee ownership? No

COSTS
Total cost: $77.4K-135.1K
Franchise fee: $9.9K
Royalty fee: 8%
Term of agreement: 10 years renewable
　　for 20% of initial fee
Franchisees required to buy multiple
　　units? No

FINANCING
No financing available

QUALIFICATIONS
Net worth: $250K+
Cash liquidity: $35K
Experience:
　　General business experience
　　Marketing skills

TRAINING
At headquarters: 2 weeks

BUSINESS SUPPORT
Internet
Newsletter
Meetings
Toll-free phone line
Field operations/evaluations
Security/safety procedures

MARKETING SUPPORT
National media campaign
Regional marketing

MAINTENANCE ▸ *Asphalt Services*

AMERICAN ASPHALT SEALCOATING CO.

Financial rating: $$$

P.O. Box 600
Chesterland, OH 44026
(888)603-7325/(440)729-8080
www.american-sealcoating.com
Asphalt maintenance services &
　　coatings
Began: 1987, Franchising: 1998
Headquarters size: 11 employees
Franchise department: 6 employees

U.S. franchises: 12
Canadian franchises: 0
Other foreign franchises: 0
Company-owned: 1

Seeking: All U.S.
Seeking in Canada? Yes
Exclusive territories? Yes
Homebased option? Yes
Employees needed to run biz: 1-3
Absentee ownership? Yes

COSTS
Total cost: $41.2K-81.6K
Franchise fee: $15K
Royalty fee: 5-7%
Term of agreement: 15 years renewable
Franchisees required to buy multiple
　　units? No

FINANCING
In-house: Inventory, startup costs
3rd-party: None

QUALIFICATIONS
Net worth: $50K
Cash liquidity: $50K
Experience:
　　General business experience
　　Marketing skills
　　Aggressive & outgoing personality

TRAINING
At headquarters: 7-10 days
At franchisee's location: 3 days
At headquarters/franchise site

BUSINESS SUPPORT
Grand opening
Internet
Newsletter
Meetings
Toll-free phone line
Field operations/evaluations
Purchasing cooperatives
Security/safety procedures

MARKETING SUPPORT
Co-op advertising
Ad slicks
Ad designs
Rate negotiations

JET-BLACK INT'L. INC.

Ranked #488 in Entrepreneur Magazine's 2007 Franchise 500   *Financial rating: $$$*

25 W. Cliff Rd., #103
Burnsville, MN 55337
(888)538-2525/(952)890-8343
www.jet-black.com
Asphalt maintenance services
Began: 1988, Franchising: 1993
Headquarters size: 10 employees
Franchise department: 4 employees

U.S. franchises: 99
Canadian franchises: 0
Other foreign franchises: 0
Company-owned: 4

Seeking: Midwest, Northeast
Seeking in Canada? Yes
Exclusive territories? Yes
Homebased option? Yes
Employees needed to run biz: 3
Absentee ownership? Yes

COSTS
Total cost: $66.9K-112K
Franchise fee: $20K
Royalty fee: 8%
Term of agreement: 7 years renewable
    for 25% of then-current fee
Franchisees required to buy multiple
    units? No

FINANCING
No financing available

QUALIFICATIONS
Net worth: $100K
Cash liquidity: $49K
Experience:
    General business experience
    People skills
    Management experience

TRAINING
At headquarters: 1 week
At franchisee's location: Ongoing
Advanced training seminars

BUSINESS SUPPORT
Grand opening
Internet
Newsletter
Meetings
Toll-free phone line
Field operations/evaluations
Purchasing cooperatives
Security/safety procedures

MARKETING SUPPORT
Co-op advertising
Ad slicks
PR
Marketing programs
Lead generation

KCS APPLICATIONS INC.

Financial rating: 0

4955 Creaser Rd.
Westmoreland, NY 13490
(315)853-4805
www.kcs1.com
Acrylic asphalt sealcoating
Began: 1992, Franchising: 1994
Headquarters size: 2 employees
Franchise department: 2 employees

U.S. franchises: 25
Canadian franchises: 0
Other foreign franchises: 0
Company-owned: 0

Seeking: Northeast
Seeking in Canada? No
Exclusive territories? No
Homebased option? Yes
Employees needed to run biz: 0
Absentee ownership? No

COSTS
Total cost: $15.5K
Franchise fee: $15K
Royalty fee: $350/yr.
Term of agreement: 3 years renewable
    at no charge
Franchisees required to buy multiple
    units? No

FINANCING
No financing available

QUALIFICATIONS
Cash liquidity: $15K

TRAINING
At headquarters: 2 days
At franchisee's location: 1 day

BUSINESS SUPPORT
Internet
Field operations/evaluations

MARKETING SUPPORT
Local marketing support

MAINTENANCE ▶ *Carpet Cleaning*

SEARS CARPET & UPHOLSTERY CARE INC.

Ranked #454 in Entrepreneur Magazine's 2007 Franchise 500   *Financial rating: $$*

8472 Cotter St.
Lewis Center, OH 43035
(740)201-3003
www.searsclean.com
Carpet, upholstery, air-duct, tile &
    grout cleaning, water extraction
Began: 1992, Franchising: 1999
Headquarters size: 18 employees
Franchise department: 3 employees

U.S. franchises: 125
Canadian franchises: 0
Other foreign franchises: 0
Company-owned: 2

Seeking: All U.S.
Seeking in Canada? No
Exclusive territories? Yes
Homebased option? Yes
Employees needed to run biz: 3-10
Absentee ownership? Yes

COSTS
Total cost: $108.1K-540.5K
Franchise fee: $5K-120K
Royalty fee: 8%
Term of agreement: 10 years renewable
    for $2.5K
Franchisees required to buy multiple
    units? No

FINANCING
In-house: Franchise fee
3rd-party: Equipment, franchise fee,
    startup costs

QUALIFICATIONS
Net worth: $75K-500K
Cash liquidity: $50K-350K
Experience:
    General business experience
    Marketing skills
    Sales experience helpful

TRAINING
At headquarters: 1 week
At franchisee's location: As needed
At regional location: 1 day

BUSINESS SUPPORT
Grand opening
Internet
Newsletter
Meetings
Toll-free phone line
Field operations/evaluations
Purchasing cooperatives
Security/safety procedures

MARKETING SUPPORT
Co-op advertising
Ad slicks
Website
Online Yellow Pages
Customer retention program
Advertising source discounts

STANLEY STEEMER CARPET CLEANER

Ranked #190 in Entrepreneur Magazine's 2007 Franchise 500   *Financial rating: $$$$*

5500 Stanley Steemer Pkwy.
Dublin, OH 43016
(800)848-7496/(614)764-2007
www.stanleysteemer.com
Carpet & upholstery cleaning
Began: 1947, Franchising: 1972
Headquarters size: 80 employees
Franchise department: 15 employees

U.S. franchises: 231
Canadian franchises: 0
Other foreign franchises: 0
Company-owned: 60

Seeking: All U.S.
Seeking in Canada? No
Exclusive territories? Yes
Homebased option? Yes
Employees needed to run biz: 16
Absentee ownership? Yes

COSTS
Total cost: $91.1K-216.3K
Franchise fee: $20K+
Royalty fee: 7%
Term of agreement: 20 years
Franchisees required to buy multiple
    units? No

FINANCING
In-house: Franchise fee, inventory,
    startup costs
3rd-party: Equipment

QUALIFICATIONS
Experience:
    General business experience
    Marketing skills

TRAINING
At headquarters: 2 weeks
Ongoing

BUSINESS SUPPORT
Internet
Newsletter
Meetings
Toll-free phone line
Security/safety procedures

MARKETING SUPPORT
Co-op advertising
Ad slicks
National media campaign

MAINTENANCE · *Commercial Cleaning*

ANAGO CLEANING SYSTEMS

Ranked #215 in Entrepreneur Magazine's 2007 Franchise 500 *Financial rating: 0*

3111 N. University Dr., #625
Coral Springs, FL 33065
(800)213-5857
www.anagousa.com
Commercial cleaning
Began: 1989, Franchising: 1991
Headquarters size: 10 employees
Franchise department: 10 employees

U.S. franchises: 840
Canadian franchises: 0
Other foreign franchises: 0
Company-owned: 0

Seeking: All U.S.
Seeking in Canada? Yes
Exclusive territories? Yes
Homebased option? Yes
Employees needed to run biz: 4-10
Absentee ownership? No

COSTS
Total cost: $8K-350K
Franchise fee: $2K-350K
Royalty fee: 5%
Term of agreement: 10 years renewable
    at no charge
Franchisees required to buy multiple
    units? No

FINANCING
In-house: Franchise fee
3rd-party: None

QUALIFICATIONS
Net worth: $10K-250K
Cash liquidity: $2K/50K
Experience:
    General business experience
    Marketing skills

TRAINING
At franchisee's location: 1 week
Ongoing

BUSINESS SUPPORT
Grand opening
Internet
Newsletter
Meetings
Toll-free phone line
Field operations/evaluations
Lease negotiations
Purchasing cooperatives
Security/safety procedures

MARKETING SUPPORT
Ad slicks
National media campaign
Regional marketing

BEARCOM BUILDING SERVICES

Financial rating: 0

7022 S. 400 West
Midvale, UT 84047
(888)569-9533/(801)569-9500
www.bearcomservices.com
Commercial cleaning
Began: 1979, Franchising: 1990
Headquarters size: 4 employees
Franchise department: 2 employees

U.S. franchises: 53
Canadian franchises: 0
Other foreign franchises: 0
Company-owned: 0

Seeking: All U.S.
Seeking in Canada? No
Exclusive territories? No
Homebased option? Yes
Employees needed to run biz: 0-2
Absentee ownership? No

COSTS
Total cost: $12.8K-39.3K+
Franchise fee: $9.99K-14.99K+
Royalty fee: 6-8%
Term of agreement: 5 years renewable
    at no charge
Franchisees required to buy multiple
    units? No

FINANCING
In-house: Accounts receivable,
    equipment, franchise fee
3rd-party: None

QUALIFICATIONS
Experience:
    Industry experience
    General business experience
    Marketing skills

TRAINING
At headquarters: 24 hours

BUSINESS SUPPORT
Internet
Newsletter
Toll-free phone line
Field operations/evaluations

MARKETING SUPPORT
Marketing training

BONUS BUILDING CARE

Ranked #31 in Entrepreneur Magazine's 2007 Franchise 500　　　*Financial rating: $$$*

P.O. Box 300
Indianola, OK 74442
(800)931-1102
www.bonusbuildingcare.com
Commercial cleaning
Began: 1996, Franchising: 1996
Headquarters size: 30 employees
Franchise department: 30 employees

U.S. franchises: 1,415
Canadian franchises: 0
Other foreign franchises: 0
Company-owned: 3

Seeking: All U.S.
Seeking in Canada? Yes
Exclusive territories? Yes
Homebased option? Yes
Employees needed to run biz: 1-5
Absentee ownership? No

COSTS
Total cost: $7.2K-13.6K
Franchise fee: $6.5K
Royalty fee: 10%
Term of agreement: 20 years renewable
　for $2K
Franchisees required to buy multiple
　units? Outside the U.S. only

FINANCING
In-house: Accounts receivable,
　equipment, franchise fee
3rd-party: Accounts receivable,
　equipment, payroll, startup costs

QUALIFICATIONS
Info not provided

TRAINING
At headquarters: As needed
At franchisee's location: As needed

BUSINESS SUPPORT
Grand opening
Internet
Newsletter
Meetings
Toll-free phone line
Field operations/evaluations
Purchasing cooperatives
Security/safety procedures

MARKETING SUPPORT
Ad slicks
National media campaign
Regional marketing
Newspaper ads
Referrals
Trade shows

BUILDINGSTARS INC.

Ranked #228 in Entrepreneur Magazine's 2007 Franchise 500　　　*Financial rating: $$$$*

11489 Page Service Dr.
St. Louis, MO 63146
(314)991-3356
www.buildingstars.com
Commercial cleaning
Began: 1994, Franchising: 2000
Headquarters size: 18 employees
Franchise department: 3 employees

U.S. franchises: 217
Canadian franchises: 0
Other foreign franchises: 0
Company-owned: 0

Seeking: Midwest, Southwest
Seeking in Canada? No
Exclusive territories? No
Homebased option? Yes
Employees needed to run biz: 5
Absentee ownership? No

COSTS
Total cost: $1.9K
Franchise fee: $995
Royalty fee: 10%
Term of agreement: 5 years
　renewable at no charge
Franchisees required to buy
　multiple units? No

FINANCING
In-house: Accounts receivable,
　equipment, inventory
3rd-party: None

QUALIFICATIONS
Cash liquidity: $1K

TRAINING
At headquarters: 1 week

BUSINESS SUPPORT
Internet
Newsletter
Meetings

MARKETING SUPPORT
Info not provided

CHAMPION CLEAN

Current financial data not available

283 Cranes Roost Blvd., #111
Altamonte Springs, FL 32701
(407)379-0041
www.championclean.com
Commercial cleaning
Began: 1997, Franchising: 2003
Headquarters size: 6 employees
Franchise department: 4 employees

U.S. franchises: 66
Canadian franchises: 0
Other foreign franchises: 0
Company-owned: 1

Seeking: All U.S.
Seeking in Canada? Yes
Exclusive territories? Yes
Homebased option? Yes
Employees needed to run biz: 2-10
Absentee ownership? Yes

COSTS
Total cost: $3.5K+/65K+
Franchise fee: $2.5K/50K+
Royalty fee: 3%/4%
Term of agreement: 10 years renewable
   at no charge
Franchisees required to buy multiple
   units? No

FINANCING
In-house: Franchise fee
3rd-party: None

QUALIFICATIONS
Net worth: $5K+
Cash liquidity: $1K+

TRAINING
At headquarters: 80 hours
At franchisee's location: 40 hours

BUSINESS SUPPORT
Internet
Toll-free phone line
Lease negotiations
Security/safety procedures

MARKETING SUPPORT
Co-op advertising

CITY WIDE MAINTENANCE FRANCHISE CO.

Ranked #360 in Entrepreneur Magazine's 2007 Franchise 500   *Financial rating: $$$$*

8460 Nieman Rd.
Lenexa, KS 66214
(913)888-5700
www.citywidefranchise.com
Maintenance services
Began: 1959, Franchising: 2001
Headquarters size: 50 employees
Franchise department: 5 employees

U.S. franchises: 11
Canadian franchises: 0
Other foreign franchises: 0
Company-owned: 1

Seeking: All U.S.
Seeking in Canada? No
Exclusive territories? Yes
Homebased option? No
Employees needed to run biz: 3
Absentee ownership? No

COSTS
Total cost: $100K-250K
Franchise fee: $75K
Royalty fee: 3-5%
Term of agreement: 15 years renewable
   for 10% of franchise fee
Franchisees required to buy multiple
   units? No

FINANCING
No financing available

QUALIFICATIONS
Net worth: $250K
Cash liquidity: $150K
Experience:
   General business experience
   Marketing skills

TRAINING
At headquarters: 2 weeks
At franchisee's location: 2 weeks
Annual training meeting

BUSINESS SUPPORT
Internet
Meetings
Toll-free phone line
Field operations/evaluations
Purchasing cooperatives
Security/safety procedures

MARKETING SUPPORT
Ad slicks
National media campaign
Marketing materials

CLEANNET USA INC.

Ranked #36 in Entrepreneur Magazine's 2007 Franchise 500   *Financial rating: $$$$*

9861 Broken Land Pkwy., #208
Columbia, MD 21046
(800)735-8838/(410)720-6444
www.cleannetusa.com
Commercial cleaning
Began: 1988, Franchising: 1988
Headquarters size: 45 employees
Franchise department: 32 employees

U.S. franchises: 3,763
Canadian franchises: 0
Other foreign franchises: 0
Company-owned: 8

Seeking: All U.S.
Seeking in Canada? Yes
Exclusive territories? Yes
Homebased option? Yes
Employees needed to run biz: 3-10
Absentee ownership? Yes

COSTS
Total cost: $3.9K-35.6K
Franchise fee: $2.95K-32K
Royalty fee: 3%
Term of agreement: 20 years renewable
for $5K
Franchisees required to buy multiple
units? No

FINANCING
In-house: Accounts receivable,
equipment, franchise fee,
inventory, startup costs
3rd-party: Payroll

QUALIFICATIONS
Net worth: $10K-300K
Cash liquidity: $5K-100K
Experience:
General business experience

TRAINING
At headquarters: 1-4 weeks
At franchisee's location: 1-4 weeks

BUSINESS SUPPORT
Grand opening
Internet
Newsletter
Meetings
Toll-free phone line
Field operations/evaluations
Purchasing cooperatives
Security/safety procedures

MARKETING SUPPORT
Regional marketing

COVERALL CLEANING CONCEPTS

Ranked #67 in Entrepreneur Magazine's 2007 Franchise 500   *Financial rating: $*

5201 Congress Ave., #275
Boca Raton, FL 33487
(800)537-3371/(561)922-2500
www.coverall.com
Commercial cleaning
Began: 1985, Franchising: 1985
Headquarters size: 262 employees
Franchise department: 182 employees

U.S. franchises: 8,994
Canadian franchises: 238
Other foreign franchises: 303
Company-owned: 0

Seeking: All U.S.
Seeking in Canada? Yes
Exclusive territories? Yes
Homebased option? Yes
Employees needed to run biz: 2
Absentee ownership? Yes

COSTS
Total cost: $6.3K-35.9K
Franchise fee: $6K-32.2K
Royalty fee: 5%
Term of agreement: 20 years renewable
at no charge
Franchisees required to buy multiple
units? Outside the U.S. only

FINANCING
In-house: Equipment, franchise fee,
inventory, startup costs
3rd-party: None

QUALIFICATIONS
Net worth: $6K-32K
Cash liquidity: $1.5K

TRAINING
At headquarters: 80 hours
At franchisee's location: 40 hours+
& ongoing
At international master office:
10 weeks

BUSINESS SUPPORT
Grand opening
Internet
Newsletter
Meetings
Toll-free phone line
Field operations/evaluations
Security/safety procedures

MARKETING SUPPORT
Co-op advertising
Ad slicks
National media campaign
Regional marketing

E.P.I.C. SYSTEMS INC.

Current financial data not available

402 E. Maryland St.
Evansville, IN 47711
(800)230-3742
Commercial cleaning
Began: 1994, Franchising: 1994
Headquarters size: 3 employees
Franchise department: 2 employees

U.S. franchises: 6
Canadian franchises: 0
Other foreign franchises: 0
Company-owned: 0

Seeking: All U.S.
Seeking in Canada? No
Exclusive territories? Info not
    provided
Homebased option? Yes
Employees needed to run biz: 4
Absentee ownership? Yes

COSTS
Total cost: $10.2K-28.5K
Franchise fee: $6.5K/25K
Royalty fee: 4-10%
Term of agreement: 10 years renewable
    for 10% of franchise fee
Franchisees required to buy multiple
    units? No

FINANCING
In-house: Franchise fee
3rd-party: Equipment, inventory

QUALIFICATIONS
Net worth: $25K
Cash liquidity: $5K
Experience:
    General business experience

TRAINING
At headquarters: 2 weeks

BUSINESS SUPPORT
Internet
Toll-free phone line
Field operations/evaluations

MARKETING SUPPORT
Ad slicks

JANI-KING

Ranked #13 in Entrepreneur Magazine's 2007 Franchise 500

Financial rating: $$$$

16885 Dallas Pkwy.
Addison, TX 75001
(800)552-5264
www.janiking.com
Commercial cleaning
Began: 1969, Franchising: 1974
Headquarters size: 100 employees
Franchise department: 100 employees

U.S. franchises: 9,933
Canadian franchises: 580
Other foreign franchises: 1,630
Company-owned: 19

Seeking: All U.S.
Seeking in Canada? Yes
Exclusive territories? Yes
Homebased option? Yes
Employees needed to run biz: Info
    not provided
Absentee ownership? No

COSTS
Total cost: $11.3K-34.1K+
Franchise fee: $8.6K-16.3K+
Royalty fee: 10%
Term of agreement: 20 years renewable
    at no charge
Franchisees required to buy multiple
    units? No

FINANCING
In-house: Accounts receivable,
    equipment
3rd-party: Equipment, franchise fee,
    startup costs

QUALIFICATIONS
Info not provided

TRAINING
At local office: 40-1/2 hours+

BUSINESS SUPPORT
Internet
Newsletter
Meetings
Toll-free phone line
Field operations/evaluations
Purchasing cooperatives
Security/safety procedures

MARKETING SUPPORT
Co-op advertising
Ad slicks
National media campaign
Regional marketing
Race car sponsorship
PR

JANTIZE AMERICA

Ranked #322 in Entrepreneur Magazine's 2007 Franchise 500   *Financial rating: $$$*

825 N. Pontiac Tr., #5
Walled Lake, MI 48390
(800)968-9182
www.jantize.com
Commercial cleaning
Began: 1988, Franchising: 1988
Headquarters size: 4 employees
Franchise department: 4 employees

U.S. franchises: 62
Canadian franchises: 0
Other foreign franchises: 0
Company-owned: 1

Seeking: All U.S.
Seeking in Canada? No
Exclusive territories? Yes
Homebased option? Yes
Employees needed to run biz: 4
Absentee ownership? No

COSTS
Total cost: $9.6K-43.1K
Franchise fee: $3.5K-35K
Royalty fee: 6-15%
Term of agreement: 10 years renewable
    at no charge
Franchisees required to buy multiple
    units? No

FINANCING
In-house: Accounts receivable,
    franchise fee
3rd-party: Equipment

QUALIFICATIONS
Net worth: $25K
Cash liquidity: $10K-50K
Experience:
    General business experience
    Marketing skills

TRAINING
At headquarters: 3 days
At franchisee's location: 2 days

BUSINESS SUPPORT
Internet
Toll-free phone line
Field operations/evaluations

MARKETING SUPPORT
National media campaign
Regional marketing

MINT CONDITION FRANCHISING INC.

Financial rating: $

1057 521 Corporate Center Dr.,
    #165
Fort Mill, SC 29715
(803)548-6121
www.mintconditioninc.com
Janitorial & building maintenance
    services
Began: 1996, Franchising: 1996
Headquarters size: 10 employees
Franchise department: 2 employees

U.S. franchises: 49
Canadian franchises: 0
Other foreign franchises: 0
Company-owned: 1

Seeking: Northeast, Southeast
Seeking in Canada? No
Exclusive territories? No
Homebased option? Yes
Employees needed to run biz: 0-4
Absentee ownership? No

COSTS
Total cost: $4.9K-45.4K
Franchise fee: $3K-22K
Royalty fee: 9%
Term of agreement: 10 years renewable
    for 10% of then-current fee
Franchisees required to buy multiple
    units? No

FINANCING
In-house: Equipment, franchise fee
3rd-party: None

QUALIFICATIONS
Cash liquidity: $500-6K

TRAINING
At headquarters: 9 hours
At franchisee's location: 8-10 hours

BUSINESS SUPPORT
Field operations/evaluations
Purchasing cooperatives
Security/safety procedures

MARKETING SUPPORT
Initial leads

OCTOCLEAN FRANCHISING SYSTEMS
Ranked #307 in Entrepreneur Magazine's 2007 Franchise 500 *Financial rating: $$$*

5225 Canyon Crest Dr., #71-339
Riverside, CA 92507
(951)683-5859
www.octoclean.com
Janitorial services
Began: 1981, Franchising: 2000
Headquarters size: 10 employees
Franchise department: 10 employees

U.S. franchises: 103
Canadian franchises: 0
Other foreign franchises: 0
Company-owned: 0

Seeking: All U.S.
Seeking in Canada? No
Exclusive territories? Yes
Homebased option? Yes
Employees needed to run biz: 2
Absentee ownership? No

COSTS
Total cost: $9.5K-182.2K
Franchise fee: $8K-57.5K
Royalty fee: 5%
Term of agreement: 15 years renewable
    at no charge
Franchisees required to buy multiple
    units? No

FINANCING
In-house: Equipment, franchise fee,
    inventory
3rd-party: None

QUALIFICATIONS
Net worth: $20K
Cash liquidity: $3K

TRAINING
At headquarters: 30 days
At franchisee's location: As needed

BUSINESS SUPPORT
Newsletter
Meetings
Toll-free phone line
Field operations/evaluations
Purchasing cooperatives
Security/safety procedures

MARKETING SUPPORT
Info not provided

OPENWORKS
Ranked #288 in Entrepreneur Magazine's 2007 Franchise 500 *Financial rating: $$$$*

4742 N. 24th St., #300
Phoenix, AZ 85016
(800)777-6736
www.openwordsweb.com
Commercial cleaning
Began: 1983, Franchising: 1983
Headquarters size: 40 employees
Franchise department: 11 employees

U.S. franchises: 344
Canadian franchises: 0
Other foreign franchises: 0
Company-owned: 0

Seeking: All U.S.
Seeking in Canada? Yes
Exclusive territories? Yes
Homebased option? Yes
Employees needed to run biz: 3
Absentee ownership? No

COSTS
Total cost: $15.2K-150K+
Franchise fee: $15.2K-67.5K
Royalty fee: 10%
Term of agreement: 10 years renewable
    at no charge
Franchisees required to buy multiple
    units? No

FINANCING
In-house: Accounts receivable,
    equipment, franchise fee, payroll
3rd-party: Inventory

QUALIFICATIONS
Cash liquidity: $7K-150K+
Experience:
    General business experience

TRAINING
At headquarters: 2-4 weeks
At franchisee's location: Ongoing
At regional location: 2 weeks+ &
    ongoing

BUSINESS SUPPORT
Newsletter
Meetings
Toll-free phone line
Field operations/evaluations
Purchasing cooperatives
Security/safety procedures

MARKETING SUPPORT
Regional marketing
Bid preparation & presentation

PRO ONE JANITORIAL INC.

Ranked #462 in Entrepreneur Magazine's 2007 Franchise 500   *Financial rating: 0*

1486 Kenwood Ctr.
Menasha, WI 54952
(920)721-1014
www.pro1janitorial.com
Commercial cleaning
Began: 1989, Franchising: 1995
Headquarters size: 20 employees
Franchise department: 3 employees

U.S. franchises: 72
Canadian franchises: 0
Other foreign franchises: 0
Company-owned: 0

Seeking: Midwest
Seeking in Canada? No
Exclusive territories? No
Homebased option? Yes
Employees needed to run biz: 2
Absentee ownership? No

COSTS
Total cost: $16.5K-156K
Franchise fee: $7.5K-50K
Royalty fee: 19%
Term of agreement: 5 years renewable
    for $1.5K
Franchisees required to buy multiple
    units? No

FINANCING
In-house: Franchise fee
3rd-party: None

QUALIFICATIONS
Info not provided

TRAINING
At headquarters: 2 days
At franchisee's location: 2 nights

BUSINESS SUPPORT
Internet
Newsletter
Meetings
Toll-free phone line
Field operations/evaluations
Purchasing cooperatives
Security/safety procedures

MARKETING SUPPORT
Co-op advertising

SERVICEMASTER CLEAN

Ranked #34 in Entrepreneur Magazine's 2007 Franchise 500   *Financial rating: $$$$*

3839 Forest Hill Irene Rd.
Memphis, TN 38125
(800)255-9687/(901)597-7500
www.ownafranchise.com
Commercial/residential cleaning &
    disaster restoration
Began: 1947, Franchising: 1952
Headquarters size: 134 employees
Franchise department: 12 employees

U.S. franchises: 2,978
Canadian franchises: 166
Other foreign franchises: 1,396
Company-owned: 0

Seeking: All U.S.
Seeking in Canada? Yes
Exclusive territories? No
Homebased option? Yes
Employees needed to run biz: 3
Absentee ownership? No

COSTS
Total cost: $19.1K-109.2K
Franchise fee: $16.9K-45K
Royalty fee: 4-10%
Term of agreement: 5 years renewable
    at no charge
Franchisees required to buy multiple
    units? Outside the U.S. only

FINANCING
In-house: Accounts receivable,
    equipment, franchise fee,
    inventory, startup costs
3rd-party: None

QUALIFICATIONS
Net worth: $50K-75K
Cash liquidity: $15K-25K
Experience:
    General business experience

TRAINING
At headquarters: 2 weeks
At franchisee's location: 1-2 days
Annual convention
Regional seminars

BUSINESS SUPPORT
Internet
Newsletter
Meetings
Toll-free phone line
Field operations/evaluations
Security/safety procedures

MARKETING SUPPORT
Co-op advertising
Ad slicks
National media campaign
Regional marketing
Intranet
Web design templates

SYSTEM4

Ranked #188 in Entrepreneur Magazine's 2007 Franchise 500   *Financial rating: $$$$*

10060 Brecksville Rd.
Brecksville, OH 44141
(440)746-0440
www.system4usa.com
Commercial cleaning
Began: 2003, Franchising: 2003
Headquarters size: 10 employees
Franchise department: 10 employees

U.S. franchises: 283
Canadian franchises: 0
Other foreign franchises: 0
Company-owned: 0

Seeking: All U.S.
Seeking in Canada? No
Exclusive territories? No
Homebased option? Yes
Employees needed to run biz: 3
Absentee ownership? Yes

COSTS
Total cost: $5.5K-37.8K
Franchise fee: $4.4K-32K
Royalty fee: 5%
Term of agreement: 20 years renewable
    at no charge
Franchisees required to buy multiple
    units? No

FINANCING
In-house: Accounts receivable,
    equipment, franchise fee
3rd-party: None

QUALIFICATIONS
Net worth: $10K
Cash liquidity: $5K

TRAINING
At franchisee's location: 3 days
Seminars

BUSINESS SUPPORT
Internet
Meetings
Toll-free phone line
Field operations/evaluations
Purchasing cooperatives
Security/safety procedures

MARKETING SUPPORT
Ad slicks
Regional marketing

VANGUARD CLEANING SYSTEMS

Ranked #81 in Entrepreneur Magazine's 2007 Franchise 500   *Financial rating: $$$$*

655 Mariners Island Blvd., #303
San Mateo, CA 94404
(800)564-6422/(650)594-1500
www.vanguardcleaning.com
Commercial cleaning
Began: 1984, Franchising: 1984
Headquarters size: 20 employees
Franchise department: 3 employees

U.S. franchises: 576
Canadian franchises: 0
Other foreign franchises: 0
Company-owned: 3

Seeking: All U.S.
Seeking in Canada? No
Exclusive territories? No
Homebased option? Yes
Employees needed to run biz: 1-2
Absentee ownership? No

COSTS
Total cost: $6.6K-32.9K
Franchise fee: $6.3K-31.95K
Royalty fee: 5%
Term of agreement: 10 years renewable
    at no charge
Franchisees required to buy multiple
    units? No

FINANCING
In-house: Equipment, franchise fee
3rd-party: None

QUALIFICATIONS
Cash liquidity: $2.8K-9K
Experience:
    General business experience

TRAINING
At headquarters: 2 weeks
At regional offices: 2 weeks

BUSINESS SUPPORT
Newsletter
Toll-free phone line
Field operations/evaluations

MARKETING SUPPORT
Regional marketing
Initial customer base

MAINTENANCE ▸ *Handyman Services*

CASE HANDYMAN & REMODELING SERVICES LLC
Ranked #348 in Entrepreneur Magazine's 2007 Franchise 500   *Financial rating: $$$$*

4701 Sangamore Rd., N. Plaza, #40
Bethesda, MD 20816
(800)426-9434
www.casehandyman.com
Handyman services
Began: 1961, Franchising: 1997
Headquarters size: 110 employees
Franchise department: 9 employees

U.S. franchises: 56
Canadian franchises: 0
Other foreign franchises: 0
Company-owned: 4

Seeking: All U.S.
Seeking in Canada? No
Exclusive territories? Yes
Homebased option? No
Employees needed to run biz: 8
Absentee ownership? No

COSTS
Total cost: $200K-300K
Franchise fee: $45K
Royalty fee: 4-6.5%
Term of agreement: 10 years renewable
   for $5K+
Franchisees required to buy multiple
   units? No

FINANCING
No financing available

QUALIFICATIONS
Net worth: $500K
Cash liquidity: $250K
Experience:
   Industry experience
   General business experience

TRAINING
At headquarters: 4 weeks
At franchisee's location: 3 days

BUSINESS SUPPORT
Grand opening
Internet
Newsletter
Meetings
Toll-free phone line
Field operations/evaluations
Security/safety procedures

MARKETING SUPPORT
Ad slicks
National media campaign
Regional marketing
Radio
Internet
Direct-mail marketing

HANDYMAN CONNECTION
Ranked #299 in Entrepreneur Magazine's 2007 Franchise 500   *Financial rating: $$$$*

10250 Alliance Rd., #100
Cincinnati, OH 45242
(800)466-5530
www.handymanconnection.com
Home repairs & remodeling services
Began: 1990, Franchising: 1991
Headquarters size: 14 employees
Franchise department: 3 employees

U.S. franchises: 135
Canadian franchises: 24
Other foreign franchises: 0
Company-owned: 1

Seeking: All U.S.
Seeking in Canada? Yes
Exclusive territories? Yes
Homebased option? No
Employees needed to run biz: 3
Absentee ownership? Yes

COSTS
Total cost: $65K-110K
Franchise fee: $25K-40K
Royalty fee: 5%
Term of agreement: 10 years renewable
   for 10% of franchise fee
Franchisees required to buy multiple
   units? No

FINANCING
No financing available

QUALIFICATIONS
Net worth: $250K
Cash liquidity: $100K
Experience:
   General business experience
   Marketing skills

TRAINING
At headquarters: 2 weeks
At franchisee's location: 1 week

BUSINESS SUPPORT
Grand opening
Internet
Newsletter
Meetings
Toll-free phone line
Field operations/evaluations
Purchasing cooperatives

MARKETING SUPPORT
Co-op advertising
Ad slicks
National media campaign
Regional marketing

HANDYMAN HQ INC.

Financial rating: $$$

9100 W. Bloomington Fwy., #126
Bloomington, MN 55431
(952)440-2124
www.help-handyman.com
Home maintenance, repairs &
    improvements
Began: 2005, Franchising: 2005
Headquarters size: 2 employees
Franchise department: 2 employees

U.S. franchises: 0
Canadian franchises: 0
Other foreign franchises: 0
Company-owned: 2

Seeking: All U.S.
Seeking in Canada? No
Exclusive territories? Yes
Homebased option? Yes
Employees needed to run biz: 2-5
Absentee ownership? No

COSTS
Total cost: $25K-40K
Franchise fee: $17.5K
Royalty fee: 6%
Term of agreement: 10 years renewable
    for $1K
Franchisees required to buy multiple
    units? No

FINANCING
In-house: Franchise fee
3rd-party: None

QUALIFICATIONS
Net worth: $50K
Cash liquidity: $25K
Experience:
    General business experience

TRAINING
At headquarters: 4 weeks

BUSINESS SUPPORT
Internet
Meetings
Toll-free phone line
Field operations/evaluations
Security/safety procedures

MARKETING SUPPORT
Co-op advertising
Ad slicks
Regional marketing

HANDYMAN MATTERS FRANCHISE INC.

Ranked #343 in Entrepreneur Magazine's 2007 Franchise 500

Financial rating: $$$

12567 W. Cedar Dr., #250
Lakewood, CO 80228
(866)448-3451
www.handymanmatters.com
Handyman services
Began: 1997, Franchising: 2001
Headquarters size: 25 employees
Franchise department: 25 employees

U.S. franchises: 113
Canadian franchises: 1
Other foreign franchises: 2
Company-owned: 0

Seeking: All U.S.
Seeking in Canada? No
Exclusive territories? Yes
Homebased option? Yes
Employees needed to run biz: 3-9
Absentee ownership? Yes

COSTS
Total cost: $48K-106.2K
Franchise fee: $30K/40K/50K
Royalty fee: 6%
Term of agreement: 10 years renewable
    for $3.5K
Franchisees required to buy multiple
    units? No

FINANCING
No financing available

QUALIFICATIONS
Net worth: $175K
Cash liquidity: $60K
Experience:
    General business experience
    Marketing skills

TRAINING
At headquarters: 1-1/2 weeks
At franchisee's location: 1 week
Ongoing

BUSINESS SUPPORT
Internet
Newsletter
Meetings
Toll-free phone line
Field operations/evaluations
Purchasing cooperatives
Security/safety procedures

MARKETING SUPPORT
Co-op advertising
Ad slicks
National media campaign
Regional marketing
Print, radio & TV ads

HANDYMAN NETWORK

Current financial data not available

1165 San Antonio Dr., #H
Long Beach, CA 90807
(562)216-9292
www.handyman-network.com
Handyman services
Began: 2000, Franchising: 2002
Headquarters size: 20 employees
Franchise department: 13 employees

U.S. franchises: 22
Canadian franchises: 1
Other foreign franchises: 0
Company-owned: 1

Seeking: All U.S.
Seeking in Canada? Yes
Exclusive territories? Yes
Homebased option? No
Employees needed to run biz: 2-3
Absentee ownership? Yes

COSTS
Total cost: $84.8K-174.3K
Franchise fee: $30K
Royalty fee: 6%
Term of agreement: 10 years renewable
    at no charge
Franchisees required to buy multiple
    units? No

FINANCING
No financing available

QUALIFICATIONS
Net worth: $150K
Cash liquidity: $60K
Experience:
    General business experience
    Marketing skills

TRAINING
At headquarters: 1 week
At franchisee's location: 4 days

BUSINESS SUPPORT
Grand opening
Internet
Newsletter
Meetings
Toll-free phone line
Field operations/evaluations
Security/safety procedures

MARKETING SUPPORT
Co-op advertising
Ad slicks
National media campaign
Regional marketing
Full-service marketing & advertising

HANDYPRO HANDYMAN SERVICES INC.

Financial rating: $

995 S. Main
Plymouth, MI 48170
(800)942-6394
www.handypro.com
Handyman services
Began: 1996, Franchising: 2000
Headquarters size: 13 employees
Franchise department: 3 employees

U.S. franchises: 4
Canadian franchises: 0
Other foreign franchises: 0
Company-owned: 1

Seeking: All U.S.
Seeking in Canada? No
Exclusive territories? Yes
Homebased option? Yes
Employees needed to run biz: 1-10
Absentee ownership? Yes

COSTS
Total cost: $36.4K-61.9K
Franchise fee: $25K
Royalty fee: Varies
Term of agreement: 7 years renewable
    for 25% of initial franchise fee
Franchisees required to buy multiple
    units? No

FINANCING
No financing available

QUALIFICATIONS
Net worth: $50K
Cash liquidity: $30K
Experience:
    General business experience
    Management experience

TRAINING
At headquarters: 1 week
At franchisee's location: 1 week
    quarterly

BUSINESS SUPPORT
Grand opening
Internet
Newsletter
Meetings
Toll-free phone line
Field operations/evaluations
Purchasing cooperatives
Security/safety procedures

MARKETING SUPPORT
Co-op advertising
Ad slicks

HOMEFIXOLOGY

Current financial data not available

14502 N. Dale Mabry Hwy., #200
Tampa, FL 33618
(877)933-3337
www.homefixology.com
Handyman services
Began: 2005, Franchising: 2005
Headquarters size: 6 employees
Franchise department: 6 employees

U.S. franchises: 5
Canadian franchises: 0
Other foreign franchises: 0
Company-owned: 1

Seeking: All U.S.
Seeking in Canada? Yes
Exclusive territories? Yes
Homebased option? Yes
Employees needed to run biz: 3
Absentee ownership? No

COSTS
Total cost: $65K-115K
Franchise fee: $19.9K-39.9K
Royalty fee: 7%
Term of agreement: 5 years renewable
    for $5K
Franchisees required to buy multiple
    units? No

FINANCING
In-house: Franchise fee, startup
    costs
3rd-party: None

QUALIFICATIONS
Net worth: $150K
Cash liquidity: $50K
Experience:
    General business experience

TRAINING
At headquarters: 1 week

BUSINESS SUPPORT
Grand opening
Internet
Newsletter
Meetings
Toll-free phone line
Purchasing cooperatives
Security/safety procedures

MARKETING SUPPORT
Co-op advertising
Ad slicks
National media campaign

HOMETASK.COM HANDYMAN SERVICES

Current financial data not available

15200 52nd Ave. S., #100
Seattle, WA 98188
(206)763-6800
www.hometask.com
Handyman services
Began: 2000, Franchising: 2002
Headquarters size: 14 employees

U.S. franchises: 30
Canadian franchises: 2
Other foreign franchises: 0
Company-owned: 0

Seeking: All U.S.
Seeking in Canada? Yes
Exclusive territories? Info not
    provided
Homebased option? Yes
Employees needed to run biz: 1
Absentee ownership? No

COSTS
Total cost: $17K-33K
Franchise fee: $15K
Royalty fee: 7%
Term of agreement: 7 years renewable
    for $5K
Franchisees required to buy multiple
    units? Info not provided

FINANCING
No financing available

QUALIFICATIONS
Experience:
    Industry experience
    General business experience

TRAINING
At headquarters: Ongoing

BUSINESS SUPPORT
Grand opening
Internet
Newsletter
Meetings
Toll-free phone line
Field operations/evaluations
Security/safety procedures

MARKETING SUPPORT
Co-op advertising
Regional marketing
PR

HOUSE DOCTORS

Ranked #457 in Entrepreneur Magazine's 2007 Franchise 500   *Financial rating: $$$$*

575 Chamber Dr.
Milford, OH 45150
(800)319-3359
www.housedoctors.com
Handyman services & home repairs
Began: 1994, Franchising: 1995
Headquarters size: 23 employees
Franchise department: 12 employees

U.S. franchises: 166
Canadian franchises: 0
Other foreign franchises: 0
Company-owned: 0

Seeking: All U.S.
Seeking in Canada? No
Exclusive territories? Yes
Homebased option? Yes
Employees needed to run biz: Info
  not provided
Absentee ownership? No

COSTS

Total cost: $31.5K-60.6K
Franchise fee: $15.9K-35.9K
Royalty fee: 6%
Term of agreement: 10 years renewable
  at no charge
Franchisees required to buy multiple
  units? No

FINANCING

In-house: Franchise fee
3rd-party: None

QUALIFICATIONS

Experience:
  General business experience

TRAINING

At headquarters: 1 week

BUSINESS SUPPORT

Internet
Newsletter
Meetings
Toll-free phone line
Field operations/evaluations

MARKETING SUPPORT

Ad slicks

MAINTENANCE MADE SIMPLE

Ranked #429 in Entrepreneur Magazine's 2007 Franchise 500   *Financial rating: $$$$*

7575 E. Redfield Rd., #237
Scottsdale, AZ 85260
(866)778-6283
www.m2simple.com
Handyman & home maintenance
  services
Began: 2003, Franchising: 2003
Headquarters size: 11 employees

U.S. franchises: 36
Canadian franchises: 0
Other foreign franchises: 0
Company-owned: 0

Seeking: All U.S.
Seeking in Canada? Yes
Exclusive territories? Yes
Homebased option? Yes
Employees needed to run biz: 3
Absentee ownership? Yes

COSTS

Total cost: $50.2K-77.5K
Franchise fee: $30K
Royalty fee: 7%
Term of agreement: 15 years renewable
  for $5K
Franchisees required to buy multiple
  units? Outside the U.S. only

FINANCING

In-house: None
3rd-party: Equipment, franchise fee,
  inventory, payroll, startup costs

QUALIFICATIONS

Experience:
  General business experience

TRAINING

At headquarters: 5-7 days
At franchisee's location: 2 days

BUSINESS SUPPORT

Grand opening
Newsletter
Meetings
Toll-free phone line
Field operations/evaluations
Purchasing cooperatives
Security/safety procedures

MARKETING SUPPORT

Co-op advertising
Ad slicks
National media campaign
Regional marketing
Inbound & outbound call center
National accounts
Marketing collateral

MR. HANDYMAN INT'L. LLC
Ranked #120 in Entrepreneur Magazine's 2007 Franchise 500   *Financial rating: $$$$*

3948 Ranchero Dr.
Ann Arbor, MI 48108
(800)289-4600
www.mrhandyman.com
Home maintenance & repairs
Began: 2000, Franchising: 2000
Headquarters size: 65 employees
Franchise department: 12 employees

U.S. franchises: 216
Canadian franchises: 14
Other foreign franchises: 0
Company-owned: 0

Seeking: All U.S.
Seeking in Canada? Yes
Exclusive territories? Yes
Homebased option? Yes
Employees needed to run biz: 8
Absentee ownership? No

COSTS
Total cost: $86.2K-127.3K
Franchise fee: $9.9K
Royalty fee: 7%
Term of agreement: 10 years renewable
   for $1.98K
Franchisees required to buy multiple
   units? No

FINANCING
No financing available

QUALIFICATIONS
Net worth: $250K+
Cash liquidity: $30K
Experience:
   General business experience
   Marketing skills

TRAINING
At headquarters: 1 week
At franchisee's location: 6-9 weeks

BUSINESS SUPPORT
Grand opening
Internet
Newsletter
Meetings
Toll-free phone line
Field operations/evaluations
Purchasing cooperatives
Security/safety procedures

MARKETING SUPPORT
Co-op advertising
Ad slicks
Press releases
Vehicle decals

ODD JOB BOB
Financial rating: $$$

503 E. Jackson St., #130
Tampa, FL 33602
(866)464-2639
www.oddjobbob.com
Residential/commercial repairs &
   renovations
Began: 2003, Franchising: 2005
Headquarters size: 6 employees
Franchise department: 3 employees

U.S. franchises: 0
Canadian franchises: 1
Other foreign franchises: 0
Company-owned: 1

Seeking: All U.S.
Seeking in Canada? Yes
Exclusive territories? Yes
Homebased option? Yes
Employees needed to run biz: 3
Absentee ownership? Yes

COSTS
Total cost: $67.2K-159.2K
Franchise fee: $25K+
Royalty fee: 6%
Term of agreement: 5 years renewable
   at no charge
Franchisees required to buy multiple
   units? No

FINANCING
No financing available

QUALIFICATIONS
Net worth: $250K
Cash liquidity: $50K
Experience:
   General business experience
   Marketing skills
   Sales & construction knowledge

TRAINING
At headquarters: 5 days
At franchisee's location: 5 days
Ongoing

BUSINESS SUPPORT
Grand opening
Internet
Meetings
Toll-free phone line
Field operations/evaluations
Purchasing cooperatives
Security/safety procedures

MARKETING SUPPORT
Co-op advertising
Ad slicks
National media campaign
Regional marketing

 **Home Repairs, Miscellaneous**

MAINTENANCE

AIRE SERV HEATING & AIR CONDITIONING INC.

Ranked #250 in Entrepreneur Magazine's 2007 Franchise 500 Current financial data not available

1020 N. University Parks Dr.
Waco, TX 76707
(800)583-2662
www.discoveras.com
Heating & air conditioning services
Began: 1993, Franchising: 1993
Headquarters size: 110 employees
Franchise department: 30 employees

U.S. franchises: 99
Canadian franchises: 0
Other foreign franchises: 1
Company-owned: 0

Seeking: All U.S.
Seeking in Canada? No
Exclusive territories? Yes
Homebased option? Yes
Employees needed to run biz: 5-6
Absentee ownership? No

COSTS
Total cost: $36K-136.5K
Franchise fee: $22K
Royalty fee: 3-5%
Term of agreement: 10 years renewable
  for $750
Franchisees required to buy multiple
  units? Outside the U.S. only

FINANCING
In-house: Franchise fee
3rd-party: Equipment, franchise fee,
  startup costs

QUALIFICATIONS
Net worth: $150K+
Cash liquidity: $35K
Experience:
  Marketing skills

TRAINING
At headquarters: 10 days
At franchisee's location: 3 days
Regional training meetings: 2 days
  (4 times per year)

BUSINESS SUPPORT
Grand opening
Internet
Newsletter
Meetings
Toll-free phone line
Field operations/evaluations
Purchasing cooperatives
Security/safety procedures

MARKETING SUPPORT
Co-op advertising
Ad slicks
National media campaign

FURNITURE MEDIC

Ranked #271 in Entrepreneur Magazine's 2007 Franchise 500   *Financial rating: $$$$*

3839 Forest Hill Irene Rd.
Memphis, TN 38125
(800)255-9687/(901)597-8600
www.furnituremedicfranchise.com
Furniture restoration & repair services
Began: 1992, Franchising: 1992
Headquarters size: 24 employees
Franchise department: 9 employees

U.S. franchises: 328
Canadian franchises: 54
Other foreign franchises: 88
Company-owned: 0

Seeking: All U.S.
Seeking in Canada? Yes
Exclusive territories? No
Homebased option? Yes
Employees needed to run biz: 1
Absentee ownership? No

COSTS
Total cost: $37K-81.9K
Franchise fee: $24.5K
Royalty fee: 7%
Term of agreement: 5 years renewable
  at no charge
Franchisees required to buy multiple
  units? Outside the U.S. only

FINANCING
In-house: Equipment, franchise fee,
  inventory, vehicle
3rd-party: None

QUALIFICATIONS
Net worth: $60K-80K
Cash liquidity: $15K-25K
Experience:
  Industry experience
  General business experience
  Marketing skills

TRAINING
At headquarters: 2 weeks
Home study/mentor program:
  2 weeks+

BUSINESS SUPPORT
Internet
Newsletter
Meetings
Toll-free phone line
Field operations/evaluations
Security/safety procedures

MARKETING SUPPORT
Ad slicks
National media campaign
Website template

GLASS DOCTOR

Ranked #303 in Entrepreneur Magazine's 2007 Franchise 500   *Financial rating: $$*

1020 N. University Parks Dr.
Waco, TX 76707
(800)280-9858
www.glassdoctor.com
Auto, residential & commercial glass
   replacement
Began: 1962, Franchising: 1981
Headquarters size: 110 employees
Franchise department: 30 employees

U.S. franchises: 147
Canadian franchises: 0
Other foreign franchises: 0
Company-owned: 1

Seeking: All U.S.
Seeking in Canada? Yes
Exclusive territories? Yes
Homebased option? No
Employees needed to run biz: 5-6
Absentee ownership? No

COSTS
Total cost: $109.7K-261.7K
Franchise fee: $22K
Royalty fee: 4-7%
Term of agreement: 10 years renewable
   for $2.5K
Franchisees required to buy multiple
   units? Outside the U.S. only

FINANCING
In-house: Franchise fee
3rd-party: Accounts receivable,
   equipment, franchise fee,
   inventory, payroll, startup costs

QUALIFICATIONS
Net worth: $100K
Cash liquidity: $50K
Experience:
   General business experience

TRAINING
At headquarters: 10 days
At franchisee's location: 3 days
Regional training meetings: Twice a
   year

BUSINESS SUPPORT
Grand opening
Internet
Newsletter
Meetings
Toll-free phone line
Field operations/evaluations

MARKETING SUPPORT
Co-op advertising
Ad slicks
National media campaign

MR. APPLIANCE CORP.

Ranked #229 in Entrepreneur Magazine's 2007 Franchise 500   *Financial rating: $$$$*

1020 N. University Parks Dr.
Waco, TX 76707
(800)290-1422
www.mrappliance.com
Household appliance services &
   repairs
Began: 1996, Franchising: 1996
Headquarters size: 110 employees
Franchise department: 30 employees

U.S. franchises: 97
Canadian franchises: 2
Other foreign franchises: 0
Company-owned: 0

Seeking: All U.S.
Seeking in Canada? No
Exclusive territories? Yes
Homebased option? Yes
Employees needed to run biz: 1-3
Absentee ownership? No

COSTS
Total cost: $36.3K-72.9K
Franchise fee: $19.95K
Royalty fee: 4-7%
Term of agreement: 10 years renewable
   for $2.5K
Franchisees required to buy multiple
   units? Outside the U.S. only

FINANCING
In-house: Franchise fee
3rd-party: Equipment, franchise fee,
   startup costs

QUALIFICATIONS
Net worth: $75K
Cash liquidity: $25K
Experience:
   Industry experience

TRAINING
At headquarters: 1 week
At franchisee's location: Varies
Regional meetings

BUSINESS SUPPORT
Internet
Newsletter
Meetings
Toll-free phone line
Field operations/evaluations

MARKETING SUPPORT
Co-op advertising
Ad slicks
National media campaign

MR. ELECTRIC

Ranked #294 in Entrepreneur Magazine's 2007 Franchise 500   *Financial rating: $$$$*

1020 N. University Parks Dr.
Waco, TX 76707
(800)805-0575
www.mrelectric.com
Electrical services
Began: 1994, Franchising: 1994
Headquarters size: 110 employees
Franchise department: 30 employees

U.S. franchises: 134
Canadian franchises: 2
Other foreign franchises: 3
Company-owned: 0

Seeking: All U.S.
Seeking in Canada? Yes
Exclusive territories? Yes
Homebased option? Yes
Employees needed to run biz: 2-3
Absentee ownership? No

COSTS
Total cost: $69K+
Franchise fee: $22K
Royalty fee: 4-7%
Term of agreement: 10 years renewable
for $2.5K
Franchisees required to buy multiple
units? No

FINANCING
In-house: Franchise fee
3rd-party: Equipment, franchise fee,
startup costs

QUALIFICATIONS
Net worth: $75K
Cash liquidity: $25K-50K
Experience:
Industry experience
General business experience

TRAINING
At headquarters: 10 days
At franchisee's location: 2-3 days
Regional locations: 2 days

BUSINESS SUPPORT
Grand opening
Internet
Newsletter
Meetings
Toll-free phone line
Field operations/evaluations
Purchasing cooperatives
Security/safety procedures

MARKETING SUPPORT
Co-op advertising
Ad slicks
National media campaign

ONE HOUR AIR CONDITIONING & HEATING

Ranked #258 in Entrepreneur Magazine's 2007 Franchise 500   *Financial rating: $$$$*

50 Central Ave., #920
Sarasota, FL 34236
(800)746-0458/(941)552-5100
www.onehourheatandair.com
HVAC replacement & services
Began: 1999, Franchising: 2003
Headquarters size: 37 employees
Franchise department: 15 employees

U.S. franchises: 139
Canadian franchises: 0
Other foreign franchises: 0
Company-owned: 27

Seeking: All U.S.
Seeking in Canada? No
Exclusive territories? Yes
Homebased option? No
Employees needed to run biz: 4-12
Absentee ownership? Yes

COSTS
Total cost: $46.5K-453.4K
Franchise fee: $15K+
Royalty fee: 5%
Term of agreement: 10 years renewable
for 50% of original fee
Franchisees required to buy multiple
units? No

FINANCING
In-house: Franchise fee
3rd-party: None

QUALIFICATIONS
Experience:
Industry experience
General business experience
Marketing skills

TRAINING
At headquarters: 3 days
At franchisee's location: 3 days
At model centers & training school
Internet training

BUSINESS SUPPORT
Internet
Newsletter
Meetings
Toll-free phone line
Field operations/evaluations
Purchasing cooperatives
Security/safety procedures

MARKETING SUPPORT
National media campaign
Regional marketing
Internet
Radio ads

PRECISION DOOR SERVICE

Ranked #311 in Entrepreneur Magazine's 2007 Franchise 500   *Financial rating: $$$$*

2395 S. Washington Ave., #5
Titusville, FL 32780
(888)833-3494/(321)225-3500
www.precisiondoor.net
Garage door repairs & installation
Began: 1997, Franchising: 1999
Headquarters size: 20 employees
Franchise department: 2 employees

U.S. franchises: 68
Canadian franchises: 1
Other foreign franchises: 0
Company-owned: 0

Seeking: All U.S.
Seeking in Canada? Yes
Exclusive territories? Yes
Homebased option? Yes
Employees needed to run biz: 3-6
Absentee ownership? No

COSTS
Total cost: $56.96K-1M
Franchise fee: $10K-800K
Royalty fee: $250/wk.+
Term of agreement: 10 years renewable
     at no charge
Franchisees required to buy multiple
     units? No

FINANCING
In-house: Franchise fee
3rd-party: None

QUALIFICATIONS
Net worth: $250K
Cash liquidity: $60K+
Experience:
     General business experience

TRAINING
At headquarters: 2 weeks
At franchisee's location: As needed

BUSINESS SUPPORT
Internet
Newsletter
Meetings
Field operations/evaluations
Purchasing cooperatives
Security/safety procedures

MARKETING SUPPORT
Co-op advertising
Ad slicks

THE SCREEN MACHINE

Current financial data not available

4173 First St.
Livermore, CA 94557
(877)505-1985
www.screen-machine.com
Mobile window screen repair &
     fabrication
Began: 1986, Franchising: 1988
Headquarters size: 3 employees
Franchise department: 3 employees

U.S. franchises: 29
Canadian franchises: 0
Other foreign franchises: 0
Company-owned: 1

Seeking: Midwest, South, Southeast,
     Southwest, West
Seeking in Canada? No
Exclusive territories? Yes
Homebased option? Yes
Employees needed to run biz: 1
Absentee ownership? No

COSTS
Total cost: $47K-72.1K
Franchise fee: $25K
Royalty fee: 5%
Term of agreement: 10 years renewable
     for $2K
Franchisees required to buy multiple
     units? No

FINANCING
No financing available

QUALIFICATIONS
Net worth: $50K
Cash liquidity: $25K
Experience:
     General business experience
     Marketing skills

TRAINING
At headquarters: 1 week
Annual meeting: 2 days

BUSINESS SUPPORT
Internet
Meetings
Toll-free phone line
Field operations/evaluations
Purchasing cooperatives
Security/safety procedures

MARKETING SUPPORT
Co-op advertising
Ad slicks

THE SCREENMOBILE

Ranked #237 in Entrepreneur Magazine's 2007 Franchise 500   *Financial rating: $$$$*

72050-A Corporate Wy.
Thousand Palms, CA 92276
(800)775-7795
www.screenmobile.com
Mobile window & door screening
Began: 1982, Franchising: 1984
Headquarters size: 8 employees
Franchise department: 3 employees

U.S. franchises: 84
Canadian franchises: 0
Other foreign franchises: 0
Company-owned: 1

Seeking: All U.S.
Seeking in Canada? No
Exclusive territories? Yes
Homebased option? Yes
Employees needed to run biz: 1
Absentee ownership? Yes

COSTS
Total cost: $69.3K-75K
Franchise fee: $25.5K
Royalty fee: 5%
Term of agreement: 10 years renewable
    for $1K
Franchisees required to buy multiple
    units? No

FINANCING
No financing available

QUALIFICATIONS
Net worth: $100K
Cash liquidity: $50K

TRAINING
At headquarters: 8 days

BUSINESS SUPPORT
Internet
Newsletter
Meetings
Field operations/evaluations
Security/safety procedures

MARKETING SUPPORT
Ad slicks
TV ads
Direct-mail fliers
Door hangers

MAINTENANCE   *Lawn Care*

BIRTHFLOWERS.COM

Financial rating: 0

161 Swint Ave.
Milledgeville, GA 31061
(478)452-0008
www.birthflowers.com
Landscape design, installation &
    maintenance
Began: 1995, Franchising: 2006
Headquarters size: 2 employees
Franchise department: 2 employees

U.S. franchises: 0
Canadian franchises: 0
Other foreign franchises: 0
Company-owned: 1

Seeking: GA
Seeking in Canada? No
Exclusive territories? Yes
Homebased option? Yes
Employees needed to run biz: 1
Absentee ownership? No

COSTS
Total cost: $29.2K-66.2K
Franchise fee: $7K
Royalty fee: 5.5%
Term of agreement: 2 years/5 years
    renewable for $1K
Franchisees required to buy multiple
    units? No

FINANCING
In-house: Franchise fee, inventory
3rd-party: None

QUALIFICATIONS
Net worth: $50K
Cash liquidity: $10K
Experience:
    2 years of college or business
    ownership

TRAINING
At headquarters: 7 days
At franchisee's location: Twice a year

BUSINESS SUPPORT
Grand opening
Internet
Newsletter
Meetings
Field operations/evaluations

MARKETING SUPPORT
Ad slicks
National media campaign
Regional marketing
Signs
PR

ENVIRO MASTERS LAWN CARE

Current financial data not available

Box 178
Caledon East, ON L0N 1E0 Canada
(905)584-9592
www.enviromasters.com
Organic lawn care
Began: 1987, Franchising: 1991
Headquarters size: 4 employees
Franchise department: 4 employees

U.S. franchises: 0
Canadian franchises: 52
Other foreign franchises: 0
Company-owned: 3

Seeking: Not available in the U.S.
Seeking in Canada? Yes
Exclusive territories? Yes
Homebased option? Yes
Employees needed to run biz: 2-4
Absentee ownership? No

COSTS
Total cost: $40K
Franchise fee: $25K-35K
Royalty fee: 5%
Term of agreement: 10 years renewable
    for 25-50% of fee
Franchisees required to buy multiple
    units? No

FINANCING
No financing available

QUALIFICATIONS
Net worth: $40K
Cash liquidity: $25K
Experience:
    General business experience
    Environmentally conscious

TRAINING
At headquarters: Varies
At franchisee's location: 2-5 days
At existing locations: Ongoing

BUSINESS SUPPORT
Grand opening
Internet
Newsletter
Meetings
Toll-free phone line
Field operations/evaluations
Purchasing cooperatives
Security/safety procedures

MARKETING SUPPORT
Co-op advertising
Ad slicks
National media campaign
Regional marketing

LAWN DOCTOR

Ranked #92 in Entrepreneur Magazine's 2007 Franchise 500   *Financial rating: $$$$*

142 Hwy. 34
Holmdel, NJ 07733-0401
(800)452-9637
www.lawndoctorfranchise.com
Lawn, tree & shrub care, pest control
Began: 1967, Franchising: 1967
Headquarters size: 80 employees
Franchise department: 3 employees

U.S. franchises: 490
Canadian franchises: 0
Other foreign franchises: 0
Company-owned: 0

Seeking: All U.S.
Seeking in Canada? No
Exclusive territories? Yes
Homebased option? Yes
Employees needed to run biz: Info
    not provided
Absentee ownership? No

COSTS
Total cost: $97.9K-108.3K
Franchise fee: $25K
Royalty fee: 10%
Term of agreement: 20 years renewable
    at no charge
Franchisees required to buy multiple
    units? No

FINANCING
In-house: Equipment, franchise fee,
    startup costs
3rd-party: Equipment, franchise fee,
    inventory, startup costs

QUALIFICATIONS
Net worth: $150K
Cash liquidity: $60K
Experience:
    General business experience

TRAINING
At headquarters: 2 weeks

BUSINESS SUPPORT
Internet
Newsletter
Meetings
Toll-free phone line
Field operations/evaluations
Security/safety procedures

MARKETING SUPPORT
Co-op advertising
Ad slicks
Regional marketing

NATURALAWN OF AMERICA INC.

Ranked #483 in Entrepreneur Magazine's 2007 Franchise 500　　　*Financial rating: $$$$*

1 E. Church St.
Frederick, MD 21701
(800)989-5444
www.nl-amer.com
Organic lawn care
Began: 1987, Franchising: 1989
Headquarters size: 14 employees
Franchise department: 2 employees

U.S. franchises: 60
Canadian franchises: 0
Other foreign franchises: 0
Company-owned: 4

Seeking: All U.S.
Seeking in Canada? No
Exclusive territories? Yes
Homebased option? No
Employees needed to run biz: 2-6
Absentee ownership? No

COSTS

Total cost: $112.8K-149.9K
Franchise fee: $29.5K
Royalty fee: 7-9%
Term of agreement: 5 years renewable
　at no charge
Franchisees required to buy multiple
　units? Outside the U.S. only

FINANCING

In-house: None
3rd-party: Equipment, franchise fee,
　inventory, startup costs

QUALIFICATIONS

Net worth: $250K
Cash liquidity: $50K
Experience:
　General business experience
　Sales experience
　Management experience

TRAINING

At headquarters: 1 week
At franchisee's location: 1 week
At regional location: 2 weeks

BUSINESS SUPPORT

Grand opening
Internet
Newsletter
Meetings
Toll-free phone line
Field operations/evaluations
Purchasing cooperatives
Security/safety procedures

MARKETING SUPPORT

Co-op advertising
Ad slicks
Regional marketing
Internet marketing

NUTRI-LAWN

Current financial data not available

191 The West Mall, #110
Toronto, ON M9C 5K8 Canada
(416)620-7100
www.nutri-lawn.com
Lawn care
Began: 1983, Franchising: 1985
Headquarters size: 4 employees

U.S. franchises: 3
Canadian franchises: 29
Other foreign franchises: 0
Company-owned: 0

Seeking: Midwest, Northeast,
　Northwest, West
Seeking in Canada? Yes
Exclusive territories? Yes
Homebased option? Yes
Employees needed to run biz: 5-25
Absentee ownership? No

COSTS

Total cost: $200K
Franchise fee: $40K
Royalty fee: 6%
Term of agreement: 5 years renewable
　at no charge
Franchisees required to buy multiple
　units? No

FINANCING

No financing available

QUALIFICATIONS

Net worth: $250K
Cash liquidity: $150K
Experience:
　General business experience
　Marketing skills
　Management experience

TRAINING

At headquarters: 5 days
At franchisee's location: 10 days
Online training
Annual & regional conferences
Conference calls

BUSINESS SUPPORT

Internet
Newsletter
Meetings
Toll-free phone line
Field operations/evaluations
Purchasing cooperatives

MARKETING SUPPORT

Co-op advertising
National media campaign

SCOTTS LAWN SERVICE
Ranked #287 in Entrepreneur Magazine's 2007 Franchise 500   *Financial rating: $$$$*

14111 Scottslawn Rd.
Marysville, OH 43041
(800)264-8973
www.scottslawnservice.com
Lawn care
Began: 1984, Franchising: 1985
Headquarters size: 53 employees
Franchise department: 8 employees

U.S. franchises: 81
Canadian franchises: 0
Other foreign franchises: 0
Company-owned: 74

Seeking: All U.S.
Seeking in Canada? No
Exclusive territories? Yes
Homebased option? Yes
Employees needed to run biz: 3-10
Absentee ownership? Yes

COSTS
Total cost: $64.4K-210K
Franchise fee: $30K-75K
Royalty fee: 6-10%
Term of agreement: 10 years
    renewable
Franchisees required to buy multiple
    units? No

FINANCING
In-house: None
3rd-party: Accounts receivable,
    equipment, franchise fee,
    inventory, payroll, startup costs

QUALIFICATIONS
Net worth: $100K
Cash liquidity: $40K-60K
Experience:
    General business experience

TRAINING
At headquarters: 1 week
At franchisee's location: 1 week
Annual business/operations training
Ongoing training available

BUSINESS SUPPORT
Internet
Newsletter
Meetings
Toll-free phone line
Field operations/evaluations
Purchasing cooperatives
Security/safety procedures

MARKETING SUPPORT
Co-op advertising
National media campaign
Regional marketing
National direct-mail campaign

SPRING-GREEN LAWN CARE
Ranked #301 in Entrepreneur Magazine's 2007 Franchise 500   *Financial rating: $$$$*

11909 Spaulding School Dr.
Plainfield, IL 60544
(800)777-8608/(815)436-8777
www.springgreenfranchise.com
Lawn & tree care
Began: 1977, Franchising: 1977
Headquarters size: 16 employees
Franchise department: 7 employees

U.S. franchises: 93
Canadian franchises: 0
Other foreign franchises: 0
Company-owned: 21

Seeking: All U.S.
Seeking in Canada? No
Exclusive territories? Yes
Homebased option? Yes
Employees needed to run biz: 0
Absentee ownership? No

COSTS
Total cost: $86.9K-98.4K
Franchise fee: $30K
Royalty fee: 6-9%
Term of agreement: 10 years renewable
    at no charge
Franchisees required to buy multiple
    units? No

FINANCING
In-house: Equipment, inventory
3rd-party: Equipment, franchise fee,
    inventory, startup costs

QUALIFICATIONS
Net worth: $125K
Cash liquidity: $40K
Experience:
    General business experience
    Marketing skills

TRAINING
At headquarters: 1 week
At franchisee's location: Ongoing

BUSINESS SUPPORT
Internet
Newsletter
Meetings
Toll-free phone line
Field operations/evaluations
Security/safety procedures

MARKETING SUPPORT
Co-op advertising
Ad slicks
National media campaign
Regional marketing
Consumer website
Call centers

U.S. LAWNS

Current financial data not available

4407 Vineland Rd., #D-15
Orlando, FL 32811
(800)875-2967
www.uslawns.com
Landscape maintenance services
Began: 1986, Franchising: 1987
Headquarters size: 20 employees
Franchise department: 3 employees

U.S. franchises: 166
Canadian franchises: 0
Other foreign franchises: 0
Company-owned: 0

Seeking: All U.S.
Seeking in Canada? No
Exclusive territories? Yes
Homebased option? Yes
Employees needed to run biz: 10-15
Absentee ownership? No

COSTS
Total cost: $48.5K-70K
Franchise fee: $29K
Royalty fee: 3-4%
Term of agreement: 10 years renewable
at no charge
Franchisees required to buy multiple
units? No

FINANCING
In-house: Franchise fee
3rd-party: Equipment, inventory,
startup costs

QUALIFICATIONS
Net worth: $100K
Cash liquidity: $35K
Experience:
General business experience
Marketing skills

TRAINING
At headquarters: 6 days
At franchisee's location: Ongoing

BUSINESS SUPPORT
Internet
Newsletter
Meetings
Toll-free phone line
Field operations/evaluations
Purchasing cooperatives
Security/safety procedures

MARKETING SUPPORT
Co-op advertising
Ad slicks
National media campaign
Regional marketing
Internet support
National sales team

WEED MAN

Ranked #143 in Entrepreneur Magazine's 2007 Franchise 500　　　*Financial rating: $$$$*

11 Grand Marshall Dr.
Scarborough, ON M1B 5N6 Canada
(888)321-9333
www.weed-man.com
Lawn care
Began: 1970, Franchising: 1976
Headquarters size: 8 employees
Franchise department: 4 employees

U.S. franchises: 192
Canadian franchises: 116
Other foreign franchises: 1
Company-owned: 0

Seeking: All U.S.
Seeking in Canada? Yes
Exclusive territories? Yes
Homebased option? Yes
Employees needed to run biz: 4-6
Absentee ownership? Yes

COSTS
Total cost: $60.1K-80.3K
Franchise fee: $20K-33.8K
Royalty fee: 6%
Term of agreement: 10 years renewable
for 50% of original fee
Franchisees required to buy multiple
units? No

FINANCING
In-house: None
3rd-party: Equipment, franchise fee,
startup costs

QUALIFICATIONS
Net worth: $60K
Cash liquidity: $30K
Experience:
General business experience

TRAINING
At headquarters: 2 weeks
At franchisee's location: 2-4 days
At various locations: 3 days

BUSINESS SUPPORT
Internet
Newsletter
Meetings
Field operations/evaluations
Purchasing cooperatives
Security/safety procedures

MARKETING SUPPORT
National media campaign

MAINTENANCE   *Pest Control*

CRITTER CONTROL INC.

Ranked #308 in Entrepreneur Magazine's 2007 Franchise 500   *Financial rating: $$$$*

9435 E. Cherry Bend Rd.
Traverse City, MI 49684
(800)699-1953
www.crittercontrol.com
Urban & rural wildlife management
Began: 1983, Franchising: 1987
Headquarters size: 10 employees
Franchise department: 4 employees

U.S. franchises: 102
Canadian franchises: 2
Other foreign franchises: 0
Company-owned: 2

Seeking: All U.S.
Seeking in Canada? Yes
Exclusive territories? Yes
Homebased option? Yes
Employees needed to run biz: 1-3
Absentee ownership? No

COSTS
Total cost: $10.3K-69K
Franchise fee: $3K-36K
Royalty fee: 6-16%
Term of agreement: 10 years
    renewable
Franchisees required to buy
    multiple units? No

FINANCING
In-house: Equipment, inventory
3rd-party: Accounts receivable,
    franchise fee, payroll, startup
    costs

QUALIFICATIONS
Experience:
    Marketing skills
    Customer service skills

TRAINING
At headquarters: 1 week
At Columbus, OH or Fort
    Lauderdale, FL franchisees'
    locations
Annual conferences

BUSINESS SUPPORT
Grand opening
Internet
Newsletter
Meetings
Toll-free phone line
Field operations/evaluations
Purchasing cooperatives
Security/safety procedures

MARKETING SUPPORT
Co-op advertising
Ad slicks
National media campaign
Regional marketing
National call center
Sporting event sponsorship

PESTMASTER SERVICES

Current financial data not available

137 E. South St.
Bishop, CA 93514
(760)873-8100
www.pestmaster.com
Pest control services
Began: 1979, Franchising: 1991
Headquarters size: 12 employees
Franchise department: 1 employee

U.S. franchises: 17
Canadian franchises: 0
Other foreign franchises: 0
Company-owned: 8

Seeking: All U.S.
Seeking in Canada? No
Exclusive territories? Yes
Homebased option? Yes
Employees needed to run biz: 2
Absentee ownership? No

COSTS
Total cost: $30K-79.3K
Franchise fee: $15K-30K
Royalty fee: 5-7%
Term of agreement: 10 years renewable
    at no charge
Franchisees required to buy multiple
    units? No

FINANCING
No financing available

QUALIFICATIONS
Net worth: $65K
Cash liquidity: $50K
Experience:
    Industry experience
    General business experience

TRAINING
At headquarters: 1 week
At franchisee's location: 2 weeks
At Pestmaster University: 1 week

BUSINESS SUPPORT
Grand opening
Internet
Newsletter
Meetings
Toll-free phone line
Field operations/evaluations
Purchasing cooperatives

MARKETING SUPPORT
Co-op advertising
Ad slicks

TRULY NOLEN

Ranked #338 in Entrepreneur Magazine's 2007 Franchise 500   *Financial rating: $$$$*

3636 E. Speedway
Tucson, AZ 85716
(800)458-3664/(520)977-5817
www.trulynolen.com
Pest/termite control & lawn care
Began: 1938, Franchising: 1996
Headquarters size: 35 employees
Franchise department: 2 employees

U.S. franchises: 16
Canadian franchises: 0
Other foreign franchises: 60
Company-owned: 65

Seeking: All U.S.
Seeking in Canada? Yes
Exclusive territories? Yes
Homebased option? Yes
Employees needed to run biz: 2
Absentee ownership? Yes

COSTS
Total cost: $61K-226.5K
Franchise fee: $2.5K-45K
Royalty fee: 7%
Term of agreement: 5 years renewable
    for up to $1.5K
Franchisees required to buy multiple
    units? No

FINANCING
In-house: None
3rd-party: Accounts receivable,
    equipment, franchise fee,
    inventory, payroll, startup costs

QUALIFICATIONS
Net worth: $50K
Cash liquidity: $10K
Experience:
    Industry experience
    General business experience
    Marketing skills

TRAINING
At headquarters: 1 week
At franchisee's location: 2 weeks
At specific training centers

BUSINESS SUPPORT
Internet
Newsletter
Meetings
Toll-free phone line
Field operations/evaluations
Purchasing cooperatives
Security/safety procedures

MARKETING SUPPORT
Co-op advertising
Ad slicks
Regional marketing

 MAINTENANCE   *Plumbing*

ACE DURAFLO SYSTEMS LLC

Ranked #390 in Entrepreneur Magazine's 2007 Franchise 500   *Financial rating: $$$*

711 W. Kimberly Ave., #100
Placentia, CA 92870
(888)775-0220
www.fixmypipes.com
Pipe restoration services
Began: 1997, Franchising: 2001
Headquarters size: 12 employees
Franchise department: 6 employees

U.S. franchises: 20
Canadian franchises: 0
Other foreign franchises: 0
Company-owned: 7

Seeking: All U.S.
Seeking in Canada? Yes
Exclusive territories? No
Homebased option? No
Employees needed to run biz: 5
Absentee ownership? Yes

COSTS
Total cost: $139.7K-390.1K
Franchise fee: $24.9K
Royalty fee: 6-8%
Term of agreement: 10 years renewable
    for $1K
Franchisees required to buy multiple
    units? No

FINANCING
In-house: None
3rd-party: Equipment

QUALIFICATIONS
Net worth: $100K
Cash liquidity: $25K
Experience:
    Industry experience
    General business experience
    Marketing skills
    Must own an existing plumbing
    business

TRAINING
At headquarters: 1 week
At franchisee's location: 2 weeks

BUSINESS SUPPORT
Internet
Newsletter
Meetings
Toll-free phone line
Field operations/evaluations
Security/safety procedures

MARKETING SUPPORT
Co-op advertising
Ad slicks
National media campaign
Regional marketing

BENJAMIN FRANKLIN PLUMBING

Ranked #423 in Entrepreneur Magazine's 2007 Franchise 500　　　*Financial rating: $*

50 Central Ave., #920
Sarasota, FL 34236
(800)695-3579/(941)552-5111
www.benfranklinplumbing.com
Plumbing services
Began: 2000, Franchising: 2001
Headquarters size: 37 employees
Franchise department: 15 employees

U.S. franchises: 184
Canadian franchises: 0
Other foreign franchises: 0
Company-owned: 0

Seeking: All U.S.
Seeking in Canada? No
Exclusive territories? Yes
Homebased option? No
Employees needed to run biz: 4-12
Absentee ownership? Yes

COSTS
Total cost: $34.5K-415.7K
Franchise fee: $20K+
Royalty fee: 5%
Term of agreement: 10 years renewable
　　for 50% of franchise fee
Franchisees required to buy multiple
　　units? No

FINANCING
In-house: Franchise fee
3rd-party: None

QUALIFICATIONS
Info not provided

TRAINING
At headquarters: 3 days
At franchisee's location: 3 days
At model centers & training school
Internet training

BUSINESS SUPPORT
Internet
Newsletter
Meetings
Toll-free phone line
Field operations/evaluations
Purchasing cooperatives
Security/safety procedures

MARKETING SUPPORT
National media campaign
Regional marketing
Internet & radio ads
Press releases

MR. ROOTER

Ranked #164 in Entrepreneur Magazine's 2007 Franchise 500　　　*Financial rating: $$$$*

1020 N. University Parks Dr.
Waco, TX 76707
(800)298-6855
www.mrrooter.com
Plumbing, drain & sewer cleaning
Began: 1968, Franchising: 1972
Headquarters size: 110 employees
Franchise department: 30 employees

U.S. franchises: 194
Canadian franchises: 20
Other foreign franchises: 65
Company-owned: 0

Seeking: All U.S.
Seeking in Canada? Yes
Exclusive territories? Yes
Homebased option? Yes
Employees needed to run biz: 5-6
Absentee ownership? No

COSTS
Total cost: $50.95K-142K+
Franchise fee: $22.5K
Royalty fee: 4-7%
Term of agreement: 10 years renewable
　　for $2.5K
Franchisees required to buy multiple
　　units? Outside the U.S. only

FINANCING
In-house: Franchise fee
3rd-party: Franchise fee, startup
　　costs

QUALIFICATIONS
Net worth: $75K
Cash liquidity: $25K
Experience:
　　Industry experience
　　General business experience

TRAINING
At headquarters: 10 days
At franchisee's location: 2 days
At regional location: 2 days

BUSINESS SUPPORT
Grand opening
Internet
Newsletter
Meetings
Toll-free phone line
Field operations/evaluations
Purchasing cooperatives
Security/safety procedures

MARKETING SUPPORT
Co-op advertising
Ad slicks
National media campaign

ROOTER-MAN

Ranked #119 in Entrepreneur Magazine's 2007 Franchise 500   *Financial rating: $$$*

268 Rangeway Rd.
North Billerica, MA 01862
(800)700-8062
www.rooterman.com
Plumbing, drain & sewer cleaning
Began: 1970, Franchising: 1981
Headquarters size: 28 employees
Franchise department: 5 employees

U.S. franchises: 321
Canadian franchises: 4
Other foreign franchises: 1
Company-owned: 0

Seeking: All U.S.
Seeking in Canada? Yes
Exclusive territories? Yes
Homebased option? Yes
Employees needed to run biz: 3-5
Absentee ownership? Yes

COSTS
Total cost: $46.8K-137.6K
Franchise fee: $3.98K
Royalty fee: Varies
Term of agreement: 5 years renewable
    for $2.5K
Franchisees required to buy multiple
    units? No

FINANCING
In-house: Franchise fee
3rd-party: Equipment, inventory,
    startup costs

QUALIFICATIONS
Net worth: $25K
Cash liquidity: $10K
Experience:
    Mechanical aptitude

TRAINING
At headquarters: 6 weeks
At franchisee's location: 2 days
Training seminar: 2 days

BUSINESS SUPPORT
Grand opening
Internet
Newsletter
Meetings
Toll-free phone line
Field operations/evaluations
Lease negotiations
Purchasing cooperatives
Security/safety procedures

MARKETING SUPPORT
Co-op advertising
Ad slicks
National media campaign
Regional marketing
Website

MAINTENANCE ► *Residential Cleaning*

THE CLEANING AUTHORITY

Ranked #203 in Entrepreneur Magazine's 2007 Franchise 500   *Financial rating: $$$$*

6994 Columbia Gateway Dr., #100
Columbia, MD 21046
(877)504-6221
www.thecleaningauthority.com
Residential cleaning
Began: 1978, Franchising: 1996
Headquarters size: 35 employees
Franchise department: 35 employees

U.S. franchises: 174
Canadian franchises: 0
Other foreign franchises: 0
Company-owned: 1

Seeking: All U.S.
Seeking in Canada? No
Exclusive territories? Yes
Homebased option? No
Employees needed to run biz: 20
Absentee ownership? No

COSTS
Total cost: $80.8K-136.6K
Franchise fee: $27K-49.5K
Royalty fee: 4-6%
Term of agreement: 10 years renewable
    at no charge
Franchisees required to buy multiple
    units? No

FINANCING
In-house: None
3rd-party: Accounts receivable,
    equipment, franchise fee,
    inventory, payroll, startup costs

QUALIFICATIONS
Net worth: $150K+
Cash liquidity: $20K
Experience:
    General business experience
    People skills

TRAINING
At headquarters: 2 weeks
Ongoing

BUSINESS SUPPORT
Internet
Newsletter
Meetings
Toll-free phone line
Field operations/evaluations

MARKETING SUPPORT
Co-op advertising
Ad slicks
National media campaign
Regional marketing
Direct-mail marketing

COTTAGECARE INC.

Financial rating: $$$

6323 W. 110th St.
Overland Park, KS 66211
(913)469-8778
www.cottagecare.com
Residential cleaning
Began: 1988, Franchising: 1989
Headquarters size: 13 employees
Franchise department: 3 employees

U.S. franchises: 47
Canadian franchises: 6
Other foreign franchises: 0
Company-owned: 1

Seeking: All U.S.
Seeking in Canada? Yes
Exclusive territories? Yes
Homebased option? No
Employees needed to run biz: 10
Absentee ownership? Yes

COSTS
Total cost: $69.5K-99.5K
Franchise fee: $12.5K-19.5K
Royalty fee: 5.5%
Term of agreement: 10 years renewable
for $3K
Franchisees required to buy multiple
units? No

FINANCING
No financing available

QUALIFICATIONS
Cash liquidity: $46K-72.5K

TRAINING
At headquarters: 10 days

BUSINESS SUPPORT
Internet
Newsletter
Meetings
Field operations/evaluations

MARKETING SUPPORT
Ongoing direct-mail program

HOME CLEANING CENTERS OF AMERICA

Financial rating: $$$

10851 Mastin Blvd., #130
Overland Park, KS 66210
(800)767-1118
www.homecleaningcenters.com
House, office, carpet & window
cleaning
Began: 1981, Franchising: 1984
Headquarters size: 2 employees
Franchise department: 2 employees

U.S. franchises: 40
Canadian franchises: 0
Other foreign franchises: 0
Company-owned: 0

Seeking: All U.S.
Seeking in Canada? No
Exclusive territories? Yes
Homebased option? No
Employees needed to run biz: 12
Absentee ownership? No

COSTS
Total cost: $28.8K-30.8K
Franchise fee: $12.5K
Royalty fee: 3-5%
Term of agreement: 10 years renewable
at no charge
Franchisees required to buy multiple
units? No

FINANCING
No financing available

QUALIFICATIONS
Info not provided

TRAINING
At franchisee's location: 1 week

BUSINESS SUPPORT
Grand opening
Internet
Newsletter
Meetings
Toll-free phone line
Field operations/evaluations
Purchasing cooperatives
Security/safety procedures

MARKETING SUPPORT
Ad slicks

MAID TO PERFECTION

Ranked #182 in Entrepreneur Magazine's 2007 Franchise 500   *Financial rating: $$$$*

1101 Opal Ct. 2nd Fl.
Hagerstown, MD 21740
(800)648-6243/(301)790-7900
www.maidtoperfectioncorp.com
Residential & light commercial
    cleaning
Began: 1980, Franchising: 1990
Headquarters size: 8 employees
Franchise department: 8 employees

U.S. franchises: 247
Canadian franchises: 23
Other foreign franchises: 0
Company-owned: 4

Seeking: All U.S.
Seeking in Canada? Yes
Exclusive territories? Yes
Homebased option? No
Employees needed to run biz: 2
Absentee ownership? No

COSTS

Total cost: $48.6K-56K
Franchise fee: $12.5K
Royalty fee: 4-7%
Term of agreement: 10 years renewable
    at no charge
Franchisees required to buy multiple
    units? Outside the U.S. only

FINANCING

In-house: Franchise fee
3rd-party: None

QUALIFICATIONS

Net worth: $80K
Cash liquidity: $50K
Experience:
    General business experience
    Marketing skills

TRAINING

At headquarters: 3 days
At franchisee's location: 7 days
Ongoing training

BUSINESS SUPPORT

Grand opening
Internet
Newsletter
Meetings
Toll-free phone line
Field operations/evaluations
Lease negotiations
Purchasing cooperatives

MARKETING SUPPORT

Co-op advertising
Ad slicks
Regional marketing
Telephone routing

MAID TO SPARKLE INC.

Current financial data not available

705 Twin Ridge Ln., #10
Richmond, VA 23235
(804)272-0723
www.maidtosparkle.net
Maid services
Began: 1998, Franchising: 2003
Headquarters size: 8 employees
Franchise department: 2 employees

U.S. franchises: 2
Canadian franchises: 0
Other foreign franchises: 0
Company-owned: 1

Seeking: All U.S.
Seeking in Canada? Yes
Exclusive territories? Yes
Homebased option? Yes
Employees needed to run biz: 5
Absentee ownership? No

COSTS

Total cost: $22.6K-53.5K
Franchise fee: $20K
Royalty fee: 7%
Term of agreement: 10 years renewable
    at no charge
Franchisees required to buy multiple
    units? No

FINANCING

No financing available

QUALIFICATIONS

Net worth: $50K-100K
Cash liquidity: $25K
Experience:
    General business experience
    Marketing skills
    Customer service skills

TRAINING

At headquarters: 1 week
At franchisee's location: 1 week

BUSINESS SUPPORT

Internet
Newsletter
Meetings
Toll-free phone line
Field operations/evaluations

MARKETING SUPPORT

Ad slicks
Regional marketing

THE MAIDS HOME SERVICE

Ranked #38 in Entrepreneur Magazine's 2007 Franchise 500   *Financial rating: $$$$*

4820 Dodge St.
Omaha, NE 68132
(800)843-6243
www.maids.com
Residential cleaning
Began: 1979, Franchising: 1981
Headquarters size: 29 employees
Franchise department: 10 employees

U.S. franchises: 897
Canadian franchises: 11
Other foreign franchises: 0
Company-owned: 29

Seeking: All U.S.
Seeking in Canada? Yes
Exclusive territories? Yes
Homebased option? No
Employees needed to run biz: 20
Absentee ownership? Yes

COSTS
Total cost: $117K-170K
Franchise fee: $10K
Royalty fee: 3.9-6.9%
Term of agreement: 20 years renewable
    at no charge
Franchisees required to buy multiple
    units? No

FINANCING
In-house: None
3rd-party: Accounts receivable,
    equipment, franchise fee,
    inventory, payroll, startup costs

QUALIFICATIONS
Net worth: $300K-500K
Cash liquidity: $70K
Experience:
    General business experience
    Marketing skills
    Management skills
    People skills

TRAINING
At headquarters: 10 days
At franchisee's location: 5 days
Phone consultation: 7-10 weeks

BUSINESS SUPPORT
Internet
Newsletter
Meetings
Toll-free phone line
Field operations/evaluations
Purchasing cooperatives
Security/safety procedures

MARKETING SUPPORT
Co-op advertising
Ad slicks
National media campaign
Regional marketing
Intranet
PR
Customized collateral pieces
Proprietary software

MERRY MAIDS

Ranked #46 in Entrepreneur Magazine's 2007 Franchise 500   *Financial rating: $$$$*

P.O. Box 751017
Memphis, TN 38175-1017
(800)798-8000
www.merrymaids.com
Residential cleaning
Began: 1979, Franchising: 1980
Headquarters size: 60 employees
Franchise department: 25 employees

U.S. franchises: 771
Canadian franchises: 71
Other foreign franchises: 427
Company-owned: 178

Seeking: All U.S.
Seeking in Canada? Yes
Exclusive territories? Yes
Homebased option? No
Employees needed to run biz: 12
Absentee ownership? Yes

COSTS
Total cost: $24.4K-55.5K
Franchise fee: $19K-27K
Royalty fee: 5-7%
Term of agreement: 5 years renewable
    at no charge
Franchisees required to buy multiple
    units? No

FINANCING
In-house: Equipment, franchise fee,
    inventory
3rd-party: None

QUALIFICATIONS
Net worth: $33.5K-50.5K
Cash liquidity: $29.7K-44.3K
Experience:
    General business experience
    Management experience

TRAINING
At headquarters: 8 days
At franchisee's location: As needed
Additional training in Memphis, TN
    & regional locations

BUSINESS SUPPORT
Internet
Newsletter
Meetings
Toll-free phone line
Field operations/evaluations
Security/safety procedures

MARKETING SUPPORT
National media campaign
Yellow Pages ads
Internet ad composition site

MOLLY MAID

Ranked #83 in Entrepreneur Magazine's 2007 Franchise 500   *Financial rating: $$$$*

3948 Ranchero Dr.
Ann Arbor, MI 48108
(800)665-5962
www.mollymaid.com
Residential cleaning
Began: 1979, Franchising: 1979
Headquarters size: 65 employees
Franchise department: 12 employees

U.S. franchises: 380
Canadian franchises: 0
Other foreign franchises: 317
Company-owned: 0

Seeking: All U.S.
Seeking in Canada? No
Exclusive territories? Yes
Homebased option? No
Employees needed to run biz: 14
Absentee ownership? No

COSTS
Total cost: $110K-150K
Franchise fee: $14.9K
Royalty fee: 6.5-3%
Term of agreement: 10 years renewable
  for $2K
Franchisees required to buy multiple
  units? No

FINANCING
No financing available

QUALIFICATIONS
Net worth: $250K+
Cash liquidity: $30K
Experience:
  General business experience
  Marketing skills

TRAINING
At headquarters: 1 week
At franchisee's location: 2 days
Regional training center: 1 week

BUSINESS SUPPORT
Grand opening
Internet
Newsletter
Meetings
Toll-free phone line
Field operations/evaluations
Purchasing cooperatives
Security/safety procedures

MARKETING SUPPORT
Co-op advertising
Ad slicks
National media campaign

MTO CLEANING SERVICES

Ranked #326 in Entrepreneur Magazine's 2007 Franchise 500   *Financial rating: $$$$*

7100 E. Pleasant Valley Rd., #260
Independence, OH 44131
(877)392-6278
www.mtoclean.com
Residential & commercial cleaning,
  pressure washing, carpet cleaning
Began: 1988, Franchising: 1992
Headquarters size: 6 employees
Franchise department: 5 employees

U.S. franchises: 53
Canadian franchises: 0
Other foreign franchises: 0
Company-owned: 0

Seeking: All U.S.
Seeking in Canada? Yes
Exclusive territories? Yes
Homebased option? No
Employees needed to run biz: 3-12
Absentee ownership? Yes

COSTS
Total cost: $23K-165K
Franchise fee: $5K-50K
Royalty fee: 5%
Term of agreement: 15 years renewable
  at no charge
Franchisees required to buy multiple
  units? No

FINANCING
In-house: Franchise fee
3rd-party: None

QUALIFICATIONS
Cash liquidity: $18K-24K

TRAINING
At headquarters: 1 week
At franchisee's location: 1-2 days

BUSINESS SUPPORT
Internet
Newsletter
Meetings

MARKETING SUPPORT
Ad slicks

MAINTENANCE ▶ *Restoration Services*

DURACLEAN INT'L.

Ranked #328 in Entrepreneur Magazine's 2007 Franchise 500   *Financial rating: $$$$*

220 Campus Dr.
Arlington Heights, IL 60004
(800)251-7070/(847)704-7100
www.duraclean.com
Disaster restoration, mold
    remediation, carpet &
    upholstery cleaning
Began: 1930, Franchising: 1945
Headquarters size: 20 employees
Franchise department: 3 employees

U.S. franchises: 196
Canadian franchises: 4
Other foreign franchises: 174
Company-owned: 20

Seeking: All U.S.
Seeking in Canada? Yes
Exclusive territories? Yes
Homebased option? Yes
Employees needed to run biz: Info
    not provided
Absentee ownership? Yes

COSTS
Total cost: $51K-91.5K
Franchise fee: $17.5K
Royalty fee: 4-8%
Term of agreement: 5 years renewable
    at no charge
Franchisees required to buy multiple
    units? Outside the U.S. only

FINANCING
In-house: Franchise fee
3rd-party: None

QUALIFICATIONS
Cash liquidity: $50K
Experience:
    General business experience

TRAINING
At headquarters: 14 days
Continuing education classes
Annual meeting

BUSINESS SUPPORT
Internet
Newsletter
Meetings
Toll-free phone line
Field operations/evaluations

MARKETING SUPPORT
Ad slicks

PAUL DAVIS RESTORATION INC.

Ranked #349 in Entrepreneur Magazine's 2007 Franchise 500   *Financial rating: $$$$*

1 Independent Dr., #2300
Jacksonville, FL 32202
(904)737-2779
www.pdrestoration.com
Insurance restoration services
Began: 1966, Franchising: 1970
Headquarters size: 30 employees
Franchise department: 30 employees

U.S. franchises: 217
Canadian franchises: 0
Other foreign franchises: 0
Company-owned: 0

Seeking: All U.S.
Seeking in Canada? No
Exclusive territories? Yes
Homebased option? No
Employees needed to run biz: 2-20
Absentee ownership? No

COSTS
Total cost: $200K-300K
Franchise fee: $52.5K
Royalty fee: 3.5%
Term of agreement: 5 years renewable
    at no charge
Franchisees required to buy multiple
    units? No

FINANCING
In-house: Franchise fee
3rd-party: None

QUALIFICATIONS
Net worth: $350K
Cash liquidity: $150K-250K
Experience:
    General business experience
    Marketing skills

TRAINING
At headquarters: 4 weeks
At franchisee's location: 2 weeks
Follow-up training at 6-month
    anniversary: 3 days

BUSINESS SUPPORT
Internet
Newsletter
Meetings
Toll-free phone line
Field operations/evaluations
Purchasing cooperatives

MARKETING SUPPORT
Co-op advertising
Ad slicks
National media campaign
Regional marketing

PUROSYSTEMS INC.

Ranked #223 in Entrepreneur Magazine's 2007 Franchise 500   *Financial rating: $$$$*

6001 Hiatus Rd., #13
Tamarac, FL 33321
(800)247-9047
www.purocleanopportunity.com
Insurance restoration services
Began: 1986, Franchising: 1991
Headquarters size: 19 employees
Franchise department: 5 employees

U.S. franchises: 125
Canadian franchises: 1
Other foreign franchises: 0
Company-owned: 0

Seeking: All U.S.
Seeking in Canada? Yes
Exclusive territories? Yes
Homebased option? Yes
Employees needed to run biz: 4
Absentee ownership? No

COSTS
Total cost: $81.5K-122.4K
Franchise fee: $35K
Royalty fee: 8-10%
Term of agreement: 20 years renewable
    at no charge
Franchisees required to buy multiple
    units? No

FINANCING
In-house: None
3rd-party: Equipment

QUALIFICATIONS
Cash liquidity: $75K
Experience:
    General business experience
    Marketing skills

TRAINING
At headquarters: 3 weeks
At franchisee's location: 1 week

BUSINESS SUPPORT
Internet
Newsletter
Meetings
Toll-free phone line
Field operations/evaluations

MARKETING SUPPORT
Regional marketing

RAINBOW INT'L. RESTORATION & CLEANING

Ranked #393 in Entrepreneur Magazine's 2007 Franchise 500   *Financial rating: $$$$*

1020 N. University Parks Dr.
Waco, TX 76707
(800)280-9963
www.rainbowintl.com
Indoor restoration & cleaning
Began: 1981, Franchising: 1981
Headquarters size: 110 employees
Franchise department: 30 employees

U.S. franchises: 166
Canadian franchises: 6
Other foreign franchises: 161
Company-owned: 0

Seeking: All U.S.
Seeking in Canada? Yes
Exclusive territories? Yes
Homebased option? Yes
Employees needed to run biz: 1-3
Absentee ownership? No

COSTS
Total cost: $101.9K-163K
Franchise fee: $22K
Royalty fee: 4-7%
Term of agreement: 10 years renewable
    for $2.5K
Franchisees required to buy multiple
    units? Outside the U.S. only

FINANCING
In-house: Franchise fee
3rd-party: Equipment, franchise fee,
    inventory, startup costs

QUALIFICATIONS
Net worth: $100K
Cash liquidity: $25K
Experience:
    Industry experience
    General business experience
    Marketing skills

TRAINING
At headquarters: 14 days
At franchisee's location: 2 days
Regional training: 2-5 days

BUSINESS SUPPORT
Grand opening
Internet
Newsletter
Meetings
Toll-free phone line
Field operations/evaluations
Purchasing cooperatives
Security/safety procedures

MARKETING SUPPORT
Co-op advertising
Ad slicks
National media campaign

SERVICE TEAM OF PROFESSIONALS INC.

Ranked #334 in Entrepreneur Magazine's 2007 Franchise 500　　　　*Financial rating: $$$$*

10036 N.W. Ambassador Dr.
Kansas City, MO 64153-1362
(800)452-8326/(816)880-4746
www.stoprestoration.com
Disaster restoration, carpet
　cleaning, mold remediation,
　door & window services
Began: 1971, Franchising: 1996
Headquarters size: 4 employees
Franchise department: 4 employees

U.S. franchises: 46
Canadian franchises: 0
Other foreign franchises: 0
Company-owned: 0

Seeking: All U.S.
Seeking in Canada? No
Exclusive territories? Yes
Homebased option? Yes
Employees needed to run biz: 0-10
Absentee ownership? Yes

COSTS
Total cost: $25.4K-99.4K
Franchise fee: $24K/34K
Royalty fee: 7-9%
Term of agreement: 10 years renewable
　at no charge
Franchisees required to buy multiple
　units? No

FINANCING
In-house: Equipment
3rd-party: Franchise fee

QUALIFICATIONS
Net worth: $50K
Cash liquidity: $50K
Management aptitude

TRAINING
At headquarters: 1 week
Training conventions: 3 per year

BUSINESS SUPPORT
Internet
Meetings
Toll-free phone line
Purchasing cooperatives

MARKETING SUPPORT
Ad slicks
Fully-integrated marketing program

SERVPRO INDUSTRIES INC.

Ranked #25 in Entrepreneur Magazine's 2007 Franchise 500　　　　*Financial rating: $$$$*

801 Industrial Dr.
Gallatin, TN 37066
(800)826-9586/(615)451-0600
www.servpro.com
Insurance/disaster restoration &
　cleaning
Began: 1967, Franchising: 1969
Headquarters size: 180 employees
Franchise department: 7 employees

U.S. franchises: 1,310
Canadian franchises: 0
Other foreign franchises: 0
Company-owned: 0

Seeking: All U.S.
Seeking in Canada? No
Exclusive territories? No
Homebased option? Yes
Employees needed to run biz: 5-10
Absentee ownership? No

COSTS
Total cost: $102.3K-162.9K
Franchise fee: $37K
Royalty fee: 3-10%
Term of agreement: 5 years renewable
　for $250
Franchisees required to buy multiple
　units? No

FINANCING
In-house: Equipment, franchise fee,
　inventory, startup costs
3rd-party: Equipment, franchise fee,
　inventory, startup costs

QUALIFICATIONS
Net worth: $100K
Cash liquidity: $60K
Experience:
　General business experience
　Marketing skills

TRAINING
At headquarters: 2-1/2 weeks
At franchisee's location: 1 week
Business development program

BUSINESS SUPPORT
Grand opening
Internet
Newsletter
Meetings
Toll-free phone line
Field operations/evaluations
Purchasing cooperatives
Security/safety procedures

MARKETING SUPPORT
Co-op advertising
Ad slicks
National media campaign
Regional marketing
National accounts marketing

AEROWEST/WESTAIR DEODORIZING SERVICES

Ranked #484 in Entrepreneur Magazine's 2007 Franchise 500   *Financial rating: $$$$*

3882 Del Amo Blvd., #602
Torrance, CA 90503
(310)793-4242
www.westsanitation.com
Restroom deodorizing services
Began: 1943, Franchising: 1978
Headquarters size: 20 employees
Franchise department: 10 employees

U.S. franchises: 45
Canadian franchises: 0
Other foreign franchises: 0
Company-owned: 21

Seeking: All U.S.
Seeking in Canada? No
Exclusive territories? No
Homebased option? Yes
Employees needed to run biz: 0
Absentee ownership? No

COSTS
Total cost: $12.5K-53.9K
Franchise fee: $6K
Royalty fee: 8%
Term of agreement: 5 years renewable
   at no charge
Franchisees required to buy multiple
   units? No

FINANCING
In-house: Equipment, franchise fee,
   inventory, startup costs
3rd-party: None

QUALIFICATIONS
Net worth: $25K+
Cash liquidity: $10K
Experience:
   General business experience
   Sales & service skills

TRAINING
At franchisee's location: 2 weeks
In-field training as required

BUSINESS SUPPORT
Internet
Newsletter
Toll-free phone line
Field operations/evaluations

MARKETING SUPPORT
Regional marketing
Sales support

AIRE-MASTER OF AMERICA INC.

Ranked #319 in Entrepreneur Magazine's 2007 Franchise 500   *Financial rating: $$$$*

1821 N. Hwy. CC, P.O. Box 2310
Nixa, MO 65714
(800)525-0957/(417)725-2691
www.airemaster.com
Restroom deodorizing &
   maintenance services
Began: 1958, Franchising: 1976
Headquarters size: 66 employees
Franchise department: 2 employees

U.S. franchises: 64
Canadian franchises: 2
Other foreign franchises: 0
Company-owned: 5

Seeking: All U.S.
Seeking in Canada? No
Exclusive territories? Yes
Homebased option? Yes
Employees needed to run biz: 2
Absentee ownership? No

COSTS
Total cost: $43.1K-111.4K
Franchise fee: $28K-50.5K
Royalty fee: 5%
Term of agreement: 20 years renewable
   at no charge
Franchisees required to buy multiple
   units? No

FINANCING
In-house: None
3rd-party: Accounts receivable,
   equipment, franchise fee,
   inventory, startup costs

QUALIFICATIONS
Experience:
   Marketing skills

TRAINING
At headquarters: 5 days
At franchisee's location: 5 days
Quarterly training available at
   headquarters

BUSINESS SUPPORT
Internet
Newsletter
Meetings
Toll-free phone line
Field operations/evaluations

MARKETING SUPPORT
Customer analysis & literature

SPARKLING IMAGE

Current financial data not available

P.O. Box 93712
Southlake, TX 76092
(866)772-7559
www.sparkling-image.com
Commercial restroom hygiene &
    related products
Began: 2002, Franchising: 2004
Headquarters size: 9 employees
Franchise department: 5 employees

U.S. franchises: 36
Canadian franchises: 2
Other foreign franchises: 0
Company-owned: 0

Seeking: All U.S.
Seeking in Canada? Yes
Exclusive territories? Yes
Homebased option? Yes
Employees needed to run biz: 6
Absentee ownership? No

COSTS
Total cost: $43.9K-85.4K
Franchise fee: $19.5K-39.5K
Royalty fee: 7%
Term of agreement: 5 years renewable
    at no charge
Franchisees required to buy multiple
    units? No

FINANCING
No financing available

QUALIFICATIONS
Net worth: $100K+
Cash liquidity: $75K
Experience:
    General business experience
    Marketing skills
    Sales skills

TRAINING
At headquarters: 5 days
At franchisee's location: 5 days

BUSINESS SUPPORT
Grand opening
Internet
Meetings
Toll-free phone line
Field operations/evaluations
Purchasing cooperatives
Security/safety procedures

MARKETING SUPPORT
Ad slicks
National media campaign
Regional marketing

MAINTENANCE ▶ *Vinyl Repair*

CREATIVE COLORS INT'L.

Ranked #356 in Entrepreneur Magazine's 2007 Franchise 500

Financial rating: $$$

19015 S. Jodi Rd., #E
Mokena, IL 60448
(800)933-2656/(708)478-1437
www.creativecolorsintl.com
Leather, vinyl & plastic
    restoration/repairs
Began: 1980, Franchising: 1991
Headquarters size: 10 employees
Franchise department: 10 employees

U.S. franchises: 54
Canadian franchises: 1
Other foreign franchises: 0
Company-owned: 11

Seeking: All U.S.
Seeking in Canada? No
Exclusive territories? Yes
Homebased option? Yes
Employees needed to run biz: 1-4
Absentee ownership? Yes

COSTS
Total cost: $37.5K-71.4K
Franchise fee: $19.5K+
Royalty fee: 6%
Term of agreement: 10 years renewable
    for 20% of current fee
Franchisees required to buy multiple
    units? No

FINANCING
In-house: Equipment, startup costs
3rd-party: None

QUALIFICATIONS
Net worth: $50K+
Cash liquidity: $20K+
Experience:
    General business experience
    Marketing skills

TRAINING
At headquarters: 3 weeks
At franchisee's location: 1 week

BUSINESS SUPPORT
Grand opening
Internet
Newsletter
Meetings
Toll-free phone line
Field operations/evaluations
Security/safety procedures

MARKETING SUPPORT
Ad slicks
Regional marketing

DR. VINYL & ASSOCIATES LTD.

Ranked #230 in Entrepreneur Magazine's 2007 Franchise 500   *Financial rating: $$$*

821 N.W. Commerce
Lee's Summit, MO 64086
(800)531-6600
www.drvinyl.com
Mobile vinyl & leather repair,
    windshield repair
Began: 1972, Franchising: 1981
Headquarters size: 14 employees
Franchise department: 9 employees

U.S. franchises: 229
Canadian franchises: 0
Other foreign franchises: 70
Company-owned: 4

Seeking: All U.S.
Seeking in Canada? Yes
Exclusive territories? Yes
Homebased option? Yes
Employees needed to run biz: 1
Absentee ownership? No

COSTS
Total cost: $48.95K-76.5K
Franchise fee: $34.95K
Royalty fee: 7%
Term of agreement: 10 years renewable
    at no charge
Franchisees required to buy multiple
    units? Outside the U.S. only

FINANCING
In-house: Franchise fee
3rd-party: None

QUALIFICATIONS
Net worth: $50K
Cash liquidity: $15K
Experience:
    General business experience
    Marketing skills

TRAINING
At headquarters: 2 weeks
At franchisee's location: 2 weeks
At corporate or in-field location

BUSINESS SUPPORT
Grand opening
Internet
Newsletter
Meetings
Toll-free phone line
Field operations/evaluations
Purchasing cooperatives

MARKETING SUPPORT
Co-op advertising
Ad slicks
National media campaign

LEATHER MEDIC

Financial rating: $$$

13891 Jet Port Loop Rd., #24
Fort Myers, FL 33913
(888)561-0423
www.leathermedic.com
Leather repair & refinishing
Began: 1989, Franchising: 2003
Headquarters size: 4 employees
Franchise department: 2 employees

U.S. franchises: 19
Canadian franchises: 0
Other foreign franchises: 0
Company-owned: 1

Seeking: All U.S.
Seeking in Canada? Yes
Exclusive territories? Yes
Homebased option? Yes
Employees needed to run biz: 1
Absentee ownership? No

COSTS
Total cost: $33.5K-38.5K
Franchise fee: $29.5K
Royalty fee: $350/mo./truck
Term of agreement: 5 years renewable
    for $2.5K
Franchisees required to buy multiple
    units? No

FINANCING
In-house: Franchise fee
3rd-party: None

QUALIFICATIONS
Cash liquidity: $20K

TRAINING
At headquarters: 6 days

BUSINESS SUPPORT
Internet
Newsletter
Meetings
Toll-free phone line
Field operations/evaluations
Purchasing cooperatives
Security/safety procedures

MARKETING SUPPORT
Ad slicks
Personalized website

DR. GLASS WINDOW WASHING

Financial rating: $$$

885 Sparta Dr.
Lafayette, CO 80026
(303)499-7759
www.docglass.com
Window cleaning
Began: 1978, Franchising: 2001
Headquarters size: 2 employees
Franchise department: 2 employees

U.S. franchises: 10
Canadian franchises: 0
Other foreign franchises: 0
Company-owned: 3

Seeking: All U.S.
Seeking in Canada? Yes
Exclusive territories? Yes
Homebased option? Yes
Employees needed to run biz: 2
Absentee ownership? No

COSTS
Total cost: $4.6K
Franchise fee: $3K
Royalty fee: 10%
Term of agreement: 10 years
Franchisees required to buy multiple
    units? No

FINANCING
No financing available

QUALIFICATIONS
Net worth: $50K
Cash liquidity: $10K
Experience:
    General business experience

TRAINING
At headquarters: 1 week

BUSINESS SUPPORT
Internet
Newsletter
Toll-free phone line
Purchasing cooperatives

MARKETING SUPPORT
Ad slicks

FISH WINDOW CLEANING SERVICES INC.

Ranked #161 in Entrepreneur Magazine's 2007 Franchise 500

Financial rating: $$$

200 Enchanted Pkwy.
Manchester, MO 63021
(877)707-3474
www.fishwindowcleaning.com
Window cleaning
Began: 1978, Franchising: 1998
Headquarters size: 23 employees
Franchise department: 15 employees

U.S. franchises: 211
Canadian franchises: 0
Other foreign franchises: 0
Company-owned: 1

Seeking: All U.S.
Seeking in Canada? No
Exclusive territories? Yes
Homebased option? No
Employees needed to run biz: 5
Absentee ownership? No

COSTS
Total cost: $54.5K-127.6K
Franchise fee: $19.9K-49.9K
Royalty fee: 8-6%
Term of agreement: 10 years renewable
    for $3K
Franchisees required to buy multiple
    units? No

FINANCING
In-house: None
3rd-party: Accounts receivable,
    equipment, franchise fee,
    inventory, payroll, startup costs

QUALIFICATIONS
Net worth: $150K-500K
Cash liquidity: $60K-120K
Experience:
    Marketing skills

TRAINING
At headquarters: 10 days
At franchisee's location: 2 days

BUSINESS SUPPORT
Grand opening
Internet
Newsletter
Meetings
Toll-free phone line
Field operations/evaluations
Purchasing cooperatives
Security/safety procedures

MARKETING SUPPORT
Co-op advertising
Ad slicks
National media campaign
Regional marketing
Sales brochures
National-account referrals

SQUEEGEE SQUAD

Financial rating: 0

10044 Flanders Ct. N.E., #300
Blaine, MN 55449
(866)927-4669
www.squeegeesquad.com
Window cleaning
Began: 1999, Franchising: 2005
Headquarters size: Info not provided

U.S. franchises: 4
Canadian franchises: 0
Other foreign franchises: 0
Company-owned: 1

Seeking: All U.S.
Seeking in Canada? No
Exclusive territories? Yes
Homebased option? Yes
Employees needed to run biz: Info
not provided
Absentee ownership? Yes

COSTS
Total cost: $45K-71K
Franchise fee: $20K
Royalty fee: 7-5%
Term of agreement: 10 years renewable
for $1.5K
Franchisees required to buy multiple
units? Outside the U.S. only

FINANCING
No financing available

QUALIFICATIONS
Cash liquidity: $45K-71K
Experience:
General business experience

TRAINING
At headquarters: 2 weeks
At franchisee's location: 4 days

BUSINESS SUPPORT
Grand opening
Internet
Meetings
Toll-free phone line
Field operations/evaluations
Purchasing cooperatives
Security/safety procedures

MARKETING SUPPORT
Regional marketing
Marketing materials

WINDOW GANG

Ranked #153 in Entrepreneur Magazine's 2007 Franchise 500

Financial rating: $$$$

1509 Ann St.
Beaufort, NC 28516
(877)946-4264
www.windowgangfranchise.com
Window & pressure cleaning
Began: 1986, Franchising: 1996
Headquarters size: 6 employees
Franchise department: 3 employees

U.S. franchises: 159
Canadian franchises: 20
Other foreign franchises: 0
Company-owned: 0

Seeking: All U.S.
Seeking in Canada? Yes
Exclusive territories? Yes
Homebased option? Yes
Employees needed to run biz: 5
Absentee ownership? Yes

COSTS
Total cost: $65K-250K
Franchise fee: $25K-150K
Royalty fee: 6%
Term of agreement: 10 years renewable
for $2.5K
Franchisees required to buy multiple
units? No

FINANCING
In-house: Franchise fee
3rd-party: Equipment, inventory,
startup costs

QUALIFICATIONS
Net worth: $50K
Cash liquidity: $10K
Experience:
Marketing skills

TRAINING
At headquarters: 7-14 days
At franchisee's location: 7 days

BUSINESS SUPPORT
Grand opening
Internet
Newsletter
Meetings
Toll-free phone line
Field operations/evaluations
Lease negotiations
Purchasing cooperatives
Security/safety procedures

MARKETING SUPPORT
Ad slicks
Regional marketing
Internet

WINDOW GENIE

Financial rating: $$$

10830 Millington Ct.
Cincinnati, OH 45242
(800)700-0022
www.windowgenie.com
Residential window cleaning, window tinting, pressure washing
Began: 1994, Franchising: 1998
Headquarters size: 9 employees
Franchise department: 3 employees

U.S. franchises: 57
Canadian franchises: 0
Other foreign franchises: 0
Company-owned: 0

Seeking: All U.S.
Seeking in Canada? No
Exclusive territories? Yes
Homebased option? Yes
Employees needed to run biz: 3
Absentee ownership? No

COSTS
Total cost: $44.7K-55.4K
Franchise fee: $19.5K
Royalty fee: 6-3%
Term of agreement: 10 years renewable at no charge
Franchisees required to buy multiple units? No

FINANCING
No financing available

QUALIFICATIONS
Net worth: $75K
Cash liquidity: $30K
Experience:
    General business experience
    Marketing skills
    Sales skills

TRAINING
At headquarters: 5 days
At franchisee's location: 5 days

BUSINESS SUPPORT
Grand opening
Internet
Meetings
Toll-free phone line
Field operations/evaluations
Purchasing cooperatives
Security/safety procedures

MARKETING SUPPORT
Ad slicks
Regional marketing

MAINTENANCE ▶ *Miscellaneous*

AMERICAN LEAK DETECTION

Ranked #115 in Entrepreneur Magazine's 2007 Franchise 500

Financial rating: $$$$

888 Research Dr., #100
Palm Springs, CA 92262
(800)755-6697/(760)320-9991
www.americanleakdetection.com
Concealed water, gas & sewer leak-detection services
Began: 1974, Franchising: 1984
Headquarters size: 34 employees
Franchise department: 1 employee

U.S. franchises: 298
Canadian franchises: 8
Other foreign franchises: 37
Company-owned: 6

Seeking: All U.S.
Seeking in Canada? Yes
Exclusive territories? Yes
Homebased option? Yes
Employees needed to run biz: 2-3
Absentee ownership? No

COSTS
Total cost: $71.3K-155.1K
Franchise fee: $57.5K+
Royalty fee: 6-10%
Term of agreement: 10 years renewable at no charge
Franchisees required to buy multiple units? Outside the U.S. only

FINANCING
In-house: Franchise fee
3rd-party: None

QUALIFICATIONS
Net worth: $200K
Cash liquidity: $65K
Experience:
    General business experience
    Marketing skills

TRAINING
At headquarters: 6-12 weeks
At franchisee's location: 1 week
Annual convention: 4 days

BUSINESS SUPPORT
Internet
Newsletter
Meetings
Toll-free phone line
Field operations/evaluations
Security/safety procedures

MARKETING SUPPORT
Ad slicks
Regional marketing

CLEAN FIRST TIME INC.

Current financial data not available

8810 Commodity Cir., #7
Orlando, FL 32819
(866)390-2532
www.cleanfirsttime.com
Construction cleaning
Began: 2003, Franchising: 2004
Headquarters size: 16 employees
Franchise department: 1 employee

U.S. franchises: 15
Canadian franchises: 0
Other foreign franchises: 0
Company-owned: 1

Seeking: All U.S.
Seeking in Canada? Yes
Exclusive territories? Yes
Homebased option? Yes
Employees needed to run biz: 3
Absentee ownership? No

COSTS
Total cost: $12K-150K
Franchise fee: $12K-150K
Royalty fee: 7%
Term of agreement: 10 years
Franchisees required to buy multiple
     units? No

FINANCING
In-house: Equipment, franchise fee,
     startup costs
3rd-party: None

QUALIFICATIONS
Net worth: $12K+
Cash liquidity: $12K
Experience:
     General business experience

TRAINING
At headquarters: 3-5 days
At franchisee's location: 3-5 days
Ongoing

BUSINESS SUPPORT
Grand opening
Internet
Meetings
Toll-free phone line
Field operations/evaluations
Lease negotiations
Security/safety procedures

MARKETING SUPPORT
Regional marketing

CRYSTAL CLEAR WINDOW WORKS USA

Financial rating: $$

475 Craighead St.
Nashville, TN 37204
(615)385-0240
www.ccwwi.com
Window restoration & defogging
Began: 2004, Franchising: 2005
Headquarters size: 12 employees
Franchise department: 4 employees

U.S. franchises: 17
Canadian franchises: 20
Other foreign franchises: 0
Company-owned: 0

Seeking: All U.S.
Seeking in Canada? Yes
Exclusive territories? No
Homebased option? Yes
Employees needed to run biz: 6
Absentee ownership? Yes

COSTS
Total cost: $91K-132.5K
Franchise fee: $50K
Royalty fee: 12.5%
Term of agreement: 5 years renewable
     at no charge
Franchisees required to buy multiple
     units? Info not provided

FINANCING
No financing available

QUALIFICATIONS
Net worth: $91K-132.5K
Experience:
     General business experience
     Marketing skills

TRAINING
At headquarters: 5 days

BUSINESS SUPPORT
Grand opening
Internet
Newsletter
Meetings
Field operations/evaluations
Security/safety procedures

MARKETING SUPPORT
Co-op advertising
Ad slicks

FILTAFRY

Ranked #233 in Entrepreneur Magazine's 2007 Franchise 500　　　*Financial rating: $$$*

5401 S. Kirkman Rd., #740
Orlando, FL 32819
(407)996-5550
www.filtafry.com
Fryer management/mobile filtration
　　services
Began: 1996, Franchising: 1997
Headquarters size: 12 employees
Franchise department: 22 employees

U.S. franchises: 142
Canadian franchises: 8
Other foreign franchises: 121
Company-owned: 0

Seeking: All U.S.
Seeking in Canada? Yes
Exclusive territories? Yes
Homebased option? Yes
Employees needed to run biz: 0
Absentee ownership? No

COSTS
Total cost: $72.3K-80.1K
Franchise fee: $27.8K
Royalty fee: to $450/mo.
Term of agreement: 5 years
　　renewable
Franchisees required to buy multi-
　　ple units? Outside the U.S. only

FINANCING
In-house: Equipment, franchise fee
3rd-party: Accounts receivable,
　　equipment, franchise fee,
　　inventory, payroll, startup costs

QUALIFICATIONS
Experience:
　　General business experience
　　required for multi-unit
　　development

TRAINING
At headquarters: 2 weeks
At franchisee's location: 2-3 weeks

BUSINESS SUPPORT
Internet
Newsletter
Meetings
Toll-free phone line
Field operations/evaluations
Security/safety procedures

MARKETING SUPPORT
National media campaign

JANBURY

　　　　　　　　　　　　　　　　　　　　　　　　　　Financial rating: $$$

5674 Marquesas Cir.
Sarasota, FL 34233
(941)927-9400
www.janbury.com
Construction support/cleaning services
Began: 2001, Franchising: 2006
Headquarters size: 8 employees
Franchise department: 8 employees

U.S. franchises: 1
Canadian franchises: 0
Other foreign franchises: 0
Company-owned: 1

Seeking: All U.S.
Seeking in Canada? No
Exclusive territories? Yes
Homebased option? No
Employees needed to run biz: 2
Absentee ownership? Yes

COSTS
Total cost: $163.6K-373K
Franchise fee: $50K
Royalty fee: 7%
Term of agreement: 7 years renewable
　　for $5K
Franchisees required to buy multiple
　　units? No

FINANCING
No financing available

QUALIFICATIONS
Cash liquidity: $75K
Experience:
　　General business experience
　　Marketing skills

TRAINING
At headquarters: 1 week
At franchisee's location: 1 week

BUSINESS SUPPORT
Internet
Toll-free phone line
Field operations/evaluations
Lease negotiations
Security/safety procedures

MARKETING SUPPORT
Ad slicks

OVENU OVEN DETAILING SERVICE

Financial rating: $$$

285 Passaic St.
Hackensack, NJ 07601
(888)296-8368
www.ovenu.com
Oven, cooktop, exhaust hood & barbecue cleaning services
Began: 1994, Franchising: 1999
Headquarters size: 3 employees
Franchise department: 2 employees

U.S. franchises: 1
Canadian franchises: 0
Other foreign franchises: 104
Company-owned: 0

Seeking: Northeast, Southeast
Seeking in Canada? Yes
Exclusive territories? Yes
Homebased option? Yes
Employees needed to run biz: 1
Absentee ownership? Yes

COSTS
Total cost: $33.5K-43.4K
Franchise fee: $17.9K
Royalty fee: $295/mo.
Term of agreement: 10 years renewable at no charge
Franchisees required to buy multiple units? No

FINANCING
No financing available

QUALIFICATIONS
Cash liquidity: $15K-20K

TRAINING
At headquarters: 5 days

BUSINESS SUPPORT
Grand opening
Internet
Meetings
Field operations/evaluations
Security/safety procedures

MARKETING SUPPORT
Ad slicks
Regional marketing
PR
Guerilla marketing template

THE POOL DOCTORS

Financial rating: 0

12 Prestwick Wy.
Trabuco Canyon, CA 92679
(949)713-7622
www.thepooldoctors.net
Swimming pool services & repairs
Began: 1981, Franchising: 2003
Headquarters size: 3 employees
Franchise department: 2 employees

U.S. franchises: 6
Canadian franchises: 0
Other foreign franchises: 2
Company-owned: 1

Seeking: Midwest, Southeast, Southwest, West
Seeking in Canada? No
Exclusive territories? Yes
Homebased option? Yes
Employees needed to run biz: 1-10
Absentee ownership? Yes

COSTS
Total cost: $12K-38K
Franchise fee: $7K
Royalty fee: 4%
Term of agreement: 5 years renewable for $1.5K
Franchisees required to buy multiple units? No

FINANCING
In-house: Franchise fee
3rd-party: None

QUALIFICATIONS
Experience:
    General business experience
    Marketing skills

TRAINING
At headquarters: 1 week
At franchisee's location: 1-3 days

BUSINESS SUPPORT
Grand opening
Internet
Newsletter
Field operations/evaluations
Purchasing cooperatives
Security/safety procedures

MARKETING SUPPORT
Co-op advertising
National media campaign
Internet

RECEIL IT CEILING RESTORATION

Current financial data not available

175-B Liberty St.
Copiague, NY 11726
(800)234-5464
www.receilit.com
Ceiling restoration
Began: 1992, Franchising: 2002
Headquarters size: 5 employees
Franchise department: 4 employees

U.S. franchises: 2
Canadian franchises: 0
Other foreign franchises: 0
Company-owned: 1

Seeking: Northeast, Southeast
Seeking in Canada? Yes
Exclusive territories? Yes
Homebased option? Yes
Employees needed to run biz: 2
Absentee ownership? No

COSTS
Total cost: $38.9K-55K
Franchise fee: $17.5K
Royalty fee: 7%
Term of agreement: 10 years renewable
    for $10K
Franchisees required to buy multiple
    units? No

FINANCING
In-house: Equipment, inventory
3rd-party: None

QUALIFICATIONS
Net worth: $100K
Cash liquidity: $53.9K
Experience:
    General business experience
    Sales background or aptitude

TRAINING
At headquarters: 6 days
At franchisee's location: 2 days

BUSINESS SUPPORT
Internet
Newsletter
Meetings
Toll-free phone line
Field operations/evaluations
Security/safety procedures

MARKETING SUPPORT
Regional marketing

SPARKLE WASH

Financial rating: $

26851 Richmond Rd.
Cleveland, OH 44146
(800)321-0770/(216)464-4212
www.sparklewash.com
On-site cleaning & restoration
Began: 1965, Franchising: 1967
Headquarters size: 10 employees
Franchise department: 2 employees

U.S. franchises: 81
Canadian franchises: 1
Other foreign franchises: 24
Company-owned: 1

Seeking: All U.S.
Seeking in Canada? Yes
Exclusive territories? Yes
Homebased option? Yes
Employees needed to run biz: 2
Absentee ownership? Yes

COSTS
Total cost: $35K-98.5K
Franchise fee: $20K-50K
Royalty fee: 3-5%
Term of agreement: 10 years renewable
    for $100
Franchisees required to buy multiple
    units? Outside the U.S. only

FINANCING
In-house: Franchise fee
3rd-party: Equipment

QUALIFICATIONS
Net worth: $100K
Cash liquidity: $35K
Experience:
    General business experience

TRAINING
At headquarters: 1 week
At franchisee's location: 1 week
Additional training available

BUSINESS SUPPORT
Internet
Newsletter
Meetings
Toll-free phone line
Field operations/evaluations
Security/safety procedures

MARKETING SUPPORT
Ad slicks
Regional marketing
Prospecting programs

ANDY ONCALL

Ranked #265 in Entrepreneur
Magazine's 2007 Franchise 500
Financial rating: $$$$
921 E. Main St.
Chattanooga, TN 37408
(423)242-0401
www.andyoncall.com
Handyman services
Financial rating: $$$$

ASP POOL & SPA CO.

3986 Lake St.
Macon, GA 31204
(478)254-4495
www.asppoolandspaco.com
Swimming pool maintenance &
    repairs
Current financial data not available

CARTEX LIMITED

42816 Mound Rd.
Sterling Heights, MI 48314
(586)739-4330
www.fabrion.net
Leather, vinyl, plastic & cloth repair
Current financial data not available

CERTIRESTORE

310 Northern Pacific Ave.
Fargo, ND 58102
(888)502-3784/(701)277-1005
www.certirestore.com
Furniture restoration & repair
Financial rating: $

CHEM-DRY CARPET DRAPERY & UPHOLSTERY CLEANING

Ranked #27 in Entrepreneur
Magazine's 2007 Franchise 500
1530 N. 1000 West
Logan, UT 84321
(877)307-8233
www.chemdry.com
Carpet, drapery & upholstery cleaning
Financial rating: $$$$

DISASTER KLEENUP INT'L.

Ranked #306 in Entrepreneur
Magazine's 2007 Franchise 500
29 S. LaSalle St., #930
Chicago, IL 60603
(630)350-3000
www.disasterkleenup.com
Insurance restoration services
Financial rating: $$$$

HEAVEN'S BEST CARPET & UPHOLSTERY CLEANING

Ranked #40 in Entrepreneur
Magazine's 2007 Franchise 500
247 N. First East, P.O. Box 607
Rexburg, ID 83440
(800)359-2095
www.heavensbest.com
Carpet & upholstery cleaning
Financial rating: $$

JAN-PRO FRANCHISING INT'L. INC.

Ranked #23 in Entrepreneur
Magazine's 2007 Franchise 500
11605 Haynes Bridge Rd., #425
Alpharetta, GA 30004
(678)336-1780
www.jan-pro.com
Commercial cleaning
Financial rating: $$$$

JANILINK

3545 McCall Pl., #D
Doraville, GA 30340
(770)216-9977
www.janilink.com
Janitorial supplies
Current financial data not available

MAID BRIGADE USA/ MINIMAID CANADA

Ranked #64 in Entrepreneur
Magazine's 2007 Franchise 500
4 Concourse Pkwy., #200
Atlanta, GA 30328
(800)722-6243
www.maidbrigade.com
Residential cleaning
Financial rating: $$$$

MAIDPRO

Ranked #249 in Entrepreneur
Magazine's 2007 Franchise 500
180 Canal St.
Boston, MA 02114
(888)624-3776/(617)742-8787
www.maidpro.com
Professional home & office cleaning
Financial rating: $$$$

MOSQUITONIX

14288 Gillis Rd.
Dallas, TX 75244
(972)934-2000
www.mosquitonix.com
Pest-control misting system
Current financial data not available

1-800-DRYCARPET CARPET CLEANING

3000 W. MacArthur Blvd., 5th Fl.
Santa Ana, CA 92704
(800)379-2277
www.drycarpet.com/franchise
Dry carpet cleaning
Current financial data not available

1-800-WATER DAMAGE

1167 Mercer St.
Seattle, WA 98109
(206)381-3047
www.1800waterdamage.com
Water-damage restoration services
Current financial data not available

ROTO-STATIC INT'L.

90 Delta Park Blvd., #A
Brampton, ON L6T 5E7 Canada
(877)586-4469/(905)458-7002
www.rotostatic.com
Carpet, upholstery, floor mainte-
    nance, ceiling & wall cleaning
Current financial data not available

SWISHER HYGIENE FRANCHISE CORP.

4725 Piedmont Row Dr., #400
Charlotte, NC 28210
(800)444-4138/(704)364-7707
www.swisherhygiene.com
Restroom-hygiene & commercial
    pest-control services & products
Financial rating: $$$$

ULTRASONIC BLIND CLEANING INC.

538 W. 5th St.
San Pedro, CA 90731
(310)372-4772
www.ubcc5star.com
Blinds/window coverings cleaning,
    sales & maintenance
Current financial data not available

PERSONAL CARE ▸ *Fitness*

ANYTIME FITNESS

Ranked #353 in Entrepreneur Magazine's 2007 Franchise 500   *Financial rating: $*

12181 Margo Ave. S.
Hastings, MN 55033
(800)704-5004
www.anytimefitness.com
Fitness center
Began: 2001, Franchising: 2002
Headquarters size: 18 employees
Franchise department: 5 employees

U.S. franchises: 323
Canadian franchises: 1
Other foreign franchises: 0
Company-owned: 12

Seeking: All U.S.
Seeking in Canada? Yes
Exclusive territories? Yes
Homebased option? No
Employees needed to run biz: 0-1
Absentee ownership? Yes

COSTS
Total cost: $32K-282K
Franchise fee: $8.99K
Royalty fee: $399
Term of agreement: 5 years renewable
    for $500
Franchisees required to buy multiple
    units? No

FINANCING
No financing available

QUALIFICATIONS
Net worth: $50K
Cash liquidity: $13.5K-70K
Experience:
    General business experience

TRAINING
At headquarters: 3 days+
At franchisee's location: 3 days+
Ongoing

BUSINESS SUPPORT
Grand opening
Internet
Newsletter
Meetings
Toll-free phone line
Field operations/evaluations
Lease negotiations
Purchasing cooperatives
Security/safety procedures

MARKETING SUPPORT
Ad slicks

BUTTERFLY LIFE

Financial rating: $$$

2404 San Ramon Valley Blvd., #200
San Ramon, CA 94583
(800)290-2977
www.butterflylife.com
Women's healthy living & fitness
    center
Began: 2003, Franchising: 2003
Headquarters size: 25 employees
Franchise department: 9 employees

U.S. franchises: 28
Canadian franchises: 0
Other foreign franchises: 1
Company-owned: 0

Seeking: All U.S.
Seeking in Canada? Yes
Exclusive territories? Yes
Homebased option? No
Employees needed to run biz: 1-2
Absentee ownership? Yes

COSTS
Total cost: $91K-109K
Franchise fee: $29.5K
Royalty fee: $1K/mo.
Term of agreement: 10 years renewable
    for $10K
Franchisees required to buy multiple
    units? No

FINANCING
In-house: None
3rd-party: Equipment, inventory,
    startup costs

QUALIFICATIONS
Experience:
    Industry experience
    General business experience
    Marketing skills

TRAINING
At headquarters: 1 week
At franchisee's location: 3 days
Annual conferences
Phone & on-site assistance

BUSINESS SUPPORT
Grand opening
Internet
Newsletter
Meetings
Toll-free phone line
Field operations/evaluations
Lease negotiations
Security/safety procedures

MARKETING SUPPORT
Co-op advertising
Ad slicks
National media campaign
Regional marketing
Direct response campaign

CATZ-COMPETITIVE ATHLETE TRAINING ZONE

Financial rating: 0

114 First Ave.
Needham, MA 02494
(781)449-2289
www.catzsports.com
Sports performance training
Began: 1997, Franchising: 2004
Headquarters size: 9 employees
Franchise department: 6 employees

U.S. franchises: 5
Canadian franchises: 0
Other foreign franchises: 0
Company-owned: 4

Seeking: All U.S.
Seeking in Canada? Yes
Exclusive territories? Yes
Homebased option? No
Employees needed to run biz: 3-7
Absentee ownership? Yes

COSTS
Total cost: $173.5K-341K
Franchise fee: $40K
Royalty fee: 6-8%
Term of agreement: 10 years renewable
    for $10K
Franchisees required to buy multiple
    units? No

FINANCING
In-house: None
3rd-party: Equipment, franchise fee,
    startup costs

QUALIFICATIONS
Net worth: $500K
Cash liquidity: $100K
Experience:
    General business experience

TRAINING
At headquarters: 3 weeks

BUSINESS SUPPORT
Grand opening
Internet
Field operations/evaluations
Security/safety procedures

MARKETING SUPPORT
Ad slicks

CONTOURS EXPRESS

Ranked #141 in Entrepreneur Magazine's 2007 Franchise 500   *Financial rating: $$$$*

156 Imperial Wy.
Nicholasville, KY 40356
(877)227-2282
www.contoursexpress.com
Women's fitness center
Began: 1998, Franchising: 1998
Headquarters size: 25 employees
Franchise department: 12 employees

U.S. franchises: 335
Canadian franchises: 15
Other foreign franchises: 105
Company-owned: 0

Seeking: All U.S.
Seeking in Canada? Yes
Exclusive territories? Yes
Homebased option? No
Employees needed to run biz: 2
Absentee ownership? Yes

COSTS
Total cost: $55.7K-95.4K
Franchise fee: $18K
Royalty fee: $395/mo.
Term of agreement: 10 years renewable
    at no charge
Franchisees required to buy multiple
    units? No

FINANCING
In-house: None
3rd-party: Equipment, franchise fee,
    startup costs

QUALIFICATIONS
Net worth: $75K
Cash liquidity: $25K

TRAINING
At headquarters: 5 days
At franchisee's location: 3 days
Ongoing training seminars

BUSINESS SUPPORT
Grand opening
Internet
Newsletter
Meetings
Toll-free phone line
Field operations/evaluations
Lease negotiations
Purchasing cooperatives
Security/safety procedures

MARKETING SUPPORT
Ad slicks
National media campaign
Regional marketing

CURVES

Ranked #15 in Entrepreneur Magazine's 2007 Franchise 500   *Financial rating: $$$$*

100 Ritchie Rd.
Woodway, TX 76712
(800)848-1096/(254)399-9285
www.buycurves.com
Women's fitness & weight-loss center
Began: 1992, Franchising: 1995
Headquarters size: 50 employees
Franchise department: 40 employees

U.S. franchises: 7,875
Canadian franchises: 737
Other foreign franchises: 1,268
Company-owned: 2

Seeking: All U.S.
Seeking in Canada? Yes
Exclusive territories? Yes
Homebased option? No
Employees needed to run biz: 2
Absentee ownership? Yes

COSTS
Total cost: $31.4K-53.5K
Franchise fee: $24.9K-39.9K
Royalty fee: 5%/6%
Term of agreement: 5 years renewable
    at no charge
Franchisees required to buy multiple
    units? No

FINANCING
In-house: Franchise fee
3rd-party: Equipment, franchise fee,
    startup costs

QUALIFICATIONS
Net worth: $75K
Cash liquidity: $50K
Financial stability

TRAINING
At headquarters: 1 week
At franchisee's location: 4 days
At regional meetings: 1 day
Convention: 3 days
Local events: 1 day

BUSINESS SUPPORT
Grand opening
Internet
Newsletter
Meetings
Toll-free phone line
Field operations/evaluations

MARKETING SUPPORT
Co-op advertising
Ad slicks
National media campaign
Regional marketing

CUTS FITNESS FOR MEN

Financial rating: $$

109 Lefferts Ln.
Clark, NJ 07066
(732)381-9300
www.cutsfitness.com
Circuit training for men
Began: 2003, Franchising: 2003
Headquarters size: 6 employees
Franchise department: 3 employees

U.S. franchises: 74
Canadian franchises: 2
Other foreign franchises: 17
Company-owned: 0

Seeking: All U.S.
Seeking in Canada? Yes
Exclusive territories? Yes
Homebased option? No
Employees needed to run biz: 1-2
Absentee ownership? No

COSTS
Total cost: $67.5K-104.7K
Franchise fee: $39.5K
Royalty fee: $400/mo.
Term of agreement: 10 years renewable
  at no charge
Franchisees required to buy multiple
  units? No

FINANCING
In-house: None
3rd-party: Equipment, franchise fee,
  startup costs

QUALIFICATIONS
Cash liquidity: $80K
Experience:
  Industry experience
  General business experience
  Marketing skills

TRAINING
At headquarters: 2 days
At franchisee's location: As needed

BUSINESS SUPPORT
Grand opening
Internet
Newsletter
Meetings
Field operations/evaluations
Purchasing cooperatives

MARKETING SUPPORT
Co-op advertising
Ad slicks
National media campaign
Regional marketing

EXPRESS TRAIN FITNESS FOR MEN

Financial rating: 0

P.O. Box 781153
Orlando, FL 32878-1156
(321)217-2325
www.expresstrainonline.com
30-minute circuit training for
  men/lifestyle coaching
Began: 2005, Franchising: 2005
Headquarters size: 3 employees
Franchise department: 3 employees

U.S. franchises: 0
Canadian franchises: 0
Other foreign franchises: 0
Company-owned: 1

Seeking: All U.S.
Seeking in Canada? Yes
Exclusive territories? Yes
Homebased option? No
Employees needed to run biz: 2-3
Absentee ownership? Yes

COSTS
Total cost: $73.7K-130K
Franchise fee: $37.95K
Royalty fee: 3%
Term of agreement: 5 years renewable
  for $5K
Franchisees required to buy multiple
  units? Yes

FINANCING
No financing available

QUALIFICATIONS
Net worth: $75K

TRAINING
At headquarters: 3 days
At franchisee's location: 3 days

BUSINESS SUPPORT
Grand opening
Internet
Newsletter
Meetings
Field operations/evaluations
Purchasing cooperatives
Security/safety procedures

MARKETING SUPPORT
Co-op advertising
Ad slicks
National media campaign
Regional marketing

FIT ZONE FOR WOMEN

Financial rating: $$$

4341 S. Westnedge Ave., #1103
Kalamazoo, MI 49008
(269)226-9564
www.fitzoneforwomen.com
Fitness center for women
Began: 2003, Franchising: 2006
Headquarters size: 6 employees
Franchise department: 2 employees

U.S. franchises: 18
Canadian franchises: 0
Other foreign franchises: 0
Company-owned: 5

Seeking: All U.S.
Seeking in Canada? No
Exclusive territories? Info not
    provided
Homebased option? No
Employees needed to run biz: 4
Absentee ownership? Yes

COSTS
Total cost: $94.6K-144.95K
Franchise fee: $19.5K
Royalty fee: Varies
Term of agreement: 5 years renewable
    at no charge
Franchisees required to buy multiple
    units? No

FINANCING
No financing available

QUALIFICATIONS
Info not provided

TRAINING
At headquarters: 7 days
At franchisee's location: 3 days

BUSINESS SUPPORT
Grand opening
Internet
Meetings
Toll-free phone line
Field operations/evaluations

MARKETING SUPPORT
Ad slicks

FITNESS TOGETHER

Ranked #77 in Entrepreneur Magazine's 2007 Franchise 500

Financial rating: $$$$

9092 Ridgeline Blvd., #A
Highlands Ranch, CO 80129
(303)663-0880
www.fitnesstogetherfranchise.com
Personal fitness training
Began: 1984, Franchising: 1996
Headquarters size: 14 employees
Franchise department: 14 employees

U.S. franchises: 261
Canadian franchises: 3
Other foreign franchises: 1
Company-owned: 0

Seeking: All U.S.
Seeking in Canada? Yes
Exclusive territories? Yes
Homebased option? No
Employees needed to run biz: 3-5
Absentee ownership? Yes

COSTS
Total cost: $150.5K-201.7K
Franchise fee: $34K
Royalty fee: 6%
Term of agreement: 10 years renewable
    for 25% of current franchise fee
Franchisees required to buy multiple
    units? Outside the U.S. only

FINANCING
In-house: None
3rd-party: Equipment, franchise fee,
    inventory, startup costs

QUALIFICATIONS
Net worth: $250K
Cash liquidity: $100K

TRAINING
At headquarters: 4-5 days

BUSINESS SUPPORT
Grand opening
Internet
Newsletter
Meetings
Toll-free phone line
Field operations/evaluations
Lease negotiations
Purchasing cooperatives
Security/safety procedures

MARKETING SUPPORT
Co-op advertising
Ad slicks
Regional marketing
Teleconferences

GOLD'S GYM FRANCHISING LLC

Ranked #63 in Entrepreneur Magazine's 2007 Franchise 500   *Financial rating: $$$$*

125 E. John Carpentar Fwy., #1300
Irving, TX 75062
(214)296-5026
www.goldsgym.com
Gym & fitness center
Began: 1965, Franchising: 1980
Headquarters size: 100 employees
Franchise department: 16 employees

U.S. franchises: 626
Canadian franchises: 10
Other foreign franchises: 94
Company-owned: 48

Seeking: All U.S.
Seeking in Canada? Yes
Exclusive territories? Yes
Homebased option? No
Employees needed to run biz: Info
    not provided
Absentee ownership? Yes

COSTS
Total cost: $300K-2M
Franchise fee: $25K
Royalty fee: 3%
Term of agreement: 10 years renewable
    for 50% of initial fee
Franchisees required to buy multiple
    units? No

FINANCING
In-house: None
3rd-party: Accounts receivable,
    equipment, franchise fee,
    inventory, payroll, startup costs

QUALIFICATIONS
Net worth: $800K
Cash liquidity: $300K
Experience:
    Industry experience
    General business experience

TRAINING
At headquarters: 1 week
Advanced training & staff training:
    1 week

BUSINESS SUPPORT
Grand opening
Internet
Newsletter
Meetings
Toll-free phone line
Field operations/evaluations
Purchasing cooperatives

MARKETING SUPPORT
Co-op advertising
Regional marketing
Marketing campaign & vendor
    program
Initial & ongoing training

THE HIT CENTER

Current financial data not available

6089 Frantz Rd., #102
Dublin, OH 43017
(866)305-5702
www.hitcentersinc.com
Athletic development, weight loss,
    fitness center
Began: 2000, Franchising: 2003
Headquarters size: 5 employees
Franchise department: 4 employees

U.S. franchises: 7
Canadian franchises: 0
Other foreign franchises: 0
Company-owned: 0

Seeking: All U.S.
Seeking in Canada? Yes
Exclusive territories? Yes
Homebased option? No
Employees needed to run biz: 12
Absentee ownership? Yes

COSTS
Total cost: $500K
Franchise fee: $40K
Royalty fee: 5%
Term of agreement: 10 years renewable
    at no charge
Franchisees required to buy multiple
    units? No

FINANCING
No financing available

QUALIFICATIONS
Experience:
    General business experience

TRAINING
At headquarters: 4 weeks
At franchisee's location: 1 week & as
    needed

BUSINESS SUPPORT
Grand opening
Internet
Newsletter
Meetings
Toll-free phone line
Purchasing cooperatives
Security/safety procedures

MARKETING SUPPORT
Co-op advertising
Ad slicks

JAZZERCISE INC.

Ranked #35 in Entrepreneur Magazine's 2007 Franchise 500   *Financial rating: $$$$*

2460 Impala Dr.
Carlsbad, CA 92008
(760)476-1750
www.jazzercise.com
Dance & exercise classes
Began: 1977, Franchising: 1983
Headquarters size: 150 employees
Franchise department: 10 employees

U.S. franchises: 5,693
Canadian franchises: 102
Other foreign franchises: 998
Company-owned: 1

Seeking: All U.S.
Seeking in Canada? Yes
Exclusive territories? No
Homebased option? Yes
Employees needed to run biz: Info
    not provided
Absentee ownership? No

COSTS
Total cost: $2.99K-33.1K
Franchise fee: $500/$1K
Royalty fee: to 20%
Term of agreement: 5 years
    renewable at no charge
Franchisees required to buy
    multiple units? No

FINANCING
No financing available

QUALIFICATIONS
Experience:
    Health & fitness background

TRAINING
At franchisee's location: 2-3 weeks
    home study
Seminars: 3 days

BUSINESS SUPPORT
Internet
Newsletter
Meetings
Toll-free phone line
Field operations/evaluations
Security/safety procedures

MARKETING SUPPORT
Co-op advertising
Ad slicks
National media campaign
Regional marketing

LA BOXING FRANCHISING CORP.

Financial rating: $$

3195-H Red Hill Ave.
Costa Mesa, CA 92626
(866)522-6946
www.laboxing.com
Cardio boxing & kickboxing classes
Began: 1992, Franchising: 2004
Headquarters size: 7 employees
Franchise department: 6 employees

U.S. franchises: 42
Canadian franchises: 0
Other foreign franchises: 0
Company-owned: 0

Seeking: All U.S.
Seeking in Canada? Yes
Exclusive territories? Yes
Homebased option? No
Employees needed to run biz: 3-5
Absentee ownership? Yes

COSTS
Total cost: $95.4K-109.7K
Franchise fee: $25K
Royalty fee: 6%
Term of agreement: 10 years renewable
    at no charge
Franchisees required to buy multiple
    units? No

FINANCING
In-house: Equipment, inventory
3rd-party: None

QUALIFICATIONS
Net worth: $150K
Cash liquidity: $25K

TRAINING
At headquarters: 1 week
At franchisee's location: 1 week
Additional training: 1 week

BUSINESS SUPPORT
Grand opening
Internet
Newsletter
Meetings
Toll-free phone line
Field operations/evaluations
Lease negotiations
Purchasing cooperatives
Security/safety procedures

MARKETING SUPPORT
Ad slicks
National media campaign
Regional marketing
TV & radio ads

LIBERTY FITNESS FOR WOMEN

Financial rating: 0

1701 Directors Blvd., #110
Austin, TX 78744
(512)623-3660
www.libertyfitness.com
30-minute women's fitness program
Began: 2002, Franchising: 2002
Headquarters size: 8 employees
Franchise department: 8 employees

U.S. franchises: 24
Canadian franchises: 0
Other foreign franchises: 0
Company-owned: 0

Seeking: All U.S.
Seeking in Canada? No
Exclusive territories? Yes
Homebased option? No
Employees needed to run biz: 2
Absentee ownership? Yes

COSTS
Total cost: $106.2K-159.4K
Franchise fee: $30.6K
Royalty fee: $495-795/mo.
Term of agreement: 10 years renewable
    at no charge
Franchisees required to buy multiple
    units? No

FINANCING
In-house: None
3rd-party: Accounts receivable,
    equipment, franchise fee,
    inventory, payroll, startup costs

QUALIFICATIONS
Net worth: $250K
Cash liquidity: $75K
Experience:
    General business experience

TRAINING
At headquarters: 5 days
At franchisee's location: 2 days
Ongoing web training

BUSINESS SUPPORT
Grand opening
Internet
Meetings
Field operations/evaluations

MARKETING SUPPORT
Ad slicks
National media campaign

NITRO FITNESS FOR MEN

Current financial data not available

12760 W. 87th St. Pkwy., #108
Lenexa, KS 66215
(913)495-5550
www.nitrofitnessformen.com
Health club
Began: 2004, Franchising: 2004
Headquarters size: 4 employees
Franchise department: 4 employees

U.S. franchises: 9
Canadian franchises: 0
Other foreign franchises: 0
Company-owned: 1

Seeking: All U.S.
Seeking in Canada? No
Exclusive territories? Yes
Homebased option? No
Employees needed to run biz: 2
Absentee ownership? No

COSTS
Total cost: $67.5K-83.8K
Franchise fee: $39.8K
Royalty fee: $498/mo.
Term of agreement: 7 years renewable
    for $5K
Franchisees required to buy multiple
    units? No

FINANCING
In-house: None
3rd-party: Accounts receivable,
    equipment, franchise fee,
    inventory, startup costs

QUALIFICATIONS
Net worth: $200K
Experience:
    Industry experience

TRAINING
At headquarters: 3 days
At franchisee's location
Corporate classroom: 1 day

BUSINESS SUPPORT
Grand opening
Internet
Newsletter
Meetings
Toll-free phone line
Field operations/evaluations
Purchasing cooperatives

MARKETING SUPPORT
Ad slicks

1-2-3 FIT

Financial rating: $$

1415 Larimer St., #500
Denver, CO 80202
(888)688-4630/(720)479-9000
www.123fit.com
Fitness club
Began: 2005, Franchising: 2005
Headquarters size: 20 employees

U.S. franchises: 30
Canadian franchises: 0
Other foreign franchises: 0
Company-owned: 0

Seeking: All U.S.
Seeking in Canada? Yes
Exclusive territories? No
Homebased option? No
Employees needed to run biz: 4-6
Absentee ownership? Info not
   provided

COSTS
Total cost: $63.4K-115.8K
Franchise fee: $20K
Royalty fee: 5%
Term of agreement: Info not provided
Franchisees required to buy multiple
   units? No

FINANCING
In-house: None
3rd-party: Accounts receivable,
   equipment, franchise fee,
   inventory, payroll, startup costs

QUALIFICATIONS
Net worth: $125K

TRAINING
At headquarters: 7 days
At franchisee's location
Self-study course

BUSINESS SUPPORT
Grand opening
Internet
Meetings
Toll-free phone line
Field operations/evaluations
Security/safety procedures

MARKETING SUPPORT
National media campaign

RETRO FITNESS

Financial rating: 0

522 Rt. 9 N., #331
Manalapan, NJ 07726
(800)738-7604
www.retrofitness.net
Fitness center
Began: 2005, Franchising: 2005
Headquarters size: 10 employees
Franchise department: 2 employees

U.S. franchises: 24
Canadian franchises: 0
Other foreign franchises: 0
Company-owned: 0

Seeking: All U.S.
Seeking in Canada? Yes
Exclusive territories? Yes
Homebased option? No
Employees needed to run biz: 10-20
Absentee ownership? Yes

COSTS
Total cost: $536.4K-875.6K
Franchise fee: $35K
Royalty fee: 5%
Term of agreement: 10 years renewable
   at no charge
Franchisees required to buy multiple
   units? No

FINANCING
In-house: None
3rd-party: Equipment, startup costs

QUALIFICATIONS
Net worth: $400K
Cash liquidity: $75K-110K
Experience:
   General business experience

TRAINING
At headquarters: 8 days
At franchisee's location: 8 days

BUSINESS SUPPORT
Grand opening
Internet
Newsletter
Meetings
Toll-free phone line
Field operations/evaluations
Lease negotiations
Purchasing cooperatives
Security/safety procedures

MARKETING SUPPORT
Co-op advertising
Ad slicks
Regional marketing

SNAP FITNESS INC.

Ranked #206 in Entrepreneur Magazine's 2007 Franchise 500   *Financial rating: $$$*

2025 Coulter Ave., #200
Chanhassen, MN 55317
(952)474-5422
www.snapfitness.com
24-hour fitness center
Began: 2003, Franchising: 2004
Headquarters size: 14 employees

U.S. franchises: 141
Canadian franchises: 0
Other foreign franchises: 0
Company-owned: 2

Seeking: All U.S.
Seeking in Canada? Yes
Exclusive territories? Yes
Homebased option? No
Employees needed to run biz: 1
Absentee ownership? Yes

COSTS
Total cost: $130K-140K
Franchise fee: $15K
Royalty fee: $399/mo.
Term of agreement: 5 years renewable
   at no charge
Franchisees required to buy multiple
   units? No

FINANCING
In-house: None
3rd-party: Accounts receivable,
   equipment, inventory, payroll,
   startup costs

QUALIFICATIONS
Net worth: $150K-200K
Cash liquidity: $50K-70K

TRAINING
At headquarters: 2 days

BUSINESS SUPPORT
Grand opening
Internet
Meetings
Toll-free phone line
Field operations/evaluations
Lease negotiations
Purchasing cooperatives
Security/safety procedures

MARKETING SUPPORT
Co-op advertising
Ad slicks
National media campaign
Regional marketing

VELOCITY SPORTS PERFORMANCE

Current financial data not available

3650 Brookside Pkwy., #300
Alpharetta, GA 30022
(866)955-0400
www.velocitysp.com
Sports performance training
Began: 1999, Franchising: 2002
Headquarters size: 20 employees
Franchise department: 3 employees

U.S. franchises: 70
Canadian franchises: 3
Other foreign franchises: 0
Company-owned: 1

Seeking: All U.S.
Seeking in Canada? Yes
Exclusive territories? Yes
Homebased option? No
Employees needed to run biz: 6-10
Absentee ownership? Yes

COSTS
Total cost: $215K-665K
Franchise fee: $30K
Royalty fee: 2-6%
Term of agreement: 10 years renewable
   at no charge
Franchisees required to buy multiple
   units? Outside the U.S. only

FINANCING
In-house: None
3rd-party: Equipment, franchise fee,
   inventory, startup costs

QUALIFICATIONS
Net worth: $500K
Cash liquidity: $200K
Experience:
   General business experience
   Marketing skills

TRAINING
At headquarters: 2 weeks
At franchisee's location: 2 days
Periodic conferences: 2 days
Sales training: 1 day/quarter

BUSINESS SUPPORT
Grand opening
Internet
Newsletter
Meetings
Toll-free phone line
Field operations/evaluations
Lease negotiations
Purchasing cooperatives
Security/safety procedures

MARKETING SUPPORT
Co-op advertising
Ad slicks
National media campaign
Regional marketing
Direct-mail pieces
Marketing brochures

PERSONAL CARE ▶ *Hair Salons*

CARRS THE TRADITIONAL BARBER

Financial rating: $$$$

4700 Millenia Blvd., #340
Orlando, FL 32839
(407)428-9300
www.carrsbarbers.com
Men's grooming services
Began: 2003, Franchising: 2004
Headquarters size: 5 employees
Franchise department: 2 employees

U.S. franchises: 11
Canadian franchises: 0
Other foreign franchises: 0
Company-owned: 1

Seeking: All U.S.
Seeking in Canada? No
Exclusive territories? Yes
Homebased option? No
Employees needed to run biz: Info
    not provided
Absentee ownership? Yes

COSTS
Total cost: $84.8K-161.3K
Franchise fee: $20K
Royalty fee: $150/chair
Term of agreement: 10 years
Franchisees required to buy multiple
    units? No

FINANCING
No financing available

QUALIFICATIONS
Cash liquidity: $25K
Experience:
    General business experience

TRAINING
At headquarters: 4-8 days
At franchisee's location: 6-10 days

BUSINESS SUPPORT
Grand opening
Internet
Newsletter
Meetings
Toll-free phone line
Field operations/evaluations
Security/safety procedures

MARKETING SUPPORT
Ad slicks
Regional marketing

CARTOON CUTS

Current financial data not available

5101 N.W. 21st Ave., #410
Fort Lauderdale, FL 33309
(800)701-2887
www.cartooncuts.com
Children's hair salon
Began: 1991, Franchising: 2000
Headquarters size: 200 employees
Franchise department: 10 employees

U.S. franchises: 5
Canadian franchises: 0
Other foreign franchises: 3
Company-owned: 21

Seeking: All U.S.
Seeking in Canada? No
Exclusive territories? Yes
Homebased option? No
Employees needed to run biz: 6-8
Absentee ownership? Yes

COSTS
Total cost: $97K-216K
Franchise fee: $25K
Royalty fee: 5%
Term of agreement: 10 years
Franchisees required to buy multiple
    units? No

FINANCING
No financing available

QUALIFICATIONS
Net worth: $250K
Cash liquidity: $40K
Experience:
    General business experience
    Marketing skills
    Customer service skills

TRAINING
At headquarters: 2 weeks
At franchisee's location: 1 week

BUSINESS SUPPORT
Grand opening
Internet
Newsletter
Meetings
Toll-free phone line
Field operations/evaluations
Purchasing cooperatives
Security/safety procedures

MARKETING SUPPORT
Ad slicks
Regional marketing

COST CUTTERS FAMILY HAIR CARE

Ranked #113 in Entrepreneur Magazine's 2007 Franchise 500   *Financial rating: $$$$*

7201 Metro Blvd.
Minneapolis, MN 55439
(888)888-7008/(952)947-7777
www.regisfranchise.com
Family hair salon
Began: 1982, Franchising: 1982
Headquarters size: 800 employees
Franchise department: 125 employees

U.S. franchises: 606
Canadian franchises: 0
Other foreign franchises: 0
Company-owned: 260

Seeking: All U.S.
Seeking in Canada? No
Exclusive territories? Yes
Homebased option? No
Employees needed to run biz: 6-8
Absentee ownership? Yes

COSTS
Total cost: $83.3K-159.6K
Franchise fee: $12.5K-22.5K
Royalty fee: 6%
Term of agreement: 15 years renewable
    at no charge
Franchisees required to buy multiple
    units? Yes

FINANCING
In-house: None
3rd-party: Equipment, franchise fee,
    inventory, startup costs

QUALIFICATIONS
Net worth: $300K
Cash liquidity: $100K
Experience:
    General business experience
    Marketing skills
    Retail/service-industry experience

TRAINING
At headquarters: 4 days
At franchisee's location: 5 days
Additional training as needed

BUSINESS SUPPORT
Grand opening
Internet
Meetings
Toll-free phone line
Field operations/evaluations
Lease negotiations
Security/safety procedures

MARKETING SUPPORT
Ad slicks
Regional marketing

FANTASTIC SAMS

Ranked #39 in Entrepreneur Magazine's 2007 Franchise 500   *Financial rating: $$$*

50 Dunham Rd., 3rd Fl.
Beverly, MA 01915
(978)232-5600
www.fantasticsams.com
Full-service hair salon
Began: 1974, Franchising: 1976
Headquarters size: 30 employees
Franchise department: 4 employees

U.S. franchises: 1,366
Canadian franchises: 12
Other foreign franchises: 15
Company-owned: 0

Seeking: All U.S.
Seeking in Canada? Yes
Exclusive territories? Yes
Homebased option? No
Employees needed to run biz: 8
Absentee ownership? Yes

COSTS
Total cost: $100.5K-225.1K
Franchise fee: $25K-35K
Royalty fee: Varies
Term of agreement: 10 years renewable
    for $6.25K
Franchisees required to buy multiple
    units? No

FINANCING
In-house: None
3rd-party: Equipment, franchise fee,
    inventory, startup costs

QUALIFICATIONS
Net worth: $250K
Cash liquidity: $50K
Experience:
    General business experience

TRAINING
At headquarters: 1 week
At franchisee's location: Ongoing
At regional office: 1 week

BUSINESS SUPPORT
Grand opening
Internet
Newsletter
Meetings
Field operations/evaluations
Security/safety procedures

MARKETING SUPPORT
Co-op advertising
Ad slicks
National media campaign
Regional marketing
Turnkey marketing
In-salon graphics & promo pieces

FIRST CHOICE HAIRCUTTERS

Current financial data not available

6465 Millcreek Dr., #210
Mississauga, ON L5N 5R6 Canada
(800)617-3961/(905)363-4105
www.firstchoice.com
Full-service family hair care
Began: 1980, Franchising: 1982
Headquarters size: Info not provided
Franchise department: 6 employees

U.S. franchises: 0
Canadian franchises: 206
Other foreign franchises: 0
Company-owned: 229

Seeking: Not available in the U.S.
Seeking in Canada? Yes
Exclusive territories? Yes
Homebased option? No
Employees needed to run biz: 6
Absentee ownership? Info not
    provided

COSTS
Total cost: $96K-167K
Franchise fee: $12.5K-22.5K
Royalty fee: 5-7%
Term of agreement: 10 years renewable
    at no charge
Franchisees required to buy multiple
    units? Outside the U.S. only

FINANCING
In-house: None
3rd-party: Accounts receivable,
    equipment, franchise fee,
    inventory, startup costs

QUALIFICATIONS
Net worth: $300K
Cash liquidity: $100K
Experience:
General business experience

TRAINING
At headquarters: 5 days

BUSINESS SUPPORT
Grand opening
Meetings
Toll-free phone line
Field operations/evaluations
Lease negotiations
Security/safety procedures

MARKETING SUPPORT
Co-op advertising
Ad slicks

GREAT CLIPS INC.

Ranked #43 in Entrepreneur Magazine's 2007 Franchise 500   *Financial rating: $*

7700 France Ave., #425
Minneapolis, MN 55435
(800)947-1143/(952)893-9088
www.greatclipsfranchise.com
Family hair salon
Began: 1982, Franchising: 1983
Headquarters size: 255 employees
Franchise department: 9 employees

U.S. franchises: 2,484
Canadian franchises: 57
Other foreign franchises: 0
Company-owned: 0

Seeking: Midwest, South, Southeast,
    Southwest, West
Seeking in Canada? Yes
Exclusive territories? Yes
Homebased option? No
Employees needed to run biz: 8-10
Absentee ownership? Yes

COSTS
Total cost: $98.9K-184.7K
Franchise fee: $25K
Royalty fee: 6%
Term of agreement: 10 years renewable
    for $1.75K
Franchisees required to buy multiple
    units? No

FINANCING
In-house: None
3rd-party: Accounts receivable,
    equipment, franchise fee,
    inventory, payroll, startup costs

QUALIFICATIONS
Net worth: $300K
Cash liquidity: $150K
Experience:
    Marketing skills
    Strong management &
    leadership skills

TRAINING
At headquarters: 5 days
At locatl training center: 3 days &
    ongoing

BUSINESS SUPPORT
Grand opening
Internet
Meetings
Toll-free phone line
Field operations/evaluations
Purchasing cooperatives
Security/safety procedures

MARKETING SUPPORT
Co-op advertising
Broadcast media

HAIR CUTTERY

Financial rating: 0

1577 Spring Hill Rd., #500
Vienna, VA 22182
(877)876-7400
www.haircuttery.com/franchise
Hair salon
Began: 1974, Franchising: 2004
Headquarters size: 200 employees
Franchise department: 25 employees

U.S. franchises: 2
Canadian franchises: 0
Other foreign franchises: 0
Company-owned: 846

Seeking: Midwest, Northwest,
    South, Southwest, West
Seeking in Canada? No
Exclusive territories? Yes
Homebased option? No
Employees needed to run biz: 10
Absentee ownership? No

COSTS
Total cost: $120.5K-283K
Franchise fee: $15K-25K
Royalty fee: 4.5-5%
Term of agreement: 10 years renew-
    able for 25% of franchise fee
Franchisees required to buy multiple
    units? Yes

FINANCING
No financing available

QUALIFICATIONS
Net worth: $500K
Cash liquidity: $250K
Experience:
    General business experience
    Multi-unit experience

TRAINING
At headquarters: 1 week
At franchisee's location: 8 weeks

BUSINESS SUPPORT
Grand opening
Internet
Newsletter
Meetings
Toll-free phone line
Field operations/evaluations
Purchasing cooperatives
Security/safety procedures

MARKETING SUPPORT
Ad slicks
Local store marketing

HAIR SALOON FOR MEN

Financial rating: $

111 W. Port Plaza, #505
St. Louis, MO 63146
(314)576-7300
www.hairsaloon.com
Men's haircutting services & products
Began: 1997, Franchising: 2002
Headquarters size: 8 employees
Franchise department: 4 employees

U.S. franchises: 7
Canadian franchises: 0
Other foreign franchises: 0
Company-owned: 4

Seeking: All U.S.
Seeking in Canada? Yes
Exclusive territories? Yes
Homebased option? No
Employees needed to run biz: 12
Absentee ownership? No

COSTS
Total cost: $198K-249K
Franchise fee: $20K
Royalty fee: 6%
Term of agreement: 10 years renewable
    for 25% of initial franchise fee
Franchisees required to buy multiple
    units? No

FINANCING
In-house: None
3rd-party: Financing available

QUALIFICATIONS
Net worth: $1M
Cash liquidity: $200K
Experience:
    General business experience
    Marketing skills

TRAINING
At headquarters: 1 week
At franchisee's location: 1 week
Ongoing

BUSINESS SUPPORT
Grand opening
Internet
Newsletter
Meetings
Toll-free phone line
Field operations/evaluations
Purchasing cooperatives
Security/safety procedures

MARKETING SUPPORT
Co-op advertising
Ad slicks
Regional marketing

THE LEMON TREE

Financial rating: $$$

One Division Ave.
Levittown, NY 11756
(800)345-9156/(516)735-2828
www.lemontree.com
Family hair care
Began: 1974, Franchising: 1976
Headquarters size: 5 employees
Franchise department: 3 employees

U.S. franchises: 61
Canadian franchises: 0
Other foreign franchises: 0
Company-owned: 0

Seeking: All U.S.
Seeking in Canada? No
Exclusive territories? Yes
Homebased option? No
Employees needed to run biz: 5-10
Absentee ownership? No

COSTS
Total cost: $68.6K-115.1K
Franchise fee: $20K
Royalty fee: 6%
Term of agreement: 15 years renewable
at no charge
Franchisees required to buy multiple
units? No

FINANCING
In-house: Equipment, franchise fee
3rd-party: None

QUALIFICATIONS
Net worth: $100K-200K
Cash liquidity: $50K-75K
Experience:
General business experience

TRAINING
At headquarters: 1 week
At franchisee's location: 1 week
Additional training available

BUSINESS SUPPORT
Grand opening
Meetings
Toll-free phone line
Field operations/evaluations
Purchasing cooperatives

MARKETING SUPPORT
Co-op advertising
Ad slicks
National media campaign
Regional marketing

MALE CARE

Current financial data not available

3936 Barrett St.
Augusta, GA 30909
(706)854-7765
www.malecarefranchise.com
Combination barber shop, car wash
& dry cleaners
Began: 1998, Franchising: 2003
Headquarters size: 2 employees
Franchise department: 2 employees

U.S. franchises: 0
Canadian franchises: 0
Other foreign franchises: 0
Company-owned: 0

Seeking: All U.S.
Seeking in Canada? Yes
Exclusive territories? Info not
provided
Homebased option? No
Employees needed to run biz: 8
Absentee ownership? Yes

COSTS
Total cost: $68K-85K
Franchise fee: $25K
Royalty fee: 6%
Term of agreement: 10 years renewable
at no charge
Franchisees required to buy multiple
units? No

FINANCING
No financing available

QUALIFICATIONS
Net worth: $100K
Cash liquidity: $25K
Experience:
General business experience
Marketing skills

TRAINING
At franchisee's location: 2 weeks

BUSINESS SUPPORT
Grand opening
Internet
Toll-free phone line
Field operations/evaluations

MARKETING SUPPORT
Ad slicks

PIGTAILS & CREWCUTS

Financial rating: $$

1100 Old Ellis Rd., #1200
Roswell, GA 30076
(770)752-6800
www.pigtailsandcrewcuts.com
Children's hair salon
Began: 2002, Franchising: 2004
Headquarters size: 4 employees
Franchise department: 3 employees

U.S. franchises: 6
Canadian franchises: 0
Other foreign franchises: 0
Company-owned: 0

Seeking: All U.S.
Seeking in Canada? No
Exclusive territories? Yes
Homebased option? No
Employees needed to run biz: Info
    not provided
Absentee ownership? Info not
    provided

COSTS
Total cost: $84.3K-168.3K
Franchise fee: $25K
Royalty fee: 5%
Term of agreement: 10 years
Franchisees required to buy multiple
    units? No

FINANCING
In-house: None
3rd-party: Equipment, franchise fee,
    inventory, payroll, startup costs

QUALIFICATIONS
Net worth: $150K
Experience:
    General business experience

TRAINING
At headquarters: 1 week

BUSINESS SUPPORT
Grand opening
Meetings
Toll-free phone line
Field operations/evaluations
Lease negotiations
Purchasing cooperatives
Security/safety procedures

MARKETING SUPPORT
Ad slicks
Regional marketing
Promotional items

PRO-CUTS

Ranked #400 in Entrepreneur Magazine's 2007 Franchise 500   *Financial rating: $$$$*

7201 Metro Blvd.
Minneapolis, MN 55439
(952)947-7777
www.regisfranchise.com
Hair salon
Began: 1982, Franchising: 1984
Headquarters size: 800 employees
Franchise department:
    125 employees

U.S. franchises: 177
Canadian franchises: 0
Other foreign franchises: 0
Company-owned: 0

Seeking: All U.S.
Seeking in Canada? No
Exclusive territories? Yes
Homebased option? No
Employees needed to run biz: 6-8
Absentee ownership? Yes

COSTS
Total cost: $84.6K-148.3K
Franchise fee: $12.5K-22.5K
Royalty fee: 6%
Term of agreement: 10 years renewable
    for $2.5K
Franchisees required to buy multiple
    units? Yes

FINANCING
In-house: None
3rd-party: Equipment, franchise fee,
    inventory, startup costs

QUALIFICATIONS
Net worth: $300K
Cash liquidity: $100K
Experience:
    General business experience

TRAINING
At headquarters: 3-5 days
At franchisee's location: 5 days
Additional training as needed

BUSINESS SUPPORT
Grand opening
Meetings
Toll-free phone line
Field operations/evaluations
Lease negotiations
Security/safety procedures

MARKETING SUPPORT
Co-op advertising
Ad slicks

SNIP-ITS

Financial rating: $

1085 Worcester Rd.
Natick, MA 01760
(508)651-7052
www.snipits.com
Children's hair care & party services
Began: 1995, Franchising: 2003
Headquarters size: 50 employees
Franchise department: 8 employees

U.S. franchises: 42
Canadian franchises: 0
Other foreign franchises: 0
Company-owned: 2

Seeking: All U.S.
Seeking in Canada? No
Exclusive territories? Yes
Homebased option? Yes
Employees needed to run biz: 10-11
Absentee ownership? Yes

COSTS
Total cost: $164.7K-273.2K
Franchise fee: $25K
Royalty fee: 6%
Term of agreement: 10 years renewable
    at no charge
Franchisees required to buy multiple
    units? No

FINANCING
In-house: None
3rd-party: Equipment, franchise fee,
    inventory, startup costs

QUALIFICATIONS
Net worth: $250K
Cash liquidity: $50K
Experience:
    General business experience

TRAINING
At headquarters: 5 days
At franchisee's location: 3-4 days

BUSINESS SUPPORT
Grand opening
Internet
Meetings
Toll-free phone line
Field operations/evaluations

MARKETING SUPPORT
Co-op advertising
Ad slicks

SPORT CLIPS

Ranked #72 in Entrepreneur Magazine's 2007 Franchise 500

Financial rating: $$$$

P.O. Box 3000-266
Georgetown, TX 78627-3000
(512)869-1201
www.sportclips.com
Men's sports-themed hair salon
Began: 1993, Franchising: 1995
Headquarters size: 40 employees
Franchise department: 6 employees

U.S. franchises: 341
Canadian franchises: 0
Other foreign franchises: 0
Company-owned: 12

Seeking: Midwest, South, Southeast,
    Southwest, West
Seeking in Canada? No
Exclusive territories? Yes
Homebased option? No
Employees needed to run biz: 6-12
Absentee ownership? Yes

COSTS
Total cost: $165K
Franchise fee: $49.5K
Royalty fee: 6%
Term of agreement: 5 years renewable
    for $3.5K
Franchisees required to buy multiple
    units? Yes

FINANCING
In-house: None
3rd-party: Equipment, franchise fee,
    inventory, payroll, startup costs

QUALIFICATIONS
Net worth: $300K
Cash liquidity: $100K
Experience:
    General business experience
    Marketing skills
    People skills

TRAINING
At headquarters: 5 days
At franchisee's location: 5 days
At existing locations: 5 days

BUSINESS SUPPORT
Grand opening
Internet
Newsletter
Meetings
Toll-free phone line
Field operations/evaluations
Lease negotiations
Purchasing cooperatives
Security/safety procedures

MARKETING SUPPORT
Co-op advertising
Ad slicks
National media campaign
Regional marketing
Ad fund
Local radio & TV
Celebrity fees

SUPERCUTS

Ranked #30 in Entrepreneur Magazine's 2007 Franchise 500

Financial rating: $$$$

7201 Metro Blvd.
Minneapolis, MN 55439
(888)888-7008/(952)947-7777
www.regisfranchise.com
Family hair care
Began: 1975, Franchising: 1979
Headquarters size: 800 employees
Franchise department: 125 employees

U.S. franchises: 932
Canadian franchises: 22
Other foreign franchises: 0
Company-owned: 1,063

Seeking: All U.S.
Seeking in Canada? Yes
Exclusive territories? Yes
Homebased option? No
Employees needed to run biz: 6-8
Absentee ownership? Yes

COSTS
Total cost: $106.8K-197.9K
Franchise fee: $12.5K-22.5K
Royalty fee: 6%
Term of agreement: Conditional &
    renewable
Franchisees required to buy multiple
    units? Yes

FINANCING
In-house: None
3rd-party: Equipment, franchise fee,
    inventory, startup costs

QUALIFICATIONS
Net worth: $300K
Cash liquidity: $100K
Experience:
    General business experience
    Marketing skills
    Retail/service-industry experience

TRAINING
At headquarters: 4 days
At company training center

BUSINESS SUPPORT
Grand opening
Internet
Newsletter
Meetings
Toll-free phone line
Field operations/evaluations
Lease negotiations
Security/safety procedures

MARKETING SUPPORT
Ad slicks
National media campaign

V'S BARBERSHOP

Current financial data not available

9311 E. Via De Ventura
Scottsdale, AZ 85258
(602)414-4800
www.vbarbershop.com
Upscale old-time barbershop
Began: 1999, Franchising: 2004
Headquarters size: 5 employees
Franchise department: 5 employees

U.S. franchises: 2
Canadian franchises: 0
Other foreign franchises: 0
Company-owned: 3

Seeking: All U.S.
Seeking in Canada? No
Exclusive territories? No
Homebased option? No
Employees needed to run biz: 5-9
Absentee ownership? Yes

COSTS
Total cost: $193.5K-339.5K
Franchise fee: $25K
Royalty fee: 5%
Term of agreement: 10 years renewable
    for 33% of then-current fee
Franchisees required to buy multiple
    units? No

FINANCING
In-house: None
3rd-party: Equipment, inventory,
    startup costs

QUALIFICATIONS
Net worth: $300K
Cash liquidity: $100K
Experience:
    General business experience
    Marketing skills

TRAINING
At headquarters
At franchisee's location: 2 days
At an existing shop

BUSINESS SUPPORT
Grand opening
Internet
Newsletter
Field operations/evaluations
Lease negotiations
Purchasing cooperatives
Security/safety procedures

MARKETING SUPPORT
Ad slicks
Regional marketing

PERSONAL CARE *Senior Services*

AEGIN PLACE

Financial rating: $$

2521 N. Main St., #1-300
Las Cruces, NM 88001
(866)659-1834/(505)382-1300
www.aeginplace.com
Live-in nonmedical care for seniors
Began: 1999, Franchising: 2005
Headquarters size: 2 employees
Franchise department: 1 employee

U.S. franchises: 12
Canadian franchises: 0
Other foreign franchises: 0
Company-owned: 0

Seeking: All U.S.
Seeking in Canada? No
Exclusive territories? Yes
Homebased option? Yes
Employees needed to run biz: 2
Absentee ownership? Yes

COSTS
Total cost: $46.3K-84.5K
Franchise fee: $30K
Royalty fee: 3%
Term of agreement: 10 years renewable
   at no charge
Franchisees required to buy multiple
   units? No

FINANCING
No financing available

QUALIFICATIONS
Net worth: $100K
Experience:
   General business experience
   Marketing skills
   Interest in helping older adults

TRAINING
At headquarters: 4 days

BUSINESS SUPPORT
Grand opening
Internet
Meetings
Toll-free phone line

MARKETING SUPPORT
Ad slicks
Regional marketing
Internet
Lead generation
Advertising materials

AGING EXCELLENCE

Financial rating: $$$

251 Congress St., P.O. Box 8660
Portland, ME 04104
(207)771-0991
www.seniorsonthego.com
Nonmedical senior-care services
Began: 1999, Franchising: 2003
Headquarters size: Info not
   provided

U.S. franchises: 3
Canadian franchises: 0
Other foreign franchises: 0
Company-owned: 1

Seeking: All U.S.
Seeking in Canada? No
Exclusive territories? Yes
Homebased option? Yes
Employees needed to run biz: 14
Absentee ownership? Yes

COSTS
Total cost: $33.7K-51.2K
Franchise fee: $15.9K
Royalty fee: 5%
Term of agreement: 5 years renewable
   at no charge
Franchisees required to buy multiple
   units? No

FINANCING
No financing available

QUALIFICATIONS
Net worth: $100K
Cash liquidity: $50K
Experience:
   General business experience
   Marketing skills

TRAINING
At headquarters: 1 week
At franchisee's location: 2 days
Ongoing training

BUSINESS SUPPORT
Grand opening
Internet
Meetings
Toll-free phone line
Field operations/evaluations
Purchasing cooperatives
Security/safety procedures

MARKETING SUPPORT
Co-op advertising
Ad slicks
Regional marketing

BRIGHTSTAR HEALTHCARE

Financial rating: 0

150 N. Michigan Ave., #2800
Chicago, IL 60601
(847)235-2580
www.brightstarfranchise.com
Medical/nonmedical home care &
  medical staffing
Began: 2002, Franchising: 2005
Headquarters size: 18 employees
Franchise department: 8 employees

U.S. franchises: 4
Canadian franchises: 0
Other foreign franchises: 0
Company-owned: 3

Seeking: All U.S.
Seeking in Canada? No
Exclusive territories? Yes
Homebased option? No
Employees needed to run biz: 4-10
Absentee ownership? Yes

COSTS
Total cost: $100K-160K
Franchise fee: $35K
Royalty fee: 5-7%
Term of agreement: 10 years renewable
  at no charge
Franchisees required to buy multiple
  units? No

FINANCING
No financing available

QUALIFICATIONS
Net worth: $250K
Cash liquidity: $75K-100K
Experience:
  General business experience
  Marketing skills

TRAINING
At headquarters: 10 days
At franchisee's location: 10 days

BUSINESS SUPPORT
Grand opening
Internet
Newsletter
Meetings
Toll-free phone line
Field operations/evaluations
Purchasing cooperatives
Security/safety procedures

MARKETING SUPPORT
Co-op advertising
Ad slicks
National media campaign
Regional marketing

CAREMINDERS HOME CARE INC.

Current financial data not available

11625 Rainwater Dr., #350
Alpharetta, GA 30004
(877)264-6337/(770)973-6400
www.careminders.com
Nonmedical personal care for
  seniors & convalescing adults
Began: 2004, Franchising: 2004
Headquarters size: 6 employees
Franchise department: 3 employees

U.S. franchises: 9
Canadian franchises: 0
Other foreign franchises: 0
Company-owned: 0

Seeking: All U.S.
Seeking in Canada? No
Exclusive territories? Yes
Homebased option? Yes
Employees needed to run biz: 1-2
Absentee ownership? Yes

COSTS
Total cost: $32.4K-62.5K
Franchise fee: $19.8K
Royalty fee: 3-5%
Term of agreement: 10 years renewable
  for $2.5K
Franchisees required to buy multiple
  units? No

FINANCING
No financing available

QUALIFICATIONS
Net worth: $75K
Cash liquidity: $20K

TRAINING
At headquarters: 1 week
At franchisee's location: 2 days

BUSINESS SUPPORT
Internet
Newsletter
Meetings
Toll-free phone line
Field operations/evaluations

MARKETING SUPPORT
Ad slicks
Manuals
Video
TV ads

CARING TRANSITIONS

Financial rating: $

10700 Montgomery Rd., #300
Cincinnati, OH 45242
(800)647-0766
www.caringtransitions.net
Sales of estates & household goods
Began: 2006, Franchising: 2006
Headquarters size: 35 employees
Franchise department: 35 employees

U.S. franchises: 1
Canadian franchises: 0
Other foreign franchises: 0
Company-owned: 0

Seeking: All U.S.
Seeking in Canada? Yes
Exclusive territories? Yes
Homebased option? Yes
Employees needed to run biz: 2
Absentee ownership? Yes

COSTS
Total cost: $28.2K-43.4K
Franchise fee: $19.9K-25.9K
Royalty fee: 6%
Term of agreement: 10 years renewable
    at no charge
Franchisees required to buy multiple
    units? Outside the U.S. only

FINANCING
In-house: Franchise fee
3rd-party: None

QUALIFICATIONS
Cash liquidity: $9.5K

TRAINING
At headquarters: 5 days
Regional & national meetings
Sales boot camps

BUSINESS SUPPORT
Grand opening
Internet
Newsletter
Meetings
Toll-free phone line
Purchasing cooperatives
Security/safety procedures

MARKETING SUPPORT
Co-op advertising
Ad slicks
National media campaign

CHOOSE HOME

Financial rating: $$$

9324 E. Raintree Dr., #100
Scottsdale, AZ 85260
(866)370-4227
www.choose-home.com
Senior-care services
Began: 1998, Franchising: 2004
Headquarters size: 10 employees
Franchise department: 6 employees

U.S. franchises: 0
Canadian franchises: 0
Other foreign franchises: 0
Company-owned: 1

Seeking: All U.S.
Seeking in Canada? No
Exclusive territories? Yes
Homebased option? No
Employees needed to run biz: Info
    not provided
Absentee ownership? Yes

COSTS
Total cost: $49.9K-90.9K
Franchise fee: $21.5K
Royalty fee: 5-3%
Term of agreement: 10 years
Franchisees required to buy multiple
    units? No

FINANCING
No financing available

QUALIFICATIONS
Net worth: $100K
Cash liquidity: $80K
Experience:
    General business experience

TRAINING
At headquarters: 1 week
At franchisee's location: Varies
Additional training available

BUSINESS SUPPORT
Grand opening
Internet
Newsletter
Meetings
Toll-free phone line
Field operations/evaluations
Purchasing cooperatives
Security/safety procedures

MARKETING SUPPORT
Ad slicks
National media campaign
Regional marketing

COMFORCARE SENIOR SERVICES INC.

Ranked #246 in Entrepreneur Magazine's 2007 Franchise 500   *Financial rating: $$$$*

2510 Telegraph Rd., #100
Bloomfield Hills, MI 48302
(800)886-4044
www.comforcare.com/franchise
Nonmedical home-care services
Began: 1996, Franchising: 2001
Headquarters size: 15 employees
Franchise department: 7 employees

U.S. franchises: 82
Canadian franchises: 0
Other foreign franchises: 0
Company-owned: 1

Seeking: All U.S.
Seeking in Canada? Yes
Exclusive territories? Yes
Homebased option? No
Employees needed to run biz: 1
Absentee ownership? Yes

COSTS
Total cost: $48K-68K
Franchise fee: $19.5K
Royalty fee: 3-5%
Term of agreement: 10 years renewable
    for $2.5K
Franchisees required to buy multiple
    units? No

FINANCING
No financing available

QUALIFICATIONS
Net worth: $100K
Cash liquidity: $30K

TRAINING
At headquarters: 1 week
At franchisee's location: Several
    times per year
Training available for key
    administrators

BUSINESS SUPPORT
Grand opening
Internet
Newsletter
Meetings
Toll-free phone line
Field operations/evaluations
Purchasing cooperatives
Security/safety procedures

MARKETING SUPPORT
Co-op advertising
Ad slicks
Regional marketing
Online ordering
Strategic alliances
PowerPoint presentations

COMFORT KEEPERS

Ranked #78 in Entrepreneur Magazine's 2007 Franchise 500   *Financial rating: $$$$*

6640 Poe Ave., #200
Dayton, OH 45414
(888)329-1368/(888)801-1121
www.comfortkeepers.com
Nonmedical in-home senior care
Began: 1998, Franchising: 1999
Headquarters size: 30 employees
Franchise department: 8 employees

U.S. franchises: 535
Canadian franchises: 25
Other foreign franchises: 5
Company-owned: 0

Seeking: All U.S.
Seeking in Canada? No
Exclusive territories? Yes
Homebased option? Yes
Employees needed to run biz: 10
Absentee ownership? No

COSTS
Total cost: $56.4K-88.8K
Franchise fee: $32.5K
Royalty fee: 5-3%
Term of agreement: 10 years renewable
    at no charge
Franchisees required to buy multiple
    units? Outside the U.S. only

FINANCING
No financing available

QUALIFICATIONS
Net worth: $150K+
Cash liquidity: $56.4K+
Experience:
    General business experience
    Marketing skills
    Understanding of importance
    of HR

TRAINING
At headquarters: 8 days
At franchisee's location: Ongoing
Monthly training available in
    financing, marketing &
    operations

BUSINESS SUPPORT
Grand opening
Internet
Newsletter
Meetings
Toll-free phone line
Field operations/evaluations
Purchasing cooperatives
Security/safety procedures

MARKETING SUPPORT
Co-op advertising
Ad slicks
Regional marketing

GRISWOLD SPECIAL CARE

Ranked #449 in Entrepreneur Magazine's 2007 Franchise 500   *Financial rating: $$$$*

717 Bethlehem Pike, #300
Erdenheim, PA 19073
(215)402-0200
www.griswoldspecialcare.com
Nonmedical home-care services
Began: 1982, Franchising: 1984
Headquarters size: 70 employees

U.S. franchises: 80
Canadian franchises: 0
Other foreign franchises: 2
Company-owned: 7

Seeking: Midwest, Northeast, South,
    Southeast, Southwest
Seeking in Canada? Yes
Exclusive territories? Yes
Homebased option? Yes
Employees needed to run biz: 1-2
Absentee ownership? No

COSTS
Total cost: $15K-39K
Franchise fee: $9K
Royalty fee: 3-4%
Term of agreement: 7 years renewable
    at no charge
Franchisees required to buy multiple
    units? No

FINANCING
In-house: None
3rd-party: Payroll

QUALIFICATIONS
Experience:
    Industry experience
    General business experience
    Marketing skills

TRAINING
At headquarters: 1 week
At franchisee's location: 2-4 days
Free annual workshops
Ongoing in-field training

BUSINESS SUPPORT
Internet
Newsletter
Meetings
Toll-free phone line
Field operations/evaluations
Purchasing cooperatives
Security/safety procedures

MARKETING SUPPORT
Co-op advertising
Ad slicks
National media campaign
Regional marketing
Ongoing phone support
Customized software

HOME HELPERS

Ranked #53 in Entrepreneur Magazine's 2007 Franchise 500   *Financial rating: $$$$*

10700 Montgomery Rd., #300
Cincinnati, OH 45242
(800)216-4196
www.homehelpers.cc
Nonmedical care services
Began: 1997, Franchising: 1997
Headquarters size: 35 employees
Franchise department: 35 employees

U.S. franchises: 601
Canadian franchises: 3
Other foreign franchises: 0
Company-owned: 0

Seeking: All U.S.
Seeking in Canada? Yes
Exclusive territories? Yes
Homebased option? Yes
Employees needed to run biz: 2
Absentee ownership? Yes

COSTS
Total cost: $36.1K-50.8K
Franchise fee: $24.9K
Royalty fee: 6-4%
Term of agreement: 10 years renewable
    at no charge
Franchisees required to buy multiple
    units? No

FINANCING
In-house: Franchise fee
3rd-party: None

QUALIFICATIONS
Cash liquidity: $9.5K

TRAINING
At headquarters: 5 days
Sales boot camps
Ongoing

BUSINESS SUPPORT
Internet
Newsletter
Meetings
Toll-free phone line
Field operations/evaluations
Security/safety procedures

MARKETING SUPPORT
Ad slicks
National media campaign
Electronic ad & presentation
    formats

HOME INSTEAD SENIOR CARE

Ranked #76 in Entrepreneur Magazine's 2007 Franchise 500   *Financial rating: $$$$*

13330 California St., #200
Omaha, NE 68154
(888)484-5759/(402)498-4466
www.homeinstead.com
Nonmedical senior-care services
Began: 1994, Franchising: 1995
Headquarters size: 60 employees
Franchise department: 9 employees

U.S. franchises: 522
Canadian franchises: 19
Other foreign franchises: 132
Company-owned: 1

Seeking: All U.S.
Seeking in Canada? Yes
Exclusive territories? Yes
Homebased option? No
Employees needed to run biz: 85
Absentee ownership? No

COSTS
Total cost: $37.1K-50.1K
Franchise fee: $25.5K
Royalty fee: 5%
Term of agreement: 10 years renewable
    at no charge
Franchisees required to buy multiple
    units? Outside the U.S. only

FINANCING
In-house: None
3rd-party: Franchise fee, startup
    costs

QUALIFICATIONS
Cash liquidity: $50K-60K
Experience:
    General business experience
    Marketing skills

TRAINING
At headquarters: 1 week
At franchisee's location: 13 weeks
Initial on-site visit

BUSINESS SUPPORT
Internet
Newsletter
Meetings
Toll-free phone line
Field operations/evaluations
Purchasing cooperatives
Security/safety procedures

MARKETING SUPPORT
Ad slicks
National media campaign
National lead development services

HOMEWATCH CAREGIVERS

Ranked #227 in Entrepreneur Magazine's 2007 Franchise 500   *Financial rating: $$$$*

7100 E. Belleview Ave., #303
Greenwood Village, CO 80111
(800)777-9770/(303)758-5111
www.homewatch-intl.com
Home-care services
Began: 1973, Franchising: 1986
Headquarters size: 13 employees
Franchise department: 13 employees

U.S. franchises: 108
Canadian franchises: 2
Other foreign franchises: 5
Company-owned: 8

Seeking: All U.S.
Seeking in Canada? Yes
Exclusive territories? Yes
Homebased option? No
Employees needed to run biz: 3-30
Absentee ownership? Yes

COSTS
Total cost: $49.2K-76.2K
Franchise fee: $28.5K
Royalty fee: 5%
Term of agreement: 10 years renewable
    for 25% of current franchise fee
Franchisees required to buy multiple
    units? No

FINANCING
No financing available

QUALIFICATIONS
Net worth: $250K
Cash liquidity: $75K
Experience:
    Industry experience
    General business experience
    Marketing skills
    Sales & management experience
    People skills
    Compassionate individual

TRAINING
At headquarters: 5 days
At franchisee's location: 2-3 days
Ongoing support

BUSINESS SUPPORT
Grand opening
Internet
Newsletter
Meetings
Toll-free phone line
Field operations/evaluations
Purchasing cooperatives
Security/safety procedures

MARKETING SUPPORT
Co-op advertising
Ad slicks
National media campaign
Regional marketing

RIGHT AT HOME INC.

Ranked #251 in Entrepreneur Magazine's 2007 Franchise 500

Financial rating: $$$$

11949 Q St., #S-100
Omaha, NE 68137
(877)697-7537
www.rightathome.net
Senior home care & medical staffing
Began: 1995, Franchising: 2000
Headquarters size: 14 employees
Franchise department: 6 employees

U.S. franchises: 91
Canadian franchises: 0
Other foreign franchises: 0
Company-owned: 0

Seeking: All U.S.
Seeking in Canada? No
Exclusive territories? Yes
Homebased option? No
Employees needed to run biz: Info
    not provided
Absentee ownership? No

COSTS
Total cost: $38.2K-69.5K
Franchise fee: $24.8K
Royalty fee: 5%
Term of agreement: 10 years renewable
    at no charge
Franchisees required to buy multiple
    units? No

FINANCING
No financing available

QUALIFICATIONS
Net worth: $100K
Cash liquidity: $50K-60K
Experience:
    General business experience

TRAINING
At headquarters: 2 weeks

BUSINESS SUPPORT
Internet
Newsletter
Meetings
Toll-free phone line
Field operations/evaluations
Security/safety procedures

MARKETING SUPPORT
Ad slicks
Website

SENIOR HELPERS

Financial rating: $$$

8601 LaSalle Rd., #208
Towson, MD 21286
(800)760-6389
www.seniorhelpers.com
Home care for seniors
Began: 2001, Franchising: 2005
Headquarters size: 15 employees
Franchise department: 5 employees

U.S. franchises: 33
Canadian franchises: 0
Other foreign franchises: 0
Company-owned: 2

Seeking: All U.S.
Seeking in Canada? No
Exclusive territories? Yes
Homebased option? No
Employees needed to run biz: 3
Absentee ownership? Yes

COSTS
Total cost: $40.6K-61.6K
Franchise fee: $25K
Royalty fee: 5-3%
Term of agreement: 10 years renewable
    at no charge
Franchisees required to buy multiple
    units? No

FINANCING
No financing available

QUALIFICATIONS
Cash liquidity: $75K
Experience:
    Industry experience
    General business experience
    Marketing skills
    Staffing skills

TRAINING
At headquarters: 1 week
At franchisee's location: 3 days
Additional on-site training
Computer-based training

BUSINESS SUPPORT
Grand opening
Internet
Newsletter
Meetings
Toll-free phone line
Field operations/evaluations
Purchasing cooperatives
Security/safety procedures

MARKETING SUPPORT
Co-op advertising
Ad slicks
Regional marketing

SPECTRUM HOME SERVICES

Financial rating: 0

9690 S. 300 West, #320G-H
Sandy, UT 84070
(800)496-5993
www.spectrumhomeservices.com
Senior care & home services
Began: 2000, Franchising: 2004
Headquarters size: Info not provided
Franchise department: 8 employees

U.S. franchises: 13
Canadian franchises: 0
Other foreign franchises: 0
Company-owned: 1

Seeking: All U.S.
Seeking in Canada? No
Exclusive territories? Yes
Homebased option? Yes
Employees needed to run biz: 4
Absentee ownership? No

COSTS
Total cost: $55.7K-100.9K
Franchise fee: $25K
Royalty fee: 5%
Term of agreement: 5 years renewable
    at no charge
Franchisees required to buy multiple
    units? No

FINANCING
No financing available

QUALIFICATIONS
Net worth: $100K
Cash liquidity: $25K
Experience:
    General business experience
    Marketing skills

TRAINING
At headquarters: 1 week
At franchisee's location: 1 week
Ongoing

BUSINESS SUPPORT
Grand opening
Internet
Newsletter
Meetings
Toll-free phone line
Field operations/evaluations
Purchasing cooperatives

MARKETING SUPPORT
Ad slicks
Regional marketing

SYNERGY HOMECARE

Financial rating: $$$$

1757 E. Baseline Rd., Bldg. 6, #124
Gilbert, AZ 85233
(888)659-7771/(480)659-7771
www.synergyhomecare.com
Nonmedical home-care services
Began: 2000, Franchising: 2005
Headquarters size: 12 employees
Franchise department: 6 employees

U.S. franchises: 14
Canadian franchises: 0
Other foreign franchises: 0
Company-owned: 0

Seeking: All U.S.
Seeking in Canada? Yes
Exclusive territories? Yes
Homebased option? No
Employees needed to run biz: 1
Absentee ownership? Yes

COSTS
Total cost: $50.2K-70.5K
Franchise fee: $30K
Royalty fee: 5%
Term of agreement: 5 years renewable
    at no charge
Franchisees required to buy multiple
    units? No

FINANCING
In-house: Franchise fee
3rd-party: Franchise fee

QUALIFICATIONS
Net worth: $75K+
Cash liquidity: $43K-61K
Experience:
    General business experience

TRAINING
At headquarters: 1 week
Initial on-site visit

BUSINESS SUPPORT
Grand opening
Internet
Newsletter
Meetings
Toll-free phone line
Field operations/evaluations
Lease negotiations
Purchasing cooperatives
Security/safety procedures

MARKETING SUPPORT
Co-op advertising
Ad slicks
National media campaign
Regional marketing
National lead development

VISITING ANGELS

Ranked #269 in Entrepreneur Magazine's 2007 Franchise 500

Financial rating: $$$

28 W. Eagle Rd., #201
Havertown, PA 19083
(800)365-4189/(610)924-0630
www.livingassistance.com
Nonmedical home-care services for
    seniors
Began: 1992, Franchising: 1998
Headquarters size: 13 employees
Franchise department: 10 employees

U.S. franchises: 248
Canadian franchises: 1
Other foreign franchises: 0
Company-owned: 0

Seeking: All U.S.
Seeking in Canada? Yes
Exclusive territories? Yes
Homebased option? Yes
Employees needed to run biz: 1
Absentee ownership? No

COSTS
Total cost: $32.99K-56.95K
Franchise fee: $19.95K-36.95K
Royalty fee: 2.95-2%
Term of agreement: 10 years renewable
    for $2.5K
Franchisees required to buy multiple
    units? No

FINANCING
No financing available

QUALIFICATIONS
Cash liquidity: $33K-59K

TRAINING
At headquarters: 5 days
5+ regional refresher meetings
    per year

BUSINESS SUPPORT
Internet
Newsletter
Meetings
Toll-free phone line
Field operations/evaluations
Purchasing cooperatives

MARKETING SUPPORT
Co-op advertising
Ad slicks
National media campaign
Regional marketing
PR
Internet marketing

PERSONAL CARE ▶ *Tanning*

DESERT SUN TANNING SALONS

Financial rating: $

P.O. Box 8470
Covington, WA 98042
(425)433-1900
www.desertsuntanning.com
Tanning services
Began: 2000, Franchising: 2005
Headquarters size: 15 employees
Franchise department: 10 employees

U.S. franchises: 29
Canadian franchises: 0
Other foreign franchises: 0
Company-owned: 11

Seeking: All U.S.
Seeking in Canada? Yes
Exclusive territories? No
Homebased option? No
Employees needed to run biz: 5
Absentee ownership? No

COSTS
Total cost: $198.5K-427.5K
Franchise fee: $50K
Royalty fee: 4-6%
Term of agreement: 10 years renewable
    at no charge
Franchisees required to buy multiple
    units? No

FINANCING
In-house: None
3rd-party: Equipment, franchise fee,
    startup costs

QUALIFICATIONS
Net worth: $250K-500K
Cash liquidity: $250K

TRAINING
At headquarters: 35 hours
At franchisee's location: 50 hours

BUSINESS SUPPORT
Grand opening
Internet
Meetings
Field operations/evaluations
Purchasing cooperatives
Security/safety procedures

MARKETING SUPPORT
Co-op advertising
Ad slicks
Regional marketing

EXECUTIVE TANS INC.

Financial rating: $$$$

165 S. Union Blvd., #785
Lakewood, CO 80228
(877)393-2826/(303)988-9999
www.executivetans.com
Tanning salon
Began: 1991, Franchising: 1995
Headquarters size: 7 employees
Franchise department: 6 employees

U.S. franchises: 47
Canadian franchises: 0
Other foreign franchises: 0
Company-owned: 0

Seeking: All U.S.
Seeking in Canada? No
Exclusive territories? Yes
Homebased option? No
Employees needed to run biz: 2-4
Absentee ownership? Yes

COSTS
Total cost: $258K-448K
Franchise fee: to $25K
Royalty fee: $795/mo.
Term of agreement: 10 years renewable
for $2K
Franchisees required to buy multiple
units? No

FINANCING
In-house: None
3rd-party: Equipment, franchise fee,
inventory, startup costs

QUALIFICATIONS
Net worth: $150K
Cash liquidity: $50K-75K
Experience:
General business experience
Marketing skills

TRAINING
At headquarters: 1 week
At franchisee's location: 1 week
At off-site locations: Periodically

BUSINESS SUPPORT
Grand opening
Internet
Newsletter
Meetings
Toll-free phone line
Field operations/evaluations
Purchasing cooperatives
Security/safety procedures

MARKETING SUPPORT
Co-op advertising
Ad slicks
National media campaign
Regional marketing
Radio

HOLLYWOOD TANS

Ranked #106 in Entrepreneur Magazine's 2007 Franchise 500

Financial rating: $$$$

11 Enterprise Ct.
Sewell, NJ 08080
(856)716-2150
www.hollywoodtans.com
Tanning services & lotions
Began: 1994, Franchising: 1998
Headquarters size: 20 employees
Franchise department: 8 employees

U.S. franchises: 300
Canadian franchises: 0
Other foreign franchises: 4
Company-owned: 7

Seeking: All U.S.
Seeking in Canada? Yes
Exclusive territories? Yes
Homebased option? No
Employees needed to run biz: 6-8
Absentee ownership? Yes

COSTS
Total cost: $310.5K-390.5K
Franchise fee: $34.5K
Royalty fee: 7%
Term of agreement: 10 years renewable
at no charge
Franchisees required to buy multiple
units? No

FINANCING
In-house: None
3rd-party: Equipment, franchise fee,
startup costs

QUALIFICATIONS
Net worth: $250K
Cash liquidity: $75K-100K
Experience:
General business experience
Marketing skills

TRAINING
At headquarters: 5 days
At franchisee's location: 2-3 days
Ongoing monthly training

BUSINESS SUPPORT
Grand opening
Internet
Newsletter
Meetings
Toll-free phone line
Field operations/evaluations
Purchasing cooperatives
Security/safety procedures

MARKETING SUPPORT
Co-op advertising
Ad slicks
National media campaign
Regional marketing

IMAGE SUN TANNING CENTERS

Ranked #375 in Entrepreneur Magazine's 2007 Franchise 500　　　*Financial rating: $$$*

5514 Metro Pkwy.
Sterling Hts., MI 48310
(800)837-1388
www.imagesun.com
Indoor tanning center
Began: 1994, Franchising: 2000
Headquarters size: 10 employees
Franchise department: 8 employees

U.S. franchises: 31
Canadian franchises: 0
Other foreign franchises: 0
Company-owned: 6

Seeking: All U.S.
Seeking in Canada? Yes
Exclusive territories? Yes
Homebased option? No
Employees needed to run biz: 5
Absentee ownership? Yes

COSTS
Total cost: $305K-867K
Franchise fee: $25K
Royalty fee: 6%
Term of agreement: 10 years renewable
    for 10% of franchise fee
Franchisees required to buy multiple
    units? No

FINANCING
In-house: None
3rd-party: Equipment, inventory,
    startup costs

QUALIFICATIONS
Net worth: $200K
Cash liquidity: $60K-70K
Experience:
    General business experience

TRAINING
At headquarters: 1 week+
At franchisee's location: Up to
    5 days
Ongoing phone support

BUSINESS SUPPORT
Grand opening
Internet
Newsletter
Toll-free phone line
Field operations/evaluations
Lease negotiations
Purchasing cooperatives

MARKETING SUPPORT
Co-op advertising
Ad slicks
Regional marketing
Media kit

THE PALMS TANNING RESORT

Current financial data not available

8577 E. Arapahoe Rd., #A
Greenwood Village, CO 80112
(866)725-6748
www.thepalmstanningresort.com
Tanning salon
Began: 2003, Franchising: 2003
Headquarters size: 7 employees
Franchise department: 7 employees

U.S. franchises: 1
Canadian franchises: 0
Other foreign franchises: 0
Company-owned: 2

Seeking: All U.S.
Seeking in Canada? No
Exclusive territories? Yes
Homebased option? No
Employees needed to run biz: 3-5
Absentee ownership? Yes

COSTS
Total cost: $440K-520K
Franchise fee: $20K
Royalty fee: 5%
Term of agreement: 10 years renewable
    for 25% of initial franchise fee
Franchisees required to buy multiple
    units? No

FINANCING
In-house: None
3rd-party: Equipment, franchise fee,
    inventory, startup costs

QUALIFICATIONS
Net worth: $500K+
Cash liquidity: $100K
Experience:
    General business experience
    Marketing skills
    Customer service skills

TRAINING
At headquarters: 1 week+
At franchisee's location: 1 week+

BUSINESS SUPPORT
Grand opening
Internet
Meetings
Toll-free phone line
Field operations/evaluations
Lease negotiations
Purchasing cooperatives
Security/safety procedures

MARKETING SUPPORT
Co-op advertising
Regional marketing
Sports teams marketing
Yellow Pages ads
Radio spots

PLANET BEACH FRANCHISING CORP.

Ranked #317 in Entrepreneur Magazine's 2007 Franchise 500   *Financial rating: $*

5161 Taravella Rd.
Marrero, LA 70072
(888)290-8266/(504)361-5550
www.planetbeach.com
Tanning spa, clothing, lotions. supplies
Began: 1995, Franchising: 1996
Headquarters size: 65 employees
Franchise department: 11 employees

U.S. franchises: 299
Canadian franchises: 19
Other foreign franchises: 2
Company-owned: 0

Seeking: All U.S.
Seeking in Canada? Yes
Exclusive territories? Yes
Homebased option? No
Employees needed to run biz: 4
Absentee ownership? Yes

COSTS
Total cost: $189.8K-504K
Franchise fee: $25K
Royalty fee: 6%
Term of agreement: 10 years renewable
  at no charge
Franchisees required to buy multiple
  units? Outside the U.S. only

FINANCING
In-house: None
3rd-party: Accounts receivable,
  equipment, franchise fee,
  inventory, payroll, startup costs

QUALIFICATIONS
Net worth: $250K
Cash liquidity: $60K
Experience:
  General business experience
  Marketing skills

TRAINING
At headquarters: 5 days
At franchisee's location: 5 days
At franchise opening
Ongoing online training

BUSINESS SUPPORT
Grand opening
Internet
Newsletter
Meetings
Toll-free phone line
Field operations/evaluations
Purchasing cooperatives
Security/safety procedures

MARKETING SUPPORT
Co-op advertising
Ad slicks
National media campaign
Regional marketing
Local ad program

THE TAN CO.

Ranked #368 in Entrepreneur Magazine's 2007 Franchise 500   *Financial rating: $$$*

11 Champion Dr.
Fenton, MO 63026
(888)688-8222
www.thetanco.com
Tanning salon
Began: 1994, Franchising: 2001
Headquarters size: 23 employees
Franchise department: 4 employees

U.S. franchises: 39
Canadian franchises: 0
Other foreign franchises: 0
Company-owned: 26

Seeking: All U.S.
Seeking in Canada? No
Exclusive territories? No
Homebased option? No
Employees needed to run biz: 5
Absentee ownership? Yes

COSTS
Total cost: $386.7K-844K
Franchise fee: $25K
Royalty fee: 6%
Term of agreement: 10 years renewable
  for $500
Franchisees required to buy multiple
  units? No

FINANCING
In-house: None
3rd-party: Equipment, franchise fee,
  inventory, startup costs

QUALIFICATIONS
Net worth: $250K
Cash liquidity: $60K-125K

TRAINING
At headquarters: 4 weeks
At franchisee's location: 1 week

BUSINESS SUPPORT
Grand opening
Internet
Newsletter
Meetings
Toll-free phone line
Field operations/evaluations
Purchasing cooperatives
Security/safety procedures

MARKETING SUPPORT
Co-op advertising
Ad slicks
National media campaign
Regional marketing

ATIR NATURAL NAIL CARE CLINIC

Financial rating: $

1303 Jamestown Rd., #101
Williamsburg, VA 23185
(757)258-0696
www.atirnaturalnailclinic.com
Natural manicures & pedicures
Began: 2004, Franchising: 2004
Headquarters size: Info not provided
Franchise department: 5 employees

U.S. franchises: 5
Canadian franchises: 0
Other foreign franchises: 0
Company-owned: 2

Seeking: All U.S.
Seeking in Canada? No
Exclusive territories? Yes
Homebased option? No
Employees needed to run biz: 6-8
Absentee ownership? Yes

COSTS
Total cost: $143K-235K
Franchise fee: $25K
Royalty fee: 5%
Term of agreement: 10 years renewable
    for $12.5K
Franchisees required to buy multiple
    units? No

FINANCING
No financing available

QUALIFICATIONS
Net worth: $215K
Experience:
    General business experience
    Sales experience
    Customer service experience

TRAINING
At headquarters: 7 days
At franchisee's location: 3 days
Supplemental training upon request

BUSINESS SUPPORT
Grand opening
Internet
Field operations/evaluations

MARKETING SUPPORT
Ad slicks

DERMACARE LASER & SKIN CARE CLINICS

Financial rating: $

4835 E. Cactus Rd., #345
Scottsdale, AZ 85254
(602)424-0788
www.dermacareusa.com
Skin-care procedures & products
Began: 2001, Franchising: 2004
Headquarters size: 24 employees
Franchise department: 12 employees

U.S. franchises: 21
Canadian franchises: 0
Other foreign franchises: 0
Company-owned: 2

Seeking: All U.S.
Seeking in Canada? Yes
Exclusive territories? Yes
Homebased option? No
Employees needed to run biz: 6-8
Absentee ownership? No

COSTS
Total cost: $167.1K-402.1K
Franchise fee: $75K
Royalty fee: 5%
Term of agreement: 10 years renewable
    for 50% of then-current fee
Franchisees required to buy multiple
    units? No

FINANCING
In-house: None
3rd-party: Accounts receivable,
    equipment, franchise fee,
    inventory, payroll, startup costs

QUALIFICATIONS
Physicians preferred

TRAINING
At headquarters: 2 weels
At franchisee's location: 1 week

BUSINESS SUPPORT
Grand opening
Internet
Newsletter
Meetings
Toll-free phone line
Field operations/evaluations
Security/safety procedures

MARKETING SUPPORT
Co-op advertising
Ad slicks
National media campaign
Regional marketing

FACELOGIC

Financial rating: $$$

1404 S. New Rd.
Waco, TX 76708
(254)757-1554
www.facelogicspa.com
Skin care
Began: 2005, Franchising: 2005
Headquarters size: 14 employees
Franchise department: 10 employees

U.S. franchises: 4
Canadian franchises: 1
Other foreign franchises: 0
Company-owned: 0

Seeking: All U.S.
Seeking in Canada? Yes
Exclusive territories? Yes
Homebased option? No
Employees needed to run biz: 10
Absentee ownership? Yes

COSTS

Total cost: $169.6K-269.8K
Franchise fee: $29.9K
Royalty fee: $895/mo.
Term of agreement: 10 years
Franchisees required to buy multiple
    units? No

FINANCING

In-house: None
3rd-party: Franchise fee, startup
    costs

QUALIFICATIONS

Experience:
    Industry experience
    General business experience
    Marketing skills

TRAINING

At headquarters: 3 days
At franchisee's location: 5 days

BUSINESS SUPPORT

Grand opening
Internet
Newsletter
Toll-free phone line
Field operations/evaluations

MARKETING SUPPORT

Ad slicks

HAND AND STONE MASSAGE SPA

Financial rating: 0

1830 Hooper Ave.
Toms River, NJ 08753
(732)255-9300
www.handandstone.com
Massage therapy spas
Began: 2004, Franchising: 2006
Headquarters size: 5 employees
Franchise department: 3 employees

U.S. franchises: 0
Canadian franchises: 0
Other foreign franchises: 0
Company-owned: 2

Seeking: Midwest, Northeast,
    Southeast, Southwest, West
Seeking in Canada? Yes
Exclusive territories? Yes
Homebased option? No
Employees needed to run biz: 6
Absentee ownership? No

COSTS

Total cost: $276K-371K
Franchise fee: $45K
Royalty fee: 5%
Term of agreement: 5 years renewable
    at no charge
Franchisees required to buy multiple
    units? No

FINANCING

No financing available

QUALIFICATIONS

Net worth: $400K
Cash liquidity: $50K
Experience:
    General business experience

TRAINING

At headquarters: 3 weeks
At franchisee's location: 1 week

BUSINESS SUPPORT

Grand opening
Internet
Meetings
Toll-free phone line
Field operations/evaluations
Purchasing cooperatives
Security/safety procedures

MARKETING SUPPORT

Co-op advertising
Ad slicks

IDEAL IMAGE

Ranked #470 in Entrepreneur Magazine's 2007 Franchise 500　　　*Financial rating: $$*

4830 W. Kennedy Blvd., #440
Tampa, FL 33609
(813)286-8100
www.idealimage.com
Laser hair removal
Began: 2001, Franchising: 2004
Headquarters size: 55 employees
Franchise department: 4 employees

U.S. franchises: 44
Canadian franchises: 0
Other foreign franchises: 1
Company-owned: 6

Seeking: All U.S.
Seeking in Canada? Yes
Exclusive territories? Yes
Homebased option? No
Employees needed to run biz: 4
Absentee ownership? Yes

COSTS
Total cost: $551.3K-903.4K
Franchise fee: $25K-35K
Royalty fee: 9%
Term of agreement: 10 years renewable
　　for $10K or 25% of current fee
Franchisees required to buy multiple
　　units? No

FINANCING
In-house: None
3rd-party: Equipment, inventory

QUALIFICATIONS
Net worth: $750K+
Cash liquidity: $450K

TRAINING
At headquarters: 2-4 weeks
At franchisee's location: As needed
Ongoing online training

BUSINESS SUPPORT
Grand opening
Internet
Newsletter
Meetings
Toll-free phone line
Field operations/evaluations
Security/safety procedures

MARKETING SUPPORT
Regional marketing
Market-specific ad campaigns

JOHN CASABLANCAS MODELING & CAREER CENTERS

Financial rating: $$$$

648 Trade Center Blvd.
Chesterfield, MO 63005
(636)536-6100
www.jcasablancas.com
Modeling school & agency
Began: 1979, Franchising: 1979
Headquarters size: 7 employees
Franchise department: 2 employees

U.S. franchises: 31
Canadian franchises: 1
Other foreign franchises: 7
Company-owned: 0

Seeking: All U.S.
Seeking in Canada? Yes
Exclusive territories? Yes
Homebased option? No
Employees needed to run biz: 4-7
Absentee ownership? No

COSTS
Total cost: $113.3K-286.3K
Franchise fee: $40K-50K
Royalty fee: 7%
Term of agreement: 10 years renewable
　　at no charge
Franchisees required to buy multiple
　　units? No

FINANCING
In-house: Franchise fee
3rd-party: None

QUALIFICATIONS
Cash liquidity: $200K-275K
Experience:
　　Industry experience
　　General business experience
　　Marketing skills
　　Sales experience

TRAINING
At headquarters: 7 days
At franchisee's location: 7 days
Ongoing field visits

BUSINESS SUPPORT
Grand opening
Internet
Newsletter
Meetings
Field operations/evaluations
Lease negotiations
Security/safety procedures

MARKETING SUPPORT
Co-op advertising
Ad slicks
National media campaign
Local advertising

MASSAGE ENVY

Ranked #149 in Entrepreneur Magazine's 2007 Franchise 500   *Financial rating: $$$$*

14350 N. 87th St., #200
Scottsdale, AZ 85260
(602)889-1090
www.massageenvy.com
Therapeutic massage services
Began: 2001, Franchising: 2003
Headquarters size: 35 employees
Franchise department: 3 employees

U.S. franchises: 151
Canadian franchises: 0
Other foreign franchises: 0
Company-owned: 0

Seeking: All U.S.
Seeking in Canada? No
Exclusive territories? Yes
Homebased option? No
Employees needed to run biz: 20
Absentee ownership? No

COSTS
Total cost: $200K-400K
Franchise fee: $39K/29K
Royalty fee: 5%
Term of agreement: 10 years renewable
  for 25% of current franchise fee
Franchisees required to buy multiple
  units? No

FINANCING
No financing available

QUALIFICATIONS
Net worth: $250K
Cash liquidity: $200K
Experience:
  General business experience
  Marketing skills

TRAINING
At headquarters: 5 days
At franchisee's location: 5 days
Additional training as needed

BUSINESS SUPPORT
Grand opening
Internet
Newsletter
Meetings
Toll-free phone line
Field operations/evaluations
Lease negotiations
Purchasing cooperatives
Security/safety procedures

MARKETING SUPPORT
Co-op advertising
Ad slicks
Regional marketing

METRONAPS

Current financial data not available

350 Fifth Ave., Empire State Bldg.,
  #2210
New York, NY 10118
(212)239-3344
www.metronaps.com
Napping facilities & napping
  products
Began: 2003, Franchising: 2005
Headquarters size: 5 employees
Franchise department: 3 employees

U.S. franchises: 1
Canadian franchises: 0
Other foreign franchises: 0
Company-owned: 2

Seeking: All U.S.
Seeking in Canada? Yes
Exclusive territories? Yes
Homebased option? No
Employees needed to run biz: 1
Absentee ownership? Yes

COSTS
Total cost: $72K-214.5K
Franchise fee: $25K
Royalty fee: 5%
Term of agreement: 5 years renewable
  at no charge
Franchisees required to buy multiple
  units? No

FINANCING
In-house: None
3rd-party: Equipment

QUALIFICATIONS
Net worth: $170K-320K
Cash liquidity: $28.3K-53.3K
Experience:
  General business experience

TRAINING
At headquarters: 10 days
At franchisee's location: 3 days

BUSINESS SUPPORT
Grand opening
Internet
Newsletter
Meetings
Toll-free phone line

MARKETING SUPPORT
Ad slicks

POSITIVE CHANGES HYPNOSIS CENTERS

Financial rating: 0

4390 Tuller Rd.
Dublin, OH 43017-5031
(800)880-0436
www.positivechanges.com
Self-improvement products &
    services
Began: 1987, Franchising: 2001
Headquarters size: 5 employees
Franchise department: 5 employees

U.S. franchises: 40
Canadian franchises: 9
Other foreign franchises: 0
Company-owned: 0

Seeking: All U.S.
Seeking in Canada? Yes
Exclusive territories? Yes
Homebased option? No
Employees needed to run biz: 7
Absentee ownership? Yes

COSTS
Total cost: $65.5K-174K
Franchise fee: $19.5K
Royalty fee: 6%
Term of agreement: 10 years renewable
    for 20% of current franchise fee
Franchisees required to buy multiple
    units? No

FINANCING
No financing available

QUALIFICATIONS
Net worth: $250K
Cash liquidity: $75K
Experience:
    General business experience

TRAINING
At headquarters: 1 week
At franchisee's location: 3 days

BUSINESS SUPPORT
Grand opening
Internet
Newsletter
Meetings
Toll-free phone line
Field operations/evaluations
Purchasing cooperatives

MARKETING SUPPORT
Ad slicks

RADIANCE MEDSPA

Ranked #495 in Entrepreneur Magazine's 2007 Franchise 500

Financial rating: $$$

15333 N. Pima Rd., #355
Scottsdale, AZ 85260
(480)661-5411
www.radiancefranchise.com
MedSpa
Began: 2004, Franchising: 2004
Headquarters size: 15 employees
Franchise department: 2 employees

U.S. franchises: 30
Canadian franchises: 0
Other foreign franchises: 0
Company-owned: 0

Seeking: All U.S.
Seeking in Canada? Yes
Exclusive territories? Yes
Homebased option? No
Employees needed to run biz: 6
Absentee ownership? Yes

COSTS
Total cost: $269.3K-533.3K
Franchise fee: $80K
Royalty fee: 4%
Term of agreement: 10 years renewable
    for 50% of current franchise fee
Franchisees required to buy multiple
    units? Outside the U.S. only

FINANCING
In-house: None
3rd-party: Accounts receivable,
    equipment, franchise fee,
    inventory, payroll, startup costs

QUALIFICATIONS
Experience:
    General business experience
    Marketing skills
    Sales experience

TRAINING
At headquarters: 2 weeks
At franchisee's location: 4 days

BUSINESS SUPPORT
Grand opening
Internet
Newsletter
Meetings
Toll-free phone line
Field operations/evaluations
Lease negotiations
Security/safety procedures

MARKETING SUPPORT
Ad slicks
National media campaign
Regional marketing

SONA MEDSPA INT'L. INC.

Current financial data not available

840 Crescent Centre Dr., #260
Franklin, TN 37067
(615)591-5040
www.sonamedspa.com
Laser hair removal & anti-aging
    products/services
Began: 1997, Franchising: 2002
Headquarters size: 26 employees

U.S. franchises: 30
Canadian franchises: 0
Other foreign franchises: 0
Company-owned: 2

Seeking: All U.S.
Seeking in Canada? Yes
Exclusive territories? Yes
Homebased option? No
Employees needed to run biz: 5-15
Absentee ownership? Yes

COSTS
Total cost: $409.2K-824.9K
Franchise fee: $59.5K
Royalty fee: 7.5%
Term of agreement: 15 years renewable
    for 25% of franchise fee
Franchisees required to buy multiple
    units? No

FINANCING
In-house: None
3rd-party: Equipment, franchise fee,
    inventory, startup costs

QUALIFICATIONS
Net worth: $750K
Cash liquidity: $250K
Experience:
    Industry experience
    General business experience
    Marketing skills
    Strong interpersonal skills

TRAINING
At headquarters: 14 days
At franchisee's location: 6 days
Regional training
Web-based training
Monthly webcasts

BUSINESS SUPPORT
Grand opening
Internet
Newsletter
Meetings
Toll-free phone line
Field operations/evaluations
Lease negotiations
Purchasing cooperatives
Security/safety procedures

MARKETING SUPPORT
Ad slicks
Regional marketing
Local marketing

TOP OF THE LINE FRAGRANCES

Current financial data not available

515 Bath Ave.
Long Branch, NJ 07740
(732)229-0014
www.tolfranchise.com
Retail discount cosmetics &
    fragrances
Began: 1983, Franchising: 1987
Headquarters size: 9 employees
Franchise department: 6 employees

U.S. franchises: 5
Canadian franchises: 0
Other foreign franchises: 0
Company-owned: 2

Seeking: All U.S.
Seeking in Canada? No
Exclusive territories? Yes
Homebased option? No
Employees needed to run biz: 5
Absentee ownership? Yes

COSTS
Total cost: $164.8K-237.8K
Franchise fee: $20K
Royalty fee: 5%
Term of agreement: 10 years renewable
    for $2.5K
Franchisees required to buy multiple
    units? No

FINANCING
No financing available

QUALIFICATIONS
Net worth: $200K
Cash liquidity: $100K
Experience:
    General business experience

TRAINING
At franchisee's location: 7-10 days

BUSINESS SUPPORT
Grand opening
Toll-free phone line
Field operations/evaluations
Lease negotiations

MARKETING SUPPORT
Ad slicks

PERSONAL CARE ▶ *Other Franchises*

AGE ADVANTAGE HOME CARE FRANCHISING INC.
9461 Grossmont Summit Dr., #E
La Mesa, CA 91941
(877)433-0141
www.ageadvantage.com
In-home senior care
Current financial data not available

ARISTOCARE
698 E. Wetmore Rd., #200
Tucson, AZ 85715
(520)577-4825
www.aristocare.net
Home health-care services
Financial rating: 0

ATWORK HELPINGHANDS SERVICES
3215 John Sevier Hwy.
Knoxville, TN 37920
(800)383-0804
www.atworkhelpinghands.com
Nonmedical in-home services &
    senior care
Financial rating: $$$$

THE BLITZ
P.O. Box 3695
Apollo Beach, FL 33572
(913)856-2424
www.timetoblitz.com
20-minute men's fitness program
Current financial data not available

ELIZABETH GRADY
222 Boston Ave.
Medford, MA 02155
(781)391-9380
www.elizabethgrady.com
Skin-care salons
Current financial data not available

HOME CARE ASSISTANCE
148 Hawthorne Ave.
Palo Alto, CA 94301
(702)204-1436
www.hcafranchise.com
Nonmedical home-care services
Current financial data not available

LUCILLE ROBERTS FITNESS EXPRESS
4 E. 80th St.
New York, NY 10021
(888)582-4553
www.lucilerobertsexpress.com
Women's fitness & weight-loss
    center
Current financial data not available

MERLE NORMAN COSMETICS
*Ranked #21 in Entrepreneur
Magazine's 2007 Franchise 500*
9130 Bellanca Ave.
Los Angeles, CA 90045
(800)421-6648/(310)641-3000
www.merlenorman.com
Cosmetics studio
Financial rating: $$$$

PALM BEACH TAN
*Ranked #253 in Entrepreneur
Magazine's 2007 Franchise 500*
13800 Senlac Dr., Ste. 200
Farmers Branch, TX 75234
(866)728-2450
www.palmbeachtan.com
Indoor tanning salon
Financial rating: $$$

PARAMOUNT HOME BEAUTY FRANCHISE
100 N. Main St., #200
Chagrin Falls, OH 44022
(440)893-0920
www.paramounthomebeauty.com
Beauty services & products for
    medically-restricted individuals
Current financial data not available

SLIM AND TONE
10 Penn Valley Dr.
Yardley, PA 19067
(215)321-6661
www.slimandtone.com
Fitness club for women
Current financial data not available

TIME FOR FITNESS LLC
667 Waterview Cove
Eagan, MN 55123
(612)703-6151
www.time4fitness.com
Health club for baby boomers &
    seniors
Current financial data not available

21 MINUTE CONVENIENCE FITNESS
1919 Mt. Diablo Blvd.
Walnut Creek, CA 94596
(925)280-8211
www.21minutefitness.com
Fitness studio
Current financial data not available

THE WOODHOUSE DAY SPA
1 O'Connor Plaza, 12th Fl.
Victoria, TX 77901
(877)570-7772
www.woodhousespas.com
Day spa services/bath & body retail
    products
Current financial data not available

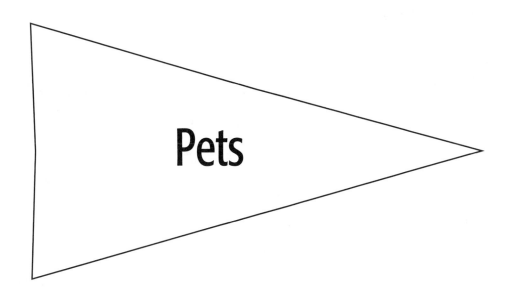

Pets

PETS   *Bird Stores*

WILD BIRD CENTERS OF AMERICA INC.
Ranked #490 in Entrepreneur Magazine's 2007 Franchise 500   *Financial rating: $$$*

7370 MacArthur Blvd.
Glen Echo, MD 20812
(800)945-3247/(301)229-9585
www.wildbird.com
Bird-watching & feeding supplies
Began: 1985, Franchising: 1990
Headquarters size: 16 employees
Franchise department: 2 employees

U.S. franchises: 83
Canadian franchises: 0
Other foreign franchises: 0
Company-owned: 0

Seeking: All U.S.
Seeking in Canada? Yes
Exclusive territories? Yes
Homebased option? No
Employees needed to run biz: 2-4
Absentee ownership? Yes

COSTS
Total cost: $94.9K-152.3K
Franchise fee: $23K
Royalty fee: 3.5-5.5%
Term of agreement: 10 years renewable
    at no charge
Franchisees required to buy multiple
    units? No

FINANCING
In-house: Equipment, franchise fee,
    inventory, startup costs
3rd-party: None

QUALIFICATIONS
Net worth: $150K
Cash liquidity: $33K-50K
Birding hobby knowledge

TRAINING
At headquarters: 6 days
At franchisee's location: 1-2 days
Annual convention: 3 days per year
Additional training available

BUSINESS SUPPORT
Grand opening
Internet
Newsletter
Meetings
Toll-free phone line
Field operations/evaluations
Purchasing cooperatives
Security/safety procedures

MARKETING SUPPORT
Co-op advertising
Ad slicks
National media campaign
Regional marketing
Local advertising support

WILD BIRDS UNLIMITED

Ranked #191 in Entrepreneur Magazine's 2007 Franchise 500   *Financial rating: $$$$*

11711 N. College Ave., #146
Carmel, IN 46032
(888)730-7108
www.wbu.com
Bird-feeding supplies & nature gift
    items
Began: 1981, Franchising: 1983
Headquarters size: 43 employees
Franchise department: 2 employees

U.S. franchises: 293
Canadian franchises: 14
Other foreign franchises: 0
Company-owned: 0

Seeking: All U.S.
Seeking in Canada? Yes
Exclusive territories? Yes
Homebased option? No
Employees needed to run biz: 4
Absentee ownership? No

COSTS
Total cost: $99K-155K
Franchise fee: $18K
Royalty fee: 4%
Term of agreement: 10 years renewable
    at no charge
Franchisees required to buy multiple
    units? No

FINANCING
In-house: Franchise fee
3rd-party: None

QUALIFICATIONS
Net worth: $150K
Cash liquidity: $30K
People skills
Must love birds & nature

TRAINING
At headquarters: 6 days
At franchisee's location: 2 days
At annual meeting: 5 days

BUSINESS SUPPORT
Grand opening
Internet
Newsletter
Meetings
Toll-free phone line
Field operations/evaluations
Purchasing cooperatives
Security/safety procedures

MARKETING SUPPORT
Co-op advertising
Ad slicks
National media campaign

PETS   *Products*

PET HABITAT

Current financial data not available

6921 Heather St.
Vancouver, BC V6P 3P5 Canada
(604)266-2721
www.pethabitat.com
Pet shop
Began: 1979, Franchising: 1981
Headquarters size: 4 employees
Franchise department: 2 employees

U.S. franchises: 0
Canadian franchises: 4
Other foreign franchises: 0
Company-owned: 0

Seeking: Not available in the U.S.
Seeking in Canada? Yes
Exclusive territories? Yes
Homebased option? No
Employees needed to run biz: 10-15
Absentee ownership? No

COSTS
Total cost: $95K
Franchise fee: $25K
Royalty fee: 5%
Term of agreement: Info not provided
Franchisees required to buy multiple
    units? No

FINANCING
No financing available

QUALIFICATIONS
Net worth: $50K
Experience:
    Industry experience
    General business experience
    Marketing skills

TRAINING
At franchisee's location

BUSINESS SUPPORT
Field operations/evaluations
Lease negotiations

MARKETING SUPPORT
Info not provided

PET SUPPLIES "PLUS"

Current financial data not available

22670 Haggerty Rd., #200
Farmington Hills, MI 48335
(866)477-7748/(248)374-1900
www.petsuppliesplus.com
Pet supplies
Began: 1987, Franchising: 1990
Headquarters size: 24 employees
Franchise department: 2 employees

U.S. franchises: 220
Canadian franchises: 0
Other foreign franchises: 0
Company-owned: 1

Seeking: All U.S.
Seeking in Canada? No
Exclusive territories? Yes
Homebased option? No
Employees needed to run biz: 18-20
Absentee ownership? Yes

COSTS
Total cost: $395.5K-611K
Franchise fee: $25K
Royalty fee: Varies
Term of agreement: 5 years renewable
    at no charge
Franchisees required to buy multiple
    units? No

FINANCING
No financing available

QUALIFICATIONS
Net worth: $400K
Cash liquidity: $200K

TRAINING
At headquarters: 4 weeks

BUSINESS SUPPORT
Grand opening
Internet
Meetings
Field operations/evaluations
Purchasing cooperatives

MARKETING SUPPORT
Co-op advertising
Ad slicks

PETLAND

Ranked #192 in Entrepreneur Magazine's 2007 Franchise 500   *Financial rating: $$$$*

250 Riverside St.
Chillicothe, OH 45601
(800)221-5935
www.petland.com
Full-service pet store
Began: 1967, Franchising: 1971
Headquarters size: 45 employees
Franchise department: 25 employees

U.S. franchises: 119
Canadian franchises: 50
Other foreign franchises: 12
Company-owned: 6

Seeking: All U.S.
Seeking in Canada? Yes
Exclusive territories? Yes
Homebased option? No
Employees needed to run biz: 18
Absentee ownership? No

COSTS
Total cost: $550.5K-1.2M
Franchise fee: $25K
Royalty fee: 4.5%
Term of agreement: 20 years renewable
    at no charge
Franchisees required to buy multiple
    units? No

FINANCING
In-house: None
3rd-party: Equipment, franchise fee,
    inventory, payroll, startup costs

QUALIFICATIONS
Net worth: $250K
Cash liquidity: $125K
Experience:
    Team-building skills

TRAINING
At headquarters: 3 weeks
At franchisee's location: 3 weeks
In-store training: 1-4 weeks

BUSINESS SUPPORT
Grand opening
Internet
Newsletter
Meetings
Toll-free phone line
Field operations/evaluations
Lease negotiations
Purchasing cooperatives
Security/safety procedures

MARKETING SUPPORT
Ad slicks
Regional marketing
Customized annual marketing plan

PETS ▶ *Services*

AUSSIE PET MOBILE
Ranked #114 in Entrepreneur Magazine's 2007 Franchise 500   *Financial rating: $$$$*

34189 Pacific Coast Hwy., #203
Dana Point, CA 92629
(949)234-0680
www.aussiepetmobile.com
Mobile pet grooming
Began: 1996, Franchising: 1996
Headquarters size: 25 employees
Franchise department: 12 employees

U.S. franchises: 320
Canadian franchises: 3
Other foreign franchises: 62
Company-owned: 6

Seeking: All U.S.
Seeking in Canada? Yes
Exclusive territories? Yes
Homebased option? Yes
Employees needed to run biz: 1-2
Absentee ownership? Yes

COSTS
Total cost: $83.2K-241.5K
Franchise fee: $35K-125K
Royalty fee: 8-5%
Term of agreement: 10 years renewable
     for 33% of original franchise fee
Franchisees required to buy multiple
     units? Outside the U.S. only

FINANCING
In-house: None
3rd-party: Equipment, franchise fee,
     inventory, startup costs

QUALIFICATIONS
Net worth: $350K
Cash liquidity: $55K
Experience:
     General business experience
     Marketing skills

TRAINING
At headquarters: 3 days
In-field training for groomers:
     2 weeks
Ongoing training for advanced
     grooming

BUSINESS SUPPORT
Grand opening
Internet
Newsletter
Meetings
Toll-free phone line
Field operations/evaluations
Purchasing cooperatives
Security/safety procedures

MARKETING SUPPORT
Ad slicks
National media campaign
Regional marketing

BARK BUSTERS HOME DOG TRAINING
Ranked #105 in Entrepreneur Magazine's 2007 Franchise 500   *Financial rating: $$$$*

250 W. Lehow Ave., #B
Englewood, CO 80110
(877)300-2275
www.barkbusters.com
In-home dog training
Began: 1989, Franchising: 1994
Headquarters size: 5 employees
Franchise department: 5 employees

U.S. franchises: 193
Canadian franchises: 17
Other foreign franchises: 78
Company-owned: 0

Seeking: All U.S.
Seeking in Canada? Yes
Exclusive territories? Yes
Homebased option? Yes
Employees needed to run biz: 0
Absentee ownership? No

COSTS
Total cost: $64.5K-91.4K
Franchise fee: $34.5K
Royalty fee: 8%
Term of agreement: 5 years renewable
     for $1.5K
Franchisees required to buy multiple
     units? No

FINANCING
In-house: None
3rd-party: Equipment, franchise fee,
     inventory, startup costs

QUALIFICATIONS
Net worth: $200K
Cash liquidity: $12.5K-39.4K
Experience:
     General business experience
     Marketing skills
     Passion for dogs

TRAINING
At headquarters: 120 hours+

BUSINESS SUPPORT
Internet
Newsletter
Meetings
Toll-free phone line
Field operations/evaluations
Security/safety procedures

MARKETING SUPPORT
Co-op advertising
Ad slicks
National media campaign
PR

CAMP BOW WOW

Financial rating: $$

1877 Broadway, #101
Boulder, CO 80302
(877)700-2275
www.campbowwowusa.com
Dog day care & boarding services
Began: 2000, Franchising: 2003
Headquarters size: 25 employees
Franchise department: 25 employees

U.S. franchises: 25
Canadian franchises: 0
Other foreign franchises: 0
Company-owned: 1

Seeking: All U.S.
Seeking in Canada? Yes
Exclusive territories? Yes
Homebased option? No
Employees needed to run biz: 8-12
Absentee ownership? Yes

COSTS
Total cost: $250K-500K
Franchise fee: $50K
Royalty fee: 6%
Term of agreement: 10 years renewable
    for $5K
Franchisees required to buy multiple
    units? No

FINANCING
In-house: None
3rd-party: Equipment, inventory,
    startup costs

QUALIFICATIONS
Net worth: $250K
Cash liquidity: $60K
Experience:
    General business experience

TRAINING
At headquarters: 2 weeks
At franchisee's location: 1 week
Home study: 1 week

BUSINESS SUPPORT
Grand opening
Internet
Newsletter
Meetings
Toll-free phone line
Field operations/evaluations
Lease negotiations
Purchasing cooperatives
Security/safety procedures

MARKETING SUPPORT
Co-op advertising
Ad slicks
National media campaign
Regional marketing

FETCH! PET CARE INC.

Ranked #498 in Entrepreneur Magazine's 2007 Franchise 500

Financial rating: $$$

2101 Los Angeles Ave.
Berkeley, CA 94707
(866)338-2463
www.fetchpetcare.com
Pet-sitting & dog-walking services
Began: 2002, Franchising: 2004
Headquarters size: 3 employees
Franchise department: 3 employees

U.S. franchises: 48
Canadian franchises: 0
Other foreign franchises: 0
Company-owned: 2

Seeking: All U.S.
Seeking in Canada? Yes
Exclusive territories? Yes
Homebased option? Yes
Employees needed to run biz: 1
Absentee ownership? Yes

COSTS
Total cost: $14.3K-30.5K
Franchise fee: $6K
Royalty fee: 5%
Term of agreement: 10 years renewable
    at no charge
Franchisees required to buy multiple
    units? No

FINANCING
No financing available

QUALIFICATIONS
Net worth: $25K
Cash liquidity: $15K
Experience:
    General business experience

TRAINING
At headquarters: 2 days (optional)
Training manual & video

BUSINESS SUPPORT
Grand opening
Internet
Newsletter
Meetings
Toll-free phone line
Field operations/evaluations
Purchasing cooperatives
Security/safety procedures

MARKETING SUPPORT
Ad slicks
National media campaign
Regional marketing
Local marketing materials

IN HOME PET SERVICES INC.

Current financial data not available

38-17 Little Neck Pkwy.
Little Neck, NY 11363
(516)553-0602
www.inhomepetservices.com
Pet-sitting & dog-walking services
Began: 2001, Franchising: 2005
Headquarters size: 8 employees
Franchise department: 1 employee

U.S. franchises: 0
Canadian franchises: 0
Other foreign franchises: 0
Company-owned: 2

Seeking: All U.S.
Seeking in Canada? No
Exclusive territories? Yes
Homebased option? Yes
Employees needed to run biz: 0-4
Absentee ownership? No

COSTS
Total cost: $5.2K-31.1K
Franchise fee: $4K
Royalty fee: 5%
Term of agreement: 10 years renewable
   for $500
Franchisees required to buy multiple
   units? No

FINANCING
No financing available

QUALIFICATIONS
Net worth: $25K
Experience:
   Industry experience
   General business experience

TRAINING
At headquarters: 1 week

BUSINESS SUPPORT
Internet
Meetings
Security/safety procedures

MARKETING SUPPORT
Co-op advertising
Ad slicks
National media campaign

PREPPY PET

Financial rating: $$$

57 W. Michigan St.
Orlando, FL 32806
(407)420-1060
www.preppypet.com
Pet boarding & day care
Began: 2003, Franchising: 2006
Headquarters size: 2 employees
Franchise department: 2 employees

U.S. franchises: 0
Canadian franchises: 0
Other foreign franchises: 0
Company-owned: 1

Seeking: All U.S.
Seeking in Canada? No
Exclusive territories? Yes
Homebased option? No
Employees needed to run biz: 4
Absentee ownership? No

COSTS
Total cost: $67.5K-147.5K
Franchise fee: $19.5K
Royalty fee: 4-6%
Term of agreement: 10 years
Franchisees required to buy multiple
   units? No

FINANCING
In-house: Franchise fee
3rd-party: Equipment, inventory,
   startup costs

QUALIFICATIONS
Net worth: $100K
Experience:
   General business experience

TRAINING
At headquarters

BUSINESS SUPPORT
Grand opening
Internet
Newsletter
Meetings
Toll-free phone line
Field operations/evaluations
Purchasing cooperatives
Security/safety procedures

MARKETING SUPPORT
Co-op advertising
Ad slicks
Regional marketing

WELLINGTON SYSTEMS INC.

Financial rating: $$$$

1016 W. Ninth Ave.
King of Prussia, PA 19406
(866)974-2267
www.wellingtonpets.com
Pet care, boarding & day care
Began: 2006, Franchising: 2006
Headquarters size: 4 employees
Franchise department: 1 employee

U.S. franchises: 0
Canadian franchises: 0
Other foreign franchises: 0
Company-owned: 0

Seeking: All U.S.
Seeking in Canada? No
Exclusive territories? No
Homebased option? No
Employees needed to run biz: 20
Absentee ownership? No

COSTS
Total cost: $450K
Franchise fee: $10K
Royalty fee: 7%
Term of agreement: 15 years
    renewable at no charge
Franchisees required to buy multiple
    units? No

FINANCING
In-house: None
3rd-party: Equipment, franchise fee,
    inventory, startup costs

QUALIFICATIONS
Net worth: $425K
Cash liquidity: $90K
Experience:
    General business experience

TRAINING
At headquarters: 3 weeks
At franchisee's location: Ongoing

BUSINESS SUPPORT
Grand opening
Internet
Newsletter
Meetings
Toll-free phone line
Field operations/evaluations
Lease negotiations
Security/safety procedures

MARKETING SUPPORT
Co-op advertising
Ad slicks
National media campaign
Regional marketing
Full-service in-house ad agency

PETS ▶ *Waste Removal*

DOODYCALLS

Financial rating: $$$

5 Burke Ct.
Palmyra, VA 22963
(800)366-3922
www.doodycalls.com
Pet waste removal
Began: 2000, Franchising: 2004
Headquarters size: 2 employees
Franchise department: 2 employees

U.S. franchises: 13
Canadian franchises: 0
Other foreign franchises: 0
Company-owned: 3

Seeking: All U.S.
Seeking in Canada? No
Exclusive territories? Yes
Homebased option? Yes
Employees needed to run biz: 1-4
Absentee ownership? No

COSTS
Total cost: $42.4K-66.7K
Franchise fee: $20K
Royalty fee: 6%
Term of agreement: 10 years renewable
    for 25% of then-current fee
Franchisees required to buy multiple
    units? Yes

FINANCING
No financing available

QUALIFICATIONS
Net worth: $50K
Cash liquidity: $25K

TRAINING
At headquarters: 30 hours
Ongoing

BUSINESS SUPPORT
Grand opening
Internet
Newsletter
Meetings
Toll-free phone line
Purchasing cooperatives

MARKETING SUPPORT
Co-op advertising
Ad slicks
National media campaign
Regional marketing
National call center

PET BUTLER

Financial rating: $$$

5300 Town & Country Blvd., #440
Frisco, TX 75034
(800)738-2885
www.petbutler.com
Pet waste removal, pet sitting, dog
    walking
Began: 1998, Franchising: 2005
Headquarters size: 15 employees
Franchise department: 8 employees

U.S. franchises: 52
Canadian franchises: 0
Other foreign franchises: 0
Company-owned: 18

Seeking: All U.S.
Seeking in Canada? No
Exclusive territories? Yes
Homebased option? Yes
Employees needed to run biz: 0
Absentee ownership? Yes

COSTS
Total cost: $49.9K-81.5K
Franchise fee: $18.9K
Royalty fee: 7%
Term of agreement: 10 years renewable
    for 25% of initial fee
Franchisees required to buy multiple
    units? No

FINANCING
In-house: Accounts receivable,
    equipment, franchise fee,
    inventory, payroll, startup costs
3rd-party: None

QUALIFICATIONS
Info not provided

TRAINING
At headquarters: 5 days
Video
Conference calls

BUSINESS SUPPORT
Grand opening
Internet
Newsletter
Meetings
Toll-free phone line
Field operations/evaluations
Purchasing cooperatives
Security/safety procedures

MARKETING SUPPORT
Co-op advertising
Ad slicks
National media campaign
Regional marketing

PETS   *Other Franchises*

AT-HEEL LEARNING CENTERS LLC
10205 Canoe Branch Rd.
Castalian Springs, TN 37031
(615)374-2141
www.at-heel.com
Dog training & boarding
Current financial data not available

HAPPY TAILS DOG SPA
8528-F Tyco Rd.
Vienna, VA 22182
(703)821-1777
www.dogfranchise.com
Dog day care & boarding
Current financial data not available

LAUND-UR-MUTT
8854 S. Edgewood St.
Littleton, CO 80130
(303)470-1540
www.laundurmutt.com
Self-service dog wash & pet center
Current financial data not available

PETS ARE INN
5100 Edina Industrial Blvd., #206
Minneapolis, MN 55439
(866)343-0086/(952)944-8298
www.petsareinn.com
Pet lodging service in private homes
Current financial data not available

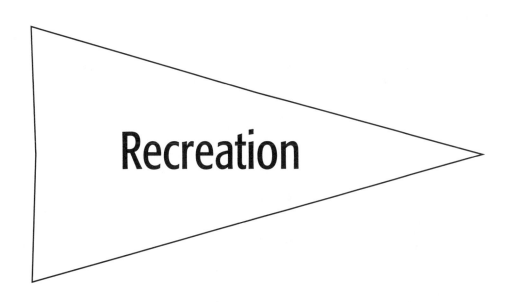

Recreation

RECREATION ▸ *Golf*

GOLF USA INC.

Ranked #433 in Entrepreneur Magazine's 2007 Franchise 500   *Financial rating: $$$$*

3705 W. Memorial Rd., #801
Oklahoma City, OK 73134
(800)488-1107/(405)751-0015
www.golfusa.com
Golf store
Began: 1986, Franchising: 1989
Headquarters size: 20 employees
Franchise department: 3 employees

U.S. franchises: 77
Canadian franchises: 7
Other foreign franchises: 26
Company-owned: 4

Seeking: All U.S.
Seeking in Canada? Yes
Exclusive territories? Yes
Homebased option? No
Employees needed to run biz: 4
Absentee ownership? Yes

COSTS
Total cost: $250K-415K
Franchise fee: $34K-44K
Royalty fee: 2%
Term of agreement: 15 years renewable
    at no charge
Franchisees required to buy multiple
    units? No

FINANCING
In-house: None
3rd-party: Accounts receivable,
    equipment, franchise fee,
    inventory, startup costs

QUALIFICATIONS
Net worth: $350K
Cash liquidity: $100K
Experience:
    Industry experience
    General business experience
    Marketing skills

TRAINING
At headquarters: 10 days

BUSINESS SUPPORT
Grand opening
Internet
Newsletter
Meetings
Toll-free phone line
Field operations/evaluations
Purchasing cooperatives
Security/safety procedures

MARKETING SUPPORT
Co-op advertising
Ad slicks
National media campaign
Regional marketing
Internet advertising

LTS LEADERBOARD

Financial rating: 0

21043-2591 Panorama Dr.
Coquitlam, BC V3E 2Y0 Canada
(800)411-4448/(604)468-2211
www.ltsleaderboard.com
Golf tournament scoring,
    administration & sponsorships
Began: 1995, Franchising: 2001
Headquarters size: 8 employees
Franchise department: 3 employees

U.S. franchises: 24
Canadian franchises: 2
Other foreign franchises: 3
Company-owned: 1

Seeking: All U.S.
Seeking in Canada? Yes
Exclusive territories? Yes
Homebased option? Yes
Employees needed to run biz: 2
Absentee ownership? No

COSTS
Total cost: $49.8K-173.9K
Franchise fee: $18K-71.1K
Royalty fee: Varies
Term of agreement: 5 years renewable
    at no charge
Franchisees required to buy multiple
    units? No

FINANCING
No financing available

QUALIFICATIONS
Net worth: $200K
Cash liquidity: $49K-102K
Experience:
    General business experience
    Marketing skills
    Golf knowledge

TRAINING
At headquarters: 2-1/2 weeks

BUSINESS SUPPORT
Internet
Newsletter
Meetings
Toll-free phone line
Field operations/evaluations

MARKETING SUPPORT
Co-op advertising
National media campaign
Regional marketing

RECREATION ▶ *Rentals*

EAGLERIDER MOTORCYCLE RENTAL
Ranked #367 in Entrepreneur Magazine's 2007 Franchise 500

Financial rating: $$$

11860 S. La Cienega Blvd.
Hawthorne, CA 90250-3461
(888)960-1500/(310)536-6777
www.eaglerider.com
Motorcycle, ATV & watercraft
    rentals
Began: 1992, Franchising: 1997
Headquarters size: 40 employees
Franchise department: 6 employees

U.S. franchises: 32
Canadian franchises: 0
Other foreign franchises: 2
Company-owned: 5

Seeking: All U.S.
Seeking in Canada? Yes
Exclusive territories? Yes
Homebased option? No
Employees needed to run biz: 5
Absentee ownership? No

COSTS
Total cost: $181.5K-775.1K
Franchise fee: $18K
Royalty fee: 5%/10%
Term of agreement: 10 years
    renewable at no charge
Franchisees required to buy
    multiple units? No

FINANCING
In-house: None
3rd-party: Equipment, franchise fee,
    inventory, startup costs

QUALIFICATIONS
Net worth: $350K
Cash liquidity: $100K
Experience:
    Industry experience
    General business experience
    Marketing skills
    Understanding of travel industry

TRAINING
At headquarters: 6 days
At franchisee's location: 2 days

BUSINESS SUPPORT
Grand opening
Internet
Newsletter
Meetings
Toll-free phone line
Field operations/evaluations
Purchasing cooperatives
Security/safety procedures

MARKETING SUPPORT
Ad slicks
National media campaign
Regional marketing
Int'l. advertising & promotions

WHEEL FUN RENTALS

Ranked #357 in Entrepreneur Magazine's 2007 Franchise 500　　　*Financial rating: $$$*

4526 Telephone Rd., #202
Ventura, CA 93003
(805)650-7770
www.wheelfunrentals.com
Recreational rentals
Began: 1987, Franchising: 2000
Headquarters size: 8 employees
Franchise department: 4 employees

U.S. franchises: 58
Canadian franchises: 0
Other foreign franchises: 0
Company-owned: 11

Seeking: All U.S.
Seeking in Canada? No
Exclusive territories? Yes
Homebased option? No
Employees needed to run biz: 3-12
Absentee ownership? No

COSTS
Total cost: $78.5K-250K
Franchise fee: $20K
Royalty fee: 6%
Term of agreement: 10 years renewable
　for $1K
Franchisees required to buy multiple
　units? No

FINANCING
In-house: None
3rd-party: Equipment, franchise fee,
　startup costs

QUALIFICATIONS
Net worth: $150K
Cash liquidity: $75K
Experience:
　General business experience

TRAINING
At headquarters: 7 days
At franchisee's location: Varies
Ongoing

BUSINESS SUPPORT
Grand opening
Internet
Newsletter
Meetings
Toll-free phone line
Field operations/evaluations

MARKETING SUPPORT
Co-op advertising
Ad slicks

RECREATION ▶ *Sports Equipment & Apparel*

THE ATHLETE'S FOOT

Financial rating: $$

1412 Oakbrook Dr., #100
Norcross, GA 30093
(800)524-6444/(770)514-4523
www.theathletesfoot.com
Athletic footwear & related sports
　accessories
Began: 1972, Franchising: 1973
Headquarters size: Info not
　provided

U.S. franchises: 251
Canadian franchises: 1
Other foreign franchises: 413
Company-owned: 0

Seeking: All U.S.
Seeking in Canada? Yes
Exclusive territories? Yes
Homebased option? No
Employees needed to run biz: 6-10
Absentee ownership? Yes

COSTS
Total cost: $196K-446K
Franchise fee: $39.9K
Royalty fee: 5%
Term of agreement: 10 years renewable
　at no charge
Franchisees required to buy multiple
　units? Outside the U.S. only

FINANCING
In-house: Equipment, inventory
3rd-party: None

QUALIFICATIONS
Net worth: $200K
Cash liquidity: $75K-100K
Experience:
　General business experience

TRAINING
At headquarters: 5 days
At franchisee's location: 5 days at
　opening

BUSINESS SUPPORT
Grand opening
Internet
Newsletter
Meetings
Toll-free phone line
Field operations/evaluations
Lease negotiations
Security/safety procedures

MARKETING SUPPORT
Ad slicks
Regional marketing

CONTE'S BICYCLE & FITNESS EQUIPMENT

Financial rating: $$$$

1205 Barn Brook Rd.
Virginia Beach, VA 23454
(757)496-6970
www.contebikes.com
Bicycle & fitness equipment
Began: 1957, Franchising: 2004
Headquarters size: 18 employees
Franchise department: 4 employees

U.S. franchises: 6
Canadian franchises: 0
Other foreign franchises: 0
Company-owned: 1

Seeking: All U.S.
Seeking in Canada? No
Exclusive territories? Yes
Homebased option? No
Employees needed to run biz: 3
Absentee ownership? No

COSTS
Total cost: $348K-531.8K
Franchise fee: $50K
Royalty fee: 3%
Term of agreement: 10 years renewable
    for $2K
Franchisees required to buy multiple
    units? No

FINANCING
In-house: None
3rd-party: Equipment, franchise fee,
    inventory, startup costs

QUALIFICATIONS
Net worth: $174K-266K
Cash liquidity: $87K-133K
Experience:
    Industry experience
    General business experience
    Retail experience preferred

TRAINING
At headquarters: 2 weeks
At franchisee's location: 2 weeks

BUSINESS SUPPORT
Grand opening
Internet
Newsletter
Meetings
Field operations/evaluations
Lease negotiations
Purchasing cooperatives
Security/safety procedures

MARKETING SUPPORT
Co-op advertising
Ad slicks
Events & sponsorship support

FLEET FEET SPORTS

Ranked #339 in Entrepreneur Magazine's 2007 Franchise 500

Financial rating: $$$$

406 E. Main St., P.O. Box 789
Carrboro, NC 27510
(919)942-3102
www.fleetfeet.com
Athletic footwear, apparel &
    accessories
Began: 1976, Franchising: 1978
Headquarters size: 11 employees
Franchise department: 11 employees

U.S. franchises: 67
Canadian franchises: 0
Other foreign franchises: 0
Company-owned: 0

Seeking: All U.S.
Seeking in Canada? No
Exclusive territories? Yes
Homebased option? No
Employees needed to run biz: 5
Absentee ownership? No

COSTS
Total cost: $161K-275K
Franchise fee: $35K
Royalty fee: 3-4%
Term of agreement: 20 years renewable
    at no charge
Franchisees required to buy multiple
    units? No

FINANCING
No financing available

QUALIFICATIONS
Info not provided

TRAINING
At headquarters: 1 week
At franchisee's location: 1 week
At existing stores: 15 days

BUSINESS SUPPORT
Grand opening
Newsletter
Meetings
Toll-free phone line
Field operations/evaluations

MARKETING SUPPORT
Info not provided

PRO IMAGE FRANCHISE LC

Ranked #440 in Entrepreneur Magazine's 2007 Franchise 500   *Financial rating: $$$$*

233 N. 1250 W., #200
Centerville, UT 84014
(801)296-9999
www.getproimage.com
Licensed sports apparel &
    accessories
Began: 1985, Franchising: 1986
Headquarters size: 9 employees
Franchise department: 9 employees

U.S. franchises: 98
Canadian franchises: 0
Other foreign franchises: 0
Company-owned: 0

Seeking: All U.S.
Seeking in Canada? No
Exclusive territories? No
Homebased option? No
Employees needed to run biz: 4
Absentee ownership? Yes

COSTS
Total cost: $120K-250K
Franchise fee: $25K
Royalty fee: 4%
Term of agreement: 10 years renewable
    at no charge
Franchisees required to buy multiple
    units? No

FINANCING
No financing available

QUALIFICATIONS
Net worth: $250K
Cash liquidity: $75K+
Experience:
    General business experience
    Marketing skills

TRAINING
At headquarters: 3 days
At franchisee's location: 2-3 days
At store opening

BUSINESS SUPPORT
Grand opening
Internet
Newsletter
Meetings
Toll-free phone line
Field operations/evaluations
Purchasing cooperatives
Security/safety procedures

MARKETING SUPPORT
Co-op advertising
Ad slicks
POP programs

RECREATION ► *Sports Programs*

AMERICAN POOLPLAYERS ASSOCIATION

Ranked #173 in Entrepreneur Magazine's 2007 Franchise 500   *Financial rating: $$$$*

1000 Lake St. Louis Blvd., #325
Lake St. Louis, MO 63367
(636)625-8611
www.poolplayers.com
Recreational billiard league
Began: 1981, Franchising: 1982
Headquarters size: 47 employees
Franchise department: 3 employees

U.S. franchises: 280
Canadian franchises: 20
Other foreign franchises: 0
Company-owned: 0

Seeking: All U.S.
Seeking in Canada? Yes
Exclusive territories? Yes
Homebased option? Yes
Employees needed to run biz: 1-3
Absentee ownership? No

COSTS
Total cost: $11.98K-14.8K
Franchise fee: $5K+
Royalty fee: 20%
Term of agreement: 2 years renewable
    at no charge
Franchisees required to buy multiple
    units? No

FINANCING
No financing available

QUALIFICATIONS
Experience:
    General business experience
    Marketing skills

TRAINING
At headquarters: 6 days

BUSINESS SUPPORT
Internet
Newsletter
Meetings
Toll-free phone line
Field operations/evaluations

MARKETING SUPPORT
Ad slicks

EXTRA INNINGS

Financial rating: $$

264 S. Main St.
Middleton, MA 01949
(978)762-0448
www.eifranchise.com
Indoor baseball/softball training
center & pro shop
Began: 1996, Franchising: 2004
Headquarters size: 35 employees
Franchise department: 7 employees

U.S. franchises: 14
Canadian franchises: 0
Other foreign franchises: 0
Company-owned: 1

Seeking: All U.S.
Seeking in Canada? No
Exclusive territories? Yes
Homebased option? No
Employees needed to run biz: 2-5
Absentee ownership? Yes

COSTS
Total cost: $179K-399.5K
Franchise fee: $25K
Royalty fee: Varies
Term of agreement: 10 years renewable
for $5K
Franchisees required to buy multiple
units? No

FINANCING
In-house: None
3rd-party: Equipment, franchise fee,
inventory, startup costs

QUALIFICATIONS
Net worth: $150K-300K
Experience:
Industry experience
General business experience
Marketing skills

TRAINING
At headquarters: 4 days
At franchisee's location: 4 days

BUSINESS SUPPORT
Grand opening
Internet
Meetings
Field operations/evaluations

MARKETING SUPPORT
Regional marketing

ι9 SPORTS

Financial rating: 0

1723 S. Kings Ave.
Brandon, FL 33511
(866)398-1137
www.i9sportsfranchise.com
Amateur sports leagues,
tournaments & events
Began: 2002, Franchising: 2003
Headquarters size: 9 employees
Franchise department: 9 employees

U.S. franchises: 80
Canadian franchises: 0
Other foreign franchises: 0
Company-owned: 2

Seeking: All U.S.
Seeking in Canada? Yes
Exclusive territories? Yes
Homebased option? Yes
Employees needed to run biz: 1
Absentee ownership? No

COSTS
Total cost: $39.5K-59.9K
Franchise fee: $12.5K-18.5K
Royalty fee: 7.5%
Term of agreement: 10 years renewable
for $2.5K
Franchisees required to buy multiple
units? Outside the U.S. only

FINANCING
In-house: None
3rd-party: Accounts receivable,
equipment, franchise fee,
inventory, payroll, startup costs

QUALIFICATIONS
Net worth: $100K
Cash liquidity: $39.5K-59.9K
Experience:
General business experience
Marketing skills

TRAINING
At headquarters: 1 week
At franchisee's location: 2 days
Optional refresher training available

BUSINESS SUPPORT
Internet
Newsletter
Meetings
Toll-free phone line
Field operations/evaluations
Purchasing cooperatives
Security/safety procedures

MARKETING SUPPORT
Co-op advertising
Ad slicks
National media campaign
Regional marketing
Administrative, billing &
commission payment support
Visits
Sales & PR guidance

RECREATION · *Travel*

ALL ABOUT HONEYMOONS

Financial rating: 0

7887 E. Belleview, #1225
Englewood, CO 80110
(800)813-9557/(720)259-4543
www.aahfranchise.com
Travel agency specializing in honey-
    moons & destination weddings
Began: 1994, Franchising: 2003
Headquarters size: 8 employees
Franchise department: 8 employees

U.S. franchises: 88
Canadian franchises: 3
Other foreign franchises: 0
Company-owned: 0

Seeking: All U.S.
Seeking in Canada? Yes
Exclusive territories? Yes
Homebased option? Yes
Employees needed to run biz: 0
Absentee ownership? Yes

COSTS
Total cost: $9.9K-36.1K
Franchise fee: $9K/19K/29K
Royalty fee: Varies
Term of agreement: 10 years
    renewable for $500
Franchisees required to buy
    multiple units? No

FINANCING
In-house: Franchise fee
3rd-party: Equipment

QUALIFICATIONS
Experience:
    Industry experience
    Customer service skills

TRAINING
At headquarters: 2 days (optional)
At franchisee's location: Optional
30-day orientation program
Internet classes

BUSINESS SUPPORT
Grand opening
Internet
Newsletter
Meetings
Toll-free phone line
Field operations/evaluations

MARKETING SUPPORT
Co-op advertising
Ad slicks
National media campaign
Regional marketing
Direct-marketing mailers & emails

CARLSON WAGONLIT TRAVEL

Ranked #204 in Entrepreneur Magazine's 2007 Franchise 500　　　*Financial rating: $$$$*

701 Carlson Pkwy., P.O. Box 59159
Minnetonka, MN 55459-8207
(866)225-9026
www.carlsontravel.com
Travel agency
Began: 1888, Franchising: 1984
Headquarters size: 1,070 employees
Franchise department: 104 employees

U.S. franchises: 622
Canadian franchises: 0
Other foreign franchises: 0
Company-owned: 23

Seeking: All U.S.
Seeking in Canada? No
Exclusive territories? No
Homebased option? No
Employees needed to run biz: 10
Absentee ownership? No

COSTS
Total cost: $1.6K-11.6K
Franchise fee: $1.5K
Royalty fee: $505-960/mo.
Term of agreement: 5 years renewable
    for $1K
Franchisees required to buy multiple
    units? No

FINANCING
In-house: Franchise fee
3rd-party: None

QUALIFICATIONS
Experience:
    Must own existing travel agency
    Industry experience
    General business experience
    Marketing skills

TRAINING
At headquarters: 3 days
At franchisee's location: Varies
Workshops: 1-2 days
Online training

BUSINESS SUPPORT
Internet
Newsletter
Meetings
Toll-free phone line
Field operations/evaluations

MARKETING SUPPORT
Co-op advertising
Ad slicks
National media campaign
Regional marketing

CRUISE HOLIDAYS

Ranked #445 in Entrepreneur Magazine's 2007 Franchise 500   *Financial rating: $$$$*

701 Carlson Pkwy., P.O. Box 59159
Minneapolis, MN 55459-8207
(800)496-2255
www.cruiseholidays.com
Cruise & land-tour vacations
Began: 1984, Franchising: 1984
Headquarters size: 961 employees
Franchise department: 96 employees

U.S. franchises: 85
Canadian franchises: 31
Other foreign franchises: 0
Company-owned: 0

Seeking: All U.S.
Seeking in Canada? Yes
Exclusive territories? No
Homebased option? No
Employees needed to run biz: 4
Absentee ownership? No

COSTS
Total cost: $139.9K
Franchise fee: $30K
Royalty fee: Varies
Term of agreement: 10 years renewable
    for $1K
Franchisees required to buy multiple
    units? No

FINANCING
No financing available

QUALIFICATIONS
Net worth: $250K
Cash liquidity: $150K
Experience:
    General business experience
    Marketing skills

TRAINING
At headquarters: 3 weeks
At franchisee's location: Varies
Cruise University: 2 weeks
Annual regional meetings: 2 days
Annual convention: 4 days

BUSINESS SUPPORT
Grand opening
Internet
Newsletter
Meetings
Toll-free phone line
Field operations/evaluations
Purchasing cooperatives

MARKETING SUPPORT
Co-op advertising
Ad slicks
National media campaign
Seminars
Internet marketing

CRUISEONE INC.

Ranked #131 in Entrepreneur Magazine's 2007 Franchise 500   *Financial rating: $$$$*

1415 N.W. 62nd St., #205
Fort Lauderdale, FL 33309
(800)892-3928
www.cruiseonefranchise.com
Cruise-only travel agency
Began: 1989, Franchising: 1993
Headquarters size: 80 employees
Franchise department: 4 employees

U.S. franchises: 470
Canadian franchises: 0
Other foreign franchises: 0
Company-owned: 0

Seeking: All U.S.
Seeking in Canada? No
Exclusive territories? No
Homebased option? Yes
Employees needed to run biz: 0
Absentee ownership? No

COSTS
Total cost: $9.8K-25.4K
Franchise fee: $9.8K
Royalty fee: 3%
Term of agreement: 5 years renewable
    at no charge
Franchisees required to buy multiple
    units? No

FINANCING
No financing available

QUALIFICATIONS
Cash liquidity: $20K

TRAINING
At headquarters: 8 days
Seminars at sea: 3-7 days

BUSINESS SUPPORT
Internet
Newsletter
Meetings
Toll-free phone line

MARKETING SUPPORT
Co-op advertising
Ad slicks
Regional marketing

CRUISE PLANNERS FRANCHISING LLC/AMERICAN EXPRESS

Ranked #79 in Entrepreneur Magazine's 2007 Franchise 500   *Financial rating: $$$$*

3300 University Dr., #602
Coral Springs, FL 33065
(888)582-2150/(954)227-2545
www.beacruiseagent.com
Cruise/tour travel agency
Began: 1994, Franchising: 1999
Headquarters size: 30 employees
Franchise department: 3 employees

U.S. franchises: 680
Canadian franchises: 0
Other foreign franchises: 0
Company-owned: 0

Seeking: All U.S.
Seeking in Canada? No
Exclusive territories? No
Homebased option? Yes
Employees needed to run biz: 1-2
Absentee ownership? Yes

COSTS
Total cost: $1.9K-19.6K
Franchise fee: $495-9.99K
Royalty fee: 3-0%
Term of agreement: 3 years renewable
    at no charge
Franchisees required to buy multiple
    units? No

FINANCING
No financing available

QUALIFICATIONS
Net worth: $17.1K
Cash liquidity: $9.99K

TRAINING
Training available

BUSINESS SUPPORT
Internet
Newsletter
Meetings
Toll-free phone line
Purchasing cooperatives

MARKETING SUPPORT
Co-op advertising
Ad slicks
National media campaign
Regional marketing

RESULTS TRAVEL

Ranked #62 in Entrepreneur Magazine's 2007 Franchise 500   *Financial rating: $$$$*

701 Carlson Pkwy., P.O. Box 59159
Minneapolis, MN 55459-8207
(888)523-2200
www.resultstravel.com
Travel services
Began: 2000, Franchising: 2000
Headquarters size: 1,070 employees
Franchise department: 104 employees

U.S. franchises: 901
Canadian franchises: 0
Other foreign franchises: 0
Company-owned: 0

Seeking: All U.S.
Seeking in Canada? No
Exclusive territories? No
Homebased option? No
Employees needed to run biz: 5
Absentee ownership? Yes

COSTS
Total cost: $25-10.7K
Franchise fee: to $1.5K
Royalty fee: $600/yr.
Term of agreement: 1 year renewable
    for $600
Franchisees required to buy multiple
    units? No

FINANCING
No financing available

QUALIFICATIONS
Experience:
    Must own existing travel agency
    Industry experience
    General business experience
    Marketing skills

TRAINING
At franchisee's location: Varies
Orientation & sales training in
    major U.S. cities: 1-2 days

BUSINESS SUPPORT
Newsletter
Meetings
Toll-free phone line

MARKETING SUPPORT
Co-op advertising
Regional marketing

SEAMASTER CRUISES

Ranked #359 in Entrepreneur Magazine's 2007 Franchise 500   *Financial rating: $$$$*

701 Carlson Pkwy.
Minnetonka, MN 55305
(763)212-4590
www.seamastercruises.com
Cruises
Began: 2004, Franchising: 2004
Headquarters size: 961 employees
Franchise department: 96 employees

U.S. franchises: 75
Canadian franchises: 0
Other foreign franchises: 0
Company-owned: 0

Seeking: All U.S.
Seeking in Canada? No
Exclusive territories? No
Homebased option? Yes
Employees needed to run biz: 1-2
Absentee ownership? No

COSTS
Total cost: $10.3K-16.9K
Franchise fee: $9.5K
Royalty fee: 3%
Term of agreement: 5 years renewable
    at no charge
Franchisees required to buy multiple
    units? No

FINANCING
No financing available

QUALIFICATIONS
Net worth: $10K
Cash liquidity: $10K
Experience:
    General business experience
    Marketing skills

TRAINING
At headquarters: 5 days
At franchisee's location
Advanced training cruise: 7-10 days
Online training

BUSINESS SUPPORT
Grand opening
Internet
Newsletter
Meetings
Toll-free phone line
Purchasing cooperatives
Security/safety procedures

MARKETING SUPPORT
Co-op advertising
Ad slicks
Regional marketing
Personal website
Turnkey marketing campaigns

RECREATION ▸ *Miscellaneous*

MONSTER MINI GOLF

Current financial data not available

755 Westminster St., #401
Providence, RI 02903
(401)437-8634
www.monsterminigolf.com
Family entertainment center featur-
    ing glow-in-the-dark mini golf
Began: 2004, Franchising: 2005
Headquarters size: 6 employees
Franchise department: 6 employees

U.S. franchises: 10
Canadian franchises: 0
Other foreign franchises: 0
Company-owned: 1

Seeking: All U.S.
Seeking in Canada? Yes
Exclusive territories? Yes
Homebased option? No
Employees needed to run biz: 6
Absentee ownership? No

COSTS
Total cost: $221K-290K
Franchise fee: $30K
Royalty fee: 8%
Term of agreement: 5 years renewable
    at no charge
Franchisees required to buy multiple
    units? No

FINANCING
No financing available

QUALIFICATIONS
Net worth: $250K
Cash liquidity: $30K
Hospitality skills

TRAINING
At headquarters: 2-4 weeks
At franchisee's location: 2 weeks

BUSINESS SUPPORT
Grand opening
Internet
Meetings
Field operations/evaluations
Purchasing cooperatives
Security/safety procedures

MARKETING SUPPORT
Co-op advertising
Ad slicks
Regional marketing
Website development

OUTDOOR CONNECTION

Ranked #443 in Entrepreneur Magazine's 2007 Franchise 500   *Financial rating: $$*

424 Neosho
Burlington, KS 66839
(620)364-5500
www.outdoor-connection.com
Fishing & hunting trips
Began: 1988, Franchising: 1990
Headquarters size: 5 employees
Franchise department: 4 employees

U.S. franchises: 81
Canadian franchises: 4
Other foreign franchises: 0
Company-owned: 3

Seeking: All U.S.
Seeking in Canada? Yes
Exclusive territories? Yes
Homebased option? Yes
Employees needed to run biz: 0
Absentee ownership? Yes

COSTS
Total cost: $13.9K-18.4K
Franchise fee: $12.9K
Royalty fee: 4%
Term of agreement: 5 years renewable
   for $1K
Franchisees required to buy multiple
   units? No

FINANCING
In-house: Franchise fee
3rd-party: None

QUALIFICATIONS
Experience:
   Marketing skills

TRAINING
At headquarters: 2 days
Annual convention: 2-3 days

BUSINESS SUPPORT
Internet
Newsletter
Meetings
Field operations/evaluations
Purchasing cooperatives

MARKETING SUPPORT
Co-op advertising
National media campaign

WORLD CHAMPIONSHIP ARMWRESTLING

Current financial data not available

111 Lynn Ave.
Ames, IA 50014
(866)232-5023
www.realitysportsent.com
Arm-wrestling tournaments
Began: 2002, Franchising: 2003
Headquarters size: 3 employees
Franchise department: 1 employee

U.S. franchises: 2
Canadian franchises: 0
Other foreign franchises: 0
Company-owned: 2

Seeking: All U.S.
Seeking in Canada? Yes
Exclusive territories? No
Homebased option? Yes
Employees needed to run biz: 1
Absentee ownership? Yes

COSTS
Total cost: $32.7K
Franchise fee: $25K
Royalty fee: $750/mo.
Term of agreement: 5 years renewable
   for $10K
Franchisees required to buy multiple
   units? No

FINANCING
In-house: Franchise fee
3rd-party: Franchise fee

QUALIFICATIONS
Cash liquidity: $5K
Experience:
   Marketing skills

TRAINING
At headquarters: 3-5 days
At franchisee's location: 3 days
Ongoing

BUSINESS SUPPORT
Internet
Newsletter
Meetings
Field operations/evaluations
Security/safety procedures

MARKETING SUPPORT
National media campaign
Regional marketing
PR

BATES MOTOR HOME RENTAL NETWORK INC.
Ranked #477 in Entrepreneur Magazine's 2007 Franchise 500
3690 S. Eastern Ave., #220
Las Vegas, NV 89109
(702)737-9050
www.batesintl.com
Motor home rentals
Financial rating: $$

FREEDOM BOAT CLUB
Ranked #335 in Entrepreneur Magazine's 2007 Franchise 500
4242 Airport Rd.
Cincinnati, OH 45226
(513)310-5515
www.freedomboatclub.com
Membership boat & yacht club
Financial rating: $$$$

GOLF ETC.
2201 Commercial Ln.
Granbury, TX 76048
(800)806-8633/(817)279-7888
www.golfetc.com
Golf supplies, equipment & services
Financial rating: $$$

PARMASTERS GOLF TRAINING CENTERS INC.
#1400, 1500 W. Georgia St.
Vancouver, BC V6G 2Z6 Canada
(800)663-2331
www.parmastersfranchise.com
Indoor golf-training center
Financial rating: 0

PLAY IT AGAIN SPORTS
Ranked #254 in Entrepreneur Magazine's 2007 Franchise 500
4200 Dahlberg Dr., #100
Minneapolis, MN 55422-4837
(800)453-7752/(763)520-8480
www.playitagainsports.com
New & used sporting goods/ equipment
Financial rating: $$$$

PRO GOLF INT'L. INC.
Ranked #464 in Entrepreneur Magazine's 2007 Franchise 500
37735 Enterprise Ct., #600
Farmington Hills, MI 48331
(800)776-4653/(248)994-0553
www.progolfdiscount.com
Golf equipment & accessories
Financial rating: $$$

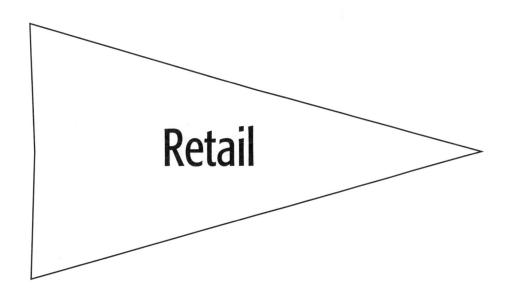

RETAIL · *Apparel*

APRICOT LANE

Financial rating: $$$

3333 Vaca Valley Pkwy., #900
Vacaville, CA 95688
(800)425-8883(707)451-6890
www.apricotlanefranchise.com
Fashion accessories, gifts, candles,
  home decor
Began: 1991, Franchising: 2004
Headquarters size: 10 employees
Franchise department: 1 employee

U.S. franchises: 17
Canadian franchises: 0
Other foreign franchises: 0
Company-owned: 1

Seeking: All U.S.
Seeking in Canada? No
Exclusive territories? No
Homebased option? No
Employees needed to run biz: 5
Absentee ownership? Yes

COSTS
Total cost: $102.4K-198.5K
Franchise fee: $25K
Royalty fee: 5.5%
Term of agreement: 10 years renewable
  at no charge
Franchisees required to buy multiple
  units? No

FINANCING
No financing available

QUALIFICATIONS
Net worth: $200K
Cash liquidity: $30K

TRAINING
At headquarters: 1 week
At franchisee's location: 1 week
Home learning program: 2 weeks

BUSINESS SUPPORT
Grand opening
Internet
Newsletter
Meetings
Toll-free phone line
Field operations/evaluations
Lease negotiations
Purchasing cooperatives
Security/safety procedures

MARKETING SUPPORT
Info not provided

PICKLES & ICE CREAM FRANCHISING INC.

Financial rating: $

5001 Spring Valley Rd., #385-W
Dallas, TX 75244
(214)742-5537
www.picklesandicecream.com
Maternity apparel store
Began: 1997, Franchising: 1999
Headquarters size: 10 employees
Franchise department: 4 employees

U.S. franchises: 4
Canadian franchises: 0
Other foreign franchises: 0
Company-owned: 2

Seeking: All U.S.
Seeking in Canada? No
Exclusive territories? Yes
Homebased option? No
Employees needed to run biz: 3
Absentee ownership? No

COSTS

Total cost: $167.2K-366K
Franchise fee: $30K
Royalty fee: 6%
Term of agreement: 7 years renewable
    for 33% of then-current fee
Franchisees required to buy multiple
    units? No

FINANCING

No financing available

QUALIFICATIONS

Cash liquidity: $50K
Experience:
    General business experience

TRAINING

At headquarters: 10 days
At franchisee's location: 2 days

BUSINESS SUPPORT

Grand opening
Internet
Newsletter
Meetings
Toll-free phone line
Field operations/evaluations
Purchasing cooperatives

MARKETING SUPPORT

National media campaign

RESTYLE

Financial rating: $$$

1404 S. New Rd.
Waco, TX 76708
(254)757-1445
www.findleygroup.com
Consignment clothing store
Began: 2005, Franchising: 2005
Headquarters size: 14 employees
Franchise department: 10 employees

U.S. franchises: 1
Canadian franchises: 0
Other foreign franchises: 0
Company-owned: 0

Seeking: All U.S.
Seeking in Canada? No
Exclusive territories? Yes
Homebased option? No
Employees needed to run biz: 3
Absentee ownership? Yes

COSTS

Total cost: $46.5K-61.7K
Franchise fee: $24.9K
Royalty fee: $500/mo.
Term of agreement: 10 years renewable
    at no charge
Franchisees required to buy multiple
    units? No

FINANCING

No financing available

QUALIFICATIONS

Net worth: $100K
Cash liquidity: $30K-40K
Experience:
    General business experience
    Marketing skills

TRAINING

At headquarters
At franchisee's location

BUSINESS SUPPORT

Grand opening
Internet
Newsletter
Meetings
Toll-free phone line
Field operations/evaluations
Security/safety procedures

MARKETING SUPPORT

Ad slicks
Regional marketing

AM/PM CONVENIENCE STORES
Ranked #51 in Entrepreneur Magazine's 2007 Franchise 500   *Financial rating: $$$$*

4101 Winfield Rd.
Warrenville, IL 60555
(888)894-2676
www.bpfranchising.com
Convenience food store
Began: 1975, Franchising: 1979
Headquarters size: Info not provided

U.S. franchises: 667
Canadian franchises: 0
Other foreign franchises: 1,987
Company-owned: 244

Seeking: West
Seeking in Canada? Yes
Exclusive territories? No
Homebased option? No
Employees needed to run biz: 10
Absentee ownership? No

COSTS
Total cost: $2.5M-6.3M
Franchise fee: $70K
Royalty fee: 5-6%
Term of agreement: 20 years renewable
    for $35K-60K
Franchisees required to buy multiple
    units? No

FINANCING
In-house: Site improvements
3rd-party: None

QUALIFICATIONS
Cash liquidity: $700K-1M
Experience:
    General business experience
    Hands-on retail experience
    Good credit history

TRAINING
At franchisee's location
In-class sessions
Hands-on training

BUSINESS SUPPORT
Grand opening
Internet
Meetings
Toll-free phone line
Field operations/evaluations
Security/safety procedures

MARKETING SUPPORT
Regional marketing
In-store promotions
TV & radio advertising

BP CONNECT

Financial rating: $$$$

4101 Winfield Rd.
Warrenville, IL 60555
(888)894-2676
www.bpfranchising.com
Convenience store & gas station
Began: 2000, Franchising: 2006
Headquarters size: Info not provided

U.S. franchises: 0
Canadian franchises: 0
Other foreign franchises: 0
Company-owned: 250

Seeking: Midwest, Northeast,
    Southeast
Seeking in Canada? No
Exclusive territories? No
Homebased option? No
Employees needed to run biz: Info
    not provided
Absentee ownership? No

COSTS
Total cost: $2.3M-6.6M
Franchise fee: $30K
Royalty fee: 3%
Term of agreement: 20 years renewable
    for then-current fee
Franchisees required to buy multiple
    units? No

FINANCING
In-house: Site improvements
3rd-party: None

QUALIFICATIONS
Cash liquidity: $700K-1M
Experience:
    General business experience
    Hands-on retail experience
    Good credit history

TRAINING
At headquarters
At franchisee's location
In-class sessions & hands-on
    training: 7 weeks

BUSINESS SUPPORT
Grand opening
Meetings
Toll-free phone line
Field operations/evaluations
Security/safety procedures

MARKETING SUPPORT
Regional marketing
In-store promotions
TV & radio ads

7-ELEVEN INC.

Ranked #4 in Entrepreneur Magazine's 2007 Franchise 500   *Financial rating: $$$$*

2711 N. Haskell Ave., Box 711
Dallas, TX 75221
(800)255-0711
www.7-eleven.com
Convenience store
Began: 1927, Franchising: 1964
Headquarters size: 1,000 employees
Franchise department: 18 employees

U.S. franchises: 3,998
Canadian franchises: 0
Other foreign franchises: 23,163
Company-owned: 2,304

Seeking: Midwest, Northeast,
    Southwest, West
Seeking in Canada? No
Exclusive territories? No
Homebased option? No
Employees needed to run biz: 7-10
Absentee ownership? No

COSTS
Total cost: Varies
Franchise fee: Varies
Royalty fee: Varies
Term of agreement: 15 years renewable
    at no charge
Franchisees required to buy multiple
    units? No

FINANCING
In-house: Accounts receivable,
    inventory, payroll
3rd-party: None

QUALIFICATIONS
Experience:
    General business experience
    Retail experience
    Customer service skills

TRAINING
At local training centers: 6 weeks

BUSINESS SUPPORT
Grand opening
Internet
Newsletter
Meetings
Toll-free phone line
Field operations/evaluations
Purchasing cooperatives
Security/safety procedures

MARKETING SUPPORT
National media campaign
Regional marketing
In-house marketing team

RETALL ◄ *Dollar Stores*

JUST-A-BUCK

Current financial data not available

301 N. Main St.
New City, NY 10956
(800)332-2229/(845)638-4111
www.just-a-buck.com
General merchandise for $1
Began: 1988, Franchising: 1992
Headquarters size: 15 employees
Franchise department: 12 employees

U.S. franchises: 32
Canadian franchises: 0
Other foreign franchises: 0
Company-owned: 8

Seeking: All U.S.
Seeking in Canada? No
Exclusive territories? Yes
Homebased option? No
Employees needed to run biz: 6
Absentee ownership? No

COSTS
Total cost: $140K-250K
Franchise fee: $25K
Royalty fee: 4%
Term of agreement: 10 years renewable
    at no charge
Franchisees required to buy multiple
    units? No

FINANCING
In-house: None
3rd-party: Equipment, franchise fee,
    inventory, startup costs

QUALIFICATIONS
Net worth: $180K
Cash liquidity: $40K-50K
Experience:
    General business experience

TRAINING
At headquarters: 2 weeks
At franchisee's location: 2 weeks

BUSINESS SUPPORT
Grand opening
Internet
Newsletter
Toll-free phone line
Field operations/evaluations
Lease negotiations
Purchasing cooperatives
Security/safety procedures

MARKETING SUPPORT
Ad slicks

YOUR DOLLAR STORE WITH MORE

Current financial data not available

102-1626 Richter St.
Kelowna, BC V1Y 2M3 Canada
(250)860-4225
www.dollarstore.ca
Dollar store
Began: 1998, Franchising: 1998
Headquarters size: 15 employees
Franchise department: 7 employees

U.S. franchises: 0
Canadian franchises: 170
Other foreign franchises: 0
Company-owned: 8

Seeking: All U.S.
Seeking in Canada? Yes
Exclusive territories? No
Homebased option? No
Employees needed to run biz: 4-12
Absentee ownership? Yes

COSTS
Total cost: $60K-200K
Franchise fee: $20K
Royalty fee: 4%
Term of agreement: 10 years renewable
for $2K
Franchisees required to buy multiple
units? No

FINANCING
No financing available

QUALIFICATIONS
Net worth: $75K
Cash liquidity: $75K
Experience:
General business experience

TRAINING
At headquarters: 5 days
At franchisee's location: 5 days
Ongoing

BUSINESS SUPPORT
Grand opening
Internet
Newsletter
Meetings
Toll-free phone line
Field operations/evaluations
Lease negotiations
Purchasing cooperatives
Security/safety procedures

MARKETING SUPPORT
Ad slicks
National media campaign
Flyers
Balloons
Gift certificates

RETAIL *Furniture*

MORE SPACE PLACE

Ranked #341 in Entrepreneur Magazine's 2007 Franchise 500

Financial rating: $$$$

5040 140th Ave. N.
Clearwater, FL 33760
(888)731-3051
www.morespaceplace.com
Space-saving furniture systems
Began: 1985, Franchising: 1993
Headquarters size: 56 employees
Franchise department: 21 employees

U.S. franchises: 37
Canadian franchises: 0
Other foreign franchises: 0
Company-owned: 3

Seeking: All U.S.
Seeking in Canada? No
Exclusive territories? Yes
Homebased option? No
Employees needed to run biz: 3
Absentee ownership? Yes

COSTS
Total cost: $128.5K-194K
Franchise fee: $18K-29.5K
Royalty fee: 4.5%
Term of agreement: 10 years renewable
for 15% of initial franchise fee
Franchisees required to buy multiple
units? No

FINANCING
In-house: None
3rd-party: Equipment, franchise fee,
inventory, startup costs

QUALIFICATIONS
Cash liquidity: $40K-65K
Experience:
General business experience
Customer-interaction skills

TRAINING
At headquarters: 2 weeks
At franchisee's location: 2 weeks+
Additional training available

BUSINESS SUPPORT
Grand opening
Internet
Newsletter
Meetings
Toll-free phone line
Field operations/evaluations
Lease negotiations
Purchasing cooperatives
Security/safety procedures

MARKETING SUPPORT
Co-op advertising
Ad slicks
National media campaign
Regional marketing
Ready-to-use materials

MOUNTAIN COMFORT FURNISHINGS

Current financial data not available

P.O. Box 1970
Frisco, CO 80443
(970)668-0502
www.mountaincomfort.net
Home furnishings
Began: 1984, Franchising: 1991
Headquarters size: 14 employees
Franchise department: 2 employees

U.S. franchises: 8
Canadian franchises: 0
Other foreign franchises: 0
Company-owned: 2

Seeking: All U.S.
Seeking in Canada? No
Exclusive territories? Yes
Homebased option? No
Employees needed to run biz: 8
Absentee ownership? Yes

COSTS
Total cost: $189.97K-410.8K
Franchise fee: $22.5K
Royalty fee: $10K/yr.
Term of agreement: 10 years
Franchisees required to buy multiple
  units? No

FINANCING
No financing available

QUALIFICATIONS
Cash liquidity: $125K
Experience:
  General business experience

TRAINING
At headquarters: 2 weeks
At franchisee's location: 1 week
Additional training available

BUSINESS SUPPORT
Grand opening
Internet
Newsletter
Meetings
Toll-free phone line
Field operations/evaluations
Lease negotiations
Purchasing cooperatives
Security/safety procedures

MARKETING SUPPORT
Ad slicks
Internet
Catalogs & brochures
TV ads

NORWALK - THE FURNITURE IDEA

Ranked #305 in Entrepreneur Magazine's 2007 Franchise 500   *Financial rating: $$$*

100 Furniture Pkwy.
Norwalk, OH 44857
(888)667-9255/(419)744-3200
www.norwalkfurnitureidea.com
Custom furniture & accessories
Began: 1902, Franchising: 1987
Headquarters size: 750 employees
Franchise department: 15 employees

U.S. franchises: 59
Canadian franchises: 6
Other foreign franchises: 0
Company-owned: 3

Seeking: All U.S.
Seeking in Canada? Yes
Exclusive territories? Yes
Homebased option? No
Employees needed to run biz: 14
Absentee ownership? No

COSTS
Total cost: $495K
Franchise fee: $35K
Royalty fee: 0
Term of agreement: 5 years renewable
  at no charge
Franchisees required to buy multiple
  units? No

FINANCING
In-house: None
3rd-party: Equipment, inventory,
  startup costs

QUALIFICATIONS
Net worth: $500K
Cash liquidity: $150K
Experience:
  Industry experience
  General business experience

TRAINING
At headquarters: 5 days
At franchisee's location: 10 days
Administrative & service-management
  support

BUSINESS SUPPORT
Grand opening
Internet
Newsletter
Meetings
Toll-free phone line
Field operations/evaluations

MARKETING SUPPORT
Ad slicks
Regional marketing

SLUMBERLAND INT'L. CO.

Financial rating: $

3060 Centerville Rd.
Little Canada, MN 55117
(651)482-7500
www.slumberland.com
Home & home-office furnishings
Began: 1968, Franchising: 1974
Headquarters size: 119 employees
Franchise department: 9 employees

U.S. franchises: 60
Canadian franchises: 0
Other foreign franchises: 0
Company-owned: 33

Seeking: Midwest
Seeking in Canada? No
Exclusive territories? No
Homebased option? No
Employees needed to run biz: 10
Absentee ownership? Yes

COSTS
Total cost: $438.5K-1.3M
Franchise fee: $30K-50K
Royalty fee: 3%
Term of agreement: 10 years renewable
  at no charge
Franchisees required to buy multiple
  units? No

FINANCING
In-house: None
3rd-party: Equipment, franchise fee,
  inventory, startup costs

QUALIFICATIONS
Net worth: $300K+
Cash liquidity: $100K+
Experience:
  Industry experience
  General business experience
  Marketing skills
  Commitment to customer service

TRAINING
At headquarters: 2-3 days
At franchisee's location: 2 weeks
Ongoing

BUSINESS SUPPORT
Grand opening
Internet
Newsletter
Meetings
Field operations/evaluations
Purchasing cooperatives

MARKETING SUPPORT
Co-op advertising
Ad slicks
National media campaign
Regional marketing

RETAIL ▸ *Hobby Stores*

HOBBYTOWN USA

Ranked #255 in Entrepreneur Magazine's 2007 Franchise 500

Financial rating: $$$$

6301 S. 58th St.
Lincoln, NE 68516
(800)858-7370
www.hobbytown.com
General hobbies & supplies
Began: 1969, Franchising: 1986
Headquarters size: 45 employees
Franchise department: 45 employees

U.S. franchises: 166
Canadian franchises: 0
Other foreign franchises: 0
Company-owned: 1

Seeking: All U.S.
Seeking in Canada? Yes
Exclusive territories? Yes
Homebased option? No
Employees needed to run biz: 4
Absentee ownership? Yes

COSTS
Total cost: $160K-720K
Franchise fee: $10K-19.5K
Royalty fee: 3-4%
Term of agreement: 10 years renewable
  for $1K
Franchisees required to buy multiple
  units? No

FINANCING
In-house: None
3rd-party: Equipment, franchise fee,
  inventory, startup costs

QUALIFICATIONS
Cash liquidity: $50K-225K

TRAINING
At headquarters: 1 week
At franchisee's location: 3 weeks

BUSINESS SUPPORT
Grand opening
Internet
Newsletter
Meetings
Toll-free phone line
Field operations/evaluations
Lease negotiations
Purchasing cooperatives
Security/safety procedures

MARKETING SUPPORT
Co-op advertising
Ad slicks
National media campaign

REMOTE CONTROL HOBBIES

Current financial data not available

5435 Boatworks Dr., #1
Littleton, CO 80126
(303)804-0470
http://franchise.rc-hobbies.com
Remote control hobby vehicles,
    parts & accessories
Began: 2003, Franchising: 2004
Headquarters size: 10 employees
Franchise department: 4 employees

U.S. franchises: 7
Canadian franchises: 0
Other foreign franchises: 0
Company-owned: 1

Seeking: All U.S.
Seeking in Canada? No
Exclusive territories? Yes
Homebased option? No
Employees needed to run biz: Info
    not provided
Absentee ownership? No

COSTS
Total cost: $98.5K-250K
Franchise fee: $15K
Royalty fee: 2.5%
Term of agreement: 10 years renewable
    at no charge
Franchisees required to buy multiple
    units? No

FINANCING
In-house: Franchise fee, inventory
3rd-party: None

QUALIFICATIONS
Net worth: $200K
Cash liquidity: $50K
Experience:
    General business experience
    Hobby interest

TRAINING
At headquarters: 7 weeks
At franchisee's location: 6 weeks

BUSINESS SUPPORT
Grand opening
Newsletter
Meetings
Toll-free phone line
Field operations/evaluations
Purchasing cooperatives

MARKETING SUPPORT
Co-op advertising
National media campaign

WOODCRAFT FRANCHISE LLC

Ranked #296 in Entrepreneur Magazine's 2007 Franchise 500   *Financial rating: $$$$*

1177 Rosemar Rd., P.O. Box 245
Parkersburg, WV 26105
(304)422-5412
www.woodcraft.com
Woodworking supply specialty store
Began: 1928, Franchising: 1997
Headquarters size: 80 employees
Franchise department: 2 employees

U.S. franchises: 79
Canadian franchises: 0
Other foreign franchises: 0
Company-owned: 3

Seeking: All U.S.
Seeking in Canada? No
Exclusive territories? Yes
Homebased option? No
Employees needed to run biz: 8-9
Absentee ownership? No

COSTS
Total cost: $461.2K-561.2K
Franchise fee: $50K
Royalty fee: 5%
Term of agreement: 10 years renewable
    at no charge
Franchisees required to buy multiple
    units? No

FINANCING
No financing available

QUALIFICATIONS
Cash liquidity: $150K
Must love woodworking

TRAINING
At headquarters: 2 weeks
At franchisee's location: 2-3 weeks

BUSINESS SUPPORT
Grand opening
Internet
Newsletter
Meetings
Toll-free phone line
Field operations/evaluations
Lease negotiations
Purchasing cooperatives
Security/safety procedures

MARKETING SUPPORT
Co-op advertising
Ad slicks
National media campaign
Regional marketing

RETAIL ▶ *Newsstands*

GATEWAY CIGAR STORE/NEWSTANDS
Ranked #168 in Entrepreneur Magazine's 2007 Franchise 500　　　　*Financial rating: $$$$*

9555 Yonge St., #400
Richmond Hill, ON L4C 9M5
　　Canada
(800)942-5351/(905)737-7755
www.gatewaynewstands.com
Newsstand & sundry store
Began: 1983, Franchising: 1983
Headquarters size: 20 employees
Franchise department: 4 employees

U.S. franchises: 145
Canadian franchises: 229
Other foreign franchises: 0
Company-owned: 0

Seeking: All U.S.
Seeking in Canada? Yes
Exclusive territories? No
Homebased option? No
Employees needed to run biz: 1-2
Absentee ownership? Yes

COSTS
Total cost: $55.9K-362.8K
Franchise fee: $15K-125K
Royalty fee: 3.5%
Term of agreement: 5, 7 or 10 years
　　renewable
Franchisees required to buy multiple
　　units? No

FINANCING
In-house: None
3rd-party: Equipment

QUALIFICATIONS
Net worth: $200K
Cash liquidity: $75K
Experience:
　　General business experience

TRAINING
At franchisee's location:
　　2 days-1 week

BUSINESS SUPPORT
Grand opening
Internet
Newsletter
Toll-free phone line
Field operations/evaluations
Purchasing cooperatives
Security/safety procedures

MARKETING SUPPORT
Head office & field support

STREET CORNER
Ranked #381 in Entrepreneur Magazine's 2007 Franchise 500　　　　*Financial rating: $$$*

2945 S.W. Wanamaker Dr.
Topeka, KS 66614
(785)272-8529
www.streetcornernews.com
Mall-based newsstand &
　　convenience store
Began: 1988, Franchising: 1995
Headquarters size: 7 employees
Franchise department: 3 employees

U.S. franchises: 52
Canadian franchises: 0
Other foreign franchises: 0
Company-owned: 0

Seeking: All U.S.
Seeking in Canada? No
Exclusive territories? Yes
Homebased option? No
Employees needed to run biz: 2
Absentee ownership? Yes

COSTS
Total cost: $150K-200K
Franchise fee: $19.9K
Royalty fee: 4.5%
Term of agreement: 7 years renewable
　　for $2.5K
Franchisees required to buy multiple
　　units? No

FINANCING
In-house: None
3rd-party: Accounts receivable,
　　equipment, franchise fee,
　　inventory, payroll, startup costs

QUALIFICATIONS
Net worth: $100K
Cash liquidity: $30K

TRAINING
At headquarters: Upon request
At franchisee's location: 1 week

BUSINESS SUPPORT
Grand opening
Internet
Newsletter
Meetings
Toll-free phone line
Field operations/evaluations
Purchasing cooperatives
Security/safety procedures

MARKETING SUPPORT
Ad slicks
National media campaign
Regional marketing
Store marketing reviews

RETAIL   *Tech*

EGISMOZ

Current financial data not available

900 Victors Way., #200
Ann Arbor, MI 48108
(734)994-9199
www.egismoz.com
Consumer electronics
Began: 2005, Franchising: 2006
Headquarters size: 25 employees
Franchise department: 15 employees

U.S. franchises: 0
Canadian franchises: 0
Other foreign franchises: 0
Company-owned: 1

Seeking: All U.S.
Seeking in Canada? No
Exclusive territories? Info not
    provided
Homebased option? No
Employees needed to run biz: 4
Absentee ownership? No

COSTS
Total cost: $175K-296K
Franchise fee: $35K
Royalty fee: 4%
Term of agreement: 10 years renewable
    for $5K or 33% of current fee
Franchisees required to buy multiple
    units? No

FINANCING
No financing available

QUALIFICATIONS
Net worth: $500K
Cash liquidity: $50K-75K

TRAINING
At headquarters: 7-10 days
At franchisee's location: 2-3 days

BUSINESS SUPPORT
Grand opening
Internet
Meetings
Toll-free phone line
Field operations/evaluations
Purchasing cooperatives
Security/safety procedures

MARKETING SUPPORT
Co-op advertising
Ad slicks
National media campaign
Regional marketing

RADIOSHACK

Current financial data not available

300 RadioShack Cir.
Fort Worth, TX 76102
(817)415-9138
www.radioshack.com
Consumer electronics
Began: 1921, Franchising: 1968
Headquarters size: 2,000 employees
Franchise department: 150 employees

U.S. franchises: 1,660
Canadian franchises: 16
Other foreign franchises: 25
Company-owned: 4,982

Seeking: All U.S.
Seeking in Canada? Yes
Exclusive territories? No
Homebased option? No
Employees needed to run biz: 2
Absentee ownership? No

COSTS
Total cost: $69.9K
Franchise fee: $39.9K
Royalty fee: 0
Term of agreement: 10 years
    renewable at no charge
Franchisees required to buy multiple
    units? No

FINANCING
No financing available

QUALIFICATIONS
Experience:
    General business experience
    Retail ownership experience

TRAINING
At franchisee's location: 1 week
Local workshops
Annual convention

BUSINESS SUPPORT
Grand opening
Internet
Newsletter
Meetings
Toll-free phone line
Field operations/evaluations

MARKETING SUPPORT
Ad slicks
National media campaign
Bimonthly customer mailings

WIRELESS TOYZ

Ranked #352 in Entrepreneur Magazine's 2007 Franchise 500　　*Financial rating: 0*

28470 W. Thirteen Mile Rd., #300
Farmington Hills, MI 48334
(866)237-2624/(248)426-8200
www.wirelesstoyz.com
Cellular phones, satellite systems,
　accessories
Began: 1995, Franchising: 2001
Headquarters size: 42 employees
Franchise department: 3 employees

U.S. franchises: 145
Canadian franchises: 0
Other foreign franchises: 0
Company-owned: 3

Seeking: All U.S.
Seeking in Canada? No
Exclusive territories? Yes
Homebased option? No
Employees needed to run biz: 4
Absentee ownership? No

COSTS
Total cost: $209K-632K
Franchise fee: $30K
Royalty fee: 13%
Term of agreement: 10 years renewable
　for $5K
Franchisees required to buy multiple
　units? No

FINANCING
In-house: None
3rd-party: Equipment, inventory,
　startup costs

QUALIFICATIONS
Net worth: $100K
Cash liquidity: $60K-90K
Experience:
　General business experience
　Sales experience

TRAINING
At headquarters: 3 weeks
At franchisee's location: 1 week
At local store: 3 weeks

BUSINESS SUPPORT
Grand opening
Internet
Meetings
Toll-free phone line
Field operations/evaluations
Lease negotiations
Purchasing cooperatives
Security/safety procedures

MARKETING SUPPORT
Co-op advertising
Ad slicks
Regional marketing

WIRELESS ZONE

Ranked #214 in Entrepreneur Magazine's 2007 Franchise 500　　*Financial rating: $$$$*

34 Industrial Park Pl.
Middletown, CT 06457
(860)632-9494
www.wirelesszone.com
Wireless communications store
Began: 1988, Franchising: 1989
Headquarters size: 67 employees
Franchise department: 24 employees

U.S. franchises: 253
Canadian franchises: 0
Other foreign franchises: 0
Company-owned: 0

Seeking: Midwest, Northeast,
　Southeast
Seeking in Canada? No
Exclusive territories? Yes
Homebased option? No
Employees needed to run biz: 4
Absentee ownership? No

COSTS
Total cost: $38.4K-148.8K
Franchise fee: $1K-25K
Royalty fee: Varies
Term of agreement: 7 years renewable
　for $7.5K
Franchisees required to buy multiple
　units? No

FINANCING
In-house: Equipment, franchise fee,
　inventory
3rd-party: Accounts receivable,
　inventory, payroll, startup costs

QUALIFICATIONS
Experience:
　Industry experience
　General business experience
　Marketing skills
　2-years wireless experience
　Customer service background

TRAINING
At headquarters: 1 day
At franchisee's location: Ongoing
At existing franchise location:
　1 week
Seminars: Twice yearly

BUSINESS SUPPORT
Grand opening
Internet
Newsletter
Meetings
Field operations/evaluations

MARKETING SUPPORT
Co-op advertising
Ad slicks
Regional marketing
PR

YAKETY YAK WIRELESS

Financial rating: $$$$

3400 Irvine Ave., #118
Newport Beach, CA 92660
(888)925-4887
www.yakitup.com
Wireless services & related products
Began: 1999, Franchising: 2005
Headquarters size: 11 employees
Franchise department: 11 employees

U.S. franchises: 10
Canadian franchises: 0
Other foreign franchises: 0
Company-owned: 0

Seeking: All U.S.
Seeking in Canada? No
Exclusive territories? Yes
Homebased option? No
Employees needed to run biz: 2
Absentee ownership? No

COSTS
Total cost: $88.5K-209.5K
Franchise fee: $15K
Royalty fee: $300
Term of agreement: 5 years renewable
at no charge
Franchisees required to buy multiple
units? No

FINANCING
In-house: None
3rd-party: Equipment, inventory,
startup costs

QUALIFICATIONS
Net worth: $50K-90K
Cash liquidity: $40K-50K
Experience:
General business experience

TRAINING
At headquarters: 2 weeks
Daily conference calls

BUSINESS SUPPORT
Grand opening
Internet
Newsletter
Meetings
Lease negotiations

MARKETING SUPPORT
Ad slicks
National media campaign
Regional marketing

RETAIL ◀ *Tools & Hardware*

ACE HARDWARE CORP.

Ranked #18 in Entrepreneur Magazine's 2007 Franchise 500   *Financial rating: $$$$*

2200 Kensington Ct.
Oak Brook, IL 60523
(630)990-6900
www.myace.com
Hardware & home improvement
store
Began: 1924, Franchising: 1976
Headquarters size: 1,100 employees

U.S. franchises: 4,140
Canadian franchises: 0
Other foreign franchises: 225
Company-owned: 17

Seeking: All U.S.
Seeking in Canada? Yes
Exclusive territories? Yes
Homebased option? No
Employees needed to run biz: 25
Absentee ownership? Yes

COSTS
Total cost: $600K-1M
Franchise fee: $5K application fee
Royalty fee: $3K-10K ad fee
Term of agreement: Info not provided
Franchisees required to buy multiple
units? No

FINANCING
In-house: None
3rd-party: Accounts receivable,
equipment, inventory, payroll,
startup costs

QUALIFICATIONS
Net worth: $400K
Cash liquidity: $250K
Experience:
General business experience

TRAINING
At headquarters: 2 weeks
At franchisee's location: Ongoing

BUSINESS SUPPORT
Grand opening
Internet
Newsletter
Meetings
Toll-free phone line
Field operations/evaluations
Purchasing cooperatives
Security/safety procedures

MARKETING SUPPORT
Co-op advertising
Ad slicks
National media campaign
Regional marketing

MATCO TOOLS

Ranked #24 in Entrepreneur Magazine's 2007 Franchise 500   *Financial rating: $$$$*

4403 Allen Rd.
Stow, OH 44224
(800)368-6651
www.matcotools.com
Tools
Began: 1979, Franchising: 1993
Headquarters size: 150 employees
Franchise department: 7 employees

U.S. franchises: 1,421
Canadian franchises: 11
Other foreign franchises: 0
Company-owned: 0

Seeking: All U.S.
Seeking in Canada? Yes
Exclusive territories? Yes
Homebased option? Yes
Employees needed to run biz: 0
Absentee ownership? No

COSTS
Total cost: $74K-169K
Franchise fee: $0
Royalty fee: 0
Term of agreement: 10 years renewable
    at no charge
Franchisees required to buy multiple
    units? No

FINANCING
In-house: Accounts receivable,
    equipment, inventory, startup
    costs
3rd-party: Accounts receivable,
    equipment, inventory, startup
    costs

QUALIFICATIONS
Net worth: $60K
Cash liquidity: $25K
Experience:
    Industry experience
    General business experience
    Marketing skills

TRAINING
At headquarters: 2 weeks
At franchisee's location: 3 weeks
District meetings: Every 5 weeks

BUSINESS SUPPORT
Grand opening
Internet
Newsletter
Meetings
Toll-free phone line
Field operations/evaluations

MARKETING SUPPORT
National media campaign
Regional marketing
Direct-sales meetings
Online support

MIGHTY DISTRIB. SYSTEM OF AMERICA

Ranked #435 in Entrepreneur Magazine's 2007 Franchise 500   *Financial rating: $$$$*

650 Engineering Dr.
Norcross, GA 30092
(800)829-3900/(770)448-3900
www.mightyfranchising.com
Wholesale distribution of auto parts
Began: 1963, Franchising: 1970
Headquarters size: 45 employees
Franchise department: 7 employees

U.S. franchises: 112
Canadian franchises: 0
Other foreign franchises: 0
Company-owned: 5

Seeking: All U.S.
Seeking in Canada? Yes
Exclusive territories? Yes
Homebased option? No
Employees needed to run biz: 1
Absentee ownership? No

COSTS
Total cost: $126.6K-254.1K
Franchise fee: $12.9K-34.8K
Royalty fee: 5%
Term of agreement: 10 years renewable
    for 20% of current license fee
Franchisees required to buy multiple
    units? No

FINANCING
No financing available

QUALIFICATIONS
Net worth: $500K
Cash liquidity: $100K
Experience:
    Industry experience
    General business experience

TRAINING
At headquarters: 4-5 days
At franchisee's location: 5-10 days

BUSINESS SUPPORT
Grand opening
Internet
Newsletter
Meetings
Toll-free phone line
Field operations/evaluations

MARKETING SUPPORT
Co-op advertising
Ad slicks
National media campaign
Regional marketing

SNAP-ON TOOLS

Ranked #61 in Entrepreneur Magazine's 2007 Franchise 500   *Financial rating: $$$$*

2801 80th St., P.O. Box 1410
Kenosha, WI 53141-1410
(877)476-2766
www.snapon.com
Professional tools & equipment
Began: 1920, Franchising: 1991
Headquarters size: 500 employees
Franchise department: 10 employees

U.S. franchises: 3,087
Canadian franchises: 332
Other foreign franchises: 846
Company-owned: 30

Seeking: All U.S.
Seeking in Canada? Yes
Exclusive territories? No
Homebased option? Yes
Employees needed to run biz: 0
Absentee ownership? No

COSTS
Total cost: $18.8K-262.9K
Franchise fee: $7.5K
Royalty fee: $63/mo.
Term of agreement: 10 years
    renewable for 50% of
    current license fee
Franchisees required to buy multiple
    units? No

FINANCING
In-house: None
3rd-party: Accounts receivable,
    franchise fee, inventory

QUALIFICATIONS
Net worth: to $30K
Cash liquidity: $18.8K-60.3K
Experience:
    Sales experience

TRAINING
At franchisee's location: 3 weeks
At branch office: 1 week
At regional centers: 1 week

BUSINESS SUPPORT
Grand opening
Internet
Newsletter
Meetings
Toll-free phone line
Field operations/evaluations
Security/safety procedures

MARKETING SUPPORT
Info not provided

RETAIL ▶ *Video Games*

PLAY N TRADE FRANCHISE INC.

Ranked #460 in Entrepreneur Magazine's 2007 Franchise 500   *Financial rating: $$$*

3400 Irvine Ave., Bldg. 118
Newport Beach, CA 92660
(949)486-6000
www.playntrade.com
New & used video games
Began: 2001, Franchising: 2003
Headquarters size: 15 employees

U.S. franchises: 20
Canadian franchises: 0
Other foreign franchises: 0
Company-owned: 0

Seeking: All U.S.
Seeking in Canada? Yes
Exclusive territories? No
Homebased option? No
Employees needed to run biz: 1-2
Absentee ownership? No

COSTS
Total cost: $120K
Franchise fee: $20K
Royalty fee: 3%
Term of agreement: 5 years
Franchisees required to buy multiple
    units? No

FINANCING
No financing available

QUALIFICATIONS
Net worth: $117K-214.5K
Cash liquidity: $52K-100K
Experience:
    General business experience
    Marketing skills

TRAINING
At headquarters

BUSINESS SUPPORT
Grand opening
Internet
Newsletter
Meetings
Toll-free phone line
Lease negotiations

MARKETING SUPPORT
Ad slicks
National media campaign

VINTAGE STOCK

Current financial data not available

202 E. 32nd St.
Joplin, MO 64804
(417)623-1550
www.vintagestock.com
DVDs, video games, music, sports
cards
Began: 1980, Franchising: 2005
Headquarters size: 9 employees

U.S. franchises: 0
Canadian franchises: 0
Other foreign franchises: 0
Company-owned: 13

Seeking: All U.S.
Seeking in Canada? No
Exclusive territories? Yes
Homebased option? No
Employees needed to run biz: 6
Absentee ownership? Yes

COSTS
Total cost: $337.7K-585.4K
Franchise fee: $30K
Royalty fee: 5%
Term of agreement: 10 years
renewable for $500
Franchisees required to buy
multiple units? Yes

FINANCING
No financing available

QUALIFICATIONS
Info not provided

TRAINING
At headquarters: 1 week
At franchisee's location: 2-3 weeks

BUSINESS SUPPORT
Field operations/evaluations

MARKETING SUPPORT
Regional marketing

RETAIL ◄ *Miscellaneous*

AARON'S SALES & LEASE OWNERSHIP

Ranked #49 in Entrepreneur Magazine's 2007 Franchise 500   *Financial rating: $$$$*

309 E. Paces Ferry Rd.
Atlanta, GA 30305-2377
(800)551-6015
www.aaronsfranchise.com
Furniture, electronics, computer &
appliance leasing/sales
Began: 1955, Franchising: 1992
Headquarters size: Info not provided
Franchise department: 35 employees

U.S. franchises: 403
Canadian franchises: 6
Other foreign franchises: 0
Company-owned: 763

Seeking: All U.S.
Seeking in Canada? Yes
Exclusive territories? Yes
Homebased option? No
Employees needed to run biz: 6
Absentee ownership? Yes

COSTS
Total cost: $269K-574K
Franchise fee: $15K-50K
Royalty fee: 6%
Term of agreement: 10 years renewable
for $2.5K
Franchisees required to buy multiple
units? Outside the U.S. only

FINANCING
In-house: None
3rd-party: Inventory

QUALIFICATIONS
Net worth: $450K
Cash liquidity: $300K
Experience:
General business experience

TRAINING
At headquarters: 3 days
At franchisee's location: Less than
30 days
At regional location: 1 week

BUSINESS SUPPORT
Grand opening
Internet
Newsletter
Meetings
Toll-free phone line
Field operations/evaluations
Purchasing cooperatives
Security/safety procedures

MARKETING SUPPORT
Co-op advertising
Ad slicks
National media campaign
Regional marketing
Race car sponsorship

BATTERIES PLUS

Ranked #133 in Entrepreneur Magazine's 2007 Franchise 500   *Financial rating: $$$$*

925 Walnut Ridge Dr.
Hartland, WI 53029
(800)274-9155
www.batteriesplus.com
Batteries & related products
Began: 1988, Franchising: 1992
Headquarters size: 70 employees
Franchise department: 3 employees

U.S. franchises: 254
Canadian franchises: 0
Other foreign franchises: 0
Company-owned: 14

Seeking: All U.S.
Seeking in Canada? No
Exclusive territories? Yes
Homebased option? No
Employees needed to run biz: 3-4
Absentee ownership? Yes

COSTS
Total cost: $143.8K-295.7K
Franchise fee: $35K
Royalty fee: 4%
Term of agreement: 10 years renewable
    for $2K
Franchisees required to buy multiple
    units? No

FINANCING
In-house: None
3rd-party: Accounts receivable,
    equipment, inventory, startup
    costs

QUALIFICATIONS
Net worth: $300K
Cash liquidity: $75K+
Experience:
    General business experience
    Marketing skills
    People skills

TRAINING
At headquarters: 3 weeks
At franchisee's location: 3 weeks
Periodic store visits
Regional meetings

BUSINESS SUPPORT
Grand opening
Internet
Newsletter
Meetings
Toll-free phone line
Field operations/evaluations
Lease negotiations
Purchasing cooperatives
Security/safety procedures

MARKETING SUPPORT
Co-op advertising
Ad slicks
TV & radio spots
POP
Catalogs & literature

CARDSMART RETAIL CORP.

Ranked #480 in Entrepreneur Magazine's 2007 Franchise 500   *Financial rating: $$$$*

430 Pine St.
Central Falls, RI 02863
(877)227-3762
www.cardsmart.com
Card & gift store
Began: 1996, Franchising: 2001
Headquarters size: 15 employees
Franchise department: 15 employees

U.S. franchises: 76
Canadian franchises: 0
Other foreign franchises: 0
Company-owned: 3

Seeking: All U.S.
Seeking in Canada? No
Exclusive territories? Yes
Homebased option? No
Employees needed to run biz: 7
Absentee ownership? Yes

COSTS
Total cost: $193.9K-263.6K
Franchise fee: $15K
Royalty fee: 2.5%
Term of agreement: 10 years
    renewable at no charge
Franchisees required to buy
    multiple units? No

FINANCING
No financing available

QUALIFICATIONS
Net worth: $200K
Cash liquidity: $75K

TRAINING
At headquarters: 2 weeks

BUSINESS SUPPORT
Grand opening
Newsletter
Meetings
Toll-free phone line
Lease negotiations

MARKETING SUPPORT
Ad slicks

CHEMSTATION

Financial rating: $$$

3400 Encrete Ln.
Dayton, OH 45439
(937)294-8265
www.chemstation.com
Industrial cleanser manufacturing &
distribution
Began: 1965, Franchising: 1983
Headquarters size: 46 employees
Franchise department: 2 employees

U.S. franchises: 49
Canadian franchises: 1
Other foreign franchises: 0
Company-owned: 5

Seeking: Midwest, Northeast, West
Seeking in Canada? Yes
Exclusive territories? Yes
Homebased option? No
Employees needed to run biz: 6
Absentee ownership? No

COSTS
Total cost: $500K-700K
Franchise fee: $45K
Royalty fee: 4%
Term of agreement: 10 years renewable
at no charge
Franchisees required to buy multiple
units? No

FINANCING
In-house: Equipment
3rd-party: None

QUALIFICATIONS
Net worth: $1M
Cash liquidity: $300K-500K
Experience:
Marketing skills

TRAINING
At headquarters: As needed
At franchisee's location: As needed

BUSINESS SUPPORT
Internet
Newsletter
Meetings
Toll-free phone line
Field operations/evaluations
Purchasing cooperatives
Security/safety procedures

MARKETING SUPPORT
Co-op advertising
Ad slicks
National media campaign
Regional marketing

COLOR ME MINE ENTERPRISES INC.

Current financial data not available

3722 San Fernando Rd.
Glendale, CA 91204
(818)291-5900
www.colormemine.com
Paint-your-own-ceramics studio
Began: 1992, Franchising: 1995
Headquarters size: 18 employees
Franchise department: 3 employees

U.S. franchises: 93
Canadian franchises: 0
Other foreign franchises: 15
Company-owned: 1

Seeking: All U.S.
Seeking in Canada? Yes
Exclusive territories? Yes
Homebased option? No
Employees needed to run biz: 2-6
Absentee ownership? Yes

COSTS
Total cost: $97.5K-185K
Franchise fee: $25K
Royalty fee: 5%
Term of agreement: For duration of
lease term, renewable at no
charge
Franchisees required to buy multiple
units? Outside the U.S. only

FINANCING
In-house: None
3rd-party: Equipment, franchise fee,
inventory, startup costs

QUALIFICATIONS
Net worth: $200K+
Cash liquidity: $30K-60K
Experience:
General business experience
Marketing skills

TRAINING
At headquarters: 10 days
At franchisee's location: 6 days
Semi-annual workshops

BUSINESS SUPPORT
Grand opening
Internet
Newsletter
Meetings
Toll-free phone line
Purchasing cooperatives
Security/safety procedures

MARKETING SUPPORT
Ad slicks
Marketing materials

COUNTRY CLUTTER

Financial rating: $$$

3333 Vaca Valley Pkwy., #900
Vacaville, CA 95688
(800)425-8883/(707)451-6890
www.countryclutterfranchise.com
Gifts, home decor, candles, fashion
   accessories
Began: 1991, Franchising: 1992
Headquarters size: 10 employees
Franchise department: 1 employee

U.S. franchises: 33
Canadian franchises: 0
Other foreign franchises: 0
Company-owned: 4

Seeking: All U.S.
Seeking in Canada? No
Exclusive territories? No
Homebased option? No
Employees needed to run biz: 5
Absentee ownership? No

COSTS
Total cost: $102.4K-198.5K
Franchise fee: $25K
Royalty fee: 5.5%
Term of agreement: 10 years
   renewable at no charge
Franchisees required to buy
   multiple units? No

FINANCING
No financing available

QUALIFICATIONS
Net worth: $200K+
Cash liquidity: $30K

TRAINING
At headquarters: 4 days
At franchisee's location: 6 days
At-home learning: 12 weeks

BUSINESS SUPPORT
Grand opening
Internet
Newsletter
Meetings
Toll-free phone line
Field operations/evaluations
Lease negotiations
Purchasing cooperatives
Security/safety procedures

MARKETING SUPPORT
Ad slicks
Customized marketing support

CROWN TROPHY INC.

Ranked #276 in Entrepreneur Magazine's 2007 Franchise 500

Financial rating: $$$$

9 Skyline Dr.
Hawthorne, NY 10532
(800)583-8228
www.crownfranchise.com
Award & recognition items
Began: 1978, Franchising: 1987
Headquarters size: 40 employees
Franchise department: 6 employees

U.S. franchises: 136
Canadian franchises: 0
Other foreign franchises: 0
Company-owned: 0

Seeking: All U.S.
Seeking in Canada? No
Exclusive territories? Yes
Homebased option? No
Employees needed to run biz: 2
Absentee ownership? No

COSTS
Total cost: $160K-185K
Franchise fee: $35K
Royalty fee: 5%
Term of agreement: 5 years renewable
   at no charge
Franchisees required to buy multiple
   units? No

FINANCING
In-house: None
3rd-party: Equipment, startup costs

QUALIFICATIONS
Cash liquidity: $50K-60K
Experience:
   Marketing skills
   People skills
   Leadership skills

TRAINING
At headquarters: 9 days
At franchisee's location: 4 days
Annual franchise meeting

BUSINESS SUPPORT
Grand opening
Internet
Newsletter
Meetings
Toll-free phone line
Field operations/evaluations
Lease negotiations
Purchasing cooperatives
Security/safety procedures

MARKETING SUPPORT
Ad slicks
Regional marketing
In-house marketing materials
Catalogs
Exclusive products

FLOWERAMA OF AMERICA

Ranked #292 in Entrepreneur Magazine's 2007 Franchise 500

Financial rating: $$$$

3165 W. Airline Hwy.
Waterloo, IA 50703
(319)291-6004
www.flowerama.com
Flowers, plants, gifts, silk items
Began: 1966, Franchising: 1972
Headquarters size: 40 employees
Franchise department: 4 employees

U.S. franchises: 96
Canadian franchises: 0
Other foreign franchises: 0
Company-owned: 12

Seeking: All U.S.
Seeking in Canada? No
Exclusive territories? No
Homebased option? No
Employees needed to run biz: 8-10
Absentee ownership? Yes

COSTS
Total cost: $209K-411
Franchise fee: $35K
Royalty fee: 5%
Term of agreement: 20 years renewable
   at no charge
Franchisees required to buy multiple
   units? No

FINANCING
In-house: None
3rd-party: Equipment, inventory,
   payroll, startup costs

QUALIFICATIONS
Cash liquidity: $50K

TRAINING
At headquarters: 4-6 weeks
At franchisee's location: 1-2 weeks
Ongoing field training & support

BUSINESS SUPPORT
Grand opening
Internet
Newsletter
Toll-free phone line
Field operations/evaluations
Lease negotiations
Purchasing cooperatives
Security/safety procedures

MARKETING SUPPORT
Co-op advertising
Ad slicks

PARTY LAND INC.

Financial rating: 0

5215 Militia Hill Rd.
Plymouth Meeting, PA 19462
(800)778-9563/(610)941-6200
www.partyland.com
Party supplies & balloons
Began: 1986, Franchising: 1988
Headquarters size: 15 employees
Franchise department: 4 employees

U.S. franchises: 42
Canadian franchises: 2
Other foreign franchises: 533
Company-owned: 0

Seeking: All U.S.
Seeking in Canada? Yes
Exclusive territories? Yes
Homebased option? No
Employees needed to run biz: 4-12
Absentee ownership? Yes

COSTS
Total cost: $299K
Franchise fee: $35K
Royalty fee: 5%
Term of agreement: 20 years renewable
   for $1K
Franchisees required to buy multiple
   units? Outside the U.S. only

FINANCING
In-house: None
3rd-party: Accounts receivable,
   equipment, franchise fee,
   inventory, payroll, startup costs

QUALIFICATIONS
Net worth: $250K
Cash liquidity: $80K
Experience:
   General business experience

TRAINING
At headquarters: 1 week
In Toronto, ON: 3 days

BUSINESS SUPPORT
Grand opening
Internet
Newsletter
Meetings
Toll-free phone line
Field operations/evaluations
Purchasing cooperatives
Security/safety procedures

MARKETING SUPPORT
Co-op advertising
Ad slicks
National media campaign
Regional marketing

7 VALLEYS CUSTOM BLENDS FARM FRESH TOBACCO

Current financial data not available

47 N. Port Royal Dr.
Hilton Head Island, SC 29928
(843)681-3966
www.customblends.com
Tobacco retail store
Began: 1993, Franchising: 2005
Headquarters size: 6 employees
Franchise department: 6 employees

U.S. franchises: 1
Canadian franchises: 0
Other foreign franchises: 0
Company-owned: 2

Seeking: All U.S.
Seeking in Canada? Yes
Exclusive territories? Yes
Homebased option? No
Employees needed to run biz: Info
    not provided
Absentee ownership? Yes

COSTS
Total cost: $112.2K-197K
Franchise fee: $30K
Royalty fee: 6%
Term of agreement: 5 years renewable
    at no charge
Franchisees required to buy multiple
    units? Outside the U.S. only

FINANCING
No financing available

QUALIFICATIONS
People skills

TRAINING
At headquarters: 10 days+
At franchisee's location: 8 days+
Additional training available

BUSINESS SUPPORT
Grand opening
Internet
Meetings
Toll-free phone line
Field operations/evaluations
Lease negotiations
Purchasing cooperatives
Security/safety procedures

MARKETING SUPPORT
Info not provided

SHEFIELD & SONS

Current financial data not available

2265 W. Railway St., P.O. Box 490
Abbotsford, BC V2T 6Z7 Canada
(604)859-1014
www.shefield.com
Tobacco products & gifts
Began: 1976, Franchising: 1976
Headquarters size: 19 employees
Franchise department: 1 employee

U.S. franchises: 0
Canadian franchises: 53
Other foreign franchises: 0
Company-owned: 3

Seeking: Not available in the U.S.
Seeking in Canada? Yes
Exclusive territories? No
Homebased option? No
Employees needed to run biz: 4
Absentee ownership? Yes

COSTS
Total cost: $110K-200K
Franchise fee: $10K
Royalty fee: 2%/8%
Term of agreement: 5 years renewable
    for $5K
Franchisees required to buy multiple
    units? No

FINANCING
No financing available

QUALIFICATIONS
Net worth: $150K
Experience:
    General business experience

TRAINING
At franchisee's location: 2 weeks

BUSINESS SUPPORT
Grand opening
Internet
Newsletter
Toll-free phone line
Field operations/evaluations
Lease negotiations
Purchasing cooperatives
Security/safety procedures

MARKETING SUPPORT
Co-op advertising
Ad slicks
National media campaign

SHEFIELD GOURMET

Current financial data not available

2265 W. Railway St., P.O. Box 490
Abbotsford, BC V2T 6Z7 Canada
(604)852-8771
www.shefield.com
Tobacco products, coffee,
  accessories
Began: 1996, Franchising: 1996
Headquarters size: 19 employees
Franchise department: 1 employee

U.S. franchises: 0
Canadian franchises: 15
Other foreign franchises: 0
Company-owned: 3

Seeking: Not available in the U.S.
Seeking in Canada? Yes
Exclusive territories? No
Homebased option? No
Employees needed to run biz: 6
Absentee ownership? Yes

COSTS
Total cost: $150K-200K
Franchise fee: $25K
Royalty fee: 5-8%
Term of agreement: 5 years renewable
  for $5K
Franchisees required to buy multiple
  units? No

FINANCING
No financing available

QUALIFICATIONS
Net worth: $150K
Experience:
  General business experience

TRAINING
At franchisee's location: 2 weeks

BUSINESS SUPPORT
Grand opening
Internet
Newsletter
Toll-free phone line
Field operations/evaluations
Lease negotiations
Purchasing cooperatives
Security/safety procedures

MARKETING SUPPORT
Co-op advertising
Ad slicks
National media campaign

RETAIL ▶ *Other Franchises*

CLOTHES MENTOR
6215 Enterprise Ct.
Dublin, OH 43016
(866)261-2030
www.clothesmentor.com
New/used women's clothing &
  accessories
Current financial data not available

DOTI DESIGN STORES
*Ranked #372 in Entrepreneur
Magazine's 2007 Franchise 500*
18-3 E. Dundee Rd., #208
Barrington, IL 60010
(888)382-7488
www.dotifranchising.com
Upscale home furnishings & design
  store
Financial rating: $$$$

1ST PROPANE FRANCHISING INC.
14670 Cantova Wy., #208
Rancho Murieta, CA 95683
(877)977-6726
www.1st-propane.com
Bulk propane distribution
Financial rating: 0

MUSIC GO ROUND
*Ranked #493 in Entrepreneur
Magazine's 2007 Franchise 500*
4200 Dahlberg Dr., #100
Minneapolis, MN 55422-4837
(800)269-4076/(763)520-8582
www.musicgoround.com
New/used musical instruments &
  sound equipment
Financial rating: $$$$

PARTY AMERICA FRANCHISING INC.
*Ranked #268 in Entrepreneur
Magazine's 2007 Franchise 500*
980 Atlantic Ave., #103
Alameda, CA 94501
(510)747-1800
www.partyamerica.com
Party supplies, balloons, cards
Financial rating: $$$$

PLATO'S CLOSET
*Ranked #150 in Entrepreneur
Magazine's 2007 Franchise 500*
4200 Dahlberg Dr., #100
Minneapolis, MN 55422-4837
(800)269-4081/(763)520-8581
www.platoscloset.com
New/used clothing for teens &
  young adults
Financial rating: $$$$

VERLO MATTRESS FACTORY STORES
P.O. Box 298
Whitewater, WI 53190
(262)473-8957
www.verlofranchise.com
Mattresses, futons, sofa sleepers,
  bedding products
Financial rating: $$$

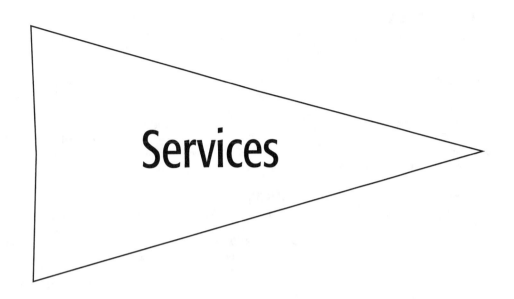

Services

SERVICES Delivery

DOOR-TO-DOOR DRY CLEANING

Financial rating: $$$

8400 E. Prentice Ave., #1500
Greenwood Village, CO 80111
(877)769-3667
www.mydoor.biz
Dry cleaning delivery
Began: 2004, Franchising: 2006
Headquarters size: 4 employees
Franchise department: 4 employees

U.S. franchises: 16
Canadian franchises: 0
Other foreign franchises: 0
Company-owned: 1

Seeking: All U.S.
Seeking in Canada? Yes
Exclusive territories? Yes
Homebased option? Yes
Employees needed to run biz: 0
Absentee ownership? No

COSTS
Total cost: $33K-54K
Franchise fee: $25K
Royalty fee: 5-7%
Term of agreement: 5 years renewable
    at no charge
Franchisees required to buy multiple
    units? No

FINANCING
No financing available

QUALIFICATIONS
Net worth: $50K
Cash liquidity: $30K-40K

TRAINING
At headquarters: 1 week
At franchisee's location: 1 week

BUSINESS SUPPORT
Grand opening
Internet
Newsletter
Meetings
Toll-free phone line
Field operations/evaluations
Lease negotiations
Purchasing cooperatives
Security/safety procedures

MARKETING SUPPORT
Co-op advertising
National media campaign
Regional marketing

1-800-DRYCLEAN

Ranked #386 in Entrepreneur Magazine's 2007 Franchise 500   *Financial rating: $$*

3948 Ranchero Dr.
Ann Arbor, MI 48108
(866)822-6115
www.1-800-dryclean.com
Dry cleaning pickup & delivery
Began: 1997, Franchising: 2000
Headquarters size: 65 employees
Franchise department: 12 employees

U.S. franchises: 109
Canadian franchises: 0
Other foreign franchises: 0
Company-owned: 0

Seeking: All U.S.
Seeking in Canada? Yes
Exclusive territories? Yes
Homebased option? Yes
Employees needed to run biz: 1
Absentee ownership? No

COSTS
Total cost: $49.9K-65K
Franchise fee: $14.9K
Royalty fee: 7%
Term of agreement: 10 years renewable
    for $1K
Franchisees required to buy multiple
    units? No

FINANCING
No financing available

QUALIFICATIONS
Net worth: $100K
Cash liquidity: $30K
Experience:
    General business experience
    Marketing skills
    Interpersonal skills

TRAINING
At headquarters: 5 days
At franchisee's location: 5 days
Pre-training by phone: 4-6 weeks

BUSINESS SUPPORT
Grand opening
Internet
Newsletter
Meetings
Toll-free phone line
Field operations/evaluations
Purchasing cooperatives
Security/safety procedures

MARKETING SUPPORT
Marketing programs

PRESSED4TIME INC.

Ranked #329 in Entrepreneur Magazine's 2007 Franchise 500   *Financial rating: $$$*

8 Clock Tower Pl., #110
Maynard, MA 01754
(800)423-8711/(978)823-8300
www.pressed4time.com
Dry cleaning pickup & delivery,
    shoe repair
Began: 1987, Franchising: 1990
Headquarters size: 5 employees
Franchise department: 2 employees

U.S. franchises: 162
Canadian franchises: 2
Other foreign franchises: 5
Company-owned: 0

Seeking: All U.S.
Seeking in Canada? Yes
Exclusive territories? Yes
Homebased option? Yes
Employees needed to run biz: 0
Absentee ownership? No

COSTS
Total cost: $26.9K-37.8K
Franchise fee: $24.9K
Royalty fee: 4-6%
Term of agreement: 10 years renewable
    for 10% of current franchise fee
Franchisees required to buy multiple
    units? No

FINANCING
No financing available

QUALIFICATIONS
Cash liquidity: $40K
Experience:
    Marketing skills

TRAINING
At headquarters: 3 days
At franchisee's location: 3 days
Follow-up at franchisee's location:
    1 day

BUSINESS SUPPORT
Grand opening
Internet
Newsletter
Meetings
Toll-free phone line
Field operations/evaluations
Purchasing cooperatives
Security/safety procedures

MARKETING SUPPORT
Ad slicks
Marketing materials
PR

SERVICES ▸ *Dry Cleaning*

CERTIFIED RESTORATION DRYCLEANING NETWORK
Ranked #313 in Entrepreneur Magazine's 2007 Franchise 500　　　*Financial rating: $$$*

2060 Coolidge Hwy.
Berkley, MI 48072
(800)520-2736
www.crdn.com
Restoration dry cleaning services
Began: 1992, Franchising: 2001
Headquarters size: 120 employees
Franchise department: 25 employees

U.S. franchises: 118
Canadian franchises: 11
Other foreign franchises: 17
Company-owned: 0

Seeking: All U.S.
Seeking in Canada? Yes
Exclusive territories? Yes
Homebased option? No
Employees needed to run biz: 10
Absentee ownership? No

COSTS
Total cost: $40.6K-230.5K
Franchise fee: $4K/8K
Royalty fee: Varies
Term of agreement: 10 years renewable
　for 20% of initial franchise fee
Franchisees required to buy multiple
　units? No

FINANCING
In-house: Franchise fee
3rd-party: None

QUALIFICATIONS
Experience:
　Industry experience
　General business experience
　Marketing skills
　Dry cleaning experience

TRAINING
At headquarters: 1 week
At franchisee's location: 1 day
At various locations: 2-4 days

BUSINESS SUPPORT
Internet
Newsletter
Meetings
Toll-free phone line
Field operations/evaluations

MARKETING SUPPORT
Co-op advertising
National media campaign
Regional marketing

COMET CLEANERS
Current financial data not available

406 W. Division St.
Arlington, TX 76011
(817)461-3555
www.cometcleaners.com
Dry cleaning & laundry services
Began: 1947, Franchising: 1967
Headquarters size: 7 employees
Franchise department: 5 employees

U.S. franchises: 272
Canadian franchises: 0
Other foreign franchises: 11
Company-owned: 10

Seeking: Midwest, South, Southeast,
　Southwest, West
Seeking in Canada? No
Exclusive territories? Yes
Homebased option? No
Employees needed to run biz: 10
Absentee ownership? Yes

COSTS
Total cost: $237.5K-472K
Franchise fee: $25K-50K
Royalty fee: 0
Term of agreement: 5 years
Franchisees required to buy multiple
　units? No

FINANCING
In-house: None
3rd-party: Equipment, franchise fee,
　startup costs

QUALIFICATIONS
Net worth: $200K
Cash liquidity: $50K
Experience:
　General business experience

TRAINING
At headquarters: 1 week
At franchisee's location: 2 weeks

BUSINESS SUPPORT
Grand opening
Internet
Newsletter
Meetings
Toll-free phone line
Field operations/evaluations
Purchasing cooperatives
Security/safety procedures

MARKETING SUPPORT
Co-op advertising
Ad slicks

DRYCLEAN USA

Ranked #396 in Entrepreneur Magazine's 2007 Franchise 500　　　*Financial rating: $$$$*

290 N.E. 68th St.
Miami, FL 33138
(800)746-4583/(305)754-9966
www.drycleanusa.com
Dry cleaning
Began: 1976, Franchising: 1978
Headquarters size: 35 employees
Franchise department: 5 employees

U.S. franchises: 168
Canadian franchises: 0
Other foreign franchises: 305
Company-owned: 0

Seeking: All U.S.
Seeking in Canada? Yes
Exclusive territories? Yes
Homebased option? No
Employees needed to run biz: 5-7
Absentee ownership? Yes

COSTS
Total cost: $237.5K-519.5K
Franchise fee: $30K
Royalty fee: $5.7K/yr.
Term of agreement: 10 years renewable
 for $5K
Franchisees required to buy multiple
 units? No

FINANCING
In-house: None
3rd-party: Equipment, franchise fee,
 startup costs

QUALIFICATIONS
Net worth: $250K
Cash liquidity: $100K-125K
Experience:
 General business experience

TRAINING
At headquarters: 1 week
At franchisee's location: 1 week
At Dryclean USA training plant

BUSINESS SUPPORT
Grand opening
Internet
Meetings
Toll-free phone line
Field operations/evaluations
Lease negotiations
Purchasing cooperatives
Security/safety procedures

MARKETING SUPPORT
Co-op advertising
Ad slicks
Regional marketing

FRSTEAM

Current financial data not available

3201 B Investment Blvd.
Hayward, CA 94545
(510)723-1008
www.frsteam.com
Restoration dry cleaning
Began: 1988, Franchising: 2006
Headquarters size: 30 employees
Franchise department: 6 employees

U.S. franchises: 0
Canadian franchises: 0
Other foreign franchises: 0
Company-owned: 8

Seeking: All U.S.
Seeking in Canada? No
Exclusive territories? Yes
Homebased option? No
Employees needed to run biz: 5-10
Absentee ownership? No

COSTS
Total cost: $168K-384.5K
Franchise fee: $25K-35K
Royalty fee: 6%
Term of agreement: 10 years renewable
 for $2.5K
Franchisees required to buy multiple
 units? No

FINANCING
No financing available

QUALIFICATIONS
Net worth: $500K
Cash liquidity: $100K
Experience:
 Industry experience
 General business experience
 Dry cleaning & laundry
 experience

TRAINING
At headquarters: 2 weeks
At franchisee's location: 1-2 days

BUSINESS SUPPORT
Internet
Meetings
Toll-free phone line
Field operations/evaluations

MARKETING SUPPORT
Ad slicks
National media campaign
Regional marketing

LAPELS

Financial rating: 0

962 Washington St.
Hanover, MA 02339
(866)695-2735
www.lapelsdrycleaning.com
Dry cleaning & pickup/delivery
    services
Began: 2000, Franchising: 2001
Headquarters size: 4 employees
Franchise department: 4 employees

U.S. franchises: 30
Canadian franchises: 0
Other foreign franchises: 0
Company-owned: 0

Seeking: All U.S.
Seeking in Canada? Yes
Exclusive territories? Yes
Homebased option? Yes
Employees needed to run biz: 4
Absentee ownership? Yes

COSTS
Total cost: $27K-343K
Franchise fee: $10K-20K
Royalty fee: 5%
Term of agreement: 10 years renewable
    for $5K
Franchisees required to buy multiple
    units? Outside the U.S. only

FINANCING
In-house: None
3rd-party: Equipment, startup costs

QUALIFICATIONS
Net worth: $100K
Cash liquidity: $50K
Experience:
    General business experience
    Customer service skills

TRAINING
At headquarters: 10 days
At franchisee's location: 2 days

BUSINESS SUPPORT
Grand opening
Internet
Newsletter
Meetings
Toll-free phone line
Field operations/evaluations
Purchasing cooperatives

MARKETING SUPPORT
Co-op advertising
Ad slicks
Regional marketing

MARTINIZING DRY CLEANING

Ranked #207 in Entrepreneur Magazine's 2007 Franchise 500   *Financial rating: $$$$*

422 Wards Corner Rd.
Loveland, OH 45140
(800)827-0345/(513)699-4243
www.martinizingfranchise.com
Dry cleaning & laundry services
Began: 1949, Franchising: 1949
Headquarters size: 7 employees
Franchise department: 4 employees

U.S. franchises: 358
Canadian franchises: 14
Other foreign franchises: 238
Company-owned: 0

Seeking: All U.S.
Seeking in Canada? Yes
Exclusive territories? Yes
Homebased option? No
Employees needed to run biz: 6
Absentee ownership? Yes

COSTS
Total cost: $275.5K-476K
Franchise fee: $35K
Royalty fee: 4%
Term of agreement: 20 years renewable
    for $1K
Franchisees required to buy multiple
    units? Outside the U.S. only

FINANCING
In-house: None
3rd-party: Accounts receivable,
    equipment, franchise fee,
    inventory, payroll, startup costs

QUALIFICATIONS
Net worth: $250K
Cash liquidity: $125K
Experience:
    General business experience

TRAINING
At headquarters: 1 week
At franchisee's location: 2 weeks

BUSINESS SUPPORT
Grand opening
Internet
Newsletter
Meetings
Toll-free phone line
Field operations/evaluations
Security/safety procedures

MARKETING SUPPORT
Co-op advertising
Ad slicks
Regional marketing
Field marketing visits & consultations

SERVICES   *eBay Drop-Off Stores*

ASSIST 2 AUCTION LLC

Current financial data not available

951 Broken Sound Pkwy. N.W., #135
Boca Raton, FL 33487
(877)727-5222
www.assist2auction.com
eBay drop-off store
Began: 2005, Franchising: 2005
Headquarters size: 8 employees
Franchise department: 2 employees

U.S. franchises: 8
Canadian franchises: 0
Other foreign franchises: 0
Company-owned: 0

Seeking: All U.S.
Seeking in Canada? No
Exclusive territories? Yes
Homebased option? Yes
Employees needed to run biz: 1
Absentee ownership? No

COSTS
Total cost: $19.8K
Franchise fee: $17.99K
Royalty fee: $75/wk
Term of agreement: 10 years
    renewable for $2.5K
Franchisees required to buy
    multiple units? No

FINANCING
No financing available

QUALIFICATIONS
Net worth: $50K
Cash liquidity: $20K
Experience:
    Marketing skills

TRAINING
At headquarters: 4 days

BUSINESS SUPPORT
Internet
Newsletter
Meetings
Toll-free phone line
Field operations/evaluations
Purchasing cooperatives
Security/safety procedures

MARKETING SUPPORT
Co-op advertising
Ad slicks
Regional marketing

THE EYARDSALE.COM

Current financial data not available

10700 Montgomery Rd., #300
Cincinnati, OH 45242
(800)291-0771
www.theeyardsale.com
eBay consignment selling services
Began: 2005, Franchising: 2005
Headquarters size: 35 employees
Franchise department: 35 employees

U.S. franchises: 2
Canadian franchises: 0
Other foreign franchises: 0
Company-owned: 0

Seeking: All U.S.
Seeking in Canada? Yes
Exclusive territories? Yes
Homebased option? Yes
Employees needed to run biz: Info
    not provided
Absentee ownership? Yes

COSTS
Total cost: $4K
Franchise fee: $3K
Royalty fee: 6%
Term of agreement: 10 years renewable
    at no charge
Franchisees required to buy multiple
    units? No

FINANCING
In-house: Franchise fee
3rd-party: None

QUALIFICATIONS
Net worth: $25K
Cash liquidity: $9.5K

TRAINING
At headquarters: 5 days
Sales boot camps
Ongoing support

BUSINESS SUPPORT
Internet
Newsletter
Meetings
Toll-free phone line
Purchasing cooperatives
Security/safety procedures

MARKETING SUPPORT
Ad slicks
National media campaign

iSOLD IT

Ranked #110 in Entrepreneur Magazine's 2007 Franchise 500   *Financial rating: $$$$*

401 Huntington Dr.
Monrovia, CA 91016
(626)739-9200
www.i-soldit.com
eBay drop-off store
Began: 2003, Franchising: 2003
Headquarters size: 40 employees
Franchise department: 5 employees

U.S. franchises: 182
Canadian franchises: 2
Other foreign franchises: 7
Company-owned: 1

Seeking: All U.S.
Seeking in Canada? Yes
Exclusive territories? Yes
Homebased option? No
Employees needed to run biz: 4
Absentee ownership? No

COSTS
Total cost: $105.5K
Franchise fee: $22K
Royalty fee: 4%
Term of agreement: 10 years renewable
    for 50% of current fee
Franchisees required to buy multiple
    units? No

FINANCING
In-house: None
3rd-party: Accounts receivable,
    equipment, franchise fee,
    inventory, payroll, startup costs

QUALIFICATIONS
Net worth: $100K
Cash liquidity: $30K-50K
Experience:
    General business experience

TRAINING
At headquarters: 1 week

BUSINESS SUPPORT
Grand opening
Internet
Newsletter
Meetings
Toll-free phone line
Field operations/evaluations
Lease negotiations
Purchasing cooperatives
Security/safety procedures

MARKETING SUPPORT
Co-op advertising
Ad slicks
National media campaign
Regional marketing

QUIKDROP

Ranked #422 in Entrepreneur Magazine's 2007 Franchise 500   *Financial rating: $$*

3151 Airway Ave., #M3
Costa Mesa, CA 92626
(714)429-1040
www.quikdropfranchise.com
eBay drop-off store
Began: 2003, Franchising: 2003
Headquarters size: 30 employees
Franchise department: 6 employees

U.S. franchises: 85
Canadian franchises: 3
Other foreign franchises: 1
Company-owned: 0

Seeking: All U.S.
Seeking in Canada? Yes
Exclusive territories? Yes
Homebased option? No
Employees needed to run biz: 4
Absentee ownership? Yes

COSTS
Total cost: $100K
Franchise fee: $25K
Royalty fee: $1.8K/mo.
Term of agreement: 15 years renewable
    for $2.5K
Franchisees required to buy multiple
    units? No

FINANCING
In-house: None
3rd-party: Equipment, franchise fee,
    inventory, startup costs

QUALIFICATIONS
Net worth: $150K
Cash liquidity: $75K
Experience:
    General business experience
    Marketing skills

TRAINING
At headquarters: 5 days
At franchisee's location: 5 days

BUSINESS SUPPORT
Grand opening
Internet
Newsletter
Meetings
Field operations/evaluations
Purchasing cooperatives
Security/safety procedures

MARKETING SUPPORT
Co-op advertising
Ad slicks
National media campaign
Regional marketing

SELL YOUR STUFF

Financial rating: $$$

437 Exchange St.
Geneva, NY 14456
(877)797-8833
www.sysfranchise.com
eBay drop-off center
Began: 2005, Franchising: 2006
Headquarters size: 3 employees
Franchise department: 3 employees

U.S. franchises: 0
Canadian franchises: 0
Other foreign franchises: 0
Company-owned: 1

Seeking: All U.S.
Seeking in Canada? Yes
Exclusive territories? Yes
Homebased option? No
Employees needed to run biz: Info
    not provided
Absentee ownership? Yes

COSTS
Total cost: $51K-73.5K
Franchise fee: $9.9K
Royalty fee: 2%
Term of agreement: 7 years renewable
    for 15% of current franchise fee
Franchisees required to buy multiple
    units? No

FINANCING
In-house: None
3rd-party: Accounts receivable,
    equipment, franchise fee,
    inventory, payroll, startup costs

QUALIFICATIONS
Net worth: $250K
Cash liquidity: $20K
Experience:
    General business experience

TRAINING
At headquarters: 5 days
At franchisee's location: 3 days

BUSINESS SUPPORT
Grand opening
Newsletter
Meetings

MARKETING SUPPORT
Co-op advertising
Ad slicks
National media campaign
Regional marketing

SNAPPY AUCTIONS

Ranked #309 in Entrepreneur Magazine's 2007 Franchise 500

Financial rating: $$

209 10th Ave. S., #322
Nashville, TN 37203
(888)490-1820
www.snappyauctions.com
eBay consignment outlet/drop-off
    store
Began: 2003, Franchising: 2003
Headquarters size: 12 employees

U.S. franchises: 55
Canadian franchises: 0
Other foreign franchises: 0
Company-owned: 4

Seeking: All U.S.
Seeking in Canada? Yes
Exclusive territories? Yes
Homebased option? No
Employees needed to run biz: 3
Absentee ownership? Yes

COSTS
Total cost: $42K-75K
Franchise fee: $25K
Royalty fee: 2-4%
Term of agreement: 5 years renewable
    for $1.5K
Franchisees required to buy multiple
    units? No

FINANCING
No financing available

QUALIFICATIONS
Cash liquidity: $75K
Experience:
    General business experience
    Marketing skills

TRAINING
At headquarters: 1 week
At franchisee's location: 1 week
Additional training as needed

BUSINESS SUPPORT
Grand opening
Internet
Newsletter
Meetings
Toll-free phone line
Field operations/evaluations
Lease negotiations
Security/safety procedures

MARKETING SUPPORT
Co-op advertising
Ad slicks
National media campaign
PR

SERVICES ▸ *Framing*

BIG PICTURE FRAMING

Financial rating: $$$

855 Highland Ave.
Needham, MA 02494
(800)315-0024
www.bigpictureframing.com
Custom picture framing &
    ready-made frames
Began: 2000, Franchising: 2003
Headquarters size: Info not provided

U.S. franchises: 3
Canadian franchises: 0
Other foreign franchises: 0
Company-owned: 5

Seeking: All U.S.
Seeking in Canada? No
Exclusive territories? Yes
Homebased option? No
Employees needed to run biz: 3-5
Absentee ownership? Yes

COSTS
Total cost: $121K-151K
Franchise fee: $25K-35K
Royalty fee: 5.5%
Term of agreement: 10 years
Franchisees required to buy multiple
    units? No

FINANCING
No financing available

QUALIFICATIONS
Info not provided

TRAINING
At headquarters: 2 weeks
At franchisee's location: 1 week

BUSINESS SUPPORT
Grand opening
Meetings
Field operations/evaluations
Purchasing cooperatives

MARKETING SUPPORT
Co-op advertising
Ad slicks
Regional marketing

DECK THE WALLS

Financial rating: $$$$

P.O. Box 1187
Houston, TX 77251-1187
(800)543-3325/(281)775-5262
www.dtwfraninfo.com
Prints, posters, framing services
Began: 1979, Franchising: 1979
Headquarters size: 25 employees
Franchise department: 5 employees

U.S. franchises: 68
Canadian franchises: 0
Other foreign franchises: 0
Company-owned: 0

Seeking: All U.S.
Seeking in Canada? No
Exclusive territories? No
Homebased option? No
Employees needed to run biz: 2-4
Absentee ownership? Yes

COSTS
Total cost: $180.9K-245.2K
Franchise fee: $30K
Royalty fee: 7%
Term of agreement: 10 years renewable
    at no charge
Franchisees required to buy multiple
    units? No

FINANCING
In-house: None
3rd-party: Accounts receivable,
    equipment, franchise fee,
    inventory, payroll, startup costs

QUALIFICATIONS
Net worth: $250K
Cash liquidity: $75K
Experience:
    General business experience
    People skills
    Customer service skills

TRAINING
At headquarters: 2 weeks
At franchisee's location: 1 week
Convention & trade shows: 3-5 days

BUSINESS SUPPORT
Grand opening
Internet
Newsletter
Meetings
Toll-free phone line
Field operations/evaluations
Purchasing cooperatives
Security/safety procedures

MARKETING SUPPORT
Co-op advertising
Ad slicks
National media campaign
Regional marketing
Local marketing support
Direct mail

FASTFRAME USA INC.

Ranked #220 in Entrepreneur Magazine's 2007 Franchise 500 *Financial rating: $$$*

1200 Lawrence Dr., #300
Newbury Park, CA 91320
(800)333-3225
www.fastframe.com
Custom picture framing & art sales
Began: 1986, Franchising: 1987
Headquarters size: 20 employees
Franchise department: 3 employees

U.S. franchises: 313
Canadian franchises: 0
Other foreign franchises: 9
Company-owned: 1

Seeking: All U.S.
Seeking in Canada? No
Exclusive territories? Yes
Homebased option? No
Employees needed to run biz: 2
Absentee ownership? Yes

COSTS
Total cost: $105.8K-150.3K
Franchise fee: $25K
Royalty fee: 7.5%
Term of agreement: 10 years renewable
    for 25% of current fee
Franchisees required to buy multiple
    units? No

FINANCING
In-house: None
3rd-party: Accounts receivable,
    equipment, franchise fee,
    inventory, payroll, startup costs

QUALIFICATIONS
Net worth: $150K
Cash liquidity: $40K
Experience:
    General business experience

TRAINING
At headquarters: 2 weeks
At franchisee's location: 1 week
At regional location: 1-2 days

BUSINESS SUPPORT
Grand opening
Internet
Newsletter
Meetings
Toll-free phone line
Field operations/evaluations
Purchasing cooperatives
Security/safety procedures

MARKETING SUPPORT
Co-op advertising
Ad slicks
National media campaign
Regional marketing
Consumer website

THE GREAT FRAME UP

Ranked #270 in Entrepreneur Magazine's 2007 Franchise 500 *Financial rating: $$$$*

P.O. Box 1187
Houston, TX 77251-1187
(800)543-3325/(281)775-5262
www.tgfufraninfo.com
Prints, posters, framing services
Began: 1971, Franchising: 1975
Headquarters size: 25 employees
Franchise department: 4 employees

U.S. franchises: 171
Canadian franchises: 0
Other foreign franchises: 0
Company-owned: 0

Seeking: All U.S.
Seeking in Canada? No
Exclusive territories? Yes
Homebased option? No
Employees needed to run biz: 2-4
Absentee ownership? Yes

COSTS
Total cost: $149K-226.3K
Franchise fee: $30K
Royalty fee: 7%
Term of agreement: 10 years renewable
    at no charge
Franchisees required to buy multiple
    units? No

FINANCING
In-house: None
3rd-party: Accounts receivable,
    equipment, franchise fee,
    inventory, payroll, startup costs

QUALIFICATIONS
Net worth: $200K
Cash liquidity: $50K
Experience:
    General business experience
    Marketing skills
    People skills
    Customer service skills

TRAINING
At headquarters: 2 weeks
At franchisee's location: 4 days
Convention & trade shows

BUSINESS SUPPORT
Grand opening
Internet
Newsletter
Meetings
Toll-free phone line
Field operations/evaluations
Lease negotiations
Purchasing cooperatives
Security/safety procedures

MARKETING SUPPORT
Co-op advertising
Ad slicks
National media campaign
Regional marketing
Direct-mail program for local markets

SERVICES ▸ *Home Inspections*

ADVANCE LOOK BUILDING INSPECTIONS
Ranked #380 in Entrepreneur Magazine's 2007 Franchise 500   *Financial rating: $$*

14 Merchant St.
Barre, VT 05641
(800)218-0283
www.advancelook.net
Building inspections &
   environmental testing
Began: 1989, Franchising: 1996
Headquarters size: 5 employees
Franchise department: 5 employees

U.S. franchises: 79
Canadian franchises: 1
Other foreign franchises: 0
Company-owned: 1

Seeking: All U.S.
Seeking in Canada? Yes
Exclusive territories? Yes
Homebased option? Yes
Employees needed to run biz: 1-3
Absentee ownership? Yes

COSTS
Total cost: $33.3K-58.1K
Franchise fee: $23.9K
Royalty fee: 7.5%
Term of agreement: 6 years renewable
   for $2K
Franchisees required to buy multiple
   units? No

FINANCING
In-house: None
3rd-party: Equipment, franchise fee,
   startup costs

QUALIFICATIONS
Cash liquidity: $7.9K-24K
Experience:
   Industry experience

TRAINING
At headquarters: 10 days
Up to 15 days of refresher courses
   per year

BUSINESS SUPPORT
Internet
Newsletter
Meetings
Toll-free phone line
Field operations/evaluations

MARKETING SUPPORT
Ad slicks
National media campaign
Regional marketing
Telephone Outreach Project (TOP)

AMERISPEC HOME INSPECTION SERVICES
Ranked #144 in Entrepreneur Magazine's 2007 Franchise 500   *Financial rating: $$$$*

889 Ridge Lake Blvd.
Memphis, TN 38120
(888)327-0269/(901)597-8500
www.amerispecfranchise.com
Home inspections
Began: 1987, Franchising: 1988
Headquarters size: 45 employees
Franchise department: 4 employees

U.S. franchises: 316
Canadian franchises: 74
Other foreign franchises: 0
Company-owned: 2

Seeking: All U.S.
Seeking in Canada? Yes
Exclusive territories? Yes
Homebased option? Yes
Employees needed to run biz: 3
Absentee ownership? No

COSTS
Total cost: $26.6K-64.8K
Franchise fee: $19.9K/29.9K
Royalty fee: 7%
Term of agreement: 5 years renewable
   at no charge
Franchisees required to buy multiple
   units? No

FINANCING
In-house: None
3rd-party: Franchise fee

QUALIFICATIONS
Net worth: $50K
Cash liquidity: $10K-15K
Experience:
   Industry experience
   General business experience
   Marketing skills

TRAINING
At headquarters: 2 weeks
At franchisee's location: 27 weeks by
   correspondence

BUSINESS SUPPORT
Internet
Newsletter
Meetings
Toll-free phone line
Field operations/evaluations
Purchasing cooperatives

MARKETING SUPPORT
Co-op advertising
Ad slicks
National media campaign
Regional marketing

1ST INSPECTION SERVICES INC.

Current financial data not available

11590 Century Blvd., #200
Cincinnati, OH 45246
(800)944-7211
www.1stinspections.com
Home & commercial inspections
Began: 2003, Franchising: 2005
Headquarters size: 4 employees
Franchise department: 2 employees

U.S. franchises: 3
Canadian franchises: 0
Other foreign franchises: 0
Company-owned: 1

Seeking: All U.S.
Seeking in Canada? Yes
Exclusive territories? Yes
Homebased option? Yes
Employees needed to run biz: 1-2
Absentee ownership? No

COSTS
Total cost: $30.4K-115K
Franchise fee: $5K-25K
Royalty fee: 8%
Term of agreement: 5 years renewable
    at no charge
Franchisees required to buy multiple
    units? No

FINANCING
In-house: Franchise fee
3rd-party: Accounts receivable,
    equipment, inventory, payroll,
    startup costs

QUALIFICATIONS
Net worth: $100K
Cash liquidity: $12.5K
Experience:
    Industry experience
    General business experience
    Marketing skills

TRAINING
At headquarters: 3 weeks
At franchisee's location: 1 week

BUSINESS SUPPORT
Grand opening
Internet
Newsletter
Meetings
Toll-free phone line
Field operations/evaluations
Lease negotiations
Purchasing cooperatives
Security/safety procedures

MARKETING SUPPORT
Ad slicks
National media campaign

HOMESAFE INSPECTION INC.

Current financial data not available

2653 W. Oxford Loop #111
Oxford, MS 38655
(662)236-1232
www.homesafeinspection.com
Home inspections using infrared
    technology
Began: 2003, Franchising: 2003
Headquarters size: 14 employees
Franchise department: 10 employees

U.S. franchises: 45
Canadian franchises: 0
Other foreign franchises: 2
Company-owned: 3

Seeking: All U.S.
Seeking in Canada? Yes
Exclusive territories? Yes
Homebased option? Yes
Employees needed to run biz: 1-3
Absentee ownership? Yes

COSTS
Total cost: $29.5K+
Franchise fee: $12K+
Royalty fee: $600-750/mo.
Term of agreement: 3 years renewable
    at no charge
Franchisees required to buy multiple
    units? No

FINANCING
In-house: Equipment, franchise fee,
    startup costs
3rd-party: None

QUALIFICATIONS
Experience:
    Industry experience
    General business experience
    Marketing skills

TRAINING
At headquarters: 2 weeks
Inspection training

BUSINESS SUPPORT
Grand opening
Internet
Newsletter
Meetings
Toll-free phone line
Field operations/evaluations
Lease negotiations

MARKETING SUPPORT
Co-op advertising
Ad slicks

THE HOMETEAM INSPECTION SERVICE

Ranked #169 in Entrepreneur Magazine's 2007 Franchise 500   *Financial rating: $$$*

575 Chamber Dr.
Milford, OH 45150
(800)598-5297
www.hometeaminspection.com
Home inspections
Began: 1991, Franchising: 1992
Headquarters size: 25 employees
Franchise department: 13 employees

U.S. franchises: 372
Canadian franchises: 15
Other foreign franchises: 0
Company-owned: 0

Seeking: All U.S.
Seeking in Canada? Yes
Exclusive territories? Yes
Homebased option? Yes
Employees needed to run biz: 1
Absentee ownership? No

COSTS
Total cost: $19.9K-49.1K
Franchise fee: $11.9K-29.9K
Royalty fee: 6%
Term of agreement: 10 years renewable
at no charge
Franchisees required to buy multiple
units? No

FINANCING
In-house: Equipment, franchise fee,
startup costs
3rd-party: None

QUALIFICATIONS
Cash liquidity: $7.5K
Experience:
Industry experience
General business experience
Marketing skills

TRAINING
At headquarters: 2 weeks
At franchisee's location: As needed
Annual meetings

BUSINESS SUPPORT
Grand opening
Internet
Newsletter
Meetings
Toll-free phone line
Field operations/evaluations
Security/safety procedures

MARKETING SUPPORT
Co-op advertising
Ad slicks
National media campaign
Regional marketing
National advertising fund

HOUSEMASTER HOME INSPECTIONS

Ranked #257 in Entrepreneur Magazine's 2007 Franchise 500   *Financial rating: $$$$*

421 W. Union Ave.
Bound Brook, NJ 08805
(800)526-3939
www.housemaster.com
Home inspections
Began: 1971, Franchising: 1979
Headquarters size: 20 employees
Franchise department: 20 employees

U.S. franchises: 325
Canadian franchises: 37
Other foreign franchises: 0
Company-owned: 0

Seeking: All U.S.
Seeking in Canada? Yes
Exclusive territories? Yes
Homebased option? Yes
Employees needed to run biz: 1-5
Absentee ownership? Yes

COSTS
Total cost: $31K-69K
Franchise fee: $19.5K
Royalty fee: 5-7.5%
Term of agreement: 5 years renewable
at no charge
Franchisees required to buy multiple
units? No

FINANCING
In-house: Franchise fee
3rd-party: None

QUALIFICATIONS
Net worth: $50K
Cash liquidity: $20K
Experience:
Marketing skills

TRAINING
At headquarters: 1 week
Technical training: 1 week

BUSINESS SUPPORT
Grand opening
Internet
Newsletter
Meetings
Toll-free phone line
Field operations/evaluations
Purchasing cooperatives
Security/safety procedures

MARKETING SUPPORT
Co-op advertising
Ad slicks
National media campaign
Regional marketing
Annual conferences
Proprietary software
Database marketing

INSPECT-IT 1ST PROPERTY INSPECTION

Current financial data not available

8541 E. Anderson Dr., #102
Scottsdale, AZ 85255
(800)510-9100/(480)355-3250
www.inspectit1st.com
Property inspections
Began: 1991, Franchising: 1998
Headquarters size: 5 employees
Franchise department: 5 employees

U.S. franchises: 66
Canadian franchises: 0
Other foreign franchises: 0
Company-owned: 0

Seeking: All U.S.
Seeking in Canada? No
Exclusive territories? Yes
Homebased option? Yes
Employees needed to run biz: 0
Absentee ownership? No

COSTS
Total cost: $34K-54.3K
Franchise fee: $24.9K
Royalty fee: 6-7%
Term of agreement: 10 years renewable
    at no charge
Franchisees required to buy multiple
    units? No

FINANCING
No financing available

QUALIFICATIONS
Net worth: $75K
Cash liquidity: $30K
Experience:
    Marketing skills

TRAINING
At headquarters: 2 weeks

BUSINESS SUPPORT
Internet
Newsletter
Meetings
Toll-free phone line
Field operations/evaluations
Security/safety procedures

MARKETING SUPPORT
Co-op advertising
Ad slicks
National media campaign

NATIONAL PROPERTY INSPECTIONS INC.

Ranked #166 in Entrepreneur Magazine's 2007 Franchise 500

Financial rating: $$$$

9375 Burt, #201
Omaha, NE 68114
(800)333-9807
www.npiweb.com
Home & commercial property
    inspections
Began: 1987, Franchising: 1987
Headquarters size: 12 employees
Franchise department: 12 employees

U.S. franchises: 269
Canadian franchises: 19
Other foreign franchises: 0
Company-owned: 0

Seeking: All U.S.
Seeking in Canada? Yes
Exclusive territories? Yes
Homebased option? Yes
Employees needed to run biz: 1
Absentee ownership? No

COSTS
Total cost: $29.5K-33K
Franchise fee: $23.8K
Royalty fee: 8%
Term of agreement: 10 years renewable
    at no charge
Franchisees required to buy multiple
    units? No

FINANCING
In-house: None
3rd-party: Accounts receivable,
    equipment, franchise fee,
    inventory, payroll, startup costs

QUALIFICATIONS
Cash liquidity: $23K
Experience:
    General business experience
    Marketing skills

TRAINING
At headquarters: 2 weeks
At franchisee's location: 1 week
Optional field training: 1 week

BUSINESS SUPPORT
Internet
Newsletter
Meetings
Toll-free phone line
Field operations/evaluations
Purchasing cooperatives

MARKETING SUPPORT
Ad slicks
Regional marketing
Corporate relocation referral
    program

PILLAR TO POST

Ranked #108 in Entrepreneur Magazine's 2007 Franchise 500   *Financial rating: $$$$*

13902 N. Dale Mabry Hwy., #300
Tampa, FL 33618
(877)963-3129
www.pillartopost.com
Home inspections
Began: 1994, Franchising: 1994
Headquarters size: 20 employees
Franchise department: 12 employees

U.S. franchises: 412
Canadian franchises: 83
Other foreign franchises: 0
Company-owned: 0

Seeking: All U.S.
Seeking in Canada? Yes
Exclusive territories? Yes
Homebased option? Yes
Employees needed to run biz: 1
Absentee ownership? No

COSTS
Total cost: $35.7K-73.7K
Franchise fee: $19.9K-35.9K
Royalty fee: 7%
Term of agreement: 5 years renewable
    for $2.5K
Franchisees required to buy multiple
    units? No

FINANCING
No financing available

QUALIFICATIONS
Net worth: $100K
Cash liquidity: $50K
Experience:
    General business experience
    Marketing skills
    Computer skills
    Presentation & communication
    skills

TRAINING
At headquarters: 2 weeks
Ongoing

BUSINESS SUPPORT
Internet
Newsletter
Meetings
Toll-free phone line

MARKETING SUPPORT
Co-op advertising
Ad slicks
National media campaign
Regional marketing

PROSPECTION LLC

Financial rating: $$$$

7100 E. Pleasant Valley Rd., #260
Independence, OH 44131
(877)392-6278
www.prospectionusa.com
Property inspections
Began: 2003, Franchising: 2003
Headquarters size: 25 employees
Franchise department: 3 employees

U.S. franchises: 15
Canadian franchises: 0
Other foreign franchises: 0
Company-owned: 0

Seeking: All U.S.
Seeking in Canada? No
Exclusive territories? Yes
Homebased option? Yes
Employees needed to run biz: 1
Absentee ownership? Yes

COSTS
Total cost: $15.8K-38.1K
Franchise fee: $6K-12K
Royalty fee: Varies
Term of agreement: 7 years renewable
    at no charge
Franchisees required to buy multiple
    units? No

FINANCING
In-house: Franchise fee
3rd-party: None

QUALIFICATIONS
Info not provided

TRAINING
At regional training facility: 6 days
Online: 4 hours

BUSINESS SUPPORT
Internet
Newsletter
Meetings

MARKETING SUPPORT
Co-op advertising
Ad slicks
National media campaign
Regional marketing

WIN HOME INSPECTION

Ranked #180 in Entrepreneur Magazine's 2007 Franchise 500   *Financial rating: $$$$*

6500 6th Ave. N.W.
Seattle, WA 98117
(800)967-8127
www.winfranchise.com
Home inspections
Began: 1993, Franchising: 1994
Headquarters size: 12 employees
Franchise department: 3 employees

U.S. franchises: 224
Canadian franchises: 0
Other foreign franchises: 0
Company-owned: 0

Seeking: All U.S.
Seeking in Canada? Yes
Exclusive territories? Yes
Homebased option? Yes
Employees needed to run biz: 0
Absentee ownership? Yes

COSTS
Total cost: $45.6K-57.6K
Franchise fee: $25K
Royalty fee: 7%
Term of agreement: 10 years renewable
 at no charge
Franchisees required to buy multiple
 units? No

FINANCING
In-house: Franchise fee
3rd-party: Equipment, inventory,
 startup costs

QUALIFICATIONS
Net worth: $40K
Cash liquidity: $25K
Experience:
 General business experience
 Marketing skills
 Construction & remodeling
 knowledge
 Working knowledge of
 Windows-based software

TRAINING
At headquarters: 2 weeks
Online pre-training: 40 hours
At training facility: 2 weeks

BUSINESS SUPPORT
Grand opening
Internet
Newsletter
Meetings
Toll-free phone line
Purchasing cooperatives
Security/safety procedures

MARKETING SUPPORT
Co-op advertising
Ad slicks
National media campaign
Regional marketing

SERVICES ▶ *Moving*

MOVE IT NOW LLC

Financial rating: $$$$

10060 Brecksville Rd., #200
Brecksville, OH 44141
(440)717-9660
www.moveitnowusa.com
Moving services & storage
Began: 2003, Franchising: 2004
Headquarters size: 4 employees
Franchise department: 4 employees

U.S. franchises: 5
Canadian franchises: 0
Other foreign franchises: 0
Company-owned: 0

Seeking: All U.S.
Seeking in Canada? No
Exclusive territories? Yes
Homebased option? No
Employees needed to run biz: 5
Absentee ownership? Yes

COSTS
Total cost: $47.8K-201.5K
Franchise fee: $24K
Royalty fee: 6.5%
Term of agreement: 10 years renewable
 for $5K
Franchisees required to buy multiple
 units? No

FINANCING
In-house: Franchise fee
3rd-party: None

QUALIFICATIONS
Net worth: $75K
Cash liquidity: $50K
Experience:
 General business experience
 Marketing skills

TRAINING
At headquarters: 1 week
At franchisee's location: 10 days
At existing location: 3 days

BUSINESS SUPPORT
Grand opening
Internet
Meetings
Toll-free phone line
Field operations/evaluations
Lease negotiations
Purchasing cooperatives
Security/safety procedures

MARKETING SUPPORT
Ad slicks
Regional marketing

MOVING SOLUTIONS FRANCHISE LLC

Current financial data not available

115 W. Eagle Road
Havertown, PA 19083
(610)853-4300
www.movingsolutions.com
Moving management & relocation
    services for seniors/working
    professionals
Began: 1996, Franchising: 2005
Headquarters size: 30 employees
Franchise department: 3 employees

U.S. franchises: 5
Canadian franchises: 0
Other foreign franchises: 0
Company-owned: 1

Seeking: All U.S.
Seeking in Canada? No
Exclusive territories? Yes
Homebased option? Yes
Employees needed to run biz: Info
    not provided
Absentee ownership? No

COSTS
Total cost: $29.3K-40.7K
Franchise fee: $17K
Royalty fee: Varies
Term of agreement: 10 years renewable
    for 25% of initial franchise fee
Franchisees required to buy multiple
    units? No

FINANCING
No financing available

QUALIFICATIONS
Experience:
    General business experience
    Marketing skills

TRAINING
At headquarters: 10 days

BUSINESS SUPPORT
Internet
Meetings
Security/safety procedures

MARKETING SUPPORT
Regional marketing
Local PR program
Brochures
Sales materials

SMARTBOX PORTABLE SELF STORAGE

Financial rating: $$$

2100 Dabney Rd.
Richmond, VA 23230
(804)282-9944
www.smartboxusa.com
Portable storage units & moving
    services
Began: 2003, Franchising: 2004
Headquarters size: 12 employees
Franchise department: 5 employees

U.S. franchises: 8
Canadian franchises: 0
Other foreign franchises: 0
Company-owned: 0

Seeking: All U.S.
Seeking in Canada? No
Exclusive territories? Yes
Homebased option? No
Employees needed to run biz: 3
Absentee ownership? Yes

COSTS
Total cost: $365.9K-849.3K
Franchise fee: $40K-150K
Royalty fee: 7%
Term of agreement: 10 years renewable
    at no charge
Franchisees required to buy multiple
    units? No

FINANCING
In-house: None
3rd-party: Equipment, franchise fee,
    inventory, startup costs

QUALIFICATIONS
Net worth: $500K
Cash liquidity: $250K
Experience:
    General business experience
    Marketing skills

TRAINING
At headquarters: 2 weeks
At franchisee's location: 1 week

BUSINESS SUPPORT
Grand opening
Internet
Meetings
Toll-free phone line
Field operations/evaluations
Purchasing cooperatives
Security/safety procedures

MARKETING SUPPORT
Co-op advertising
Ad slicks
TV & radio
Direct mail

TWO MEN AND A TRUCK INT'L. INC.

Ranked #171 in Entrepreneur Magazine's 2007 Franchise 500   *Financial rating: $$$$*

3400 Belle Chase Wy.
Lansing, MI 48911
(800)345-1070/(517)394-7210
www.twomenandatruck.com
Moving services
Began: 1985, Franchising: 1989
Headquarters size: 50 employees
Franchise department: 4 employees

U.S. franchises: 136
Canadian franchises: 5
Other foreign franchises: 0
Company-owned: 7

Seeking: All U.S.
Seeking in Canada? Yes
Exclusive territories? Yes
Homebased option? No
Employees needed to run biz: 7
Absentee ownership? Yes

COSTS
Total cost: $112.3K-407.2K
Franchise fee: $37K
Royalty fee: 6%
Term of agreement: 5 years renewable
    for 10% of original franchise fee
Franchisees required to buy multiple
    units? No

FINANCING
In-house: None
3rd-party: Accounts receivable,
    equipment, franchise fee,
    inventory, payroll, startup costs

QUALIFICATIONS
Net worth: $300K
Cash liquidity: $100K
Experience:
    General business experience

TRAINING
At headquarters: 15 days
At franchisee's location: As needed
At regional location: 2 days
Online

BUSINESS SUPPORT
Grand opening
Internet
Newsletter
Meetings
Toll-free phone line
Field operations/evaluations

MARKETING SUPPORT
Ad slicks
National media campaign
Online marketing assistance

SERVICES   *Photography*

CLIX

Financial rating: $$$$

501 Johnson Ferry Rd., #250
Marietta, GA 30068
(678)213-2549
www.getyourclix.com
Portrait photography & digital
    scrapbooking
Began: 1999, Franchising: 2005
Headquarters size: 7 employees
Franchise department: 2 employees

U.S. franchises: 13
Canadian franchises: 0
Other foreign franchises: 0
Company-owned: 0

Seeking: All U.S.
Seeking in Canada? No
Exclusive territories? Yes
Homebased option? No
Employees needed to run biz: 4
Absentee ownership? No

COSTS
Total cost: $241K-399K
Franchise fee: $29.5K
Royalty fee: 6%
Term of agreement: 10 years renewable
    for 50% of current franchise fee
Franchisees required to buy multiple
    units? No

FINANCING
In-house: None
3rd-party: Accounts receivable,
    equipment, franchise fee,
    inventory, payroll, startup costs

QUALIFICATIONS
Net worth: $275K
Cash liquidity: $80K
Experience:
    General business experience
    Marketing skills

TRAINING
At headquarters: 3 weeks
At franchisee's location: 1 week
Ongoing

BUSINESS SUPPORT
Grand opening
Internet
Newsletter
Meetings
Toll-free phone line
Field operations/evaluations
Lease negotiations
Purchasing cooperatives
Security/safety procedures

MARKETING SUPPORT
Co-op advertising
Ad slicks
National media campaign
Regional marketing

GRINS 2 GO

Financial rating: 0

6969 Corte Santa Fe, #A
San Diego, CA 92121
(866)464-7467
www.grins2go.com
Photography & custom framing
Began: 2004, Franchising: 2005
Headquarters size: Info not provided

U.S. franchises: 14
Canadian franchises: 0
Other foreign franchises: 0
Company-owned: 0

Seeking: All U.S.
Seeking in Canada? No
Exclusive territories? Yes
Homebased option? No
Employees needed to run biz: Info
    not provided
Absentee ownership? Info not
    provided

COSTS
Total cost: $99.4K-299.1K
Franchise fee: $21K/24K/50K
Royalty fee: 7%
Term of agreement: Info not provided
Franchisees required to buy multiple
    units? Info not provided

FINANCING
In-house: None
3rd-party: Available

QUALIFICATIONS
Info not provided

TRAINING
Info not provided

BUSINESS SUPPORT
Info not provided

MARKETING SUPPORT
Info not provided

IMAGES 4 KIDS

Ranked #389 in Entrepreneur Magazine's 2007 Franchise 500   *Financial rating: $$*

12200 Ford Rd., #108
Dallas, TX 75234
(972)484-5437
www.images4kids.com
Children's photography
Began: 1983, Franchising: 2004
Headquarters size: 8 employees
Franchise department: 2 employees

U.S. franchises: 74
Canadian franchises: 0
Other foreign franchises: 0
Company-owned: 0

Seeking: All U.S.
Seeking in Canada? No
Exclusive territories? Yes
Homebased option? Yes
Employees needed to run biz: 2
Absentee ownership? No

COSTS
Total cost: $37.8K-40K
Franchise fee: $25K
Royalty fee: 0
Term of agreement: 10 years renewable
    at no charge
Franchisees required to buy multiple
    units? No

FINANCING
No financing available

QUALIFICATIONS
Experience:
    General business experience

TRAINING
At headquarters: 4 days

BUSINESS SUPPORT
Internet
Newsletter
Meetings
Toll-free phone line
Security/safety procedures

MARKETING SUPPORT
Info not provided

LIL' PALS PET PHOTOGRAPHY

Financial rating: 0

4041 Hatcher Cir.
Memphis, TN 38118
(901)682-9566
www.lilpalsphoto.com
Pet photography
Began: 2004, Franchising: 2005
Headquarters size: 50 employees
Franchise department: 5 employees

U.S. franchises: 5
Canadian franchises: 0
Other foreign franchises: 0
Company-owned: 0

Seeking: All U.S.
Seeking in Canada? No
Exclusive territories? Yes
Homebased option? Yes
Employees needed to run biz: 1-2
Absentee ownership? Yes

COSTS
Total cost: $54.7K-102.2K
Franchise fee: $10K
Royalty fee: $200/wk.
Term of agreement: 10 years
Franchisees required to buy multiple
  units? No

FINANCING
In-house: None
3rd-party: Equipment, franchise fee,
  inventory, startup costs

QUALIFICATIONS
Info not provided

TRAINING
At headquarters: 1 week
At franchisee's location: 2-3 days

BUSINESS SUPPORT
Internet
Newsletter
Meetings
Toll-free phone line
Field operations/evaluations
Security/safety procedures

MARKETING SUPPORT
Promotional products & services

TSS PHOTOGRAPHY

Ranked #261 in Entrepreneur Magazine's 2007 Franchise 500   *Financial rating: $$$*

2150 Boggs Rd., #200
Duluth, GA 30096
(866)877-4746
www.tssphotography.com
Youth, sports, school & event
  photography
Began: 1983, Franchising: 1984
Headquarters size: 130 employees
Franchise department: 35 employees

U.S. franchises: 228
Canadian franchises: 0
Other foreign franchises: 12
Company-owned: 0

Seeking: All U.S.
Seeking in Canada? Yes
Exclusive territories? Yes
Homebased option? Yes
Employees needed to run biz: 2-4
Absentee ownership? No

COSTS
Total cost: $24.7K-61.6K
Franchise fee: $12.9K-33.9K
Royalty fee: 0
Term of agreement: 10 years renewable
  for $1K
Franchisees required to buy multiple
  units? Outside the U.S. only

FINANCING
In-house: Franchise fee
3rd-party: Equipment, franchise fee

QUALIFICATIONS
Cash liquidity: $16.4K-51K
Experience:
  Marketing skills
  Sales experience

TRAINING
At headquarters: 3 days
At franchisee's location: 5 days

BUSINESS SUPPORT
Grand opening
Internet
Newsletter
Meetings
Toll-free phone line
Field operations/evaluations
Security/safety procedures

MARKETING SUPPORT
Co-op advertising
Ad slicks
Regional marketing
Relationships w/national
  organizations

THE VISUAL IMAGE INC.

Financial rating: 0

100 E. Bockman Way
Sparta, TN 38583
(800)344-0323
www.thevisualimageinc.com
Preschool & pet photography
Began: 1984, Franchising: 1994
Headquarters size: 3 employees
Franchise department: 3 employees

U.S. franchises: 21
Canadian franchises: 0
Other foreign franchises: 0
Company-owned: 1

Seeking: All U.S.
Seeking in Canada? Yes
Exclusive territories? Yes
Homebased option? Yes
Employees needed to run biz: 1-2
Absentee ownership? Yes

COSTS

Total cost: $42K
Franchise fee: $23.5K
Royalty fee: 0
Term of agreement: 3 years renewable
  for $2K
Franchisees required to buy multiple
  units? No

FINANCING

In-house: Equipment, franchise fee
3rd-party: None

QUALIFICATIONS

Net worth: $50K
Cash liquidity: $35K
Experience:
  General business experience
  Sales skills
  People skills

TRAINING

At headquarters: 2 weeks
At franchisee's location: 1 week

BUSINESS SUPPORT

Internet
Newsletter
Meetings
Toll-free phone line
Field operations/evaluations
Purchasing cooperatives

MARKETING SUPPORT

Co-op advertising
Ad slicks
Regional marketing
Website

SERVICES ▶ *Postal & Business Centers*

AIM MAIL CENTERS

Ranked #236 in Entrepreneur Magazine's 2007 Franchise 500   *Financial rating: $$$*

15550-D Rockfield Blvd.
Irvine, CA 92618
(800)669-4246/(949)837-4151
www.aimmailcenters.com
Postal & business services
Began: 1985, Franchising: 1989
Headquarters size: 17 employees
Franchise department: 3 employees

U.S. franchises: 109
Canadian franchises: 0
Other foreign franchises: 0
Company-owned: 0

Seeking: All U.S.
Seeking in Canada? No
Exclusive territories? Yes
Homebased option? No
Employees needed to run biz: 1-2
Absentee ownership? No

COSTS

Total cost: $120K-190K
Franchise fee: $26.9K
Royalty fee: 5%
Term of agreement: 15 years renewable
  for $5K
Franchisees required to buy multiple
  units? No

FINANCING

In-house: None
3rd-party: Equipment, franchise fee,
  inventory, startup costs

QUALIFICATIONS

Net worth: $200K
Cash liquidity: $45K
Experience:
  General business experience
  Marketing skills

TRAINING

At headquarters: 10 days
At franchisee's location: 3 days
Regional meetings
Annual convention

BUSINESS SUPPORT

Grand opening
Internet
Newsletter
Meetings
Toll-free phone line
Field operations/evaluations
Purchasing cooperatives

MARKETING SUPPORT

Co-op advertising
Ad slicks
National media campaign
Regional marketing

GOIN' POSTAL

Ranked #414 in Entrepreneur Magazine's 2007 Franchise 500

Financial rating: $$

4941 4th St.
Zephyrhills, FL 33542
(813)782-1500
www.goinpostal.com
Retail shipping & business services
Began: 2002, Franchising: 2004
Headquarters size: 8 employees
Franchise department: 8 employees

U.S. franchises: 189
Canadian franchises: 0
Other foreign franchises: 0
Company-owned: 1

Seeking: All U.S.
Seeking in Canada? Yes
Exclusive territories? Yes
Homebased option? No
Employees needed to run biz: 2
Absentee ownership? Yes

COSTS
Total cost: $36.7K-86.3K
Franchise fee: $15K
Royalty fee: $200/mo.
Term of agreement: 15 years renewable
at no charge
Franchisees required to buy multiple
units? No

FINANCING
In-house: None
3rd-party: Equipment, franchise fee,
inventory, startup costs

QUALIFICATIONS
Cash liquidity: $10K

TRAINING
At headquarters: 1 week & ongoing
At franchisee's location: 1 week

BUSINESS SUPPORT
Grand opening
Internet
Newsletter
Meetings
Toll-free phone line
Field operations/evaluations

MARKETING SUPPORT
Co-op advertising
Ad slicks
Regional marketing

PAK MAIL

Ranked #157 in Entrepreneur Magazine's 2007 Franchise 500

Financial rating: $$$$

7173 S. Havana St., #600
Centennial, CO 80112
(800)833-2821
www.pakmail.com
Packaging, shipping, mailboxes,
business support
Began: 1983, Franchising: 1984
Headquarters size: 20 employees
Franchise department: 3 employees

U.S. franchises: 359
Canadian franchises: 9
Other foreign franchises: 91
Company-owned: 0

Seeking: All U.S.
Seeking in Canada? Yes
Exclusive territories? Yes
Homebased option? No
Employees needed to run biz: 1-5
Absentee ownership? Yes

COSTS
Total cost: $117.2K-150.9K
Franchise fee: $29.95K
Royalty fee: to 5%
Term of agreement: 10 years
renewable for up to $2.5K
Franchisees required to buy multi-
ple units? Outside the U.S. only

FINANCING
In-house: Accounts receivable,
equipment, franchise fee,
inventory, payroll, startup costs
3rd-party: Accounts receivable,
equipment, franchise fee,
inventory, payroll, startup costs

QUALIFICATIONS
Net worth: $150K
Cash liquidity: $50K

TRAINING
At headquarters: 14 days
At franchisee's location: 3 days
At existing center: 2 days+

BUSINESS SUPPORT
Grand opening
Internet
Newsletter
Meetings
Toll-free phone line
Field operations/evaluations
Lease negotiations
Purchasing cooperatives
Security/safety procedures

MARKETING SUPPORT
Co-op advertising
Ad slicks
National media campaign
Regional marketing
PR
Desktop publishing
Marketing materials

PARCEL PLUS

Financial rating: $$$$

12715 Telge Rd.
Cypress, TX 77429
(888)638-8722
www.parcelplus.com
Packing, shipping & cargo services
Began: 1986, Franchising: 1988
Headquarters size: 155 employees
Franchise department: 100 employees

U.S. franchises: 70
Canadian franchises: 0
Other foreign franchises: 0
Company-owned: 0

Seeking: All U.S.
Seeking in Canada? Yes
Exclusive territories? Yes
Homebased option? No
Employees needed to run biz: 3
Absentee ownership? No

COSTS
Total cost: $154.3K-219.3K
Franchise fee: $35K
Royalty fee: 6%
Term of agreement: 15 years renewable
    at no charge
Franchisees required to buy multiple
    units? Outside the U.S. only

FINANCING
No financing available

QUALIFICATIONS
Cash liquidity: $45K
Experience:
    General business experience
    Marketing skills

TRAINING
At headquarters: 2-1/2 weeks
At franchisee's location: 1-1/2 weeks
Operational visit: 1-2 days

BUSINESS SUPPORT
Grand opening
Newsletter
Toll-free phone line
Field operations/evaluations

MARKETING SUPPORT
Ad slicks
National media campaign
Marketing, mailing & telemarketing
    services

POSTAL ANNEX+

Ranked #116 in Entrepreneur Magazine's 2007 Franchise 500

Financial rating: $$$$

7580 Metropolitan Dr., #200
San Diego, CA 92108
(800)456-1525/(619)563-4800
www.postalannex.com
Packaging, shipping, postal &
    business services
Began: 1985, Franchising: 1986
Headquarters size: 25 employees
Franchise department: 15 employees

U.S. franchises: 345
Canadian franchises: 0
Other foreign franchises: 2
Company-owned: 0

Seeking: All U.S.
Seeking in Canada? Yes
Exclusive territories? Yes
Homebased option? No
Employees needed to run biz: 3
Absentee ownership? Yes

COSTS
Total cost: $65.8K-191.7K
Franchise fee: $29.95K
Royalty fee: 5%
Term of agreement: 20 years renewable
    for $5K
Franchisees required to buy multiple
    units? No

FINANCING
In-house: None
3rd-party: 70% of total costs
    including working capital

QUALIFICATIONS
Net worth: $200K
Cash liquidity: $50K
Must speak English

TRAINING
At headquarters: 10 days
At franchisee's location: 4 days
At regional conferences: 3 days

BUSINESS SUPPORT
Grand opening
Internet
Newsletter
Meetings
Toll-free phone line
Field operations/evaluations
Purchasing cooperatives
Security/safety procedures

MARKETING SUPPORT
Co-op advertising
Ad slicks
National media campaign
Regional marketing
Marketing resource guide

POSTAL CONNECTIONS OF AMERICA
Ranked #330 in Entrepreneur Magazine's 2007 Franchise 500   *Financial rating: $$$$*

1081 Camino Del Rio S., #109
San Diego, CA 92108
(800)767-8257/(619)294-7550
www.postalconnections.com
Postal & business centers, internet
   services
Began: 1985, Franchising: 1995
Headquarters size: 12 employees
Franchise department: 7 employees

U.S. franchises: 75
Canadian franchises: 0
Other foreign franchises: 0
Company-owned: 0

Seeking: All U.S.
Seeking in Canada? Yes
Exclusive territories? Yes
Homebased option? No
Employees needed to run biz: 1
Absentee ownership? Yes

COSTS
Total cost: $119.1K-153.9K
Franchise fee: $23.9K
Royalty fee: 4%
Term of agreement: 10 years renewable
   for $5K
Franchisees required to buy multiple
   units? Outside the U.S. only

FINANCING
In-house: None
3rd-party: Accounts receivable,
   equipment, inventory, startup
   costs

QUALIFICATIONS
Net worth: $200K
Cash liquidity: $36K
Experience:
   General business experience
   Marketing skills

TRAINING
At franchisee's location: 4 days
At regional training stores: 5 days

BUSINESS SUPPORT
Grand opening
Internet
Newsletter
Meetings
Toll-free phone line
Field operations/evaluations
Purchasing cooperatives

MARKETING SUPPORT
Co-op advertising
Ad slicks
Nationally-produced promo
   campaigns

POSTNET POSTAL & BUSINESS SERVICES
Ranked #101 in Entrepreneur Magazine's 2007 Franchise 500   *Financial rating: $$$$*

1819 Wazee St.
Denver, CO 80202
(800)841-7171/(303)771-7100
www.postnet.com
Business & communications center
Began: 1985, Franchising: 1993
Headquarters size: 35 employees
Franchise department: 30 employees

U.S. franchises: 448
Canadian franchises: 8
Other foreign franchises: 332
Company-owned: 0

Seeking: All U.S.
Seeking in Canada? Yes
Exclusive territories? Yes
Homebased option? No
Employees needed to run biz: 2-5
Absentee ownership? No

COSTS
Total cost: $175.9K-197.6K
Franchise fee: $29.9K
Royalty fee: 5%
Term of agreement: 15 years renewable
   for 15% of current franchise fee
Franchisees required to buy multiple
   units? Outside the U.S. only

FINANCING
In-house: None
3rd-party: Equipment, franchise fee,
   inventory, startup costs

QUALIFICATIONS
Net worth: $300K
Cash liquidity: $55K
Experience:
   General business experience
   Marketing skills
   Good people & communication
   skills

TRAINING
At headquarters: 2 weeks
At franchisee's location: 1 week
At store location: 2-3 days

BUSINESS SUPPORT
Grand opening
Internet
Newsletter
Meetings
Toll-free phone line
Field operations/evaluations
Purchasing cooperatives
Security/safety procedures

MARKETING SUPPORT
Co-op advertising
Ad slicks
National media campaign

THE UPS STORE/MAIL BOXES ETC.

Ranked #5 in Entrepreneur Magazine's 2007 Franchise 500   *Financial rating: $$$$*

6060 Cornerstone Ct. W.
San Diego, CA 92121
(877)623-7253
www.theupsstore.com
Postal, business & communications
    services
Began: 1980, Franchising: 1980
Headquarters size: 300 employees
Franchise department: 84 employees

U.S. franchises: 4,428
Canadian franchises: 286
Other foreign franchises: 1,046
Company-owned: 0

Seeking: All U.S.
Seeking in Canada? Yes
Exclusive territories? Yes
Homebased option? No
Employees needed to run biz: 3-5
Absentee ownership? Yes

COSTS
Total cost: $153.95K-266.8K
Franchise fee: $29.95K
Royalty fee: 5%
Term of agreement: 10 years renewable
    for 25% of current franchise fee
Franchisees required to buy multiple
    units? No

FINANCING
In-house: Equipment, inventory,
    startup costs
3rd-party: Accounts receivable,
    equipment, franchise fee,
    inventory, payroll, startup costs

QUALIFICATIONS
Net worth: $150K
Cash liquidity: $60K
Experience:
    General business experience
    Computer skills

TRAINING
At headquarters: 2 weeks
At franchisee's location: 2 weeks
Ongoing

BUSINESS SUPPORT
Grand opening
Internet
Newsletter
Meetings
Toll-free phone line
Field operations/evaluations
Purchasing cooperatives
Security/safety procedures

MARKETING SUPPORT
Co-op advertising
Ad slicks
National media campaign
Regional marketing
Local store marketing

SERVICES ▶ *Printing*

ALLEGRA NETWORK

Ranked #235 in Entrepreneur Magazine's 2007 Franchise 500   *Financial rating: $$$$*

21680 Haggerty Rd.
Northville, MI 48167
(248)596-8600
www.allegranetwork.com
Printing center
Began: 1976, Franchising: 1977
Headquarters size: 50 employees
Franchise department: 8 employees

U.S. franchises: 374
Canadian franchises: 28
Other foreign franchises: 7
Company-owned: 0

Seeking: All U.S.
Seeking in Canada? Yes
Exclusive territories? No
Homebased option? No
Employees needed to run biz: 4
Absentee ownership? No

COSTS
Total cost: $162.9K-441.2K
Franchise fee: $30K
Royalty fee: 3.6-6%
Term of agreement: 20 years renewable
    at no charge
Franchisees required to buy multiple
    units? No

FINANCING
In-house: None
3rd-party: Accounts receivable,
    equipment, franchise fee,
    inventory, payroll, startup costs

QUALIFICATIONS
Net worth: $250K-500K
Cash liquidity: $100K-200K
Experience:
    General business experience
    Marketing skills
    Sales experience

TRAINING
At headquarters: 2 weeks
At franchisee's location: 1 week
Ongoing

BUSINESS SUPPORT
Grand opening
Internet
Newsletter
Meetings
Toll-free phone line
Field operations/evaluations
Lease negotiations

MARKETING SUPPORT
Co-op advertising
Ad slicks
Regional marketing
Direct mail
Lead generation program

ALPHAGRAPHICS

Ranked #336 in Entrepreneur Magazine's 2007 Franchise 500   *Financial rating: $$$$*

268 S. State St., #300
Salt Lake City, UT 84111
(800)955-6246/(801)595-7270
www.alphagraphics.com
Digital publishing, internet services,
   printing
Began: 1970, Franchising: 1980
Headquarters size: 98 employees
Franchise department: 6 employees

U.S. franchises: 227
Canadian franchises: 0
Other foreign franchises: 34
Company-owned: 0

Seeking: All U.S.
Seeking in Canada? Yes
Exclusive territories? Yes
Homebased option? No
Employees needed to run biz: 6
Absentee ownership? No

COSTS
Total cost: $225.7K-366.7K
Franchise fee: $25.9K/10K
Royalty fee: to 1.5-8%
Term of agreement: 20 years renewable
   at no charge
Franchisees required to buy multiple
   units? No

FINANCING
In-house: None
3rd-party: Accounts receivable,
   equipment, franchise fee,
   inventory, payroll, startup costs

QUALIFICATIONS
Net worth: $300K
Cash liquidity: $75K
Experience:
   General business experience
   Marketing skills

TRAINING
At headquarters: 4 weeks
At franchisee's location: 2 weeks
At regional location: Varies

BUSINESS SUPPORT
Grand opening
Internet
Newsletter
Meetings
Toll-free phone line
Field operations/evaluations
Purchasing cooperatives
Security/safety procedures

MARKETING SUPPORT
Co-op advertising
Ad slicks
Integrated sales & marketing
Direct mail

BUSINESS CARDS TOMORROW INC.

Ranked #467 in Entrepreneur Magazine's 2007 Franchise 500   *Financial rating: $$$$*

3000 N.E. 30th Pl., 5th Fl.
Fort Lauderdale, FL 33306
(800)627-9998
www.bct-net.com
Wholesale thermography, rubber
   stamps, custom labels
Began: 1975, Franchising: 1977
Headquarters size: 35 employees
Franchise department: 1 employee

U.S. franchises: 70
Canadian franchises: 8
Other foreign franchises: 0
Company-owned: 4

Seeking: CA, MA, MD, MI, NC, NJ
Seeking in Canada? No
Exclusive territories? Yes
Homebased option? No
Employees needed to run biz: Info
   not provided
Absentee ownership? No

COSTS
Total cost: $511K-565.8K
Franchise fee: $35K
Royalty fee: 6%
Term of agreement: 25 years renewable
   at no charge
Franchisees required to buy multiple
   units? No

FINANCING
In-house: None
3rd-party: Accounts receivable,
   equipment, franchise fee,
   inventory, payroll, startup costs

QUALIFICATIONS
Experience:
   General business experience

TRAINING
At headquarters: 2 weeks
At franchisee's location: 4 weeks

BUSINESS SUPPORT
Internet
Newsletter
Meetings
Toll-free phone line
Field operations/evaluations
Purchasing cooperatives
Security/safety procedures

MARKETING SUPPORT
Info not provided

KWIK KOPY BUSINESS CENTERS INC.

Financial rating: $$$$

12715 Telge Rd.
Cypress, TX 77429
(888)280-2053
www.kkbconline.com
Printing, copying, packing, shipping
Began: 2001, Franchising: 2001
Headquarters size: 155 employees
Franchise department: 100 employees

U.S. franchises: 16
Canadian franchises: 0
Other foreign franchises: 5
Company-owned: 1

Seeking: All U.S.
Seeking in Canada? Yes
Exclusive territories? Yes
Homebased option? No
Employees needed to run biz: 2
Absentee ownership? No

COSTS
Total cost: $237.2K-270.99K
Franchise fee: $35K
Royalty fee: 7%
Term of agreement: 15 years renewable
at no charge
Franchisees required to buy multiple
units? Outside the U.S. only

FINANCING
No financing available

QUALIFICATIONS
Cash liquidity: $100K
Experience:
General business experience

TRAINING
At headquarters: 4 weeks
At franchisee's location: 1 week

BUSINESS SUPPORT
Grand opening
Internet
Toll-free phone line
Field operations/evaluations

MARKETING SUPPORT
Marketing program
Vendor relations
Market analysis
Technology research

MINUTEMAN PRESS INT'L. INC.

Ranked #55 in Entrepreneur Magazine's 2007 Franchise 500

Financial rating: $$$$

61 Executive Blvd.
Farmingdale, NY 11735
(800)645-3006/(631)249-1370
www.minutemanpress.com
Full-service printing center
Began: 1973, Franchising: 1975
Headquarters size: 125 employees
Franchise department: 125 employees

U.S. franchises: 754
Canadian franchises: 67
Other foreign franchises: 126
Company-owned: 0

Seeking: All U.S.
Seeking in Canada? Yes
Exclusive territories? No
Homebased option? No
Employees needed to run biz: 3
Absentee ownership? No

COSTS
Total cost: $122K-242K
Franchise fee: $45.5K
Royalty fee: 6%
Term of agreement: 35 years renewable
at no charge
Franchisees required to buy multiple
units? No

FINANCING
In-house: Equipment
3rd-party: Equipment

QUALIFICATIONS
Cash liquidity: $50K
Experience:
Good work ethic

TRAINING
At headquarters: 2-1/2 weeks
At franchisee's location: 1-2 weeks
Ongoing

BUSINESS SUPPORT
Grand opening
Internet
Newsletter
Meetings
Toll-free phone line
Field operations/evaluations
Lease negotiations
Security/safety procedures

MARKETING SUPPORT
Ad slicks
Regional marketing
Ongoing in-field training

PIP PRINTING & DOCUMENT SERVICES

Ranked #409 in Entrepreneur Magazine's 2007 Franchise 500   *Financial rating: $$$$*

26722 Plaza Dr., #200
Mission Viejo, CA 92691
(800)894-7498
www.pip.com
Business printing products & services
Began: 1965, Franchising: 1968
Headquarters size: 25 employees

U.S. franchises: 196
Canadian franchises: 0
Other foreign franchises: 7
Company-owned: 0

Seeking: All U.S.
Seeking in Canada? No
Exclusive territories? Yes
Homebased option? No
Employees needed to run biz: 3-5
Absentee ownership? Yes

COSTS
Total cost: $262K-290K
Franchise fee: $25K
Royalty fee: 0.25-6.5%
Term of agreement: 20 years renewable
    at no charge
Franchisees required to buy multiple
    units? No

FINANCING
In-house: None
3rd-party: Accounts receivable,
    equipment, franchise fee,
    inventory

QUALIFICATIONS
Net worth: $300K
Cash liquidity: $125K-150K
Experience:
    General business experience
    Marketing skills

TRAINING
At headquarters: 2 weeks
At franchisee's location: 2 weeks
Regional meetings: 1-3 days

BUSINESS SUPPORT
Grand opening
Internet
Newsletter
Meetings
Toll-free phone line
Field operations/evaluations
Purchasing cooperatives
Security/safety procedures

MARKETING SUPPORT
Co-op advertising
Ad slicks
National media campaign
Regional marketing
Direct mail
Marketing collateral

SIGNAL GRAPHICS BUSINESS CENTER

Ranked #350 in Entrepreneur Magazine's 2007 Franchise 500   *Financial rating: $$$$*

852 Broadway, #300
Denver, CO 80203
(800)852-6336/(303)779-6789
www.signalgraphics.com
Printing, copying, packaging,
    shipping
Began: 1974, Franchising: 1982
Headquarters size: 13 employees
Franchise department: 7 employees

U.S. franchises: 36
Canadian franchises: 0
Other foreign franchises: 0
Company-owned: 3

Seeking: All U.S.
Seeking in Canada? No
Exclusive territories? Yes
Homebased option? No
Employees needed to run biz: 2-4
Absentee ownership? Yes

COSTS
Total cost: $159K-201K
Franchise fee: $25K
Royalty fee: 5%
Term of agreement: 20 years renewable
    at no charge
Franchisees required to buy multiple
    units? No

FINANCING
In-house: None
3rd-party: Accounts receivable,
    equipment, franchise fee,
    inventory, payroll, startup costs

QUALIFICATIONS
Net worth: $150K
Cash liquidity: $50K
Experience:
    General business experience
    Marketing skills

TRAINING
At headquarters: 12 days
At franchisee's location: 5 days

BUSINESS SUPPORT
Grand opening
Internet
Newsletter
Meetings
Toll-free phone line
Field operations/evaluations
Lease negotiations
Security/safety procedures

MARKETING SUPPORT
Co-op advertising
Ad slicks
National media campaign
Regional marketing

SIR SPEEDY INC.

Ranked #248 in Entrepreneur Magazine's 2007 Franchise 500　　　*Financial rating: $$$$*

26722 Plaza Dr.
Mission Viejo, CA 92691
(949)348-5000
www.sirspeedy.com
Printing, copying, document services
Began: 1968, Franchising: 1968
Headquarters size: 70 employees
Franchise department: 59 employees

U.S. franchises: 386
Canadian franchises: 5
Other foreign franchises: 101
Company-owned: 0

Seeking: All U.S.
Seeking in Canada? Yes
Exclusive territories? Yes
Homebased option? No
Employees needed to run biz: 3-5
Absentee ownership? Yes

COSTS
Total cost: $262K-290K
Franchise fee: $25K
Royalty fee: 4-6%
Term of agreement: 20 years renewable
　　at no charge
Franchisees required to buy multiple
　　units? No

FINANCING
In-house: None
3rd-party: Accounts receivable,
　　equipment, franchise fee,
　　inventory

QUALIFICATIONS
Net worth: $300K
Cash liquidity: $125K-150K
Experience:
　　General business experience
　　Marketing skills

TRAINING
At headquarters: 2 weeks
At franchisee's location: 2 weeks
At regional meetings: 1-3 days

BUSINESS SUPPORT
Grand opening
Internet
Newsletter
Meetings
Toll-free phone line
Field operations/evaluations
Purchasing cooperatives
Security/safety procedures

MARKETING SUPPORT
Ad slicks
National media campaign
Direct-mail & marketing collateral

SERVICES *Real Estate*

ADVANCE REALTY

Financial rating: $$$

8640 Ridgleys Choice Dr., #201
Baltimore, MD 21236
(888)925-0004/(410)256-8700
www.advancerealtyusa.com
Real estate
Began: 2001, Franchising: 2005
Headquarters size: 60 employees
Franchise department: 2 employees

U.S. franchises: 11
Canadian franchises: 0
Other foreign franchises: 0
Company-owned: 1

Seeking: All U.S.
Seeking in Canada? No
Exclusive territories? Yes
Homebased option? No
Employees needed to run biz: 1
Absentee ownership? No

COSTS
Total cost: $55.6K-129K
Franchise fee: $17.5K
Royalty fee: 5%
Term of agreement: 5 years renewable
　　for 10% of franchise fee
Franchisees required to buy multiple
　　units? No

FINANCING
No financing available

QUALIFICATIONS
Net worth: $100K
Cash liquidity: $25K
Experience:
　　Industry experience
　　General business experience
　　Marketing skills

TRAINING
At headquarters: 5 days
At franchisee's location: 2 days

BUSINESS SUPPORT
Grand opening
Internet
Newsletter
Meetings
Toll-free phone line
Field operations/evaluations
Purchasing cooperatives
Security/safety procedures

MARKETING SUPPORT
Co-op advertising
Ad slicks
Regional marketing
Print, radio & TV spots
Recruitment materials

ASSIST-2-SELL
Ranked #48 in Entrepreneur Magazine's 2007 Franchise 500　　　*Financial rating: $$$$*

1610 Meadow Wood Ln.
Reno, NV 89502
(800)528-7816/(775)688-6060
www.assist2sell.com
Discount real estate services
Began: 1987, Franchising: 1993
Headquarters size: 30 employees
Franchise department: 30 employees

U.S. franchises: 620
Canadian franchises: 7
Other foreign franchises: 0
Company-owned: 1

Seeking: All U.S.
Seeking in Canada? Yes
Exclusive territories? Yes
Homebased option? No
Employees needed to run biz: 3-5
Absentee ownership? No

COSTS
Total cost: $50K-101.5K
Franchise fee: $25K
Royalty fee: 5%
Term of agreement: 5 years renewable
　for $2.99K
Franchisees required to buy multiple
　units? No

FINANCING
No financing available

QUALIFICATIONS
Cash liquidity: $40K+
Experience:
　2 years+ real estate sales experience

TRAINING
At headquarters: 5 days

BUSINESS SUPPORT
Internet
Newsletter
Meetings
Toll-free phone line

MARKETING SUPPORT
Ad slicks

AVALAR
Ranked #321 in Entrepreneur Magazine's 2007 Franchise 500　　　*Financial rating: $$*

6430 Medical Center St., #100
Las Vegas, NV 89148
(877)895-8988
www.avalar.biz
Real estate
Began: 1999, Franchising: 1999
Headquarters size: 14 employees
Franchise department: 6 employees

U.S. franchises: 110
Canadian franchises: 0
Other foreign franchises: 0
Company-owned: 8

Seeking: All U.S.
Seeking in Canada? Yes
Exclusive territories? Yes
Homebased option? No
Employees needed to run biz: Info
　not provided
Absentee ownership? Yes

COSTS
Total cost: $53.4K-330.9K
Franchise fee: $15K
Royalty fee: 5%
Term of agreement: 5 years renewable
　at no charge
Franchisees required to buy multiple
　units? No

FINANCING
No financing available

QUALIFICATIONS
Net worth: $250K/500K
Cash liquidity: $50K-100K
Experience:
　Industry experience
　General business experience
　Marketing skills

TRAINING
At headquarters: 6 weeks
At franchisee's location: Varies
Monthly broker orientation:
　1-2 days

BUSINESS SUPPORT
Grand opening
Internet
Newsletter
Meetings
Purchasing cooperatives

MARKETING SUPPORT
Based on franchisee's needs

BUG REALTY USA INC.

Financial rating: $$$

38 S. Main St.
Buffalo, WY 82834
(307)684-8600
www.bugrealty.com
Real estate brokerage
Began: 2004, Franchising: 2006
Headquarters size: 1 employee
Franchise department: 1 employee

U.S. franchises: 0
Canadian franchises: 0
Other foreign franchises: 0
Company-owned: 2

Seeking: All U.S.
Seeking in Canada? No
Exclusive territories? Yes
Homebased option? Yes
Employees needed to run biz: 0-2
Absentee ownership? Yes

COSTS
Total cost: $39.5K-78.2K
Franchise fee: $18.5K
Royalty fee: 5%
Term of agreement: 5 years renewable
    at no charge
Franchisees required to buy multiple
    units? No

FINANCING
No financing available

QUALIFICATIONS
Net worth: $30K-50K
Cash liquidity: $10K-20K
Experience:
    Industry experience
    General business experience
    Marketing skills
    Must have real estate broker's
    license or hire a licensed broker

TRAINING
At franchisee's location: 2 days
Annual convention & retreat:
    2-3 days

BUSINESS SUPPORT
Grand opening
Internet
Newsletter
Meetings
Field operations/evaluations
Purchasing cooperatives

MARKETING SUPPORT
Co-op advertising
Ad slicks
Regional marketing
Auto wrap branding package

CENTURY 21 REAL ESTATE LLC

Ranked #16 in Entrepreneur Magazine's 2007 Franchise 500

Financial rating: $$$$

1 Campus Dr.
Parsippany, NJ 07054
(877)221-2765
www.century21.com
Real estate
Began: 1971, Franchising: 1972
Headquarters size: Info not provided

U.S. franchises: 4,460
Canadian franchises: 368
Other foreign franchises: 3,268
Company-owned: 0

Seeking: All U.S.
Seeking in Canada? Yes
Exclusive territories? Yes
Homebased option? No
Employees needed to run biz: Info
    not provided
Absentee ownership? No

COSTS
Total cost: $11.8K-522.8K
Franchise fee: to $25K
Royalty fee: 6%
Term of agreement: 10 years not
    renewable
Franchisees required to buy multiple
    units? No

FINANCING
In-house: Franchise fee
3rd-party: Franchise fee

QUALIFICATIONS
Net worth: $75K
Experience:
    Industry experience
    General business experience
    Marketing skills

TRAINING
Ongoing via Century 21 Learning
    System
Conventions & workshops

BUSINESS SUPPORT
Internet
Newsletter
Meetings
Toll-free phone line
Field operations/evaluations

MARKETING SUPPORT
Co-op advertising
Ad slicks
National media campaign
Regional marketing

COLDWELL BANKER REAL ESTATE CORP.

Financial rating: $$$$

1 Campus Dr.
Parsippany, NJ 07054
(973)428-9700
www.coldwellbanker.com
Real estate
Began: 1906, Franchising: 1982
Headquarters size: 100 employees
Franchise department: 30 employees

U.S. franchises: 2,369
Canadian franchises: 228
Other foreign franchises: 295
Company-owned: 943

Seeking: All U.S.
Seeking in Canada? Yes
Exclusive territories? No
Homebased option? No
Employees needed to run biz: Info
    not provided
Absentee ownership? No

COSTS
Total cost: $23.5K-490.5K
Franchise fee: $13K-25K
Royalty fee: 6%
Term of agreement: 10 years renewable
Franchisees required to buy multiple
    units? No

FINANCING
In-house: Franchise fee
3rd-party: None

QUALIFICATIONS
Net worth: $25K
Experience:
    Industry experience

TRAINING
At headquarters: 4 days
At franchisee's location: 1-2 days
Ongoing

BUSINESS SUPPORT
Grand opening
Internet
Newsletter
Meetings
Toll-free phone line
Field operations/evaluations

MARKETING SUPPORT
Ad slicks
National media campaign
Regional marketing
Website

ERA FRANCHISE SYSTEMS INC.

Financial rating: $$$$

1 Campus Dr.
Parsippany, NJ 07054
(800)869-1260
www.era.com
Real estate
Began: 1971, Franchising: 1972
Headquarters size: Info not provided

U.S. franchises: 1,234
Canadian franchises: 0
Other foreign franchises: 1,704
Company-owned: 0

Seeking: All U.S.
Seeking in Canada? Yes
Exclusive territories? No
Homebased option? No
Employees needed to run biz: Info
    not provided
Absentee ownership? Yes

COSTS
Total cost: $42.7K-205.9K
Franchise fee: to $20K
Royalty fee: 6%
Term of agreement: 10 years
Franchisees required to buy multiple
    units? No

FINANCING
In-house: Equipment, franchise fee,
    startup costs
3rd-party: Equipment

QUALIFICATIONS
Net worth: $75K
Experience:
    Industry experience
    General business experience

TRAINING
At headquarters: 1 week
At franchisee's location: 1 week

BUSINESS SUPPORT
Internet
Newsletter
Meetings
Toll-free phone line
Field operations/evaluations

MARKETING SUPPORT
Ad slicks
National media campaign
Regional marketing

HOMES 4SALE BY OWNER NETWORK

Financial rating: $$

5151 Monroe St., #106
Toledo, OH 43623
(419)824-9983
www.homes4salebyownernetwork.com
Web-based real estate marketing
    services for homeowners
Began: 2002, Franchising: 2004
Headquarters size: 5 employees
Franchise department: 2 employees

U.S. franchises: 0
Canadian franchises: 0
Other foreign franchises: 0
Company-owned: 1

Seeking: All U.S.
Seeking in Canada? No
Exclusive territories? Yes
Homebased option? Yes
Employees needed to run biz: 2-5
Absentee ownership? Yes

COSTS
Total cost: $32.5K-68K
Franchise fee: $14.8K
Royalty fee: 7.5%
Term of agreement: 10 years renewable
    for 25% of current franchise fee
Franchisees required to buy multiple
    units? No

FINANCING
No financing available

QUALIFICATIONS
Experience:
    General business experience
    Marketing skills

TRAINING
At headquarters: 2-1/2 days
At franchisee's location
Ongoing

BUSINESS SUPPORT
Grand opening
Internet
Newsletter
Meetings
Toll-free phone line

MARKETING SUPPORT
Ad slicks
National media campaign
TV/radio spots
Ongoing tech development

HUNTING LEASE NETWORK

Current financial data not available

11516 Nicholas St., P.O. Box 542016
Omaha, NE 68154
(800)346-2650
www.nationalhuntingleases.com
Land leasing for hunting & fishing
Began: 2002, Franchising: 2004
Headquarters size: 75 employees
Franchise department: 5 employees

U.S. franchises: 9
Canadian franchises: 0
Other foreign franchises: 0
Company-owned: 2

Seeking: All U.S.
Seeking in Canada? No
Exclusive territories? Yes
Homebased option? Yes
Employees needed to run biz: 1
Absentee ownership? No

COSTS
Total cost: $23.5K-39K
Franchise fee: $15K
Royalty fee: 5%
Term of agreement: 10 years renewable
    for $1K
Franchisees required to buy multiple
    units? No

FINANCING
No financing available

QUALIFICATIONS
Net worth: $100K
Cash liquidity: $30K
Experience:
    General business experience
    Marketing skills
    Hunting & landowner experience

TRAINING
At headquarters: 3 days
At franchisee's location: As needed

BUSINESS SUPPORT
Grand opening
Internet
Meetings
Lease negotiations

MARKETING SUPPORT
Co-op advertising
National media campaign
Regional marketing
National TV marketing

KELLER WILLIAMS REALTY

Ranked #44 in Entrepreneur Magazine's 2007 Franchise 500   *Financial rating: $$$$*

807 Las Cimas Pkwy., #200
Austin, TX 78746
(512)327-3070
www.kw.com
Real estate
Began: 1983, Franchising: 1987
Headquarters size: 175 employees
Franchise department: 15 employees

U.S. franchises: 578
Canadian franchises: 12
Other foreign franchises: 0
Company-owned: 0

Seeking: All U.S.
Seeking in Canada? Yes
Exclusive territories? Yes
Homebased option? No
Employees needed to run biz: 3-4
Absentee ownership? Yes

COSTS
Total cost: $123K-459K
Franchise fee: $25K
Royalty fee: 6%
Term of agreement: 5 years
Franchisees required to buy multiple
    units? No

FINANCING
No financing available

QUALIFICATIONS
Cash liquidity: $150K+
Experience:
    Industry experience
    General business experience

TRAINING
At headquarters: Ongoing
At franchisee's location: Ongoing

BUSINESS SUPPORT
Internet
Newsletter
Meetings
Field operations/evaluations

MARKETING SUPPORT
National media campaign
In-house marketing department

PARKER FINCH MANAGEMENT

Financial rating: $$$

3838 N. Central Ave., #1100
Phoenix, AZ 85012
(877)508-1974
www.parkerfinch.com
Property management services for
    condos & homeowners
    associations
Began: 1993, Franchising: 2006
Headquarters size: 26 employees
Franchise department: 10 employees

U.S. franchises: 3
Canadian franchises: 0
Other foreign franchises: 0
Company-owned: 2

Seeking: All U.S.
Seeking in Canada? No
Exclusive territories? Yes
Homebased option? No
Employees needed to run biz: 3-5
Absentee ownership? No

COSTS
Total cost: $43.3K-82.9K
Franchise fee: $25K
Royalty fee: 3%
Term of agreement: 10 years renewable
Franchisees required to buy multiple
    units? No

FINANCING
No financing available

QUALIFICATIONS
Net worth: $250K
Cash liquidity: $150K
Experience:
    General business experience

TRAINING
At headquarters: 2 weeks

BUSINESS SUPPORT
Internet
Meetings
Toll-free phone line
Field operations/evaluations

MARKETING SUPPORT
Ad slicks
National media campaign
Regional marketing

RE/MAX INT'L. INC.

Ranked #11 in Entrepreneur Magazine's 2007 Franchise 500　　　*Financial rating: $$$$*

P.O. Box 3907
Englewood, CO 80155-3907
(800)525-7452/(303)770-5531
www.remax.com
Real estate
Began: 1973, Franchising: 1975
Headquarters size: 350 employees
Franchise department: 10 employees

U.S. franchises: 4,100
Canadian franchises: 614
Other foreign franchises: 1,824
Company-owned: 33

Seeking: All U.S.
Seeking in Canada? Yes
Exclusive territories? No
Homebased option? No
Employees needed to run biz: 2
Absentee ownership? Yes

COSTS
Total cost: $25K-199K
Franchise fee: $12.5K-25K
Royalty fee: Varies
Term of agreement: 5 years renewable
Franchisees required to buy multiple
    units? No

FINANCING
In-house: Franchise fee
3rd-party: None

QUALIFICATIONS
Experience:
    Industry experience
    General business experience
    Marketing skills

TRAINING
At headquarters: 5 days
Semiannual convention &
    conference

BUSINESS SUPPORT
Grand opening
Internet
Newsletter
Meetings
Toll-free phone line
Field operations/evaluations
Purchasing cooperatives

MARKETING SUPPORT
Ad slicks
National media campaign
Regional marketing
Brochures, magazines & videos
Online support
Business satellite network

REAL ESTATE FOR 2

Financial rating: $$$

4850 Harrison Blvd., #1
South Ogden, UT 84403
(801)394-5200
www.re42.com
Real estate
Began: 2004, Franchising: 2005
Headquarters size: 3 employees
Franchise department: 3 employees

U.S. franchises: 3
Canadian franchises: 0
Other foreign franchises: 0
Company-owned: 1

Seeking: All U.S.
Seeking in Canada? No
Exclusive territories? Yes
Homebased option? No
Employees needed to run biz: 1-3
Absentee ownership? Yes

COSTS
Total cost: $39.9K-188K
Franchise fee: $14.5K
Royalty fee: 4%
Term of agreement: 10 years renewable
    for 25% of then-current fee
Franchisees required to buy multiple
    units? No

FINANCING
No financing available

QUALIFICATIONS
Cash liquidity: $30K
Experience:
    Industry experience
    General business experience

TRAINING
At headquarters: 3 days
At franchisee's location: 3 days
Ongoing

BUSINESS SUPPORT
Grand opening
Internet
Newsletter
Meetings
Toll-free phone line
Field operations/evaluations
Lease negotiations

MARKETING SUPPORT
Ad slicks
Regional marketing
Company website & agent websites

REAL LIVING INC.

Current financial data not available

77 E. Nationwide Blvd.
Columbus, OH 43215
(614)459-7400
www.realliving.com
Residential real estate
Began: 2001, Franchising: 2002
Headquarters size: 60 employees
Franchise department: 25 employees

U.S. franchises: 61
Canadian franchises: 0
Other foreign franchises: 0
Company-owned: 62

Seeking: All U.S.
Seeking in Canada? No
Exclusive territories? Yes
Homebased option? No
Employees needed to run biz: Info
    not provided
Absentee ownership? No

COSTS
Total cost: $9.4K-107.5K
Franchise fee: $20K-40K
Royalty fee: 6%
Term of agreement: 10 years renewable
    at no charge
Franchisees required to buy multiple
    units? No

FINANCING
No financing available

QUALIFICATIONS
Net worth: $150K
Experience:
    Industry experience
    General business experience
    Marketing skills

TRAINING
At headquarters: Varies
At franchisee's location: Varies
Biannual meetings

BUSINESS SUPPORT
Internet
Newsletter
Meetings
Toll-free phone line
Field operations/evaluations
Security/safety procedures

MARKETING SUPPORT
Co-op advertising
Corporate marketing support
Office vists
TV & radio spots
PR campaigns
Direct-mail campaign

REALTY DIRECT FRANCHISE CORP.

Ranked #459 in Entrepreneur Magazine's 2007 Franchise 500   *Financial rating: $$$*

7 Pidgeon Hill Dr.
Sterling, VA 20165
(800)359-5220/(703)327-2428
www.realtydirectfranchise.com
Real estate
Began: 2001, Franchising: 2003
Headquarters size: 20 employees
Franchise department: 4 employees

U.S. franchises: 28
Canadian franchises: 0
Other foreign franchises: 0
Company-owned: 0

Seeking: All U.S.
Seeking in Canada? No
Exclusive territories? Yes
Homebased option? No
Employees needed to run biz: 5
Absentee ownership? Yes

COSTS
Total cost: $32.9K-46.9K
Franchise fee: $19.9K
Royalty fee: 5%
Term of agreement: 6 years renewable
    for $2K
Franchisees required to buy multiple
    units? No

FINANCING
No financing available

QUALIFICATIONS
Net worth: $100K
Cash liquidity: $50K
Experience:
    Industry experience
    General business experience
    Marketing skills

TRAINING
At headquarters: 4 days
At franchisee's location: 1 day

BUSINESS SUPPORT
Internet
Newsletter
Meetings
Toll-free phone line
Purchasing cooperatives

MARKETING SUPPORT
Co-op advertising
National media campaign
Templates

REALTY EXECUTIVES INT'L. INC.

Current financial data not available

2398 E. Camelback Rd., #900
Phoenix, AZ 85016
(800)252-3366/(602)957-0747
www.realtyexecutives.com
Real estate
Began: 1965, Franchising: 1973
Headquarters size: 15 employees
Franchise department: 4 employees

U.S. franchises: 736
Canadian franchises: 45
Other foreign franchises: 30
Company-owned: 0

Seeking: All U.S.
Seeking in Canada? Yes
Exclusive territories? Yes
Homebased option? No
Employees needed to run biz: Info
    not provided
Absentee ownership? Yes

COSTS
Total cost: $18.6K-88.1K
Franchise fee: $1K-26K
Royalty fee: $50/licensee
Term of agreement: 5 years renewable
    at no charge
Franchisees required to buy multiple
    units? No

FINANCING
No financing available

QUALIFICATIONS
Cash liquidity: $20K
Experience:
    Industry experience
    General business experience
    Marketing skills

TRAINING
At headquarters: 5 days
Ongoing at semi-annual meetings

BUSINESS SUPPORT
Grand opening
Internet
Newsletter
Meetings
Toll-free phone line
Field operations/evaluations
Security/safety procedures

MARKETING SUPPORT
Co-op advertising
Ad slicks
National media campaign
Regional marketing

SELL4FREE REAL ESTATE SYSTEMS INC.

Financial rating: $$$

10412 Allisonville Rd., #103
Fishers, IN 46038
(317)716-3733
www.sell4free.com
Real estate
Began: 1996, Franchising: 2002
Headquarters size: 3 employees
Franchise department: 2 employees

U.S. franchises: 16
Canadian franchises: 0
Other foreign franchises: 0
Company-owned: 0

Seeking: All U.S.
Seeking in Canada? Yes
Exclusive territories? Yes
Homebased option? Yes
Employees needed to run biz: Info
    not provided
Absentee ownership? Yes

COSTS
Total cost: $28.5K-86K
Franchise fee: $20K
Royalty fee: Varies
Term of agreement: 10 years renewable
    for $1K
Franchisees required to buy multiple
    units? No

FINANCING
In-house: None
3rd-party: Accounts receivable,
    equipment, franchise fee,
    inventory, payroll, startup costs

QUALIFICATIONS
Net worth: $30K
Cash liquidity: $25K
Experience:
    Industry experience
    General business experience
    Marketing skills

TRAINING
At headquarters: 2 days
At franchisee's location: 2 days

BUSINESS SUPPORT
Internet
Newsletter
Toll-free phone line

MARKETING SUPPORT
Ad slicks

SIMPLYSOLD REAL ESTATE

Financial rating: $$$

7421 Douglas Blvd., #N
Douglasville, GA 30135
(678)715-4000
www.simplysold.com
Real estate
Began: 2003, Franchising: 2006
Headquarters size: 8 employees
Franchise department: 5 employees

U.S. franchises: 5
Canadian franchises: 0
Other foreign franchises: 0
Company-owned: 1

Seeking: All U.S.
Seeking in Canada? No
Exclusive territories? Yes
Homebased option? No
Employees needed to run biz: 2
Absentee ownership? No

COSTS
Total cost: $75.3K-187.9K
Franchise fee: $12.5K-25K
Royalty fee: Varies
Term of agreement: 5 years renewable
 for $5K
Franchisees required to buy multiple
 units? No

FINANCING
In-house: Franchise fee
3rd-party: None

QUALIFICATIONS
Experience:
 Industry experience
 General business experience
 Marketing skills

TRAINING
At headquarters: 5 days

BUSINESS SUPPORT
Grand opening
Internet
Toll-free phone line
Field operations/evaluations

MARKETING SUPPORT
Ad slicks
Brochures
Presentations

WEICHERT REAL ESTATE AFFILIATES INC.

Ranked #152 in Entrepreneur Magazine's 2007 Franchise 500   *Financial rating: $$$*

225 Littleton Rd.
Morris Plains, NJ 07950
(973)359-8377
www.weichert.com
Real estate
Began: 1969, Franchising: 2000
Headquarters size: 52 employees
Franchise department: 52 employees

U.S. franchises: 226
Canadian franchises: 0
Other foreign franchises: 0
Company-owned: 220

Seeking: All U.S.
Seeking in Canada? No
Exclusive territories? Yes
Homebased option? No
Employees needed to run biz: 5
Absentee ownership? Yes

COSTS
Total cost: $45K-254K
Franchise fee: $25K
Royalty fee: 6%
Term of agreement: 10 years renewable
 for $1K
Franchisees required to buy multiple
 units? No

FINANCING
No financing available

QUALIFICATIONS
Experience:
 Industry experience
 General business experience
 Marketing skills

TRAINING
At headquarters: 4 days
At franchisee's location: Ongoing
Annual conference
Quarterly local workshops

BUSINESS SUPPORT
Grand opening
Internet
Newsletter
Meetings
Toll-free phone line
Field operations/evaluations
Purchasing cooperatives

MARKETING SUPPORT
Co-op advertising
Ad slicks
National media campaign
Regional marketing
PR program
Customized marketing materials

WORLD PROPERTIES INT'L.

Ranked #451 in Entrepreneur Magazine's 2007 Franchise 500   *Financial rating: $$$$*

111 Founders Plaza, 19th Fl.
East Hartford, CT 06108
(800)809-1963
www.thewpi.com
Real estate
Began: 2005, Franchising: 2005
Headquarters size: 64 employees
Franchise department: 15 employees

U.S. franchises: 78
Canadian franchises: 0
Other foreign franchises: 0
Company-owned: 0

Seeking: All U.S.
Seeking in Canada? Yes
Exclusive territories? Yes
Homebased option? Yes
Employees needed to run biz: 2
Absentee ownership? Yes

COSTS
Total cost: $1.9K-65.9K
Franchise fee: $599-50K
Royalty fee: $130/mo.
Term of agreement: 5 years renewable
    for $500
Franchisees required to buy multiple
    units? No

FINANCING
In-house: Franchise fee
3rd-party: None

QUALIFICATIONS
Experience:
    Industry experience

TRAINING
At headquarters: 1 week
At franchisee's location: Varies
Weekly online training

BUSINESS SUPPORT
Grand opening
Internet
Meetings
Field operations/evaluations
Security/safety procedures

MARKETING SUPPORT
Co-op advertising
Ad slicks
National media campaign

SERVICES ▶ *Screen Printing & Embroidery*

EMBROIDME

Ranked #123 in Entrepreneur Magazine's 2007 Franchise 500   *Financial rating: $$$*

2121 Vista Pkwy.
West Palm Beach, FL 33411
(800)727-6720
www.embroidme.com
Embroidery, screen printing, ad
    specialties
Began: 2000, Franchising: 2001
Headquarters size: 50 employees
Franchise department: 5 employees

U.S. franchises: 312
Canadian franchises: 17
Other foreign franchises: 29
Company-owned: 0

Seeking: All U.S.
Seeking in Canada? Yes
Exclusive territories? Yes
Homebased option? No
Employees needed to run biz: 2
Absentee ownership? No

COSTS
Total cost: $46.6K-222.3K
Franchise fee: $39.5K
Royalty fee: 6%
Term of agreement: 35 years renewable
    for $1.5K
Franchisees required to buy multiple
    units? No

FINANCING
In-house: None
3rd-party: Equipment, inventory

QUALIFICATIONS
Cash liquidity: $40K+
Experience:
    General business experience

TRAINING
At headquarters: 2 weeks
At franchisee's location: 2 weeks
Ongoing training

BUSINESS SUPPORT
Grand opening
Internet
Newsletter
Meetings
Toll-free phone line
Field operations/evaluations
Lease negotiations
Purchasing cooperatives
Security/safety procedures

MARKETING SUPPORT
Co-op advertising
Ad slicks
National media campaign
Regional marketing

HOMETOWN THREADS

Current financial data not available

1825 Main St.
Weston, FL 33326
(877)893-3393
www.hometownthreads.com
Personalized gift & retail
    embroidery service
Began: 1998, Franchising: 2001
Headquarters size: 10 employees
Franchise department: 10 employees

U.S. franchises: 48
Canadian franchises: 0
Other foreign franchises: 0
Company-owned: 0

Seeking: All U.S.
Seeking in Canada? No
Exclusive territories? Yes
Homebased option? No
Employees needed to run biz: 4
Absentee ownership? No

COSTS
Total cost: $165K
Franchise fee: $29K
Royalty fee: 6%
Term of agreement: 10 years renewable
    for $5K
Franchisees required to buy multiple
    units? Yes

FINANCING
In-house: None
3rd-party: Accounts receivable,
    equipment, franchise fee,
    inventory, payroll, startup costs

QUALIFICATIONS
Net worth: $200K
Cash liquidity: $50K
Experience:
    General business experience

TRAINING
At headquarters: 3 weeks
At franchisee's location: 2 weeks

BUSINESS SUPPORT
Grand opening
Internet
Newsletter
Meetings
Toll-free phone line
Field operations/evaluations
Lease negotiations
Purchasing cooperatives
Security/safety procedures

MARKETING SUPPORT
Co-op advertising
Ad slicks
National media campaign
Regional marketing

INSTANT IMPRINTS

Ranked #432 in Entrepreneur Magazine's 2007 Franchise 500

Financial rating: 0

9808 Waples St.
San Diego, CA 92121
(800)542-3437
www.instantimprints.com
Imprinted sportswear, promotional
    products, signs
Began: 1992, Franchising: 2001
Headquarters size: 20 employees
Franchise department: 12 employees

U.S. franchises: 84
Canadian franchises: 0
Other foreign franchises: 1
Company-owned: 2

Seeking: All U.S.
Seeking in Canada? Yes
Exclusive territories? Yes
Homebased option? No
Employees needed to run biz: 3
Absentee ownership? No

COSTS
Total cost: $58K-224K
Franchise fee: $32.5K
Royalty fee: 5%
Term of agreement: 15 years renewable
    for $2.5K
Franchisees required to buy multiple
    units? Outside the U.S. only

FINANCING
In-house: None
3rd-party: Accounts receivable,
    equipment, franchise fee,
    inventory, startup costs

QUALIFICATIONS
Net worth: $200K
Cash liquidity: $40K
Experience:
    General business experience
    Marketing skills

TRAINING
At headquarters: 2 weeks
At franchisee's location: 1 week

BUSINESS SUPPORT
Grand opening
Internet
Newsletter
Meetings
Toll-free phone line
Field operations/evaluations
Purchasing cooperatives

MARKETING SUPPORT
Co-op advertising
Ad slicks
National media campaign
Regional marketing

PRINTWEAR XPRESS

Financial rating: 0

416 Security Blvd.
Green Bay, WI 54313
(920)884-7380
www.printwearxpress.com
Embroidery, screen printing,
    promotional products,
    personalized gifts
Began: 2004, Franchising: 2005
Headquarters size: 4 employees
Franchise department: 4 employees

U.S. franchises: 7
Canadian franchises: 0
Other foreign franchises: 0
Company-owned: 0

Seeking: All U.S.
Seeking in Canada? No
Exclusive territories? Yes
Homebased option? No
Employees needed to run biz: 2-3
Absentee ownership? No

COSTS
Total cost: $159K
Franchise fee: $25K
Royalty fee: 5%
Term of agreement: 20 years renewable
    for $12.5K
Franchisees required to buy multiple
    units? No

FINANCING
No financing available

QUALIFICATIONS
Net worth: $250K
Cash liquidity: $30K

TRAINING
At headquarters: 1 week
At franchisee's location: 1 week

BUSINESS SUPPORT
Grand opening
Internet
Newsletter
Purchasing cooperatives

MARKETING SUPPORT
Ad slicks
Regional marketing

SERVICES ◄ *Security*

MONITORCLOSELY.COM

Financial rating: $$$

4555 Lake Forest Dr., #650
Cincinnati, OH 45242
(800)797-7505
www.monitorclosely.com
Digital surveillance systems
Began: 2006, Franchising: 2006
Headquarters size: 12 employees
Franchise department: 3 employees

U.S. franchises: 28
Canadian franchises: 0
Other foreign franchises: 0
Company-owned: 0

Seeking: All U.S.
Seeking in Canada? Yes
Exclusive territories? Yes
Homebased option? Yes
Employees needed to run biz: 1
Absentee ownership? No

COSTS
Total cost: $23.2K-37.9K
Franchise fee: $19.9K-24.9K
Royalty fee: 8%
Term of agreement: 10 years renewable
    at no charge
Franchisees required to buy multiple
    units? No

FINANCING
In-house: Franchise fee, inventory
3rd-party: None

QUALIFICATIONS
Info not provided

TRAINING
At headquarters: 4 days

BUSINESS SUPPORT
Grand opening
Internet
Newsletter
Meetings
Toll-free phone line
Field operations/evaluations
Purchasing cooperatives
Security/safety procedures

MARKETING SUPPORT
Co-op advertising
Ad slicks
National media campaign
Regional marketing

SIGNATURE ALERT SECURITY

Financial rating: 0

746 E. Winchester St., #110
Salt Lake City, UT 84107
(800)957-1030/(801)743-0101
www.signaturealert.com
Security systems & monitoring
Began: 1999, Franchising: 2003
Headquarters size: 7 employees
Franchise department: 3 employees

U.S. franchises: 36
Canadian franchises: 0
Other foreign franchises: 0
Company-owned: 3

Seeking: All U.S.
Seeking in Canada? No
Exclusive territories? Yes
Homebased option? Yes
Employees needed to run biz: 1
Absentee ownership? No

COSTS
Total cost: $42.95K-50.5K
Franchise fee: $21K
Royalty fee: $2/customer/mo.
Term of agreement: 10 years renewable
   for $3K
Franchisees required to buy multiple
   units? No

FINANCING
In-house: Franchise fee
3rd-party: None

QUALIFICATIONS
Net worth: $100K
Cash liquidity: $40K
Experience:
   General business experience
   Marketing skills

TRAINING
At headquarters: 5 days
At franchisee's location: 2 days

BUSINESS SUPPORT
Grand opening
Internet
Newsletter
Meetings
Toll-free phone line
Field operations/evaluations
Purchasing cooperatives
Security/safety procedures

MARKETING SUPPORT
Co-op advertising
Ad slicks

SERVICES ▸ *Miscellaneous*

DIRECTBUY INC.

Ranked #186 in Entrepreneur Magazine's 2007 Franchise 500   *Financial rating: $$$$*

8450 Broadway, P.O. Box 13006
Merrillville, IN 46411-3006
(800)827-6400/(219)736-1100
www.directbuyfranchising.com
Consumer buying club
Began: 1971, Franchising: 1972
Headquarters size: 330 employees
Franchise department: 6 employees

U.S. franchises: 108
Canadian franchises: 20
Other foreign franchises: 0
Company-owned: 1

Seeking: All U.S.
Seeking in Canada? Yes
Exclusive territories? Yes
Homebased option? No
Employees needed to run biz: 9-12
Absentee ownership? No

COSTS
Total cost: $290K-1.2M
Franchise fee: $55K
Royalty fee: 22%
Term of agreement: 12 years renewable
   at no charge
Franchisees required to buy multiple
   units? No

FINANCING
In-house: Franchise fee
3rd-party: Equipment, startup costs

QUALIFICATIONS
Net worth: $150K
Cash liquidity: $100K
Experience:
   Marketing skills

TRAINING
At headquarters: 4 weeks
At franchisee's location: 5 weeks
At regional meetings

BUSINESS SUPPORT
Internet
Newsletter
Meetings
Toll-free phone line
Field operations/evaluations

MARKETING SUPPORT
Co-op advertising
Ad slicks
National media campaign

ELIZA J

Current financial data not available

Box 99
Harwich, MA 02645
(508)430-0037
www.elizaj.com
Portable restrooms for outdoor
events
Began: 1997, Franchising: 2004
Headquarters size: 9 employees
Franchise department: 7 employees

U.S. franchises: 1
Canadian franchises: 0
Other foreign franchises: 0
Company-owned: 1

Seeking: All U.S.
Seeking in Canada? No
Exclusive territories? Yes
Homebased option? Yes
Employees needed to run biz: 2
Absentee ownership? No

COSTS
Total cost: $64.7K-112.4K
Franchise fee: $25K
Royalty fee: 10%
Term of agreement: 5 years
renewable
Franchisees required to buy multiple
units? No

FINANCING
In-house: Franchise fee
3rd-party: Equipment, startup costs

QUALIFICATIONS
Net worth: $250K
Cash liquidity: $50K
Experience:
General business experience
Marketing skills
Customer-service skills

TRAINING
At headquarters: 5 days
At franchisee's location: 2 days

BUSINESS SUPPORT
Internet
Newsletter
Meetings
Toll-free phone line
Field operations/evaluations
Purchasing cooperatives
Security/safety procedures

MARKETING SUPPORT
National media campaign
Regional marketing

ENVIRONIX INC.

Current financial data not available

20728 56th Ave. W.
Lynnwood, WA 98036
(425)250-0488
www.environix.com
Mold inspection & removal,
allergen control, indoor
air-quality solutions
Began: 2003, Franchising: 2007
Headquarters size: 10 employees
Franchise department: 2 employees

U.S. franchises: 0
Canadian franchises: 0
Other foreign franchises: 0
Company-owned: 1

Seeking: All U.S.
Seeking in Canada? No
Exclusive territories? Yes
Homebased option? No
Employees needed to run biz: 2
Absentee ownership? No

COSTS
Total cost: $175K
Franchise fee: $55K
Royalty fee: 10%
Term of agreement: 5 years renewable
for 67% of then-current fee
Franchisees required to buy multiple
units? No

FINANCING
In-house: None
3rd-party: Equipment, franchise fee,
inventory, startup costs

QUALIFICATIONS
Net worth: $250K
Cash liquidity: $90K-95K
Experience:
General business experience
Marketing skills
Strong sales skills

TRAINING
At headquarters: 2 weeks
Technician training at corporate
office: 2-3 days

BUSINESS SUPPORT
Grand opening
Internet
Meetings
Toll-free phone line
Field operations/evaluations
Lease negotiations
Security/safety procedures

MARKETING SUPPORT
Co-op advertising
Ad slicks
National media campaign
Website support & campaign

FAST-FIX JEWELRY & WATCH REPAIRS

Ranked #290 in Entrepreneur Magazine's 2007 Franchise 500　　　　*Financial rating: $$$$*

1300 N.W. 17th Ave., #170
Delray Beach, FL 33445
(800)359-0407/(561)330-6060
www.fastfix.com
Jewelry & watch repairs
Began: 1984, Franchising: 1987
Headquarters size: 16 employees

U.S. franchises: 148
Canadian franchises: 2
Other foreign franchises: 0
Company-owned: 0

Seeking: All U.S.
Seeking in Canada? Yes
Exclusive territories? Yes
Homebased option? No
Employees needed to run biz: 3-4
Absentee ownership? No

COSTS
Total cost: $123K-250K
Franchise fee: $35K
Royalty fee: 5%
Term of agreement: 10 years renewable
　　for $15K
Franchisees required to buy multiple
　　units? Outside the U.S. only

FINANCING
In-house: None
3rd-party: Accounts receivable,
　　equipment, inventory, startup
　　costs

QUALIFICATIONS
Cash liquidity: $50K
Experience:
　　General business experience
　　Financial stability

TRAINING
At headquarters: 10 days
At franchisee's location: 3 days at
　　opening
Annual convention

BUSINESS SUPPORT
Grand opening
Internet
Newsletter
Meetings
Toll-free phone line
Field operations/evaluations
Lease negotiations
Purchasing cooperatives
Security/safety procedures

MARKETING SUPPORT
Ad slicks
Opening marketing support
In-store graphics & promo materials
Ongoing marketing programs

L & W INVESTIGATIONS

Financial rating: 0

3140 Red Hill Ave., #270
Costa Mesa, CA 92626
(949)305-7383
www.lwfranchise.com
Private investigation services
Began: 2002, Franchising: 2002
Headquarters size: 14 employees
Franchise department: 1 employee

U.S. franchises: 34
Canadian franchises: 0
Other foreign franchises: 0
Company-owned: 2

Seeking: All U.S.
Seeking in Canada? Yes
Exclusive territories? Yes
Homebased option? Yes
Employees needed to run biz: 1
Absentee ownership? No

COSTS
Total cost: $100K-200K
Franchise fee: $70K-200K
Royalty fee: 7%
Term of agreement: 10 years renewable
　　at no charge
Franchisees required to buy multiple
　　units? No

FINANCING
No financing available

QUALIFICATIONS
Net worth: $100K
Cash liquidity: $100K
Experience:
　　General business experience
　　Marketing skills
　　Strong leadership skills

TRAINING
At headquarters: 1 week
Optional seminars

BUSINESS SUPPORT
Internet
Newsletter
Meetings
Field operations/evaluations
Security/safety procedures

MARKETING SUPPORT
Ad slicks
National media campaign
Regional marketing
Business development department

LOGOCRETE SYSTEMS LLC

Financial rating: $$$

2110 N. Ocean Blvd., #10E
Fort Lauderdale, FL 33305
(800)233-3298
www.logocretesystems.com
Concrete-blasting logo & signage
  system
Began: 2002, Franchising: 2006
Headquarters size: 10 employees
Franchise department: 10 employees

U.S. franchises: 0
Canadian franchises: 0
Other foreign franchises: 0
Company-owned: 0

Seeking: All U.S.
Seeking in Canada? No
Exclusive territories? Yes
Homebased option? Yes
Employees needed to run biz: 1-2
Absentee ownership? Yes

COSTS
Total cost: $105.4K-159.9K
Franchise fee: $69.9K
Royalty fee: 8%
Term of agreement: 5 years renewable
  for $5K
Franchisees required to buy multiple
  units? No

FINANCING
No financing available

QUALIFICATIONS
Experience:
  General business experience
  Marketing skills

TRAINING
At headquarters: 1 week
At franchisee's location: 2-3 days
  (optional)

BUSINESS SUPPORT
Internet
Toll-free phone line
Security/safety procedures

MARKETING SUPPORT
Co-op advertising
National media campaign
Professional sports team licensing

NATIONAL WATER SURVEYING

Financial rating: 0

P.O. Box 1307
Centralia, WA 98531
(866)740-6446
www.findwellwater.com
Usable groundwater locating system
Began: 2001, Franchising: 2002
Headquarters size: 7 employees
Franchise department: 3 employees

U.S. franchises: 25
Canadian franchises: 1
Other foreign franchises: 1
Company-owned: 2

Seeking: All U.S.
Seeking in Canada? Yes
Exclusive territories? No
Homebased option? Yes
Employees needed to run biz: 1
Absentee ownership? No

COSTS
Total cost: $66.4K-99K
Franchise fee: $25K
Royalty fee: 6-10%
Term of agreement: 10 years renewable
  at no charge
Franchisees required to buy multiple
  units? No

FINANCING
In-house: None
3rd-party: Accounts receivable,
  equipment, franchise fee,
  inventory, payroll, startup costs

QUALIFICATIONS
Net worth: $35K
Excellent credit

TRAINING
At headquarters: 2 weeks
Ongoing corporate support

BUSINESS SUPPORT
Grand opening
Internet
Newsletter
Meetings
Toll-free phone line
Field operations/evaluations
Purchasing cooperatives
Security/safety procedures

MARKETING SUPPORT
Co-op advertising
Ad slicks
National media campaign
Print & radio materials

1-800-GOT-JUNK?

Ranked #97 in Entrepreneur Magazine's 2007 Franchise 500   *Financial rating: $$$*

1523 W. 3rd Ave., 3rd Fl.
Vancouver, BC V6J 1J8 Canada
(877)408-5865
www.1800gotjunk.com
Junk removal service
Began: 1989, Franchising: 1998
Headquarters size: 150 employees
Franchise department: 8 employees

U.S. franchises: 208
Canadian franchises: 25
Other foreign franchises: 0
Company-owned: 6

Seeking: All U.S.
Seeking in Canada? Yes
Exclusive territories? Yes
Homebased option? No
Employees needed to run biz: 3
Absentee ownership? Yes

COSTS
Total cost: $73.1K-98.98K
Franchise fee: $20K+
Royalty fee: 8%
Term of agreement: 5 years renewable
    for up to $5K (legal fees)
Franchisees required to buy multiple
    units? No

FINANCING
In-house: Franchise fee
3rd-party: Equipment, franchise fee,
    inventory, startup costs

QUALIFICATIONS
Net worth: $150K
Cash liquidity: $70K
Experience:
    General business experience
    Marketing & sales skills
    Experience in management &
    operations

TRAINING
At headquarters: 1 week
At franchisee's location: 3 days
Annual training at franchisee's
    location: 2-3 days
Annual conference: 2-3 days

BUSINESS SUPPORT
Grand opening
Internet
Newsletter
Meetings
Toll-free phone line
Field operations/evaluations
Purchasing cooperatives
Security/safety procedures

MARKETING SUPPORT
Co-op advertising
Ad slicks
National media campaign
Regional marketing

THE ORIGINAL BASKET BOUTIQUE

Ranked #494 in Entrepreneur Magazine's 2007 Franchise 500   *Financial rating: $$*

#16, 363 Sioux Rd.
Sherwood Park, AB T8A 4W7
    Canada
(877)622-8008
www.originalbasketboutique.com
Gifts, gift baskets, corporate gifts
Began: 1989, Franchising: 1989
Headquarters size: 4 employees
Franchise department: 4 employees

U.S. franchises: 11
Canadian franchises: 24
Other foreign franchises: 0
Company-owned: 0

Seeking: All U.S.
Seeking in Canada? Yes
Exclusive territories? Yes
Homebased option? Yes
Employees needed to run biz: 1-2
Absentee ownership? Yes

COSTS
Total cost: $33K
Franchise fee: $25K
Royalty fee: 4%
Term of agreement: 5 years renewable
    for $500
Franchisees required to buy multiple
    units? No

FINANCING
No financing available

QUALIFICATIONS
Net worth: $40K
Experience:
    General business experience
    Marketing skills
    Sales experience

TRAINING
At headquarters: 3-4 days

BUSINESS SUPPORT
Internet
Newsletter
Meetings
Toll-free phone line
Field operations/evaluations
Purchasing cooperatives

MARKETING SUPPORT
Regional marketing
Sales leads

PIRTEK

Ranked #447 in Entrepreneur Magazine's 2007 Franchise 500   *Financial rating: $$$$*

501 Haverty Ct.
Rockledge, FL 32955
(321)504-4422
www.pirtekusa.com
Hydraulic hose center
Began: 1980, Franchising: 1987
Headquarters size: 35 employees
Franchise department: 6 employees

U.S. franchises: 33
Canadian franchises: 0
Other foreign franchises: 239
Company-owned: 2

Seeking: All U.S.
Seeking in Canada? No
Exclusive territories? Yes
Homebased option? No
Employees needed to run biz: 6
Absentee ownership? Yes

COSTS
Total cost: $210K-538K
Franchise fee: $45K
Royalty fee: 1.5-4%
Term of agreement: 10 years renewable
    for $5K
Franchisees required to buy multiple
    units? No

FINANCING
In-house: None
3rd-party: Accounts receivable,
    equipment, franchise fee,
    inventory, payroll, startup costs

QUALIFICATIONS
Net worth: $500K
Cash liquidity: $100K
Experience:
    General business experience
    Marketing skills

TRAINING
At headquarters: 3 weeks
At franchisee's location: As needed

BUSINESS SUPPORT
Grand opening
Internet
Newsletter
Meetings
Toll-free phone line
Field operations/evaluations
Purchasing cooperatives
Security/safety procedures

MARKETING SUPPORT
Co-op advertising
Ad slicks
National media campaign
Regional marketing

POP-A-LOCK FRANCHISE SYSTEM

Ranked #148 in Entrepreneur Magazine's 2007 Franchise 500   *Financial rating: $$$$*

1018 Harding St., #101
Lafayette, LA 70503
(337)233-6211
www.pop-a-lock.com
Locksmithing & roadside assistance
    services
Began: 1991, Franchising: 1994
Headquarters size: 14 employees
Franchise department: 3 employees

U.S. franchises: 158
Canadian franchises: 0
Other foreign franchises: 0
Company-owned: 2

Seeking: All U.S.
Seeking in Canada? No
Exclusive territories? Yes
Homebased option? Yes
Employees needed to run biz: 3-10
Absentee ownership? Yes

COSTS
Total cost: $120K+
Franchise fee: $29K
Royalty fee: 6%
Term of agreement: 10 years renewable
    at no charge
Franchisees required to buy multiple
    units? No

FINANCING
In-house: None
3rd-party: Equipment, franchise fee,
    inventory, startup costs

QUALIFICATIONS
Net worth: $250K
Cash liquidity: $45K+
Experience:
    General business experience
    Marketing skills

TRAINING
At headquarters: 1 week
At franchisee's location: 1-2 weeks
Tech/employee training: 1-2 weeks

BUSINESS SUPPORT
Grand opening
Internet
Newsletter
Meetings
Toll-free phone line
Field operations/evaluations
Purchasing cooperatives
Security/safety procedures

MARKETING SUPPORT
Ad slicks
Regional marketing
Mentor program
National accounts
DVDs
PR

SWEET BEGINNINGS

Financial rating: 0

2607 McBain Ave.
Vancouver, BC V6L 2C7 Canada
(866)730-5553/(604)738-9552
www.asweetbeginning.com
Wedding consulting & event
    planning
Began: 1997, Franchising: 2004
Headquarters size: 4 employees
Franchise department: 3 employees

U.S. franchises: 1
Canadian franchises: 15
Other foreign franchises: 0
Company-owned: 0

Seeking: All U.S.
Seeking in Canada? Yes
Exclusive territories? Yes
Homebased option? Yes
Employees needed to run biz: 2-3
Absentee ownership? No

COSTS
Total cost: $29.1K-44.7K
Franchise fee: $10K-20K
Royalty fee: $300/mo.
Term of agreement: 5 years renewable
    for $5K
Franchisees required to buy multiple
    units? Outside the U.S. only

FINANCING
In-house: None
3rd-party: Franchise fee, inventory

QUALIFICATIONS
Net worth: $50K-100K
Cash liquidity: $35K
Experience:
    General business experience

TRAINING
At headquarters: 5 days
At franchisee's location: 3 days

BUSINESS SUPPORT
Internet
Newsletter
Meetings
Purchasing cooperatives

MARKETING SUPPORT
Ad slicks

VOLVO RENTS

Ranked #354 in Entrepreneur Magazine's 2007 Franchise 500   *Financial rating: $$$*

One Volvo Dr.
Asheville, NC 28803
(866)387-3687
www.volvorents.com
Construction equipment rentals
Began: 1986, Franchising: 2001
Headquarters size: Info not provided

U.S. franchises: 59
Canadian franchises: 4
Other foreign franchises: 62
Company-owned: 4

Seeking: All U.S.
Seeking in Canada? Yes
Exclusive territories? Yes
Homebased option? No
Employees needed to run biz: 7-12
Absentee ownership? Yes

COSTS
Total cost: $3.5M-8.2M
Franchise fee: $45K
Royalty fee: 4%
Term of agreement: 15 years renewable
    at no charge
Franchisees required to buy multiple
    units? No

FINANCING
In-house: Accounts receivable,
    equipment, inventory, startup
    costs
3rd-party: None

QUALIFICATIONS
Net worth: $800K
Cash liquidity: $500K
Experience:
    Industry experience
    General business experience
    Marketing skills

TRAINING
At headquarters: 2-3 weeks
At franchisee's location: Varies
Financial/cash-flow training
Sales & marketing training

BUSINESS SUPPORT
Grand opening
Internet
Newsletter
Meetings
Toll-free phone line
Field operations/evaluations
Purchasing cooperatives
Security/safety procedures

MARKETING SUPPORT
Ad slicks
National media campaign
Regional marketing

SERVICES ▶ *Other Franchises*

AUCTION IT TODAY
301 Appian Wy.
Brighton, MI 48116
(810)225-0555
www.auctionittoday.com
eBay auction drop-off store
Financial rating: 0

AUCTION MOJO
14000 Commerce Pkwy., #G
Mt. Laurel, NJ 08054
(856)642-0130
www.auctionmojo.com
Online auction drop-off store
Current financial data not available

THE BRICKKICKER HOME INSPECTION
849 N. Ellsworth St.
Naperville, IL 60583
(888)339-5425
www.brickkicker.com
Property inspections
Current financial data not available

COLBERT/BALL TAX SERVICE
Ranked #320 in Entrepreneur
Magazine's 2007 Franchise 500
2616 S. Loop W., #110
Houston, TX 77054
(713)592-5555
www.colbertballtax.com
Tax preparation & electronic filing
Financial rating: $$$$

COMPLETE MUSIC
Ranked #264 in Entrepreneur
Magazine's 2007 Franchise 500
7877 L St.
Omaha, NE 68127
(800)843-3866/(402)339-0001
www.cmusic.com
Mobile DJ entertainment service
Financial rating: $$$$

CRATERS & FREIGHTERS
331 Corporate Cir., #I-8
Golden, CO 80401
(800)949-9931
www.cratersandfreighters.com
Specialty freight-handling services
Current financial data not available

CRYE-LEIKE FRANCHISES INC.
Ranked #365 in Entrepreneur
Magazine's 2007 Franchise 500
5111 Maryland Wy., #202
Brentwood, TN 37027
(866)603-2470/(615)221-0449
www.crye-leike.com
Real estate
Financial rating: $$$

DRY CLEANING STATION
Ranked #231 in Entrepreneur
Magazine's 2007 Franchise 500
8301 Golden Valley Rd., #240
Minneapolis, MN 55427
(800)655-8134
www.drycleaningstation.com
Dry cleaning
Financial rating: $$$

DRY CLEANING TO-YOUR-DOOR
1121 N.W. Bayshore Dr.
Waldport, OR 97394
(800)318-1800
www.dctyd.com
Dry cleaning pickup & delivery
Current financial data not available

FAST COPI
10165 USA Today Wy.
Miramar, FL 33025
(954)431-1414
www.fastcopi.com
Copy center
Current financial data not available

HELP-U-SELL REAL ESTATE
Ranked #47 in Entrepreneur
Magazine's 2007 Franchise 500
3333 Michelson Rd., #450
Irvine, CA 92612
(800)366-1177
www.helpusell.com
Real estate
Financial rating: $$$$

HOMEVESTORS OF AMERICA INC.
Ranked #252 in Entrepreneur
Magazine's 2007 Franchise 500
10670 N. Central Expwy., #700
Dallas, TX 75231
(972)761-0046
www.homevestors.com
Home buying, repair & selling system
Financial rating: $$$

HOUSEWATCH U.S.
Box 576
Greenport, NY 11944
(631)765-8348
www.housewatchus.com
House-watching services for vacation homes
Current financial data not available

IT'S JUST LUNCH INT'L. LLC
Ranked #225 in Entrepreneur
Magazine's 2007 Franchise 500
75-430 Gerald Ford Dr., #207
Palm Desert, CA 92211
(760)779-0101
www.itsjustlunch.com
Dating service
Financial rating: $$$$

LIL' ANGELS PHOTOGRAPHY
4041 Hatcher Cir.
Memphis, TN 38118
(800)358-9101
www.angelsus.com
Preschool & day-care photography
Current financial data not available

MY GIRL FRIDAY
120 E. 4th St., #215
Cincinnati, OH 45202
(513)531-4475
www.egirlfriday.com
Personal concierge services
Current financial data not available

NUMARKETS
816 Tennessee Ave.
Etowah, TN 37331
(423)263-5211
www.numarkets.com
eBay drop-off & shipping center
Current financial data not available

THE ONLINE OUTPOST FRANCHISING CORP.
5301 W. Cypress St., #105
Tampa, FL 33607
(813)470-7094
www.theonlineoutpost.com
Internet auction drop-off store
Current financial data not available

OXXO CARE CLEANERS
1874 N. Young Cir.
Hollywood, FL 33020
(954)927-7410
www.oxxousa.com
Dry cleaning & laundry services
Current financial data not available

PROFESSIONAL HOUSE DOCTORS INC.
1406 E. 14th St.
Des Moines, IA 50316
(800)288-7437
www.prohousedr.com
Environmental & building-science
  services
Current financial data not available

SHOWHOMES
758 St. Michael St., #D
Mobile, AL 36602
(251)690-9090
www.showhomes.com
Home management & staging
  services
Current financial data not available

SUNSHINE PACK & SHIP RETAIL CENTERS
6408 Parkland Dr., #104
Sarasota, FL 34243
(877)751-1513/(941)746-9825
www.sunshinepackandship.com
Commercial packing, shipping &
  freight brokering
Current financial data not available

24/7 AUCTIONS
1037 E. Vista Wy.
Vista, CA 92084
(800)468-7655
www.247auctions.com
eBay drop-off store
Current financial data not available

VIP CLEANERS
777 Passaic Ave., 3rd Fl.
Clifton, NJ 07012
(973)779-1100
www.myvipcleaners.com
Dry cleaning pickup & delivery
Current financial data not available

WE THE PEOPLE USA INC.
1436 Lancaster Ave., #340
Berwyn, PA 19312
(866)429-2785
www.wethepeopleusa.com
Legal document preparation services
Current financial data not available

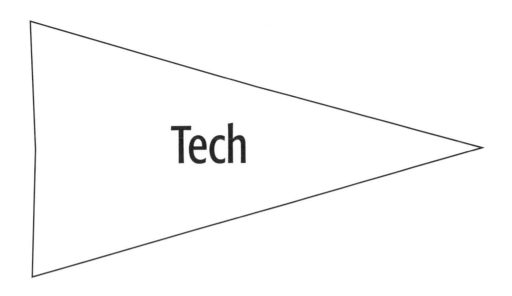

TECH

CM IT SOLUTIONS

Financial rating: 0

1701 Directors Blvd., #300
Austin, TX 78744
(512)692-3710
www.cmitsolutions.com
On-site computer support for small
  businesses
Began: 1994, Franchising: 1998
Headquarters size: 14 employees
Franchise department: 5 employees

U.S. franchises: 102
Canadian franchises: 0
Other foreign franchises: 0
Company-owned: 0

Seeking: All U.S.
Seeking in Canada? No
Exclusive territories? Yes
Homebased option? Yes
Employees needed to run biz: 5-10
Absentee ownership? No

COSTS
Total cost: $63.5K-101K
Franchise fee: $39.5K+
Royalty fee: Varies
Term of agreement: 10 years renewable
  for $500
Franchisees required to buy multiple
  units? No

FINANCING
In-house: None
3rd-party: Franchise fee, startup
  costs

QUALIFICATIONS
Net worth: $250K
Cash liquidity: $100K
Experience:
    General business experience
    Marketing skills
    Management experience

TRAINING
At headquarters: 1 week

BUSINESS SUPPORT
Internet
Newsletter
Meetings
Toll-free phone line

MARKETING SUPPORT
Ad slicks
Direct mail

COMPUTER MEDICS OF AMERICA INC.

Current financial data not available

10901 Mausel St., #106
Eagle River, AK 99577
(907)694-0371
www.computermedicsofamerica.com
Mobile computer repair services
Began: 2000, Franchising: 2003
Headquarters size: 2 employees
Franchise department: 2 employees

U.S. franchises: 50
Canadian franchises: 0
Other foreign franchises: 0
Company-owned: 3

Seeking: All U.S.
Seeking in Canada? Yes
Exclusive territories? Yes
Homebased option? Yes
Employees needed to run biz: 0
Absentee ownership? No

COSTS
Total cost: $16K-18K
Franchise fee: $15K
Royalty fee: 0
Term of agreement: 5 years renewable
  for $2K
Franchisees required to buy multiple
  units? No

FINANCING
In-house: Franchise fee
3rd-party: None

QUALIFICATIONS
Experience:
  Industry experience
  General business experience
  Basic computer repair
  knowledge & certifications

TRAINING
At headquarters: 1 week

BUSINESS SUPPORT
Internet
Meetings

MARKETING SUPPORT
Info not provided

COMPUTER RENAISSANCE

Ranked #463 in Entrepreneur Magazine's 2007 Franchise 500   *Financial rating: $$$$*

500 S. Florida Ave., #400
Lakeland, FL 33801
(863)669-1155
www.compren.com
Used & new computer sales/services
Began: 1988, Franchising: 1993
Headquarters size: 8 employees

U.S. franchises: 78
Canadian franchises: 0
Other foreign franchises: 0
Company-owned: 1

Seeking: All U.S.
Seeking in Canada? Yes
Exclusive territories? Yes
Homebased option? No
Employees needed to run biz: 5
Absentee ownership? No

COSTS
Total cost: $193K-284K
Franchise fee: $27.5K
Royalty fee: 6%
Term of agreement: 10 years renewable
  for $10K
Franchisees required to buy multiple
  units? No

FINANCING
In-house: None
3rd-party: Equipment, payroll,
  startup costs

QUALIFICATIONS
Net worth: $250K
Cash liquidity: $50K

TRAINING
At headquarters: 2 weeks
At franchisee's location: 1 week

BUSINESS SUPPORT
Grand opening
Internet
Newsletter
Meetings
Field operations/evaluations
Lease negotiations

MARKETING SUPPORT
Ad slicks

COMPUTER TROUBLESHOOTERS

Ranked #187 in Entrepreneur Magazine's 2007 Franchise 500　　　*Financial rating: $$$*

755 Commerce Dr., #412
Decatur, GA 30030
(877)704-1702/(404)477-1300
www.comptroub.com
Computer repairs & technology
　　consulting
Began: 1997, Franchising: 1997
Headquarters size: 4 employees
Franchise department: 4 employees

U.S. franchises: 240
Canadian franchises: 20
Other foreign franchises: 210
Company-owned: 1

Seeking: All U.S.
Seeking in Canada? Yes
Exclusive territories? Yes
Homebased option? Yes
Employees needed to run biz: 1
Absentee ownership? Yes

COSTS
Total cost: $19.8K-30.5K
Franchise fee: $14.5K
Royalty fee: $290/mo.
Term of agreement: 10 years renewable
　　at no charge
Franchisees required to buy multiple
　　units? No

FINANCING
In-house: Franchise fee
3rd-party: Equipment, inventory,
　　startup costs

QUALIFICATIONS
Net worth: $10.5K
Cash liquidity: $7K
Experience:
　　Industry experience
　　General business experience
　　Marketing skills
　　Technical skills

TRAINING
At headquarters: 2 days
At franchisee's location: 2 days
In New York City: 2 days
In Lansing, MI: 2 days

BUSINESS SUPPORT
Internet
Newsletter
Meetings
Toll-free phone line
Field operations/evaluations

MARKETING SUPPORT
Co-op advertising
Ad slicks
National media campaign
Regional marketing

CONCERTO NETWORKS INC.

Ranked #439 in Entrepreneur Magazine's 2007 Franchise 500　　　*Financial rating: $$$*

610 W. Ash St., #1501
San Diego, CA 92101
(866)551-4007/(619)501-4530
www.concertonetworks.com
Computer & IT services
Began: 2002, Franchising: 2003
Headquarters size: 8 employees
Franchise department: 4 employees

U.S. franchises: 42
Canadian franchises: 0
Other foreign franchises: 10
Company-owned: 0

Seeking: All U.S.
Seeking in Canada? Yes
Exclusive territories? No
Homebased option? Yes
Employees needed to run biz: 1-5
Absentee ownership? Yes

COSTS
Total cost: $57.1K-66.2K
Franchise fee: $25K
Royalty fee: 14%/12%
Term of agreement: 10 years renewable
Franchisees required to buy multiple
　　units? No

FINANCING
In-house: None
3rd-party: Franchise fee, startup
　　costs

QUALIFICATIONS
Net worth: $100K
Cash liquidity: $75K
Experience:
　　Industry experience
　　General business experience
　　Marketing skills

TRAINING
At headquarters: 5 days

BUSINESS SUPPORT
Grand opening
Internet
Newsletter
Meetings
Toll-free phone line
Field operations/evaluations
Purchasing cooperatives
Security/safety procedures

MARKETING SUPPORT
Co-op advertising
Ad slicks
National media campaign
Regional marketing
Teleconferences
Conventions
Vendor discounts
R&D
Intranet support site

DATA DOCTORS

Current financial data not available

2090 E. University, #101
Tempe, AZ 85281
(480)921-2444
www.datadoctors.com
Computer sales & services, web
　　services
Began: 1988, Franchising: 2002
Headquarters size: 37 employees

U.S. franchises: 69
Canadian franchises: 0
Other foreign franchises: 0
Company-owned: 4

Seeking: All U.S.
Seeking in Canada? Yes
Exclusive territories? Yes
Homebased option? No
Employees needed to run biz: 2-3
Absentee ownership? No

COSTS

Total cost: $83.4K-114.7K
Franchise fee: $35K
Royalty fee: 5%
Term of agreement: 20 years renewable
　　for 5% of then-current fee
Franchisees required to buy multiple
　　units? No

FINANCING

In-house: None
3rd-party: Equipment, franchise fee,
　　inventory, payroll, startup costs

QUALIFICATIONS

Cash liquidity: $150K-175K
Experience:
　　General business experience
　　Marketing skills
　　Tech experience not required

TRAINING

At headquarters: Varies
At franchisee's location: Varies
Ongoing video & internet training

BUSINESS SUPPORT

Grand opening
Internet
Newsletter
Meetings
Toll-free phone line
Field operations/evaluations
Lease negotiations
Purchasing cooperatives
Security/safety procedures

MARKETING SUPPORT

Co-op advertising
Ad slicks
Regional marketing
Weekly radio show & newspaper
　　column

EXPETEC

Current financial data not available

P.O. Box 487
Aberdeen, SD 57401
(888)297-2292
www.expetecfranchise.com
Computer, printer & telecommuni-
　　cations sales & services
Began: 1992, Franchising: 1996
Headquarters size: 20 employees
Franchise department: 3 employees

U.S. franchises: 32
Canadian franchises: 1
Other foreign franchises: 0
Company-owned: 1

Seeking: All U.S.
Seeking in Canada? No
Exclusive territories? Yes
Homebased option? No
Employees needed to run biz: 1-2
Absentee ownership? Yes

COSTS

Total cost: $71.8K-121.5K
Franchise fee: $35K-45K
Royalty fee: 12%
Term of agreement: 10 years renewable
　　at no charge
Franchisees required to buy multiple
　　units? No

FINANCING

In-house: None
3rd-party: Accounts receivable,
　　equipment, franchise fee,
　　inventory, payroll, startup costs

QUALIFICATIONS

Cash liquidity: $100K
Experience:
　　General business experience
　　Marketing skills

TRAINING

At headquarters: 1 week
At franchisee's location: 5 days
Regional meetings
Ongoing

BUSINESS SUPPORT

Grand opening
Internet
Newsletter
Meetings
Toll-free phone line
Field operations/evaluations

MARKETING SUPPORT

Ad slicks
Regional marketing
Direct-mail program

FAST-TEKS ON-SITE COMPUTER SERVICES

Ranked #385 in Entrepreneur Magazine's 2007 Franchise 500   *Financial rating: $$$*

15310 Amberly Dr., #185
Tampa, FL 33647
(800)262-1671
www.fastteks.com
On-site computer repair services
Began: 2003, Franchising: 2004
Headquarters size: 38 employees
Franchise department: 13 employees

U.S. franchises: 57
Canadian franchises: 0
Other foreign franchises: 0
Company-owned: 0

Seeking: All U.S.
Seeking in Canada? Yes
Exclusive territories? Yes
Homebased option? Yes
Employees needed to run biz: 1
Absentee ownership? Yes

COSTS
Total cost: $34.5K-57.95K
Franchise fee: $19.5K-39.5K
Royalty fee: 7%
Term of agreement: 7 years renewable
    at no charge
Franchisees required to buy multiple
    units? No

FINANCING
No financing available

QUALIFICATIONS
Experience:
    General business experience

TRAINING
At headquarters: 2 days
At franchisee's location: 2 days
Ongoing

BUSINESS SUPPORT
Internet
Newsletter
Meetings
Toll-free phone line
Purchasing cooperatives

MARKETING SUPPORT
Ad slicks
National media campaign
Regional marketing
Internet ads

FRIENDLY COMPUTERS

Ranked #283 in Entrepreneur Magazine's 2007 Franchise 500   *Financial rating: $$$*

3440 W. Cheyenne, #100
North Las Vegas, NV 89032
(800)656-3115
www.friendlycomputers.com
Computer repairs, services & sales
Began: 1992, Franchising: 1999
Headquarters size: 12 employees
Franchise department: 12 employees

U.S. franchises: 83
Canadian franchises: 0
Other foreign franchises: 0
Company-owned: 3

Seeking: All U.S.
Seeking in Canada? Yes
Exclusive territories? Yes
Homebased option? Yes
Employees needed to run biz: 1-2
Absentee ownership? Yes

COSTS
Total cost: $59.3K-219K
Franchise fee: $14.9K/25K
Royalty fee: 5%
Term of agreement: 10 years renewable
    for $2.5K
Franchisees required to buy multiple
    units? No

FINANCING
No financing available

QUALIFICATIONS
Cash liquidity: $22K-157.5K

TRAINING
At headquarters: 1 week
Monthly technical & marketing
    round tables & conference calls

BUSINESS SUPPORT
Internet
Newsletter
Meetings
Toll-free phone line
Lease negotiations
Security/safety procedures

MARKETING SUPPORT
Ad slicks
National media campaign
Client retention program
Email marketing program
Custom franchisee websites
Branded software
Website
Pre-opening marketing plan

1 800 905 GEEK

Ranked #103 in Entrepreneur Magazine's 2007 Franchise 500   *Financial rating: $$$$*

(formerly known as Geeks on Call)
814 Kempsville Rd., #106
Norfolk, VA 23502
(757)466-3448
www.geeksoncallfranchise.com
On-site computer support services
Began: 1999, Franchising: 2001
Headquarters size: 60 employees
Franchise department: 4 employees

U.S. franchises: 305
Canadian franchises: 0
Other foreign franchises: 0
Company-owned: 0

Seeking: All U.S.
Seeking in Canada? Yes
Exclusive territories? Yes
Homebased option? Yes
Employees needed to run biz: 1-2
Absentee ownership? Yes

COSTS
Total cost: $55.9K-357.7K
Franchise fee: $25K
Royalty fee: 11%
Term of agreement: 10 years renewable
    at no charge
Franchisees required to buy multiple
    units? No

FINANCING
No financing available

QUALIFICATIONS
Cash liquidity: $18K-20K
Experience:
    Industry experience
    General business experience

TRAINING
At headquarters: 1 week
At franchisee's location: 1 week

BUSINESS SUPPORT
Grand opening
Internet
Newsletter
Meetings
Toll-free phone line
Field operations/evaluations
Purchasing cooperatives

MARKETING SUPPORT
Regional marketing

RESCUECOM

Ranked #213 in Entrepreneur Magazine's 2007 Franchise 500   *Financial rating: $$$$*

2560 Burnet Ave.
Syracuse, NY 13206
(800)737-2837
www.rescuecom.com
Computer repair & technology
    management
Began: 1997, Franchising: 1998
Headquarters size: 40 employees
Franchise department: 40 employees

U.S. franchises: 116
Canadian franchises: 0
Other foreign franchises: 0
Company-owned: 0

Seeking: All U.S.
Seeking in Canada? No
Exclusive territories? Yes
Homebased option? Yes
Employees needed to run biz: 1-3
Absentee ownership? No

COSTS
Total cost: $26.5K-45.5K
Franchise fee: $14.8K-16.8K
Royalty fee: 18%
Term of agreement: 5 years renewable
    for 50% of current fee
Franchisees required to buy multiple
    units? No

FINANCING
In-house: None
3rd-party: Accounts receivable,
    equipment, franchise fee,
    inventory, payroll, startup costs

QUALIFICATIONS
Net worth: $50K-100K
Cash liquidity: $26K
Experience:
    Industry experience
    General business experience
    Marketing skills

TRAINING
At headquarters: 1 week
At franchisee's location: 1 week

BUSINESS SUPPORT
Grand opening
Internet
Newsletter
Meetings
Toll-free phone line
Field operations/evaluations
Purchasing cooperatives

MARKETING SUPPORT
Co-op advertising
Ad slicks

SILUTION FRANCHISE CORP.

Financial rating: $$$

3738 E. Colorado Blvd.
Pasadena, CA 91107
(877)745-8846
www.silution.com
Computer services & support
Began: 1998, Franchising: 2006
Headquarters size: 4 employees

U.S. franchises: 0
Canadian franchises: 0
Other foreign franchises: 0
Company-owned: 0

Seeking: All U.S.
Seeking in Canada? No
Exclusive territories? Yes
Homebased option? Yes
Employees needed to run biz: 1-2
Absentee ownership? No

COSTS
Total cost: $39.95K-71.8K
Franchise fee: $22K
Royalty fee: 10%
Term of agreement: 10 years renewable
for $5K
Franchisees required to buy multiple
units? No

FINANCING
In-house: None
3rd-party: Accounts receivable,
equipment, franchise fee,
inventory, payroll, startup costs

QUALIFICATIONS
Net worth: $50K

TRAINING
At headquarters: 5 days
At franchisee's location: 1 day

BUSINESS SUPPORT
Grand opening
Internet
Newsletter
Meetings
Toll-free phone line
Field operations/evaluations
Security/safety procedures

MARKETING SUPPORT
Ad slicks
Regional marketing
Technical assistance

TEAM LOGIC IT

Financial rating: 0

26722 Plaza Dr.
Mission Viejo, CA 92691
(949)582-6300
www.teamlogicit.com
Computer consulting, maintenance
& repairs
Began: 2004, Franchising: 2005
Headquarters size: 60 employees
Franchise department: 5 employees

U.S. franchises: 20
Canadian franchises: 0
Other foreign franchises: 0
Company-owned: 0

Seeking: All U.S.
Seeking in Canada? No
Exclusive territories? Yes
Homebased option? No
Employees needed to run biz: 2-5
Absentee ownership? Yes

COSTS
Total cost: $58.5K-121K
Franchise fee: $12.5K-25K
Royalty fee: 10%
Term of agreement: 10 years renewable
for $2K
Franchisees required to buy multiple
units? No

FINANCING
In-house: None
3rd-party: Accounts receivable,
franchise fee, inventory

QUALIFICATIONS
Net worth: $75K-125K
Cash liquidity: $40K-60K
Experience:
General business experience
Tech experience helpful

TRAINING
At headquarters: 1 week

BUSINESS SUPPORT
Internet
Newsletter
Meetings
Toll-free phone line
Purchasing cooperatives
Security/safety procedures

MARKETING SUPPORT
Ad slicks
Direct mail
Keyword purchasing program
Brochures
TV & radio spots
Sales training

TRUEPRESENCE LLC

Financial rating: $$

10 E. Baltimore St., 10th Fl.
Baltimore, MD 21210
(410)649-2164
www.truepresence.com
Web design/development & internet
marketing
Began: 2003, Franchising: 2005
Headquarters size: 25 employees
Franchise department: 2 employees

U.S. franchises: 10
Canadian franchises: 0
Other foreign franchises: 0
Company-owned: 0

Seeking: All U.S.
Seeking in Canada? No
Exclusive territories? Yes
Homebased option? Yes
Employees needed to run biz: 0
Absentee ownership? No

COSTS
Total cost: $43.3K-106.3K
Franchise fee: $34.9K
Royalty fee: 6%
Term of agreement: 10 years renewable
Franchisees required to buy multiple
units? No

FINANCING
No financing available

QUALIFICATIONS
Net worth: $50K
Cash liquidity: $20K
Experience:
Industry experience
General business experience
Marketing skills

TRAINING
At headquarters: 5 days
At franchisee's location: 3 days

BUSINESS SUPPORT
Internet
Newsletter
Meetings
Toll-free phone line
Field operations/evaluations
Purchasing cooperatives

MARKETING SUPPORT
Ad slicks

WSI INTERNET

Ranked #42 in Entrepreneur Magazine's 2007 Franchise 500

Financial rating: $$$$

5580 Explorer Dr., #600
Mississauga, ON L4W 4Y1 Canada
(888)678-7588/(905)678-7588
www.wsicorporate.com
Internet services
Began: 1995, Franchising: 1996
Headquarters size: 100 employees
Franchise department: 25 employees

U.S. franchises: 804
Canadian franchises: 69
Other foreign franchises: 890
Company-owned: 2

Seeking: All U.S.
Seeking in Canada? Yes
Exclusive territories? No
Homebased option? Yes
Employees needed to run biz: 1
Absentee ownership? No

COSTS
Total cost: $49.7K-147K
Franchise fee: $39.7K-137K
Royalty fee: 10%
Term of agreement: 5 years renewable
at no charge
Franchisees required to buy multiple
units? No

FINANCING
No financing available

QUALIFICATIONS
Net worth: $68K-82K
Cash liquidity: $5K
Experience:
General business experience

TRAINING
At headquarters: 7 days

BUSINESS SUPPORT
Internet
Newsletter
Meetings
Toll-free phone line
Purchasing cooperatives

MARKETING SUPPORT
Co-op advertising
Ad slicks
Marketing materials

TECH   *Other Franchises*

DEBUGIT COMPUTER SERVICES

417 Stokes Rd.
Medford, NJ 08055
(609)953-8055
www.debugitfranchise.com
Computer maintenance services
Current financial data not available

Top 10 Franchises
for 2007

1. Subway	www.subway.com	Submarine sandwiches & salads
2. Dunkin' Donuts	www.dunkinfranchising.com	Donuts & baked goods
3. Jackson Hewitt Tax Service	www.jacksonhewitt.com	Tax preparation services
4. 7-Eleven Inc.	www.7-eleven.com	Convenience store
5. The UPS Store/. Mail Boxes Etc	www.theupsstore.com	Postal, business & communications services
6. Domino's Pizza LLC	www.dominos.com	Pizza, breadsticks, buffalo wings
7. Jiffy Lube Int'l. Inc.	www.jiffylube.com	Fast oil change
8. Sonic Drive In Restaurants	www.sonicdrivein.com	Drive-in restaurant
9. McDonald's	www.mcdonalds.com	Hamburgers, chicken, salads
10. Papa John's Int'l. Inc.	www.papajohns.com	Pizza

Source: *Entrepreneur* magazine's 2007 Franchise 500®

Top 10 Homebased Franchises for 2007

(Franchise opportunities that can be run from home)

1. Jani-King — www.janiking.com — Commercial cleaning

2. Jan-Pro Franchising Int'l. Inc. — www.jan-pro.com — Commercial cleaning

3. Matco Tools — www.matcotools.com — Tools

4. Servpro — www.servpro.com — Insurance/disaster restoration & cleaning

5. Chem-Dry Carpet Drapery & Upholstery Cleaning — www.chemdry.com — Carpet, drapery & upholstery cleaning

6. Budget Blinds Inc. — www.budgetblinds.com — Window coverings

7. Bonus Building Care — www.bonusbuildingcare.com — Commercial cleaning

8. ServiceMaster Clean — www.ownafranchise.com — Commercial/residential cleaning & disaster restoration

9. Jazzercise Inc. — www.jazzercise.com — Dance & exercise classes

10. CleanNet USA Inc. — www.cleannetusa.com — Commercial office cleaning

Source: *Entrepreneur* magazine's 2007 Franchise 500°

Top 10 New Franchises for 2007

(Companies that have been franchising since 2002)

1. iSold It	www.i-soldit.com	eBay drop-off store
2. United Shipping Solutions	www.usshipit.com	Transportation services
3. Massage Envy	www.massageenvy.com	Therapeutic massage services
4. Super Suppers	www.supersuppers.com	Do-it-yourself home meal preparation
5. Dream Dinners Inc.	www.dreamdinners.com	Do-it-yourself home meal preparation
6. WineStyles Inc.	www.winestyles.net	Wine store
7. System4	www.system4usa.com	Commercial cleaning
8. N-Hance	www.nhancefranchise.com	Wood floor & cabinet renewal systems
9. The Growth Coach	www.thegrowthcoach.com	Small-business coaching & mentoring
10. Instant Tax Service	www.instanttaxservice.com	Retail tax preparation & electronic filing

Source: *Entrepreneur* magazine's 2007 Franchise 500®

Top 10 Low-Cost Franchises for 2007

(Franchises with minimum total investments of less than $50,000)

1. Jackson Hewitt Tax Service	www.jacksonhewitt.com	Tax preparation services
2. RE/MAX Int'l. Inc.	www.remax.com	Real estate
3. Jani-King	www.janiking.com	Commercial cleaning
4. Curves	www.buycurves.com	Women's fitness & weight-loss center
5. Liberty Tax Service	www.libertytaxfranchise.com	Income-tax preparation services
6. Merle Norman Cosmetics	www.merlenorman.com	Cosmetics studio
7. Kumon Math & Reading Centers	www.kumon.com	Supplemental education
8. Jan-Pro Franchising Int'l. Inc.	www.jan-pro.com	Commercial cleaning
9. Chem-Dry Carpet Drapery & Upholstery Cleaning	www.chemdry.com	Carpet, drapery & upholstery cleaning
10. Bonus Building Care	www.bonusbuildingcare.com	Commercial cleaning

Source: *Entrepreneur* magazine's 2007 Franchise 500®

State Franchise Authorities

CALIFORNIA

California Department of Corporations
The Commissioner of Corporations
Department of Corporations
320 West 4th St., #750
Los Angeles, CA 90013
(866) 275-2677; (213) 576-7500
www.corp.ca.gov

HAWAII

Business Registration Division
Securities Compliance
Department of Commerce and
	Consumer Affairs
335 Merchant St., Room 201
Honolulu, HI 96813
(808) 587-2727
www.hawaii.gov/dcca

ILLINOIS

Franchise Division Office of the
	Attorney General
Chief, Franchise Division
Office of the Attorney General

500 South Second St.
Springfield, IL 62706
(217) 782-4465
www.ag.state.il.us/consumers

INDIANA

Securities Commissioner
Indiana Securities Division
302 W. Washington St., Room E 111
Indianapolis, IN 46204
(317) 232-6681
www.in.gov/sos/securities

MARYLAND

Office of the Attorney General
Securities Division
200 St. Paul Pl., 20th Fl.
Baltimore, MD 21202-2020
(410) 576-6360
www.oag.state.md.us/securities

MICHIGAN

Antitrust and Franchise Unit
Department of the Attorney General

Director, Consumer Protection Division
525 W. Ottawa St.
Lansing, MI 48909
(517) 373-7117
www.michigan.gov/ag

MINNESOTA

The Commissioner of Commerce
Minnesota Department of Commerce
85 7th Place E., #500
St. Paul, MN 55101-2198
(651) 296-6025
www.commerce.state.mn.us

NEW YORK

New York State Department of Law
Bureau of Investor Protection and Securities
120 Broadway, 23rd Fl.
New York, NY 10271
(212) 416-8222
www.state.ny.us

NORTH DAKOTA

The Commissioner of Securities
North Dakota Office of Securities Commissioner
Office of the Securities Commissioner
600 East Blvd., Fifth Fl.
Bismarck, ND 58505-0510
(701) 328-2910
www.ndsecurities.com

RHODE ISLAND

Rhode Island Division of Securities
Director, Division of Securities
233 Richmond St., #232
Providence, RI 02903

(401) 222-3048
www.dbr.state.ri.us

SOUTH DAKOTA

South Dakota Division of Securities
Director, Division of Securities
445 East Capitol Ave.
Pierre, SD 57501
(605) 773-4823
www.state.sd.us/drr2/reg/securities

VIRGINIA

State Corporation Commission
Division of Securities and Retail Franchising
1300 East Main St., 9th Fl.
Richmond, VA 23219
(804) 371-9187
www.state.va.us/scc

WASHINGTON

Department of Financial Institutions
Securities Division
P.O. Box 9033
Olympia, WA 98507-9033
(360) 902-8760
www.dfi.wa.gov

WISCONSIN

The Commissioner of Securities
Wisconsin Securities Commission
P.O. Box 1768
Madison, WI 53701
(608) 266-1064
www.wdfi.org

Other Information Sources

BETTER BUSINESS BUREAU

www.bbb.org
Also look for your local office of the Better Business Bureau in the phone book or on the web.

ENTREPRENEUR'S FRANCHISE ZONE

www.entrepreneur.com/franchise
Contains articles and resources on how to buy and research a franchise, plus the latest franchise information on more than 1,200 franchise opportunities.

FEDERAL TRADE COMMISSION (FTC)

Federal Trade Commission, Attn: Consumer Response Center, Washington, DC 20580Consumer Response Center at (877) 382-4357
www.ftc.gov

Contact the Federal Trade Commission (FTC) for general investment information if you are interested in buying a franchise or business opportunity venture. The website is well worth a visit, and the FTC encourages investors to contact the agency if they discover an unlawful franchise practice.

INTERNATIONAL FRANCHISE ASSOCIATION (IFA)

www.franchise.org
(202) 628-8000

Glossary

Arbitration. Formal dispute resolution process that is legally binding on the parties.

Business Format Franchise. See the definition of "franchise."

Business Opportunity. A package of goods and materials that enables the buyer to begin or maintain a business. The Federal Trade Commission and 25 states regulate the concept.

Copyright. The legal right protecting an original work of authorship that is fixed in a tangible form.

Earnings Claim. A statement by a franchisor regarding the financial performance of existing franchisees or a projection of how a particular investor/franchisee will perform. Earnings claims may be made by a franchisor, but if so, they must be presented in item 19 of the UFOC.

Federal Trade Commission's Franchise Rule. The 1979 trade regulation rule by which all franchisors in the United States are required to deliver a presale disclosure document.

First Personal Meeting. A disclosure trigger under the Federal Trade Commission Rule; not a casual or chance meeting but a detailed discussion about a specific franchise opportunity.

Franchise. The law defines a franchise as the presence of three factors: 1) the grant of trademark rights, 2) a prescribed marketing plan, or significant control or assistance in the operation, or a community of interest, and 3) payment of a franchise fee for the right to participate. In business terms, the franchisee receives full training in the operation, follows a detailed set of business techniques, uses the franchisor's trademark and pays a continuing royalty for participation in the program.

Franchise Agreement. The contract by which a franchisor grants franchise rights to a franchisee.

Franchisee. One who receives the rights to a franchise. The owner and operator of a franchised business.

Franchise Fee. The money a franchisee is required to pay for the right to participate in the franchise program. Under the federal rules the minimum amount of franchise fee payment allowed before disclosure is required is $500. A franchise fee includes any lump sum initial payment and ongoing royalty payments.

Franchise Investment Laws. The laws of the Federal Trade Commission and 14 states that regulate the sale of a franchise.

Franchise Relationship Laws. State franchise statutes in 19 jurisdictions that generally restrict terminations or nonrenewals of franchise agreements in the absence of "good cause."

Franchisor. The person or company that grants franchise rights to a franchisee.

Limited Liability Company. A relatively new form of business organization with the liability-shield advantages of a corporation and the flexibility and tax pass-through advantages of a partnership.

Mediation. Professionally assisted negotiation. Now frequently used as a first step to resolve a dispute between a franchisor and franchisee. Mediation is generally nonbinding, unless the parties agree to a resulting settlement.

Patent. An inventor's right protecting an invention, new device, or innovation.

Product Franchise. The legal definition is the same as a "franchise." In business terms, it is a system for the distribution of a particular line of products, usually manufactured and/or supplied by the franchisor.

Renewal. Most franchise agreements grant the franchisee the right to renew the initial contract term for additional time at the end of the initial term. The contract may impose conditions on the right to renew, such as providing timely written notice, signing a new form of agreement, and paying a renewal fee.

Royalty Fee. The continuing payment paid by a franchisee to the franchisor. Usually calculated as a percentage of the franchisee's gross sales.

Territory. The rights granted to a franchisee that offer a restriction on competition within a stated area.

Trademark. A word, phrase, or logo design that identifies the source or quality of a product. A service mark means the same thing, but identifies a service.

Trade Show. An exhibition of businesses offering franchises and/or business opportunity packages.

Transfer. The sale of franchise rights by a franchisee to the buyer of all or a portion of the franchisee's business.

UFOC. Uniform Franchise Offering Circular, the specialized franchise disclosure statement that franchisors must deliver to prospective franchisees at the earlier of (1) the first personal meeting for the purpose of discussing the sale or possible sale of a franchise, or (2) ten business days (14 calendar days in Illinois) before the prospect signs a franchise agreement or pays money for the right to be a franchisee.

Index

Listings Index

Key: $ = Low cost (under $50,000)

Key: $ = Low cost (under $50,000)

Key: $ = Low cost (under $50,000)

Key: $ = Low cost (under $50,000)

Key: $ = Low cost (under $50,000)

Key: $ = Low cost (under $50,000)

Key: $ = Low cost (under $50,000)

Key: $ = Low cost (under $50,000)

Key: $ = Low cost (under $50,000)

Key: $\mathcal{S}$ = Low cost (under $50,000)

Key: *$* = Low cost (under $50,000)

Key: *$* = Low cost (under $50,000)

Key: _$_ = Low cost (under $50,000)

Key: $ = Low cost (under $50,000)

Key: $ = Low cost (under $50,000)

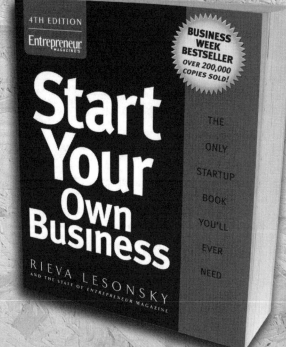

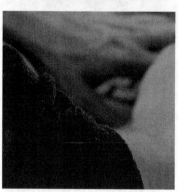